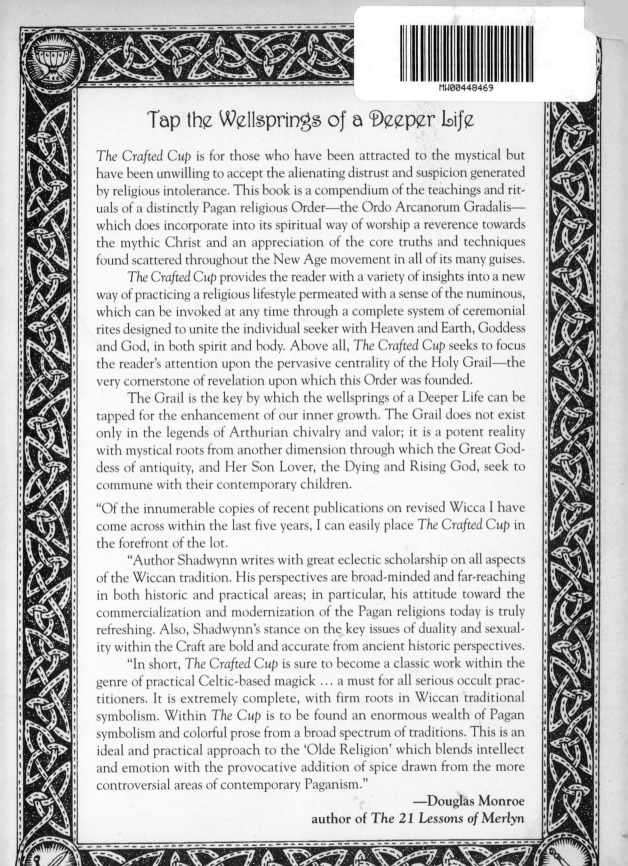

Tap the Wellsprings of a Deeper Life

The Crafted Cup is for those who have been attracted to the mystical but have been unwilling to accept the alienating distrust and suspicion generated by religious intolerance. This book is a compendium of the teachings and rituals of a distinctly Pagan religious Order—the Ordo Arcanorum Gradalis—which does incorporate into its spiritual way of worship a reverence towards the mythic Christ and an appreciation of the core truths and techniques found scattered throughout the New Age movement in all of its many guises.

The Crafted Cup provides the reader with a variety of insights into a new way of practicing a religious lifestyle permeated with a sense of the numinous, which can be invoked at any time through a complete system of ceremonial rites designed to unite the individual seeker with Heaven and Earth, Goddess and God, in both spirit and body. Above all, *The Crafted Cup* seeks to focus the reader's attention upon the pervasive centrality of the Holy Grail—the very cornerstone of revelation upon which this Order was founded.

The Grail is the key by which the wellsprings of a Deeper Life can be tapped for the enhancement of our inner growth. The Grail does not exist only in the legends of Arthurian chivalry and valor; it is a potent reality with mystical roots from another dimension through which the Great Goddess of antiquity, and Her Son Lover, the Dying and Rising God, seek to commune with their contemporary children.

"Of the innumerable copies of recent publications on revised Wicca I have come across within the last five years, I can easily place *The Crafted Cup* in the forefront of the lot.

"Author Shadwynn writes with great eclectic scholarship on all aspects of the Wiccan tradition. His perspectives are broad-minded and far-reaching in both historic and practical areas; in particular, his attitude toward the commercialization and modernization of the Pagan religions today is truly refreshing. Also, Shadwynn's stance on the key issues of duality and sexuality within the Craft are bold and accurate from ancient historic perspectives.

"In short, *The Crafted Cup* is sure to become a classic work within the genre of practical Celtic-based magick … a must for all serious occult practitioners. It is extremely complete, with firm roots in Wiccan traditional symbolism. Within *The Cup* is to be found an enormous wealth of Pagan symbolism and colorful prose from a broad spectrum of traditions. This is an ideal and practical approach to the 'Olde Religion' which blends intellect and emotion with the provocative addition of spice drawn from the more controversial areas of contemporary Paganism."

—Douglas Monroe
author of *The 21 Lessons of Merlyn*

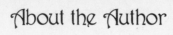

About the Author

Shadwynn has always been fascinated by the teachings and mystical aura surrounding religious faith. For over twenty years, he studied and taught as an amateur Christian theologian and student of comparative religion. His search for spiritual satisfaction led him through a varied succession of church affiliations, including Seventh-day Adventist, American Baptist, the Lutheran Church, the "Jesus Movement," the Charismatic Renewal, and Roman Catholicism. In 1984, after realizing how much of Catholic ritual mysticism was rooted in ancient Pagan practice, Shadwynn responded to the call of the Goddess by leaving Christianity for the open spiritual vistas of Neo-Paganism and Wicca.

Shadwynn is the editor of *Hallows*, a Pagan quarterly journal. He is also the founder and archpriest of the Ordo Arcanorum Gradalis, and is presiding priest of Keepers of the Cauldron. He is employed as a word processing specialist and resides in the outlying suburbs of Richmond, Virginia.

To Write to the Author

If you wish to contact the author or would like more information about this book, please write to the author in care of Llewellyn Worldwide, and we will forward your request. Both the author and publisher appreciate hearing from you and learning of your enjoyment of this book and how it has helped you. Llewellyn Worldwide cannot guarantee that every letter written to the author can be answered, but all will be forwarded. Please write to:

Shadwynn
c/o Llewellyn Worldwide
P.O. Box 64383-739, St. Paul, MN 55164-0383, U.S.A.

Please enclose a self-addressed, stamped envelope for reply, or $1.00 to cover costs.
If outside the U.S.A., enclose international postal reply coupon.

Free Catalog from Llewellyn

For more than 90 years Llewellyn has brought its readers knowledge in the fields of metaphysics and human potential. Learn about the newest books in spiritual guidance, natural healing, astrology, occult philosophy, and more. Enjoy book reviews, new age articles, a calendar of events, plus current advertised products and services. To get your free copy of *Llewellyn's New Worlds of Mind and Spirit*, send your name and address to:

Llewellyn's New Worlds of Mind and Spirit
P.O. Box 64383-739, St. Paul, MN 55164-0383, U.S.A.

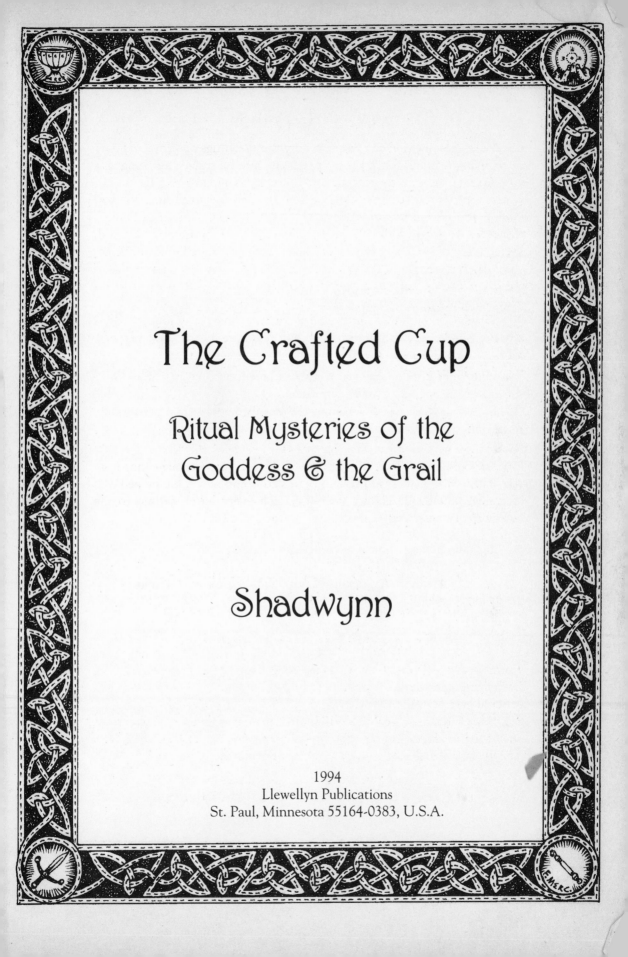

The Crafted Cup

Ritual Mysteries of the Goddess & the Grail

Shadwynn

1994
Llewellyn Publications
St. Paul, Minnesota 55164-0383, U.S.A.

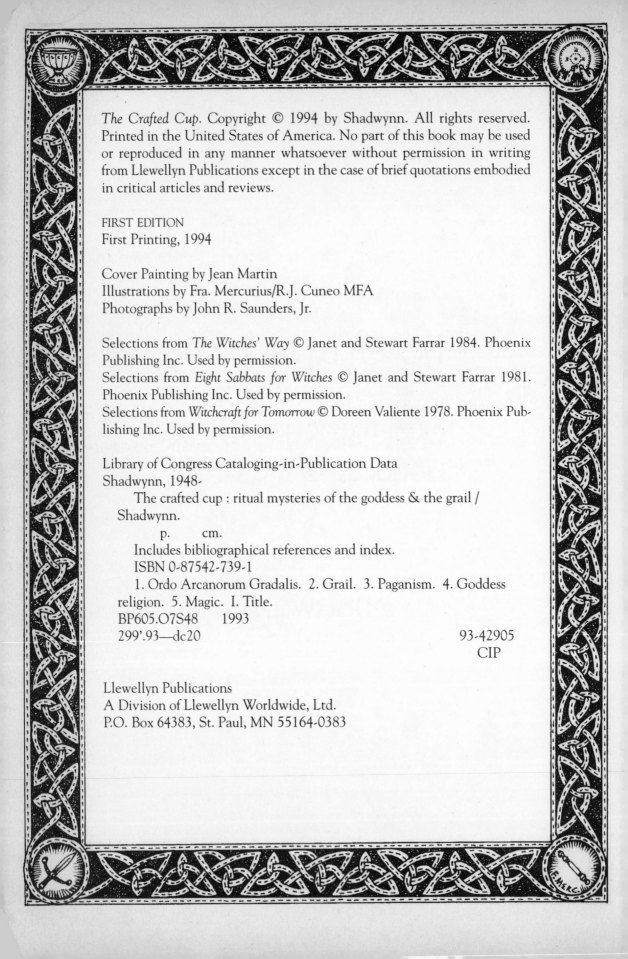

FIRST EDITION
First Printing, 1994

Cover Painting by Jean Martin
Illustrations by Fra. Mercurius/R.J. Cuneo MFA
Photographs by John R. Saunders, Jr.

Selections from *The Witches' Way* © Janet and Stewart Farrar 1984. Phoenix Publishing Inc. Used by permission.
Selections from *Eight Sabbats for Witches* © Janet and Stewart Farrar 1981. Phoenix Publishing Inc. Used by permission.
Selections from *Witchcraft for Tomorrow* © Doreen Valiente 1978. Phoenix Publishing Inc. Used by permission.

Library of Congress Cataloging-in-Publication Data
Shadwynn, 1948-
      The crafted cup : ritual mysteries of the goddess & the grail /
Shadwynn.
            p.   cm.
      Includes bibliographical references and index.
      ISBN 0-87542-739-1
      1. Ordo Arcanorum Gradalis. 2. Grail. 3. Paganism. 4. Goddess
religion. 5. Magic. I. Title.
BP605.O7S48   1993
299'.93—dc20   93-42905
                                                                CIP

Llewellyn Publications
A Division of Llewellyn Worldwide, Ltd.
P.O. Box 64383, St. Paul, MN 55164-0383

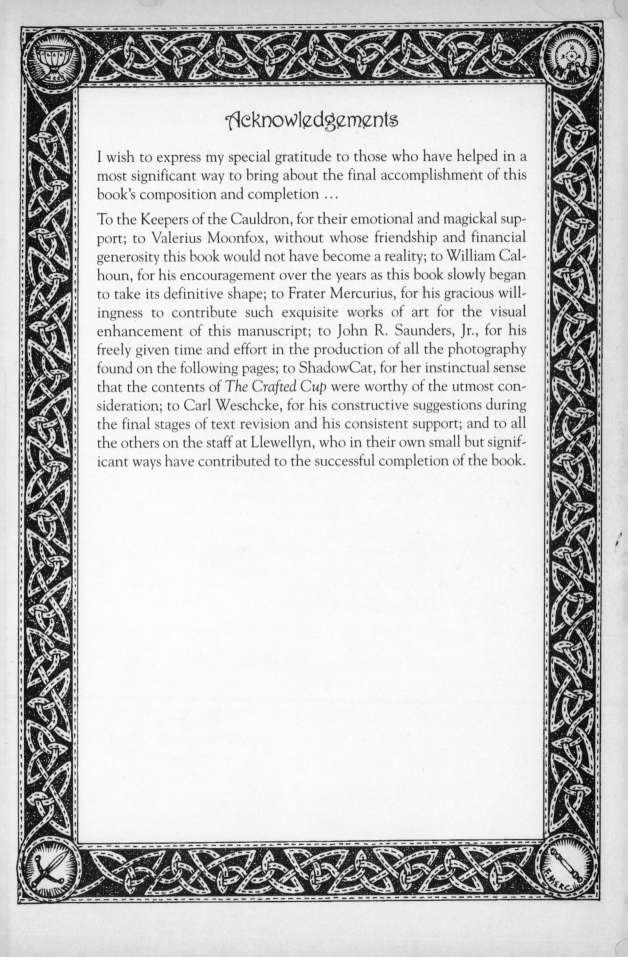

Acknowledgements

I wish to express my special gratitude to those who have helped in a most significant way to bring about the final accomplishment of this book's composition and completion …

To the Keepers of the Cauldron, for their emotional and magickal support; to Valerius Moonfox, without whose friendship and financial generosity this book would not have become a reality; to William Calhoun, for his encouragement over the years as this book slowly began to take its definitive shape; to Frater Mercurius, for his gracious willingness to contribute such exquisite works of art for the visual enhancement of this manuscript; to John R. Saunders, Jr., for his freely given time and effort in the production of all the photography found on the following pages; to ShadowCat, for her instinctual sense that the contents of *The Crafted Cup* were worthy of the utmost consideration; to Carl Weschcke, for his constructive suggestions during the final stages of text revision and his consistent support; and to all the others on the staff at Llewellyn, who in their own small but significant ways have contributed to the successful completion of the book.

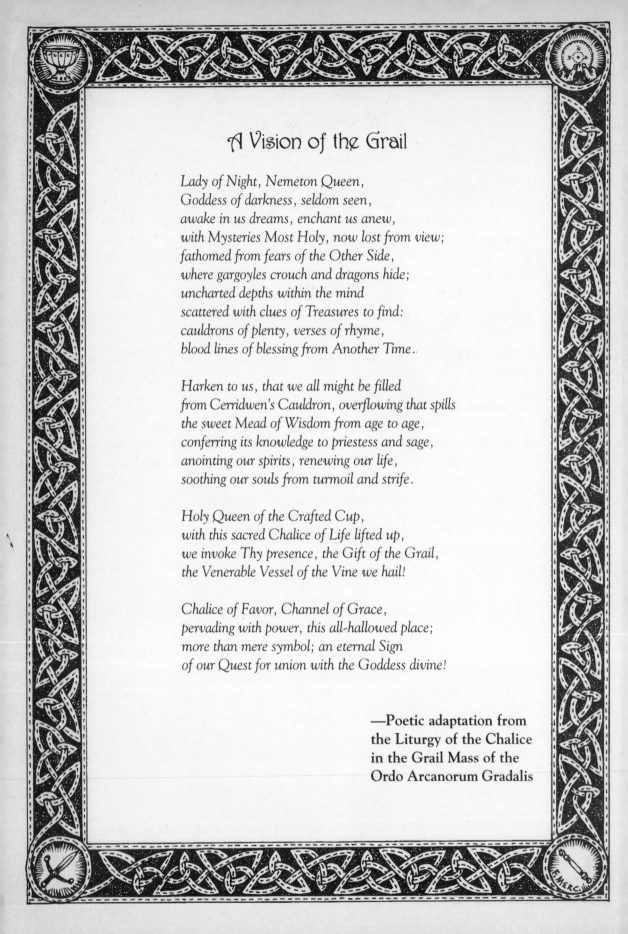

A Vision of the Grail

Lady of Night, Nemeton Queen,
Goddess of darkness, seldom seen,
awake in us dreams, enchant us anew,
with Mysteries Most Holy, now lost from view;
fathomed from fears of the Other Side,
where gargoyles crouch and dragons hide;
uncharted depths within the mind
scattered with clues of Treasures to find:
cauldrons of plenty, verses of rhyme,
blood lines of blessing from Another Time.

Harken to us, that we all might be filled
from Cerridwen's Cauldron, overflowing that spills
the sweet Mead of Wisdom from age to age,
conferring its knowledge to priestess and sage,
anointing our spirits, renewing our life,
soothing our souls from turmoil and strife.

Holy Queen of the Crafted Cup,
with this sacred Chalice of Life lifted up,
we invoke Thy presence, the Gift of the Grail,
the Venerable Vessel of the Vine we hail!

Chalice of Favor, Channel of Grace,
pervading with power, this all-hallowed place;
more than mere symbol; an eternal Sign
of our Quest for union with the Goddess divine!

—Poetic adaptation from
the Liturgy of the Chalice
in the Grail Mass of the
Ordo Arcanorum Gradalis

Table of Contents

Introduction

n recent years, more and more seeking individuals have made a personal religious commitment to follow the teachings of the Pagan path and the Wiccan way. Many see within this spiritual system the potentials for a late twentieth-century rejuvenation of holistic worship; a romanticized reflection of what many perceive to be the earliest and most sacred roots indigenous to Western religion.

For others, Wicca and Paganism offer the hope of interior integration, healing the Hellenistic dichotomy of the spiritual versus the physical by asserting the inherent interrelationship of Nature and Spirit. As such, it touches an inner animistic sensitivity within their psyche. To them, the Craft is seen as ecological in its scope of vision, a positive channeling force for the Earth's renewal.

Paganism and Wicca have been attractive to many precisely because of their lack of dogmatism and proselytizing. Generally speaking, the Craft does not seek to convert others to its way; rather, it is there as a teacher waiting for the approach of those already drawn to its wisdom. As it has been ideally envisioned, the Craft is not primarily focused upon the business basics of money collections and building programs. It has no popes or boards of directors to dictate its every form of expression. Its sanctuaries are vine-trellised yards, shadowed groves of trees, and the sea-lapped shores of sandy beaches; and most important, its supreme hierophant is the human spirit within.

The Craft is a magickal door, which, once we have walked through it, changes our perceptions of reality. Through rituals and observances we suspend our technologically encumbered psyches in an enacted passion play of gods and seasons, coming and going, growing and dying; all part of the planet rhythms of the Great Goddess.

Foremost among the highest expectations of what we hope to gain from a Pagan path of study is an attunement with the magick that is in all of life's levels of perception; a fulfilling form of worship that makes the seeker feel "at-one-ment" with the universe and its primal spirit; a deeper, internalized revelation of Goddess and God; and the ability to use magick in conjunction with others (as in a grove or coven) to bless, uplift, and heal those in need as well as to stand for justice, natural harmony, and truth as we can best perceive it in our struggle against the forces of psychic imbalance.

However, this book has not been written to serve as an introduction to the basics of the modern Neo-Pagan and Wiccan revival. Other volumes such as Margot Adler's *Drawing Down the Moon* and Starhawk's *The Spiral Dance* have more than adequately rendered this service to a spiritually seeking segment of the public which refuses to be satisfied with the rigidity of religious orthodoxy. And while we recommend these and other books for the elementary education of novice inquirers into Paganism, we must stress that we do not necessarily agree with all of their perspectives or theological viewpoints, as will be made increasingly clear in the following pages of this book. In fact, the underlying purpose of *The Crafted Cup* is to convey as plainly and forthrightly as possible a body of teaching and ritual which had its inception within the magickal world view of Wicca, but which, through an evolutionary process of spiritual development, has expanded far beyond the initial confines of contemporary Craft perspectives.

Essentially, we have come to realize that despite our affection and indebtedness to the early Neo-Pagan/Wiccan phenomenon in the recent religious life of Western society, the word "Wicca" can no longer serve as an adequate designation for what our system of ritual and belief truly represents. As an example, we have recently noticed an increasing tendency among many Wiccans, both groups and individuals, to be almost unconsciously slipping into a fairly distinct frame of reference which is more and more becoming defined by what is currently considered to be "politically correct" (PC). As much as many Neo-Pagans and Wiccans tout the slogan that diversity is their strength, and that we are all free to believe what we wish, often the unspoken "fine print" on the bottom line is that diversity should stay within the strictures of "PC" Pagan expectations if it is to be a legitimate expression of the Wiccan religion. These expectations are subtle but strong. While political and theological correctness within the spectrum of Wiccan religion is usually of the "Starhawkian" variety, it also makes easy adaptations to other traditions' needs as well. Its influence is becoming subtly pervasive.

Examples of "PC" attitudes spreading their influence throughout the larger Craft community are not difficult to find. Increasingly, many Wiccans tend to get demonstrably uncomfortable when any of their compatriots cross over the line of what are considered to be "acceptable" expectations. For instance, if you happen to oppose abortion on demand, you are immediately seen as taking an inappropriate stand for an anti-patriarchal Pagan. If you incorporate any amount of esoteric Christian imagery into your ritual format, you are suspect of being a betrayer of the "Old Ways" and a sell-out to the "enemy." If you see transcendence as a natural collary to the attributes of Deity, you are seen as subversive to the cherished immanence of the Goddess. If your views of sexual ethics value monogamy and question the philosophy of a free-wheeling, promiscuous lifestyle, you are accused of compromising the "freedom" and "natural casualness" of the Neo-Pagan approach to eroticism. If you conduct your ceremonial routine by a set and structured ritual framework, many will object to such "rigidity" as a stifling of their freedom to be anarchistically extemporaneous. Other examples could easily be conjured up, but the fact of the matter is that for those of us within the Ordo Arcanorum Gradalis, many of the prevalent expectations among other Wiccans as to what constitutes a "PC" standard for mainstream Craft are subtly oppressive as well as theologically constricting. Our own tradition has always sought to incorporate aspects from all of the various facets of the mystical gem of the Western Mystery Tradition, which glimmers its radiance to us from the distant reaches of antiquity. These include Pagan Celtic, Roman, Greek, and Mediterranean influences, along with the rich streams of Gnosticism and esoteric Christianity. But for many within the Wiccan spectrum of belief, this kind of religious syncretism is threatening, for it forces them to acknowledge the validity of the Judeo-Christian mystical traditions, something which many Wiccans and Neo-Pagans are most reluctant to do, due to their latent Christophobia.

As the rest of this book will seek to explain, the Ordo Arcanorum Gradalis is a Pagan religious order based upon the revelatory significance of the Holy Grail. The marvelous truth about the Grail is that it is neither Pagan nor Christian; it partakes of the richness of both spiritual systems. So also with the Western Mystery Tradition itself, it is built upon the bedrock of Pagan antiquity, but its temple on the inner planes is constructed with the sturdy supports and columns of Judeo-Christian spirituality.

The Western Mystery Tradition is the sum total of all the archetypal truths gleaned from the different eras and expressions of our religious history—Pagan, Christian, Jewish, and (to some extent) Islamic. However, the big problem with many who profess allegiance to the Wiccan way is their anachronistic attempt to perpetuate a form of "Paleolithic Pagan separatism" which rejects every last vestige of Christian imprint upon our culture. Instead, some of them continue to ignorantly promote the myth of their mission as being the re-establishment of the "true" Western faith of our ancestors: the "Old Religion." Of course, the concept of modern Wicca being the contemporary repository of an unbroken line of traditions, teachings, and rituals directly inherited from the most ancient priesthoods of pre-

Christian Europe is in itself a palpable myth to which many Neo-Pagans have succumbed. Wicca is not a religion rescued from Paleolithic obscurity. It is a recent twentieth-century invention of a few brilliant (some would say eccentric) occultists such as Gerald Gardner, et al., who managed to quite successfully create a *new* religion based upon an ingenious amalgamation of ceremonial magick, and the folkloric memories of the witchcraft indigenous to the British Isles.

It is important to emphasize at this point that none of the foregoing has been expressed in an attempt to in any way denigrate the positive and wondrously uplifting contributions of contemporary Wicca to the revitalization of Nature spirituality and the renewal of the latent religious creativity within the human spirit. Religion does not have to be ancient or Paleolithic in order to express the realities of spiritual truth. Every great religion of the world originally had its inception as a new and freshly-blossomed revelation, and Wicca is no exception. As a spiritual pathway, Wicca is like a youth among the revered sages of antiquity, and therein lies its vigor and vitality as a religion; but we cannot afford to turn our backs upon the accumulated wisdom of Western religious thought and practice, especially that which has been bequeathed to us by the mystics of church and synagogue alike. Recognition of the Truth comes in the realization of mystical oneness beneath the guises of religious diversity. Whether in the circle or the synagogue, we must be open to the oracular voice of the One beyond all images and symbols Who speaks to the inner depths of our spirit. To this end, it is the firm belief of those within the Ordo Arcanorum Gradalis that the mystery of the Grail which is our iconographic focus, cannot be given the full rein of spiritual expression in our ritual worship as long as we are exclusively associated with only the Wiccan aspect of the modern mystical revival.

Since we have implemented this decision in our esoteric approach, we have sensed that our focus of purpose has taken on an expanded dimension. Our horizons are broader, and our sense of unity through the Grail with the diverse streams which flow into the mighty river of the Western Way is stronger.

At this juncture, the reader may wonder just what actually constitutes the core of this Order's tradition. In answer to this silent query, I direct your attention to the words of William Calhoun, an ordained Grailpriest of this Order, whose succinct yet powerful summation of the basic, foundational premises of our vision are both poetic and sweeping as they convey the faith and focus of the Ordo Arcanorum Gradalis ...

Foreword

A New Garment Woven from Ancient Threads

rdo Arcanorum Gradalis can best be described as Gnostic in its spiritual orientation, a fellowship with regard to its ecclesiastical polity, and Arthurian in the focus of its tradition.

We are *Gnostic* in that we focus on knowledge (gnosis), the divine knowledge found in the Western Mystery Tradition. This tradition is a continuum of wisdom and practice arcing through the soul of the West. It was born in the painted caves of Liseaux and the Garden of Eden, encompassing the circle of Stonehenge, the songs of ancient bards, the goddess shrines of Old Europe, the Marian altars of Notre Dame, the visions of Camelot and Logres, the cathedral at Chartres, the laboratories of alchemists and workrooms of hermetic magicians. It plumbs the depths of the Jewish Kabbalah and the heights of esoteric Christianity to manifest in the rebirth of Paganism in America. The gnosis of the Western Mystery Tradition is the gift of the Great Goddess, as are the minds and spirits with which we receive it.

We are a *fellowship* organized as a religious Order, a union of assemblies and individuals constituting both laity and clergy, gathered for worship; worship of the Great Goddess and Her Consort, the God; our sources of life, sustenance and wisdom. Our ritual calendar honors the manifestations of the Goddess in the Earth and its seasons (the High and Low Earth Rites) and the Moon and its cycles (the Lunar Rites). The pinnacle of our worship is the Grail Mass, or Mass of the Goddess. This central mystery unites us with the Goddess through the communion of bread and wine, manifesting the eternal unity of spirit and matter.

Our priesthood is open to all men and women who are called by the Goddess. Most responsibilities, ritual and administrative, are shared by clergy and laity equally. Only the central mystery of the Grail Mass and related matters of theology and policy are reserved to priests and priestesses. Those who assume these offices are marked not by the glory of privilege, but by the burden of responsibility.

We are *Arthurian*. The tales of King Arthur, seen by many as children's stories or escapist fantasy, actually make up a complete and living spiritual tradition. The stories of Arthur, Guinevere, Merlin, Morgan, and Camelot form a body of multi-layered and faceted richness, rewarding all who dig deeply and look closely. The Arthurian mythos, through both Pagan and esoteric Christian interpretations, has much to teach us, from worship and mysticism to chivalry and personal honor. But the crown of the mythos, the heart of Avalon, the golden thread running through the entire Western Mystery Tradition is the *Holy Grail*. The Grail is the touchstone. The meeting point of Pagan and Christian, Goddess and God, male and female, Otherworld and Middle Earth, spirit and matter. It takes many forms through time and legend: the Cauldron of Cerridwen, the Chalice of the Last Supper, the Cup of Arthur's Quest, the Sword in the Stone, the Hallows of Avalon. The Grail is the center of our work, the focus of our quest, the path which guides us through the complexities of the Western Mystery Tradition.

We honor the wisdom and practice of *tradition*. Although open to the new and creative, we hold that the truths of tradition have survived for a reason, that they have value, deserve respect, and may require long and difficult work, especially by those raised in an ethos of "everything is negotiable." Thus, while more open to members' creativity than some other voices of the Western Mystery Tradition, we hold certain core practices, such as the Grail Mass, and certain teachings, such as the nature of the Goddess and God, to be non-negotiable axioms. These act as anchors to allow us a solid guide when buffeted by the constant shift and flash of the market place of spiritual ideas.

We are a new garment woven from ancient threads to a centuries-old pattern. We wish to function like the Round Table of Arthur. Like those knights and ladies, we gather to study, worship, and celebrate. We share our strengths and talents, healing one another's weaknesses. We stand as equals before the Goddess, great in our diversity, unified at our center. When called by the Lady, we each go out alone, bearing the strength and tools acquired from the fellowship of the Table; stepping out into the deep forest to seek the Grail along the path unique to each of us.

—William Douglas Calhoun
Grailpriest, O.A.G.
The Grail Chapel
Athens, Ohio

Part I

The Teachings and the Tradition

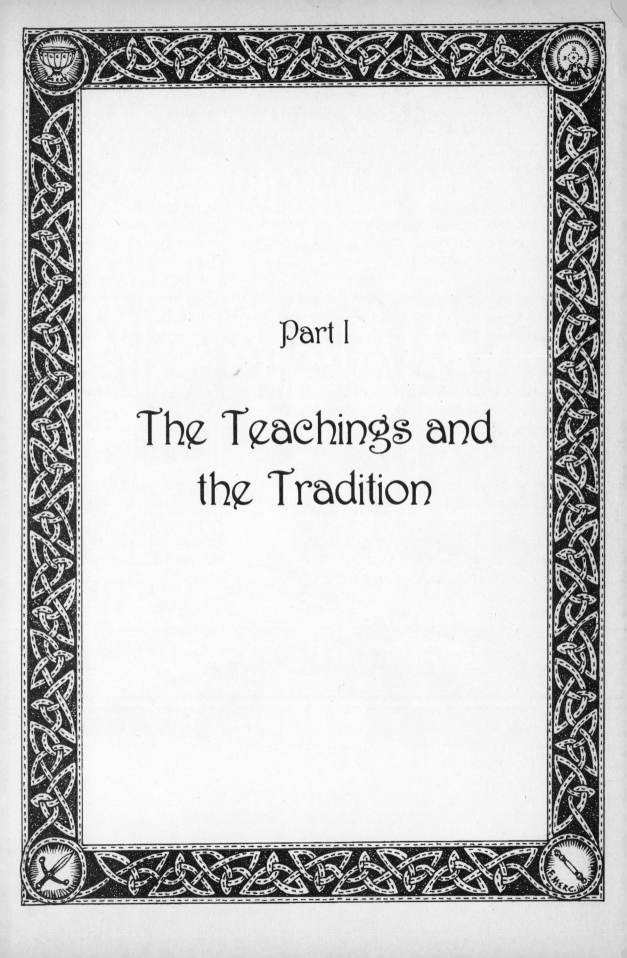

Chapter One

Ordo Arcanorum Gradalis: Overview of an Order

he *Ordo Arcanorum Gradalis* is a branch of the modern mystic revival which contains within its framework of teaching and practice an esotericism firmly grounded in the Western Mystery Tradition and the Nature-oriented spirituality of our pre-Christian heritage. It is an expression of magickal spirituality which stresses ceremonial ritual in its approach to the worship of the Deity in both masculine and feminine aspects. The primary focus of this Order is upon the value of worship itself as the most important tool for rekindling an awareness of the very essence of Deity lying dormant within us. In this fellowship of the Grail Quest, worship is perceived as being the highest manifestation of magick; a means of self-transformation by which we amplify our sense of connectedness with the ultimate Divinity.

The *Ordo Arcanorum Gradalis* adheres to a Christo-Celtic tradition, meaning that it recognizes the concept of the Cosmic Christ as one of the highest revelations of the Deity, periodically manifested in the primordial traditions of the Dying and Rising God mythos so common in most ancient religious expressions of faith (including Christianity). Much of this Order's ritual imagery is also based upon the Arthurian Grail legends rooted in the soil of Celtic myth and history.

The *Ordo Arcanorum Gradalis* is distinguished by an emphasis upon the celebration of a liturgical Eucharist centering around the mysteries of the Holy Grail.

The concept of Eucharistic communion as a means of assimilating the attributes of the gods predates Christianity far back into the misty beginnings of human religious practice, and is genuinely rooted in the most mystical of Pagan spiritual conceptualizations. The Grail Mass, which we celebrate at every gathering, is our most focal act of worship. It is a Mass addressed to the Divine Feminine as the Goddess, memorializing the many epiphanies and incarnations of Her Son/Lover, the Dying and Rising Lord. The Lord is invoked to tabernacle as the sacrificial Host under the appearance of consecrated bread, even as the Spirit of the Lady is also invoked through sacred words of power that She might become for us the true wine of the chalice, permeating the cup with Her life-changing presence. We regard the symbology of this chalice to be one of the highest mysteries of the Goddess; the chalice being a descendant from its prototype, the Womb Cauldron of the Great Mother. From our perspective, perhaps no other legacy of Western esoterica has such a potent power as that of the Holy Grail, for it can unite both Pagan and Christian before its shrine in wonder and reverence. In our Order, the Grail Mass becomes the sacramentally tangible essence of the presence of the Deity as both Goddess and God in our midst, having become a key for us in the revitalization and deepening of the Mysteries in their ever-unfolding awesomeness.

The *Ordo Arcanorum Gradalis* is a Gnostic Order in that it adheres to the maxim that true spiritual knowledge cannot be gained by mere conformance to the rules and regulations of an established ecclesiastical hierarchy. The pilgrimage to Goddess consciousness and self-realization must begin within, stirred by the promptings of that "still, small voice" which whispers to our own inner awareness with oracles of guidance towards the goal that is the Grail.

The *Ordo Arcanorum Gradalis* designates its working and worshipping groups as either groves or chapels. It must be emphasized that our system is a syncretistic fusion of mystical teachings originating from a variety of religious sources, including both Paganism and esoteric Christianity, for we are primarily A RELIGION OF THE GRAIL, and—like the Grail—we have assimilated within our hierology the arcane legends and myths of both religions, yet are owned by neither. In the same way, the designation of either "grove" (a word derived from Pagan religious usage) or "chapel" (a word of Christian derivation) is equally applicable to any group within our Order, since our liturgical ceremonies and theology partake of the occult richness of both spiritual systems.

The *Ordo Arcanorum Gradalis*, in common with certain other Nature-oriented expressions of religious faith, observes the eight great seasonal festivals (Earth Rites) of the old pre-Christian calendar as a means of attuning its members with the Earth-tides and ecological rhythms of this living planet. These observances include Hallowmas, Candlemas, Balemas, and Lammas, as well as the solstices and equinoxes. Monthly gatherings (Lunar Rites) are also celebrated in honor of the triple-aspected Goddess as symbolized by the changing phases of the Moon. Most Earth Rites are open to newcomers and guests at the discretion of the presiding priest/esses. The Lunar Rites, however, are usually closed to public participation in order to facilitate these occasions as times for the training and teaching of committed grove/chapel members.

The *Ordo Arcanorum Gradalis* has developed a non-hierarchical structure, in that there is no central authority over the Order itself other than the common myths, theology, and rituals as set forth in this book of teachings and rites. The founder of the Ordo Arcanorum Gradalis is invested with the title of Archpriest, but his authority is limited to seeing that the essential integrity of the Order's teachings, sacraments, and rituals remains the yardstick by which the theological coherence of this tradition is maintained. However, each local grove or chapel is overseen by a presiding priest and/or priestess who has been duly ordained according to the rubrics of the Order. Upon the discretion of each grove or chapel, these two leadership positions may be filled on a rotating basis as often as the group determines (or through the casting of lots) by any members who have been duly recognized as ordained according to the requirements of the Order. All matters of theology and ritual practice are determined by the priest/esses of each grove or chapel in conjunction and conformance with the guidelines and requirements as set forth in this book. All other matters of the local grove/chapel are decided by consensus or democratic vote of the entire membership.

The *Ordo Arcanorum Gradalis* does not subscribe to the three degree system of initiation common in certain magickal orders and various other esoteric groups. Entrance into the priesthood of the Order is achieved through a single, once-for-all rite of *ordination*. On the other hand, *initiation* is also a single, once-for-all rite, but it is reserved only for those who wish to become a *non-ordained* member of a local grove or chapel. Such an initiation simply marks an individual's voluntary decision to follow the Grail quester's path. Each local group shall determine its own requirements for those who seek initiatory admission as a lay grove or chapel member. (Ordination requirements are uniformly set for the Order as a whole. See Appendix A.)

The *Ordo Arcanorum Gradalis* works robed for all ceremonial occasions, and all ordained priest/esses are required to wear vestments indicative of their office. Newcomers and special guests in attendance are allowed to wear normal street clothes.

The *Ordo Arcanorum Gradalis* does not conduct any kind of explicitly sexual rites within its ceremonial system. The Great Rite is enacted at all of the eight annual Earth Rites, but only in its symbolic form with the chalice and the glaive (athame). We do not believe that ritualized sexual intercourse in group gatherings is spiritually enhancing, but inappropriate, awkward, and morally dubious. Those who may wish to become involved with the fellowship of this Order because they think it is a free ticket to orgies, drug use, and general debauchery are NOT welcome.

The *Ordo Arcanorum Gradalis* follows its own cycle of myths and sacred imagery in portraying the activities of Deity (manifested as Goddess and God) interacting in Nature through the seasonal changes celebrated during the course of the Wheel of the Year. Unlike some well-known Neo-Pagan paths, we do not subscribe to the concept that the Goddess has preeminence over the spring and summer months, while the God has preeminence over the fall and winter months. Instead, we honor the Triple Goddess in our rituals as presiding over the *entire* year in perpetual preeminence, reigning in spring and early summer as the Maiden; from late summer through early fall as the Great Mother; and from late fall through the whole of winter as the ancient Crone. Likewise, the God also reigns throughout the year as the Consort of the Goddess. In His luminous aspect, He mates with the Maiden as Satyr Pan. He is the god of sexuality and the lord of life. Reigning with the Goddess through the spring and summer, He finally dies in the fall and returns to the wintry womb of the Earth Mother to await His return with the new spring of the coming year. In His chthonic aspect, the God is revered as Kernunnos, the Horned One. He is the Sacred Stag: god of sacrifice, death, and the Underworld, reigning as the Consort of the Crone through the fall and winter months. Since in our tradition the God in His terrestrial manifestation is seen in a dual role as Satyr Lord and Sacred Stag, this mythic scenario takes the place of the Holly King/Oak King struggle for supremacy so common in the rituals of some Neo-Pagan groups.

The *Ordo Arcanorum Gradalis* reveres the Deity as both Goddess and God, but this Order teaches that the Lady should have the primacy of place as the focus of our ceremonial worship. We give veneration to the God as Lord; not as Her equal, but as Her Son, Lover, and Consort. We are, however, opposed to any form of extremist thought (such as separatist Dianic Wicca) which would attempt to obliterate the God from its system of belief due to the over-reactionism of radical feminist philosophy.

The *Ordo Arcanorum Gradalis* differs from most other magickal traditions in that "widdershins" (counterclockwise) ritual movements are used for the casting of all seasonal and lunar ceremonial circles. We do not consider the use of the "widdershins" direction in circle-casting to be in any sense a sinister or negative magickal gesture. Quite to the contrary, the custom of casting the sacred circle in the counterclockwise direction is viewed by this Order as part of an inheritance from the lore of Pagan antiquity which, in general, has been overlooked by most modern practitioners of the magickal arts and Earth-oriented spirituality.

The *Ordo Arcanorum Gradalis*, in a unique practice of its own, varies the directional positioning of the altar in the center of the circle depending upon the season of the year; facing east in the spring, south in the summer, west in the fall, and north in the winter. This, we feel, reinforces our awareness of the basic elemental relationship to the ever-changing progression of the seasons.

The *Ordo Arcanorum Gradalis* teaches that the intricate and delicate global ecosystem of our planet is in desperate need of being reclaimed and cleansed for the Goddess, for it is, in reality, analogous as the planetary body of the Earth Mother. We advocate active political participation on behalf of clean air and other environmental anti-pollution measures. We also believe in the effectiveness of ritual Earth-cleansing ceremonies toward these same ends.

The *Ordo Arcanorum Gradalis* disavows any relation to, and condemns the expression of any form of Satanism, ritual abuse or sacrifice, malicious sorcery, violence, or sexually irresponsible behavior that is falsely claimed to be a legitimate expression of occult or esoteric spirituality. Such groups and/or individuals who advocate these deplorable practices are in no way connected to the true Craft of the Wise.

The *Ordo Arcanorum Gradalis* is but one of many beautiful and legitimate traditions of the modern mystical revival being experienced within a broad spectrum of religious backgrounds. Some of our theological and liturgical approaches are unique, while in many other ways our philosophic agreement with other esoteric Christian, Gnostic, and Neo-Pagan schools of thought far outweighs our differences. What you have just read is a short and fragmentary overview of our Order. In the pages that follow, we will examine in greater detail many of these briefly stated beliefs and practices.

Chapter Two

Goddess and God: A Revelation of the Mystery

or many Neo-Pagans and Wiccans, a serious, detailed exploration into the "fine points" of theology is rarely a part of their religious experience or education. Too often, many in the Neo-Pagan community fall victim to superficially vague and confusingly muddled ways of describing their own belief systems, especially when it comes to describing their understanding of the essence of Deity and the inherent properties of the Divine Nature.

What follows is an admittedly incomplete examination of the theological aspects relating to the Goddess, the God, and what (or who) lies beyond Them both. It is incomplete, in that the subject is just too vast and overwhelming to be adequately encapsulated within the parameters of one lengthy, yet limited, article such as this. However, it is the author's fervent hope that this treatise will engender renewed interest in the intrinsic relevance of the relationship between how we perceive the attributes of Deity and how we respond to the movings and promptings of Divinity as a direct result of these perceptions.

In the Ordo Arcanorum Gradalis, we take these issues seriously, for they help to define for us our relationship with the universe and that which lies beyond. The observations which follow are not to be taken as ironclad pronouncements of an inflexible tradition, but rather processes of thought which point to a reinforcement of a basic tenet within this tradition of the Grail Quest: to achieve balance and

9

inner harmony as individuals, we must see ourselves as the offspring of a holistically equilibrated Deity which radiates a reflection of its essence in the ocean of multi-dimensional being which surrounds, and is, indeed, a part of us. To such ends, this chapter is reverently dedicated.

One of the unique features of Wiccan theology and its place within the Western religious tradition is the fact that its rites and ceremonies are centered around the concept of not only a God, but also a Goddess. Most bastions of Judeo-Christian orthodoxy are exclusively monotheistic in nature and emphasis.[1] In contrast, Wicca and the larger Neo-Pagan movement, while technically polytheistic, in actuality tend toward a ditheistic or dyadic theology which focuses on both the masculine and feminine aspects of Deity.

Many Wiccans vary in their ways of explanation regarding that which is supposed to be the focus of their worship. Some call themselves pantheists; others simply say that they "worship Nature." Still others claim they worship nothing, but are just using the gods and goddesses of Pagan antiquity as archetypal symbols by which they can better probe the depths of their own consciousness. These "post-Wiccans" have gone so far as to suggest that the Old Religion has outgrown the need to call itself a religion at all, since its main purpose (from their viewpoint) is to function as a psychic system facilitating the acquisition of personal power; in other words, a synonym for sorcery.[2] For these individuals, worship of anything is simply "passe." From this elitist perspective, "progressive" human beings should have advanced to the point where they have actualized themselves as the center of their universe. In their mind, actual religious devotion towards anything outside or beyond themselves is for the "primitives."

The Pitfalls of Pantheism

Perhaps the most popular Neo-Pagan approach to the nature of the Deity is the teaching known as *pantheism*, roughly translated from its Greek derivatives as "all or everything is God." Distilled to its basic essence, pantheism postulates that the Deity is the universe itself in all of its multiplicity of forms and energies—nothing more, nothing less. The Deity, therefore, can be neither personal nor transcendent. Divinity can only manifest through immanence in the material things around us. There can be no distinction between matter and spirit, since the material universe and its subtle energies are all there is. This form of belief is very popular among Neo-Pagans, but it is woefully inadequate in its ability to tackle those sticky questions such as "What was the origin of the universe?" "What original cause preexisted the postulated Big Bang?" "If there was a time when the universe did not exist, then who brought it into being?" Essentially, pantheism can be seen as an intellectually fashionable concept used by some who are too confirmed in their agnosticism to think exhaustively on this most profound subject ever to awe the human mind; those who can't be bothered with those "irrelevant abstracts of outmoded beliefs" use this philosophical approach to cover up their own inherent skepticism. For this reason, Wicca runs the risk of becoming, for some, not a living faith, but rather a system of rituals used to induce some form of consciousness raising serving as a trendy, "earthy" technique for self-improvement. Pantheism is popular especially among those Neo-Pagan intellectuals who insist on retaining their faith in the non-existence of the supernatural while at the same time appropriating the trappings of religious Pagan ritual which appeals to their sense of the romantic. The almost wholesale acceptance of pantheism by many modern Neo-Pagans in actuality jeopardizes their movement's generalized claim of being a revivalist continuation of ancient Pagan theology. This is because of the fact that the historical Paganism of the ancients was not pantheistic at all, but rather *theistic*, and with an emphasis on the duality of realms: the world of spirit(s) and the domain of Nature under the control of these celestial beings. The Gods, then, were conceived of in traditional Pagan theology as beings which belonged to the realm of objective, spiritual reality:

> By far the majority of people in all strata of (Pagan) society held a supernaturalistic conception of the universe that presupposed the existence of a spirit world above and beyond the world known to ordinary sense perception. In the presence of the mystery which lies back of all human experience, even the most ordinary, there were few in the Julian or Flavian periods who were content to maintain a position of agnosticism and say, "The mystery cannot be understood: therefore it may be ignored." The more curious majority sought in one way or another to penetrate the mystery and were satisfied that it held the key to an understanding of the meaning of existence. *Furthermore, so far as the ordering of the universe was concerned, the supernatural realm was conceived to be far more important then the natural world; for the ultimate forces which controlled all things were believed to be the occult spiritual powers above and not the forces of nature operative in the world below.*[3]

Of course, this is not meant to imply that Pagans did not see all of Nature as being animated with the spirit (or spirits) of the divine, unseen world (a belief known as *animism*). In fact, they did. (More often than not, many contemporary Neo-Pagans mistakenly equate their acceptance of animism with that of pantheism, but in actuality the two teachings are separate and distinct.) However, unlike modern pantheist thought, they did not equate Nature with their gods and goddesses. These deities controlled and pervaded Nature, but they were not perceived as being identical with it. Historical Pagan thought was generally polytheistic, not pantheistic, in its spiritual world view of the forces which control the natural world-plane of existence.

Unfortunately, in many Neo-Pagan periodicals, we see time and again articles which assert the *identical oneness and complete identity* of the Goddess with the Earth or Nature.[4] In essence, the term "Goddess" has become for them simply a poetic metaphor for the impersonal energies and force fields which make up our environment; a form of "divinized biology" which deifies the physical processes of life in their global totality as "Gaia." But this kind of conceptualization is far removed from the devotional thinking of early preliterate as well as later Pagan cultures. In fact, the most recent scholarly consensus has established several important conclusions regarding the so-called "worship of Nature." These include the following facts:

1. *Primitive peoples had no concept of Nature as a unified totality.* Instead, these preliterate tribes venerated only the individually distinct objects of natural phenomena such as the heavenly bodies, the forces of wind and rain, and the animals which were seen as embodiments of magickal and mysterious powers.
2. Pantheism as it has been promulgated in modern theology and philosophy cannot properly be applied to the study of the beliefs of preliterate cultures without anachronistic distortion.
3. *No documentation has yet been found of Nature being worshipped by ancient peoples as an omnipotent entity.*[5]

Devotional literature of the early historical cultures of the Fertile Crescent reveals that the Goddess was perceived as being the *creatrix* of the cosmos and the Earth; a theological concept antithetical to the tenets of pantheism, which postulates the Deity exclusively in terms of immanence. Referring to the Babylonian goddess Ishtar, one ancient prayer intones these following attributes to the heavenly lady:

> Who dost make the green herb to spring up, mistress of mankind! *Who hast created everything*, who dost guide aright all creatures! Mother Ishtar, whose power no god can approach![6]

Similar attributions appear in prayers to the Egyptian goddess Isis:

> Thou turnest the earth in its orb; Thou givest light to the sun; Thou rulest the world; Thou treadest Death underfoot. To Thee the stars are responsive; by Thee the seasons turn and the gods rejoice and the elements are in subjection …[7]

Here we see that Isis was represented, *not* as being identical with the Earth itself, *but over and above it*, as well as enveloping and controlling the very universe itself— in other words, the Goddess in Her *transcendent* aspect as Queen of the Cosmos.

Yet in the midst of these acclamations of implied transcendence, the Goddess also makes reference to Her intimate relationship with Her own creation—Nature:

> I am she that is the natural mother of all things, mistress and governor of all the elements, the initial progeny of worlds, chief of divine powers, queen of heaven, the principle of the gods celestial, the light of the goddesses, at my will are disposed the planets of the air, the wholesome winds of the seas; and the silences of the unseen world ...[8]

In fact, in some translations, the first phrase of the above quoted passage is rendered simply as "I am Nature ...," not in any sense of pantheistic self-identification, but rather as an analogous title which the Goddess claims by virtue of Her mystical intimacy with Her own creation; an intimacy which must, however, be interpreted in light of Her own simultaneous claims to a creative and controlling transcendence of the physical elements themselves. In this passage Isis reveals Her *immanence* throughout the manifested world around us by designating Herself as "Nature" or Nature's Mother, signifying Her presence in all things by virtue of Her originating, cosmic productiveness which has given rise to all that is.

We see then, in the above excerpts, that much of classical and mystery-cult Paganism viewed the Goddess (by whatever name) in Her highest form of theophany to be omnipotent *over and above* the creation, as well as being the living, *personal* embodiment of all that is inspiringly called Nature. But here we find no evidence of the Goddess as being a mere pantheistic metaphor. *She is a real, personal manifestation of the creative, sustaining intelligence who moves the universe.* This point was underscored by an individual writing in a Northwest Wiccan publication about a related topic:

> We are Wiccans and Pagans. We believe in these varied spirits, not just one feminine spirit of three faces. We cooperate and are familiar with spirit beings ...
>
> My Goddess is a separate entity from me. She is also part of me and I am part of her, for I am part of the Universe with a role to play. Nonetheless, She is Herself. She demands worship ...
>
> The Great Goddess is a goddess of great beauty and power, and deserves special treatment. So do the myriad gods, goddesses and other spirits, according to their positions and authorities. They are part of our heritage. We can not pick and choose, but must accept their existence along with the rest of our ancient ways ...[9]

The almost naive statement of some in the ranks of Neo-Paganism to the effect that they "worship Nature," is just another form of pantheism for those whose ecological mind-set has led them into a philosophical quandary which can ultimately become quite embarrassing. Bill McKibbon in his recent book *The End of Nature*, graphically demonstrates both the fragility and *imminent demise* of that which we know as Nature at the hands of a greedy, Earth-gouging humanity unless there is a drastic reversal of trends. Reviewing McKibbon's book, Robert Engleman made the following ominous statement, "McKibbon contends that we will miss nature when it's gone, the way we miss dead parents we once rebelled against, and he may be right."[10] The realization that the combination of human technology and greed could be lethal for that which we have so reverently called Nature, puts its self-proclaimed worshippers on notice that their object of veneration is not the Deity at all, but just as subject to rape, pillage, and destruction as any other part of this planetary biosphere. This, in the end, generates no hope for the future apart from human effort to turn the tide of ecological disaster. If Nature alone is our God/dess (a concept alien to historic Paganism), and we fail in our attempt to save it, then our "Deity" dies with us.

The kind of conclusions engendered by this mode of thinking can only result in a psychic pessimism of religiously cataclysmic proportions. However, from the standpoint of our own tradition, pantheistic Nature-worship is not an adequate substitute for the intimation of an ultimate, deathless Deity inherent in the most sublime teachings of the Western Mysteries.[11]

Constructing a Framework

While distinctly a modern expression of a syncretistic fusion of historical Pagan mysticism and Western esoteric mystery teachings, the Ordo Arcanorum Gradalis has a specific theological framework within which all of its subsequent teaching regarding the Deity is grounded. Since the main emphasis of our Order is the transformative power of worship, it is imperative that we know two things: *who* we worship and *how* we worship. The theology and methodology of these two spiritual correlatives is the cornerstone of all our Grail Quest perspectives as they affect our perceptions of the Cosmic Mystery and the part we play in its ever-unfolding plan. What follows, therefore, is a systematic examination of the foundational framework within which we may more easily formulate our finite conceptualizations of the Deity. Of course, this is not meant to be interpreted as an inerrant proclamation of Truth spoken "ex cathedra" from a Pagan papal throne! We realize that any dogmatic definitions about the infinite Deity determined through the limited lens of our finite, mortal visualization can be easily fraught with the fallacious fantasies of inadequate comprehension. But we do believe that what follows provides a careful and useful context for a better understanding of what so often is perceived to be a hopeless maze of theological intangibles.

In the beginning of the early Christian era, there were a wide variety of Gnostic sects both within and without the Church. Many of them were characterized by the acceptance of a doctrine of the Aeons (Ages) by which they taught their beliefs regarding the nature of God (or the gods), the different spheres and levels of the manifested intensity of the Divine Presence, and how they could be reached through spiritual discipline. In a similar way, the Ordo Arcanorum Gradalis teaches that in order to understand the multifaceted essence of the Deity, one must understand its *levels of emanation*. Being unaware of the advantages inherent in this approach, some Neo-Pagans have misguidedly railed against all Christians, Jews, etc., for being monotheistic; thinking that a belief in one supreme Deity must be antithetical to the tolerance, openness, and plurality of Paganism. This, however, is an unfortunate misconception. It has been well-documented that modified forms of monotheistic thought were widespread in Pagan religious thinking in various areas of the ancient world.[12] Further, it is worth noting that more and more thoughtful Wiccans are coming to realize that there is no necessary antipathy between monotheism and polytheism:

> At first glance a monotheistic Pagan seems a contradiction in terms. But it really isn't. The ancient Greeks believed in a Prime Cause beyond the Gods of Olympus. In Egypt, land of a thousand deities, they recognized Neter: That Which Created the Gods. So, a monotheistic Pagan is not an anomaly. What makes us Pagans is not that we worship many gods, but that we worship many aspects of the One.[13]

Because of its teaching regarding these levels of emanation, the Ordo Arcanorum Gradalis can confidently proclaim its simultaneous belief in monotheism, ditheism, and polytheism without any sense of conflict or tension between these understandings of the Divine Nature.

The Ordo Arcanorum Gradalis Is Monotheistic

In the most sublime, trans-cosmic apex of our religious conceptualizations, we perceive the supreme essence of the Deity as infinite, ineffable, holy; the One, the ground of all being, the eternal Mind; the omnipotent, omnipresent, and omniscient Numen; beyond all worlds, whose essential nature is indeed THE MYSTERY, hidden in the unmanifest beyond the approachable scrutiny of our finite comprehension.

The Ordo Arcanorum Gradalis Is Ditheistic

From this highest level of the Deity's causal generation emanates the most exalted *personas* of the manifest Divinity in its feminine and masculine aspects of cosmic polarity pre-eminently embodied as *Goddess* and *God*. This is the dual nature of the Deity most revered by the Craft. It is by means of these dual personas that the incomprehensible Deity assumes the characteristics of interrelational personality by which communion with the cosmic orders of its created intelligences is made possible. Goddess and God in turn have three levels of emanation: the *physical*, the *psychic*, and the *pneumatic*, which will be examined in more detail later.

The Ordo Arcanorum Gradalis Is Polytheistic

On this third and closest level to the sphere of human existence, the distinct and sometimes separately distinguishable attributes of the Deity are prismatically reflected through the embodied filter of the collective unconscious (*archetypes*), elemental intelligences (*lesser deities* of wind, air, water, and earth), and human incarnations of Divinity (*saviors* and *avatars*). These various god/desses, spirits, and supernatural heroes are not worshipped in a high, exalted sense as much as they are venerated as channels and/or reservoirs of divine energies, or, as in the case of various dying and rising gods, incarnate microcosms of spiritual fullness; epiphanies of the Deity on a level closer to the grasp of human understanding.

The Ordo Arcanorum Gradalis Is Both Theistic and Panentheistic

The Ordo Arcanorum Gradalis is *theistic* in the sense that we perceive the supernal Deity as the essence of eternal reality and being, and the source of all that is; the preexisting cause of all manifestation. This concept is not new to Paganism. It was shared by many of the Greek philosophers of old, who "were all seeking after the One who was yet greater than the gods."[14]

As already discussed, pantheism is the belief that the universe itself is "God." However in contradistinction to this, both certain forms of Pagan theism and *panentheism* teach that the supernal Deity pervades all things, yet simultaneously *transcends* them:

> PANENTHEISM … The belief that the Being of God (sic) includes and penetrates the whole universe, so that every part of it exists in Him (sic), but (as against Pantheism, q.v.) that His (sic) Being *is more than, and is not exhausted by*, the universe.[15]

This is the essential difference between the two teachings of pantheism and panentheism.

When we say that the Deity pervades all things, we are teaching the doctrine of *immanence* (which we share in common with pantheism); the belief that the Deity is made known to us in and through all the manifested creation, including the wonder of our own personal being and the interior depths of its self-identity. The doctrine of immanence forever banishes the notion that the Divine Nature shares nothing in common with the physical cosmos, for from our standpoint, the universe itself was originated from within the creative mind of the Deity. Some have even gone so far as to intimate that the Goddess and God have somehow gone through a process of *cosmic incarnation* by which they exude Divinity through the creative activity of manifesting universal being.[16]

When we state that the Supreme Deity transcends the material universe (as its creator would logically have to do), we affirm, (in opposition to pantheism), that the essential qualities and attributes of the godhead are ultimately transcendent of the manifested cosmos, since the Divine Presence contains the entire expanse of the creation within itself. This, in simplified form, is known as the doctrine of *transcendence*.

This teaching was surprisingly well-expressed and embraced in an article appearing recently in a Neo-Pagan/Wiccan publication *The Silver Chalice*:

> The One exists in what It created, yet It also goes beyond that ...
>
> Embodied in all existence, Divinity goes beyond Its creation and can never be known in Its entirety. Yet because It exists in nature, nature reveals certain truths about It.[17]

There are many within the ranks of Neo-Paganism who have a knee-jerk, negative reaction to any kind of teaching which even hints of transcendence. It would appear that the main problem in this area is a confusion of the teaching of the transcendence of the Deity with the lopsided overemphasis upon a distorted doctrine of transcendence often espoused by the Church throughout its history. Many misconceptions regarding the real theological meaning of transcendence have arisen precisely because of our exposure in a predominantly Christian culture to the popular, pious exaggerations of God's "otherness" by the established Church.

For many, a Deity who is transcendent signifies a god/dess shrouded in remoteness, aloofness, and detached distance from the world of humanity. This, however, is an unfortunate misunderstanding based upon the Church's attempt to make people feel a sense of acute alienation from the Deity in order to solidify the power of the ecclesiastical hierarchy as exclusive mediators of salvation for a fallen and sinful race. But in reality, *transcendence has to do with the infinite extent of the being and consciousness of Deity*. It has nothing to do with a huffy "attitude problem" on the part of the God/dess towards us! *Immanence, on the other hand, has to do with the interior and immediate proximity of the presence of Deity*. For lack of a better pair of terms, it can be inferred that transcendence describes the *macrocosmic* aspects of divinity, whereas immanence has reference to the means by which the Deity manifests within the *microcosmic* levels of existence. To have one without the other is like imagining Yin being complete without Yang, or the Goddess without the God. From the teaching standpoint of the Ordo Arcanorum Gradalis, the key to this issue is the concept of a BALANCED Deity. It is an old occult axiom that manifested evil is, in actuality, unbalanced force. To deprive the Divine Nature of either transcendence or immanence would be to create in our conceptualizations a truly imbalanced Deity which can only give rise to distorted perceptions of divinity. A perfect example can be seen in the effect of the Church's overemphasis upon transcendence as virtually the primary attribute of Deity. This in turn gave rise to all sorts of popular misconceptions of a remote God "out there" who couldn't really get close to us. But an exclusive emphasis in the other direction, proclaiming immanence as the sole ontological attribute of Deity, can only in turn give rise to the gross theological mutation of the quintessential Deity deprived of the basic attributes which inspire us to both awe and reverence: omnipresence, omniscience, and omnipotence. As already described above, the God/dess of pantheism is both incomplete and imbalanced, having no sense of multidimensional wholeness, being held captive by a finite universe beyond which it can neither perceive nor transcend.

For others, transcendence is totally unnecessary as a descriptive appellation of the Divine Nature, since from a pantheistic viewpoint, the Deity is manifested exclusively as immanent being. But this assumption also has its pitfalls and limitations.

In Pagan theism as well as pan<u>en</u>theism, we do not confuse the creation with its creative source, as does pantheism. We readily acknowledge that we and the entire universe are the conceptual and generative offspring of divine origination, brought forth through the instrumentality of the Goddess and the God as agents of the Supernal Deity's creative intentions. It is true that there are some Neo-Pagans and Wiccans who have a problem in accepting the idea of a god/dess who actually *created* the cosmic boundaries of physical and finite reality, because they can readily understand that the very act of creation implies an inherent transcendence above and beyond that which is created. Acceptance of a Deity who creates the dimensions, form, and substance of the universe would therefore necessarily puncture the logic of their commitment to an exclusively immanence-oriented pantheism. But the acceptance of a transcendent, creating Deity posed no problem for most ancient Pagans, as can be discerned in the following quote from the Stoic Balbus: "For what can be more clear and manifest, when we observe the heavens and contemplate the heavenly bodies, than that there exists some divinity of supreme intelligence by whom these are governed?"[18] However, we need to underscore the fact that the act of creation is not antithetical to a belief in divine immanence, for, in reality, *creation is a PROCESS OF MANIFESTATION by which the Goddess and God incarnate a measure of their infinite intelligence and intricate energies into the very warp and woof of the substantive universe.* Seen from this vantage point, the Deity involved in the act of cosmic creation can no longer be validly challenged as an obstacle to the simultaneous acceptance of immanence within the divine attributes. From this perspective, it is actually the attribute of transcendence which enables the Deity to creatively mould the form and fashion of the material cosmos as a channel for its own transformation from the invisible transcendent to the visible immanent.

On the other hand, pantheism has no teaching of transcendence because it has no concept of actual Deity in any intrinsic sense. In fact, it has been described by some theologians as simply another form of material atheism:

> … The popular definition (of pantheism) does not go beyond the etymology of the word, God is all, or the all is God; but this defines nothing until we know either what God is, or what the all is. If the universe is material,

taking matter in its ordinary sense, then according to this definition God is matter, *or, what is the same thing, there is no God*; if, on the other hand, the universe is spirit, then God is spirit and matter is only an illusion. There is, then, no material universe, and what we call matter is only appearance, the image or shadow of Being. Hence two classes of Pantheists wholly distinct from each other, the material and the spiritual. *The one is without a real God, the other has only a phenomenal world.*[19]

Obviously, neither alternative within the pantheistic framework is very palatable for those who perceive the construct of reality as an interpenetration of dimensions woven with threads of spirit and material substance into the fabric which makes up the tapestry of cosmic existence.

... pantheism is merely naturalism provided with a religious flavour by the description of the whole system of finite things as being necessary and divine ... *Naturalistic pantheism, of course, is merely an undeclared variety of atheism.* The remedy for ... pantheism is a rational recognition, both of the experienced reality of finite things, and of the validity of the inference from them to infinite being; then we are able to preserve a right balance between the complementary truths of the divine immanence and the divine transcendence.[20]

Further elaborating upon this vein of thought, one theologian perceptibly wrote:

No more is there any reason to regard as irreconcilable the coexistence of the divine immanence and transcendence. It is rather to be affirmed that they are as inseparable as distinct. The immanence is but the complement of the transcendence. Immanence without transcendence would be effect virtually without cause. Transcendence without immanence would be cause without corresponding effect. (He goes on to say that a balanced theism) thus stands for the valid unification of the immanent and transcendent in the divine Personality which is revealed in nature as we know it, and therefore presumably throughout the universe beyond our knowledge. Hence it is ... saved from the disabilities which attach to the pantheistic suggestion of an impersonal and therefore insufficient deity the God (sic) who was identical with nature (the concept of pantheism) could be no more truly divine than a God helplessly severed from nature (the concept of Enlightment Deism). The unity of nature, in the widest reach accessible to our observation, is but the expression of the will of God (sic) who is at once in nature and beyond nature. The in-ness and the beyond-ness are both alike manifestations of the divine, even though the one to us is visible and the other invisible. So far as our vision extends, God (sic) is at once the distinct Source of nature's grandest unified totality, and the everpresent secret spring of its minutest workings. *Thus one may venture upon the suggestion, nor would less be true, that nature is but the unified totality of the sphere of which God Himself (sic) is alike centre and radii, circumfer-*

ence and contents. Analogy confessedly fails, but the reality to which it imperfectly points endures. "In Him, we live and move and have our being." (Quotation from an early Pagan poet.)[21]

We therefore see that from a Pagan theistic/panentheistic perspective, there is no real need to perceive immanence and transcendence as two incompatible theological beliefs, since both are complementary to one another; immanence being the internal manifestation of divinity within the cosmic spectrum of multileveled, interior realities, and transcendence being the trans-spatial limitlessness of the infinite Numen which by its nature and consciousness is not capable of being contained.

The Three Levels of Emanation

As stated previously, the Ordo Arcanorum Gradalis teaches that there are three distinct levels by which both the Goddess and the God reveal the mysteries of the divine, ontological reality to our finite comprehensions by means of the *physical*, the *psychic*, and the *pneumatic* levels of emanation.

The Goddess

In Her *physical* or *terrestrial* emanation, She is the Mother of the Earth, infusing Her very life into the planet itself with all of its myriad forces and sentient forms: the winds, the crash of ocean waves, the cyclic parade of passing seasons, the mysteries of life and death, and all the rest of the kaleidoscopic profusion that constitutes the totality of our physical environment, pure and unrefined from the bounty of the Mother of all Nature. In this we see and sense the geological, geographical, and biological pervasiveness of the animating presence of the Goddess throughout the Earth, which is, in a sense, analogous as Her incarnate body in the realm of the physical. It is important to note here that we do not pantheistically worship the Earth itself, but the spirit of the Goddess, who, through the creative processes of the cosmic Logos, materialized this whirling globe as a planetary habitation for Her presence.

In Her *psychic* or *celestial* emanation, She is the Lunar Goddess; the Moon being a symbol of all that is intuitive, magickal, and filled with occult mystery. It is this particular self-revelation of the Goddess which so captured the imagination of the ancients, even as it does today in countless covens and groves where the names of Diana, Selene, and Hekate are invoked beneath the silver light of the swift-sailing Moon. The almost overwhelming tidal swell of interest in the realms of the occult and the desire for psychic experiences is the symptomatic manifestation of our patriarchal society's unconscious yearning for a relationship with the Goddess. For it is through the channels of ESP and the inexplicable, intuitive discernment exercised from time to time in our daily experiences that the Goddess makes known to us that corresponding spark of Her presence within our own psyche. It is through Her psychic communication with us that we begin to see ourselves as more than mere mortals who through Her guidance can pass beyond the limitations of the five physical senses. Through Her psychic communion with us, the Goddess strengthens our sense of hidden realities and sacred mysteries yet to be explored.

In Her *pneumatic* or *cosmic* emanation, the Goddess is seen in our tradition as Hagia Sophia, Holy Wisdom, the Shekinah of the Presence. This we perceive to be the highest vibratory revelation of the Lady, and as such, it is the primary focus of our worship, for on this level of being, She communes with us, spirit to spirit as the immanent breath of life, the wind of the most holy (i.e., the Holy Spirit). In Her pneumatic epiphany, She subsumes all of Her other aspects under this all-encompassing glory as the Shekinah-Sophia, the feminine manifestation of the Cosmic Christ, known to many of the Gnostics as the Bride of the Logos.

> Sophia is within Herself the Holy Spirit, insightful, unique yet manifold … almighty and all-surveying … she pervades and permeates all things … Sophia is the breath of the power of the Ultimate, a pure emanation of Its glory. She is a reflection of the eternal Light. She is indeed more splendid than the sun, and She outshines all the constellations.[22]

The God

In His *physical* or *terrestrial* emanation, the God is revealed as the Horned One (horns being symbolic of virility), the regenerative and fertilizing life-force who ever seeks to spill the seed of His vital energies into the waiting womb of Nature, teeming with unlimited potentialities for growth and development. Through His presence in the natural order, we see through the God's example that sexuality is a celebration of life and an act of creative consummation, a sacrament of sensual self-awareness by which the species perpetuate their continued survival. As the God of sexuality and life, His presence in our world carries with it the imprinted stamp of divine approval upon the very nature of that which constitutes the physical or material plane of existence. Unlike other religious traditions, Wicca does not see the physical as something to be degraded, but rather as a vehicle for enhancing our incarnational enjoyment of life itself.

In His *psychic* or *celestial* emanation, the God is symbolized as the Solar Lord; the radiance of religious revelation inspiring us with a greater hunger for knowledge, understanding, and personal truth. The horns of His terrestrial form are on this higher level transformed into the unveiling and emanating rays of the Sun of Righteousness.[23] It is on the plane of this celestially psychic level that all male saviors, avatars, and redeemers reveal the compassion and self-sacrificial love of the Deity in their many guises as the sacrificed Dying and Rising God.

In His *pneumatic* or *cosmic* emanation, the God is revealed as the primordial Word, the eternal Logos, who through His creative utterance brings forth into substantive form the plans and projections of Shekinah-Sophia, the continuously self-generating wisdom of the Deity. She is the architect of the universe, conceiving the cosmos in its origination as the blueprint of the Divine Idea. But it is the God as Logos, the masculine manifestation of the Cosmic Christ, who translates these pristine ideas from the infinite source into the constructs of creation's form and substance as its master builder.

Conclusion

Seen from these perspectives, the Goddess and the God are not mere poetic metaphors for existence itself. They are, rather, a multileveled manifestation of the quintessential Deity, the divine Mind, the Source of all being. The Goddess and God are revelatory windows, as it were, through which we catch fleeting and often fragmentary glimpses into the nature of THE MYSTERIUM TREMENDUM. They are the personas by which the Deity makes itself known to us through the relational dynamics intelligible to human, finite consciousness. For these reasons, the major thrust of the rituals and worship of the Ordo Arcanorum Gradalis is to prepare ourselves for the presence of the holy which they so profoundly convey. In order to accomplish this most effectively, we must be prepared to understand the sequence of steps necessary for the implementation of an effective worship which accomplishes its magick through inner transformation of the human spirit. These steps will be explored in the next chapter entitled "The Wisdom of Worship."

Footnotes

1. It has been argued by some that, in reality, Christianity is actually a veiled form of tritheism because of its emphasis on God as a Trinity of Divine Persons.
2. Earthwind. "Witchcraft—A Viewpoint," *The Grove of the Goddess*, Vol. 2, No. 1 (Highland Springs, Virginia: October, 1989), p. 17.
3. Harold R. Willoughby, *Pagan Regeneration*. (Chicago, IL: The University of Chicago Press, 1929), p. 4. (Emphasis mine.)
4. Otter and Morning Glory Zell. "Who on Earth Is the Goddess?" *Green Egg*, Vol. XXIII, No. 89 (Ukiah, California: Beltane, 1990), pp. 6-8.
5. "Systems of Religious and Spiritual Belief," *The New Encyclopedia Britannica*, 15th Edition, Vol. 26 (Chicago, IL: 1990), p. 570.

6. *Assyrian and Babylonian Literature, Selected Translations*. (D. Appleton and Co., 1901), p. 434. (Emphasis mine.)

7. Barbara G. Walker. "Isis," *The Woman's Encyclopedia of Myths and Secrets*. (San Francisco, CA: Harper & Row, 1983), p. 453.

8. John Hunt, D.D., *Pantheism and Christianity*. (Port Washington, New York: Kennikat Press, 1884; reissued 1970), p 38.

9. Timothea. "The Other Gods," *Panegyria* (The Newsletter of the Aquarian Tabernacle Church), Vol. 6, No. 5 (Seattle, Washington: Samhain, 1989), p. 9. (Emphasis mine.)

10. Robert Engleman. "Author Examines Greenhouse Effect," *Richmond Times-Dispatch* (Richmond, Virginia: October 22, 1989), D-5.

11. See Caitlin and John Matthews, *The Western Way, Volume II—The Hermetic Tradition*. (Boston, MA: Arkana, 1986).

12. Javier Teixidor, *The Pagan God—Popular Religion in the Greco-Roman Near East*. (Princeton, NJ: Princeton University Press, 1977), pp. 13-17.

13. Ashi. "Ritual Ways: Wildcroft Coven," *The Silver Chalice*, Vol. I, Issue III (Thorofare, New Jersey; December, 1990), p. 19.

14. Hunt, p. 51.

15. *The Oxford Dictionary of the Christian Church*. Ed. by F.L. Cross. (Oxford University Press, 1974), p. 1027. Used by permission of Oxford University Press.

16. M.B. Wulf. "A Mystery of Grain and Grape," *Hallows*, Vol. 2, No. 4 (Glen Allen, Virginia: Lammas, 1990), p. 15.

17. Ashi, p. 19.

18. David Rokeah, *Jews, Pagans and Christians in Conflict*. (Jerusalem: The Magnes Press, The Hebrew University, E.J. Brill, 1982), p. 84. Quoted from Cicero's *De natura deorum*, 2, 2:4.

19. Hunt, p. 1. (Emphasis mine.)

20. D.J.B. Hawkins, *The Essentials of Theism*. (New York, NY: Sheed and Ward, 1950), pp. 108-109. (Emphasis mine.)

21. Frank Ballard, D.D., *The True God—A Modern Summary of the Relations of Theism to Naturalism, Monism, Pluralism, and Pantheism*. (London: Robert Culley, 1907), pp. 155-157. (Emphasis mine.)

22. Loosely adapted from Wisdom 7:22-29, *Holy Bible*.

23. See, for instance, the pictorial reliefs of Aton, the unique solar deity worshipped by Pharaoh Amenhotep IV, shown with life-giving rays radiating from the orb of the god with extended hands at their tips which reached the earth—a symbol of divine benevolence and loving preservation of the Creation.

Chapter Three

The Wisdom of Worship

or most people the idea of "going to worship" conjures up the not-too-appealing vision of sitting in uncomfortable pews on Sunday morning, made fidgety by a boring sermon, and counting the minutes until the final benediction and the recessional hymn. Worship, for many, is purely a matter of "putting in your time" at the local church. This, at least, is the case for multitudes of nominal Christians.

On the other hand, for those in the varied and often confusing spectrum of the Neo-Pagan movement, the word "worship" has sort of an ambiguous atmosphere about it, when and if it is ever used. For many Wiccans and other Neo-Pagans, to worship is synonymous with conducting a circle ceremony. In essence, for many of them, worship has come to be seen as simply another synonym for ritual. Worship as the outgrowth or intensification of one's personal relationship with the God/dess is an almost non-existent concept in some Neo-Pagan traditions. Unfortunately, for a significant number of Wiccans, worship does not enter into their theology at all for the simple reason that the gods are seen as mere symbolic abstracts or power sources to be tapped into via ritual means. In other words, the God and Goddess, even in their highest form, still have no "actual" existence in objective reality, or if they do, they are so remote as to make worship useless.[1] So for a growing percentage of Wiccans, the concept of actually "worshipping" the Deity is pointless and primitive. This, however, poses an interesting problem: a religion without worship is not a religion at all! "*Religion* ... belief in and reverence for a supernatural power recognized as the creator and governor of the universe ... *worship* ... the reverent love and allegiance accorded a deity ... "[2] Therefore, Neo-Pagans who insist on calling their beliefs (or lack thereof) the practice of the "Old Religion," yet see reverence and worship as a superfluous embarrassment for modern minds, put themselves squarely in the quandary of a self-contradiction.

For the Ordo Arcanorum Gradalis, worship is the central focus of our spiritual aspirations. Something stated in the first chapter of this book, "The Ordo Arcanorum Gradalis: Overview of an Order," is so important that it bears repeating here:

> Our primary focus is upon the value of worship itself as the preeminent tool for rekindling an awareness of the very essence of Deity lying dormant within us. In this tradition, worship is perceived as being the highest manifestation of magick; a means of self-transformation by which we amplify our sense of connectedness with the ultimate Divinity.

In order to properly worship, we must first have a sense of the *reality* of who we worship. This is where some contemporary "post-Wiccans" have "thrown the baby out with the bath water" by denying the place of the supernatural in their construct of ultimate reality. Wise seekers of the holy, however, know the dangers of such presumption:

> Never, ever, take the Gods, Goddesses, angels, powers, or any of these invisible forces for granted, THEY ARE REAL, and though the forms we perceive them in may not be their own true shape (for we are no longer trained to see them as they are), the powers of life and death, change and decay they wield are enormous. We cannot stand against them, any more than we can command the Sun to stand still or the seasons change to suit our whim.[3]

The prerequisite for worship is a belief in the power and reality of the unseen world. Without such a faith or openness to the possibility of the Deity's existence, the Old Religion becomes a sham; a pretense of ritualistic piety apart from the substance of genuine spirituality, reminiscent of the Christian apostle Paul's reference to those "who have a form of godliness, but deny the power thereof."[4]

In the teachings of our Order, the magick of transformative worship is accomplished through adherence to a series of successive steps which lead ultimately to a personal transformation which places one upon the threshold of growth into god/desshood. These steps consist of *adoration, absorption, assimilation,* and *apotheosis*. We will now proceed to examine these aspects in greater detail.

Adoration

Adoration is the cornerstone and essential ingredient of all true religion. It is the only means by which we can express the awe-filled sensation of being in the presence of that which is far greater than our own isolated island of individual consciousness; the presence of the infinite and the holy. On a secondary level, adoration is the means by which we channel our honor, veneration, and sense of spiritual mystification to the Deity which manifests the sacred aura of the numinous. Apart from adoration, any pretense of religion becomes an empty show:

> To exclude adoration, to say that adoration does not, or should not, form any part of worship, seems alike contrary to the very meaning of the word "worship" and to be at variance with a large and important body of the facts recorded in the history of religion. The courts of a god are customarily entered with the praise which is the outward expression of the feeling of adoration with which the worshippers spiritually gaze upon the might and majesty of the god whom they approach … Even to polytheists, the god who is worshipped at the moment, is, at that moment, one than whom there is no one, and nought, greater, *quo nihil maius*. A god who should not be worshipped thus—a god who was not the object of adoration—would not be worthy of the name, and would hardly be called a god … Worship without adoration is worship only in name, or rather is no worship at all. Only with adoration can worship begin: "hallowed be Thy name" expresses the emotion with which all worship begins, even where the emotion has not yet found the words in which to express itself.[5]

Adoration is the first step on the spiritual stairway of self-transformation, for it is a most effective means of acknowledging that our own egos are not the center of the sentient universe. Through adoration the consciousness of one's self bends the knee of voluntary reverence and interior speechlessness before the Divine theophany which has indelibly touched the heart-strings of the human spirit. It is an attitude of heart and soul that spontaneously pours forth from the inner wellsprings of the spirit which has to any degree been exposed to a personal revelation of godhead, irrespective of its forms, names, or visionary nature.

Adoration is also a personal expression of love. Adoration cannot rise from the heart of one who has never had a personal vision of the universal splendor of the spirit. It is just such experiences which have opened up the portals of inner sight enabling one to behold, in some veiled way, the manifested awesomeness which radiates from the interior essence of Divinity. An excellent example of this is found in one of the penned prayers of Lucius of Patrae, a first-century devotee of Isis, whose prayerful meditations had led him into an experiential revelation of the Goddess; a sense of being overwhelmed by the wonderment of Her loving care for the world and a corresponding desire on his part to be a channel for Her praise and worship.

O Thou holy and eternal Savior of the human race … Thou bestowest a mother's tender affections on the misfortunes of unhappy mortals … Thou dispellest the storms of life and stretchest forth Thy right hand of salvation, by which Thou unravelest even the inextricably tangled web of Fate … Thou turnest the earth in its orb; Thou givest light to the sun; Thou rulest the world; Thou treadest Death underfoot. To Thee the stars are responsive; by Thee the seasons turn and the gods rejoice and the elements are in subjection … I am too feeble to render Thee sufficient praise … but, a pious though poor worshipper, I shall essay to do all within my power; Thy divine countenance and most holy deity I shall guard and keep forever hidden in the secret place of my heart.[6]

This kind of experience was, of course, replicated in the lives of other sages and saints whose personal encounters with the Divine were awe-full moments which graphically enhanced a personal sense of insignificance and inadequacy when confronted with the numinous and the holy. Isaiah, upon seeing an exalted vision of Yahweh "high and lifted up" was reduced to speechlessness and an incomprehensible sense of dread at being in the presence of the Divine. Arjuna, upon seeing the infinite godhead revealed in Krishna, was affected in a similar way.[7]

Awe is the essence of all adoration. That before which we do not stand in awe, we cannot adore. As contemporary Pagans, this should make us stop and think: How much in awe are we of the God and Goddess to whom we pay ritualized lip service within the confines of our circles? Have we become too cavalier and presumptuous in the way we approach the altar of our deities? If we do not view them as realities from another dimension of time and space, we cannot take them seriously. If we don't take them seriously, adoration is impossible, and our religion is a palpable falsehood. It is ironic that in this time when it is becoming the fashion of New Age trendiness to go on a "vision quest" for one's personal totem animal or magickal name, etc. through the agency of commercialistic, pseudo-shamanic seminars, we are all but neglecting the greatest vision quest of all: the personal search for the experience of the holy which emanates from the very heart of godhead.[8]

But how does one enter into an experiential apprehension of the Deity which elicits an involuntary reaction of amazement and incredulous awe? There are many avenues to the realization of this experience: seeking out the wondrous works of creation; those unbelievably intricate designs of DNA and atomic particles as well as the mind-boggling patterns of a blossoming wildflower or the vast expanse of interstellar space. We need to take time to meditate on the marvels all around us, asking the Goddess to open up our hearts to an attitude of thanksgiving and wonderment at the almost incomprehensible magnificence of it all, and most especially, the concept-shattering awesomeness of the Lady and Lord who spun the threads of existence into the cloth of the material cosmos. But we should not stop there. The Goddess and the God as dual faces of the Deity are found not only in the intricacies of Nature, but also in the high ceremonials of all the Earth's religions. For us, being surrounded in Western culture as we are with the predominant influence of Judaism and Christianity, it might serve us spiritually to temporarily put aside our prejudices and disagreements with church and synagogue, and take the time on a Sunday morning to attend the most elaborate High Mass we can find (usually the best examples can be found in Greek Orthodox, High Anglican, or certain Catholic parishes which allow for the celebration of the Tridentine Mass in Latin), or on a Friday night seek out a Jewish service complete with the melodious chanting of the cantor. We can make up our mind to attend with our spirit open to the voice of the Goddess and God as they begin to show us the manifestation of their presence, even in the midst of the most patriarchal of religions. If we can make the attempt to try and capture a little of what the earliest founders and the later mystics of these religions became enraptured over in their spiritual ecstasies, we will begin to touch the edges of numinous experience which eventually issues forth in an inner attitude of awe and adoration of the ultimate Deity as manifested through the many guises of Goddess and God.

We can also seek out the holy places of the ancients still extant in the land around us. If we live in Britain, the time-defying mysteries of the standing stones can powerfully convey to us the power of the gods which was recognized and celebrated by the builders of these ancient shrines and observatories. The same holds true with those of us who inhabit the American continent, where the sleeping vestiges of snake-like mounds in the Midwest and South, as well as the large ceremonial kivas of the almost forgotten Indian inhabitants of the old Southwest can permeate our consciousness with a sense of the reverence with which the peoples of the past paid homage to their deities.

Of course, all of us do not live in close proximity to the spectacular ruins of ancient religious edifices. But the land is always haunted by the psychic energies of people's past adoration and worship. It might be profitable if we seek to tune in to those remnants of Native Indian reverence which invisibly reside in the morning mists of country meadows, the dark stillness of subterranean caves long silent from the last chants of worship to the Earth Mother, and the breeze-blown plains where the Great Spirit was invoked in purity of heart.

The opportunities for us to seek out the presence of the Goddess and God all around us are limited only by our own imagination. In the words of the most famous Hebrew teacher, "Seek and you shall find, knock and the door shall be opened to you."[9] We need to ask the Goddess in Her revelatory aspect as Sophia and the God in His manifesting aspect as the Logos to implant in our spirit a desire to delve more deeply into the depths of the Divine Nature. It is the answer to this request which will undoubtedly lead us into the presence of the holy before which our speechlessness shall turn into unutterable yearnings for the ability to express our adoration which we will find spontaneously welling up from the sanctuary of our soul.

Absorption

When we worship the deities, we are thereby acknowledging that they possess both archetypal and quintessential qualities of personhood that far surpass any similar qualities within ourselves which are mere pale reflections in comparison. The Goddess and God, then, in their numerous guises and manifestations, are the collective embodiment of all the essential and definitive attributes which in their totality constitute the epitome of perfection, balance, and harmony toward which we should strive if we are to in any way walk in the footsteps of the deities who have preceded us in the magickal landscape of history and mythology.

In order to walk the seldom-trod path towards god/desshood, one must determine to do more than try and imitate the attributes of the deities. Imitation is exactly that: imitation—not the real thing. Divine attributes cannot be authentically imitated any more than an orange can imitate an apple. The key to developing one's potential god/desshood lies in the secret of *absorption*. In the Ordo Arcanorum Gradalis, our goal is to literally transfer or extend the essence of divine attributes from the Deity to the worshipper by means of exposing ourselves to the blessings, promises, and mystery-sacraments of the gods and goddesses which have been made available to us in the numerous religio-magickal systems of antiquity. How do we do this? It is not an overnight process, nor is it a procedure which guarantees instant transformation. It is a way of life which must be developed and cultivated through praise, prayer, study, meditation, and discipline.

One of the first steps towards the absorption of the divine attributes is a personal commitment to intensive study of the myths and sacred stories which give us the most vivid pictures of the god/desses to whose character and spiritual traits we are most drawn. As is often the case among many nominal Neo-Pagans, individuals tend to use the names of various deities in their invocations and ritual enactments without any real appreciation or knowledge of their essential nature and individual uniquenesses. While it is admirable to have a fair-to-thorough knowledge of the many pantheons now being resurrected from ancient cultures and history for the purposes of Neo-Pagan ritual, it is far more needful for our inner spiritual transformation that we begin to seek the cultivation of a *personal relationship* with the deities towards whom we are most drawn in our devotions. This requires time and diligence, but the end result will be the ability to more accurately *visualize* and *commune* with these god/desses through meditation and prayer.

Secondly, we need to study the spoken words of the Goddess and God in their many manifestations as they have been recorded through the mediumship and sensitive receptivity of the ancient mystics. Examples of this can be found in the mystery cult of Isis, which preserved certain sayings and promises of the Goddess which were meant for the instruction and edification of the faithful. The traditional Charge of the Goddess is also a good source for such current revelations of Goddess-speak. (The Bible is not the only source of divine promises!) The more we become familiar with the sacred sayings and recorded myths which formed the nucleus of the Pagan Mysteries, the more we will be exposed to the formulas for self-transformation inherent in the promises of the gods.

If we exhaustively begin to research for every piece of information we can find on a particular aspect of the goddess or god to which we are attracted, we will find that our times of meditation will slowly become extended moments of spiritual *communion* with that specific deity. The more we commune with them, we will find that our own spirit will begin to psychically absorb the attributes radiating from the presence of these god/desses. This will initiate a process of transformation alluded to by Paul, the apostle of the Christians, who no doubt had been influenced in this understanding by his exposure to the Hellenistic mystery cults:

> And we, who with unveiled faces all contemplate the Lord's glory, are being *transformed into his likeness* with ever-increasing glory, which comes from the Lord, who is the Spirit.[10]

From his standpoint, absorption of the actual "glory" of the Lord (i.e., the very extension and intensity of the being of the Deity) was an essential by-product of the act of worship. Worship is not just some religious exercise to appease the inflated ego of the the Goddess and God; it is, rather, the means by which we divest ourselves of spiritual blindness and progressively become aware of the light (glory) of the Deity radiating from within us as we invite the presence of the divinities which we have invoked to saturate us in an ever-expanding experience of spiritual union.

Worship itself is a form of deep meditation (notice Paul's usage of the word "contemplate" in the above passage) that facilitates one's psychic saturation with the spirit of the deity which is visualized. Initially, it begins with the classic "I/Thou" relationship within the lower consciousness; gradually it progresses to a point where the infinity of spirit consciousness overshadows the finite comprehension of the worshipper, resulting in a high psychic transfusion of energy, substance, and thought from god/dess to mortal. The end product of this process, if followed to its ultimate culmination, is the *divinization of human nature* to the extent that mere mortals are eventually transformed into virtual *incarnations of various aspects of the Goddess and God.* This is why it is so important for us to conceive of worship as a process where we open ourselves to the high spirit realm, absorbing the presence of the ultimate Deity through the meditative invocation of the various attributes and aspects of gods and goddesses, conversational prayer, and sacramental ritual where the presence of the Divine is Eucharistically invoked.

Assimilation

The purpose of the ancient mysteries was not a goal of "being good" in order to attain immortality. It was, rather, a blueprint for the divinization of human nature through identification with the god or goddess which was the focus of the cult.

It is the human spirit which instinctively reaches out during times of worship to absorb the emanations from the psyche of the gods, but the only means by which the effects of their influence can be made tangibly manifest in our everyday life is through the process of *assimilation*. Assimilation relates directly to the influence of these emanating attributes of the deities upon conscious thought and behavior. For instance, if we venerate Thoth, our spirit (to the extent of its receptivity) will begin to absorb the qualities of his nature when he is invoked, but we will not be able to literally walk in his wisdom in everyday situations until our spirit has the time to allow the filtering down of Thoth's attributes into the conscious mind for practical application.

It is also in the process of assimilation that worship takes its most tangible form as an expression of words and deeds which reflect the higher Goddess attributes resident within the individual psyche as a result of the earlier steps of adoration and absorption. In this way, personal behavior will be transformed, not by a set of external rules designed to suppress the impulses of our baser nature, but by an inner transformation of the human spirit initiated by the deities through the transformed residue of their nature residing within us. This is, in reality, a process of *incarnational transmutation* through which aspects of the very nature of the Goddess and God are indelibly imprinted into the essence of the human psyche. The more often we meditatively contemplate the Goddess and God through their various spiritual apparitions and aspects, to the same extent we will be conforming ourselves to divine patterns which we will begin to reflect as we become continuously exposed to the nature of the god or goddess whose presence we invoke in worship. This is especially true as we become more acutely tuned in to ritual dynamics within the ceremonial circle as a result of this absorption-assimilation process. We will discover that our words and actions within a ritual context will sound and appear more like the gods themselves because of our progressive, on-going incarnation of their attributes.

Apotheosis

The ultimate, transformative goal of personal worship is *apotheosis*—attainment unto god/desshood, when we in actuality become a *fully* incarnate extension of the very nature of Deity which has been the focus of our adoration. While this is not impossible to attain within one's lifetime, it is, however, usually assumed that such individual transmutation into an exalted state of divinity is either the product of a perfected condition resulting from multiple lifetimes of experience and soul-progression, or else from further learning and advancement in the spirit-world after death. In fact, more often than not, when the term "apotheosis" is used, it is usually in the context of ancient victims of human sacrifice (especially Sacred Kings), who, upon their death were believed to ascend to the mount of the gods, having become a god themselves through their sacrificial transition to the life beyond. However, the most dynamic and exciting possibility is that apotheosis is the fulfillment of the entire process of worship itself, beginning with those first, faint glimmers of adoration for the Deity welling forth from within the human breast. In point of fact, the hope held out by the Hellenistic mystery cults as exemplified by the devotions to Isis was the possibility of personal and spiritual identification with a living deity which would be so complete within the context of one's humanity that the devotee could legitimately be addressed in ritual as the god who was himself the focus of the mysteries. Speaking of the final ritual of initiation into the Isiac mysteries, Harold Willoughby writes:

> In the secret of the sanctuary the initiate participated in a repetition of the ancient drama, himself the central figure, the new Osiris whom Isis, by her power, exalted to an immortal regeneration ... *THIS WAS ESSENTIALLY A RITE OF DEIFICATION* ... *Hitherto he had been treated as a human being. Now he was regarded as divine* ... Figuratively, the Isiac initiation was represented as a process of regeneration and initiates were referred to as men who had been reborn (*renati*). This was the regular cult formula. *Actually, the rites were believed to accomplish the transformation and divinization of human nature* ... Reborn through the rite of initiation, the mystic believed himself born again to a superhuman life, the immortal life of the gods.[11]

While very few of us would be so presumptuous as to assume that we have already arrived, or, for that matter, that we were even on the verge of personal deification; we do nevertheless, have held out to us as seekers of mystical truths, the potentiality for inner transformation in a continuing spiritual process which will increasingly conform us to one of the many sacred images of divinity reflected by the gods and goddesses of our varied pantheons.

Conclusion

The wisdom of worship lies in the discernment to perceive that in itself worship is not an act of religious piety, but a process of divine-human interaction by which the myriad sparks of spirit encapsulated in the human race can be reunited with the cosmic flame of Deity which is their source. For each individual this journey will be uniquely different. However, the insight which appreciates the essence of worship as a gift from the Goddess and God for both spiritual communion and consummation will inevitably result in substantive ceremonies and reverential ritual in the practice of the Craft. Worship will not be seen as a type of mere religious format, but as the life-blood of one's spirituality.

For those of us in the Ordo Arcanorum Gradalis, worship is made most personally present in the life of each individual when we seriously begin to implement a lifestyle of praise, study, and meditation as briefly outlined in this installment. Not that we wish to reduce the deep mysteries of the worship dynamic into some mechanistic simplicity, for at the heart of the essence of worship is love: the love of the seeker for the Lady and Lord, and their love returned, coming full circle in a completeness of Divine-human interaction. But when we begin to fully explore the ritual, mystical, and personal pathways of worship, we will begin to experience Goddess and God in a new sense of depth and relatedness. This is the goal of the Ordo Arcanorum Gradalis and the high calling of every priest and priestess. To the extent that we respond to it, to that degree will we rend the heavens and draw down the Divine.

Footnotes

1. Margot Adler, *Drawing Down the Moon.* (Boston, MA: Beacon Press, 1986), pp. 126-127.

2. Copyright © 1985 by Houghton Mifflin Company. Reprinted by permission from *The American Heritage Dictionary, Second College Edition.*

3. Marian Green, *The Gentle Arts of Aquarian Magic.* (London: Thorsons [an imprint of HarperCollins Publishers Ltd.], 1987), pp. 140-142.

4. 2 Timothy 3:5, *Holy Bible.*

5. Frank B. Jevons, *The Idea of God in Early Religions.* (Cambridge University Press, 1910), pp. 108-109.

6. Barbara G. Walker. "Isis," *The Woman's Encyclopedia of Myths and Secrets.* (San Francisco, CA: Harper & Row, 1983), p. 453.

7. Isaiah 6:1-8, *Holy Bible.*
   The Bhagavad Gita, Chapter 11.

8. Rudolph Otto, *The Idea of the Holy.* (Oxford University Press, 1950).

9. Luke 11:9, *Holy Bible.*

10. 2 Corinthians 3:18 (NIV, margin), *Holy Bible.*

11. Harold Willoughby, *Pagan Regeneration.* (Chicago, IL: University of Chicago Press, 1929), pp. 190, 191, 192, 194. (Emphasis mine.)

Chapter Four

The Christ and the Craft

ot long ago, one of the fledgling groves within our Order under-
went a drastic upheaval resulting in the exodus of a majority of
those novices and students who were considering becoming affiliated with our tradition. The reason for this frenzied flight from the
group was their exposure to the celebration of the liturgy of the
Grail Mass, the most potent and exalted liturgy of the Ordo
Arcanorum Gradalis; but a liturgy nevertheless which includes three references to
the Christ: once as "The Cosmic Christ," once as "Jesu, the Suffering Servant," and
once as "The Crucified God."[1] For them, any reference to Jesus or the Christ sent
chills of fear and apprehension down their spines. Never mind that these references
to the Christ were always interspersed among the names of the other dying and rising gods of ancient Paganism, Jesus simply being included in the liturgy as the culmination and ultimate synthesis of all that these gods represented in their highest
attributes and mythic foreshadowings.

This underscores one thing unique to this tradition of the Grail Quest: we
have not been afraid to incorporate within our rituals certain mystic aspects of the
mythic Christ. The Ordo Arcanorum Gradalis is not anti-Christ or anti-Christian
because we understand that in its proper esoteric context, Christianity is a relevant
and valid path of the mysteries. (We are, however, totally at odds with the traditional, guilt-ridden shackles of the institutional Church and its narrow-minded

dogmas.) This is one reason we have little difficulty in using the Grail mythos directly, despite its many overt Christian trappings.

Modern Neo-Pagans generally seem to be very adept in assimilating pantheons, rituals, and concepts from nearly every Western religious path *except* Christianity. This we find to be rather unobjectively prejudicial. While realizing that the Church has historically been both politically and socially intolerant during the eras of its greatest power, that can in no way invalidate the truths of timeless mysticism which it possesses in the inner resources of its spiritual vitality. As a priesthood of the Grail, those within our Order can be just as comfortable with the Sun of Righteousness (Solar Hero/Christ) as we are with the Moon Maiden or Isis. It is just a matter of applying a truly Pagan eclecticism to what is valid and magickally helpful in Christianity as much as we do with all the other ancient faiths which Neo-Pagans and Wiccans have so blatantly raided in order to retrieve the treasures of their spiritual mysteries for the enrichment of their own newly formed traditions.

Yet the fact of the matter remains that many within the ranks of Neo-Paganism and Wicca are downright afraid of Jesus Christ. No matter how hard the modern Craft revival may try, it cannot escape the shadow of the Cross which pervades the spirituality of Western culture. Nor should it attempt to do so.

As related in the above incident, many Neo-Pagans' nerves get set on edge whenever the name of Jesus is mentioned; almost as if they would prefer to pretend that he just doesn't exist as a spiritual reality in our religious culture. Others even question the validity of anything within the pale of Christian mysticism.

Unfortunately, the anti-Christian bias of many individuals within the Craft is a symptom of their own unresolved conflicts and subsequent rebellion against the established Church of their upbringing. Actually, a lot of these people have not delved deeply into the eclecticism of authentic, historic Paganism which would enable them to see the wisdom of embracing the positive and uplifting aspects of the Christian mysteries along with the sacred stories of other cultures and ancient religions of both past and present. Instead, they are still so busy running from the Church that they have not had the time to truly embrace either Wicca or Neo-Paganism for reasons independent of their religious rebellion against Christianity. It is obvious that some have come to the Craft as a form of reactionism by which they are attempting to "get back at" the Church for all the hurt and unneeded guilt it has caused them in the past. By becoming involved in what is considered by many to be a counter-cultural fringe religious cult, they are hoping to reek revenge upon the many uninformed Christians around them through the sheer shock-effect of announcing their identity as Witches, knowing all the while that they will be perceived as dastardly "servants of the Devil." But we must keep in mind that if we are to ever truly grow spiritually, we must leave such negative motivations behind. Otherwise, many Wiccans and Neo-Pagans run the risk of degenerating into a perpetual, paranoid condition which can only be described as "Christophobia." Usually, this is symptomatic of their own inner confusion of the Christ with the authoritarian, hierarchical institution of our culture's ecclesiastical establishment. It is essential for them to make a distinction between the personage, identity, and myth of the Christ as opposed to the later oppressive tyranny of the historical Church, if this religiously parochial condition is to be rectified in a positive manner.

The Christ is the most potent archetypal figure of Western history and religion. Those who consider themselves to be part of the Craft of the Wise cannot afford to ignore his power and influence, nor should they let their knee-jerk reactions against fundamentalist narrow-mindedness create an artificial barrier between the complements of Pagan and Christian truths.

Many Wiccans seem to be under the mistaken impression that in order to be a Witch or a Pagan, they must either renounce or greatly distance themselves from the Christ. This is totally fallacious. Gerald Gardner himself, the founder of modern Wicca, declared just the opposite:

> It is usually said that to be made a witch one must abjure Christianity; this is not true; but they naturally would not receive into their ranks anyone who was a very narrow Christian. They do not think that the real Jesus was literally the Son of God, but are quite prepared to accept that he was one of the Enlightened Ones, or Holy Men. That is the reason why witches do not think they were hypocrites "in time of persecution" for going to church and honoring Christ, especially as so many of the old Sun-hero myths have been incorporated into Christianity; while others might bow to the Madonna, who is closely akin to their goddess of heaven.[2]

Doreen Valiente, another pioneer in the modern Craft revival, even related that she knew of one Wiccan priestess who had a picture of Jesus in her private sanctuary because of the honor and esteem in which she held him.[3] Another witch, interviewed by Margot Adler in her book *Drawing Down the Moon*, went so far as to declare her belief that the Christ was "an avatar of the Great Mother—a Dionysus incarnation," and she further stated her belief in the validity of the sacrificial character of the Mass, even to the extent that she would occasionally attend church in order to partake of the body and blood of the risen god.[4] This simply demonstrates that there are at least some within the Neo-Pagan and Wiccan communities who have attempted to come to terms with Jesus and his theological implications in their own personal walk of faith without resorting to negative rejection of anything that even hints at Christian influence. But alas, they do, nevertheless, seem to be in the minority.

In perhaps one of the most well thought out, yet concisely expressed comments on the Christ/Craft issue, well-known author Alan Richardson has penned some words which should give Christophobic Neo-Pagans pause for thought:

> It is a question, also, of whether we accept Jesus as *the* Son of God or a Son of Light. This in itself points out a peculiar advantage enjoyed by Pagans that not many of them realize: By regarding Jesus as a Son of Light—one

of many—they can actually work with and appreciate much of the Christian Mystery Tradition while at the same time they never need to surrender their own pantheons. Christians, on the other hand, must necessarily accept the exclusivity of their God, and are forever denied the use of Pagan altars. It was because the followers of the Old Religion saw in the image of Jesus another example of a Divine King and Sacrificed God that they were quite happy to let the new religion put down roots ... Jesus, as a Thorned God, was just one more in a long line of such beings ...[5]

For those purists who labor under the zealot-like conviction that for the Craft to be an authentic expression of the Old Religion it must never pollute its rites and ceremonies with anything of Christian origin, I would suggest a careful reading of Aidan Kelly's latest contribution to the history of the origins of modern Wicca entitled *Crafting the Art of Magic, Book I.* In it he proves how that nearly every ritual used by Gerald Gardner was taken directly from the grimoires of Judeo-Christian ceremonial magick; and only at a later time were the distinctly Christian elements of the conjurations deleted or revised.[6] So we can see that even the so-called "Old Religion" (as Kelly observes in his book, there is no concrete evidence that Wicca existed in any organized form prior to 1939) is greatly indebted to the influence and rituals of Christian occultism in the formation of its earliest Book of Shadows!

The identity of the real historical Jesus has both intrigued and obsessed scholars and theologians for centuries. But what is important from a contemporary Pagan perspective is to discern the difference between the dogmatic claims of the Church and the evidence of history regarding this greatest of all Hebrew teachers.

For fundamentalist Christians, the true identity of Jesus is easily solved by a simplistic application of Biblical "proof texts." In their minds, Jesus can only be defined on the basis of the words attributed to him within the canonical gospels of the New Testament. This naive, uncritical acceptance of these traditional utterances of Jesus makes their "research" for the truth quite easy. The fundamentalist oversimplification rests upon the bedrock of these sayings' assumed authenticity. Building upon this shaky foundation, they begin their argument along the lines of an either/or approach: "Either Jesus was telling the truth about himself (as recorded in the Gospels), or else you must accuse him of being a liar!" From this line of reasoning they conclude that any words attributed to him in the New Testament can be used as proof of his divinity, his messiahship, and his supposed status as the only way-shower to salvation. Such a superficial approach totally neglects the problem of which sayings of Jesus recorded in the Gospels can be considered authentic from the standpoint of valid Biblical scholarship and responsible textual criticism. Once authenticity has been established, *then* begins the job of adequately interpreting these sayings in light of the contemporary culture, society, and political atmosphere, as well as the religious climate of Jesus' day. This involves a lot more than opening up the Bible and pointing to a selected passage to "prove" something about the identity or divine nature of Jesus!

From a more responsible approach, the historical Jesus has been variously interpreted by scholars as being a reform-minded rabbi whose teachings were based loosely upon the more liberal Pharisaical traditions of first-century Judaism.[7] Others have seen him as an itinerant teacher who drew largely upon the mystical and magickal lore of the Essenes, Therapeuts, and other Egyptian esoteric sources.[8] Perhaps both are right in that Jesus was very possibly a charismatic character who combined the best of both religious sources into a uniquely attractive as well as controversial reform movement which threatened the complacency and entrenched political power of the Jewish rabbinical establishment, the ramifications of which eventually led to his crucifixion at the hands of the Roman authorities. Of course, many other theories about his life and death abound; some both fanciful and intriguing, including the one which asserts that Jesus did not die on the cross, but was revived and later traveled with Mary Magdalene and their child to the shores of southern France![9]

The fact of the matter is that we may never know the total truth. Contrary to the claims of the Church, Jesus was not some kind of omniscient demigod. He made mistakes in both judgement and prophetic calculation. He never claimed to be omniscient.[10] He made mistakes in judgement based upon the apocalyptic expectations of his day, assuming that he would return again in glory before the disciples had even finished preaching the Gospel in the surrounding towns of Israel![11] He no doubt saw himself as the fulfillment of various prophetic expectations which had infected the populace like a religious fever, and as a result he left an indelible imprint upon both the religious history of the Jewish people and the Western world.[12] Yet ironically, it would appear that Jesus' vision of the extent of his personal ministry did not extend beyond the boundaries of Israel itself.[13] Jesus believed that some of his disciples would never die until his second return.[14] He further declared at his own trial to the Jewish High Priest that he would see him coming again in the clouds of heaven.[15] Needless to say, the High Priest died without ever witnessing such a return.

None of these observations are meant to belittle either the intelligence or integrity of Jesus, but to establish that he was a product of his religious environment and had the same human limitations in judgement and foreknowledge as any other person. This, however, can in no way detract from the unique spiritual message which he conveyed in the course of his teaching ministry. Because of the unerasable imprint which he has made upon the history of the world through both word, deed, and the larger-than-life character of his dynamic personality, his followers understandably came to see in him the crystalization of a new composite image of the Deity which stressed the value and centrality of unconditional love ("For God so loved the world … ") as the undergirding foundation for all authentic religious experience and the definitive standard for genuinely transformative ethics in a New Age.

What was it, then, which made of this first-century rabbi/prophet/theurgist a worldwide Savior and incarnate God? To exhaustively pursue the involved path of this evolutionary development would be impossible here; others have more than adequately dealt with these religio-historical developments.[16] But suffice it to say that this was the result of an on-going process of theological mythologizing of bits and pieces of historical remembrances about Jesus into an interwoven tapestry of religious syncretistic thought which brought forth a new manifestation of the ancient Dying and Rising God, but this time in the form of Jesus Christ, Savior of the world.

From a modern Pagan perspective, the real identity of the historical Jesus is not as important as the subsequent mythical development around his personage as the Christ; an amalgam of Jewish, Hellenistic, and Pagan eschatological hope; the inheritor of all the previous myths of the solar, chthonic, and vegetative dying and rising gods which seemed to coalesce in Jesus as a fullness of all towards which the earlier gods had pointed; a manifestation of the Christ at the dawning of the Piscean Age.

It is not generally known that the earlier dying and rising gods of antiquity also functioned as literal Christs (i.e., anointed saviors) to their own devotees.[17] The titles which most Christians consider to be unique to Jesus Christ were actually appropriated from these gods of earlier Pagan mystery cults. Appellations of divinity such as Logos, Light of the World, Good Shepherd, True Vine, King of Kings, Bridegroom, and the Resurrection and the Life were all earlier devotional designations of Hermes, Mithra, Osiris, Dionysus, Attis, Adonis, Tammuz, and others. In point of fact, the composite image we have of the Christ in orthodox Church dogma is in reality not just a picture of the Jewish teacher from Galilee. It is, instead, a theological collage of the most enlightened and exalted of Pagan symbol and myth blended into the expectations of first century, apocalyptic Judaism which combined to produce the most awesome character of the mythic Christ. To some extent and degree, he is a composite of all the earlier Pagan deities which preceded but seemingly foreshadowed his appearance upon the stage of history. Interestingly enough, it was the intolerant and often unscrupulous Church which utilized the titles and sacred stories of these older gods to enhance the glory of their new successor, while at the same time condemning them as demonic entities![18] The hypocrisy here was squarely upon the shoulders of the Church, not the Christ. Nearly all of Christianity's holidays were stolen directly from earlier Pagan seasonal celebrations. The seven sacraments of the Church were patterned to some degree after the seven sacraments of Mithraism. The vestments and miters and other adornments of the Christian priests were borrowed from the pre-existing Pagan Mystery religions.[19] Even the central Mystery of the Christian religion—the Mass—was developed from earlier Pagan Eucharistic precedents.[20] Is it any wonder that a well-known Anglican priest frankly admitted that Christianity was merely a manifestation of reformed Paganism with just enough intolerance to give it a bad name?[21]

It is also important that we not forget the influence of the Gnostics within the early Church, for they brought with their beliefs a blend of Pagan and Hellenistic theology which inspired the writing of many non-canonical gospels which were considered subversive by the hierarchy of the early Church, but which some scholars believe contain original sayings of Jesus which were never allowed to surface in the later accepted Gospels of the New Testament due to their controversial implications.[22] The Gnostics had no problem incorporating the concept of the Christ into their larger spiritual cosmology, which often included different orders of celestial beings (gods and angels), as well as a focus upon the Divine Feminine.[23] In short, it is the Gnostics who give us an example of how contemporary Pagan theology can comfortably integrate the highest of the archetypal images and insights of the Christ within its own eclectic system of belief without compromising its integrity or its polytheism.

According to the teachings of the Ordo Arcanorum Gradalis, even the traditions of the Holy Grail—the central focus of our spiritual Quest—are incomplete without the mysticism of the Christ which permeates and superimposes upon the earlier Celtic context of its original derivation in the mysteries of arcane lore. What is more, the entire Western Mystery Tradition would only be a shell devoid of any sense of substantial fullness apart from the richness of esoteric Christianity which has infused it over the centuries with precious treasures of spiritual insight and aspiration.

As practitioners of the Craft, we have nothing to fear from the Christ. He, together with his apostles, consisted of a coven of thirteen.[24] He was careful as a guardian of the mysteries not to divulge the secrets of his teachings to the uninitiated, but only to the inner circle of his disciples.[25] He employed the techniques of divine magick for the healing and betterment of others.[26] He aggressively lashed out against the hypocritical religious establishment of his day.[27] He recognized the handiwork of Deity in even the most seemingly insignificant beauties of Nature.[28] He shunned the self-righteous asceticism of religious piety in favor of eating, drinking, and celebrating the joys of life with the common people most in need of his message of hope.[29] He instituted mystical rites designed to enhance our oneness with the Deity.[30] Like Tammuz, he died. Like Osiris, he descended into the realms of the dead. Like Attis, he rose again, and like Mithra, he ascended into the light of the glorious immortals. For modern Pagans to refrain from embracing at least a celebratory recognition of his ageless significance within the highest religious and mystical aspirations of Western spirituality would be to simultaneously disgrace all the previous gods of Pagan antiquity who, through the process of theological evolution, were themselves assimilated into the composite mystery which is the Christ.

Footnotes

1. See the actual text of the Grail Mass elsewhere in this book.
2. Gerald Gardner, *The Meaning of Witchcraft.* (New York, NY: Magickal Childe, Inc., 1982), p.27.
3. Doreen Valiente, *An ABC of Witchcraft.* (Custer, WA: Phoenix Publishing, Inc., 1988), p. xvi.
4. Margot Adler, *Drawing Down the Moon.* (Boston, MA: Beacon Press, 1986), p. 139.

5. Alan Richardson, *Earth God Rising*. (St Paul, MN: Llewellyn Publications, 1990), p. 141.

6. Aidan Kelly, *Crafting the Art of Magic, Book I*. (St. Paul, MN: Llewellyn Publications, 1991), pp. 50, 67.

7. Harry Emerson Fosdick, *The Man From Nazareth*. (New York, NY: Harper & Brothers, 1949).

8. Morton Smith, *Jesus the Magician*. (San Francisco, CA: Harper & Row, 1981).

9. Michael Baigent, *Holy Blood, Holy Grail*. (New York, NY: Delacorte Press, 1982).

10. Matthew 24:36, *Holy Bible*.

11. Matthew 10:23, *Holy Bible*.

12. Hugh J. Schonfield, *The Passover Plot*. (New York, NY: Bernard Geis Associates, 1965).

13. Matthew 15:24, *Holy Bible*.

14. Matthew 16:27-28, *Holy Bible*.

15. Mark 14:61-64, *Holy Bible*.

16. Father John Rossner, *In Search of the Primordial Tradition and the Cosmic Christ*. (St. Paul, MN: Llewellyn Publications, 1989).

17. J.M. Robertson, *Pagan Christs*. (New York, NY: Dorset Press, 1987).

18. Arthur Weigall, *The Paganism in Our Christianity*. (New York, NY: G. P. Putnam's Sons, 1928).

19. Barbara G. Walker, *The Woman's Encyclopedia of Myths and Secrets*. (San Francisco, CA: Harper & Row, 1983), p. 663.

20. Weigall, pp. 147-159.

    Annie Besant, *Esoteric Christianity*. (Wheaton, IL: The Theosophical Publishing House, 1982), pp. 243-244.

21. Rossner.

22. Elaine Pagels, *The Gnostic Gospels*. (New York, NY: Vintage Books, 1981).

    Robert Winterhalter, *The Fifth Gospel*. (San Francisco, CA: Harper & Row, 1988).

23. Pagels, pp. 57-83.

    Caitlin and John Matthews, *The Western Way, Volume II—The Hermetic Tradition*. (Boston, MA: Arkana, 1986), pp. 60-95.

24. Luke 6:12-16, *Holy Bible*.

25. Mark 4:10-12, *Holy Bible*.

26. John 9:6-7, *Holy Bible*.

27. Matthew 23:13-32, *Holy Bible*.

28. Matthew 6:25-34, *Holy Bible*.

29. Matthew 11:16-19, *Holy Bible*.

30. Matthew 26:26-29, *Holy Bible*.

Chapter Five

Pagan Priesthood and the Mystery of Melchizedek

very Sunday and, indeed, every day throughout the world, a strange and obscure personage is ritually remembered at the altars of the Catholic faithful:

Father, we celebrate the memory of Christ, your Son.
We, your people and your ministers,
recall his passion,
his resurrection from the dead,
and his ascension into glory;
and from the many gifts you have given us
we offer to you, God of glory and majesty,
this holy and perfect sacrifice:
the bread of life
and the cup of eternal salvation.
Look with favor on these offerings
and accept them as once you accepted
the gifts of your servant Abel,
the sacrifice of Abraham, our father in faith,
and the bread and wine offered by your priest
    Melchisedech.[1]

For the most part, even Catholics, by and large, have little knowledge as to the identity of the Biblical context of the story, which to some degree, gives a brief and tantalizing glimpse into the life of Melchizedek.

Who was he? The well-informed among the pious will answer, "He was a priest of the Most High God." What did he do? "He offered bread and wine to Abraham." Other than this bare shred of information regarding a single incident in the life of this mysterious man, we are left with a historical and Biblical blank. What does it matter? For Christians, his identity carries with it important implications which affect one of the very foundational tenets of their faith. For Pagans, Wiccans, and those of us in the Ordo Arcanorum Gradalis in particular, the political and priestly position, the religion, and the later theological exaltation of Melchizedek at the hands of both Jewish and Christian writers, represents the key by which the Pagan priesthood can once again assert its superiority over the sometimes intolerant and prejudicial claims of the ecclesiastical establishment of the Church.

The earliest and only information regarding this ancient figure from an almost forgotten past is contained in Genesis, the very first book of the Bible. Biblical scholars have long recognized the fact that Genesis, as well as the rest of the Pentateuch, is a compilation from at least two divergent sources of oral and written tradition, known respectively as "J" and "P"; "J" standing for the Yahwist narrative and "P" designating the Priestly source. But fragmentarily sandwiched in between these diverse streams of literary source material are occasional stories which have embedded themselves here and there in the manuscripts, but whose origins are distinctly more ancient than those of "J" and "P," and originating from often obscure and independent sources in Hebrew antiquity. Genesis 14:17-20 is a vivid case in point:

> When Abram (Abraham) came back after the defeat of Chedor-laomer and the kings who had been on his side, the king of Sodom came to meet him in the Valley of Shaveh (that is, the Valley of the King). Melchizedek king of Salem brought bread and wine; he was a priest of God Most High. He pronounced this blessing: "Blessed be Abram by God Most High, creator of heaven and earth, and blessed be God Most High for handing over your enemies to you." And Abram gave him a tithe of everything.[2]

On the basis of this extremely brief passage, some of the most mistaken assumptions in Judeo-Christian theology have been made which have affected the traditional perceptions of the nature and superiority of Christ and the Christian priesthood. To begin with, later Jewish commentators unwittingly initiated what would subsequently become a "domino effect" of seemingly legitimate conclusions based upon inaccurate linguistic interpretations and a faulty historical exegesis of the above scriptural text.

Outside of Genesis, reference to Melchizedek is made only one other time in the entire canon of Hebrew scripture: Psalm 110:4., "Yahweh has sworn an oath which he never will retract, 'You are a priest of the order of Melchizedek, and for ever.' "[3] Here we see that by the time of the composition of this psalm (1000 BCE-600 BCE?), the writer, speaking for Yahweh, was no longer aware of the true identity of Melchizedek. He was obviously under the impression that this priest-king who blessed the patriarch of the Hebrew nation was a member of a priesthood which from the dim mists of antiquity had been in the service of Israel's god Yahweh. It is this colossal misidentification of Melchizedek which later became the fallacious cornerstone for the Christian teachings regarding Eucharistic archetypes and the doctrine of the superiority of the priesthood of the Church over the Levitical priesthood of the Jewish people:

> You remember that Melchizedek, king of Salem, a priest of God Most High, went to meet Abraham who was on his way back after defeating the kings, and blessed him; and also that it was to him that Abraham gave a tenth of all that he had. By the interpretation of his name, he is, first, "king of righteousness" and also king of Salem, that is "king of peace"; he has no father, mother or ancestry, and his life has no beginning or ending; he is like the Son of God. He remains a priest forever. Now think how great this man must have been, if the patriarch Abraham paid him a tenth of the treasure he had captured … this man (Melchizedek), who was not of the same descent (as the Levitical Jewish priesthood), took his tenth from Abraham, and he gave his blessing to the holder of the promises (Abraham). *Now it is indisputable that a blessing is given by a superior to an inferior* … It could be said that Levi himself (the ancestor of the tribe which composed the Jewish priesthood), who receives tithes (through the priesthood of his descendants), *actually paid them, in the person of Abraham, because he was still in the loins of his ancestor (Abraham) when Melchizedek came to meet him*.[4]

This passage from the New Testament Epistle to the Hebrews goes on to designate Christ as the next in line to inherit the prerogatives of Melchizedek's superior priesthood by virtue of applying to Him the previously quoted prophecy of Psalm 110:4, "You are a priest of the order of Melchizedek, and for ever."

The writer of this early scripture to Hebrew Christians was "making as much hay" as possible from the legendary narratives of Genesis as well as the involved, sacrificial instructions contained in the Levitical regulations of the Jewish priesthood as a foreshadowing of the atoning sacrifice of the Christ. Secondarily paramount was the writer's intention to show the superiority of the Christian priesthood of apostles and prophets (having received their authority from Christ Himself, the very embodiment and fulfillment of Melchizedek's priesthood) over the "superceded" priesthood of the Jewish temple.

Part of the writer's argument hinged on the identity of Melchizedek. Admittedly, he or she knew the Old Testament extremely well, and was quite adept in bringing forth an interpretation of the scriptures which fit into the mold of his/her spiritual preconceptions. As seen from the above passage, Melchizedek is described in no uncertain terms as being like the Son of God, the original King of Peace, and even by implication, a deathless and eternal being. No doubt the author saw in Melchizedek the cast shadow which prophetically pointed to the substantive continuation of his priesthood in Jesus, the new Priest-King Messiah. It is possible the writer even conceived of Melchizedek as a literal manifestation of the pre-incarnate Christ or primordial Logos. In fact, latching on to this idea, there were those in the later Church who went so far as to assert that Melchizedek was a greater manifestation of the Logos than was Jesus![5]

Many shades of interpretation colored these verses, depending on who was expounding from this epistle. But one thing is certain: the argument of the early Christians was clear enough. The fact that Abraham, in whose loins were the later progeny of the Hebrew people, paid voluntary tithes to this mysterious priest-king of ancient Salem (Jerusalem) was proof that the messianic priesthood of Christ, being after the Order of Melchizedek, was superior to the later priesthood of the Jews, who through Abraham their supreme patriarch, were paying tithes to Melchizedek! Or so ran the argument throughout the rest of the seventh chapter of the Epistle to the Hebrews.

However, upon closer examination of these evolutionary interpretations of Genesis 14, we will discover that, far from validating the ecclesiastical preeminence of the Christian clergy, this Biblical passage actually strengthens the historical and sacramental superiority of the Pagan priesthood in relation to both church and synagogue. The thrust of this chapter is not, however, an attempt to establish one religion as being better than another. It is, rather, an effort to apply the logic used by early Christian interpreters drawn out to its ultimate conclusions when based on the historical facts surrounding the mystery of Melchizedek instead of the unfounded assumptions of the early Church fathers.

Ironically, the first mistake was made originally by the Hebrew commentators themselves with regard to the meaning of certain pivotal words in the original text itself. In Genesis 14:18, Melchizedek is described as being a priest of "God Most High." While technically speaking, this rendition of the words "el 'elyon" is not a mistranslation, it is most definitely reflective of the translators' historical ignorance relative to the contemporary culture of which Melchizedek was a part. Scholars have now learned that Melchizedek was a Canaanite priest-king who reigned over the city of Jerusalem long before it ever came under the control and supremacy of the Hebrews. The words "el 'elyon," while technically permitting the translation of "God Most High" according to later Hebrew usage, were originally a designation of either one or possibly two Canaanite deities, apparently among the most exalted gods of the Canaanite pantheon! What has become abundantly clear to discerning Biblical scholars is that Melchizedek was a *Pagan* priest, who, after the great battle between the kings, blessed Abraham, the father and patriarch of the Hebrew people, in the name of the Canaanite god(s) El 'Elyon for his victory over their common city-state enemies! Melchizedek was neither a priest nor a worshipper of the god of Abraham, known to later generations as Yahweh. Instead, he worshipped and served the god(s) of his own Pagan, Canaanite religion:

> Finally, the notice about Melchizedek merits a measure of confidence in its own right. *He invokes an authentic Canaanite deity ... as a good Canaanite priest would be expected to do.* Abraham, on the other hand, refers to Yahweh, using the Canaanite name or names in suitable apposition, which is no less appropriate in his particular case ... The narrative itself has all the ingredients of historicity ... Now that this chapter (Genesis 14) is amply attested as a source unto itself, it is not only unnecessary but fallacious to harmonize its contents with other portions of the OT (Old Testament). *As a Canaanite priest, Melchizedek would invoke his deity or deities by name; and this is what the above translation has sought to reproduce.* Abraham, on the other hand, would just as naturally turn to Yahweh, especially in an oath ...[6]

> We cannot ... be certain about Melchizedek's historical context, but it is likely that his kingdom of "Salem" was Jerusalem, *and that the "God Most High" whom he served was the Canaanite god El-Elyon* ...[7]

> Melchizedek is an old Canaanite name meaning *"My King Is (the god) Sedek"* or "My King Is Righteousness" (the meaning of the similar Hebrew cognate). Salem, of which he is said to be king, is very probably Jerusalem ... *The god whom Melchizedek serves as priest is "El 'Elyon," again a name of Canaanite origin, probably designating the high god of their pantheon ... For Abraham to recognize the authority and authenticity of a Canaanite priest-king is startling and has no parallel in biblical literature.*[8]

As just stated above, the very name itself—Melchizedek—literally means from the Canaanite usage, "My King is (the god) Sedek." So this priest-king of early Salem (later Jerusalem) was even dedicated by his own name to yet another Pagan deity!

The theological implications of these facts are nothing short of staggering. The later Hebrews saw in Melchizedek the archetype of the perfect priest of their Lord, Yahweh. They had totally lost sight of his actual identity as a Pagan priest of the very Canaanite peoples which the invading Israelites under Moses and Joshua had sworn to destroy due to the "abominations" of their Pagan religion (Deuteronomy 7:1-6)!

The Christians, in their turn, continued to compound this same scriptural misinterpretation by making Melchizedek either a pre-incarnate manifestation of the Christ, or else a foreshadowing type of the Messiah who would continue his ancient priesthood through the apostolic succession of the Church. But when we understand the historical facts surrounding the original events described in Genesis 14, we see that not only are the Jewish and Christian theologies relating to

Melchizedek totally fallacious in their basic assumptions, but they play perfectly into the hands of those of us who are instrumental in the contemporary re-establishment of the Pagan priesthood.

If we use, in our turn, the same interpretive approach as did the writer of the Epistle to the Hebrews, we will easily come to some most astounding conclusions. To begin with, Melchizedek was a Pagan priest. He did not serve the god of Abraham, but rather his own Canaanite deity(ies), El 'Elyon. Abraham paid his tithes to the chief priest of a Pagan religion, so, if like the early Christian interpreters, we see Abraham as symbolically containing in his loins the later spiritual progeny of the Jewish priesthood, and succeeding them (in Christian teaching), the priesthood of the Church, then we can just as consistently argue that in paying his tithes to Melchizedek, Abraham and through him all the later generations of Jewish and Christian clergy were acknowledging the superiority of Melchizedek's priesthood, which, as has been clearly established, was PAGAN! Furthermore, Jesus Christ is said by the New Testament writers to be an eternal High Priest of the Order of Melchizedek (Hebrews 7:17, 24). If we use the same kind of interpretive analysis, this makes Christ the successor and embodiment of an ancient and venerable Pagan priesthood! Therefore, it can be said that modern Pagans have more of a legitimate claim upon the deified priest-king Christ than does the Christian Church itself, for His priesthood is derived, not from the Jewish Temple, but from the Pagan priest-king Melchizedek!

Neither should it be forgotten that Melchizedek is seen as the great archetype of the divine origination of the Eucharist giving as he did bread and wine to Abraham. For this reason, as is quoted at the beginning of this chapter, Melchizedek is memorialized daily in the traditional Canon of the Roman Catholic Mass. Now again, when we use the same interpretive logic as did the early Church, we can confidently assert, in light of the historical facts, that the very elements of sacred bread and wine—the Eucharist in the making—were a gift to Abraham and his spiritual descendants (i.e., the Christian priesthood of apostolic succession) from one of the most venerable Hierophants of ancient Paganism: Melchizedek, priest of El 'Elyon! "Melchizedek is hermetically considered to be an inner master because he had neither 'beginning of days nor end of life.' His motif is woven into the Grail legends. His is a strong and high contact which will bring the reader into the presence of eternal things."[9] For those of us in the Ordo Arcanorum Gradalis, for whom the Eucharistic mystery of the Grail Mass is of central importance within the confines of our tradition, this all the more reinforces our long-standing belief that, far from being alien to the Pagan way, Eucharistic worship is indeed inextricably bound into the heart of Pagan antiquity. It was not stolen from the Church. Actually, it was the Church, which, through Abraham, received it as a gift from the chief priest of Canaanite Paganism!

Contemporary Pagans, Wiccans, and other esoterically-minded occultists need to realize that it often pays off theologically to closely examine the teachings, claims, and dogmas of the Church, for very often we will find that they have built upon the foundation of the pre-Christian Pagan mysteries whose original meaning has been distorted for the purposes of furthering certain claims of Christian exclusivity and theological intolerance. But it is in the process of this kind of investigation that we occasionally come across "a pearl of great price" like Melchizedek, a man whose mysterious obscurity has long held the key for authenticating the spiritual precedence and antiquity of the Pagan priesthood over later Judeo-Christian claims of religious and ecclesiastical superiority.

This knowledge is important for us because it reinforces the realization that through Melchizedek, Pagan, Jewish, and Christian clergy stand on an equally valid footing derived from the same source of blessing and empowerment. For this reason (as well as a host of others), it is needful for those who function as priest/esses of covens, groves, and chapels of the Pagan way to ponder deeply upon their calling as ministers of the sacred.

During much of the recent upsurge of the Wiccan and Neo-Pagan movements, there was often what can only be described as a much too cavalier and/or casual attitude towards being a high priest or high priestess. For some it was the means of obtaining power over a small group for immature ego gratification. Titles of priesthood among modern Neo-Pagans have often been "a dime a dozen." In some groups, any pretense of priesthood has degenerated into a travesty; the means of initiation often depending upon who slept with who. As one Grailpriest reflected:

> All too often in American Neo-Paganism, the steps leading to office and title can be all too easy ("I read Starhawk, so I'm a High Priest!"), all too immature ("Okay, I slept with you, where's my 2nd degree?"), or irrelevant ("The initiate shows proper magical attitude by washing the High Priest's car"). The steps to title and office must be challenging, mature and relevant. Plus they must refer back to a tradition, to connect us with our past.[10]

In the past lies our religious and historical authentication; in the future lies the fulfillment of our priestly potential, if we learn a lesson from the example of Melchizedek. As contemporary Paganism comes of age, there is dawning upon many in the positions of its leadership a corresponding yearning for more serious structuring of both practical and theoretical training for those who feel compelled to follow the call to service and responsibility as a member of the ranks of Pagan clergy. This is a necessary imperative in the right direction if we are to reflect in our society at large a reputation as representatives of serious theological substance and religious relevance. Historically, members of any priesthood have been expected to function as intercessors for their people before the gods, to minister to the spiritual needs of their people, and to stand courageously in resolute defense of their deities, traditions and sacred truths. In the Ordo Arcanorum Gradalis we also take seriously our priestly stewardship as the dispensers of sacramental grace through the celebration of the Grail Mass. If we want the public at large to view the priesthoods of modern Paganism with the same sense of validity as they do both Jewish and Christian clergy, we must be able to expound not only the realities of our links with the revered faiths of ancient antiquity, but also upon the seriousness with which we take our vows of ordination in order to serve the spiritual needs of our people and the ecological imperatives of our planet. It is a most astounding commentary for our consideration that Melchizedek as a Pagan priest-king was so respected even by those—like Abraham—who were of other religious faiths, that they willingly received upon themselves and their posterity the blessings which he bestowed. Let us pray to the Goddess that the Pagan priesthood can become worthy of being held in such high esteem by Jews, Christians, and all other faiths within our pluralistic society, that they will willingly listen to the wisdom of our counsel and respect the integrity of our convictions.

Footnotes

1. Excerpts from the English translation of *The Roman Missal* © 1973, International Committee on English in the Liturgy, Inc. All rights reserved.

2. Genesis 14:17-20, *The Jerusalem Bible*. (Garden City, NY: Doubleday & Company, Inc., 1966).

3. Psalm 110:4, *The Jerusalem Bible*.

4. Hebrews 7:1-4, 6-7, 9-10, *The Jerusalem Bible*. (Emphasis mine.)

5. *The Oxford Dictionary of the Christian Church.* Ed. by F. L. Cross. (New York, NY: Oxford University Press, 1974), p. 899.

6. *The Anchor Bible: Genesis.* A New Translation with Introduction and Commentary by Ephraim A. Speiser. (New York, NY: Doubleday & Company, Inc., 1981), pp. 109, 104. (Emphasis mine.)

7. Richard Coggins, *Who's Who in the Bible*. (London: B.T. Batsford Ltd., 1981), p. 100. (Emphasis mine.)

8. From "Melchizedek" in *Encyclopaedia Britannica*, 15th edition (1985), 7:1029. (Emphasis mine.)

9. Caitlin and John Matthews, *The Western Way, Volume II—The Hermetic Tradition*. (London: Arkana, 1986), p. 178.

10. William Calhoun. "Vigil and Question," *Hallows* (Glen Allen, VA, Fall, 1990), p. 11.

Chapter Six

The Cup and the Cauldron

regorian chant hypnotically wafts its way invisibly through the sanctuary. Incense spirals in undulating patterns through the air, encircling the high candles of the altar, wrapping the concelebrants in cloaks of aromatic haze. The priest lifts up the wheaten Host and a chalice filled with wine. Small bells are rung by kneeling altar boys announcing to all assembled that the God has been made visibly present in their midst. The congregation bows before Him—He who has become for them a theophany of bread and wine.

In this scene we encounter a sense of the mystery of the Catholic Mass; a two thousand-year tradition which Pagan writer Isaac Bonewits has described as at one time being "the most powerful ritual in the Western world."[1] But what, you may ask, has this to do with modern Paganism and the Craft revival? Everything, is the answer, if we but have the spiritual sense to perceive the hidden presence of the Goddess even in the most potent magick of the Christian religion.

The secrets of the Goddess are never readily apparent to the untrained seeker. They often remain shrouded in vaguely inexplicable legends and seemingly quaint stories which frequently gather themselves around place names and localities that ever evoke a sense of lost times and forgotten wonders. So it is with Glastonbury, Avalon, and Ynys-witrin. Ancient Albion, the Britain of enchantment and mystery, existed in the "real" world and simultaneously beyond its boundaries. The Celtic manifestation of the Goddess in Her many guises ruled free and unfettered in these time-warped isles, presiding over woodlands, pastures, and misty lakes, while other kindred gods roamed the breadth of these realms undisturbed, animating both countryside and village with the residue of their natural magick. The Pagan spirit held sway; these islands were the habitation of the Goddess, the home of Her cauldron.

But changes were coming from the East. Rome was in decline and turmoil, and a new god was capturing the world's collective eye of faith. Already, luminous strangers were rumored to have landed upon the shores long haunted by Gwyn ap Nudd, below the Glastonbury Tor which guarded the gate to the Underworld. These pilgrims brought with them gifts from the new god: the Holy Thorn, the Precious Vials ... the Chalice of the Grail.

With the dawn of the Piscean Age reflecting the rising glory of the Christian God, the Old Ones prepared to depart into more distant dimensions far from the reach of the conquering Church. This was not meant to be construed as some retreat from conflict with the increasingly influential Judean Savior. It was a resignation based on understanding. The native traditions of the land were entering their predetermined twilight in preparation for the coming of the newly crowned Christ. But this was not an overnight process; it was gradual, and finally accomplished only after the passage of generations destined to be caught in the chaotic confluence of two overlapping ages. Such was the time of Arthur, Merlin, and the Lady of the Lake.

Yet in this period of emerging ecclesiastical patriarchy through the aegis of the Church, the Goddess and Her gentler mysteries were not without their witnesses. The flame of mystic knowledge which burned within Her breast was spread abroad, but underground and secretly.

The Old Gods knew well how the growing Church was preordained to engulf the Western Isles. As the centuries began to pass, it became clear to the Guardians on the Inner Planes that the only means by which the Exalted Lady could ensure the survival of Her deepest mysteries would be within the protective confines of the sacred sanctuaries of the Piscean Christ. The sign of the fish had long been a symbol of Her "fish-teeming womb" of fertility; now it was being redefined as a symbol of the One who called His disciples to be "fishers" for the future faithful.[2]

Through its rigid sense of developing hierarchicalism, the Christian Church was sowing the seeds of entrenched, religious patriarchy throughout the Western civilized world. The remnants of the remaining Goddess-centered mystery cults were fast disintegrating before the missionary onslaught of the unyielding Cross. It seemed as though all traces of the worship of the Great Lady of Heaven and Earth would soon be obliterated. But the Goddess was never without a witness, however feeble.

It was at Ephesus in Asia Minor that the spirit of the Goddess prevailed *within* the established Church without its prelates even faintly comprehending the import of Her devious victory. Early in the first century the Christian zealot, Paul of Tarsus, sought to preach his exclusively monotheistic gospel throughout the area of Ephesus. In this city was located one of the seven wonders of the ancient world: the great Temple of Diana. The inhabitants of Ephesus were fiercely loyal to Her worship, and Paul soon found himself surrounded by a sea of angry citizens who did not take kindly to his message which indirectly denigrated the Goddess.[3] But as the years passed, the later generations of the city would succumb with the rest of the Empire to the ultimatums of Christian proclamation. Yet the influence of the Lady still lingered in the city of Her former glory. After more than a century of worshipping in the purely male-oriented deity system of the Church, people began to yearn for the tender closeness of a Divine Mother to whom they could resort in prayer and adoration. The stern, male Christ portrayed by the teachings of the Christian priesthood was beginning to become too forbidding and far-away in the religious perceptions of the multitudes. This slowly gave rise to a spontaneous emphasis upon the adoration of the Blessed Virgin, Mother of Christ.

Finally, at the Council of Ephesus in 431 CE, the Church opened wide its gates to the Goddess, albeit in a disguised and subjugated form. Mary, the humble Jewish maiden who had given birth to Jesus, was now so highly exalted by the Church that it conferred upon her the august title of *Theotokos*—Mother of God. She, in essence, had become the Piscean mask by which the Great Goddess was enabled to perpetuate Her worship as Queen of Heaven and Mother of Gods. The later hairsplitting of theologians to the effect that Mary was not a goddess, nor was she adored on a level with God (latria), but rather given the highest veneration possible without, technically speaking, becoming a manifestation of worship reserved alone for the Holy Trinity (hyperdulia), was lost upon the perceptions of rank-and-file Catholics (as it still is in parts of Latin America).

The cultus of the Virgin Mary began to subvert the focus of faith away from the male, Christocentric emphasis of the Church. To be sure, the repression, misogyny, and tyrannical intolerance of Christianity's developing rigidity continued through these centuries basically unabated. But despite it all, the Roman Church especially, began to allow wholesale appropriation of Pagan custom and ritual for application in liturgical contexts. This in conjunction with the exaltation of the Virgin Goddess in Her Christian cloak of masquerade, insured the survival of a semblance of the earlier pre-Christian Mysteries for those who had the spiritual insight to discern them strategically placed within the body of oral, written, and liturgical Church tradition.

Parallel with this evolutionary Mariological development, the Mass itself was undergoing a steady transformation from the simple Love Feast of the first-century Christians into the mystical epitome of ecclesiastical, incantatory magick. This, ironically, was not totally out of keeping with Jesus' probable adaptation of the Eucharistic concept from certain hermetic teachings of Egyptian magick.[4] Such communion rites had served the purpose of sealing the magician's personal identification with the power and personality of the god being invoked. Jesus probably utilized this as a mystical means by which his followers could commune with his dynamic presence long after he had departed from them physically. We know that any form of literal Eucharistic belief was alien to first-century Judaism.[5] However, it would appear that Jesus adeptly mixed certain metaphors regarding the sacrificial Passover lamb (applying them to himself) with the concept of some form of magickal "transubstantiation" derived from these esoteric Egyptian practices. The end result was a communal ritual centered around a sacred Cup of Mystery which became a means of identification and oneness with Jesus as the risen God; a sacrament which never ceased to inspire a mystical sense of wonderment and contemplation in his followers. This preoccupation with the Eucharist, described by the devout as the "medicine of immortality," eventually became the guise through which the deep esoteric truths of the Holy Grail began to be disseminated in their later literary forms.

It would truly be an oversimplification to say that the concept of the Grail is of Christian origin. While the later writers of the twelfth century can fairly be credited with the transformation of the Grail into the supposed wonder-working chalice used by Jesus at the Last Supper, it is plain upon investigation that the original substratum of the Grail imagery is situated in the bedrock of pre-Christian Celtic mythology, where it is described as a mysterious Cauldron of the miraculous and the supernatural.[6]

The transference of the mystifying otherworldliness of the Pagan cauldron to the sanctified aura of the Christian cup required little concentrated effort on the part of the medieval descendants of British Celtic Christianity; a branch of the Church which, according to historian Geoffrey Ashe, was always underscored by an unsettling "Sense of Something Else" lurking in the shadows of its inner, hidden identity.[7] The Celts had an uncanny knack for religious eclecticism to the point where gods, goddesses, saints, and spirits seemed to have a rather eerie and uncontentious coexistence with one another, despite the official temporal and religious ascendancy of the Church.[8] The Old Ones had receded into the timeless mists of Avalon, but as the Celts silently surmised, they had never fully deserted their ancient haunts. Where once had stood their age-honored shrines, there now were erected upon those ruined foundations splendid edifices of Christian worship. The Old Ones may have been forgotten by many, but beneath these altars of the Christ there still lives the faintly detectable presence of Cerridwen, Sul, Nodens, Woden, and Gwyn ap Nudd.

In both Pagan and Christian versions, the Grail was always the focus for a Quest. Whether it was Arthur and his adventurous companions seeking the magick Cauldron in the perilous regions of Annwn, or Galahad seeking the depths of his spiritual longing for the Holy Cup of the Beautific Vision, the message conveyed was basically the same: the Grail serves as a symbol of that which is both the source and the ultimate satisfaction of our personal, spiritual odyssey.

For ages long before the coming of Christianity, the cauldron was the most universal symbol of that goal towards which we all must journey in our own way. Throughout the many lands settled by Celtic peoples, the cauldron always played a prominent place as a manifestation of the miraculous as well as of the divine presence of the Goddess in her aspect as the Great Mother, Source of Life, and Womb-Bearer of Creation. The Cauldron of the Goddess was seen as that mysterious container of the Mother's magickal, life-giving blood by which She held the secrets of death and the certainty of rebirth. Some of the hero-gods of old were even said to have stolen draughts of this living liquid from Her Cauldron deep within the earth.[9]

The cauldron has always been a symbolic metaphor for the generative womb of the Earth Mother, the very source of our incarnational existence. In later mythology, the cauldron slowly evolved into a representation of reincarnation: all that dies goes back into the dark, subterranean womb/tomb of the Mother's Earth to be given new birth in yet another life. The cauldron therefore came to be synonymous with what was perceived as the cyclical wheel of eternal life.[10] Scenes from the Gundestraup Cauldron found in Denmark also are remarkable for their depiction of this vessel as a symbol of sacrificial death, transformation, and apotheosis.[11] The cauldron, then, was far more than the occasional brewing pot of Shakespearean witches, as popular misconceptions have often portrayed.

Certain of the Medieval writers poetically identified the Grail with the Virgin Mary, calling her, oddly enough, by a Pagan appellation of honor: the "Cauldron of purest descent."[12] In this they accurately discerned a vital truth: the Quest for the Grail is, in reality, a Quest for the Goddess. By whatever name She may be called, Christian or Pagan, the glorious Lady is the embodiment of the ancient Cauldron of Life, Death, and Regeneration. This is the secret which gives insight into the interpenetrating symbolism of the Cup and the Cauldron.

The relationship of the Cup to the Cauldron therefore becomes apparent. The Cup as an archetype of the life-force of the feminine has its origin in, as we have seen, the even more ancient symbol of the Cauldron of the Goddess. The Communion Cup has often been a central mystery of religious practice, both Christian and Pagan. From the sacred barley drink of the Eleusinian mysteries and the water and wine of the Mithraic sacrament to the elevated Chalice of the Roman Mass, the Eucharistic Cup has figured prominently in historic religious devotions.

The chalice or cup has long been perceived as being symbolic of the archetypal feminine in culture, psychology, and spirituality. Feminist author Riane Eisler has even gone so far as to categorize the historic antithesis between matrifocal and patriarchal cultures as a conflict between the chalice and the blade, respectively.[13] In a more positive context, it is interesting to note that in the Ordo Arcanorum Gradalis, as well as most modern Neo-Pagan and Wiccan Traditions, the Great Rite in its symbolic form has always been enacted by lowering the blade of the glaive (athame) into the ritual cup of wine; the obvious and widely accepted symbolism having always been one of thanksgiving for the fertility which produces life: a representation of male (the blade) and female (the chalice) in sexual union.

In the developing growth of Christian Eucharistic theology, however, the Cup of the Sacrament lost any feminine connotations whatsoever. The focus of the Church "fathers" was, not surprisingly, on the male sacrificial victim, Son of the Father-God. All but forgotten was the theological understanding that the body and blood of their crucified Savior (i.e., His humanity) came exclusively from His

Mother via the Virgin Birth, not from the Spirit. His blood was indirectly Her own. She alone was the source of His human manifestation. The Christian Mass, then, could not be possible apart from Her initial mediation of His incarnation.

In the *Queste del Saint Graal*, the glory of the Grail was made manifest to Galahad in a "Mass of the Mother of God" (i.e., a Mass of the Christian Goddess).[14] In this respect, one of the most important contributions of certain Grail romances was their subtle equation of the sacramental vessels, especially the Chalice, with the special presence of the Mother of God, the Divine Feminine.[15] Just as Mary was the sacred vessel who carried Jesus in Her virgin womb, so also, there was the implication of an existing esoteric Mass where the Christian Cup became the archetypal manifestation *par excellence* of the divine maternal womb, the holy receptacle for the body and blood of Her Son, which She dispensed forth daily into the world in an ever-recurring incarnation of bread and wine. Essentially then, in the minds of some Grail mystics, the cup was once again restored as a living, multidimensional icon of the Great Mother within the Grail concepts of a Higher Mass. Unfortunately, such depths of revelation were lost upon the vast majority of those who wielded the spiritual authority of the Church.

Long predating the advent of the Grail adventures and its related literature, the implications of this kind of theological meditation were not lost upon the more perceptive Gnostics of the fledgling Church, some of whom celebrated a secret Mass where the Deity as the Divine Feminine was invoked. The Eucharistic Cup was believed by them to be the grace-dispensing "blood" of She who is *Charis*: "May She who is before all things, the incomprehensible and indescribable Grace, fill you within, and increase in you Her own knowledge."[16]

Interestingly enough, the hierarchical stratification of the early Church was developed primarily as a defensive measure in order to render the Eucharistic celebrations of all other competing Gnostic groups "invalid." Any Mass not authorized by the bishop or his priestly representatives was not a "true" Mass.[17] This should make it clear that early Catholicism was not the sole possessor of the concept of the Eucharist. This type of sacrament was being observed by different competing sects with widely varying interpretations.

Before the rise of Christianity, the Mystery religions had long observed similar ritualistic enactments. In drinking the sacred *kykeon*, the participants in the Eleusinian mysteries were enabled to partake in the mystical fellowship of the grieving goddess Demeter. In the Mysteries of Mithra, tiny loaves of bread marked with a cross (!) were distributed to the initiates along with the sacramental cup, recalling the final meal this Persian sun-god had with his friends before his final ascension into heaven.[18] (Christians were often accused by learned Pagans of having copied their rites from the previous practices of far older cults. It would seem that there was some truth to the accusations!) The rites of Attis and Cybele were replete with Eucharistic trappings, as were those of Osiris in Egypt. Annie Besant mentions similar rituals involving the use of bread and wine being observed by the Druids,

Greeks, Egyptians, Tibetans, and pre-Columbian Mexican cultures.[19] From this and other available evidence, we can see that Eucharistic communion as a means of assimilating the attributes of the gods predates Christianity far back into the dim beginnings of civilized religious practice, and is genuinely rooted in the most mystical of Pagan spiritual conceptualizations.

Despite the fact that the earlier feminine connotations of the Cup had been virtually eclipsed in the exoteric teachings of the Church, it is curious that among those most addicted to the praise of the Virgin Mary with Her accompanying devotions (such as the rosary), there almost always springs a spontaneous love for the Mass itself. It is as if, in some strange way, the archetypal Goddess being manifest through Mary has been conveying to Her devotees a precious truth which most have yet to perceive in its full implications: "See Me in the Cup. I am the Vessel of the Blood of Life. Contained within My womb have been all the Sons and Saviors of antiquity … Adonis, Attis, Osiris, Jesus. They came forth from Me. They were loved by Me. They died and were restored to life by Me."

We have now arrived at a juncture in time when the Piscean Age of orthodox Christianity is drawing to a close. The Aquarian Age of the Spirit is about to begin a new era inaugurated by worldwide change and spiritual transformations. As a result, fundamentalism as a Western religious phenomenon has begun to raise its clenched and ugly fist in an intolerant challenge against any influence which could conceivably weaken the established dogmatic and hierarchical structures of the Western ecclesiastical establishments, be they Christian, Jewish, or Islamic.

Today the Church cannot hold within its bosom the questing spirits of those thirsty souls who seek for water from deeper wells. The Old Ones are returning. The worship of the Great Goddess is being restored through the Neo-Pagan and Wiccan revival, together with a refocusing upon the spiritual relevancy of Avalon within the consciousness of Western mystical awareness. The fog of centuries is finally beginning to lift from the occult landscapes of mythic legend. In books and channeled teachings, Merlin speaks his prophecies once more. Arthur prepares for his long-rumored return into the collective psyche of our seeking society, and the Grail is being seen in the morning mists of a New Age, shifting shape from cup to cauldron and back again.

This slow but continual shift in spiritual climate and consciousness indicates that the time is ripe for a liturgically restructured, post-Christian Eucharist which restores the Goddess to Her rightful role as the ultimate Mystery of the Mass. However much we may deplore the often theologically fascist record of Catholic Christianity over the past two thousand years, it has nevertheless bequeathed to us in the Mass a form and format for the most potent magickal rite uniquely at the apex of the Western Mystery Tradition.

According to some Grail legends, there were certain secret words of consecration known only to a selected few who apparently celebrated a High Mass that was not known to the vast majority of the established Church. Theories of missing

Grail missals and heterodox conspiracies have abounded for generations but with no final literary solution ever confirmed. Whatever the original authors had in mind at the time they penned these cryptic compositions of imaginative verse, it is clear to most who have studied the arcane lore of the Grail, that there was a hidden message lurking "between the lines" revealing a mystery of deeper significance than the official interpretations of the Mass of the Catholic Church.

It is for the glory of this higher Mass that we seek; the Mass of the Mother of Gods which bestows upon us the mystic sight by which we behold the transforming vision hidden in the Cauldron's Cup; the vision which transcends the limitations of Christian orthodoxy and liberates the sacrament from the stale bread and sour wine of parochial, patriarchal theology. In the Ordo Arcanorum Gradalis we have determined to reestablish the Mass of the Goddess once again within the hallowed shrines of modern, mystical Paganism. Within our sacred circles, the Cup and the Cauldron merge together once more as magickal extensions of one another in an ecumenical Eucharist which is not afraid to celebrate the sacrifice of the Dying and Rising God: He who is the Christ of Christians and the Corn King of the Old Religion. And in the Chalice of the Grail we dare to taste the holy liquid of life, retrieved from the everlasting Cauldron of the Living Lady by words of power infused with tenacious faith.

In many ways, this is not unlike the visionary hope of Taliesin as related in Marion Zimmer Bradley's spellbinding Arthurian novel, *The Mists of Avalon*:

> The voice of Taliesin was low and gentle. "Know you my dearest wish, my lord and king?"
>
> "'What, Lord Merlin?"
>
> "That one day—not now, for the land is not yet ready for it, and neither are those who follow Christ—but one day, Druid and priest should worship as one; that within their great church, their sacred Eucharist should be celebrated with yonder cup and dish to hold their bread and wine, in token that all the Gods are as One."[20]

Casual cakes and wine does wonders for helping to cement the social cohesiveness of a grove or coven, but from the point of view of this Order, it is lacking in the awesome undertones of Holy Mystery which are present in a genuine Eucharist. For this reason, we have incorporated the best of both worlds within our circle ceremonies, focusing upon the Mass of Our Lady as food for the spirit, yet celebrating our social bonding through the joy of cakes and wine.

There are some within the Craft who may feel that by establishing a distinctively Pagan Eucharist, we would merely be copying at best, or making a parody at worst of Christian rituals; thereby diluting the purity of revivalist Paganism.

One well-known Wiccan authority has even gone so far as to discourage any reference to the Wiccan altar cup as a "chalice," fearing it may foster the impression of having Eucharistic connotations.[21] However, Wiccans and Neo-Pagans have been notorious for appropriating into their metaphysical arsenal whatever works best for them as a religious body of people. In fact there is no such thing as "pure Paganism." There is nothing "pure" about what is anachronistically referred to as the Old Religion, for it is a wondrous blend of the inventive and eclectic magickal mind. Many of its rituals come from a variety of divergent sources. Some, for instance, are directly derived from the Victorian lodges of ceremonial magick; not, as the romantics would like to believe, the cave chants of Neolithic shamans!

Most of the Wiccan/Pagan community has reveled at one time or another, in the mystique of Merlin and the allure of Arthurian "otherworldliness," but more often than not, they have sidestepped their own personal Quest for the Grail, being afraid of it as "too Christian." Perhaps now we can lay aside such fearful reservations. Christians do not have a monopoly on the Mass, nor is the Eucharist the exclusive possession of any one religion. As a living priesthood of the Goddess, our Order believes it has a responsibility to reclaim the Eucharistic heritage that is ours as recipients and guardians of the Ancient Mysteries. The call of the Goddess is upon us. Her words ring clear with symbolic language reminiscent of the Eucharist. It is Hagia Sophia, Holy Lady Wisdom, who speaks:

> In Me are all graces, all ways, all truths. In Me is every hope for life and strength ... Approach Me, you who would desire My presence, fill yourselves from the abundance of My fruits ... All those who eat Me will hunger for more, all those who drink Me will thirst for more ... Come now, and recline at table with Me; eat My bread, and drink the wine I have prepared![22]

Footnotes

1. Philip Emmons Issac Bonewits, *Real Magic*. (Berkeley, CA: Creative Arts Book Company, 1971, 1979), p. 149.

2. Barbara G. Walker, *The Secrets of the Tarot*. (San Francisco, CA: Harper & Row, 1984), pp. 141-142.

3. Acts 19:23-41, *Holy Bible*.

4. Morton Smith, *Jesus the Magician*. (San Francisco, CA: Harper & Row, 1978), pp. 58, 122-123.

5. Leviticus 17:11-12; John 6:52-66, *Holy Bible*.

6. Geoffrey Ashe, *King Arthur's Avalon*. (E.P. Dutton & Co. Inc., 1957), pp. 226-228.

7. Ibid., p. 152.

8. John Carey. "Listening to the Celts," *Gnosis*, No. 9 (Fall, 1988), pp. 16-19.

9. Barbara G. Walker. "Cauldron," *The Woman's Encyclopedia of Myths and Secrets* (San Francisco, CA: Harper & Row, 1983), p. 150.

10. Ibid., p. 151.

11. Ibid, p. 153.

12. Ashe, pp. 268-269.

13. Riane Eisler, *The Chalice and the Blade*. (San Francisco, CA: Harper & Row, 1987).

14. Ashe, p. 267.

15. Ibid., pp. 270-271.
   See also William G. Gray, *Evoking the Primal Goddess*. (St. Paul, MN: Llewellyn Publications, 1989), pp. 33-64.

16. Elaine Pagels, *The Gnostic Gospels*. (New York, NY: Vintage Books, 1979, 1981), p. 60.

17. Ignatius of Antioch, Philadelphians 1:9-12; Smyrnaeans 2:16; 3:4-5.

18. Harold R. Willoughby, *Pagan Regeneration*. (Chicago, IL: The University of Chicago Press, 1929), p. 162.

19. Annie Besant, *Esoteric Christianity*. (Wheaton, IL: The Theosophical Publishing House, 1901, 1966), pp. 243-244.

20. Marion Zimmer Bradley, *The Mists of Avalon*. (New York, NY: Ballantine Books, 1982), p. 206. Reprinted by permission of the author and the author's agents, Scott Meredith Literary Agency, Inc., 845 Third Avenue, New York, NY 10022.

21. Raymond Buckland, *Buckland's Complete Book of Witchcraft*. (St. Paul, MN: Llewellyn Publications, 1986), p. 23.

22. Adapted from Ecclesiasticus 24:18-22; Proverbs 9:5, *Holy Bible*.

Chapter Seven

The Significance of Sin

ncreasingly, we see in many articles, books, and publications purporting to educate the public as to the essentials of what actually constitutes the basics of Goddess-worship, a tendency to recite what the authors often contend is a summary list of its theological characteristics. Foremost on this list is the insistence that Wicca and Neo-Paganism are completely devoid of any concept of sin in their religious belief system. De-Anna Alba, a well-known Wiccan writer and high priestess, has gone so far as to say, "There is no concept of sin in Goddess worship, no external set of rules that make sin possible … "[1] Starhawk, one of the most famous figures in the modern Wiccan revival, has echoed the same sentiments in her popular book *The Spiral Dance*.[2] All these and other references in recent Neo-Pagan apologetics underscore a grave misconception which assumes that "sin" is somehow an invention of Judeo-Christian oppressiveness, an anachronistic appendage of Victorian prudishness, or worse, the last vestiges of patriarchal, religious manipulation designed to keep the human spirit in chains of guilt and fear. As I will shortly make plainly evident, nothing could be farther from the truth. (In his best-selling book *Whatever Became of Sin?*, Dr. Karl Menninger has also demonstrated the shallowness of such assumptions.)[3]

The concept of sin in human relationships with one another and with the Deity pre-existed the advent of both Judaism and Christianity. Its origins lie in early *Pagan* theologies of moral ethics and ritual purity. A consciousness of sin, in one form or another, can be found to be pervasive in ancient religious preoccupations with sacrifice and salvation. In Pagan Babylon, the penitential psalms were characterized by sentiments which affirmed that none of the human race was exempt from sin, and that, indeed, *all* had committed offenses against the gods: "(Human)kind as many as there be (commit) sin ... "[4] Confession of sins was one of the liturgical requirements for initiation into the Mysteries of Samothrace.[5] The consciousness of sin found expression again and again in the plethora of Pagan religions throughout the ancient world: the Egyptians, Hittites, Babylonians, Sumerians, and Greeks all had concrete conceptualizations of sin and its effect upon the human/human and human/divine relationships, though their approach and emphasis often varied from culture to culture.[6] Even among Native American tribes, the custom of public confession of personal sins at special times gave evidence to their understanding that sin could be a barrier to harmonious relationships between individuals and their deities.[7] As a matter of fact, many of the liturgical invocations to the Goddess, whether they were addressed to Isis or Ishtar, implored Her to forgive their sins and look upon the penitent with the favor of Her mercy: "O my Mistress, make me to know my deed, establish for me a place of rest! *Absolve my sins*, lift up my face!"[8] The point being made here is simply that "the concept of sin," far from being absent or alien in Pagan religions, was deeply embedded in certain areas of their theological consciousness. To just assume that a preoccupation with sin was the sole province of Judeo-Christian, ecclesiastical "guilt-tripping" is to ignore the abundant evidence of our own Pagan antiquity.

In light of this evidence, for modern Neo-Pagan and Wiccan spokespersons to glibly assert that today's Goddess-worship "has no concept of sin" is to separate its modern manifestation from any sense of continuity with Paganism's historical precursors from the past. Furthermore, a religion which has no sense of sin within its theological consciousness betrays its subservience to introspective blindness and ethical bankruptcy. Every major religion of the world has a concept of sin within its belief system and morality. For Wiccans to pretend they can sidestep this thorny issue as an example of their liberation from personality-inhibiting rules and regulations will be to confirm to observers from other religious faiths that our claims to spiritual authenticity are fraught with shallowness and deceptive thinking.

Having a theology of sin is most important, because it will force some "Pollyanna Pagans" among us to confront and consider the brutal reality of evil and negativity which pervades the world, the human collective unconscious, and the submerged shadows of our own individual psyches. All the "power of positive thinking" and New Age pseudo-Gnosticism which proclaims that evil is only a figment of our matter-bound imaginations will not mitigate the chilling spectre of a sin-sick civilization polluting itself in the noxiousness of its own miasma.

The most insidious obstacle to seriously considering this whole matter of sin and evil is the negative conditioning that we have received from the religious establishment which usually equated "sins" with such petty practices as playing cards, drinking a beer, going to the theater on Sunday, dancing, smoking, petting, using condoms, or having sex in any other than the missionary position. What this actually represents, however, is the Church's puritanical trivialization of its own definition of sin. The teaching of the early Church regarding the meaning of sin was not as variant from that of its Pagan competitors as one might be led to believe. In the New Testament, the influential writer John penned quite a bit about the "sin question." Among other things, he wrote what is perhaps the most succinct definition of sin available: "Sin is the transgression of law" (1 John 3:4). From the context it is obvious that he was not referring to any specific legal code such as the Law of Moses, but rather he was painting upon the canvas of a much broader picture which conceived of law in the wider, generic sense, such as "moral law," "natural law," etc. In one Bible version, John's words are translated as "sin is lawlessness." In this there is conveyed a strong sense that sin is moral anarchy which exercises no consideration and submits to no constraints. In the original Greek, the word translated as "sin" actually has the literal meaning of "to miss the mark" like someone who misses the bull's eye on the target, or similar to our colloquial phrase describing a person as being "off the track." Anyone who has objectively looked at the panorama of human history with its parade of continual carnage, geographical greed, institutional oppression, and insensitive arrogance would have no problem admitting that somewhere along the line many millenniums ago, the human race definitely "got off the track"!

When it comes to listing specific kinds of sins, St. Paul both utilized and incorporated parts from the list of vices used by the Pagan Stoics in their own moral apologetics.[9] Greed, murder, and theft were listed among their vices and/or sins—hardly anything which respectable Pagans should have a problem in viewing as evil manifestations of human behavior.

But what should be the significance of sin from a Pagan perspective? In order to answer this, we must first squarely face the uncomfortable fact that "sin happens," to paraphrase a notorious bumper sticker. SIN IS REAL. It screams at us from the headlines of the daily paper and the heart-wrenching scenes on the evening news. It has infected our society from head to toe. Like a virus that spreads through the bloodstream of civilization, sin has debilitated human culture with a seemingly incurable sickness which has been with us since the dawn of history.

I have no intention here of getting entangled in the abstract arguments of some who would insist that sin is indefinable and totally relative, since what is considered taboo or a moral/social offense varies from culture to culture. Suffice it to say that, indeed, there *are* some religious and social taboos which have relevance only within the context of their own native culture. Obviously, these cannot be applied in any kind of universal imposition upon the human race as a whole. But there are some who would use such a philosophical approach as an argumentative tactic designed to divert our attention from the real issue at hand: deep down within the human conscience there is an inherent knowledge of the most basic distinctions between right and wrong which sets us apart from the rest of the animal realm, and when we transgress those most basic standards of decency, we have succumbed to the sway of sin.

Sin is a violation of respect-in-community, respect of self, and respect of Nature; a desecration of the Law of Love, whether it be defined as the Golden Rule, the Wiccan Rede, or the Threefold Law. Clearly, from this perspective (which is, incidentally, the most *basic* of practical definitions), it would be both ethically specious and morally indefensible to refuse to classify as sin such offenses against our common and individual humanity as murder, genocide, torture, theft, sexual deceit and infidelity, greed, cruelty, and child abuse, to name but a few. And it is from these and other traits of evil tainting the human race that we see the rising manifestation of sins against Mother Earth. Because of their greed for money and land, people are daily *sinning against the Goddess* as they strip the rain forests from Her terrestrial skin, pollute Her planetary atmosphere, and poison Her rivers and seas. *The ecological catastrophe facing this planet is the direct result of human sin*. Likewise, the nuclear conflagration that has long hovered upon the horizon of our future is also the offspring of our liaison with evil: the greed for world domination, power and territory, and the devaluation of human life as a means to the end of such geo-political selfishness. Closer to home, we are constantly bombarded with the reality of sin as it seeps into the fabric of our own communities: crime, drug trafficking, domestic violence, racism, gay bashing, the plight of the victimized homeless; the list could go on *ad infinitum*. It seems to me incredible that in the face of these evils, we could be so socially and ethically naive as to declare that the Old Religion "has no concept of sin."

De-Anna Alba, quoted earlier in this article, went on to emphasize that though Goddess-worshippers supposedly "have no concept of sin, no set of external rules that make sin possible," they do, nevertheless, adhere to the tenet of the Threefold Law. In this one sentence she has succeeded in contradicting herself, for to violate by our actions the intent of the Threefold Law would be to *sin* against that law (remember the earlier definition: "sin is the transgression of law"). If, as Neo-Pagans/Wiccans, we accept the ethical intent of the Threefold Law, the Golden Rule, and/or the Wiccan Rede, then our basic definition of sin would have to be the willful thwarting of these moral principles. It is ridiculous to insist that we have no concept of sin while at the same time we declare our allegiance to these revered laws of the Craft!

What I detect as I read Wiccan literature which touches upon this sensitive subject, is the strong aversion to any words or moral concepts which even hint at being leftover Christian baggage. No better example could be found than the legalistic nonsense of puritanical prudery which is often attached to the concept of sin in the minds of people who left the Church because of its preoccupation with instilling a sense of personal guilt as a means of manipulation through fear. However, we need to realize that Victorian, fundamentalist and overly legalistic, orthodox distortions of the sin concept have contributed to a warped understanding of the real gravity of sin as both a collective and personal manifestation of evil in our world. But if, in reaction, we pretend that sin doesn't exist merely by not calling it "sin," we have succeeded only in temporarily obscuring its presence from the direct gaze of our consciousness, but its reality will remain, just the same. We cannot afford to "throw the baby out with the bath water" by drowning our awareness of humanity's instrumentality as a vehicle for the proliferation of societal evil.

What then, should be a Neo-Pagan approach to the moral dilemma of sin and evil? Needless to say, a thorough discussion of all the intricate labyrinths to be found in such a profound topic is not possible in the space limitations of this chapter. But there are several foundational perspectives which need to be emphasized if we are to develop a serious and realistic teaching on this matter. First, we need to honestly acknowledge the reality of evil instead of trying to minimize it or "make it go away" through the clever usage of philosophical abstractions which attempt to relativize it out of existence as a mere negative concept of the mind. New Age protestations notwithstanding, all we need do is take a hard look and we will be unable to avoid the sight of sin's ravages all around us. As previously mentioned, sin and evil are real, and we need to be realistic in our approach to its presence both within and among us. We start by admitting that it exists.

Secondly, we need to perceive the truth that sin is not just something "out there" done by other people. None of us are immune from its tyranny over our wills and weaknesses. The mistake of the Church at this point was to use this fact as a baseball bat with which to clobber us into believing that we are depraved and evil to the very core of our being. However, from the perspective of the Ordo Arcanorum Gradalis, such conclusions are overbearing and unnecessary. The Babylonians held to a far more realistic view: evil was coextensive with the first generation of deities, corrupting even the minor gods. The first humans did not bring sin into the world (as in the Hebrew rewriting of this story found in Genesis), rather *they were born into a world previously permeated with evil, and as such, they were victims of an environment already infected by the sin of fallen gods.*[10] Rather than blaming the human race as the originating instigator of all evil, we should instead simply acknowledge that we have been placed by the higher powers into a world where we are subject to manifold choices and temptations to do that which is destructive to both ourselves and our common humanity. I believe that we have been placed here by the Deity to grow into god/desshood by virtue of what we learn through our response to the opportunities presented by both good and evil. (Remember the statement of the Serpent [originally a symbol of Goddess-wisdom] to Adam and Eve: "And ye shall be as gods, knowing good and evil.") Of course, being humans victimized by an environment infected by supernaturally evil influences, we often succumb to various degrees of sin. Let's face it: we're all sinners, we've all made wrong choices and done things which were hurtful to others and ourselves. Why should that be so hard for us to admit? As has been stated before this was a commonly held belief among many of the ancient Pagan religions, though it may have been expressed through various and diverse mythological explanations. The idea that "all have sinned and come short of the glory of God" was not an idea new with the coming of Christianity, nor should we jettison such an insight from the accumulated wisdom of our theology because of such a misconception.

But what about guilt? Won't the acknowledgement of sin in ourselves and others be a certain stepping stone to living in a continuous state of guilt? Isn't that why we left the Church in the first place? For some, it may be the reason why they left the Church, but an acknowledgement of sin is in no way antithetical to a healthy, Pagan way of life. In the first place, there is nothing wrong with guilt. It is a natural reaction of the conscience, a higher function of the human psyche. If you murdered someone or burglarized their home, what would be wrong with feeling guilty? If you lie, cheat, or steal, yet feel no sense of guilt or remorse, such a callous attitude is symptomatic of a psychological sociopath, not a well-adjusted person! The way we constructively deal with guilt is to make amends with those we have wronged, ask the forgiveness of the Goddess, and most importantly of all, *learn to forgive ourselves for our own faults and failings*, for in so doing we minister the absolution of the Lady to our own conscience. When a sense of inner forgiveness prevails, the individual conscience is freed from the condemnatory burden of guilt. Furthermore, the idea of overemphasizing sin and guilt as a means of converting the masses through fear is alien to the theology of our religion. Hence, the pitfalls of Christian doctrinal abuse in this area would have a difficult time making any foothold within a Neo-Pagan/Wiccan framework of teaching. Therefore, the fear that talking and teaching about sin will somehow introduce a constant sense of interior moral oppression within our community is totally unfounded.

In historical retrospect, it is interesting to note that the early Church was extremely successful in its propagation of faith because it did not shrink from declaring a message which called for personal introspection and repentance. "Repentance" is a relatively unpopular word today because it conjures up visions of sackcloth and ashes and people striking their breasts in outpourings of personal remorse. However, in the original Greek, "repentance" is translated from the word "metanoia," and literally means to turn around, to go the other direction, and by extension, to have a change of heart. The purpose of speaking about collective or personal sin within the context of our religious beliefs is to elicit a response of repentance; a change of heart which issues forth in a transformed way of life. This process was embodied in the very first words Jesus ever uttered at the beginning of his career: "Repent, for the Kingdom of God is at hand!"[11] In other words, "Wake up! Turn around! Take a hard look at yourselves and the world's negative state of affairs, but realize that there is hope for change if we but take hold of the Divine potential that is within us when we have the spiritual eye of faith!" His was a message of transformation.

But what has this to do with the way we proclaim our Paganism today? Actually, infinitely more than most of us have realized! The more prophetic aspects of the contemporary Pagan movement are often on the front line for ecological reform, animal rights, and world peace, to name but a few of the pertinent causes which modern Earth religions have highlighted in their fight against humankind's insensitive and destructive course towards global and evolutionary catastrophe. "Radical" groups such as Earth First!, Greenpeace, The Sea Shepherd Society, Pagans for Peace, The Thomas Morton Alliance, and other anti-nuclear organizations are all in their own way calling our civilization to a collective *ecological and moral repentance* for its sins against the environment, the land, endangered species, and humanity itself. Pagans, by both word and deed, are sounding forth a call to repent (i. e., have a change of heart) about the way we look at Nature, life, and one another. When Jesus first said, "Repent, for the Kingdom of God is at hand!," he was ushering in the spiritual changes which were to be characteristics of the Piscean Age. Today, without realizing it, modern Paganism is fulfilling a similar function by calling the masses to repentance from the multitudinous sins of self-destruction which threaten to doom the planet: "Have a change of-heart, for the Realm of the Goddess is all around you, and yet you have not realized its sanctity!" And so we serve as prophetic lightning rods illuminating the urgency for planetary change and personal transformation ushering in the first fringes of the Aquarian Age, which, if our message is heeded, will become a millennium of harmony and peace.

Of course, this brief chapter on sin cannot even begin to scratch the surface of a topic so rich in potential for moral scrutiny and evaluation. Not every personal or political act can be considered automatically "black" or "white." Shades of grey always lurk in the shadows of our moral dilemmas, and life is not filled with easy answers, but the significance of sin lies in the fact that it keeps us acutely aware of the weaknesses which are common to humanity, and it is an essential element in the cosmic plan which experientially facilitates the fulfillment of the Serpent's promise: "Ye shall be as gods, knowing good and evil." When we have been sufficiently transformed through the process of spiritual growth to the point where we have learned to avoid the lure of evil through the knowledge of its deception, then sin as an ongoing reality may truly be relegated to a mere memory in the annals of human history. But until that Golden Age arrives, we dare not proclaim its demise or irrelevancy. To do so would be to deceive ourselves and prolong the ordeal of humankind's moral and spiritual adolescence.

In the Ordo Arcanorum Gradalis, each and every time we celebrate the Grail Mass we are consciously offering up the self-sacrifice of the Goddess and God in Their earthen guise as bread and wine for the sustenance of our spiritual growth and the healing of the sin-scarred wasteland which the world has become. Our Order is a Pagan priesthood which offers sacramental sacrifice for sin, that spiritual eyes might be enlightened and multitudes may have a change of heart about their environment, their neighbors, and themselves. And like the questing knights of old, we must attempt to teach those who seek the Grail to ask the right questions in order that the healing of our worldwide wasteland might be hastened.

Footnotes

1. De-Anna Alba. "The Goddess Emerging," *Gnosis* (Fall, 1989), p. 28.

2. Starhawk, *The Spiral Dance*. (San Francisco, CA: Harper & Row, 1979), p. 11.

3. Karl Menninger, M.D., *Whatever Became of Sin?* (New York, NY: Hawthorn Books, 1973).

4. *The Encyclopedia of Religion*, Vol. 13. Ed. by Mircea Eliade. (New York, NY: Macmillan Publishing Company, 1987), p. 327.

5. *Ibid.*, Vol. 12, p. 339.

6. S.G.F. Brandon, *Dictionary of Comparative Religion*. (New York, NY: Charles Scribner's Sons, 1970), p. 578.

7. *Encyclopedia of Religion and Ethics*, Vol. 11. Ed. by James Hastings. (New York, NY: Charles Scribner's Sons, 1926), pp. 528-531.

8. *Assyrian and Babylonian Literature, Selected Translations*. (D. Appleton and Co., 1901), p. 434.

9. *The International Standard Bible Encyclopedia*. Vol. 4. Ed. by Geoffrey W. Bromiley. (Grand Rapids, MI: William B. Eerdmans, 1988), p. 621.

10. *The Encyclopedia of Religion*, Vol. 5, p. 259.

11. Matthew 4:17, *Holy Bible*.

Chapter Eight

Magick, Meditation, and Maturity

here is something about the word "magick" that strikes a deep, inner resonance with our own inherent need to experience the terrifying exhilaration of being in some way a co-creator with the wonder-filled presence that is the moving power behind the universe. As children, magick was the thread which wove enchantment through our most cherished fairy tales. Our first experiences of "shape-shifting" owe much to the vividness of our childhood imagination which allowed us to become the ghost, witch, or fairy queen of our desire on that most magickal of nights—Halloween. A simple bed sheet became the ectoplasm of Casper's manifestation; a little make-up, an old black dress, and a worn-out broom turned us into night-flying specters in the moon-drenched sky.

In our youth, magick was the inexplicable evidence of an alternative reality which never ceased to amaze us with wonderment, but as we progressed through the stages of "growing up, " ascending the heady plateau of adolescent hubris and hormonal seduction, we eagerly sought to leave behind the last vestiges of childhood; attempting instead to propel ourselves into an adult maturity characterized by "rationality" and "common sense." However, in a world society permeated for nearly a century by the competing ideologies of capitalistic materialism on the one hand, and atheistic communism on the other, Western sociological projections of just what constitutes "maturity" have focused on a personal consciousness strapped by the straitjacket of scientific empiricism. This has led to an almost consistent denial of the supernatural, the paranormal, and the viability of unseen, parallel realities within our cosmological environment. In the long run, this societal homage to the golden calf of materialistic rationality has taken its toll upon the younger generation, whose most ambitious goals have reached their apex in the fevered frenzy for money and "the things that matter": a BMW in the garage, designer clothes, and membership in the most prestigious of the "body beautiful" health spas catering to the physical fantasies of the yuppie elite and other aspiring "corporate climbers."

In our modern, technologically oriented culture, "magic" has been reduced to an emasculated, circus-like caricature for Las Vegas stage shows, whose only substantial claim to reality is in the illusion of mirrors, rabbits in hats, and deceptive, slight-of-hand artistry. Yet running deep within the yearning of the human breast is an inexplicable desire to reclaim the lost heritage of our first estate, lingering within our soul as subtle shadings from pre-incarnate memories of faery and fantasy which persist in their interior insistence on a place within our conscious construct of reality, however perplexing or paradoxical they may seem. Much to the consternation of most accepted psychological perspectives, authentic spiritual maturity is incomplete without the assimilation of magick as an essential ingredient in its make-up.

The actual definition of magick is sometimes just as elusive as the reality which it attempts to convey. It has been described as everything from the interpenetration of parallel dimensions to the art of changing consciousness at will.[1] However, the technicalities of wording and phraseology are insignificant in comparison to the impact that true magick has had upon all of us who have been drawn to the paradoxical wisdom of the occult sciences. Whether we realize it or not, magick has often impacted upon the parameters of our consciousness, causing subtle changes in our spiritual vision and psychic senses of perception through such disciplines as ritual, meditative visualization, and prayer.

It is important that we keep in mind that there are different kinds of magick. For purposes of conciseness and brevity, we shall briefly examine four general classifications: religious, natural, ceremonial, and negative magick.

Religious Magick

Religious magick is also known in some circles as "High Theurgy, " and it is the magick with which the Ordo Arcanorum Gradalis is most involved. Its primary purpose is to bring the power and authority of the spiritual realm into manifestation on the physical as well as astral planes. It is evoked most effectively through the ritual trappings of worship, such as sacraments, chants, mantras, prayers, and inspirational music. Through these channels, worship becomes a spiritual process by which the individual psyche is tuned in to the ever-present will of the Divine Mind (i.e., *a transformation of consciousness*).

Religious magick invokes the power of gods and goddesses for the purpose of both enhancing and intensifying the strength of our spiritual natures; a means towards the ultimate end of personal *theosis*; in other words, a process which can eventually result in the deification of the individual human spirit. This (as was previously discussed in an earlier chapter) is one of the central values inherent in the philosophy of theurgic worship: oneness with Divinity; and indeed, nothing could be more magickal than the personal accomplishment of such a spiritual process.[2]

Natural Magick

Natural magick is the way in which many who style themselves as "kitchen witches" succeed in cooperating with the living force fields of their surrounding environment. This is especially true of those who specialize in the arcane and medicinal use of plants and herbs.[3] Being able to attune oneself to the elemental energies of wind, rivers, plants, Moon, stars, seasons, and Sun in such a way as to literally and *magickally* be one with the Earth is the legacy of a most venerable wisdom handed down from the dimmest recesses of antiquity. The natural magick known to the medieval midwives and wise-women of those dark and troubled times kindled both fear and envy in the perverse hearts of the corrupted Church establishment, giving rise eventually to the horrors of the Burning Times and the tortures of the Inquisition.

While religious magick is primarily a tool for the transformation of the human spirit, natural magick is a means of attuning to the subtle rhythms of the Earth and Cosmos which environmentally envelop us in order to psychically and physically cooperate with this vast web of energies for the optimum benefit of all involved. More and more good books on this fascinating subject have been published in recent years and they are highly recommended for those who wish to pursue their interests in this "earthy" facet of the magickal studies.[4]

Ceremonial Magick

Ceremonial magick is practiced most prevalently today in a number of magickal orders widespread throughout the Western world. They are usually initiatory and secretive, and they are not directly related to either Neo-Paganism or Wicca, although there are some who practice the Craft while they simultaneously pursue the teachings and rituals of ceremonial magick. Groups such as the Hermetic Order of the Golden Dawn have enjoyed immense popularity among the esoteric intelligentsia of the last century, and indeed, their influence even upon some of the basics of Neo-Pagan ritual is considerably more than minimal.

Significant portions of some of the traditions and rituals of the magickal orders and lodges owe much to the grimoires of medieval magicians who utilized various names and words of power ultimately derived from Judeo-Christian origins. The purposes of these magickal operations were often less than salutary, including the conjuring up of demons to do the bidding of the magician. Rites of sorcery were the stock and trade of many. However, in all fairness to the present-day practitioners of ceremonial magick, and especially the more reputable of the various orders and lodges, it should be pointed out that there are very legitimate groups which seek to use the time-honored techniques of their particular magickal traditions to achieve greater communion with the higher self and ancient hierarchy of the more advanced principalities on the angelic planes, and in these attempts they are to be highly commended. Yet the fact remains that novice dabblers new to the occult who participate in unsupervised experimentation with the rituals of ceremonial magick as a playground for their curious psychic exploration are in reality flirting with a deadly fire which could consume them. Ceremonial magick is not some form of psychic novelty game. It is serious, and without a thorough understanding of its working principles, utilizing these rituals in a cavalier manner can sometimes result in the nasty side effects of psychic disorientation, paranoia, and spiritual oppression. Only the psychically experienced and mature should actually contemplate participation in a magickal lodge, and then only after meticulous study and research to insure that whichever lodge or order they wish to approach for training is solely involved in the more sublime of the spiritual arts.[5]

Negative Magick

Perhaps the most famous (or infamous) kind of magick to capture the imagination of the Western psyche is sorcery, or negative magick. From the depiction of Mickey Mouse as the sorcerer's apprentice to the landscape of fairy tales replete with evil sorcerers, we are exposed to sorcery from the time of childhood when it begins to instill within us a sense of both fascination and dread. Unfortunately, now that many older teenagers and college-age students are once again discovering that magick does have an authentic frame of reference in the context of psychological and psychic reality, they have begun to flock in increasingly significant numbers to occult bookstores, driven by a curiosity regarding the "arcane arts, " which they often associate with sorcery. I personally know a proprietor of a local New Age/occult bookstore in my own community who has told me that many times he has witnessed the influx of magickally inexperienced high school students who come into his shop for the first time and immediately ask him where they can find the writings of Aleister Crowley;

something which for them could be likened to the equivalent of playing with burning brimstone![6] Despite any discouragement which he would express to them, their minds were made up to procure for themselves copies of Crowley's rituals and his other writings. This can easily be compared with a kindergartner insisting on reading a textbook on advanced trigonometry! However, people attracted to the occult for all the wrong reasons will often attempt a "crash course" in sorcery techniques for the purpose of instantly gratifying their psychic lust for power over others through hexes, curses, spells, and the darker aspects of ceremonial magick in order to make up for their own inner feelings of powerlessness and frustration.

As in all areas of the occult sciences, definitions as to exactly what constitutes sorcery are varied. Suffice it to say that for the purposes of this book sorcery is viewed as the intentional manipulation of psychic and spirit forces through ritual means for either selfish, intolerant, ego-centered, or malicious aggrandizement. Whereas religious and natural magick are forms of ceremonial *cooperation* with the deities and lower elemental forces, sorcery, on the other hand, is the attempted *coercion* of cosmic or natural energies for the accomplishment of personal and group ambitions. This is, unfortunately, one of the greatest attractions for young people drawn to the occult. Instead of wanting to progress in their own spiritual growth as a being in harmony with the universe, most are eager only for the "thrills and chills" of what they imagine to be the impregnability which accompanies psychic power. However, in the Ordo Arcanorum Gradalis, such base and egocentric attitudes are not tolerated, for they are antithetical to the aims and ethics of this Order.

Magick, then, in the O.A.G. is pervasive, yet paradoxically, strictly placed within limitations. It is pervasive to the extent that the highest forms of sacramental theurgy are practiced in all of our rituals to facilitate the interpersonal dynamic of spiritual communion between god/desses and humans; but when the context is shifted from worship to the manifestation of personal will in relationship to others, magick is placed within the tried and true limitations of ethical morality based upon respect and love.

Magickal spells and rituals designed to manipulate another individual against his/her will, or seeking to harm an enemy are invitations to the accumulation of disastrous karma. The Threefold Law of Witchcraft is of utmost importance in this connection: whatever you send out to others will return back to you threefold. If you are using magickal practices to hex, manipulate, or curse another, rest assured that you will eventually become the recipient of your own malicious vindictiveness![7]

Fundamentalist Sorcery

The practice of sorcery or negative magick is not the sole province of those less scrupulous members of the occult community at large. In the June, 1990, issue of the now defunct Wiccan publication *The Crone Papers*, the editor, Grey Cat, made a most astute observation about the psychic peril which is arrayed in force against the Neo-Pagan/Wiccan movement, but about which they as a whole seem almost oblivious:

> It is easy to observe that this year is being hard on groups in the Craft and Neo-Pagan world. So many groups I know or have heard about have been going through great changes, upsets, political battles and so on, that there does have to be something particular affecting us. Whether it is the stars *or that some of the fundamentalists' prayer groups are working effective magick against Goddess energy*, I don't know. I just know that it's happening to so many groups that it seems unlikely that it's caused by separate faults of the many leaders concerned![8]

Fundamentalists are familiar to most of us as more of a nuisance and/or political "thorn in the flesh" rather than a formidable army of psychic sorcerers. But it is my contention that Grey Cat has zeroed in on a most potent realization: fundamentalist and charismatic Christians have the magickal ability to wreak havoc within the ranks of contemporary Neo-Paganism *because they are masters of the art of prayer-sorcery*. Of course, good "born-againers" (especially charismatics and Pentecostals) would be mortally horrified at such a description of themselves, but the fact remains: if the shoe fits, wear it! And the shoe, indeed, *does* fit!

With regard to all of this, I speak from a wealth of experience. Having been within the inner circles of both moderate as well as fringe-fanatical charismatic churches for over fifteen years, I can write authoritatively about this subject, for I know extremely well about that in which I was once so intimately involved as a spiritual endeavor.

In the more aggressive charismatic groups spreading their influence among the Christian faithful, prayer is not some kind of moaning and groaning verbal exercise of religiosity which begs the Deity for trivial favors and vague generalities ending with the "fire-escape" clause of "if it be Thy will." Instead, prayer is perceived by them as being a trigger by which the supernatural powers and abilities of God are loosed into active creativity in the world. Prayer is not a begging for divine favors; it is the mental and verbal means of manifesting the Divine Will in the earth, based upon the promises given in the Scriptures. Of course, we all know that Bible passages have often been hopelessly taken out of context by fundamentalists, but that is irrelevant in this instance, for it is their faith and belief which makes their prayers effective magick, not the historical or Biblical accuracy of their theology.

From the fundamentalist viewpoint, Witchcraft, Paganism, and the occult are all directly related to the "End Times" as a manifestation of Satanic activity. The will of God for the "Church Militant" is therefore to be the agency by which the destructive judgments of the Lord are going to be visited upon the "ungodly," much in the same way as Moses brought Egypt to its knees by pronouncing the plagues upon them for their resistance. To this end, both prayer and prophetic utterances are utilized as the channels through which the human instrumentality of the Church will accomplish this "purification" of America so that they can once again become a nationalistic theocracy modeled upon the harshness of Old Testament outlooks with regard to "deviance" and "idolatry."

What the fundamentalists believe as part of their often warped theology might be basically irrelevant to us if it weren't for the fact that through the exercise of what they call the "Gifts of the Spirit" they have begun to function quite adeptly as psychics ("the word of knowledge"), oracles ("the word of wisdom"), mediums for channeled ecstatic utterances ("the gifts of tongues and interpretation"), exorcists ("discerning of spirits"), and shape-shifters of times and events ("the gift of prophecy"). In their own minds, of course, charismatic Christians consider these abilities to be an anointing of the Holy Spirit far superior to the "counterfeit" marvels of psychic phenomena which they consider to be all demonically inspired. Poor things, if only they realized that they were moving in the same extrasensory realms as those who they so heartily condemn! But the fact remains that in their vaulted spiritual egotism and exclusivity they have managed to master many occult gifts in the service of their religious paranoia and intolerance. When it comes to Neo-Pagans and Wiccans, that makes them extremely dangerous.

I can remember being in the midst of prayer services where the "judgments of the Lord" were invoked upon certain individuals in the public sector which their intolerance had labeled as enemies of God. In one such case, within two or three weeks after this modern-day "apostle" decreed the judgment, the person was dead. Other victims of such pronouncements often ended up in the hospital from heart attacks, etc.

Few people can imagine the psychic intensity which permeates a church which is moving in a strong psychic (charismatic) element. Physically, it feels like you are swimming in a sea of electricity all around you being generated by worship rising spontaneously from the people *and from the intensity of their prayer focus*. Imagine over 500 people in just one local church focusing these energies simultaneously towards the object of their wrath (Wiccans and Neo-Pagans) as they proclaim our disintegration and disarray in the name of the triumphant Christ! Now multiply that scene untold thousands of times for all the charismatic, fundamentalist, and Pentecostal churches sharing such a similar focus of prayer on a typical Wednesday night prayer meeting! Do not think even for a moment that Witches alone raise cones of power. Charismatics are most experienced in this practice, they just call it by other names.

The use (or in their case, the *misuse*) of the name of Christ can be a most potent force, for he is one of the strongest Archetypes of Western spirituality. To be sure, they are abusing the power of his name, but the negative effect of such Christian hexing should be a source of concern for most of us involved in non-traditional, spiritual pathways. The bottom line of all this is that these psychically oriented "true believers" are beginning to work effective sorcery against us, and one of the biggest factors is the lack of spiritual awareness and discipline among Pagans in general which keeps them in the dark regarding the concerted onslaught of charismatic cursings and the power of their negative prayer projections.

Lest anyone think accusing fanatical Christians of sorcery to be "far-fetched," a little Biblical refresher course would be in order. In the *Acts of the Apostles* is recorded an incident where Paul uses his own unexplained magickal means to convey temporary blindness upon a rival sorcerer who was trying to discredit him.[9] In one of his epistles to the church in Corinth, Paul went so far as to pronounce a death-judgment upon a wayward member of the congregation who had lapsed into the practice of incest:

> For though absent in body I am present in spirit, and as if present, *I have already pronounced judgment* in the name of the Lord Jesus on the man who has done this thing (married his stepmother). When you (the local church) are assembled, and my spirit is present (it would seem that Paul was adept at leaving his body at will), with the power of our Lord Jesus, you are to deliver this man to Satan *for the destruction of his flesh*, that his spirit may be saved in the day of the Lord.[10]

Regarding this, some theologians have candidly admitted that "Paul calls for the invoking of a curse that will bring about the man's death."[11] When the apostle Peter caught two members of the Jerusalem church in a lie about how much they had donated to the congregation, he proclaimed upon them the judgment of the Holy Spirit and they both fell dead at his feet, and it says that "great fear came upon them all" (that is what I would call rather drastic church discipline!).[12] Neither was the apostle Paul above pronouncing curses upon anyone (including angels) who disagreed with his particular interpretation of the Gospel.[13] According to Jewish tradition, Moses was also well-schooled in the magickal arts of Egypt, which would readily explain his ability to foil the abilities of the Pharaoh's priests. Daniel is also described as being in charge of, and chief over, all the court astrologers and magicians of ancient Babylon, and the most proficient among them in dream interpretation.[14] All of this was not lost on certain popes who were avid practitioners of the magickal arts!

None of this information is meant to imply that contemporary charismatic and fundamentalist Christians are consciously trying to practice forms of known sorcery, but it *is* produced as obvious examples of what kind of attitudes and psychic force can be engendered by people who are convinced that they are in league with the "only true God" and are being used as his prophetic instruments to combat evil and transform the Earth in preparation for Christ's coming again. So, as we have seen, everything in the pages of the New Testament is not all "gentle Jesus, meek and mild," as much Christian propaganda would have us believe. When they get serious about "casting out the power of Satan" and "binding the enemy" (presumably "demonic religions" like Neo-Paganism and Wicca), they will stop at nothing to accomplish what they believe to be their God-appointed mission, including using every psychic weapon at their disposal from the arsenal of the "Gifts of the Holy Spirit." I have personally witnessed prayer meetings where the dire judgments of God were invoked upon those who practice Witchcraft in the land, and believe me, you would not have wanted to be on the receiving end of the death and destruction they were "prayerfully" aiming our way!

What then should be a constructive Craft response to this specter of spiritual sorcery? Our approach should be threefold. First, it is imperative to realize that we are involved, whether we like it or not, in *spiritual and psychic warfare* with these sworn, fanatical enemies of our religion, and this is exactly the way they view their relationship with us. When we are spiritually, politically, and psychically attacked, our defenses undermined, and our movement as a whole debilitated by a continuous barrage of negative prayer and destructive oracular energies generated by literally hundreds of thousands of fundamentalist, charismatic, and Pentecostal Christian "soldiers, " it is time we wake up to the peril that threatens our progress.

Psychic self-defense should be the first of our priorities not only as individuals, but also for the preservation and strengthening of our covens and groves. There are already numerous books which can be obtained that give valuable instructions about erecting barriers for deflecting psychic attack.[15] It is time that Neo-Pagan and Wiccan groups begin to take this advice seriously and start putting it into practice.

While it is of the utmost importance that we tune ourselves into a "defense awareness" for our protection, it is also mandatory that we begin to take the offensive against these enemy soldiers of religious intolerance. One of the best offenses is an aggressive campaign of *education*, where we take every opportunity to dispel the ignorance which gives rise to gross superstitions and fears about the Craft among the uninformed. This would include the formation of speakers bureaus in the local Pagan communities which would be ready to speak to churches, community organizations, and any other interested groups regarding the truth about Wicca, Earth religions, and Nature-oriented spirituality. When the public at large begins to understand that we are not evil, demented devil-worshippers, but simply representatives of a holistic approach to natural spirituality based upon ancient precedent, then a lot of the "fright-rhetoric" of fundamentalist firebrands will be unable to find a lodging within the rationality of most thoughtful citizens.

We also need to revitalize our own oracular abilities and recognize the calling within the Pagan priesthood to prophetic positions where channeled words of spoken prophecy and guidance are part and parcel of the seer's responsibility. The charismatics have discovered that words have inherent power to create that to which they give verbal form. But in reality, much of this concept regarding the power of the spoken word was inherited by Christianity from earlier Pagan religions as well as the Hebrew prophetic tradition. As Pagans, we need to reclaim our own traditions of seership. (A more detailed analysis of this subject will be forthcoming later in this chapter.)

Third and finally, we must find a way of strengthening our own commitment to a form of Pagan spirituality which permeates our entire lifestyle and facilitates a continual flow of divine energy through us as a channel for the healing of people and the planet. Prayer and intense meditative communion with our deities are the key to the reinforcement of our own inner strength. Without it, "fair-weather" Pagans who embrace the Old Religion as a form of romantic escapism from the status quo of society's establishment mentality will soon wither on the vine when the heat of persecution from the psychic aggression of committed Christian "soldiers" begins to tear apart the fabric of Neo-Pagan cohesiveness. How we respond to the threat of fundamentalist sorcery will help to determine the future health of our religious expression and the vitality of our spiritual focus. The challenge is upon us and the solution is ours to create.

Meditation

A metaphysical trendsetter in recent years among both New Age and Neo-Pagan practices has been the rapid dissemination of various techniques for the practice of personal meditation, creative visualization, and astral projection. In many ways, meditation has become a "buzz word" among large numbers of esoteric groupies. Of course, there is nothing wrong with meditation, per se. In fact, its positive, psychic, spiritual, and even physical side effects have been well-documented and described by numerous books on the subject which are available in most New Age bookstores.

To be sure, there are different kinds of meditation, ranging from the practices of Eastern yoga and metaphysics and Zen tradition to those of the Christian hermits and mystics. It is not my intention to rehash the details and comparisons between these meditative variations, but rather to simply suggest a few pertinent guidelines which can help those new to such concepts to avoid certain pitfalls which could be psychically disruptive to their inner growth.

Unfortunately, most people associate meditation solely with a type of mind-quieting passivity where the individual allows his/her consciousness to become a slate-cleaned blank devoid of thoughts and distractions; and although this is not necessarily an accurate portrayal of meditation either in its goals or techniques, the stereotype of one sitting in a yoga position chanting "OM" is a misleading caricature which has lead most marginally informed people into associating meditation exclusively with a form of metaphysical self-lobotomy. Actually, the most established of meditative techniques, when properly followed, can only result in physical health, inner growth, and spiritual serenity. However, there are other loosely related techniques aimed at inducing trance states designed to facilitate out-of-body experiences which, when practiced by inexperienced novices who have not been properly trained, can open up the psyche to a state of passive vulnerability which can make the mind a potential channel or mediumistic conduit for just about any kind of disembodied entity who decides to take up temporary residence.

A good example of this danger can be found in the New Age obsession with "channeling," which is really nothing more than a trendy word substitute for old-fashioned spirit mediumship with one important difference: in years gone by, the mediums in the Spiritualist Churches were usually much more experienced and ethical. Today it is obvious that the New Age movement, ravaged as it is with unsuspecting gullibility, has become a target for plenty of manipulating and deceitful spirit entities who revel in their ability to use these unquestioning channelers for the propagation of bogus oracles and misleading messages pertaining to life's greatest mysteries. Sometimes these entities are simply taking advantage of the psychic openness of those who often experiment with altered states of consciousness and various kinds of trance workings in order to satisfy their yen for the recognition and prestige which were denied them in their embodied state. Too often we make the mistake of assuming that all the dead who have passed on into the invisible realms are automatically elevated to high levels of cosmic knowledge and spiritual purity. Such is simply not the case. The early Christians had a saying which was certainly grounded in healthy discernment: "Trust not every spirit, but test the spirits to see if they be of God."[16] (This is a little gem of wisdom based on obvious experience, and we should be open enough to take truth wherever we find it—even in the Christian scriptures.)

The plethora of New Age channelers taking their mediumistic show on the road with high-priced seminars promising people the secrets of spirituality through new revelations of cosmic insight from their own "familiar spirits" is yet another indication of the moral dubiousness of those who use their channeled "gifts" as a vehicle for selling the supernatural. It should also not go without notice that a comparison of some of the channeled statements of various competing entities will occasionally reveal an uncomfortable amount of contradictions surrounded in a verbal haze of vagueness. You would assume that if all these spirits had access to Higher Truth, their revelations would not be at odds with one another! (There is also the possibility that some of these New Age entrepreneurs are only channeling the fantasies of their own fertile imaginations, which further complicates the search for oracular authenticity.)

These reflections are not meant to imply that the channeling of loving and truthful entities is not a possibility. Indeed, it is plain that Beings of Light have been impinging on the parameters of human consciousness with far greater frequency than in the past, even in some of the more reputable quarters of the New Age movement; but it is essential that we learn to develop our faculties of spiritual discernment in order to protect ourselves from the barrages of metaphysical deception sometimes transmitted by the denizens of darkness via the astral airwaves to the unsuspecting minds of the spiritually naive. For this reason it is strongly recommended that those who choose to practice some of the more involved meditative or trance techniques be careful to first reinforce their auric fields through specific psychic exercises designed to protect both spirit and body from unwanted interference from negative entities.[17] This also holds true for those who practice various forms of creative visualization, since some of the more advanced of these exercises can occasionally culminate in actual out-of-body experiences where protection on the astral plane would be most needful.

Meditation, of course, should not be grounded in the over-generalized premise that it is always a precursor to trance states and resulting psychic vulnerability. Such is simply not the case. Another form of meditation that is often overlooked by present-day New Age adherents consists of exercises in the time-honored techniques of active contemplation. This kind of meditation is also well-suited for those whose busy schedules afford them little time for the luxuries of extended peace and quiet. For instance, one can meditate or actively contemplate certain inspiring texts from the rituals of the O.A.G. (see the last half of this book), or mentally dwell upon the underlying, mystic meanings of the Major Arcana of the Tarot, or upon descriptions and characteristics of the high gods and goddesses of antiquity, just to give a few examples. When you meditate in this way it does not necessarily require a serene setting undisturbed by the business of daily life. This kind of contemplation can continue on throughout the course of a day within your mind. As another example, many evangelical Christians have a meditational regimen where they utilize daily "scripture cards." Each one has the text of a Bible verse printed upon it. Their aim is to memorize and meditate upon one verse each day, thereby building up their knowledge of scripture recall as well as being edifying to their own spirit. In the same way, we can mentally dwell upon the deeper aspects of the sacred mysteries by following similar techniques of contemplation. This kind of active meditation also has the added benefit of being virtually immune from any of the dangers posed by certain forms of deep trance states when irresponsibly practiced by spiritual novices.

The bottom line to this concern over the use of various psychic techniques as a tool for spiritual growth is the need for exercise on the part of each individual of precautionary and protective measures to keep both one's spirit and aura intact from the damage which can be inflicted by manipulating and unscrupulous entities which are all around us on the invisible planes. Trance and astral projection work, like magick, must be approached with the utmost respect and carefulness in order to extract from its processes the ultimate reward of the Gnosis—that interior knowledge of the self and its place in the cosmic scheme.

Maturity and the Spiritual Gifts

Magick, as well as meditation and all the other related fields of esoteric practice, should have as their ultimate aim the equipping of the practitioner with the means to facilitate the full manifestation of his/her spiritual maturity. Maturity is achieved only through a growth process whereby the individual learns to balance the competing internal drives of his/her own personhood. In some theologies, a human being possesses three major components which make up the totality of the individual: body (physical appetites and functions), soul (emotions and feelings), and spirit (the eternal seat of our spiritual individuality [i.e., the Higher Self]). Sad to say, most of humanity lives in a perpetual state of imbalance between these different aspects of personal make-up. For far too many, the physical desires of the body and its cravings (such as food and sex) take center stage as obsessive priorities. Others live entrapped by the snares of their soulish nature, riding a continual roller coaster of careening emotions, mood swings, and attitudes dictated by the fluctuating state of their feelings. Far too few, unfortunately, have even discovered the reality of their own spiritual consciousness, buried as it often is beneath the blankets of physical and emotional preoccupations. But the key to achieving maturity lies in one's ability to *balance* these three aspects of human personality.

The body is a beautiful creation of divine craftmanship, and its desires are healthy and beneficial *when indulged in a moderation* which does not allow for its dominance over the fully wholesome expression of one's soul and spirit. The same holds true for our soulish or emotional nature. Of course, the ideal state for which we should all be striving is one in which we are so in tune with our higher self that its wisdom and guidance produces interrelated, harmonious balance between body, soul, and spirit, enabling us to attain the complete expression of all that we were meant to be as mature human beings made in the image of the Goddess and the God.

Maturity, however, should not be seen only as an individual state of development. One of the most important issues yet to be plumbed to its depths is the need for a magickal growth process which can succeed in bringing about a real manifestation of communal maturity within the Neo-Pagan/Wiccan community at large. Ironically, one of the keys for the inauguration of such a transformative process can be found in the early epistles of the Christian apostle, Paul. As we touched upon earlier in this chapter, charismatic Christians have become a potent force as a religious community due to their effective use of what is commonly termed by them as the "Gifts of the Spirit." What most of the Pagan community does not realize, however, is the integral fact that these psychic/spiritual gifts were not the exclusive property of the early Church:

> It is very important that Christians today understand the universal sources from which the mosaic of Judeo-Christian revelation and inspiration were taken. Indeed the ancient Jews originated in Mesopotamia, passed through the civilization of Egypt, entered Canaan, were dominated by other nations including Persia, Greece and Rome. They absorbed, modified, and re-presented in new cultural forms of their own (in the Yahwist cult) many of the Primordial insights of pagan wisdom. Intuitive sources of ancient-sacral knowledge, such as prophecy, trance phenomena, oracular consultations and other psychic experiences, were used by Israelite and pagan alike. A

whole common typology of intuitive wisdom deriving from such sources may be found among mystical Jewish groups well before the Christian era.[18]

Paul listed these special gifts in his epistle to the local church in Corinth around 55 CE, and they are as follows: the Word of Wisdom, the Word of Knowledge, Prophecy, Miracles, Healing, Discerning of Spirits, Faith, Tongues, and Interpretation of Tongues. Most all of these singular abilities were familiar to pre-Christian Pagans as manifestations of the divine *charis*, or *grace*, of the Goddess within the context of many of their own priesthoods, and it clear that these gifts were of a decidedly psychic nature, even as practiced within the early Church:

> St. Paul enumerates other psychic gifts of the Spirit as including prophecy, miracle working, and healing. Prophecy in the early Christian community clearly included what we would today call clairvoyance, clairaudience, precognition, and distant viewing; and miracle working included psychokinetic phenomena of various types as signs of the divine presence in the works of apostles and other Christian missionaries.[19]

Since these gifts were common to the religious phenomena of Pagans as well as Christians, it would definitely be advantageous to us if we briefly examined the nature of each of these special graces to see if we as contemporary Neo-Pagans and Wiccans have adequately sought after a proficiency in these spiritual talents.

"THE WORD OF WISDOM"—(i.e., the gift of being able to convey divine wisdom through the medium of personal counsel and inspired speech). Long before the rise of the Church, wise sages throughout the Pagan world were often sought after because of their gifted insight. But in a Pagan context, perhaps the best examples of this kind of wisdom were dispensed through the oracular shrines dedicated to the various gods and goddesses, and whose function was to give answers of divine guidance to those who came as pilgrims with perplexing and important questions which required replies of unusual depth and discernment.

"THE WORD OF KNOWLEDGE"—(i.e., the ability of telepathic discernment as well as "mind-reading" and the gift of knowing a person's past, complete with specific incidents, even though no prior contact or communication with the person has ever taken place). It can be quite unnerving to have a priest/ess meet you for the first time and yet be able to tell you things about yourself which only you could possibly know! Jesus, for instance, illustrated this psychic ability on more than one occasion.[20] This talent was often seen in ancient times as an indication that one was possessed by the mind of a god.

While there has been little, if any, emphasis upon this gift in modern Neo-Paganism, it is a subject which needs to be seriously studied so that aspiring priest/esses can strive to walk in this age-old ability anciently attributed to the Sight. I have personally seen it practiced within a charismatic Christian context, and its effect has been particularly impressionable upon the minds of those touched by the experience, especially the skeptical. This is a psychic gift which can be instrumental in confirming to others the authenticity of a divine presence actively at work within the Pagan priesthood.

"PROPHECY"—Prophecy has never been the exclusive property of Christian clairvoyance. Oracular shrines dispensing glimpses into the activities of future generations as well as granting insight into individual motives and future life-choices were well-known throughout the Pagan religious landscape of the ancient world, foremost among them being such shrines as the one at Delphi. Others included Claros, Didyma, and Patara.[21] Prophets and prophetesses were also common in the Pagan priesthood.[22]

Literally, prophecy is the art of "forth-telling." It is not merely a predictive type of oracular revelation, but can also have reference to any form of speech which is so weighted with the heaviness of divine inspiration that it conveys within its words an inherently creative force able to bring about the accomplishment of that which it envisions. It would be wise indeed for contemporary priests and priestesses of the Neo-Pagan/Wiccan revival to more actively entertain the concept of their own spoken words at certain auspicious times becoming virtual oracles of prophetic inspiration which empower their hearers with the guidance and insight to bring into actual manifestation these divinely channeled directives sent to us via the good daemons (messengers) of the Goddess and the God.

Our words have the potential of being a creative force for change towards good or evil, or they can simply be dissipated in directionless chatter and general verbal wastefulness. Our alternative is to contend within the unexplored recesses of our latent spirituality for the faith that we can truly speak for the Mighty Ones when moved upon by the divine Spirit. We need to have the farsightedness to envision the reality of Pagan prophets and prophetesses speaking as living oracles throughout the land, encouraging the hearts of those loyal to the love of the Lady.

"MIRACLES"—This gift needs little elaboration. Suffice it to say that miracles have been known, experienced, and recorded in the annals of every major religion of the world, both ancient and modern. Obviously, they are not as commonplace in religious experience as are many other spiritual gifts, but they usually surface unpredictably in ways which confirm to those who witness or experience such a seemingly inexplicable event that the numinous presence and power of Deity is a reality which still impinges upon the consciousness of human history.

Miracles are not necessarily the result of tediously strained efforts at personal psychic development; they are, more than likely, the product of a life lived in intimate proximity with the heart-soul of the divine will, enabling an individual to become a channel of tremendous psychic and spiritual energies which can transcend the seeming limitations of our physical environment with transformative occurrences which can be described as nothing short of miraculous. As Neo-Pagans and Wiccans, this possibility should challenge us to a deeper walk with the god/desses of our respective pantheons that we might be graced with their abilities and insights to accomplish those "greater works" which will redound to the glory and worship of that Holy Presence which demonstrates its love for us through such actions.[23]

"HEALING"—Psychic abilities of a spiritually gifted person being used for the physical healing of others' ailments and debilitations are well attested throughout religious history from the distant past right up to the present time. Of all the grace-gifts of the Goddess, this one seems to be the most popular and sought after.

The Church has always had those within its ranks who cured and raised up the sick in accordance with apostolic injunction, despite the irritating presence in every age (especially ours) of evangelical charlatans and charismatic fakes whose primary ministry is that of leeching from the gullible and the trusting every dollar bill which they can extract through the application of deceptive emotionalism and sophisticated trickery. Of course, like the other gifts, Christians have never had a monopoly on the effective use of psychic healing powers. Over the last decade, the New Age movement has encouraged the resurgence of this most compassionate gift. With techniques ranging from the reading of auras to the use of crystals, many people in need are being touched with the extrasensory technologies of physical wholeness.

To a great extent, Neo-Pagans in general have also become very attuned to the reality of healing through herbs as well as meditation, demonstrating that this one gift has a variety of ways in which it can be applied in order to meet individual needs. Those who feel a drawing towards the possibility of becoming a healer should follow their intuitive instincts in this regard, for healing is one of the most charitable and love-manifesting of all the gifts; a magickal balm for the sores of a sickness-ravaged world.

"DISCERNING OF SPIRITS"—The ability to discern the true nature of spirits and all sorts of invisible entities is one of the most important of all spiritual gifts, for it is essentially protective in its nature. It is the divinely given means by which any religious community can guard itself from the intrusion and deceptive designs of malevolent or evil spirits. Sad to say, there are some in the ranks of New Age believers who scoff at the very idea of evil spirits, assuming that true spiritual beings can only be pure and good; evil being merely the creation of deluded and negative thinking. While this is not the place for an in-depth examination of the question of evil, even a superficial overview of the many religions of the world from the advent of antiquity to the present reveals a consistent belief in the existence of evil spirit forces in the invisible realms. We should therefore be most reticent to ignore thousands of years of human religious testimony in this matter.

One of the most important aspects related to the discerning of spirits is exorcism. This is a subject barely broached in contemporary Neo-Paganism, mainly because of an uncomfortableness in dealing face-to-face with the specter of incarnate evil, spirit possession and oppression, or any kind of actual confrontation with negative entities. To be sure, those who have difficulty believing in the reality of the supernatural or demonic beings of any form would have even more trouble in accepting the validity of exorcism! However, for those Pagans who have progressed beyond the stage of trying to explain away the objective existence of the spirit realm with psychological double-talk, the time is overdue for an in-depth examination of the proper place and purpose of exorcism within our religious community.

While Christians have recourse to priests and ministers specially trained in the area of exorcism, Neo-Pagans and Wiccans, on the other hand, cannot simply thumb through the Yellow Pages for a priest or priestess proficient in the art of casting out spirits! This is not meant to imply that possession is somehow rampant among us, but for an occult religion which utilizes techniques and rituals designed to interconnect with invisible worlds of gods and spirits, it would behoove us to take an open-eyed, second look at this subject.

Exorcism is not applicable only to situations involving possessive evil entities. Sometimes there are cases of disoriented, Earth-bound spirits oppressively haunting a certain house, area, or person. In such cases it would be advantageous if we had recourse to those who were knowledgeable in these often perplexing situations, and who had the spiritual ability to deal with them.

Exorcism is, needless to say, not the most popular ministerial profession to which one can be called! However, for those who feel a leading to explore this area further, make sure that you are first spiritually and emotionally grounded with a sense of stability and the protective armor of a reinforced aura. Paganism has had exorcists within its priestly ranks since time immemorial, and the time is ripe for us to assert our proficiency in this ability once more, in order to insure for those few who become entrapped victims of spirit harassment the means of their liberation.

The discerning of spirits can be an invaluable aid in consolidating the spiritual cohesiveness of Neo-Pagan and Wiccan groups. No doubt, many priests and priestesses charged with the responsibility of guiding, nurturing, and teaching fledgling groups of novices have at times unconsciously made use of this gift in several different ways for their own or their group's protection. Many Pagan leaders have experienced a situation where someone wanted to become involved with the grove or coven, but there was just that certain "something" which they couldn't put their finger on, but it caused a sense of wariness or uncomfortableness to arise within them to such an extent that the person was declined an invitation to attend the group's activities. This is an indication of the first stirrings of the gift within a leader, for the gift is for the discerning, not only of other spirit entities, but also for discerning the condition of another *person's* spirit, or spiritual condition. Without the development of such psychic intuition, many Neo-Pagan and other magickal groups would be prime targets for any number of weirdos and unbalanced "creeps" whose presence in group gatherings would tend to be both distracting and disruptive.

The gift of discerning spirits can often be used extensively within the ritual circle. Occasionally before a ritual, the priest/ess may sense the presence of negative forces which for some reason have been attracted to the circle area. This will immediately alert him/her to the potential disruptive danger in time to perform an extra-strong banishing before the circle begins.

At other times, during the course of a ritual one can sometimes perceive the presence of certain elementals, angels, or lesser divinities, as well as spirits of the dead (especially at Samhain) in attendance. Many times they are drawn by the worship itself and are simply lending their protective presence, but if one through the discerning of spirits is enabled to become aware of them, it can enhance the power of the ritual in a most positive way.

The ability to see into the spirit realm is truly a gift of the Sight, and should be cultivated wherever the seeds of its inception are found scattered within the soil of the psyche.

"FAITH"—All of us at one time or another have known someone who had the inner self-assurance that things would work out for the best, despite the dour appearances of the immediate crisis or situation through which they were passing. The gift of faith has nothing to do with Pollyanna expectations based upon little more than the naive hope that "everything will be all right." True gift-faith has a direct relationship with that phenomenon often alluded to as an "inner knowing"; a personal experience of the omniscience in however faint a measure, which infuses within the human spirit a sense of the ultimate reality undergirding all things, its purpose and its goal. This in turn stabilizes one's spiritual perspective, and inspires the power to persevere through the turbulence and transience of daily life. Such a gift is often not recognized for what it truly is because it does not issue forth in the miraculous or the psychically spectacular, but without the hope generated by living faith, our religious sense of purpose and destiny would be sorely weakened and undernourished.

"TONGUES AND INTERPRETATION OF TONGUES"—This is without a doubt the most controversial and misunderstood of all the spiritual gifts. In Christianity, differences in doctrine over this topic have led to fierce feuding and the rending of church membership rolls because of flared theological tempers. Neo-Pagans, on the other hand, have barely even thought about the nature of tongues and its possible relationship to Pagan worship, assuming it to be a purely fringe phenomenon confined to certain sects of Christianity. History, however, is full of surprises for both Neo-Pagans and Christians when it comes to discovering the religious roots of this "tongues" issue.

Speaking in tongues, or *glossolalia*, as it is often called in scholarly theological quarters, can best be described as the unexplained ability of a person to speak a language hitherto unlearned. It could be a contemporary language such as Japanese or Italian, or a technically "dead" tongue of an ancient culture such as Etruscan or Sumerian. But in by far the majority of instances where speaking in tongues has been heard by observers, these utterances, while spoken in a verbal flow resembling the audible characteristics attributable to a language, defy identification with any known spoken dialect. Taking this into consideration, one Bible translation rendered the word "tongues" in Paul's listing of spiritual gifts as "ecstatic utterances."[24]

What most Neo-Pagans have failed to grasp regarding this subject is that the origins of "tongue-speaking" lie squarely within the sacral contexts of ancient Pagan religious fervor and ritual, not in the innovations of Christian piety:

> ... it had never been pointed out to me until I prowled through historical commentaries that glossolalia had pre-Christian antecedents and that the phenomenon was by no means uncommon in ancient rituals where pagan gods were worshipped.[25]

In fact, some fundamentalists who are opposed to the phenomenon of glossolalia, have not hesitated to point out the historical connections of speaking in tongues with Pagan cultic practices in their attempt to malign this spiritual gift.[26] As an example, it is known that the worshippers of Hermes, the Syrian goddess Juno, and other Pagan deities were often reputed to speak in unknown ecstatic utterances as part of their religious expression.[27] This was especially true in Corinth, to which, as mentioned earlier, Paul addressed his epistle, and where even a "language of ghosts" was said to have been spoken in the religious rituals of the city.[28] This brings into clearer focus why he spent so much time discussing the issue of glossolalia in his writing to them, for he was taking great pains to try and give guidelines to that church which would carefully distinguish the way Christians practiced this gift as opposed to its use by the Pagan Greeks in their own temple services. The relationship of magickal formulae for the invocation of deities with Pagan tongue-speaking has also not gone unnoticed by historical researchers:

> Besides the writings ascribed to individuals there are formulae and unintelligible lists of names and letters used in magical papyri for the invoking of gods and spirits and thought by some to derive from glossolalia. In these there are echoes of oriental languages mingled with gibberish, thought to have originated in allegedly supra-terrestrial tongues used by gods and spirits, each class being allocated its peculiar language or dialect.[29]

Speaking in other tongues has been verified as a recurring practice among many religions, both sophisticated and primitive, from around the world.[30] It is with good reason, then, that we examine the pertinent rationale which warrants a renewal of focus upon this almost forgotten *Pagan* religious practice in the life of contemporary Neo-Paganism.

Basically speaking, there are two kinds of glossolalia within a Pagan religious context. One is activated in an individual when that person is temporarily possessed by the spirit of a god or goddess, and begins to speak ecstatically in the language of the deity, usually unintelligible to those who are listening. This often necessitates the presence of a prophet or prophetess who can give an interpretation of the inspired message. This was normally the way in which the sacred oracles were revealed through the resident priest or priestess of a shrine.[31] In fact, in these particular situations there was often the simultaneous activity of several spiritual gifts, including tongues, interpretation of tongues, prophecy, and the word of wisdom.

> … the path of glossolalia led from the festivals at Eleusis to Delphi where the oracle set in the sulphurous mist, her throne the tripod of Apollo, whose messenger she was. Her temple was in a cleft of the rocks near a holy hill, close to a sacred stream on the southwest slopes of Mt. Parnassus. Here she was visited by rulers and citizens from far and near. Here she prophesied and often when the ecstasy came upon her, her voice was taken over by Apollo and her words would be unknown even to herself. Men said she was intoxicated with the presence of the god, but a city grew up around Delphi because of her. Delphi—where men drank of the sacred stream and stood at the water's edge and spoke in tongues.[32]

The other and much more common aspect of speaking in tongues occurs with worshippers, either individually or in groups, who become overwhelmed or moved upon by the spirit of divine ecstasy. This is usually not oracular in nature necessitating any kind of interpretation, for it is primarily a form of personal praise ascending from the lips of the worshipper to the throne of the Deity.

> Clearly glossolalia had its origin in unrecorded history … Long before the coming of churches and temples, before men were certain about the object of their worship, an inner awareness of something higher and greater than themselves filled their hearts with rapture and their tongues with praise. This became an accepted practice wherever people gathered in religious and prophetic observances.[33]

The Christian apostle Paul described the very same phenomenon as a gift whose primary purpose was praise of the Deity and the resulting personal edification of the human spirit. "When a man is using the language of ecstasy he is talking with God, not with men, for no man understands him; he is no doubt inspired, but he speaks mysteries."[34] Speaking in tongues is a way of worship which enables one's spirit to bypass dependence upon the conscious mind as a filtering vehicle for the directing and focusing of praise. Instead, the higher faculties of the human spirit, in conjunction with the overshadowing presence of Divinity, takes control of the tongue, and through it speaks forth the ecstasy of spiritual communion: spirit with spirit. For those who have ever spoken in tongues, it is a never-to-be-forgotten experience which reinforces belief in the reality of a personal interaction with the numinous.

Over twenty years ago, Marcus Bach, an ecumenical religious pioneer of his day, wrote a fascinating book about his own Pentecostal experience which resulted in his "baptism in the Holy Spirit" and subsequent speaking in tongues; but what makes his book such a gem of religious insight was his realization that glossolalia, whether spoken in a Pentecostal revival meeting or in the ancient mystery cult rit-

uals of the Hellenistic world, were all examples of a spiritual gift emanating ultimately from the same supernatural source. Recalling the time shortly after this realization had dawned upon him as the result of his historical research, he wrote:

> I went about my work in the printery and directed the orchestra at the ser-
> vices and sometimes spoke in tongues, but never now without a new iden-
> tification. Now when "tongues" broke out in ecstatical Pentecostal
> meetings honoring God and Jesus, I heard it in Phrygian festivals praising
> Attis and Cybele, in Syrian services paying homage to Adonis and
> Aphrodite, in Egyptian rituals where Isis and Osiris were worshipped, and
> in Roman festivals where, on the occasion of the Saturnalia held in late
> December, it inspired the exchange of gifts.
>
> … When would they (Pentecostal Christians) learn that the nature of
> ecstasy increases by virtue of its universality? When would they recognize
> that since glossolalia was demonstrated in pagan times, it took on added
> significance when the Apostles "Christianized" it?[35]

These words should give us pause to reflect upon the opportunities we have to
carry on the gift of glossolalia as expressed in the annals of historic Pagan tradition.
As Bach admits, the early Church did little more than "Christianize" a prevalent
practice found in Pagan worship. We need to reclaim many of the psychic and spiritual gifts that are part of our forgotten religious legacy, and speaking in tongues is
certainly one of them.

Finally, it should be noted with intense interest in the Neo-Pagan and Wiccan
communities that speaking, or even singing in other tongues, can be a most powerful way of raising the energies necessary for a "cone of power" within a ritual context. The power of praise raised through the medium of glossolalia can create some
of the most intense magick energies imaginable. Anyone who has ever witnessed a
charismatic congregation "singing in the spirit" (i.e., tongues) will certainly nod in
agreement. If we consciously begin to manifest these same Goddess-given gifts
within the Neo-Pagan community at large, the effects could be absolutely staggering in their transformative implications.

Conclusion

This briefly sketched outline of spiritual grace-gifts, or *charismata*, demonstrates the
pervasive usage of these abilities everywhere in the ancient world, irrespective of
partisan religious contexts. These "gifts of the Spirit" transcend the petty divisive-
ness of religious competition. The reservoir of their power has been tapped by Christian, Jew, and Pagan alike. Of course, true to their intolerant little hearts, early
Christians as well as present-day charismatics have self-righteously pointed the fin-

ger of accusation at any group or sect not in agreement with their own, insisting that any manifestation of such extraordinary gifts outside of their "only true Faith" was a deceptive form of supernatural trickery on the part of Satan in order to lead others astray from the Christian message.[36] It is truly unfortunate that such a parochial theological mindset has so infected many quarters of the Christian Church.

Much to the disappointment of some, there is no set pattern which one can follow in order to receive or develop these spiritual gifts. While some Pentecostal and charasmatic Christians have formulated a specific sequence of steps which must be taken by the individual seeker in order to receive the "baptism of the Holy Spirit," and subsequently these gifts; nevertheless, the experience of many has tended to support the belief that the ways we each come into an appropriation of these extraordinary abilities is as varied as those who seek them. There are, however, a few general guidelines which could be helpful. First, focus your priority upon a religious walk with the Goddess and the God which is daily strengthened through conversational prayer and a heartfelt attitude of reverence and worship. Secondly, be sensitive to the inner promptings of your own spirit as to which of these gifts you should seek to develop, for sometimes they can be lying dormant within you just waiting for your own spiritual desire to awaken and bring them to life. Thirdly, there are some gifts which are sovereignly given by the Lady to those of Her own choosing. So if we wish to be used by Her as a willing cooperator in Her sometimes inscrutable plans, we should let our willingness to be blessed with such a calling be known in personal prayer, for prayer activates a sense of communion with the Goddess, making us more receptive to closer encounters with the Divine, and malleable to the wishes of Her will.

This short overview of the relevance of spiritual gifts to the contemporary Pagan populace as a whole has been undertaken in order to inspire a vision of our potentials for maturing as a magickally empowered community. These gifts are channels through which our lives are infused with the numinosity of the divine attributes, investing us with both the power and authority to help guide, forewarn, and heal one another as we progress towards the growth and perfection of our religious community as a vehicle for the eventual global epiphany of the Goddess upon the consciousness of human society. It is therefore essential that we begin to perceive ourselves as potential conveyors of spiritual rejuvenation through the medium of these charismata; servants of the Goddess as She pours forth *through us* by means of these gifts streams of transforming grace upon the world in preparation for the dawning of the New Age.

Footnotes

1. Philip Emmons Isaac Bonewits, *Real Magic*. (Berkeley, CA: Creative Arts Book Company, 1971, 1979), pp. 25-33.

2. Caitlin and John Matthews, *The Western Way, Volume II—The Hermetic Tradition*. (Boston, MA: Arkana, 1986), p. 80.

3. Paul Beyerl, *The Master Book of Herbalism*. (Custer, WA: Phoenix Publishing Co., 1984).

4. Marian Green, *The Gentle Arts of Aquarian Magic*. (Wellingborough: The Aquarian Press, 1987).
   Doreen Valiente, *Natural Magic*. (Custer, WA: Phoenix Publishing Co., 1975).
   Scott Cunningham, *Earth, Air, Fire & Water*. (St. Paul, MN: Llewellyn Publications, 1991).

5. For an excellent introduction to the concepts and theology of high ceremonial magick, consult the following books by Melita Denning and Osborne Phillips: *Robe and Ring, The Apparel of High Magick, The Sword and the Serpent, The Triumph of Light*, and *Mysteria Magica* (St. Paul, MN: Llewellyn Publications.)

6. Aleister Crowley is easily the most infamous of all who have practiced the Magickal Arts in this century. The man was brilliant, and he possessed insights into the occult which were truly remarkable. However, there is an old saying that often there is a very fine line between genius and insanity, and in Crowley's case this may have some limited validity. After all, a man who styles himself as the Anti-Christ "Beast" of the Book of Revelation, and who has no moral qualms about invoking demonic entities within a ritual context is decidedly not the kind of person a magickal novice should seek out for a teacher! There are some good books about the life and teachings of Crowley, and they would make good reading for those interested in knowing more about him, but I would strongly recommend against trying to "cut one's teeth" on the magickal experience by attempting to perform any of his rituals.

7. This does not, however, prevent one from employing exercises and rituals of psychic self-defense in response to malicious metaphysical attack by an enemy. In cases such as this, a person has every right to make use of whatever magickal means necessary to defend him/herself.

8. Grey Cat, *The Crone Papers* June, 1990 (P. O. Box 181, Crossville, TN).

9. Acts 13:4-12, *Holy Bible*.

10. 1 Corinthians 5:3-5 from the Revised Standard Version of the Bible, © 1946, 1952, 1971 by the Division of Christian Education of the National Council of the Churches of Christ in the U.S.A.

11. From *The Interpreter's Bible, Volume X*, p. 62. Copyright renewal © 1981 by Abingdon. Used by permission.

12. Acts 5:1-11, *Holy Bible*.

13. Galatians 1:8-9, *Holy Bible*.

14. Daniel 2:48, *Holy Bible*.

15. Melita Denning and Osborne Phillips, *Psychic Self-Defense & Well-Being*. (St. Paul, MN: Llewellyn Publications, 1982).

16. 1 John 4:1, *Holy Bible*.

17. See Denning and Phillips, *Psychic Self-Defense and Well-Being*.

   Also see Janet and Stewart Farrar, *The Witches' Way*. (Custer, WA: Phoenix Publishing Co., 1986), pp. 82-94.

   The fact that not all channeled spirits are harmless "guides" has been confirmed by critics within the occult sciences who have, for instance, characterized "Ramtha," a well-known channeled spirit whose pronouncements have been received as "gospel truth" by numerous New Age groupies, as being a "less (than) benign entity." (Arthur and Joyce Berger, *The Encyclopedia of Parapsychology and Psychical Research*. [New York, NY: Paragon House, 1991], p. 348.) In further confirmation of this, Anderson Reed, in her book entitled *Shouting at the Wolf: A Guide to Identifying and Warding Off Evil in Everyday Life* (New York, NY: Citadel Press, 1990), describes in detail the dangers inherent in the "channeling" process and the unscrupulous spirits only too eager to take advantage of such passive states of mind in order to gain a foothold within the unsuspecting psyches of novice practitioners (see pp. 249-254).

18. Father John Rossner, *In Search of the Primordial Tradition and the Cosmic Christ*. (St. Paul, MN: Llewellyn Publications, 1989), p. 248.

19. *Ibid.*, pp. 68-69.

20. John 4:15-21, *Holy Bible*.

21. Robin Lane Fox. "The Language of the Gods," *Pagans and Christians* (New York, NY: Alfred A. Knopf, Inc., 1989), pp. 168-261.

22. *Ibid.*, p. 253.

23. Even most Christians are not aware that their own Savior is reputed to have declared that those who came after him would do even greater works (i.e., marvels of the miraculous) than he himself had performed (see John 14:12).

24. 1 Corinthians 14:2, *New English Bible*.

25. From *The Inner Ecstasy*. Copyright © 1969 by Marcus Bach. Reprinted by permission of The World Publishing Company. Apex edition published 1971. Excerpted here by permission of Abingdon Press.

26. Robert Glenn Gromacki, *The Modern Tongues Movement*. (Philadelphia, PA: The Presbyterian and Reformed Publishing Co., 1967), pp.5-6.

27. *Ibid.*, p. 8.

   See also David Christie-Murray, *Voices From the Gods*. (London: Routledge & Kegan Paul, 1978), p. 3.

28. Christie-Murray, p. 2.

29. *Ibid.*, p. 3.

30. *Ibid.*, pp. 4-13.

31. Fox, pp. 168-261.

32. Bach, pp. 74-75.

33. *Ibid.*, pp. 75-76.

34. 1 Corinthians 14:2, *New English Bible*.

35. Bach, pp. 76-77.

36. See Footnote 26.

Chapter Nine

Whisperings from the Whirling Wheel

olidays have always held a special place in the hearts of people the world over. In our culture, and in Western society in general, the predominant holidays were determined centuries ago under the influence of the Christian Church. Christmas and Easter, the two most well-known celebrations of the year, were instituted ostensibly to celebrate the events of the birth and resurrection of Christ, respectively. Card companies will make doubly sure that the public at large is not allowed the luxury of forgetting those other annual days of social obligation such as Valentine's Day, St. Patrick's Day, and Halloween, complete with symbols of hearts, shamrocks, and pumpkins. Most people, however, celebrate these times by virtue of the historically accumulated pressure of social and religious convention; not from any innate sense of understanding just why previous generations have chosen to observe them. As a result, a great percentage of these festivities have degenerated into a commercialistic orgy of gift-giving and card-buying instigated by enterprising merchants interested in exploiting the calendrical habits of a tradition-bound culture.

For those of us who have embraced the tenets and lifestyle of Pagan teachings, holidays are of a much deeper and Nature-oriented significance. The holidays (or holy days) of the Old Religions are rooted in the whispering rhythms of annual Earth cycles, the endlessly turning Wheel of the Year which whirls through time, slowly transporting us from one season to another.

Our sacred times of celebration are determined by the hemisphere in which we live, the climate, and the flora and fauna of the given geography which we inhabit, for in these various factors are formulated the ways in which Mother Earth manifests her own yearly cycles by which we sow the seed, reap the harvest, and rest through the season of dormancy in preparation for the seasonal Wheel to begin again.[1]

Later Christian culture, in creating its calendar of holidays, drew heavily upon the preexisting layer of Pagan festivals and sacred days, coating them with a thin veneer of Church myth and pious legends invented to supply an "acceptable" reason for the continuation of these observances. Christmas evolved from the earlier Pagan celebration of the Winter Solstice, or Yule. Easter descended from the spring fertility rites of ancient religious faiths. St. Valentine's Day was the heir to the earlier (and bawdier) riotousness of the Roman Lupercalia. The list could go on and on. But suffice it to say that the REAL meanings of these ancient observances are hidden in the teachings and insights, not of the Church, but of the Old Religions and their modern esoteric revivals.

In most Neo-Pagan traditions, there are eight major holy days spaced somewhat equally from one another around the calendrical Wheel of the Year. In most traditions, these holidays are designated by the term *Sabbats*. However, in the Ordo Arcanorum Gradalis, they are usually referred to as the *Earth Rites*, for they are meant to celebrate the changing of the seasons which in turn effect the life-tides of Nature. These Earth Rites are divided between the four major holidays (the High Rites), and the four minor holidays (the Low Rites). The Low Rites always designate the beginning of one of the four seasons of the year. These include the equinoxes and the solstices. The High Rites always occur at the midpoint or apex of the respective seasons. These include Hallowmas (fall), Candlemas (winter), Balemas (spring), and Lammas (summer).

Many Wiccan or Neo-Pagan Traditions have their own slightly differentiated interpretation as to the exact significance of each of the eight Earth Rites. But it can be safely said that many groups tend to follow a mythic system which divides the Wheel of the Year equally between the rulership of the Goddess in spring and summer, and the rulership of the God in fall and winter. As a result, many of their Sabbat rituals reflect this orientation. But our Order's differences with this mythic scenario, even though already touched upon in the first chapter, bears repeating here once again:

> The Ordo Arcanorum Gradalis follows its own cycle of myths and sacred imagery in portraying the activities of Deity (manifested as Goddess and God) interacting in Nature through the seasonal changes celebrated during the course of the Wheel of the Year. Unlike some well-known Neo-Pagan paths, we do not subscribe to the concept that the Goddess has preeminence over the spring and summer months, while the God has preeminence over the fall and winter months. Instead, we honor the Triple

Goddess in our rituals as presiding over the *entire* year in perpetual preeminence, reigning in spring and early summer as the Maiden; from late summer through early fall as the Great Mother; and from late fall through the whole of winter as the ancient Crone. Likewise, the God also reigns throughout the year as the Consort of the Goddess. In His luminous aspect, He mates with the Maiden as Satyr Pan. He is the god of sexuality and the lord of life. Reigning with the Goddess through the spring and summer, He finally dies in the fall and returns to the wintry womb of the Earth Mother to await His return with the new spring of the coming year. In His chthonic aspect, the God is revered as Kernunnos, the Horned One. He is the Sacred Stag: god of sacrifice, death, and the Underworld, reigning as the Consort of the Crone through the fall and winter months. Since in our tradition the God in His terrestrial manifestation is seen in a dual role as Satyr Lord and Sacred Stag, this mythic scenario takes the place of the Holly King/Oak King struggle for supremacy so common in the rituals of some Neo-Pagan groups.

First of all—and it is very important to keep this in mind—we do not take issue with other traditions' seasonal myths as being in any way *wrong* or inaccurate. If it works for them, then it is a viable and valid system—for the Seax-Wica or whoever else may subscribe to such a system.

It is interesting to note that some of the other traditions have replied to our criticism of the idea that the God and Goddess each rule one half of the year respectively, by responding that Raymond Buckland (a well-respected Wiccan author who has done much to popularize this concept) does not believe that either the Goddess or the God is supreme over the other during a given season of the year; in fact, he states as much in *Buckland's Complete Book of Witchcraft*.[2] However, it took the criticism of this seeming relegation of one deity over another during specified seasons of the year by Janet and Stewart Farrar in their excellent volume entitled *Eight Sabbats for Witches* to encourage Buckland to elaborate his belief in more depth, which he did in his above-mentioned book.[3] But the fact remains that the perception of this teaching of the Goddess having predominance during the summer and the God having predominance in the winter is seen as a form of abdication temporarily by one in favor of the other: "It (Halloween) is also the time when the summer goddess … *relinquishes her power* to the … winter god."[4] This kind of understanding of Buckland's teaching (or misunderstanding, whichever the case may be) is totally at odds with the basic concepts and deity mythos which we follow in this tradition, for several reasons. To begin with, we are *moderately* Dianic in our theology, since the Ordo Arcanorum Gradalis teaches that the Lady should always have the *primacy of place* as the primary focus of our ceremonial worship. As also stated in the first chapter, we give veneration to the Horned Lord, not as Her equal, but as Her Son, Lover, and Consort. Therefore, from the perspective of our own mythos, for the Goddess at any time to retreat, relinquish, abdicate, or mitigate Her place, prerogatives, or power would be unthinkable. Buckland nevertheless still insists on the *emphasis* on the Goddess in the summer months and an *emphasis* on the God in the winter months. While this approach is certainly not as drastic, to us it unnecessarily creates a subtle equation of the Goddess with a part of the year and likewise with the God.

In the Ordo Arcanorum Gradalis, the changing of the year's seasons is matched by a changing of the various *aspects* of the Goddess in Her triple manifestation as Maiden, Mother, and Crone. In this mythic understanding, it therefore becomes unnecessary for either the Goddess or the God "to take a vacation" or go into seclusion for half the year, for the Lady always reigns and is always the focus of our rites. The essential difference between the two systems lies in the fact that one sees the change of seasons as reflecting a role reversal between the Goddess and the God at the old Celtic dividing of the year; whereas, in our own system, the essential role and rulership of Goddess and God never change or fluctuate; *only their aspects do*. So while at various seasons the Goddess will reign as either the Spring Maiden, the Mother of Harvest, or the Crone of Winter's Death, Her primacy of place and position is never abdicated or altered.

Likewise, the Horned God always reigns with the Goddess as Her Consort, but in a dual aspect which is divided loosely between the two halves of the year. In spring and summer, He is the Satyr Lord, in fall and winter He is the Sacred Stag. (In this connection, it is worth mentioning that while Buckland does not personally adhere to the theory of a dual-natured Horned God, he *does* see a validity in its concept as expounded by the Farrars: "This is an excellent book (*Eight Sabbats for Witches*) and should be studied both for this interesting theory of theirs, on *a duality* of the Horned God, and for the structuring and composition of sabbat rituals as a whole."[5] While different on the surface and in the names we use, the basic concept of a duality in the Horned One is shared by both the Farrars and our own Order.

From our perspective, the mythology of the Ordo Arcanorum Gradalis with regards to the Goddess and the God is most logical as a variant way of explaining the seasonal turning of the Wheel of the Year. This whole issue has been dealt with here in some detail precisely because it is inextricably bound up in the themes of our Earth Rites, and we have found that they work for us admirably.

We need to keep in mind that this is not meant to be some kind of mean-spirited theological "battle." If we were studying to become an initiate of either the Seax-Wica or Gardnerian traditions, we would naturally adapt to their own chosen mythological structure and theological stratification in order to be able to fully perceive the cosmos and this terrestrial creation from their unique way of telling its story. *No tradition is right and another wrong; we simply have different ways of telling the same basic, eternally recurring story.*

In the same way, when we choose to become a student of the Ordo Arcanorum Gradalis, we will find that by learning to see the validity of its particular way of describing the supernatural forces of the universe, we will simply be expanding our spiritual perspective in a continually growing anthology of religious story-telling. The stories themselves are an aspect of the creativity of the gods within us. Each story told by each tradition has something special to teach us, irrespective of whether it may technically contradict another. *Our myths are not meant to convey totally literal truth, but to be ways in which we can see all life in some form of metaphysical perspective.*

In order to gain a more sequential and thorough understanding of each annual Earth Rite and its primary significance within this Order, we will now begin a brief examination of them, beginning with the traditional starting point of the yearly cycle of seasons: Hallowmas.[6]

Hallowmas

*The Dark Mother comes
from time long past the setting sun …*

It may seem strange to some that most Craft traditions begin their new year when everything around us seems to be dying, but for those acclimated to the changing climes and the vegetative cycles of the seasons, it was most logical to perceive the death of the year with the falling of autumn leaves. The harvest had been gathered and the first frosts of winter's breath were being felt in the chill morning air. It is therefore not surprising that the Celts saw fall as a time of transitions between the dying of one year and the beginning of another. But it was a time of transition for more than just the changing of years. As it was a time of death for the old year and the nascent beginning of the new, so also it was a season when one's thoughts turned inward and retrospective; a time of remembering our loved ones who, like the leaves of autumn, had fallen asleep upon the gentle breeze of death, being carried down into the dimensions of the dead below. To the Celts, this was the season of Samhain; a moment in time when the psychic veil between the worlds of the living and the dead was transparently thin. Samhain or, as it is also called, All Hallows, was a time when the departed dead could unexpectedly appear to us, impinging upon the periphery of the physical realm. It was, in essence, a celebration which remembered the deceased ancestors of family and tribe, for it was believed that the dead returned to their familiar haunts at this time. Hence, the focus upon ghosts at Halloween in the garbled mixture of holiday traditions still popular.

In the Ordo Arcanorum Gradalis, Hallowmas (All Hallows) is the highest holy day of the year, and the ritual for its observance is, accordingly, the most elaborate and involved of any Earth Rite in our tradition. For us, Hallowmas marks the beginning of the reign of the Triple Goddess in Her aspect as the Crone, the Harbinger of Death, presiding over the demise of the old year as well as being the Spectral Sovereign of the shades of the dead. On the surface, the Crone is a most frightening presence to encounter for the unprepared, but in reality, She is the necessary doorway through which all things must pass in order to enter new phases of life.

Hallowmas also designates the beginning of the reign of Kernunnos as the Consort of the Crone. In the ritual for Hallowmas, Kernunnos describes himself: *"Dark Twin of Pan am I, wraith-raiser of the waning seasons!"* In our tradition, Kernunnos is the dark aspect of the Horned One; the Lord of the Underworld, and the winter manifestation of the God's sacrificial aspect. For it is the antlered God who is revealed during this season as the Sacred Stag, reminding us that in ancient times when winters were harsh, it was only through the rewards of the hunt that the people were enabled to survive. So the Sacred Stag Kernunnos becomes a symbol of the self-sacrifice of Nature willingly giving up the life of one species for the survival of another (our own). As the God who is sacrificed as the victim of the hunt, He is therefore associated with death and the Underworld, and is a most sacred theophany of the God. Together with the Crone (most often referred to in our rituals as Hekate), Kernunnos also reigns as the Lord of the Dead, and as such, is a central focus of our Order's Hallowmas (Samhain) ritual.

The question of when we should actually celebrate Hallowmas is a matter of divergent opinion. There are those who I would classify as the "calendrical purists" (among whom I once classified myself) who insist that this Earth Rite should always be observed on the actual date of October 31st, since that is supposedly the date which was always celebrated by the Druids in Britain. And it is true that there always seems to be a special "presence" in the actual date of particular holidays. But many do not realize that All Hallows is not limited to a day. In reality, the Season of the Dead has long been recognized by many divergent cultures as being that time from later October through mid November (in the Northern Hemisphere). For example, in ancient Egypt, the festival celebrating Isis' raising up of Osiris and his status as Lord of the Dead was celebrated around November 1-4. Furthermore, another feast was observed by them around the 13th of November in honor of all the dead, known as the Feast of Lamps.[7] In fact, if we were to still follow the pre-Gregorian calendar used by the Witches of olden times, we would be celebrating Hallowmas around the 12th or 13th of November! Interestingly, some of the old Samhain customs in certain areas of England have been transferred to St. Martin's Day: November 13th! So we feel that we can safely say that as long as we place our celebration sometime between October 31st and November 20th, we are still most definitely in that season of the year when the memory and occasional manifestation of the dead is very much alive.

One of the problems with actually observing it on Halloween night has to do with the constant interruptions of "trick-or-treaters" at the door. This means that your ritual would of necessity be late in order to avoid such distractions. The Farrars have wisely suggested that we fully participate in the festive customs of Halloween (as people would expect Witches to do) and wait for the closest weekend after the 31st for the observance of the actual Earth Rite ritual.[8] In this we would most heartily concur.

When all is said and done, the best advice on the matter of Earth Rite dates was given by John and Caitlin Matthews: "Although a (Celtic) festival may be assigned to a particular date, calendrical shift and seasonal inclemency should be taken into account when deciding the right time to celebrate. In inner terms, the right time is more important than the right date."[9]

… And the Wheel of the Year begins to whirl once more, whispering in the dreams of the dead visions of the Grail of Immortality.

Winter Solstice

Behold the light that can never die,
reborn anew in the Solstice sky!

The Winter Solstice, while being one of the Low Rites of the year, nevertheless has the distinction of being one of the most festive Sabbats of them all. This is due in large part to the carry-over of our society's obsession with the beautiful customs of Christmas. There is something almost contagious about the celebratory atmosphere of this season. Much of this harks back to the most ancient times, when humankind looked longingly forward to the reborn hope of warmer times to come symbolized by the Solstice Sun on or around December 21st. The Winter Solstice (or Yule, as it was called among the Norse) is, of course, the primary solar holiday on the Wheel of the Year. It is, actually, the real beginning of the Solar New Year, for the Sun at that moment is in a sense "reborn" as it begins its annual growth and ascent back to its former strength and glory, culminating in the Summer Solstice.

For Pagans, the fun part of the Christmas celebrations so popular at this time lies in our knowledge that most of the "good Christian" populace is observing a plethora of Pagan customs during their holiday revelries, but without any understanding of why they are observing them! However, for those of us well-educated in the lore of pre-Christian religion, these various, cherished customs have a deeper meaning than the general public will ever grasp. The Christmas tree is a universal symbol of this blessed season, but for Pagans its significance is important as an ancient emblem of the life that does not die. Evergreens always remind us throughout the winter that there is hope in the midst of barrenness and bleakness. Holly has ever been sacred to both the Goddess and the Sun God. Wreaths were old symbols of the solar disc. Mistletoe was revered by the Druids as a manifestation of the male energies of the God. The Yule Log was an old Norse custom ("Yule" meaning "Wheel," a symbol of the Sun). Christians therefore had a relatively easy time "dressing up" these customs with trappings of Jesus-centered piety. After all, for nominal Christians just recently converted from Paganism, the theological hair-splitting between the Sun God and God the Son was too fine for their serious concern!

In the Ordo Arcanorum Gradalis, the Winter Solstice, or Christmas, is a time to celebrate the advent of winter, the new birth of the Sun, and the illumination of the Light of the Cosmic Christ of which the rising light of the Solstice Sun is indeed a potent and living symbol.

It is an interesting fact that scholars now know that Jesus was not born in the winter season at all! He was more than likely born during early autumn. But the Church decided to celebrate his birth at the time of the Winter Solstice for the obvious reasons of close correlation between the Pagan symbology of the season and the myth of the birth of the new Christ, the "Sun of Righteousness." And in this, we as Pagans should not take offense, for in so doing, the Church has paid Paganism a great historical compliment by admitting that without the help of the Winter Solstice mystery-symbols of solar rebirth and its accompanying festivities, rejoicing and merriment, Christianity would have had a much harder time making a foothold in the consciousness of the newly converted "heathens" of the European realms.

In actual practice, the circle decorations for the Winter Solstice ritual are probably the most beautiful of the entire year. With branches of fir, pine, spruce, and sprigs of mistletoe framed by glowing candles, the ceremonial place of ritual is usually transformed into a winter's fairy tale setting for the appearance of Father Frost!

With regards to the proper date for the celebration of the Solstice, it is always preferable to observe the actual date of the Winter Solstice (usually December 21st or 22nd). However, in light of the social realities posed by our society, we find that most of the time all of us are pulled here and there by family obligations, especially as we more closely approach the actual date of Christmas. We have therefore found it more amenable to celebrate this Solar Rite on the closest weekend before the actual Solstice date. This enables grove members to be able to travel or spend necessary social times with relatives during the actual period of Christmas Eve, Christmas Day, etc.

… And the Wheel of the Year begins to whirl once more, whispering fantasies from the Grail of Promise upon frosted window panes crystallized in the glorious glow of new-born light.

Candlemas

Draw near unto Me,
ye who seek
for dawn beyond the dark,
and light thy candles …

In the Ordo Arcanorum Gradalis, Candlemas is exactly that: a Mass of the Candles. It is a celebration of the coming of spring's warming light, which, even though it is still afar, can be faintly discerned in the slightly lingering light of the slowly strengthening Sun. Originally known as Imbolc among the ancient Celts, this Earth Rite is actually situated in the very midst of the winter season, when the weather conditions can often be at their most frigid. But this sacred convocation, as a celebration of light, has as its main focus the coming of the bright half of the year heralded by the Maiden aspect of the Goddess. Ironically, even though Candlemas marks the peak of the winter season, it is, nevertheless, an Earth Rite which bespeaks *transition*, for while the Goddess as Crone technically presides over this Earth Rite, its most vivid liturgical imagery is saved for the Maiden in her prophetic evocations of spring.

In our tradition, the Maiden Goddess as Holy Brigit is the primary name of the Lady by which we address Her at this time. This is for good reason: Brigit is a Celtic goddess of fire, inspiration, and childbirth; fire for light and purity (the Christian Feast of the Purification is annually held on the 2nd of February—again, another borrowing from Pagan imagery), and childbirth for the bringing forth of new life and by extension, new beginnings, even as the seeds stir in the earth with the foreshadowings of spring's vegetative rebirth.

Four of the annual Earth Rites are generally considered to be fire festivals of Pagan antiquity, but among them it is Candlemas alone which stands for the abstract purity, beauty, and symbolic potency that is Light itself. In all the other Earth Rites, the lighting of candles or fires connotes varying shades of meaning, from being representative of the newborn or waxing Sun to being flaming beacons to light the way for spirits to return to their ancestral homes. But at Candlemas, we celebrate the glory of the light and all the blessings which have been bestowed upon us by virtue of its gift to the world from the hands of the Lady.

February 2nd has traditionally been the date set by modern Neo-Pagans for the observance of Candlemas. However, the closest weekend after that date (if it occurs during the week) would be the most convenient time for its celebration.

… And the Wheel of the Year begins to whirl once more, whispering hymns to Brigit, bright with radiant hope overflowing from the Grail of Light.

Spring Equinox

We bid Thee welcome,
returning Maiden of many Names;
green-gowned Goddess
awakening the drowsy year
from its seasonal, wintry sleep!

Spring Equinox (March 20-23rd) is probably the least emphasized Earth Rite of all in our liturgical calendar, not because of any intentional disparagement, but due to the fact that it is simply a solar signpost announcing the beginning of spring. It is celebrated by a ritual which encourages the earth to break forth in blossom with the first, full flushes of flowered adornment, but which, nevertheless, still looks forward to the fullness of spring which is yet to come.

The equinoxes and solstices are times for recalling the cyclic progress of the Solar Hero as he goes through the various stages of his birth, growth, zenith, decline, and death. The Spring Equinox is a time of seeing the youthful vigor of the maturing Sun Lord as he begins his rayed infatuation with the Goddess in Her seasonal manifestation as the Maiden.

Colored eggs are a standard part of this Earth Rite celebration to symbolize the emerging fertility of the season. But the *real* revelry over the fertility that is spring itself is not liturgically observed until the next holy day on the turning spokes of the Wheel of the Year—Balemas. Hence, Spring Equinox functions more like a *precursor* to the plenitude of the season which is still to come.

This particular Earth Rite has also been referred to as the "Pagan Easter" because most of the trappings traditional to the Easter season (i.e., bunnies, eggs, flowers, etc.) are all carry-overs from the early pre-Christian fertility myths and rites. Furthermore, at Spring Equinox our thoughts naturally begin to turn towards thoughts of resurrection and new life, for it is indeed the seasonal resurrection of all annual vegetation which points us to the Mysteries of the Dying and Rising God in His many names and forms. From the new sprouting "baskets of Adonis" planted by the ancient Syrians in honor of their beloved god, to the alabaster lilies florally framing the Christian altars at Easter, the hope and faith that death is not the seal of finality, but merely the prelude to the beginning of another chapter in the cycle of unending life, has continued to be the theme of these many sacred festivals of spring.

... And the Wheel of the Year begins to whirl once more, whispering echoes of revivifying life through the dormant chambers of slumbering Death as the Grail of Resurrection beckons both seeds and spirits to rise anew.

Balemas

Holy Pan of the shepherds' shrine,
Goat-footed God,
Faunus of the forest glades,
we beseech Thee to be here among us
as we revel in Beltane abandon ...

Balemas (also popularly known as Beltane) is considered by most to be one of the two highest holidays of the pre-Christian Celtic calendar (the other being Hallowmas [Samhain]). The time generally coinciding with the first week of May was thought of as the real beginning of the summer season. (In Celtic reckoning the year was divided into two main seasons: summer and winter.)

The celebration of this Earth Rite was always accompanied by great festivity and freewheeling frolic. The fertility of Nature and the lure of romantic attraction was the focus of the observances, and balefires were lit on the hilltops as symbols of the ever-strengthening God of Light.

In the Ordo Arcanorum Gradalis, Balemas is celebrated as a revelation of the union of Goddess and God as the Grail of Love. This is the Earth Rite which conveys the intensity of desire between the Goddess and the God in their terrestrial manifestations as Maiden and Satyr Lord. It is an unabashed celebration of the physical, the erotic, and the sensual seductiveness by which life ever regenerates itself.

Whereas the Spring Equinox was still anticipatory in its expectation for the full flowering of spring, Balemas is jubilant in the realization of its arrival. It is supremely an annual reaffirmation of the wondrous and intricately interrelated web of life as manifested in ourselves and the living environment around us.

Balemas signifies not only the mating of the Lady and Lord to produce the luscious verdancy of spring, but also Their marriage as well. It is at Balemas that the God in His aspect as Satyr Lord officially becomes the *Consort* of the Maiden Goddess. Again, this is the celebration of the *terrestrial* consummation of the fertile union of the Goddess and the God. Balemas is a Sabbat of *earthiness*; a reveling in the joys of the physical in both Nature's beauty and the substantive physicality of our own wholistic *bodiliness*.

Despite the attempts of the Church to stifle the more blatant aspects of this ancient Pagan festivity, it miserably failed. The phallic legacy of the Maypole and the assimilated custom of crowning a young maid as the "May Queen" are still with us to this day. Even Catholicism had to capitulate to the extent that the month of May is dedicated to the Virgin Mary, the spiritual "May Queen" of Christianity.

... And the Wheel of the Year begins to whirl once more, whispering entrancements from the Grail of Love's Desire.

Summer Solstice

Solstice Sovereign,
Sol of a thousand rays,
we greet Thee with praise
as Thou takest Thy place
upon the high throne of the firmament!

The Earth Rite of Summer Solstice (June 20-23) is almost totally solar in its emphasis. It is the recognition of the highest glory of the Sun in its annual progression through the seasons. What began as the infant Sun at the Winter Solstice, matured into young manhood at the Spring Equinox and finally, now, at this astronomically propitious occasion, he has become invested by the summer with all the glory and regality of his annual enthronement as the High Lord of the Heavens.

Of course, as we are well aware, these titles and descriptive appellations are primarily mytho-poetic means by which we see in the natural phenomena around us an outer reflection of the inner divinity of existence which manifests in the many guises of Goddess and God.

In the case of the Sun Lord, his moment of shining solstice splendor makes him a literal heavenly icon through which we are able to glimpse the explosive intensity and cosmic purity of that creative Light from which all light originates: the Light which emerged from the still darkness of an as yet uncreated cosmos, only to explode in a spiral of eternally existent energy, flinging form and substance into the womb of the waiting Void; the beginnings of the birth of Creation.

The Sun is also a symbol of the truths and revelations which emanate from the Spirit of the High and Holy Deity which has periodically anointed the many Christs and avatars who have conveyed the sense of the numinous being somehow immanent in our midst. At the Summer Solstice we should be reminded that the Sun is but a galactic symbol of the God in His celestial aspect; He who through the Christ said to all who had ears to hear, "I am the Light of the World!"

The Summer Solstice is the magickal moment of a season's solar fulfillment. In it we witness the apex of celestial glory; but with the corresponding and sobering knowledge that from this time on in the months to follow, the light will be in decline ever so slowly, waning into a faint reflection of its former intensity.

… And the Wheel of the Year begins to whirl once more, whispering its solstice secret: "The glimpse of the Grail of Glory is only for a moment, but its memory lingers beyond a lifetime."

Lammas

*We wave before Thee in somber presentation
the seasonal sheaf of sacrifice,
the body of the Corn King ...*

Lammas literally means in old Anglo-Saxon usage, "Loaf-Mass." It was an observance of thankfulness for the first grain harvest of the year. Without it, bread would have been an impossibility, not to mention beer! So it is readily understandable why this was anciently considered to be one of the four most important Celtic holidays.

Many Neo-Pagan groups refer to this Earth Rite as "Lughnassad," emphasizing the Celtic mythology dealing with the god Lugh as being appropriate to the season. This, however, is something which our Order has decided to bypass for its central theme, because of the fact that the thanksgiving for the grain harvest incorporates some of the most primal symbols of sacrificial meaning, making the additional overlay of other mythological elements almost a distractive influence deflecting from what is, at least to us, the Earth Rite's most meaningful message.

Waves of breeze-blown wheat often present an artist's landscape rendition of late summer's serenity. But the scythes of the reapers are about to be sharpened for the first harvest; the God in the grain willingly waits for the moment of His impending sacrifice. In the mowings of the harvesters' scythe we reap the death of the immanent God as He gives Himself up to the flashing blade in order that we may be physically nourished through the baking of bread and intoxicated into altered consciousness by the magickal fermentation of brew and beer—a gift from the spirit of the Corn King.

Such lessons, once learned, can make indelible imprints upon the psyche about the nature of life itself as a form of perpetual sacrifice. Lammas is an Earth Rite which touches us with the magick and the mystery of the cycles of death for life in the inherent processes of Nature's way. It makes us truly thankful for the crunch of a whole kernel of grain in a fresh-baked slice of wheat bread, or for the foamy head gracing the chilled glass of lager at the bar. In this celebration we are made aware of the basic lesson that the sacrifice of life—be it plant or animal—is necessary for the continuation of physical existence: life feeds upon life. It can be almost morbidly sobering, but when we reflect deeply upon the mystery, we cannot but realize that in the daily and annual sacrifice of life for food we are witnessing a theophany of the God in perpetual self-sacrifice for the nourishment and growth of His own earthly creation, and in that brief flash of recognition, we see in the Grail of Sacrifice both Corn King and Christ merged as One in common cause: "I am the Bread of Life."

... And the Wheel of the Year begins to whirl once more, whispering in the sultry breezes of the season joyous requiems through the barley, the oats, and the rye.

Fall Equinox

Summer now retreats
into the perennial parade of passing seasons …
at this last Sabbat of the dying year,
the love of the Lady
and the gifts of the God
surround us in a multicolored cornucopia
of autumn's abundance …

Officially, the Fall Equinox (September 20-23) is the astronomical herald of autumn's arrival; and even though leaves may not yet be turning, an occasional yellow or red splash of color upon selected spots of foliage clues us in to the approaching hues of the season. Though the weather may still be warm, summer is on the wane: the gardens have been picked clean and the fields are being harvested. Now we begin to rejoice in the cornucopian blessings of harvest bounty which the Great Mother has bestowed upon the land.

At this Equinox, once again, it is a moment equally dividing the light from the dark; but it is this Earth Rite which marks the ascendancy of night, for the dark half of the year will shortly be upon us. This is the last or closing Earth Rite upon the Wheel of the Year. It is, therefore, naturally a time for thanksgiving, for not only the abundance which the earth has yielded, but also for the personal growth and wisdom which we have gained in whirling through another year towards greater personal maturity.

At the Fall Equinox, we come to recognize that the bounteous Goddess of summer's growth is now enacting through the changes of the season a passion play as She ages with the beginning of fall, passing from being the Mother who has brought forth the offspring of Her harvest, on through the menopause of Her aging year in preparation for Her seasonal culmination as the Crone, the Hag Queen, the Aged Wise One.

It is during this time of life that much wisdom is gained, for we pause to reflect and look backward through the year; and, despite the pain and pressure, to be thankful for our lives and what we have learned. The Earth Rite of the Fall Equinox is an observance marking our recognition of the cycles, seasons, and changes, not only within the year, but also within our own selves; and for all of this we give thanks to the Lady and the Lord.

… And the Wheel of the Year begins to whirl once more, whispering memories from the lessons of life in the depths of the Grail of Wisdom.

Footnotes

1. For an example of how the observance of Earth Rites (Sabbats) can differ from one hemisphere to another, see Janet and Stewart Farrar, *The Witches' Way* (Custer, WA: Phoenix Publishing Co., 1984), pp. 268-275. The ritual texts for the Earth Rites which constitute the latter portion of this book are reflective of the seasonal cycles of the Northern hemisphere above the tropical belt. In the future, the O.A.G. has plans for expanding its ritual corpus to include seasonal ceremonies which incorporate God and Goddess myths based upon the weather patterns of the tropics and the Southern Hemisphere as well.

2. Raymond Buckland, *Buckland's Complete Book of Witchcraft*. (St. Paul, MN: Llewellyn Publications, 1986), p. 15.

3. Janet and Stewart Farrar, *Eight Sabbats for Witches*. (Custer, WA: Phoenix Publishing Co., 1984), p. 29.

4. Erica Jong, *Witches*. (New York, NY: New American Library, 1981), p. 122. All rights reserved. (Emphasis mine.)

5. Buckland, p. 67. (Emphasis mine.)

6. The portions of ritual text which precede each Earth Rite's description are taken directly from the O.A.G. ceremonies which appear in their entirety in the second part of this book.

7. Arthur Weigall, *The Paganism in Our Christianity*. (New York, NY: G.P. Putnam's Sons, 1928), pp. 125-126.

8. Farrar, pp. 128-129.

9. Caitlin and John Matthews, *The Western Way, Volume I—The Native Tradition*. (London: Arkana, 1985), p. 47.

Chapter Ten

Casting the Ceremonial Circle

rom time immemorial, humans have sought ways to distinguish the sacred from the mundane. Temples and sanctuaries have been edifices traditionally set apart for the worship of the gods alone. Permanent structures built for the express purpose of worship are rare among the many and varied groups who practice the numerous forms of contemporary Paganism in today's society. Instead, we meet in private homes, backyards, beaches, forests, and open fields—in short, wherever is available, practical, and aesthetically convenient. This, naturally, calls for a simple, concise ritual method by which common, ordinary places can temporarily (for the duration of a designated celebration) be cleansed of psychic negativity and set apart for the specific religious purpose of the rite to be performed. In the Craft this is known as the Casting of the Circle. Its main objective is, as the Wiccan author Starhawk so aptly described it, "creating sacred space."[1]

Since ancient times a circle has been a symbol of containment, wholeness, and the endless cycle of eternity—the mythic serpent swallows its own tail in the circular motif of endlessness. Through the ages, the casting or drawing of a ritual circle has been done for two primary purposes: the setting apart of a designated area for sacred use, or the erecting of a protective psychic shield around an established area in order to protect those involved in ceremonial or magickal practices from harmful attack by malevolent entities which might be summoned as the result of certain rites of sorcery.

In the Ordo Arcanorum Gradalis, as in most other Craft and Neo-Pagan traditions, the primary intent of casting a circle is making a place suitable for spiritual worship, rather than a walled fortress for defense in psychic warfare. This is not to say, however, that the circle is never used for other purposes than worship. Quite to the contrary, when the coven or grove performs any kind of magickal rites, healing, or even meditation exercises, a circle should always be created through ritual visualization in order to keep any psychically unhealthy vibrations or unwanted entities from entering the area.

Actually, the term "casting a circle" is technically a misnomer, even though its usage is well-entrenched in Craft terminology. In reality, when one casts a circle, the circle should be viewed in the mind's eye as being simply the circumference of a psychic sphere that envelops a designated space both above and below like a transparent bubble of light. The outer limits of its spatial radius is what we would commonly call the boundary line; the circular marking of which is usually drawn upon the ground. This is explained most thoroughly by the Farrars:

> … it is important to have a very clear idea of just what a Magic Circle is … In the first place, it is in fact not a Circle at all, but a sphere; and it should always be so envisaged. The Circle is merely its equator, the line where the sphere cuts the ground. When one is casting it, one should picture an upright axis in the centre, with a semicircular arc running from its top, through the ground at the edge of the intended Circle, and so on down to its bottom. As one casts the Circle with sword or athame, one should feel one is pulling this semicircular arc round like the edge of a curtain, building up the sphere segment by segment like a reconstructed orange, until one comes back to the starting point and the sphere is complete … The sphere itself should be envisaged as a glowing, transparent, electric-blue or violet globe, brightening to a fiery line of the same colour where it cuts the ground.[2]

It stands to reason that if one were to literally cast only a circular wall of psychic protection around a designated area, it would still be unable to contain the group-energy which might be raised, or to keep out negative influences due to an unprotected, open "ceiling," as you will, above the cast wall of a circular enclosure. Only an envisioned sphere can totally encapsulate a place or person(s) from negative force-fields and guarantee an effective "leak-proof" enclosure for the containment of raised power until the proper time is signalled for its release from the sphere to its ultimate destination.[3]

Perhaps the most controversial divergence of the Ordo Arcanorum Gradalis from other Craft and Pagan systems is the direction in which we believe the circle should be cast. Anyone who begins to study Neo-Pagan and Wiccan teachings in general will inevitably come across those strange words "deosil" and "widdershins" used among them to describe directional movements within the magick circle.

Almost without exception, nearly all contemporary authors on Craft ritual vehemently insist that a circle should be drawn or cast deosil, meaning literally in old Gaelic, "to the right," or clockwise, and by strong implication, "going the way of the Sun." Raymond Buckland, long well known as a pioneer in the field of traditional Wicca, exemplifies this seemingly strange insistence: "The drawing of the circle ... is *always* drawn clockwise, or *deosil*."[4] This assertion is echoed by most other Wiccan writers, including Starhawk, Marion Weinstein, and Doreen Valiente.[5] The widespread assumption seems to be that to trace out a magick circle in imitation of the Sun's seeming directional movements is the most positive way to create one's sacred space, because, as Starhawk declares, "When we move 'sunwise' or clockwise, 'deosil,' we follow the direction the sun appears to move in the sky, and draw in power. Deosil is the direction of increase, of fortune, favor and blessing."[6] The obvious implication is that casting a circle or making other ritual movements within the circle in an opposite or widdershins direction is going to be detrimental to the practitioner's "fortune, favor and blessing," or else that such discarding of deosil directioning within the context of ritual space sanctification, if done consciously, must surely be for the purpose of negative magickal intent toward others through black magick. The Farrars, who are most prominent as teachers in the Wiccan revival, also generally go along with this mood of thought:

> An anti-clockwise movement is known as "widdershins" (Middle High German *widersinnes*, "in a contrary direction") ... A widdershins magical movement is considered black or malevolent, unless it has a precise symbolic meaning such as an attempt to regress in time, or a return to the source preparatory to rebirth; in such cases it is always in due course "unwound" by a deosil movement ...[7]

Inherent in this belief is an almost superstitious avoidance of widdershins motions. I have even known some Wiccans who were horrified when another coven member might mistakenly or forgetfully walk in an anti-clockwise direction within the ritual circle after it had been cast! Such fear and trepidation among modern Wiccans and Neo-Pagans concerning widdershins movements is one of the most glaring and incredulous examples of a "blind spot" in the thinking of contemporary Pagans which makes it possible for them to uncritically accept a societal superstition whose origin is to be found in the erosive, patriarchal denigration of ancient matriarchal precedents. It is supremely ironic that Craft leadership in general, priding itself with a matrifocal and <u>thea</u>logical emphasis, should so easily be "hoodwinked" into accepting the ritualistic axioms of religious patriarchy!

The left-hand position and the leftward, widdershins direction were often considered sacred to the Goddess in early cultures which exalted the Divine Feminine.[8] Conversely, the place of the right-hand was considered as the position of favor in relation to the male, patriarchal God (remember the words of the creed: "He is seated at the *right hand* of God the Father Almighty"); and by extension, the right-ward direction from east to west which traced the journey of the Solar Lord through his daily celestial navigation of the azure firmament was thought to be most worthy of ritualistic emulation. Hence, the popularity of "sun-wise" directional movements in patriarchal Pagan as well as Christian ceremony. (In this connection, it should not be forgotten that the Christ is also given the title of the "*Sun* of Righteousness.")

With the historical advent of patriarchal intolerance and its fear of feminine supremacy, either in society or the heavenly pantheon, the widdershins ways of the Mother were usually debased through slanderous superstitions which declared such practices evil and unlucky. In this way, the ascendancy of the father-gods was strengthened through revision of both religious thought and ritual routine.

Wiccan traditionalists will no doubt seek to justify their current habit of casting the circle clockwise by an appeal to the prevalent popularity of later Celtic folk practices which often specified deosil movements for magickal and protective purposes. However, it should not be forgotten that the Celts themselves were patriarchal, and there are stories in Celtic literature which suggest that such customs as the deosil rite were meant to supplant earlier, possibly matriarchal, incantatory practices which incorporated the use of counterclockwise circumambulation.[9]

Today there are a small number of covens and groves that do, apparently, cast their circles widdershins without attaching any sense of negativity to such a practice. Doreen Valiente, in her book *Witchcraft for Tomorrow*, while strongly emphasizing the "correctness" of casting the circle in a deosil movement, nevertheless makes a most candid and revealing admission: "*Some covens draw their magic circle widdershins*; but personally I think this is rather too negative a way of drawing the magic circle for general working purposes."[10]

In this context, it is most interesting to note that Sybil Leek, one of the most famous Witches of the early Craft revival who did much to popularize Wicca in both England and the United States, did not share Valiente's opinion. In one of her most famous and popular books, she refers to the casting of the circle: "The drawing of the circle in which witches meet when they are initiated has been written about many hundreds of times. The circle is a protective measure for its inhabitants, who wish to perform their ceremony undisturbed by outside influences ... *The circle is cut counterclockwise*."[11]

Actually, the logic for drawing the sacred circle counterclockwise or leftward, is based upon observations from astronomy, astrology, and a much older body of occult antiquity than many Wiccans and Neo-Pagans realize. It is most interesting to take into account the fact that Wiccans and Neo-Pagans in general often refer to their faith as being an "Earth Religion." Yet, ironically, in their ritual practice they have ignored the example of Mother Earth herself, who daily casts her own revolutions in space, constantly spinning *counterclockwise*. Our logic is straightforward on this point: as members of an Earth Religion, what better pattern could there be to imitate than the celestial motions of our own planet? Scientific confirmation of this also demonstrates that the Moon—one of the most revered and potent sky-symbols of the Goddess—also rotates in the widdershins direction:

> Viewed from the celestial north pole, the Moon's geocentric orbital motion, the Earth-Moon's heliocentric motion, and the axial rotations of both Earth and Moon are all *counterclockwise*. Because the Earth spins west to east in a time that is short compared to the month, the Moon, like the sun and the stars, appears to rise in the east and set in the west, even though its true motion relative to the celestial north pole is from west to east.[12]

Furthermore, astrologically speaking, the movement of the Moon during its monthly course through the twelve signs is also *counterclockwise*. Even the Sun, in its annual journey through the zodiacal Wheel of the Year, travels *counterclockwise* through the signs. On the basis of these facts alone, one Wiccan astrologer has indicated to this author that "indeed, a case *could* be made for widdershins circle-casting for Esbats and Sabbats both.[13]

But there is even more evidence to consider. Barbara Walker, in her monumental and often controversial work of scholarly compilation entitled *The Woman's Encyclopedia of Myths and Secrets*, has researched a formidable array of evidence to show that most modern Wiccan practice with regard to ritual circumambulation is contrary to that of their spiritual forebears:

> Europe's pagan customs, embodied in "witchcraft," maintained the virtues of left-sidedness against prevailing patriarchal opinion ... Witches' dances circled to the left, counterclockwise ... The medieval church said dancing, turning, or circumambulation in this direction was heresy. During the centuries of persecution, countless people were burned alive for dancing widdershins ... *The pagans were firmly in favor of the widdershins direction*. Pre-Christian kings in Scandinavia were expected to lay magic circles of protection around their cities by circumambulating them widdershins. Irish druidic law insisted on the same counterclockwise movement around the holy omphalos at Tara, a shrine of Mother Earth: "Thou shalt not go righthandwise around Tara." Tantric influence also directed Middle-Eastern Sufis to circumambulate their shrines in the widdershins direction.
>
> The Christians reversed the direction of all turning charms ...[14]

In light of this mounting accumulation of relevant observations and ancient Pagan precedence, the Ordo Arcanorum Gradalis casts all of its monthly Lunar Rite and annual Earth Rite circles in the widdershins direction in imitation of both the Moon and the Sun in their respective cycles through the circle of the zodiac, and in conformance with the daily counterclockwise rotation of the Earth herself.

The popular argument put forward by many contemporary Wiccans to the effect that casting a circle deosil or clockwise is more advantageous since it follows the perceived daily path of the Sun through the sky, loses much of the force of its argumentation when it is pointed out that when we observe the eight Earth Rites, we are celebrating, *not* the *daily* direction of the Sun as it appears to travel above us from dawn to dusk, but rather the path of the Sun through the signs of the zodiac; the Earth Rites being, from a Pagan astrological perspective, the *annual* progression points or calendrical markers of the Sun's *counterclockwise* journey around the Wheel of the Year. Likewise, when we observe the Lunar Rites, we are celebrating another completion of the Moon's lunar cycle, which also circles *counterclockwise* through the astrological signs during the course of its monthly movements. As modern Pagans, our Earth Rites and Lunar Rites celebrate the *annual* and *monthly* cycles of the Sun and Moon. However, deosil or clockwise ritual gestures used by many Wiccans to cast their circles, do not in any way reflect the respective annual or monthly astrological movements of the Sun and Moon; and for this reason alone, ritualized deosil directioning for the casting of the circle can be seen as an inadequate representation of these particular solar and lunar patterns marking the passage of cyclic time.[15]

Another point for consideration is the fact that whenever a grove or coven forms a circle facing inward to the center with the right palm of each individual under the top of the next person's left hand, the raising of power or odic force is generated in a *counterclockwise* motion. This is because, as many occult practitioners have demonstrated, we best conduct the flow of energies receiving through our left hand and channeling them on to the next person through our right hand. So we see that even the spiral of a cone of power can be closely connected with the widdershin waves of counterclockwise phenomena.[16]

As far as the original reasons as to why the Pagans of the past insisted on their preference for widdershins movements in both ceremony and dance, we can only begin to guess. While it is possible that some of their logic can be attributed to a few of the reasons we have put forward, there is undoubtedly a deeper layer of logic and/or esoteric lore upon which they drew for confirmation of their practice which we have yet to discover. Many of these ancient religio-magickal understandings of the universe and the planet on which we live may never be fully fathomed, but from the standpoint of the Ordo Arcanorum Gradalis, the fact that they did have what they considered to be more than substantial reasons, is sufficient justification for us that we continue their practice and preference for the widdershins direction in circle-casting.

The usage of the widdershins, counterclockwise movement in ritual activity can go a long way in eliminating the unhealthy patriarchal superstition that rightward (deosil) equals good and leftward (widdershins) equals evil, as well as help us to be more in touch with some of the ancient customs of the Old Religions regarding circle-casting long forgotten by many modern practitioners of the Craft.

Footnotes

1. Starhawk, *The Spiral Dance*. (San Francisco, CA: Harper & Row, 1979), p. 55.

2. Janet and Stewart Farrar, *The Witches' Way*. (Custer, WA: Phoenix Publishing Inc., 1984), pp. 83-84.

3. It should be understood, of course, that not all gatherings within the circle are for the purpose of raising and sending magickal power.

4. Raymond Buckland, *Buckland's Complete Book of Witchcraft*. (St. Paul, MN: Llewellyn Publications, 1986), p. 43. (Emphasis by Buckland.)

5. Marion Weinstein, *Positive Magic*. (Custer, WA: Phoenix Publishing Inc., 1981), p. 77.

6. Starhawk, p. 61.

7. Janet and Stewart Farrar, *Eight Sabbats for Witches*. (Custer, WA: Phoenix Publishing Inc., 1981), p. 38.

8. Barbara G. Walker, *The Woman's Encyclopedia of Myths and Secrets*. (San Francisco, CA: Harper & Row, 1983), pp. 530-534.

9. "Perhaps the oldest Irish written description of the *Desiul* occurs in the 'Book of Ballymote,' where it is recorded that a celebrated poet, King of Leinster, had a magical well in his garden, to which no one, save the monarch and his three cupbearers, could approach without being instantly deprived of sight. The queen, determined to test the mystical powers of its waters, not only approached the well, *but passed three times round it to the left, as was customary in ancient incantations.* Upon the completion of the third round, the spring burst forth in a raging torrent, and three enormous waves dashed over the hapless queen, who was thus carried right out to the ocean." (W.G. Wood-Martin, *Pagan Ireland*. [New York, NY: Longmans, Green, and Co., 1895], p. 147.)

   The part which I have emphasized in the above quoted passage makes it plain that the underlying purpose of this story was the stigmatization of an already popular incantatory practice which utilized leftward, counterclockwise movements. It is obvious from the context of this tale that the queen is purposely being associated with these older, more ancient practices, and the king with an implied opposition to them; making this an excellent example of how patriarchal propaganda was used in an effort to eradicate any sympathy for the remnants of preexisting matriarchal customs.

10. Doreen Valiente, *Witchcraft for Tomorrow*. (Custer, WA: Phoenix Publishing Inc., 1978), p. 87. (Emphasis mine.)

11. From *The Complete Art of Witchcraft* by Sybil Leek. Copyright © 1971 by Sybil Leek. Used by permission of New American Library, a division of Penguin Books USA Inc. (Emphasis mine.)

12. From "Solar System" in *Encyclopaedia Britannica*, 15th edition (1985), 27:534. (Emphasis mine.)

13. Excerpt from personal correspondence with Wiccan astrologer Ms. M.B. Wulf.

14. Walker, p. 532. (Emphasis mine.)

15. Of course, it can also be logically argued that circles which have nothing to do with Lunar or Earth Rite observances, but are used instead for purposes of personal meditation and/or magick on a random day-to-day basis, can appropriately be cast in the deosil direction since deosil reflects the *daily* chart movements of both Sun and Moon. Individuals who would choose to follow such a practice could possibly find some justification in this reasoning, although the majority in the Ordo Arcanorum Gradalis prefer to cast their circles widdershins in imitation of the Earth Mother's daily counterclockwise rotation.

16. For a similar example of this kind of counterclockwise energy raising, see Diane Mariechild, *Mother Wit—A Feminist Guide to Psychic Development* (Trumansburg, NY: The Crossing Press, 1981), p 31.

Chapter Eleven

The Altar and the Sacred Tools

he altar is the central focal point for worship within the sacred circle. Upon it are placed all the essential tools necessary for ceremonial ritual. Among the ancient Pagans, an altar was considered to be the appropriate place for sacrifice to their deities. Even in Judeo-Christian usage, the emphasis placed upon the concept of an altar was that of sacrificial worship.[1] The same emphasis has been preserved in the Catholic tradition, where the Mass is always celebrated upon the altar as an ongoing "unbloody sacrifice" pleasing to God the Father.

Most movements within the Neo-Pagan revival continue the age-old tradition of having some kind of altar for use within their ritual areas, though the interpretation of its theological significance may vary widely from that of a merely utilitarian nature to one of a highly mystical importance. The Ordo Arcanorum Gradalis falls within this latter category with regard to its perception of the altar as a visible meeting place between deities and mortals, and therefore worthy of a significant reverence. In our own Order, the altar is the place of Eucharistic theophany where the Goddess and God grace us with Their sacramental presence each time we celebrate the Grail Mass. The altar, then, becomes for us more than a mere resting place for the ritual tools, for it is, moreover, the mystical Throne of the Lady and the Lord.

Many well-known Neo-Pagan and Wiccan traditions are in the habit of placing their altar in the north quarter of the circle. For them, the northern direction is imbued with the qualities of mystery and a sense of spiritual permanence symbolized by the North or Polar Star. In some cultural mythologies the realms of the north were considered to be the dwelling place of goddesses and gods. In the Ordo Arcanorum Gradalis, however, the altar is not set permanently in one directional position. The altar (usually situated in the center of the circle) is arranged so that it changes direction within the circle depending upon the season of the year.

The four quarters of the circle correspond to the four seasons of the year in the context of our Order's magickal symbology. Each season contains within its time-frame two of the eight annual Pagan Earth Rites (Sabbats).

For the Earth Rites of the Spring Equinox and Balemas, the altar is set up facing the quarter light burning at the eastern periphery of the circle. The east is the direction of Eos, goddess of the dawn, and the place of the rising Sun; the time of morning and new beginnings. Its color is yellow/gold. The eastern direction corresponds to the season of spring, when the new growth of vegetation is flowering forth as the rising warmth of the Sun dispels the last vestiges of winter.

For the Earth Rites of the Summer Solstice and Lammas, the altar is set up facing the quarter light burning at the southern periphery of the circle. The south is the direction of the solar intensity at its seasonal zenith. Its color is red, the scarlet blaze of fire. It corresponds to the season of summer, when the Sun reigns in glory across the sky, bathing the land with its searing heat.

For the Earth Rites of the Fall Equinox and Hallowmas (Halloween), the altar is set up facing the quarter light burning at the western periphery of the circle. The west is the direction of the setting Sun and the closing of the day; a fitting symbol for autumn, that splendid, color-splashed season of the declining year. It is most appropriate that the Earth Rite of Hallowmas commemorating the dead should occur during this time of year. The color of the west is dark blue; the hue of late twilight and peaceful waters, inviting us to rest and repose in preparation for the coming of winter's sleep upon the land.

For the Earth Rites of Winter Solstice and Candlemas, the altar is set up facing the quarter light burning at the northern periphery of the circle. North is the direction of the polar axis of the planet and the fixed Northern Star, symbolizing all that is massive, stationary, and solid in the element of Earth. North is also the direction from which comes the icy chill of winter and the dormancy of the land during this cold season of hibernation and inactivity. Its colors are green (the primary color) and brown, colors of both the living and dormant Earth, the holly and the withered leaf.

If at all possible, the altar should be facing these particular directions during their appropriate seasons. There are, of course, always exceptions to the general rule. At outdoor gatherings or celebrations in very large rooms of a house where the furniture is not cluttered, and especially in an area that has been set aside as a permanent temple, these stipulations with regard to altar directional alignment in the circle should always be followed. However, many of us as urban-dwellers are not so fortunate as to own rural property or spacious homes where large-scale Earth Rites or Lunar Rites could be celebrated. Most of us have to put up with small apartments where the luxury of space to accommodate a moveable altar is virtually non-existent.

You may have your personal altar stationed by necessity in whatever corner or area of the room is available, and moving your altar around a room that is confining or cramped for space may be a bit unwieldy. In these situations it may be the best procedure to simply leave the altar in its stationary location and then cast your ceremonial circle visually in such a way as to have the altar included within the ritual area. However, in recognition of the Quarter-Regent (known in other traditions as the Lord of the Watchtowers) which has the preeminence for the season, you would still begin the Assembling of the Quarter-Regents (see "The Opening and Closing Rites") starting with whatever direction the altar should, under ideal circumstances, be facing. For instance, if you were celebrating the Summer Solstice, you would begin to assemble the Quarter-Regents by first addressing the Regent of the South who has the preeminence for the summer season.

In the Ordo Arcanorum Gradalis, the size and shape of the altar is purely optional. However, a circular wooden altar is considered to be the standard. Aesthetically speaking, and on mystical grounds alone, a round altar is symbolic of the never-ending circle of eternity, life, death, and rebirth. As a point of interest, the Saxon Tradition of Seax-Wica also encourages the use of a circular altar.[2]

The most unique altar used by this Order is known as the Altar of the Pentagram. The diameter of its circular top is a minimum of 36 inches across. Its height is approximately 16 to 17 inches from the floor. This enables people to sit comfortably around the altar and talk to one another without their view of each other being blocked by its height.

The Altar of the Pentagram has either a white or silver pentagram painted upon it and enclosed by a circle which borders the edge of the altar top. This circular border is divided into four sections. In the middle of each section is the zodiacal sign which marks the beginning of one of the seasons of the year. Each section of this border is painted with the appropriate seasonal color which corresponds to one of the quarters of the circle. The seasonal sections of this border follow one another in the natural order of their progression through the Wheel of the Year: spring, summer, fall, and winter (see the illustration on the following page). In each section there is also a magickal symbol for the season it represents as well as a symbol of the element to which it corresponds. So each section would contain the symbols for the following:

Yellow Section	Air	Aries	Spring
Red Section	Fire	Cancer	Summer
Blue Section	Water	Libra	Fall
Green Section	Earth	Capricorn	Winter

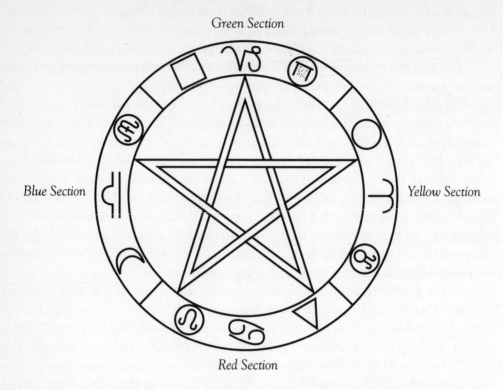

Green Section

Blue Section

Yellow Section

Red Section

The Symbols and Colors of the Altar of the Pentagram

When the Altar of the Pentagram is set up in the middle of the circle area, the point of the pentagram which touches the color of the corresponding season in which you are celebrating is set directly facing the appropriate quarter light burning at the edge of the circle. For instance, if you were celebrating the Earth Rite of Balemas, the point of the altar's pentagram touching the yellow section of the seasonal border would be set facing the eastern quarter light, since east and yellow correspond with spring, the time of Balemas. If you were celebrating the Earth Rite of Lammas, the point of the altar's pentagram touching the red section of the seasonal border would be set in the direction of the red southern quarter light, since south and red correspond with summer, the time of Lammas. This same procedure would be followed for the Earth Rites of fall and winter corresponding to the pentagram's points situated in the blue and green sections of the border.

For more information regarding these seasonal and elemental symbols, please consult the following books: *Natural Magic* by Doreen Valiente (Phoenix, 1975), p. 37; and *The Art & Practice of Talismanic Magic* by Ophiel (Samuel Weiser, Inc., 1973), "Elemental Forces," pp. 47-55.

On the other hand, you may prefer the more rustic look of a wooden altar engraved with these designs by, perhaps, a wood-burning set, but devoid of any painted colors. In such a case, you would align your altar during the year according to the point of the pentagram that touches the section of the seasonal border with the appropriate zodiacal sign which marks the beginning of the season in which you are celebrating. As an example, for the Earth Rite of Balemas, the point of the pentagram touching that section of the circular border which has in it the sign of spring/Aries/Air would be pointed toward the eastern quarter light.

Instead of actually engraving the wood of the altar itself, you may wish to sew or embroider a circular altar cloth with these designs. For some, this might be easier and less time-consuming. Again, the final decision will be up to you or your grove.

There will always be some who prefer the widely used rectangular altars common in other Neo-Pagan and Wiccan traditions. You may use anything from a coffee table to something which you construct yourself. The choice is yours.

These kind of altars would probably look best when covered by an altar cloth. If you use an altar cloth, your creative imagination is the limit as far as design and/or emblems with which you may wish to embellish it. The only requirement is that the altar cloth be of the appropriate color for the season during which you are celebrating. (Obviously, you would need a minimum of four altar cloths to cover the entire seasonal spectrum of the Wheel of the Year: yellow for spring, red for summer, blue for fall, and green for winter.)

It should go without saying that the candles used for quarter lights should be in glass containers or "votive style" holders, each one colored according to the quarter direction in which it will be placed: east/yellow, south/red, west/blue, and north/green. When the quarter lights, altar candles, and altar cloth (if one is used) are in their properly colored alignment, it sends a powerful signal to one's magickal self, grounding the focus of attention in an awareness of the subtle seasonal vibrations at work upon the psyche.

Most often, the altar is placed in the center of the circle. However, if you would rather have an altar of regular table height so that the Grail Mass and other rituals may be performed while standing, without recourse to kneeling, then such an altar should be placed near the edge of the circle in whichever quarter has the seasonal preeminence at the time. This enables the grove members to sit in the circle area during times of teaching, magickal work, or informal discussion without their view of one another being obstructed by a tall altar. If you have a tall altar, it is usually best to drape it with a long altar cloth, unless, of course, it is the Altar of the Pentagram which requires none, since it is already painted and engraved.

The set-up and arrangement of the ritual implements and sacred tools are rather simple and practical to enable the celebrants of the Earth Rites and Lunar Rites easy access to everything upon the altar without any sense of awkwardness. But there is one important divergence in the Ordo Arcanorum Gradalis altar arrangement from that of other magickal and Wiccan traditions: the Grail Chalice is always positioned in the center of the altar to emphasize it as the object of highest sanctity and the liturgical focus of the altar layout.

Arrangement of Tools upon the Altar of the Pentagram

1. Chalice
2. Paten
3. Sceptre
4. Glaive(s)
5. Censer and Incense
6. Bell(s)
7. Salt & Water Bowls (the addition of a small water cruet or pitcher is optional)
8. Altar Candlesticks
9. Goddess and God Statues
10. Three-Branched Candle-holder (Lunar Rites only)

```
8              11              8
        9          9
                        10

    5          1
               2            7
        6      3      7
               4            7
```

Arrangement of Tools upon the Standard Rectangular Altar

1. Chalice
2. Paten
3. Sceptre
4. Glaive(s)
5. Censer and Incense
6. Bell(s)

7. Salt & Water Bowls (the addition of a small water cruet or pitcher is optional)
8. Altar Candlesticks
9. Goddess and God Statues
10. Missal Stand (optional)
11. Three-Branched Candle-holder (Lunar Rites only)

The four most important sacred tools are known as the Hallows of the Altar and the Holy Regalia of the Grail. They are the chalice, the paten (dish), the sceptre (or staff), and the glaive(s). These serve as visible representations of the archetypal Grail Hallows which gave their names and symbols to the traditional Tarot: Cups, Pentacles, Wands, and Swords. The Hallows of the Altar are always laid out in a straight line in the center of the altar. We shall now proceed with an in-depth examination of these most revered sacred tools of the Craft.

The Chalice

In the Ordo Arcanorum Gradalis, this is the most spiritually potent symbolic object upon the altar. The kind, size, and style design of the chalice is totally a matter of personal taste. However, certain things should be kept in mind when venturing out to find your own Grail Chalice. Several options are open to you or your grove when deciding on the selection of the chalice to be used for the Grail Eucharist.

If you or your grove have money to spare, you can go the route of purchasing two chalices one gold (plated, of course!) and the other silver (or silvery pewter finish). This would give your grove the option of using the gold cup for the Earth Rite celebrations as a symbol of their solar orientation, while the silver chalice would be used at all Lunar Rite gatherings as symbolic of the Moon-oriented nature of these rituals.[3]

You could also go to the other extreme and use only an earthenware pottery or even a wooden chalice. Most anything is acceptable as long as it appeals to the group's or your own sense of the mystical. But perhaps the best route to go is the "middle path" of simply buying some form of silver chalice to be used at all times as the Grail Chalice for the altar. This has several good reasons to recommend it. First of all, in most Craft traditions, silver is the metal of the Goddess, while gold is the metal sacred to the God. Therefore, it would make more sense to have the chalice—which is itself the ultimate symbol of the watery womb of the Lady—always as a silver cup; that is, if you wish to have a chalice made of metal. Pottery chalices are just as appropriate however, for the color of the cup is merely an addition to the symbolism that is already there inherent in the shape of the cup itself. The metallic aura of silver or gold is just not necessary unless you feel you need it.

As with most other tools of the Craft, church supply or antique shops, silversmiths or flea markets are excellent sources for finding your own personal Grail Chalice. Needless to say, any object like this should be ritually and psychically cleansed and consecrated before it is placed upon your altar for religious use.

I wish to stress here that the chalice is the most venerable object upon the altar of this Order's rites. Choose it carefully and make sure that you sense a mystical rapport bonding between yourself and your cup. With the passage of time and sacred use, it will acquire an aura of holiness and divine mystery. In the words of Caitlin and John Matthews concerning the Grail:

> The vessel of redemption, knowledge and fulfilment. It is sought everywhere on quest, but achieved by few. It is not a physical object, *although real cups, chalices and cauldrons partake of its virtues as the inner symbol superimposes over them by means of worship or cult focus.*[4]

It is best to keep a special cloth draped over the chalice when it is not actually in ritual use. It also serves as a symbol of the "Veil of Isis" (i.e., the outer manifestation of the Goddess in Her Earth Body which nevertheless still conceals the inner Wisdom and Spirit of She Who is the Source of All; the wondrous, invisible Cauldron of Creation).

Finally there is one more issue that needs to be explained in order for a newly forming grove to make an informed decision on which philosophy they will adopt regarding the range and functions to be served by the Grail Chalice. Most groups will prefer to use the Grail Chalice *only* for the actual Eucharistic Mass itself, feeling that reserving this cup solely for such sacramental communion with the Mother enhances its sacredness and the holiness of its magickal vibrations. They will therefore choose to have a separate, usually larger, chalice of ceramic pottery for the purpose of sharing the wine between one another during the informalities which follow the opening of the circle at the close of the ritual. This happens to be the author's preference as well. However, admittedly, this tendency is no doubt inherited from the beliefs of traditional Western mystery schools of ceremonial magick (as well as the medieval Church) which insist that reserving your magickal tools only for ceremonial purposes intensifies their power and potency. Hence, the using of these ritual tools for mere mundane purposes is seen as a dangerous dissipation of their stored magickal energies.

On the other hand, there are those who take the view that full spiritual and experiential insight into the Goddess Who is Herself the Grail cannot be actualized in a religious vacuum cut off from everyday activities that sustain us. From their perspective, sharing with one another the basic building blocks of physical sustenance in the informal atmosphere of the Cakes and Wine ceremony is in reality a continuation of the Grail Mystery itself, for by it the Goddess is seen to be nourishing our bodies and spirits simultaneously through the cakes, wine, and the mutual sharing of close fellowship, building in us a growing recognition of the Lady in all things; Her divinity permeating both food and friendship in a "mundane epiphany," if you will, of what has just previously transpired on a highly ritual level in the Grail Mass. Members of our Order who favor this persuasion have no objections whatsoever to using the Grail Chalice for the communal cup as well. In fact, they feel that having two cups tends to take away from the centrality of worshipful focus upon a single chalice on the altar.[5]

Both theological approaches can be seen as reverentially honoring the Goddess and the concept of the Grail in their own ways. We should never lose sight of the fact that there is not one "true and only way." In the last analysis, to each his/her own. The choice is up to you and your local grove.

The Paten

The paten, or holy dish, is the necessary complement of the Grail Chalice, for they both are the venerated receptacles for the respective Eucharistic offerings of bread and wine. The paten loosely corresponds to the dish or metal disc called the pentacle in some Wiccan traditions. Many even inscribe them with a pentagram in the bottom of the dish as a symbol of Earth, and various items are blessed and consecrated by being placed on the pentacle. However, in the Ordo Arcanorum Gradalis, the paten is used for only one purpose: the placement of the Host for the Grail Mass, for it serves as its temporary tabernacle during the Eucharistic Rite itself. Nor do we inscribe it with a pentagram as do some other groups, since for us the wheaten bread of the Host superbly serves as a most natural symbol of elemental Earth. Also, since many groves will choose to use the Altar of the Pentagram for their rituals, the whole circular altar itself becomes a "disc of blessing" inscribed with the potency of the Five-Pointed Mystic Star, voiding any need for a pentacle dish as used by other traditions.

If you are planning to get a traditional style Grail Chalice of silver, I would strongly recommend that you look through some Catholic or Anglican altarware catalogues at your local religious supply store, for most chalices also come with a matching paten for the Host. The purchase of these may run into several hundred dollars or more, but if you find that special chalice and paten set that seems to exude that distinctive aura of magickal sanctity, then it will be worth it. Often the whole grove can chip in monetarily, making it a collective group project and thereby lighten any individual financial burdens caused by the purchase.

Of course, the alternative would be the obtaining of a ceramic chalice and paten (as already mentioned). You can usually find local potter craftpersons who will be glad to make a matching chalice and paten according to the design and specifications which you require, and at a reasonable price. Whatever your preference, it is suggested that you make certain that your chalice and paten are a matched set, for it better signifies their unity of Eucharistic purpose as well as causing the altar arrangement to look more aesthetically pleasing.[6]

Some patens are of the type which can easily fit almost like a cover on the top of the chalice. In this case, it would be most proper to leave them this way upon the altar until the point in the Mass where the Liturgy of the Chalice begins, at which time the celebrant would take the paten and Host from the top of the chalice and place it in back or to the side of the chalice's base in preparation for the beginning of this segment of the Mass.

As regards the acquisition of wheaten wafers for the Host, the best place (of course) is any Catholic religious supply house. You should measure the diameter of your paten to make sure that you purchase the right size wafer which will fit nicely in the paten. If your paten has a circular well or indentation, make certain that the wafer does not exceed the diameter of the interior well.[7]

Finally, while searching through catalogues of Christian altarware companies, you will frequently notice that many chalice and paten sets are designed with various religious symbols to enhance their appearance. You may be surprised to find out that not all of these emblems are unique to Christianity. The cross far predates the Church as a symbol of the sacrificed God in Paganism as well as the union of male and female. The Labarum or Chi Rho was borrowed by Christians from the followers of Mithra, the Persian Sun-god.[8] Even the sign of the fish was considered sacred to the Goddess long before it was appropriated by the Church to refer to Christ.[9] This is important to know, for when you realize that many symbols in Christianity were literally stolen from Paganism, you may not feel nearly as uncomfortable in reclaiming some of these designs for your own ritual use if they happen to be engraved on the chalice or paten. Other designs which incorporate motifs of wheat and grapes on the vine would be most appropriate for the Eucharistic vessels.

The Sceptre and Staff

The ritual tool known as the *wand* in other Pagan traditions is called the *sceptre* in the terminology of the Ordo Arcanorum Gradalis. The magick wand has a long and venerable history of popular awe now permanently embedded in the myths and legends of our Western culture. Good fairies and devious sorcerers alike have used its power for good or evil.

The power of the sceptre is resident in the *authority* which it represents. One of the dictionary definitions for a wand is "a staff of authority; a sceptre." It was often carried before high dignitaries in public processions as an indication of their rank and power.

In our Order, the sceptre and staff both partake of the same essence derived from the archetypal spear/staff/rod of the Grail Hallows, being separate extensions for the accomplishment of the same ceremonial purpose. They are actually two variant manifestations of the same spiritual tool.

The sceptre is usually no longer than between 18 and 21 inches. It can be made of wood (trees such as holly and willow have long been favored by some) or metals such as silver or copper, often tipped with a quartz crystal or other gem. The sceptre can be as ornate or as plain as you like. The same can be said for the staff; though most often made of wood, it too can be adorned with crystals and a wide variety of metal ornamentation. Serpent carvings wrapping around the staff are also popular and stand for the authoritative wisdom of the Goddess.

Each ordained member of this Order should have either a sceptre or a staff, or both, since they are the symbolic emblem of the office of the priesthood; and since every ordained member of the Ordo Arcanorum Gradalis is considered to be either priestess or priest, it is imperative that they have in their possession the visible, ritual tool which manifests and represents their authority.

The sceptre and staff are the tangible instruments which literally embody within them the vested authority of the priesthood. The blossoming rods so often pictured in most Tarot decks had their legendary origin in stories such as that of the Staff of Aaron, High Priest of the Israelites, which was said to have miraculously budded as a divine confirmation of his priestly authority to lead the Hebrews in the official worship.[10] His staff was seen as the embodiment of a living power which symbolized spiritual vitality. The Christian counterpart is seen in the bishop's crosier, which some authorities candidly admit "has been traced by some to the rod used by Roman augurs in their divinations."[11] The pervasive use of the sceptre (wand) and staff among Pagan priesthoods of the past has ample testimony from historians:

> The staff or *Lituus* was of magical import. Wands of tamarisk were in the hands of Magian priests. The tops of such augur rods were slightly hooked. One, found in Etruria, had budded in the hand. The *barsom*, or bundle of twigs, is held by Parsee priests. Strabo noted twigs in hand at prayer. The *Thyrsus* had several knots. Prometheus hid the fire from heaven in his rod.[12]

The magickal Staff of Office was most essential in the regalia of the Irish Druids. In fact, without it, it was said "a Druid could do but little."[13]

Like the mythological rod of Prometheus, the sceptre and staff are powerful symbols of the spiritual fire of divine power brought down from heaven to earth through the magickal mediation of the Pagan priesthood. In the ritual practice of this Order, the sceptre and staff are used most often by the priestess and the priest when invoking the Goddess and the God. They lift it up when praying or invoking as a reminder to the residents of the heavenly realm that they come before the gods by right of the sacred authority of their priesthood. The staff is also used to bar entrance to the circle area by members of the grove until the proper response is elicited from each individual to the priest's ceremonial challenge during the Opening Rite.

More often than not, the use of the sceptre is favored by the priestess, while the use of the staff for the same purposes is generally preferred by the priest, although there is no set of rules regarding this matter.

While the sceptre is always laid upon the altar just in front of the paten (or chalice, if the paten is placed on top of it), the staff, on the other hand, usually has a special place designated for it within the circle area. Sometimes a staff holder is made so that the staff can be placed in it standing upright so that it will not have to be laid upon the ground.

The sceptre and staff are occasionally used to cast the ceremonial circle instead of the glaive; especially in situations like a handfasting (wedding), where numerous guests from other religious backgrounds may be present who could easily misinterpret the significance of a ritual knife or be frightened by its use.

The Glaive

Of all the ritual implements within the modern Neo-Pagan revival, none is more famous or universally valued than the ceremonial knife, known widely within the Craft as an *athame*, though in the Ordo Arcanorum Gradalis it is called the *glaive*. Technically speaking, the ritual sword which is sometimes owned by a grove for the casting of outdoor circles is called the *Glaive Major*, while the ceremonial knife is known as the *Glaive Minor*. But for all practical purposes, what is usually referred to as the glaive is the ceremonial knife, since it is used far more often than is the ritual sword.

With the glaive, the sacred circle is created, cast by the very will of its owner flowing through its blade. Invisible pentacles of protection are traced in the air with the glaive for the banishment of negative energies, and the symbolic consummation of the Great Rite is performed by the descent of its blade into the Grail Chalice. The glaive is the single, most important active ritual instrument that a priest/ess possesses.

There is a threefold nature to the glaive which underlies its immense significance. It is a tool, a weapon, and the symbol of a most potent reality. As a handmade tool, it is a reminder of that which was one of the first evidences of human distinctiveness from the other species: the ability through developed application of intelligence to be toolmakers—something that distinguishes us from all other primates in the Earth's chain of evolutionary development. It speaks to us of our unique abilities as humans to *create*, and the responsibility we have as a species to use our creative inventions in a way which is in harmony with the rest of the living environment. When we use our glaives, we most often utilize them for the creation of sacred space; the actual carving out of psychic boundaries and barriers. The glaive as a tool is a symbol and a visible vehicle for our capacity to create our own spiritual environment.

The glaive is, secondly, a weapon. A weapon in the hands of a skilled combatant commands instant respect and instinctive fear in those who may be in the position of a potential adversary. This ceremonial blade is primarily a ritual weapon, and is necessarily used in the banishing of negative forces from any given area. When a priest/ess casts a magick circle and commands all unwanted entities to depart, it is not the actual physical knife that frightens these nefarious beings into submission, but the spiritual authority of the priest/ess in alignment with the Goddess and the God, which the glaive conveys to lower orders of the spirit realm. In this capacity, the glaive is supremely a weapon of command and a tangible symbol of a priest/ess' power when in union with the higher forces of the spiritual universe. The glaive, then, is a magickal weapon not merely to be recognized, but *obeyed*.

Thirdly, the glaive is an obvious phallic representation of the masculine polarity in the cosmic energies, especially in the context of the symbolic ritual act of the Great Rite, which is ceremonially enacted by our Order at every Earth Rite during the revolving of the Wheel of the Year. In this rite, the glaive is the corresponding complement to its feminine, yonic counterpart represented by the Grail Chalice. In this context, the glaive in conjunction with the chalice functions as a powerful symbol of sexuality on this plane as well as the whole structure of cosmic cohesion evidenced as the universal Yin/Yang manifestation of polarity.

In the Craft, the glaive has traditionally been specified as being a black-handled, double-edged knife. But as we shall discover, such tradition, far from being uniformly established, is in reality most relative depending on the particular school or group of magickal spirituality one consults as a guide. In fact, contradictions to this generally held "axiom for athames" abound in profusion.

As an example, while most Wiccans practice their magickal art with black-handled athames, there are others who instead have handles of deer feet or natural wood finishes. And, standing out in glaring contradiction to the accepted rule is Gavin and Yvonne Frost's Church and School of Wicca, which insists that the handle of the ceremonial knife be of white or natural-colored twine wrap. The Frosts also have an unusual design to their knives (usually of bronze or aluminum) with only a single-edged blade.

Many popular Wiccan traditions specify that the blade be of magnetized steel, while other groups think that only nonferrous metals should be used. Certain traditions engrave various magickal sigils on their blades or handles, while others leave their knives plain, without engraving of any kind.

To add to all of this confusion, there are differences among covens and groves as to what is the proper way for a newly initiated member to obtain his/her own personal athame. In some of the more established traditions, the athame is presented to the neophyte upon his/her initiation into the Craft. Other magickal schools stand upon the premise that the best and most effective ritual knife is one that is personally made by the individual. The list of variations and discrepancies in Craft philosophy on this subject could even be extended further to broaden the spectrum of diversity, but suffice it to say that at least all seem to agree that the athame or glaive is always a knife or dagger of some kind!

In the Ordo Arcanorum Gradalis, the approach to this question is most lenient and flexible. The number one "rule of thumb" is almost proverbial in its applicability to any question of propriety relating to Craft customs and traditions: *whatever feels most magickal and right for you is best for you.* Do you prefer to make your own glaive from scratch? Well and good! Would you rather use an ordinary hunting knife of some kind? Then follow your feelings! Would you rather search for a modern replica of a medieval dagger? Then start looking!

In the Ordo Arcanorum Gradalis, whether you have a double- or single-edged blade; a black, white, red, or deer-foot handle; or esoteric engravings on your glaive is relatively unimportant. What is essential is that the person who wishes to follow this particular path of the Grail Quest take the time to find, purchase, or make a ritual glaive which appeals to the "younger self"—that aspect of our personality which has the childlike capacity for being inspired with wonder-filled imagination and awe when looking upon that personal glaive of your very own. Each individual will know when he/she has found or created a glaive that is uniquely right for him/her; that is why we do not feel it proper to force upon all alike the dictum of having the same type of glaive, as do some Craft traditions.

The glaive, like any other ritual tool or vessel, must be ceremonially cleansed and consecrated before it is actually used. Nearly all Pagan and Wiccan traditions have their own variations in procedures for cleansing and consecration, and most of them are just as effective as any other. At the conclusion of this chapter there is a standard consecration invocation for ritual tools. In fact, it can be used for all of your ceremonial implements simply by making the appropriate minor changes in wording to apply to the particular tool or object which you are consecrating.

The Censer

Perhaps nothing is more mystically evocative than the smell and sight of incense wafting its way in circular, undulating spirals as it dissipates into the invisibility of higher vibrations in the atmosphere. The burning of fragrant resins and spices as part of religious rites is one of humanity's oldest means of bringing an acceptable offering to the deities which they worshipped. In Western religion, this custom is still retained in the Anglican, Roman Catholic, and Eastern Orthodox branches of Christianity, though unfortunately, since Vatican II, it is far less practiced than it used to be.

Neo-Paganism in general and Wicca in particular have always incorporated the censer as an essential piece of altarware, representing (as it does so graphically) that wispy, ethereal element of Air. Incense is one of the most effective ways to cleanse and consecrate a selected area for sacred purposes. It was also the belief of the ancients that incense carried our prayers to the gods. Many occultists also believe that burning incense can help certain spirit entities to materialize during the evocations of ceremonial magick, though this is very seldom the purpose for incense in the religious rites of this Order.

It is recommended that every priest/ess of this Order have a personal censer for his/her own private altar. The kind of censer or thurible chosen is thoroughly up to the discretion of the individual. There are church censers which hang from chains for walking about the altar at Mass. These can usually be purchased through any Catholic or Anglican church supply house. They are beautiful, and sometimes expensive, but are best suited for censing the periphery of the circle, especially in outdoor ceremonies.

Finding an incense burner can actually be a lot of fun, because it calls for the exercise of one's inner sense of magickal creativity. Of course, censers come in many and varied forms, depending on the type of incense you are planning to use.

While we may desire to buy anything which is aesthetically pleasing to the eye, keep in mind that your incense burner must be large enough to hold a fair amount of sand in its bottom in order to facilitate the burning of incense upon lighted pieces of charcoal made especially for that purpose. These usually get quite hot, and sand needs to be in the burner to help absorb the heat as well as prevent damage to the censer itself or the altar upon which it is sitting.

In most stores, the only kind of incense burners readily available are those small brass ones from India which are primarily for the insertion of your common stick or cone incense. While they are permissible to use in ceremonies, they are certainly not preferable. Most of the best occult incenses for ceremonial purposes require the use of those little circular charcoals in order to be properly burned. These, too, can be obtained at any Catholic or occult supply house. However, apart from the swinging chained thuribles previously mentioned, it is an extremely difficult task to find any suitable burners which are made to accommodate charcoal-burning incense, since churches are about the only source of demand for such censers. Your best bet is to take the time to search the musty corners of antique shops and second-hand "knickknack" shops for something suitable for adaptation as a censer. The object could be anything from an earthen pottery bowl to a small metal cauldron. Your imagination is the limit. The only stipulations are that it be sturdy, able to withstand heat, and visually appealing to you.

After purchasing your censer, you will need to obtain some fine, clean white sand on which the coals are to rest in order to burn the incense. (Swinging church censers do not require sand due to their special construction.) This kind of sand can best be found in hardware or home improvement stores where it is usually merchandised as children's play sand. It can be bought very cheaply, and a twenty pound bag will last you at least a year! A helpful hint to keep your sand clean is to place a small, squared piece of aluminum foil on top of the sand and then place the charcoal on the wrap before you ignite it.

The most excellent incense for ritual use can only be found in specialty establishments such as occult stores and (again) Catholic supply houses. If you have none of these kinds of businesses in your area, there are some occult shops which would gladly respond to your mail-order requests. In your choice of incenses, you can be as lavish or as simple as you wish. Some Pagans burn different kinds of incense for various purposes and occasions. Others prefer to have just a few good "all-purpose" incenses for their standard ceremonial practice. If you wish to spend the investment in time and study, you may even want to make your own incense "from scratch." There are some excellent books available on this subject in your local bookstores.

A few hints of caution are in order, however, before you begin to burn incense upon charcoals made especially for that purpose. First of all, do not put any incense upon the coal until it has been lit for at least five to ten minutes. This gives it time to heat up so that the fragrant resins will burn more efficiently and cleanly once they are placed upon the coal. In an outside ritual, a small teaspoon of incense placed upon the coal may be fine, since it produces more of an effect in the cere-mony, but dissipates quickly in the open air. However, in small apartments or enclosed areas, use only a very small amount of granulated incense grains so that you will not end up suffocating yourself in a sea of smoke which has no place to escape. (Smoke detectors sounding off in the midst of ritual enactments are defi-nitely not to be desired!) You may have to experiment several times in order to find out the right amount to use on each occasion without running the risk of causing your celebrants the discomfort of practically choking to death!

For those who live in very close quarters, you may prefer incense which comes in powdered form and can be burned on a sand base without the use of ignited coals. This type of incense can also be purchased through certain occult supply houses.

Besides group rituals, the lighting of incense can cause a superb meditative effect upon the mind and spirit when you are doing any personal contemplation or prayerful worship. For those who venture into the deeper realms of magick, the use of different kinds of incense for certain spells and rites almost requires a knowledge which is close to a form of metaphysical, scientific precision. There are also some excellent published studies and handbooks for those who may wish to pursue this study of incense more deeply.

Salt and Water Bowls

The use of water and salt for purposes of purification in religious rites goes back mil-lenniums to the dawning of human history. From the holy water found at the entrance to every Roman Catholic sanctuary to the salt and sulfur circles some-times used in certain forms of ceremonial magick, these two elements essential to the continuation of life have always exerted an enormous influence upon the spir-itual psyche of our culture's collective religious development precisely because of their seemingly magickal properties.

Water is the literal life which ever flows through the river-veins of the Earth by which the infinite variety of her offspring are sustained. Water is also the emblem in miniature of the primordial deep, the mysteriously generative womb of life's beginnings in the earliest eras of our planet's evolution. The cleansing effect of water upon the body has long been another reason why it has been universally used as an outward symbol of the inner spiritual purification of heart necessary if one is to approach the gods with confidence.

Salt, especially from the sea, was often likened to the tasty residue left from the ebbing tide of the Earth's ocean-blood. Because blood has a salty taste, salt itself was seen, at least symbolically, as a derivative of the life-giving properties of the Goddess. Without its use in the diet, no one could live. It has always been one of the most important ingredients foundational to any civilization.

Salt was also discovered to have preservative properties which retarded the spoilage of meat. In Biblical times, covenants between people as well as gods were sealed ceremonially by the use of salt as a symbol of blood. It is therefore not surprising to realize the reverential awe with which this magickal, crystalline substance was held.

When salt and water are combined in our rituals, it is the ceremonial continuation of a most ancient practice by which the flowing blood of the sacred Earth is ritually reproduced by the mixture of these elements as a reminder of our origins in the protective, watery safety of the maternal womb of the Goddess. As such, it is used (after the proper blessings) as a charged mixture which brings both blessing and protection to the designated sacred space where it is utilized in ritual aspersion.

Just about any dish or bowl can be used for the salt and water upon the altar. They need not be large. In fact, antique salt servers with matching salt spoons would be an excellent choice along with some suitable silver bowl (the smaller the better). Of course, simple miniature pottery bowls could be used as well as sea shells (as long as they are deep enough to hold a minimal amount of water and have a sturdy base to prevent spillage).

One important note to remember is that if you are using silver-plated bowls it is imperative that you empty both bowls as soon as possible after the completion of the ritual and rinse them thoroughly in order to avoid destruction of the silver plating from prolonged exposure to the chemical abrasiveness of the salt.

In the Ordo Arcanorum Gradalis, we often use a salt spoon for mixing the salt into the water rather than the blade of the glaive as is done in some other Neo-Pagan and Wiccan traditions. If you have ever had to chase around little grains of salt with the blade of a knife, you will quickly realize the sense of futility and frustration that can ensue!

Some people prefer to use a cruet on the altar which is filled with the water. They pour this into the bowl just prior to its blessing, and then simply drop a tiny pinch of salt into the water. Use whichever procedure you like the best; either way the symbolism remains the same.

In our Order, we use sea salt for the symbolic reasons already mentioned, especially the larger crystals which can be purchased in most health food or gourmet stores. Some also prefer to use distilled or bottled spring water rather than chemically treated and fluoridated tap water, since water is a symbol of purity. But in the last analysis, the use of whatever you feel most comfortable with is the best policy. When I have used tap water for rituals, I never noticed any sense of diminished spiritual presence as a result!

As with all other altarware, your salt and water bowls should be cleansed and consecrated before ritual use.

Altar Candles

The type and size of candleholders you acquire is purely a matter of personal taste. Some Pagans like very simple candleholders made of pottery or wood. Others lean towards the more ornate brass or silver-plated varieties. Of course, brass or silver will periodically require more work due to the need for polishing that inevitably arises.

In the Ordo Arcanorum Gradalis, two main candles are always placed upon the altar (see the altar illustrations). Not only do they seem to add a sense of balance to the altar itself, but they are primarily symbols of the Lady and Her Lord.

The color of the altar candles should always correspond to the color of the quarter of the circle towards which the altar is facing. During spring, the altar faces east. The color of the eastern quarter is yellow. Therefore the altar candles are also yellow. During summer, the altar faces south. The color of the southern quarter is red. Therefore the altar candles are also red. During fall, the altar faces west. The color of the western quarter is blue. Therefore the altar candles are also blue. During winter, the altar faces north. The color of the northern quarter is green. Therefore the altar candles are also green.

Another item which is needed within the circle is a candle-lantern. It is used to salute the Quarter-Regents of the south and in all the Solstice and Equinox Earth Rites in honor of the Sun, as well as for the more mundane purpose of helping others in the grove read their ritual lines in the dark. Such lanterns can often be found at craft shows, specialty shops, or patio supply businesses. If you cannot locate one to your satisfaction, you can either make your own or else just use another candle with a large sturdy base which can be placed at the southern quarter area.

It is important to caution about the dangers of coming too close to open candle flames during the course of a ritual while wearing flowing, swirling robes. Always be aware of the burning candles around and take the proper precautions. If you have a permanent temple in your home, one way of doing this is to place the quarter lights on the walls of the room according to the directional points of a proper compass reading. If outdoors, you can always make the circle larger than will actually be needed so that the quarter lights on the periphery will be well away from the grove participants' garments.

For your Lunar Rite altar arrangement, you will need a three-branched candlestick (or three separate, single candleholders) which should be placed in a center position midway between the two main altar candlesticks. These will hold a white, red, and black taper, standing respectively for the Goddess in Her lunar phases as waxing Maiden, full-orbed Mother, and waning Crone. (Please see "The Lunar Rite" for further details.)

Goddess and God Statues

Having a statue of the Goddess and the God upon your altar is always an aesthetically pleasing addition to your sacred area. Religious images have a long and venerable history in most religions of the world, for they have served from before the dawn of recorded time as psychic reservoirs receiving the energies of the worshipper as they use the image as a physical focusing point and outward symbol of a deity. In no way, of course, do we ever confuse the image with the spiritual reality of the deity itself, but the longer such an image and/or object remains the center of an area set apart for devotional and meditative practices, the more it begins to absorb the religious vibrations as well as the emanations of the Goddess/God energies which are invoked periodically at your altar.

The types of statues from which you can choose have only your imagination for their limit. If you are artistically inclined in either painting or sculpture, you could even create your own image or icon. Most Pagans, however, seem to prefer classic reproductions of the Venus de Milo, Aphrodite Rising from the Sea, or other works of art from the turn of the century which seemed to capture certain essences of the archetypal energies of the Goddess.

Through some occult stores you can occasionally find reproductions of other classic sculptures of Greek and Roman goddesses such as Diana or Artemis. With the steady growth of the Neo-Pagan and Wiccan movements in the United States and Canada, there has risen a sizeable number of Craft craftpersons skilled in all manner of artwork and image making specifically applicable to our kind of altar arrangements.

As with many other items necessary for your altar, images of the Goddess and God are not always easy to find. Your best bets, other than occult supply stores, are antique shops or flea markets. It is sometimes absolutely amazing what one can come across in these mercantile treasure-troves of the old, the forgotten, and the discarded. The author has discovered everything from plaster reliefs of Middle Eastern goddesses to bronze statues of Pan. Most of the time the proprietors of these stores have little idea of the mystical significance of these objects; it is only the trained Pagan or occultist's eye that spots the sacred lying in the midst of assorted antique chaos!

Another fabulous place to obtain suitable altar images as well as other items of general Pagan interest, are the local Renaissance Faires held in many states throughout the country, including California, Maryland, Pennsylvania, and New York. In many of these festive gatherings, often a majority of the craftpersons are Pagan-oriented as their works of art so amply demonstrate. But save up your money far in advance; if you do not have a strong will to resist, you will probably leave the Faire a pauper—but a happy one!

Whether you have a statue of *both* the Goddess and the God upon your altar is purely a personal decision or a group decision, depending on whether or not you are referring to your own altar or the altar for a grove. Some feel it is essential to have both represented as a symbol of balanced gender representation of Deity. Others are contented with just an image of the Goddess, since they feel that she holds the quintessential place of honored primacy for the purposes of worship. Still others are content with no image or physical representation of either the Lady or Lord, or else a very small cauldron which they set upon the altar as one of the most ancient and "witchy" symbols of the Goddess.

In the final analysis, the whole issue of a statue or statues for an altar following the rubrics of this Order is optional. There is certainly nothing essential about such a practice, and incidentally, even without a Lady image, the Goddess is still supremely represented on the altar by the Grail Chalice, the ultimate and most femininely graceful of all the ritual tools of the Craft.

The Cauldron

The cauldron has long been one of the oldest and most well known symbols of the Craft. It was the prototype of most of the feminine spiritual ideas now associated with the Grail Chalice. It is also the most ancient embodiment of all that has been associated with the lore of fertility, regeneration, and the source of life as being the womb of the Great Goddess.

In our Order, the cauldron is often situated in the southern quarter of the circle, and is used to hold the candle(s) of the Candlemas ritual and the Balemas candle (symbolic of the balefire) if that particular Earth Rite happens to be held indoors. It is also utilized as the holder for the Hallowmas candle (symbolic of the traditional Samhain bonfires) when that ritual is held indoors.

Cauldrons of the classic "Halloween" style with the tripod feet, potbellied and black, are rather hard to find. Antique stores should be your first place to explore. Sometimes you can even place an order for one with an antique dealer so that he/she will keep an eye out for you. If you happen to live in the areas of the eastern United States, cauldrons are often easier to be found in the rural, country regions where in years gone by they were utilized for various cooking purposes.

Bells

Bells are used to signal the beginning of every ritual of the Order. They are also rung during the Grail Mass at the elevation of both the Host and the Grail Chalice.

These bells can be purchased at Catholic supply stores or through Buddhist religious supply houses which usually advertise in various New Age magazines. Actually, any kind of bell is acceptable as long as it appeals to you or your grove.

The Broomstick

The broomstick is only actively used for ritual purposes during the Earth Rite of Candlemas, for the ceremonial sweeping away of winter. The rest of the year it rests beside the altar or in some other place in the circle area where it can be easily seen as a reminder of our roots in the arcane lore of the mysteries of the Old Religions.

Some of the best brooms can be found at crafts fairs, country stores or fireplace shops, where the popular style of brooms has reverted to the old "witchy" home-made look.

The Consecration of Tools

By Diana,
By Selene,
By Hecate,
By Cernunnos
    and
By Pan,

I, (here insert your Pagan name),
consecrate and dedicate this (here name the tool)
for all the positive work of Wiccan and Pagan Craft.

In the Name of She Who is the Triune Glory:
    Maiden,
    Mother,
    and Crone,

Be thou pregnant with the power of the Moon!
Be thou emblazoned with the energies of the Sun!
Be thou cleansed of all impurities of spirit!

Be thou set apart for the celebration
    of the Secret Mysteries.
Be thou permeated with the presence
    of the Lady and the Lord,
    ready for thy appointed work
    within the rites of the Craft.

In the Name of the Mighty Goddess
    and Her Horned Consort,

So Mote It Be!

Footnotes

1. Leviticus; Hebrews 13:10-13, *Holy Bible*.

2. Raymond Buckland, *The Tree: The Complete Book of Saxon Witchcraft*. (York Beach, ME: Samuel Weiser, 1974), pp. 30-31.

3. The one Earth Rite of exception to the rule of having a gold chalice would be Hallowmas (Samhain), since it is the Feast of the Dead, the time of the psychic and paranormal which has many traits in common with the Lunar Mysteries. Therefore a silver chalice would be used.

4. Caitlin and John Matthews, *The Western Way, Volume II—The Hermetic Tradition*. (Boston, MA: Arkana, 1986), p. 174.

5. However, the predominant practice still favors the use of two separate cups, since the Cakes and Wine ceremony usually takes place around a dining table away from the ritual area to signify the beginning of the evening's informalities (see "Cakes and Wine"), whereas it is preferable to leave the Grail Chalice on the altar at all times.

6. Some priest/esses of the Order, however, prefer to have their paten made from some form of stone, wood, or pottery, and distinctly different from the chalice in order to signify its elemental correspondence with Earth in contrast to the chalice's elemental affinity with Water.

7. Of course, if you have any grove members who are known for their baking abilities, you can make your own unleavened bread for each sacramental occasion. However, you would still have to take care that your wheaten cake did not exceed the diameter of the paten.

8. Barbara G. Walker, *The Woman's Encyclopedia of Myths and Secrets*. (San Francisco, CA: Harper & Row, 1983), pp. 188-190, 522.

9. Barbara G. Walker, *The Secrets of the Tarot*. (San Francisco, CA: Harper & Row, 1984), pp. 141-143.

10. Numbers 17:16-26, *Holy Bible*.

11. *The Oxford Dictionary of the Christian Church*. Ed. by F.L. Cross. (Oxford University Press, 1974), p. 361. Used by permission of Oxford University Press.

12. James Bonwick, *Irish Druids and Old Irish Religions*. (Dorset Press, 1986), p. 9.

13. *Ibid.*, p. 281.

Part II

Missale Mysteriorum

Introduction

The rituals which follow are a compilation of the primary ceremonial liturgies which in traditional Wiccan terminology would constitute the "Book of Shadows" of this Order and the tradition to which it adheres. However, in the Ordo Arcanorum Gradalis, this collection is known as the Missale Mysteriorum (the Missal of the Mysteries), for although the rites are varied in their celebration and commemoration of times, events, and personal passages, they all revolve around the centrality of the Grail Mass itself. Furthermore, if we delve deeper into the larger esoteric context, there will be found a constant thread running through all of these rites which reflects our awe of THE MYSTERY which is the Deity, as well as the Mysteries which were instituted from ancient times to keep before our spiritual consciousness a continuing awareness of the numinous and the holy. (It should be noted that this Missal is also unofficially referred to by some within our priesthood as the Missale Arcanorum [Missal of the Secrets], being roughly synonymous with Missale Mysteriorum, but carrying with it the identifying mark of one of the words which make up the name of the Order itself.)

Before continuing on into the rituals, a few technical comments are in order. In many newly-formed groups, a large number of the ritual parts in any given Earth Rite or Lunar Rite will most likely be read from the text of this Missal (although as time goes on, members will inevitably gravitate towards memorization of their parts to make for a more effective ritual). Participants in these ceremonies will soon realize that a lot of awkwardness can result if people don't know beforehand who should be holding the Missal for whom! We have learned this from sometimes humorous experiences. Each study circle or grove will have to determine for itself what way it thinks will best take care of this problem. In our own grove, we have found that by appointing someone to kneel and hold the Missal before the reader, it thereby frees the one reading from the book to gesture appropriately with his/her hands. Also, since we usually invoke the Goddess and God with either the sceptre or the staff, we need to be free from the necessity of having to hold the Missal at the same time! What way will work best can only be determined through group experimentation.

As a further point of information, it must be remembered that most of these rituals were written with a grove in mind; therefore, those who must follow a solitary practice of the Craft would have to either eliminate or modify those parts of the text which clearly necessitate various forms of communal participation. Solitary practitioners should also notice that many of the ceremonial invocations use "we" in reference to the assembled worshippers. Since the solitary obviously works alone, it may seem strange at first to be using plurals in the ritual text, but we find it easier and wiser to continue the usage of "we," "our," and other forms of plural usage as symbolic of our unity with all Pagans, Gnostics, and Wiccans everywhere who are one with us in spirit (even if we practice solitary) as we celebrate the Mysteries of the Goddess and the God. This "we" can also refer to the invisible realm of Orders and spirits in union with us as we perform the rituals, much as in the Christian concept of the Church Triumphant: the "spirits of the just made perfect" and the "heavenly cloud of witnesses" who are believed to always be present at every observance of the Eucharist.

Most of the rites which follow are accompanied by commentary, and the reader should understand that what is revealed in the fine print of these footnotes can be essential to the proper perception of the rituals themselves as a means to a closer communion with the Divine. With this in mind, you are now invited to turn these pages and enter into the magickal world of worship.

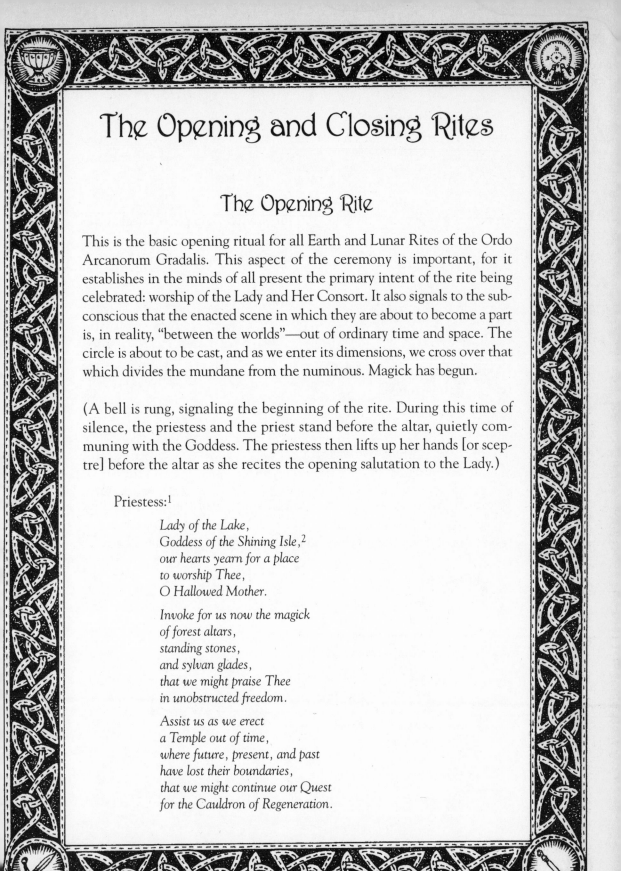

The Opening and Closing Rites

The Opening Rite

This is the basic opening ritual for all Earth and Lunar Rites of the Ordo Arcanorum Gradalis. This aspect of the ceremony is important, for it establishes in the minds of all present the primary intent of the rite being celebrated: worship of the Lady and Her Consort. It also signals to the subconscious that the enacted scene in which they are about to become a part is, in reality, "between the worlds"—out of ordinary time and space. The circle is about to be cast, and as we enter its dimensions, we cross over that which divides the mundane from the numinous. Magick has begun.

(A bell is rung, signaling the beginning of the rite. During this time of silence, the priestess and the priest stand before the altar, quietly communing with the Goddess. The priestess then lifts up her hands [or sceptre] before the altar as she recites the opening salutation to the Lady.)

Priestess:[1]

> *Lady of the Lake,*
> *Goddess of the Shining Isle,[2]*
> *our hearts yearn for a place*
> *to worship Thee,*
> *O Hallowed Mother.*
>
> *Invoke for us now the magick*
> *of forest altars,*
> *standing stones,*
> *and sylvan glades,*
> *that we might praise Thee*
> *in unobstructed freedom.*
>
> *Assist us as we erect*
> *a Temple out of time,*
> *where future, present, and past*
> *have lost their boundaries,*
> *that we might continue our Quest*
> *for the Cauldron of Regeneration.*

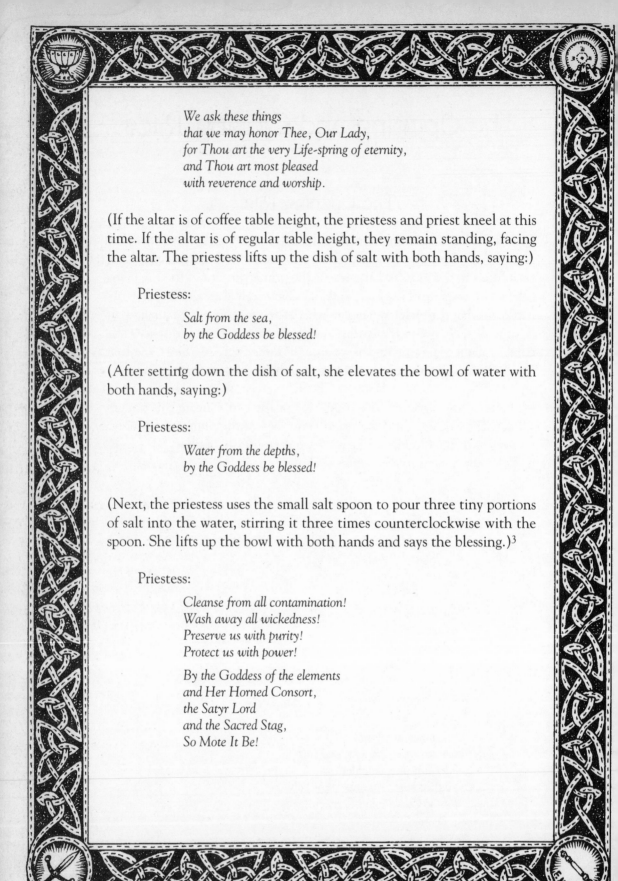

We ask these things
that we may honor Thee, Our Lady,
for Thou art the very Life-spring of eternity,
and Thou art most pleased
with reverence and worship.

(If the altar is of coffee table height, the priestess and priest kneel at this time. If the altar is of regular table height, they remain standing, facing the altar. The priestess lifts up the dish of salt with both hands, saying:)

Priestess:

Salt from the sea,
by the Goddess be blessed!

(After setting down the dish of salt, she elevates the bowl of water with both hands, saying:)

Priestess:

Water from the depths,
by the Goddess be blessed!

(Next, the priestess uses the small salt spoon to pour three tiny portions of salt into the water, stirring it three times counterclockwise with the spoon. She lifts up the bowl with both hands and says the blessing.)[3]

Priestess:

Cleanse from all contamination!
Wash away all wickedness!
Preserve us with purity!
Protect us with power!

By the Goddess of the elements
and Her Horned Consort,
the Satyr Lord
and the Sacred Stag,
So Mote It Be!

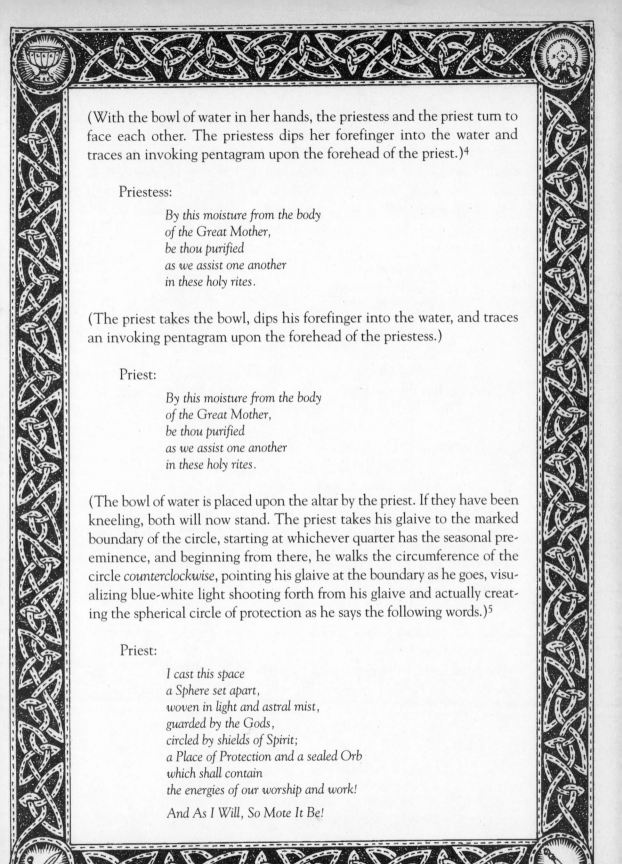

(With the bowl of water in her hands, the priestess and the priest turn to face each other. The priestess dips her forefinger into the water and traces an invoking pentagram upon the forehead of the priest.)[4]

Priestess:

> By this moisture from the body
> of the Great Mother,
> be thou purified
> as we assist one another
> in these holy rites.

(The priest takes the bowl, dips his forefinger into the water, and traces an invoking pentagram upon the forehead of the priestess.)

Priest:

> By this moisture from the body
> of the Great Mother,
> be thou purified
> as we assist one another
> in these holy rites.

(The bowl of water is placed upon the altar by the priest. If they have been kneeling, both will now stand. The priest takes his glaive to the marked boundary of the circle, starting at whichever quarter has the seasonal pre-eminence, and beginning from there, he walks the circumference of the circle *counterclockwise*, pointing his glaive at the boundary as he goes, visualizing blue-white light shooting forth from his glaive and actually creating the spherical circle of protection as he says the following words.)[5]

Priest:

> I cast this space
> a Sphere set apart,
> woven in light and astral mist,
> guarded by the Gods,
> circled by shields of Spirit;
> a Place of Protection and a sealed Orb
> which shall contain
> the energies of our worship and work!
>
> And As I Will, So Mote It Be!

(The priest returns to the altar holding his glaive upright before him while the priestess takes up the bowl of salted water from the altar along with the bunch of herbs used for aspersion.[6] Then, beginning at the same quarter of seasonal preeminence, she will slowly walk *counterclockwise* around the circle, dipping the herbs in the water and sprinkling it around the edge of the circle as she speaks the following words.)

Priestess:

> *Sphere be blessed!*
> *Circle be consecrated!*
> *Sphere be blessed!*
> *Circle be consecrated!*
> *Sphere be blessed!*
> *Circle be consecrated!*

(When she has returned full-circle to the point where she began the aspersion, she will then turn to face the priest at the altar and say:)

Priestess:

> *By all the Names of the mighty Goddess*
> *and Her Horned Consort*
> *the Satyr Lord*
> *and the Sacred Stag,*
> *So Mote It Be!*

(The priest shall then respond:)

Priest:

> *So Mote It Be!*

(The priest replaces his glaive back upon the altar and takes up either his sceptre or staff. He then raises it high as he speaks the following words of dedication.)

Priest:

> *I dedicate this Circle*
> *to the Great Goddess*
> *in all of Her many manifestations:*
> *She Who is the Triple Will,*

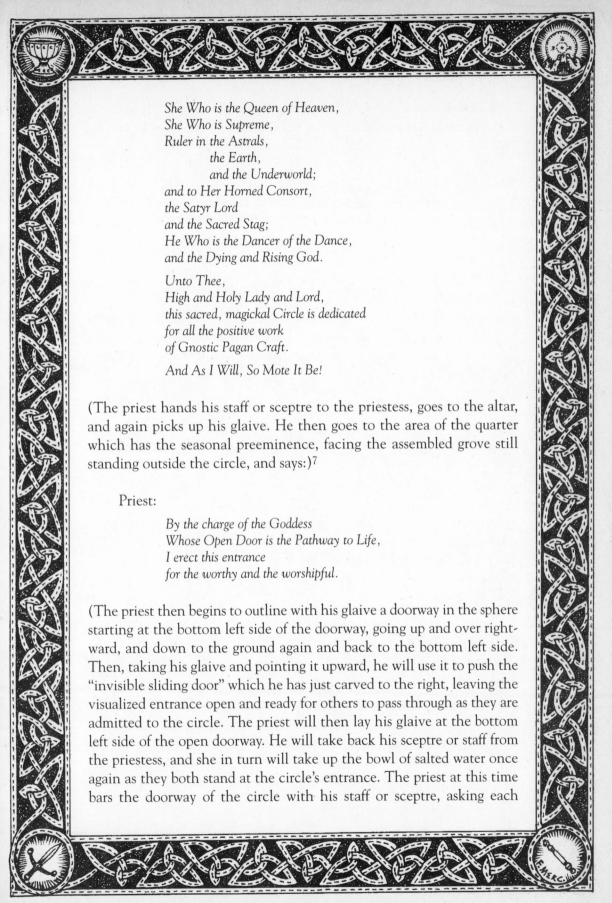

She Who is the Queen of Heaven,
She Who is Supreme,
Ruler in the Astrals,
　　　the Earth,
　　　and the Underworld;
and to Her Horned Consort,
the Satyr Lord
and the Sacred Stag;
He Who is the Dancer of the Dance,
and the Dying and Rising God.

Unto Thee,
High and Holy Lady and Lord,
this sacred, magickal Circle is dedicated
for all the positive work
of Gnostic Pagan Craft.

And As I Will, So Mote It Be!

(The priest hands his staff or sceptre to the priestess, goes to the altar, and again picks up his glaive. He then goes to the area of the quarter which has the seasonal preeminence, facing the assembled grove still standing outside the circle, and says:)[7]

    Priest:

        By the charge of the Goddess
        Whose Open Door is the Pathway to Life,
        I erect this entrance
        for the worthy and the worshipful.

(The priest then begins to outline with his glaive a doorway in the sphere starting at the bottom left side of the doorway, going up and over right-ward, and down to the ground again and back to the bottom left side. Then, taking his glaive and pointing it upward, he will use it to push the "invisible sliding door" which he has just carved to the right, leaving the visualized entrance open and ready for others to pass through as they are admitted to the circle. The priest will then lay his glaive at the bottom left side of the open doorway. He will take back his sceptre or staff from the priestess, and she in turn will take up the bowl of salted water once again as they both stand at the circle's entrance. The priest at this time bars the doorway of the circle with his staff or sceptre, asking each

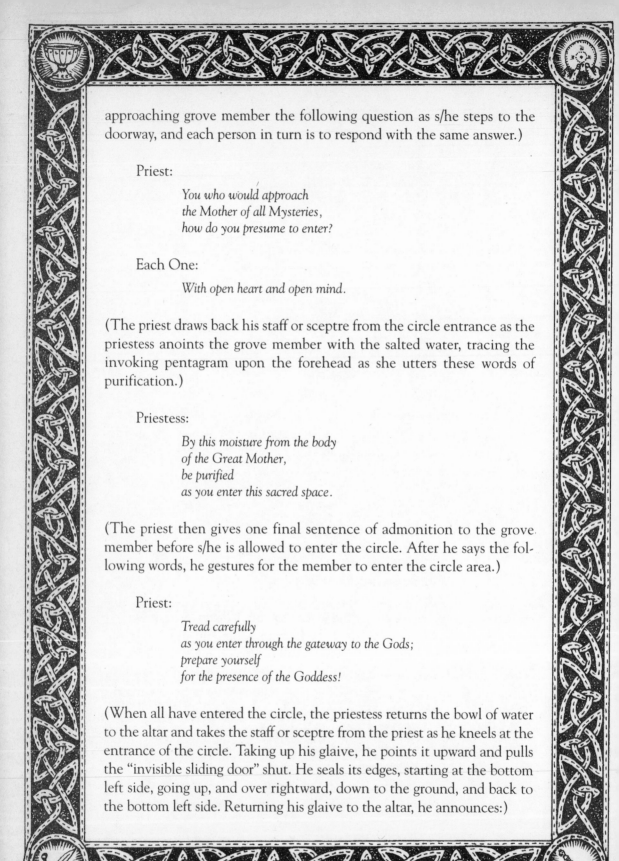

approaching grove member the following question as s/he steps to the doorway, and each person in turn is to respond with the same answer.)

Priest:

You who would approach
the Mother of all Mysteries,
how do you presume to enter?

Each One:

With open heart and open mind.

(The priest draws back his staff or sceptre from the circle entrance as the priestess anoints the grove member with the salted water, tracing the invoking pentagram upon the forehead as she utters these words of purification.)

Priestess:

By this moisture from the body
of the Great Mother,
be purified
as you enter this sacred space.

(The priest then gives one final sentence of admonition to the grove member before s/he is allowed to enter the circle. After he says the following words, he gestures for the member to enter the circle area.)

Priest:

Tread carefully
as you enter through the gateway to the Gods;
prepare yourself
for the presence of the Goddess!

(When all have entered the circle, the priestess returns the bowl of water to the altar and takes the staff or sceptre from the priest as he kneels at the entrance of the circle. Taking up his glaive, he points it upward and pulls the "invisible sliding door" shut. He seals its edges, starting at the bottom left side, going up, and over rightward, down to the ground, and back to the bottom left side. Returning his glaive to the altar, he announces:)

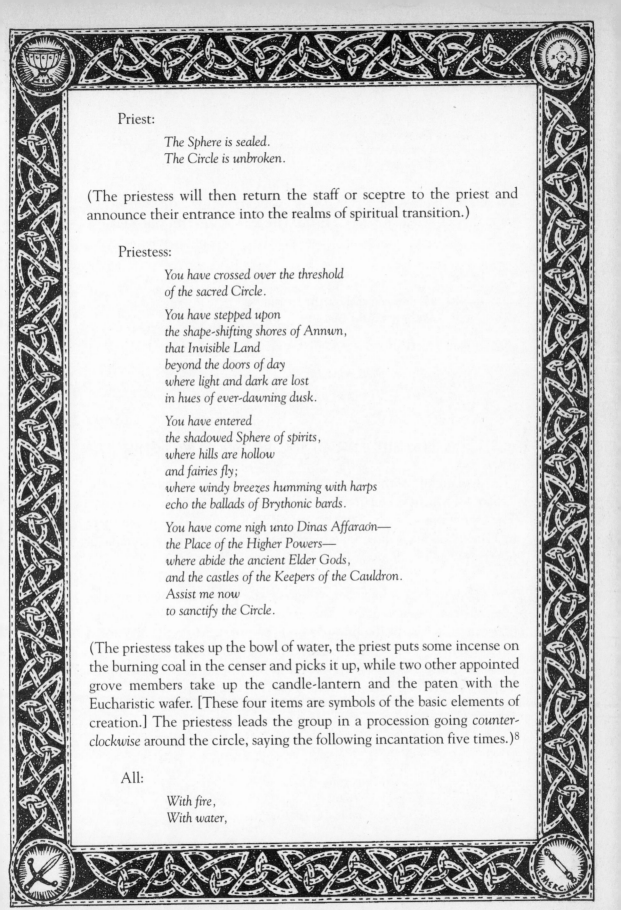

Priest:

> The Sphere is sealed.
> The Circle is unbroken.

(The priestess will then return the staff or sceptre to the priest and announce their entrance into the realms of spiritual transition.)

Priestess:

> You have crossed over the threshold
> of the sacred Circle.
>
> You have stepped upon
> the shape-shifting shores of Annwn,
> that Invisible Land
> beyond the doors of day
> where light and dark are lost
> in hues of ever-dawning dusk.
>
> You have entered
> the shadowed Sphere of spirits,
> where hills are hollow
> and fairies fly;
> where windy breezes humming with harps
> echo the ballads of Brythonic bards.
>
> You have come nigh unto Dinas Affaraòn—
> the Place of the Higher Powers—
> where abide the ancient Elder Gods,
> and the castles of the Keepers of the Cauldron.
> Assist me now
> to sanctify the Circle.

(The priestess takes up the bowl of water, the priest puts some incense on the burning coal in the censer and picks it up, while two other appointed grove members take up the candle-lantern and the paten with the Eucharistic wafer. [These four items are symbols of the basic elements of creation.] The priestess leads the group in a procession going *counter-clockwise* around the circle, saying the following incantation five times.)[8]

All:

> With fire,
> With water,

With earth,
And with air,
We invoke from the Goddess
Her protection and care!

(When the procession is completed, everyone will put their elemental symbols back where they found them. The priestess and the priest take up their respective glaives, as will everyone else, as the priest announces:)

Priest:

It is time now that our rite be witnessed
to the glory of the Goddess!

Let us assemble the Regents,
call forth the spirits,
and evoke the elementals!

The Assembling of the Quarter-Regents

(The Assembling of the Quarter-Regents begins with a salutation to the Regents of whichever quarter has the seasonal preeminence at the time.[9] The salutations to each of the Quarter-Regents will proceed from there in a *counterclockwise* direction around the circle. Below is an example of how this would be done for the Earth Rite of Balemas.)

(An appointed grove member will go to the altar while everyone else takes their glaives and points them skyward towards the eastern quarter, following the lead of the priestess and the priest, while the appointed grove member takes up the censer [having put fresh incense on the already-burning coals] and elevates it in offering to the Regents of the east as s/he invokes Them with the following salutation.)

Caller of the East:

Regents of the East,
Sovereigns of Wind and Air,
by the Holy Pentagram of Balance,
sacred to the Goddess,
Queen of the Cardinal Quarters,

we call Thee to this Circle,
charging Thee to witness and watch over
these rites of Balemas
in this sacred space between the worlds
and out of time.

(All of the grove members with the exception of the one holding aloft the censer shall then make the invoking pentagram with their glaives, after which, the person with the censer shall put it back upon the altar and return to his/her place with the others.)

(The same procedure will be followed for the calling of the northern quarter, except that the appointed grove member will hold aloft the paten with the wafer of bread as s/he recites the following salutation.)

Caller of the North:

Regents of the North,
Sovereigns of elemental Earth,
by the Holy Pentagram of Balance,
sacred to the Goddess,
Queen of the Cardinal Quarters,
we call Thee to this Circle,
charging Thee to witness and watch over
these rites of Balemas
in this sacred space between the worlds
and out of time.

(All of the grove members with the exception of the one holding aloft the paten and wafer shall then make the invoking pentagram with their glaives, after which, the person with the paten and wafer shall put it back upon the altar and return to his/her proper place with the others.)[10]

(The same procedure will be followed for the calling of the western Quarter-Regents, except that the appointed grove member will hold aloft the bowl of salted water as s/he recites the following salutation.)

Caller of the West:

Regents of the West,
Sovereigns of all Watery Realms,

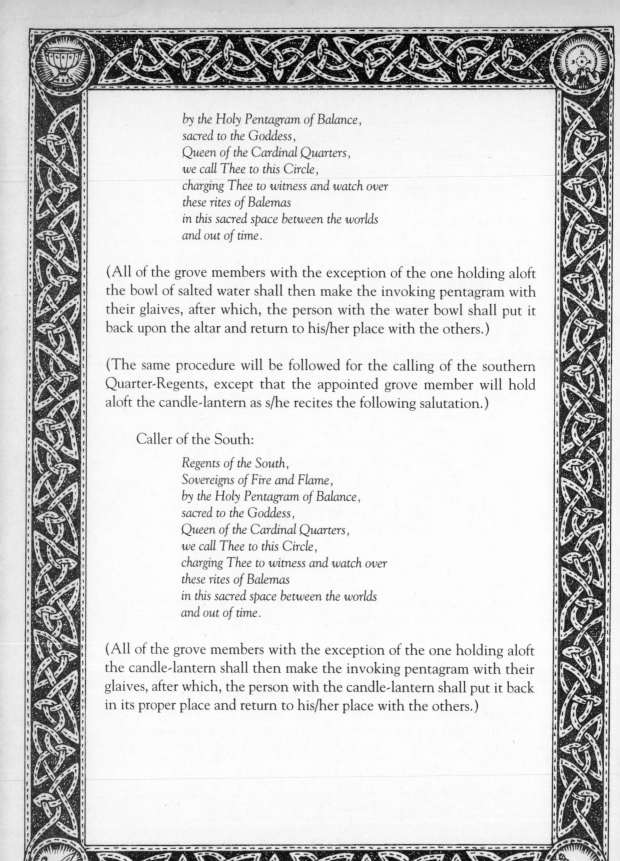

by the Holy Pentagram of Balance,
sacred to the Goddess,
Queen of the Cardinal Quarters,
we call Thee to this Circle,
charging Thee to witness and watch over
these rites of Balemas
in this sacred space between the worlds
and out of time.

(All of the grove members with the exception of the one holding aloft the bowl of salted water shall then make the invoking pentagram with their glaives, after which, the person with the water bowl shall put it back upon the altar and return to his/her place with the others.)

(The same procedure will be followed for the calling of the southern Quarter-Regents, except that the appointed grove member will hold aloft the candle-lantern as s/he recites the following salutation.)

Caller of the South:

Regents of the South,
Sovereigns of Fire and Flame,
by the Holy Pentagram of Balance,
sacred to the Goddess,
Queen of the Cardinal Quarters,
we call Thee to this Circle,
charging Thee to witness and watch over
these rites of Balemas
in this sacred space between the worlds
and out of time.

(All of the grove members with the exception of the one holding aloft the candle-lantern shall then make the invoking pentagram with their glaives, after which, the person with the candle-lantern shall put it back in its proper place and return to his/her place with the others.)

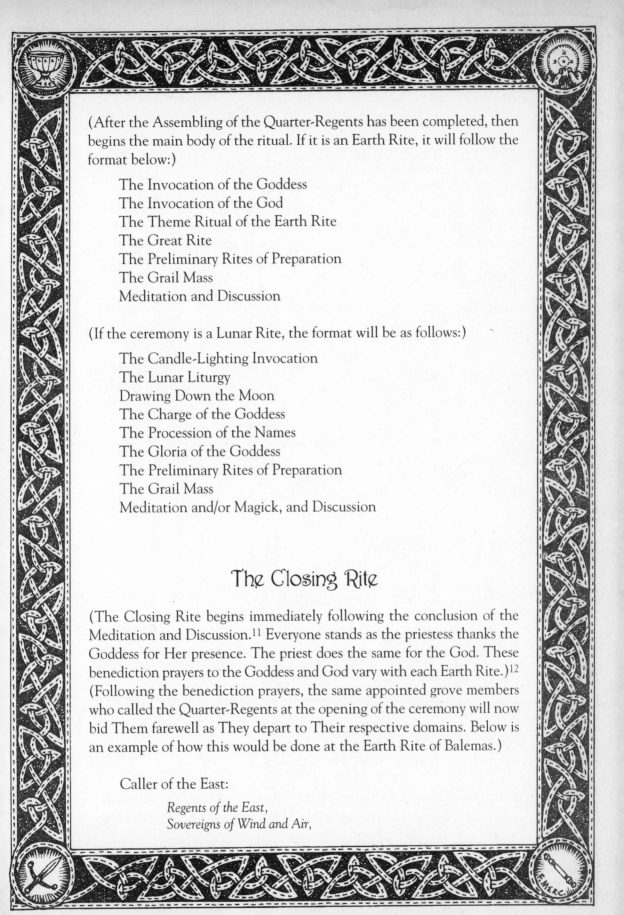

(After the Assembling of the Quarter-Regents has been completed, then begins the main body of the ritual. If it is an Earth Rite, it will follow the format below:)

> The Invocation of the Goddess
> The Invocation of the God
> The Theme Ritual of the Earth Rite
> The Great Rite
> The Preliminary Rites of Preparation
> The Grail Mass
> Meditation and Discussion

(If the ceremony is a Lunar Rite, the format will be as follows:)

> The Candle-Lighting Invocation
> The Lunar Liturgy
> Drawing Down the Moon
> The Charge of the Goddess
> The Procession of the Names
> The Gloria of the Goddess
> The Preliminary Rites of Preparation
> The Grail Mass
> Meditation and/or Magick, and Discussion

The Closing Rite

(The Closing Rite begins immediately following the conclusion of the Meditation and Discussion.[11] Everyone stands as the priestess thanks the Goddess for Her presence. The priest does the same for the God. These benediction prayers to the Goddess and God vary with each Earth Rite.)[12] (Following the benediction prayers, the same appointed grove members who called the Quarter-Regents at the opening of the ceremony will now bid Them farewell as They depart to Their respective domains. Below is an example of how this would be done at the Earth Rite of Balemas.)

Caller of the East:

> *Regents of the East,*
> *Sovereigns of Wind and Air,*

we thank Thee
for witnessing our rites
and watching the Circle,
and by the Queen of the Cardinal Quarters
we signal to Thee our fond farewell!

(At this time, following the lead of the Caller of the East, all will make the banishing pentagram towards the East in the air above with their glaives. The same procedure will be followed with each of the remaining quarters.)[13]

Caller of the North:

Regents of the North,
Sovereigns of elemental Earth,
we thank Thee
for witnessing our rites
and watching the Circle,
and by the Queen of the Cardinal Quarters
we signal to Thee our fond farewell!

Caller of the West:

Regents of the West,
Sovereigns of all Watery Realms,
we thank Thee
for witnessing our rites
and watching the Circle,
and by the Queen of the Cardinal Quarters,
we signal to Thee our fond farewell!

Caller of the South:

Regents of the South,
Sovereigns of Fire and Flame,
we thank Thee
for witnessing our rites
and watching the Circle,
and by the Queen of the Cardinal Quarters,
we signal to Thee our fond farewell!

(After the last of the Quarter-Regents have been dismissed, the priest will then take his glaive to the marked boundary of the circle, and starting at the same quarter from which he initially began to cast the circle, he will once again walk the circumference of the circle, pointing his glaive at the boundary as he goes, visualizing the dissipation of the blue-white spherical walls of the sacred space as he says the following words.)

Priest:

> Circle round of the sacred Sphere,
> may Thy boundaries be dissolved.
> Thy purpose is accomplished,
> Thy work well done.
> Blessed Be!

(The priestess [or an appointed grove member] then makes the final proclamation of ceremonial dismissal.)

Priestess:

> This rite of Balemas is ended!
> May the love of the Maiden
> and the Satyr Lord
> go with us as we venture onward
> into the warming fullness of Summer's promise!
> Merry Meet and Merry Part![14]

Footnotes

1. The designations of "priestess" or "priest" in the assigning of the spoken parts are only what we considered to be logical suggestions. Actually, the spoken parts are divided up in such a way so as to enable the celebrating priestess and priest to "trade off" their lines with each other when they so desire. If there is only one celebrant (either priest or priestess), then all of the parts would be performed by that individual. All parts of these Opening and Closing Rites are memorized by the celebrants to allow for the most effective spiritual flow of the ritual.

2. The "Shining Isle" mentioned here is a reference to Avalon itself.

3. Sea salt should always be used in this ritual, for it is a symbol of the Earth Mother's life-giving, planetary blood: the ocean. You can usually purchase sea salt in most grocery stores or your local health food store. We usually use the larger salt crystals rather than those which

are finely ground. Some people prefer to use a cruet on the altar which is filled with water. They then pour this into the bowl prior to its blessing. The need for the spoon is eliminated by simply taking a tiny pinch of salt crystals and dropping them into the water (this is done three times in honor of the Triple Goddess). Use whichever procedure you like the best; either way the symbolism remains the same.

4. The invoking pentagram is traced as follows:

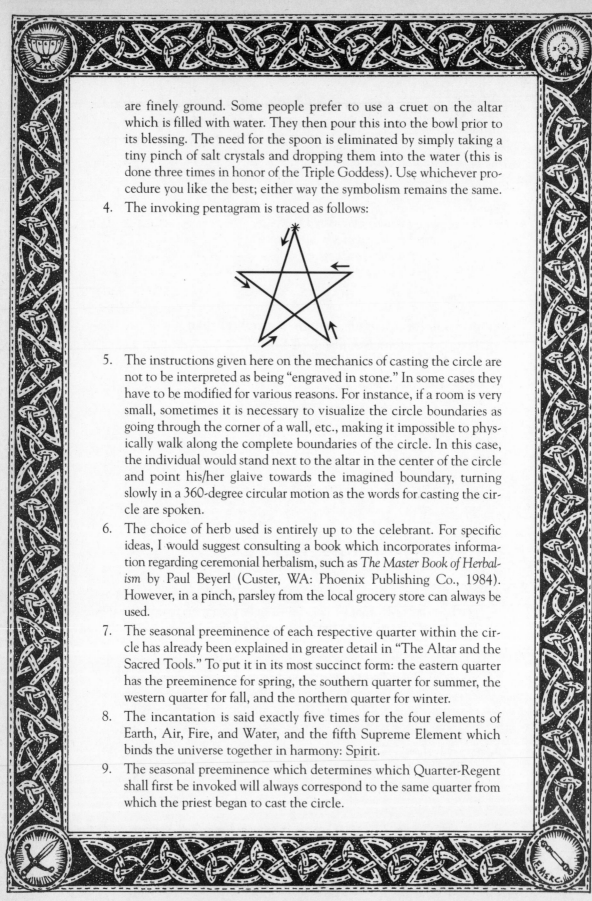

5. The instructions given here on the mechanics of casting the circle are not to be interpreted as being "engraved in stone." In some cases they have to be modified for various reasons. For instance, if a room is very small, sometimes it is necessary to visualize the circle boundaries as going through the corner of a wall, etc., making it impossible to physically walk along the complete boundaries of the circle. In this case, the individual would stand next to the altar in the center of the circle and point his/her glaive towards the imagined boundary, turning slowly in a 360-degree circular motion as the words for casting the circle are spoken.

6. The choice of herb used is entirely up to the celebrant. For specific ideas, I would suggest consulting a book which incorporates information regarding ceremonial herbalism, such as *The Master Book of Herbalism* by Paul Beyerl (Custer, WA: Phoenix Publishing Co., 1984). However, in a pinch, parsley from the local grocery store can always be used.

7. The seasonal preeminence of each respective quarter within the circle has already been explained in greater detail in "The Altar and the Sacred Tools." To put it in its most succinct form: the eastern quarter has the preeminence for spring, the southern quarter for summer, the western quarter for fall, and the northern quarter for winter.

8. The incantation is said exactly five times for the four elements of Earth, Air, Fire, and Water, and the fifth Supreme Element which binds the universe together in harmony: Spirit.

9. The seasonal preeminence which determines which Quarter-Regent shall first be invoked will always correspond to the same quarter from which the priest began to cast the circle.

10. In the case of a Grail Quest Study Circle with no one empowered to celebrate the Grail Mass, the cup and dish for Cakes and Wine shall take the place of the Grail Chalice and paten upon the altar. Accordingly, in this circumstance, the dish of cakes would be lifted up in salutation to the northern Quarter-Regents instead of the paten and wafer.

11. This is generally true, with the prominent exception of Hallowmas, where part of the theme ritual for the Earth Rite is continued after the divination, meditation, and discussion, prior to the actual commencement of the Closing Rites.

12. While the Earth Rites have specific written prayers of benediction, the Lunar Rite has no such specific prayers. Instead, whoever is chosen to lead such a prayer is expected to do so with a spontaneous expression of his/her own devotional praise.

13. The banishing pentagram is traced as follows:

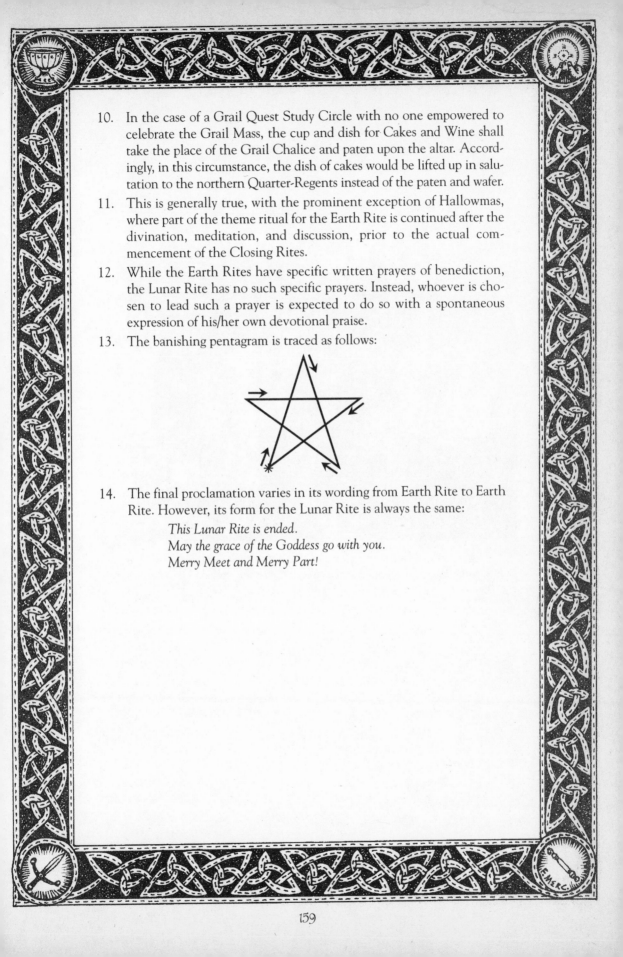

14. The final proclamation varies in its wording from Earth Rite to Earth Rite. However, its form for the Lunar Rite is always the same:

> *This Lunar Rite is ended.*
> *May the grace of the Goddess go with you.*
> *Merry Meet and Merry Part!*

The Opening Rites: The casting of the circle. "I cast this space a Sphere set apart ..."

The Great Rite

In the Ordo Arcanorum Gradalis, the Great Rite is considered to be the most elevated of the rites which celebrate the mysteries of Middle Earth. For us, it is the symbolic enactment of the literal union of male and female within the realms of the physical creation as well as an affirmation of the mystical union of these same forces on a cosmic level, which became the catalyst for the manifestation of life itself at the very beginning of time.

Among certain Wiccan traditions, the Great Rite is literally performed as an act of sexual intercourse between the priest and the priestess within the sacred circle while the rest of the coven withdraws to another room to smoke cigarettes and make small talk until the rite is consummated.[1] This is a practice which our Order tenaciously avoids for a variety of reasons. First of all, the underlying thought behind a literal, sexual enactment of the Great Rite is rooted in the idea of perpetuating the practice of the *hiero gamos*, or sacred marriage, in certain ancient religions, where the priest and priestess of the official cult sexually consummated their union as literal embodiments of the God and Goddess annually coming together to produce fertility for both land and people in the coming year. Of course, we now know that such a practice is not essential to the perpetuation of fertility for crops, livestock, or people. And while, in the religio-social context of these cultures, there was certainly nothing immoral about this practice, it is very questionable whether the restoration of such a literal sexual practice within the context of the Neo-Pagan/Wiccan revival can succeed in doing but little more than inserting a religious/sexual anachronism into a modern culture where sexual union is viewed primarily in terms of the privately erotic rather than in the context of survival through fertility. Also questionable is the ability of modern Wiccans to objectively participate in such a rite as a purely religious practice, given the very different societal attitudes and understanding of sexuality inherent in our present culture and imbedded deeply within our psyche, our protests to the contrary notwithstanding. In fact, there are inherent dangers latent within the attempt by some to restore the Great Rite as a high point of revived ritual sexuality. John and Caitlin Matthews addressed this and related topics in a strong, yet restrained warning to the Neo-Pagan/Wiccan community:

Whilst revival Craft will always attract the childish adult, the fervent (usually male) servant of the Goddess and the power-seeking High Priestess, as well as the sexually immature and the religiously undecided, it is a force to be reckoned with when it is truly in touch with its native potency. *Yet here also lies the danger of revival. What was common custom in the Fore-time—blood-sacrifice, ritual mating, etc.—does not obtain today. And while the Craft as a whole does not subscribe to these practices, those for whom these memories ring strong can be easily seduced from their spiritual evolution into inappropriate atavism.* [2]

No doubt, while there are some who have quite successfully been able to feel fully comfortable with the practice of ritual intercourse, it is nevertheless an embarrassing fact that many have attempted to enter the ranks of Wicca because of the lure of this religion as an excuse for participation in overt sexual practices of any kind. The fact that Gerald Gardner specifically tailored many aspects of his Craft rituals with an eye to the satisfaction of his own sexual fetishes certainly cannot be construed as an indication of the positive wholesomeness of overt sexuality within contemporary Pagan religious rites. [3]

Secondly, inserting sexual intercourse into the central aspect of rituals introduces a sense of awkwardness into a ceremony that tends to interrupt the orderly raising of the level of the grove's focus, intensity, and power during the course of a ritual. To cast a circle and follow through the progress up to a literal sexual enactment of the Great Rite, where the circle is then opened to allow all other coven members to leave, wait, and then come back into the circle for the continuation of the ritual after the sex act has been completed between the priest and priestess, can from our viewpoint, only serve to fragment the ceremony and dissipate its energy.

In our Order, the Great Rite is always performed in sacred symbol with glaive and chalice. One essential difference between the practice of our Order and that of other Wiccan traditions is the fact that for most traditions, the Great Rite (whether actual or symbolic), is the high point of the circle ceremony, whereas in our Order the Great Rite is the epitome of the actual Earth Rite being celebrated, but in itself it merely constitutes the prelude to the apex of all our rituals: the Grail Mass. In our ceremonial system, the Great Rite designates the point of transition from the outer court to the inner sanctum of the Temple of Wisdom. In the Great Rite we are witnessing in symbol the polarities by which the Divine immanence is made manifest throughout the creation, whereas in the Mass of the Grail we become part of a visitation of the transcendent which deigns to consubstantially commune with us through the consecrated elements of bread and wine conveying the mystery of the Deity's simultaneous earthen immanence. The Great Rite, then, serves a most important and vital role in the ritual of every seasonal celebration as a gateway to the higher mysteries of the Grail itself, upon which our Order is forever focused.

The Prefaces

(After the ceremonial theme of the Earth Rite has been enacted or ritually performed, everyone will stand around the circle facing the altar in the center. The priestess and the priest will both be standing at the altar itself, facing the other grove members. The priestess, priest, or another appointed reader will then recite the opening preface to the Great Rite which corresponds with the theme of the Earth Rite being celebrated.)

Hallowmas

> All Hallows is a feast in honor of the dead,
> but death is not a final end;
> merely a period
> of the spirit's rest and reflection
> preparatory to yet another incarnation,
> another time-encapsulated adventure
> on the periphery of eternity.
>
> Reincarnation demands a re-entry into flesh,
> a baptism anew
> into the perimeters of the physical
> that can only be initiated
> by that compelling union of body with body
> in sheer, erotic rapture;
> the Great Rite
> of life-creating sexuality.
>
> Only in this way
> are the disembodied
> able to be born again into a new body

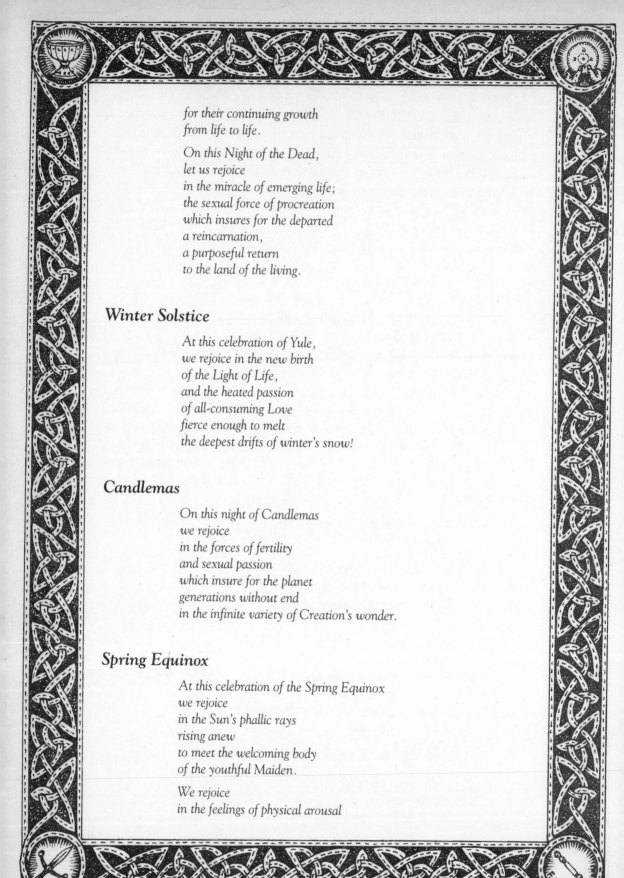

for their continuing growth
from life to life.

On this Night of the Dead,
let us rejoice
in the miracle of emerging life;
the sexual force of procreation
which insures for the departed
a reincarnation,
a purposeful return
to the land of the living.

Winter Solstice

At this celebration of Yule,
we rejoice in the new birth
of the Light of Life,
and the heated passion
of all-consuming Love
fierce enough to melt
the deepest drifts of winter's snow!

Candlemas

On this night of Candlemas
we rejoice
in the forces of fertility
and sexual passion
which insure for the planet
generations without end
in the infinite variety of Creation's wonder.

Spring Equinox

At this celebration of the Spring Equinox
we rejoice
in the Sun's phallic rays
rising anew
to meet the welcoming body
of the youthful Maiden.

We rejoice
in the feelings of physical arousal

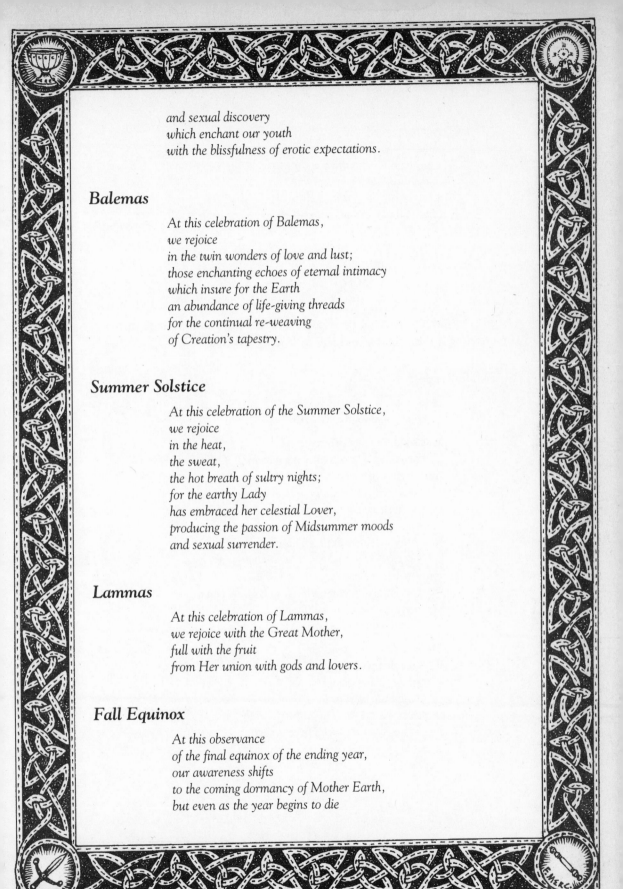

and sexual discovery
which enchant our youth
with the blissfulness of erotic expectations.

Balemas

At this celebration of Balemas,
we rejoice
in the twin wonders of love and lust;
those enchanting echoes of eternal intimacy
which insure for the Earth
an abundance of life-giving threads
for the continual re-weaving
of Creation's tapestry.

Summer Solstice

At this celebration of the Summer Solstice,
we rejoice
in the heat,
the sweat,
the hot breath of sultry nights;
for the earthy Lady
has embraced her celestial Lover,
producing the passion of Midsummer moods
and sexual surrender.

Lammas

At this celebration of Lammas,
we rejoice with the Great Mother,
full with the fruit
from Her union with gods and lovers.

Fall Equinox

At this observance
of the final equinox of the ending year,
our awareness shifts
to the coming dormancy of Mother Earth,
but even as the year begins to die

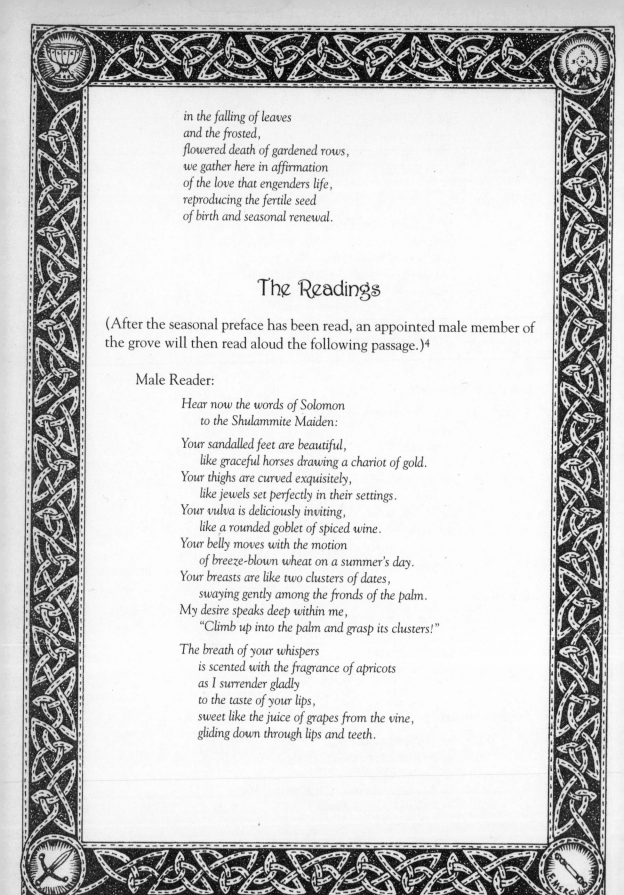

in the falling of leaves
and the frosted,
flowered death of gardened rows,
we gather here in affirmation
of the love that engenders life,
reproducing the fertile seed
of birth and seasonal renewal.

The Readings

(After the seasonal preface has been read, an appointed male member of the grove will then read aloud the following passage.)[4]

Male Reader:

Hear now the words of Solomon
to the Shulammite Maiden:

Your sandalled feet are beautiful,
like graceful horses drawing a chariot of gold.
Your thighs are curved exquisitely,
like jewels set perfectly in their settings.
Your vulva is deliciously inviting,
like a rounded goblet of spiced wine.
Your belly moves with the motion
of breeze-blown wheat on a summer's day.
Your breasts are like two clusters of dates,
swaying gently among the fronds of the palm.
My desire speaks deep within me,
"Climb up into the palm and grasp its clusters!"

The breath of your whispers
is scented with the fragrance of apricots
as I surrender gladly
to the taste of your lips,
sweet like the juice of grapes from the vine,
gliding down through lips and teeth.

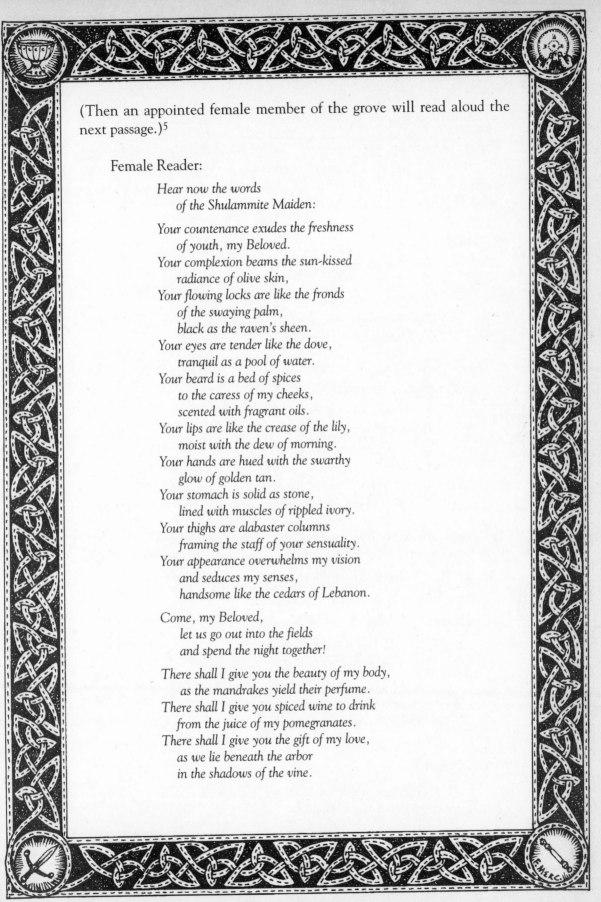

(Then an appointed female member of the grove will read aloud the next passage.)[5]

Female Reader:

Hear now the words
    of the Shulammite Maiden:

Your countenance exudes the freshness
    of youth, my Beloved.
Your complexion beams the sun-kissed
    radiance of olive skin,
Your flowing locks are like the fronds
    of the swaying palm,
    black as the raven's sheen.
Your eyes are tender like the dove,
    tranquil as a pool of water.
Your beard is a bed of spices
    to the caress of my cheeks,
    scented with fragrant oils.
Your lips are like the crease of the lily,
    moist with the dew of morning.
Your hands are hued with the swarthy
    glow of golden tan.
Your stomach is solid as stone,
    lined with muscles of rippled ivory.
Your thighs are alabaster columns
    framing the staff of your sensuality.
Your appearance overwhelms my vision
    and seduces my senses,
    handsome like the cedars of Lebanon.

Come, my Beloved,
    let us go out into the fields
    and spend the night together!

There shall I give you the beauty of my body,
    as the mandrakes yield their perfume.
There shall I give you spiced wine to drink
    from the juice of my pomegranates.
There shall I give you the gift of my love,
    as we lie beneath the arbor
    in the shadows of the vine.

The Words of Union

(The priestess takes up the Grail Chalice from the altar and holds it forth before the priest. The priest then takes his glaive, lifting it point-down above the chalice as the priestess recites the sacred Words of Union.)[6]

Priestess:

> *Behold Shakti and Shiva,*[7]
> *El and Asherah,*[8]
> *Solomon and the Shulammite.*[9]
>
> *Behold in symbol the sacred rite of Aphrodite,*[10]
> *the Threefold Six in manifestation:*[11]
> *Goddess and God,*
> *Yin and Yang,*
> *Male and Female.*
>
> *Behold the creative polarities of the Universe*
> *in the endless union of cosmic ecstasy!*

The Words of Consummation

(The priest now lowers the blade of his glaive into the wine of the chalice as he recites the Words of Consummation, which are always unique to the Earth Rite being celebrated.)

Hallowmas

> *Behold the fertile consummation,*
> *the quickening womb.*
>
> *Behold the sacred act of sexuality,*
> *restoring flesh to the formless,*
> *substance to the spirit.*

Winter Solstice

> *Behold the Darkened Mistress of December*
> *Who guards Her holly chalice*

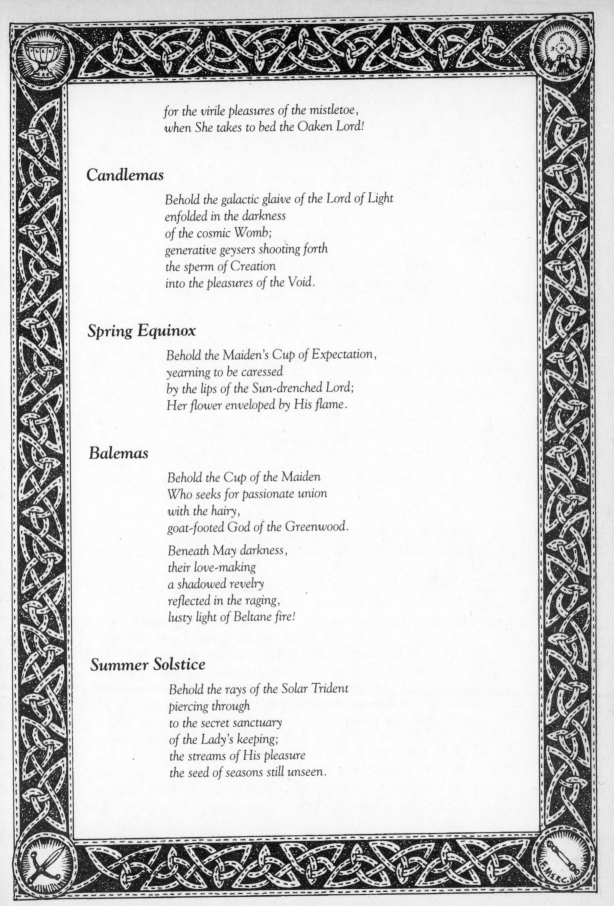

for the virile pleasures of the mistletoe,
when She takes to bed the Oaken Lord!

Candlemas

Behold the galactic glaive of the Lord of Light
enfolded in the darkness
of the cosmic Womb;
generative geysers shooting forth
the sperm of Creation
into the pleasures of the Void.

Spring Equinox

Behold the Maiden's Cup of Expectation,
yearning to be caressed
by the lips of the Sun-drenched Lord;
Her flower enveloped by His flame.

Balemas

Behold the Cup of the Maiden
Who seeks for passionate union
with the hairy,
goat-footed God of the Greenwood.

Beneath May darkness,
their love-making
a shadowed revelry
reflected in the raging,
lusty light of Beltane fire!

Summer Solstice

Behold the rays of the Solar Trident
piercing through
to the secret sanctuary
of the Lady's keeping;
the streams of His pleasure
the seed of seasons still unseen.

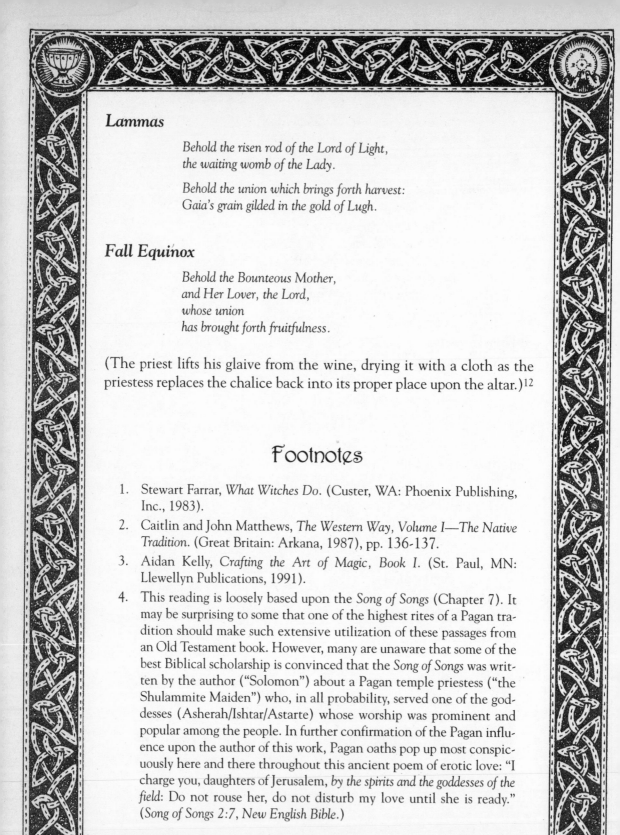

Lammas

> *Behold the risen rod of the Lord of Light,*
> *the waiting womb of the Lady.*
>
> *Behold the union which brings forth harvest:*
> *Gaia's grain gilded in the gold of Lugh.*

Fall Equinox

> *Behold the Bounteous Mother,*
> *and Her Lover, the Lord,*
> *whose union*
> *has brought forth fruitfulness.*

(The priest lifts his glaive from the wine, drying it with a cloth as the priestess replaces the chalice back into its proper place upon the altar.)[12]

Footnotes

1. Stewart Farrar, *What Witches Do.* (Custer, WA: Phoenix Publishing, Inc., 1983).

2. Caitlin and John Matthews, *The Western Way, Volume I—The Native Tradition.* (Great Britain: Arkana, 1987), pp. 136-137.

3. Aidan Kelly, *Crafting the Art of Magic, Book I.* (St. Paul, MN: Llewellyn Publications, 1991).

4. This reading is loosely based upon the *Song of Songs* (Chapter 7). It may be surprising to some that one of the highest rites of a Pagan tradition should make such extensive utilization of these passages from an Old Testament book. However, many are unaware that some of the best Biblical scholarship is convinced that the *Song of Songs* was written by the author ("Solomon") about a Pagan temple priestess ("the Shulammite Maiden") who, in all probability, served one of the goddesses (Asherah/Ishtar/Astarte) whose worship was prominent and popular among the people. In further confirmation of the Pagan influence upon the author of this work, Pagan oaths pop up most conspicuously here and there throughout this ancient poem of erotic love: "I charge you, daughters of Jerusalem, *by the spirits and the goddesses of the field*: Do not rouse her, do not disturb my love until she is ready." (*Song of Songs 2:7, New English Bible.*)

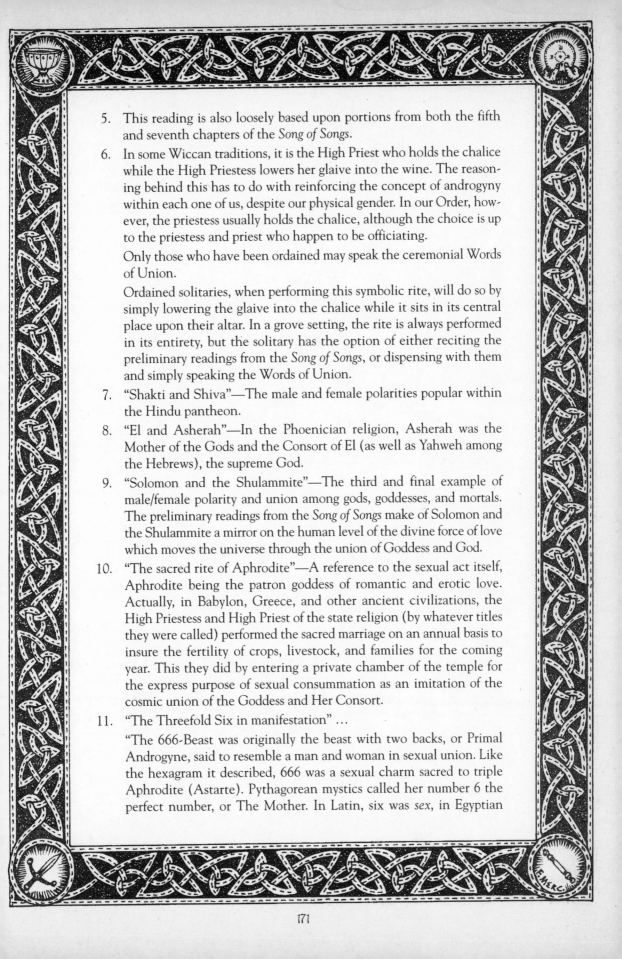

5. This reading is also loosely based upon portions from both the fifth and seventh chapters of the *Song of Songs*.

6. In some Wiccan traditions, it is the High Priest who holds the chalice while the High Priestess lowers her glaive into the wine. The reasoning behind this has to do with reinforcing the concept of androgyny within each one of us, despite our physical gender. In our Order, however, the priestess usually holds the chalice, although the choice is up to the priestess and priest who happen to be officiating.

   Only those who have been ordained may speak the ceremonial Words of Union.

   Ordained solitaries, when performing this symbolic rite, will do so by simply lowering the glaive into the chalice while it sits in its central place upon their altar. In a grove setting, the rite is always performed in its entirety, but the solitary has the option of either reciting the preliminary readings from the *Song of Songs*, or dispensing with them and simply speaking the Words of Union.

7. "Shakti and Shiva"—The male and female polarities popular within the Hindu pantheon.

8. "El and Asherah"—In the Phoenician religion, Asherah was the Mother of the Gods and the Consort of El (as well as Yahweh among the Hebrews), the supreme God.

9. "Solomon and the Shulammite"—The third and final example of male/female polarity and union among gods, goddesses, and mortals. The preliminary readings from the *Song of Songs* make of Solomon and the Shulammite a mirror on the human level of the divine force of love which moves the universe through the union of Goddess and God.

10. "The sacred rite of Aphrodite"—A reference to the sexual act itself, Aphrodite being the patron goddess of romantic and erotic love. Actually, in Babylon, Greece, and other ancient civilizations, the High Priestess and High Priest of the state religion (by whatever titles they were called) performed the sacred marriage on an annual basis to insure the fertility of crops, livestock, and families for the coming year. This they did by entering a private chamber of the temple for the express purpose of sexual consummation as an imitation of the cosmic union of the Goddess and Her Consort.

11. "The Threefold Six in manifestation" …

    "The 666-Beast was originally the beast with two backs, or Primal Androgyne, said to resemble a man and woman in sexual union. Like the hexagram it described, 666 was a sexual charm sacred to triple Aphrodite (Astarte). Pythagorean mystics called her number 6 the perfect number, or The Mother. In Latin, six was *sex*, in Egyptian

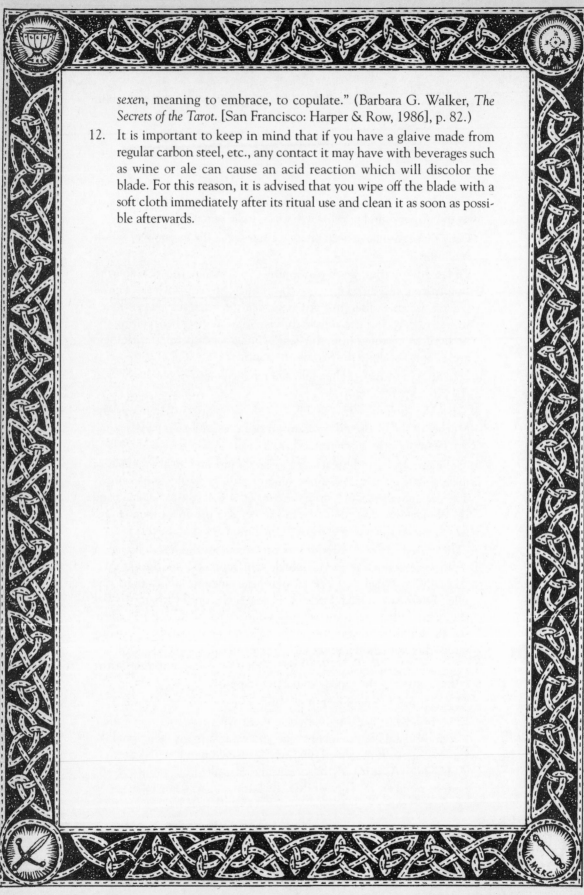

sexen, meaning to embrace, to copulate." (Barbara G. Walker, *The Secrets of the Tarot*. [San Francisco: Harper & Row, 1986], p. 82.)

12. It is important to keep in mind that if you have a glaive made from regular carbon steel, etc., any contact it may have with beverages such as wine or ale can cause an acid reaction which will discolor the blade. For this reason, it is advised that you wipe off the blade with a soft cloth immediately after its ritual use and clean it as soon as possible afterwards.

The Great Rite: The Words of Union. "Behold Shakti and Shiva, El and Asherah, Solomon and the Shulammite ..."

The Preliminary Rites of Preparation

The Announcement of Solemn Approach

(After the chalice and glaive have been replaced upon the altar, concluding the Great Rite, the priestess will then prepare the grove members for the next, more exalted level of ritual as she speaks the following words.)

Priestess:

> As seekers of the Ancient Way,
> we have celebrated these Sabbat rites[1]
> through which we marvel at the myths
> of the Mysteries of Middle Earth,[2]
> veiled in stories,
> symbols and seasonal signs;
> but now shall we venture
> beyond the enchantments of the Hollow Hills,
> into the awesome presence of the Hidden Hallows.[3]

The Prefatory Invocation

(The priest now raises his staff as he begins the first invocation, slowly turning himself deosil [clockwise] as he exclaims:)[4]

Priest:

> Raphael, Michael, Gabriel and Uriel,[5]
> Holy Angels of Higher Realms,
> we invoke Thee!
>
> Amergin, Taliesin, Merlin and Morgaine,[6]
> Stewards of the Sacred Secrets,
> we invoke thee!

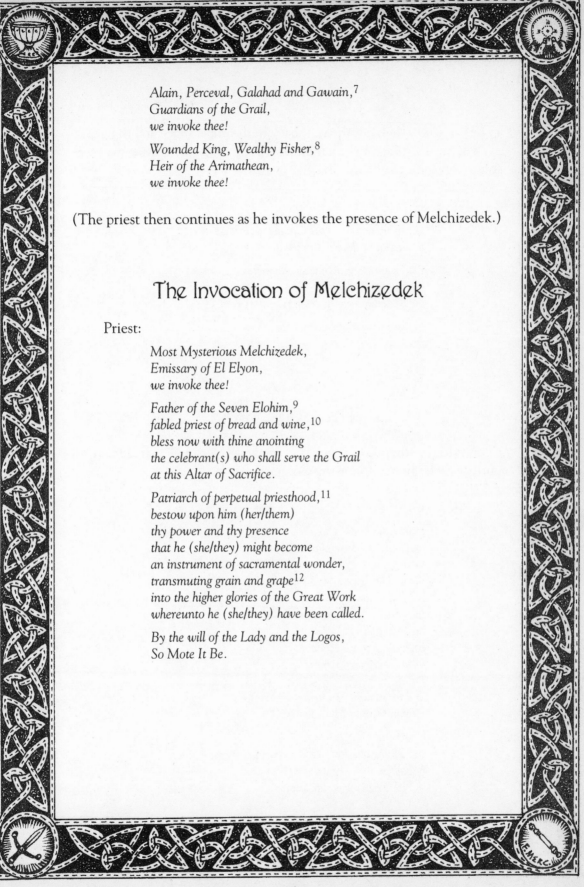

Alain, Perceval, Galahad and Gawain,[7]
Guardians of the Grail,
we invoke thee!

Wounded King, Wealthy Fisher,[8]
Heir of the Arimathean,
we invoke thee!

(The priest then continues as he invokes the presence of Melchizedek.)

The Invocation of Melchizedek

Priest:

Most Mysterious Melchizedek,
Emissary of El Elyon,
we invoke thee!

Father of the Seven Elohim,[9]
fabled priest of bread and wine,[10]
bless now with thine anointing
the celebrant(s) who shall serve the Grail
at this Altar of Sacrifice.

Patriarch of perpetual priesthood,[11]
bestow upon him (her/them)
thy power and thy presence
that he (she/they) might become
an instrument of sacramental wonder,
transmuting grain and grape[12]
into the higher glories of the Great Work
whereunto he (she/they) have been called.

By the will of the Lady and the Logos,
So Mote It Be.

The Preparatory Admonition

(The priest will then put the staff back in its proper place and the priestess will set the tone for the actual beginning of the Grail Mass with the following words of exhortation.)

Priestess:

> *Let us ascend unto the Citadel of Sarras[13]*
> *in pursuit of the Pilgrim's Path.*
>
> *Let us enter through the gates of Joyous Guard*
> *that we might behold*
> *the Sanctuary of the Secrets of the Grail.[14]*
>
> *Let us prepare ourselves with purity,*
> *that our worship may be filled with wonder.*

The Confession

(The priestess then continues the theme of personal preparation for purity by reciting the following Confession.)

Priestess:

> *Before the Lady who loves us*
> *and calls us Her children,[15]*
> *we acknowledge*
> *the fallible nature of our humanity:*
> *our limitations,*
> *our faults,*
> *and our failures;*
> *because in this lifetime*
> *we are here for learning,*
> *for overcoming,*
> *and for making of our imperfections*
> *stepping-stones to wholeness.[16]*
>
> *Therefore,*
> *we ask the all-glorious Queen of Heaven*
> *to baptize us*
> *in Her forgiving compassion*

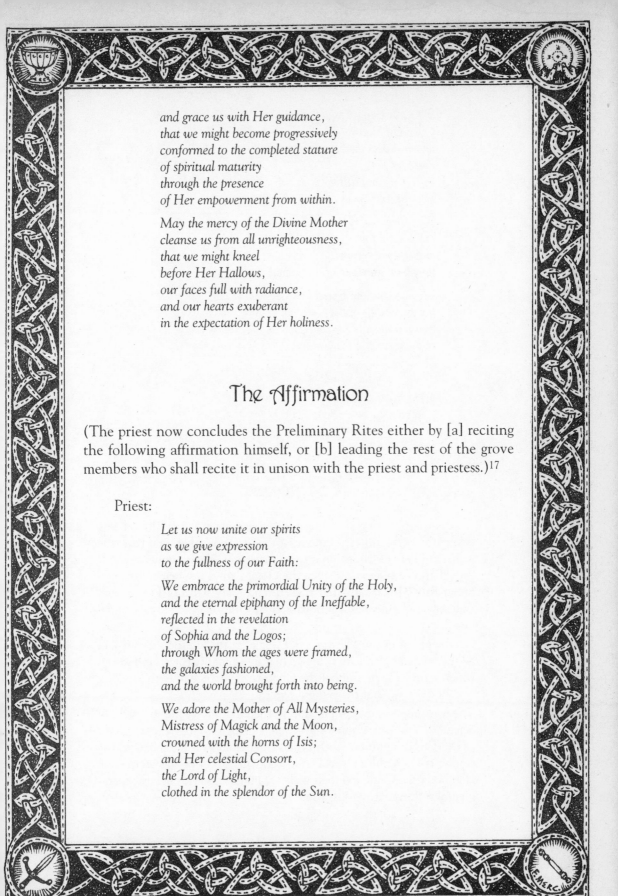

and grace us with Her guidance,
that we might become progressively
conformed to the completed stature
of spiritual maturity
through the presence
of Her empowerment from within.

May the mercy of the Divine Mother
cleanse us from all unrighteousness,
that we might kneel
before Her Hallows,
our faces full with radiance,
and our hearts exuberant
in the expectation of Her holiness.

The Affirmation

(The priest now concludes the Preliminary Rites either by [a] reciting the following affirmation himself, or [b] leading the rest of the grove members who shall recite it in unison with the priest and priestess.)[17]

Priest:

Let us now unite our spirits
as we give expression
to the fullness of our Faith:

We embrace the primordial Unity of the Holy,
and the eternal epiphany of the Ineffable,
reflected in the revelation
of Sophia and the Logos;
through Whom the ages were framed,
the galaxies fashioned,
and the world brought forth into being.

We adore the Mother of All Mysteries,
Mistress of Magick and the Moon,
crowned with the horns of Isis;
and Her celestial Consort,
the Lord of Light,
clothed in the splendor of the Sun.

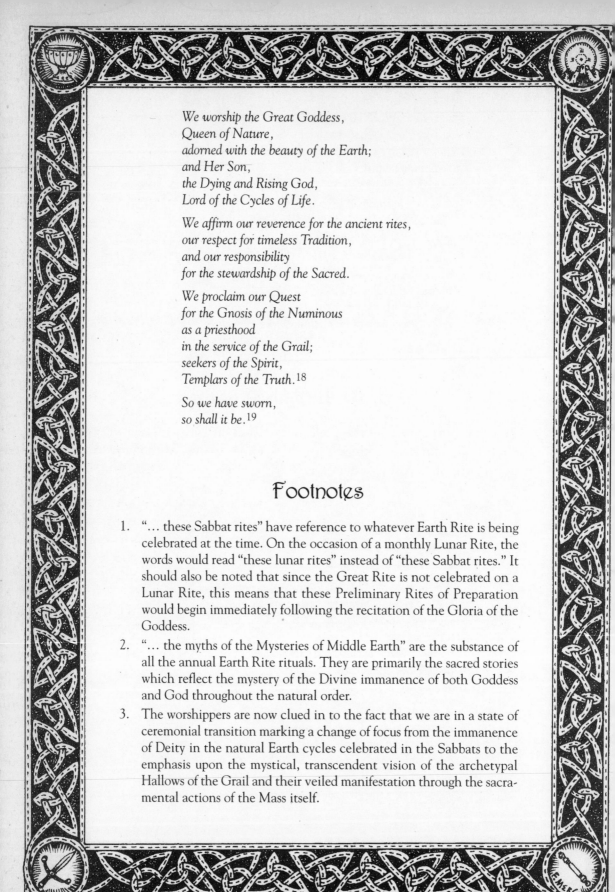

We worship the Great Goddess,
Queen of Nature,
adorned with the beauty of the Earth;
and Her Son,
the Dying and Rising God,
Lord of the Cycles of Life.

We affirm our reverence for the ancient rites,
our respect for timeless Tradition,
and our responsibility
for the stewardship of the Sacred.

We proclaim our Quest
for the Gnosis of the Numinous
as a priesthood
in the service of the Grail;
seekers of the Spirit,
Templars of the Truth.[18]

So we have sworn,
so shall it be.[19]

Footnotes

1. "… these Sabbat rites" have reference to whatever Earth Rite is being celebrated at the time. On the occasion of a monthly Lunar Rite, the words would read "these lunar rites" instead of "these Sabbat rites." It should also be noted that since the Great Rite is not celebrated on a Lunar Rite, this means that these Preliminary Rites of Preparation would begin immediately following the recitation of the Gloria of the Goddess.

2. "… the myths of the Mysteries of Middle Earth" are the substance of all the annual Earth Rite rituals. They are primarily the sacred stories which reflect the mystery of the Divine immanence of both Goddess and God throughout the natural order.

3. The worshippers are now clued in to the fact that we are in a state of ceremonial transition marking a change of focus from the immanence of Deity in the natural Earth cycles celebrated in the Sabbats to the emphasis upon the mystical, transcendent vision of the archetypal Hallows of the Grail and their veiled manifestation through the sacramental actions of the Mass itself.

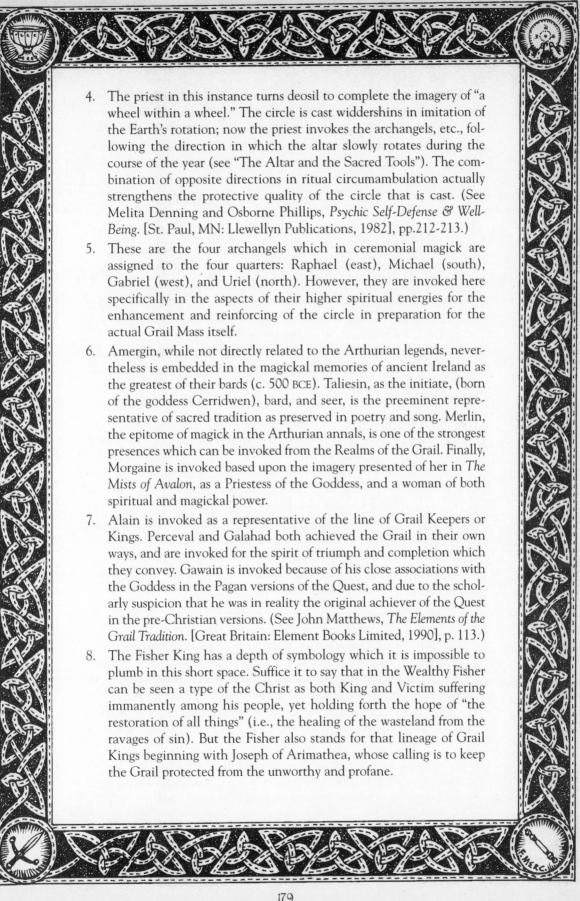

4. The priest in this instance turns deosil to complete the imagery of "a wheel within a wheel." The circle is cast widdershins in imitation of the Earth's rotation; now the priest invokes the archangels, etc., following the direction in which the altar slowly rotates during the course of the year (see "The Altar and the Sacred Tools"). The combination of opposite directions in ritual circumambulation actually strengthens the protective quality of the circle that is cast. (See Melita Denning and Osborne Phillips, *Psychic Self-Defense & Well-Being.* [St. Paul, MN: Llewellyn Publications, 1982], pp.212-213.)

5. These are the four archangels which in ceremonial magick are assigned to the four quarters: Raphael (east), Michael (south), Gabriel (west), and Uriel (north). However, they are invoked here specifically in the aspects of their higher spiritual energies for the enhancement and reinforcing of the circle in preparation for the actual Grail Mass itself.

6. Amergin, while not directly related to the Arthurian legends, nevertheless is embedded in the magickal memories of ancient Ireland as the greatest of their bards (c. 500 BCE). Taliesin, as the initiate, (born of the goddess Cerridwen), bard, and seer, is the preeminent representative of sacred tradition as preserved in poetry and song. Merlin, the epitome of magick in the Arthurian annals, is one of the strongest presences which can be invoked from the Realms of the Grail. Finally, Morgaine is invoked based upon the imagery presented of her in *The Mists of Avalon*, as a Priestess of the Goddess, and a woman of both spiritual and magickal power.

7. Alain is invoked as a representative of the line of Grail Keepers or Kings. Perceval and Galahad both achieved the Grail in their own ways, and are invoked for the spirit of triumph and completion which they convey. Gawain is invoked because of his close associations with the Goddess in the Pagan versions of the Quest, and due to the scholarly suspicion that he was in reality the original achiever of the Quest in the pre-Christian versions. (See John Matthews, *The Elements of the Grail Tradition.* [Great Britain: Element Books Limited, 1990], p. 113.)

8. The Fisher King has a depth of symbology which it is impossible to plumb in this short space. Suffice it to say that in the Wealthy Fisher can be seen a type of the Christ as both King and Victim suffering immanently among his people, yet holding forth the hope of "the restoration of all things" (i.e., the healing of the wasteland from the ravages of sin). But the Fisher also stands for that lineage of Grail Kings beginning with Joseph of Arimathea, whose calling is to keep the Grail protected from the unworthy and profane.

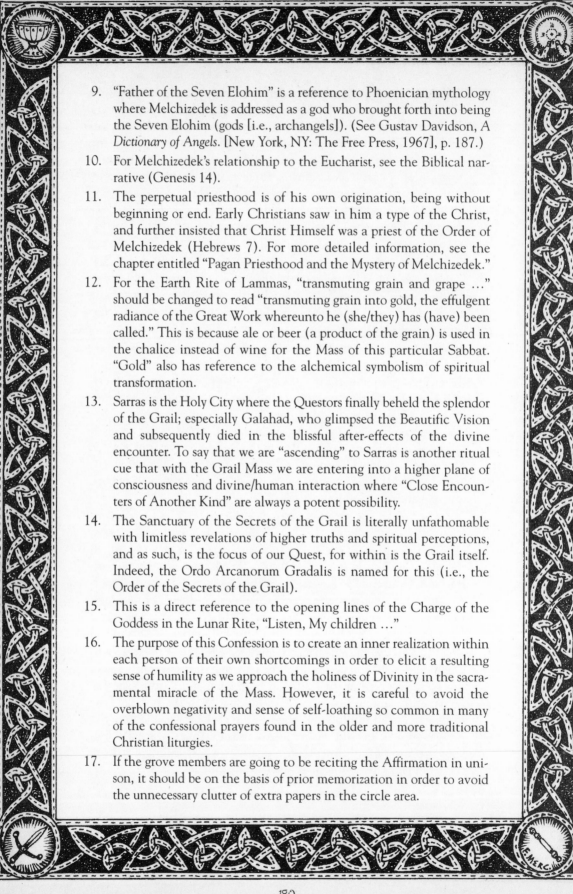

9. "Father of the Seven Elohim" is a reference to Phoenician mythology where Melchizedek is addressed as a god who brought forth into being the Seven Elohim (gods [i.e., archangels]). (See Gustav Davidson, *A Dictionary of Angels*. [New York, NY: The Free Press, 1967], p. 187.)

10. For Melchizedek's relationship to the Eucharist, see the Biblical narrative (Genesis 14).

11. The perpetual priesthood is of his own origination, being without beginning or end. Early Christians saw in him a type of the Christ, and further insisted that Christ Himself was a priest of the Order of Melchizedek (Hebrews 7). For more detailed information, see the chapter entitled "Pagan Priesthood and the Mystery of Melchizedek."

12. For the Earth Rite of Lammas, "transmuting grain and grape …" should be changed to read "transmuting grain into gold, the effulgent radiance of the Great Work whereunto he (she/they) has (have) been called." This is because ale or beer (a product of the grain) is used in the chalice instead of wine for the Mass of this particular Sabbat. "Gold" also has reference to the alchemical symbolism of spiritual transformation.

13. Sarras is the Holy City where the Questors finally beheld the splendor of the Grail; especially Galahad, who glimpsed the Beautific Vision and subsequently died in the blissful after-effects of the divine encounter. To say that we are "ascending" to Sarras is another ritual cue that with the Grail Mass we are entering into a higher plane of consciousness and divine/human interaction where "Close Encounters of Another Kind" are always a potent possibility.

14. The Sanctuary of the Secrets of the Grail is literally unfathomable with limitless revelations of higher truths and spiritual perceptions, and as such, is the focus of our Quest, for within is the Grail itself. Indeed, the Ordo Arcanorum Gradalis is named for this (i.e., the Order of the Secrets of the Grail).

15. This is a direct reference to the opening lines of the Charge of the Goddess in the Lunar Rite, "Listen, My children …"

16. The purpose of this Confession is to create an inner realization within each person of their own shortcomings in order to elicit a resulting sense of humility as we approach the holiness of Divinity in the sacramental miracle of the Mass. However, it is careful to avoid the overblown negativity and sense of self-loathing so common in many of the confessional prayers found in the older and more traditional Christian liturgies.

17. If the grove members are going to be reciting the Affirmation in unison, it should be on the basis of prior memorization in order to avoid the unnecessary clutter of extra papers in the circle area.

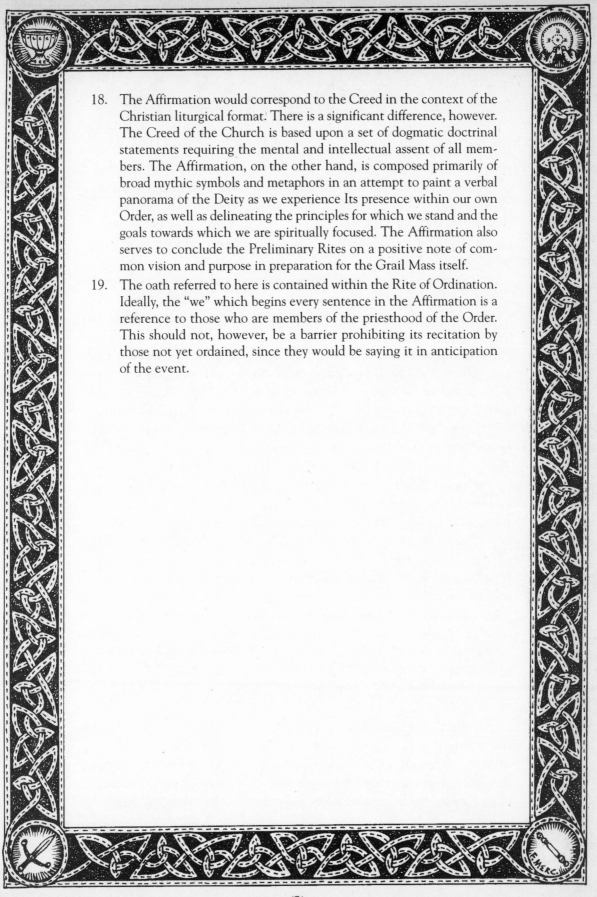

18. The Affirmation would correspond to the Creed in the context of the Christian liturgical format. There is a significant difference, however. The Creed of the Church is based upon a set of dogmatic doctrinal statements requiring the mental and intellectual assent of all members. The Affirmation, on the other hand, is composed primarily of broad mythic symbols and metaphors in an attempt to paint a verbal panorama of the Deity as we experience Its presence within our own Order, as well as delineating the principles for which we stand and the goals towards which we are spiritually focused. The Affirmation also serves to conclude the Preliminary Rites on a positive note of common vision and purpose in preparation for the Grail Mass itself.

19. The oath referred to here is contained within the Rite of Ordination. Ideally, the "we" which begins every sentence in the Affirmation is a reference to those who are members of the priesthood of the Order. This should not, however, be a barrier prohibiting its recitation by those not yet ordained, since they would be saying it in anticipation of the event.

The Grail Mass

What follows is the text and commentary on the most sacred rite within the liturgical system of the Ordo Arcanorum Gradalis. The Grail Mass is the central focus of our Order, and as such, it is worthy of much meditation upon the mystical meaning which it sacramentally conveys to our inmost spiritual selves.

It should be noted that the ritual arrangement of the Grail Mass differs in a most striking way from that of the Roman Catholic Mass. In the Christian Eucharist, the gifts of bread and wine are consecrated together as a whole, being considered as a unity of one divinity in the body and blood of Christ. However, in the Grail Mass, there are two separate liturgies: one for the Host, the embodiment of the God, and another for the chalice, the sacramental embodiment of the Goddess. Because of this, each liturgy contains its own Anamnesis, Consecration, and Elevation.

Both the Grail Mass and the Great Rite can only be ritually celebrated by those who have been duly ordained as a priest/ess of the Ordo Arcanorum Gradalis. For those who wish to become students in preparation for final ordination, the entire text of the Mass should be slowly and thoroughly committed to memory as a prerequisite for entrance into the Order as a fully functioning priest/ess.

One final word: it is always best if the celebration of the Grail Mass (as well as the entire Earth or Lunar Rite) be accompanied by the appropriate chants and/or background music. Since some priest/esses practice solitary, and those in groves often encounter the difficulty of finding musically or instrumentally inclined members, it is often best to obtain a number of cassette recordings of suitable music (New Age, Gregorian chant, and certain forms of classical are all possibilities) which can be played softly in the background throughout the ritual. (For a more detailed listing of appropriate musical recordings, see Appendix E.)

(After the Preliminary Rites of Preparation have been completed, both the priestess and priest will face the altar together, either kneeling or standing, depending upon the height of the altar. If they kneel to celebrate the Mass, then the rest of the grove will do the same. Special incense is placed within the lighted censer by the priestess. The priest then takes the censer and censes above the chalice and paten in a circular motion three times widdershins and three times deosil. [The Liturgy of the Host is usually performed by the priest, while the Liturgy of the Chalice is usually performed by the priestess, since each in their own gender represent the God and Goddess, respectively. However, in view of our androgynous nature as human beings, this assignment of liturgical roles is not seen as an inflexible necessity. In fact, the priestess and priest can "trade off" their usual parts whenever they so desire. If there is only one celebrant—either priest or priestess—then all of the following parts would be recited by that individual. As mentioned before, all parts of this Eucharist are memorized by the priest/esses to allow for the most effective spiritual flow of the rite.])

Introductory Dialogue

(The priestess now officially begins the Mass by saying the words of the opening salutation.)

Priestess:

> *The grace of the Goddess be with you!*

All:

> *And also with you!*

Priestess:

> *Let us lift up our spirits to the Lady of Life!*

The Preface

Priestess:

> *In union with all the faithful from ages past,*
> *seekers of the Way,*
> *companions on the Quest;*
> *We give honor unto Thee,*
> *O High and Holy Lady,*

for Thou art the Triune Glory[1]
of heaven and earth:
Virgin Maiden,
Mother of Gods,
Crone of Ageless Wisdom,
Who hast revealed Thyself as
Dana to the Celts,
Isis to the Egyptians, and
Gaia to the Greeks.[2]

Thou art the divine Shekinah
Who shineth forth
from above the Seat of Mercy.[3]

Thou art Hagia Sophia,
the unfathomable Wisdom
of the Cosmic Christ.[4]

Thou art (Miriam) the Queen of Heaven,
Who givest hope
to all who call upon Thy Name.[5]

Therefore,
with gods and celestials, spirits and elementals,
We invoke Thee to be here
within these sacred precincts
as we hail Thee in joyous salutation:

IO EVOHE DANA!
IO EVOHE ISIS!
IO EVOHE GAIA![6]

May our prayers be made one
with the petitions
of those who have gone before us[7]
as we prepare a pathway to Thy Presence
with this Sacrifice of Praise.[8]

The Epiclesis

(The priestess and the priest then extend their hands over the chalice and paten as the priest begins the following prayer.)

Priest:

Gracious Goddess and Glorious God,
be pleased to accept these offerings
from the staples of life,
that by Thy magickal touch
they may become for us
True Bread and True Wine;
(He signs the bread with the Sign of the Cross [for the God] and the chalice with the Sign of the Pentagram [for the Goddess].)
the Body and Blood of Thy Divinity,[9]
granting sustenance to the soul
and strength to the spirit;
and as I will, so mote it be.

The Liturgy of the Host

(The priest now lifts up his hands in an attitude of reverence and supplication as he begins the Liturgy of the Host.)

The Anamnesis

Priest:

Holy Mother,
we make manifest here
the Memorial Mystery
of Thy Beloved Son and Lover,
known from of old by innumerable names:
Adonis, Attis,
Dionysus, Tammuz, Osiris, Orpheus,
Jesu and Pan.[10]

We offer this Mystery
in memory of their dying:[11]

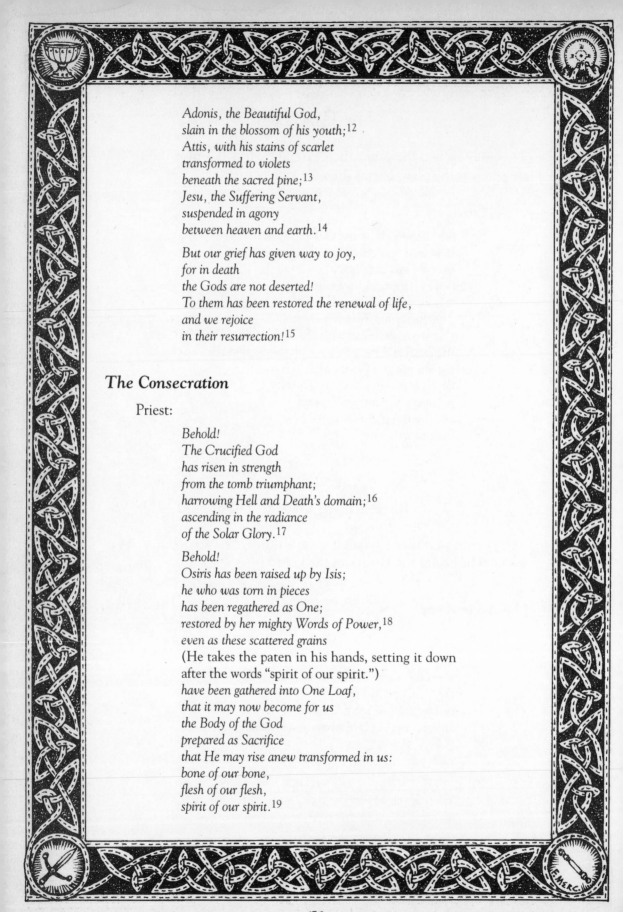

Adonis, the Beautiful God,
slain in the blossom of his youth;[12]
Attis, with his stains of scarlet
transformed to violets
beneath the sacred pine;[13]
Jesu, the Suffering Servant,
suspended in agony
between heaven and earth.[14]

But our grief has given way to joy,
for in death
the Gods are not deserted!
To them has been restored the renewal of life,
and we rejoice
in their resurrection![15]

The Consecration

Priest:

Behold!
The Crucified God
has risen in strength
from the tomb triumphant;
harrowing Hell and Death's domain;[16]
ascending in the radiance
of the Solar Glory.[17]

Behold!
Osiris has been raised up by Isis;
he who was torn in pieces
has been regathered as One;
restored by her mighty Words of Power,[18]
even as these scattered grains
(He takes the paten in his hands, setting it down
after the words "spirit of our spirit.")
have been gathered into One Loaf,
that it may now become for us
the Body of the God
prepared as Sacrifice
that He may rise anew transformed in us:
bone of our bone,
flesh of our flesh,
spirit of our spirit.[19]

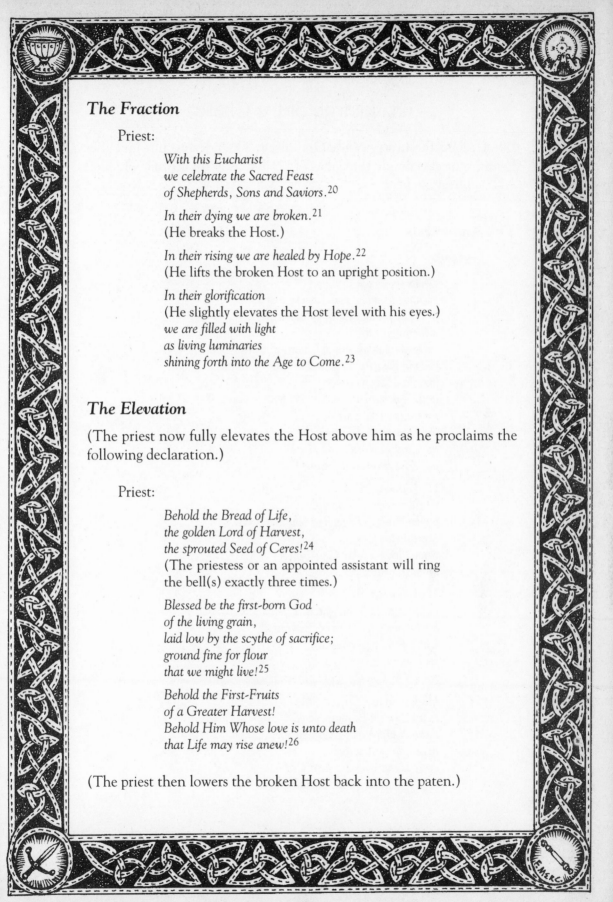

The Fraction

Priest:

> With this Eucharist
> we celebrate the Sacred Feast
> of Shepherds, Sons and Saviors.[20]
>
> In their dying we are broken.[21]
> (He breaks the Host.)
>
> In their rising we are healed by Hope.[22]
> (He lifts the broken Host to an upright position.)
>
> In their glorification
> (He slightly elevates the Host level with his eyes.)
> we are filled with light
> as living luminaries
> shining forth into the Age to Come.[23]

The Elevation

(The priest now fully elevates the Host above him as he proclaims the following declaration.)

Priest:

> Behold the Bread of Life,
> the golden Lord of Harvest,
> the sprouted Seed of Ceres![24]
> (The priestess or an appointed assistant will ring
> the bell(s) exactly three times.)
>
> Blessed be the first-born God
> of the living grain,
> laid low by the scythe of sacrifice;
> ground fine for flour
> that we might live![25]
>
> Behold the First-Fruits
> of a Greater Harvest!
> Behold Him Whose love is unto death
> that Life may rise anew![26]

(The priest then lowers the broken Host back into the paten.)

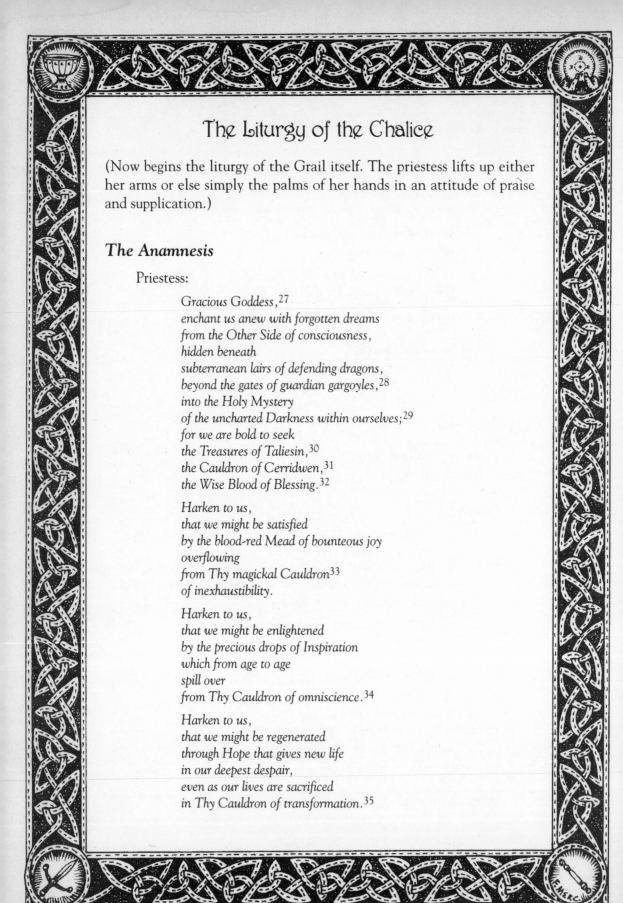

The Liturgy of the Chalice

(Now begins the liturgy of the Grail itself. The priestess lifts up either her arms or else simply the palms of her hands in an attitude of praise and supplication.)

The Anamnesis

Priestess:

Gracious Goddess,[27]
enchant us anew with forgotten dreams
from the Other Side of consciousness,
hidden beneath
subterranean lairs of defending dragons,
beyond the gates of guardian gargoyles,[28]
into the Holy Mystery
of the uncharted Darkness within ourselves;[29]
for we are bold to seek
the Treasures of Taliesin,[30]
the Cauldron of Cerridwen,[31]
the Wise Blood of Blessing.[32]

Harken to us,
that we might be satisfied
by the blood-red Mead of bounteous joy
overflowing
from Thy magickal Cauldron[33]
of inexhaustibility.

Harken to us,
that we might be enlightened
by the precious drops of Inspiration
which from age to age
spill over
from Thy Cauldron of omniscience.[34]

Harken to us,
that we might be regenerated
through Hope that gives new life
in our deepest despair,
even as our lives are sacrificed
in Thy Cauldron of transformation.[35]

The Consecration

(The priestess begins the most solemn part of the prayer. When she starts to speak, she says the words very reverently, and with an emphasis in awestruck undertones. If they are both standing at the altar, then at this point the priest kneels. If they are both already kneeling, the priest simply remains in that position.)

Priestess:

> *Holy Queen of the Glorious Grail,*
> *we offer unto Thee here*
> *this humble, crafted Cup,*[36]
> (She lifts up the chalice.)
> *that it may become for us*
> *a manifestation of THE MYSTERY;*
> *the Womb of the Wine of Wisdom;*
> *the Holy and Venerable Vessel of the Vine.*[37]
> (She lowers the chalice back to the altar.)
> *Descend, we pray,*
> (She lifts up her hands and then lowers them upon the chalice.)
> *upon this Cup which we offer,*
> *that it may become for us*
> *the Channel of Thy Grace,*
> (She makes the Sign of the Pentagram over the chalice.)
> *the Dispenser of Thy Favor,*
> (She makes the Sign of the Pentagram again.)
> *the Tabernacle of Thy Precious Presence.*[38]
> (She makes the final Sign of the Pentagram over the chalice.)

The Elevation

(The priestess now takes up the chalice and lifts it high above her head as she makes the following proclamation.)

Priestess:

> *Behold in symbol the Vision of Galahad,*[39]
> *the Hope of Glastonbury,*[40]
> *the Shrine of Avalon!*[41]

(A bell is rung three times by either the priest or
an appointed assistant.)

(The priestess will then lower and hold out the chalice towards those
assembled as she gives the following "intoxicating" invitation.)

Priestess:

> *Drink now from the Grail*
> *the Elixir distilled*
> *from the knowledge of Good*
> *and the discernment of Evil;*
> *the very condensation of the Gnosis.*[42]
>
> *Taste now the forbidden Fruit of Eden;*
> *a Gift from the Goddess*
> *for the fullness of Life*
> *and the experience of Immortality.*[43]

The Communion

(As soon as she finishes speaking these words of invitation, the priestess
will set the chalice upon the altar. The priest will then take up the paten
after he has broken the Host into small pieces and pass it deosil around
the circle, saying: "Blessed be the Bread of Life," and each person, as s/he
takes a piece of the Host, will say the same to the next person and pass on
the paten. Each person will consume his/her portion after passing on the
paten. When the paten has returned full-circle to the priestess, she will
take a piece of the Host and pass the paten to the priest, saying the same
words, and he will at last partake of all that remains of the Host. The
priestess will then take up the chalice and pass it widdershins around the
circle, saying: "Blessed be the Grail of the Goddess," and each person, as
s/he takes a sip from the chalice, will say the same to the next person and
pass on the chalice. When the chalice has returned full-circle to the
priest, he will take a sip and say these words to the priestess as she takes
the chalice and finishes the rest of the wine. She will then set the chalice upon the altar. At this time all will be seated to begin a short time of
silent or guided meditation (usually with music in the background).

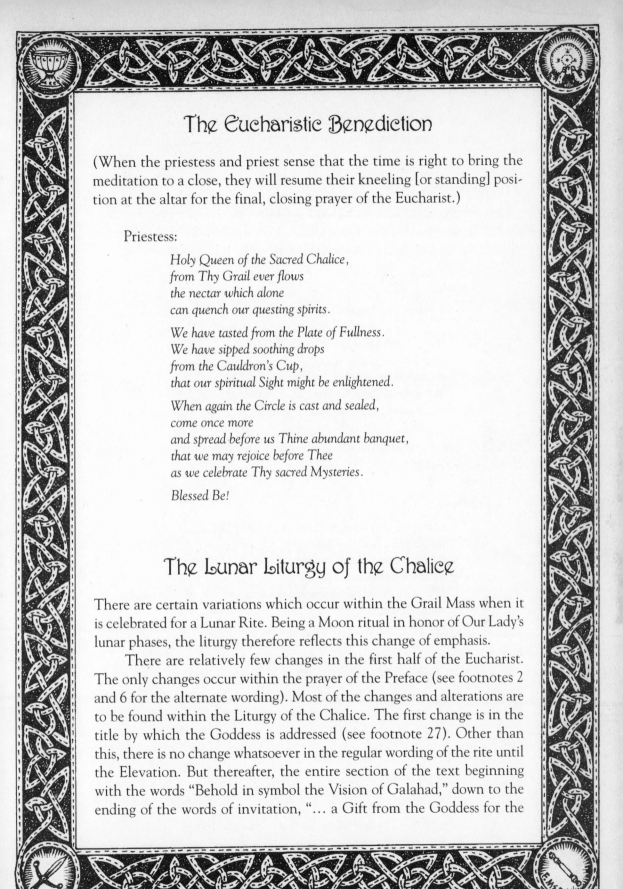

The Eucharistic Benediction

(When the priestess and priest sense that the time is right to bring the meditation to a close, they will resume their kneeling [or standing] position at the altar for the final, closing prayer of the Eucharist.)

Priestess:

Holy Queen of the Sacred Chalice,
from Thy Grail ever flows
the nectar which alone
can quench our questing spirits.

We have tasted from the Plate of Fullness.
We have sipped soothing drops
from the Cauldron's Cup,
that our spiritual Sight might be enlightened.

When again the Circle is cast and sealed,
come once more
and spread before us Thine abundant banquet,
that we may rejoice before Thee
as we celebrate Thy sacred Mysteries.

Blessed Be!

The Lunar Liturgy of the Chalice

There are certain variations which occur within the Grail Mass when it is celebrated for a Lunar Rite. Being a Moon ritual in honor of Our Lady's lunar phases, the liturgy therefore reflects this change of emphasis.

There are relatively few changes in the first half of the Eucharist. The only changes occur within the prayer of the Preface (see footnotes 2 and 6 for the alternate wording). Most of the changes and alterations are to be found within the Liturgy of the Chalice. The first change is in the title by which the Goddess is addressed (see footnote 27). Other than this, there is no change whatsoever in the regular wording of the rite until the Elevation. But thereafter, the entire section of the text beginning with the words "Behold in symbol the Vision of Galahad," down to the ending of the words of invitation, "… a Gift from the Goddess for the fullness of Life and the experience of Immortality" is completely deleted. At all Lunar Rites it is instead replaced with the text as given below.

The Elevation

(After the Words of Consecration have been spoken, the priestess takes up the chalice and moves it in a circular, widdershins motion above the altar as she makes the following exclamation.)

Priestess:

> *Observe the cloudless Crescent,*
> > *the silvered Circle,*
> > *the lunar Dark;*
> *the Moon Goddess moving*
> *through raven-black star-caverns*
> *above the sleeping horizon,*
> *skirting in silence the vault of heaven.*

(The priestess now lifts the chalice high above her as she proclaims to those assembled:)

Priestess:

> *Cast your eyes upon the Drinking Cup of Diana,*
> *the Sacred Chalice of Selene,*
> *the Hermetic Bowl of Hekate;*
> *shrouded in moonmist,*
> *filled with the nectar of Night-knowledge,*
> *subtle sensing,*
> *and psychic shadow-play.*
> (A bell is rung three times by either the priest or
> an appointed member of the grove.)

(The priestess then lowers the chalice and holds it out towards the assembled grove members as she speaks to them the following invitation.)

Priestess:

> *Drink deeply from*
> > *the Sacred Spring of Rejuvenation,*
> > *the Womb-Cup of Fruitfulness,*
> > *the Hidden Well of Wisdom's Mystery.*

Footnotes

1. The Trinity was originally a characteristic of the Great Goddess from the most ancient times, long before it was appropriated by later patriarchal religions to refer to their male deities. The true Holy Trinity is that of the Goddess as Maiden, Mother, and Crone. We therefore have restored the reference to Her trinitarian nature in the Grail Mass liturgy.

2. Three different goddesses are listed in the Lunar Rite version of this liturgy: Diana, Selene, and Hekate; all lunar aspects of the Goddess. The Lunar Rite version of this section is given below:

   Virgin Maiden,
   Mother of Gods,
   Crone of Ageless Wisdom,
   Who hast revealed Thyself as
   Diana to the Romans,
   Selene to the Greeks, and
   Hekate to the Carians.

3. The Shekinah is one of the highest spiritual manifestations of the Goddess. Those within the inner circles of the Kabbalah understand the significance of Her sublime presence within the godhead. It is an amazing testimony to the tenacity of the Goddess in that She has retained a semblance of her glory among the mystics of one of the West's most patriarchal religions: Judaism. The reference to Her shining forth from above the Seat of Mercy indicates the healing, loving character of Maternal Providence.

4. The Goddess in Her manifestation as Sophia is, in conjunction with the Shekinah, the most mystically majestic theophany of the Lady. Hagia Sophia (Greek for "Holy Wisdom") is, in reality, the feminine manifestation of the androgynous Cosmic Christ, just as the Logos, so commonly called "The Word" in Christian theology, is the masculine manifestation of the Cosmic Christ. In essence, the fullness (Greek: *Pleroma*) of the Christ is found only in the union of Goddess and God. In Gnosticism this was described as the *apocatastasis*. (See Caitlin and John Matthews, *The Western Way, Volume II*. [London: Arkana, 1986], pp. 222-223.)

5. "Queen of Heaven" is one of the most popular and devotional titles given the Goddess from the days of antiquity. Ishtar was called Queen of Heaven as were many other goddesses in the ancient world. Even the Hebrews who worshipped the goddess Asherah (much to the consternation and rage of their patriarchal prophets) addressed her as the Queen of Heaven (Jeremiah 44:15-19). The name in parentheses

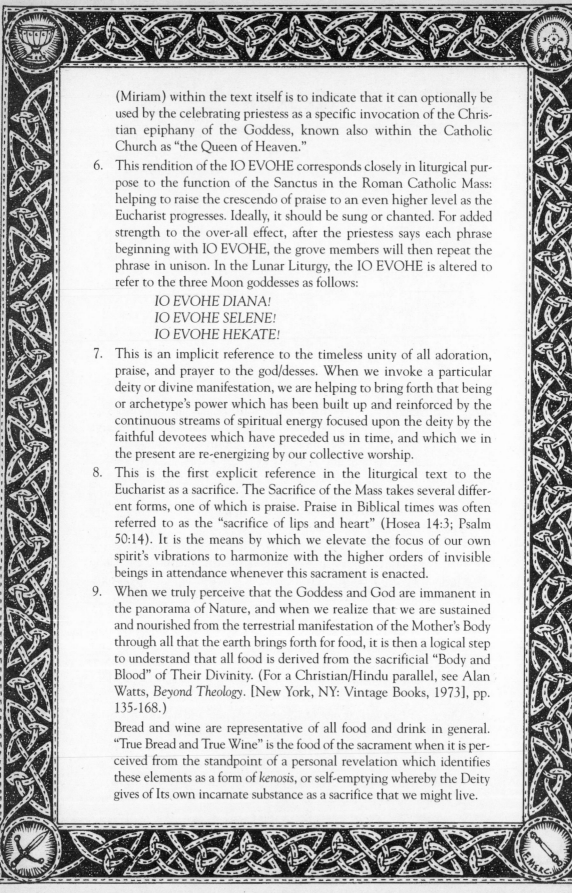

(Miriam) within the text itself is to indicate that it can optionally be used by the celebrating priestess as a specific invocation of the Christian epiphany of the Goddess, known also within the Catholic Church as "the Queen of Heaven."

6. This rendition of the IO EVOHE corresponds closely in liturgical purpose to the function of the Sanctus in the Roman Catholic Mass: helping to raise the crescendo of praise to an even higher level as the Eucharist progresses. Ideally, it should be sung or chanted. For added strength to the over-all effect, after the priestess says each phrase beginning with IO EVOHE, the grove members will then repeat the phrase in unison. In the Lunar Liturgy, the IO EVOHE is altered to refer to the three Moon goddesses as follows:

    IO EVOHE DIANA!
    IO EVOHE SELENE!
    IO EVOHE HEKATE!

7. This is an implicit reference to the timeless unity of all adoration, praise, and prayer to the god/desses. When we invoke a particular deity or divine manifestation, we are helping to bring forth that being or archetype's power which has been built up and reinforced by the continuous streams of spiritual energy focused upon the deity by the faithful devotees which have preceded us in time, and which we in the present are re-energizing by our collective worship.

8. This is the first explicit reference in the liturgical text to the Eucharist as a sacrifice. The Sacrifice of the Mass takes several different forms, one of which is praise. Praise in Biblical times was often referred to as the "sacrifice of lips and heart" (Hosea 14:3; Psalm 50:14). It is the means by which we elevate the focus of our own spirit's vibrations to harmonize with the higher orders of invisible beings in attendance whenever this sacrament is enacted.

9. When we truly perceive that the Goddess and God are immanent in the panorama of Nature, and when we realize that we are sustained and nourished from the terrestrial manifestation of the Mother's Body through all that the earth brings forth for food, it is then a logical step to understand that all food is derived from the sacrificial "Body and Blood" of Their Divinity. (For a Christian/Hindu parallel, see Alan Watts, *Beyond Theology*. [New York, NY: Vintage Books, 1973], pp. 135-168.)

Bread and wine are representative of all food and drink in general. "True Bread and True Wine" is the food of the sacrament when it is perceived from the standpoint of a personal revelation which identifies these elements as a form of *kenosis*, or self-emptying whereby the Deity gives of Its own incarnate substance as a sacrifice that we might live.

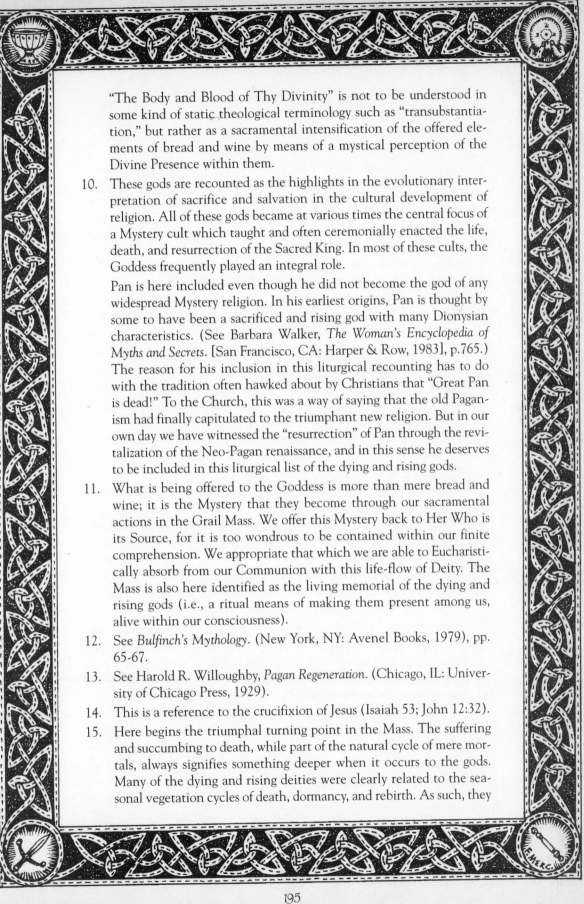

"The Body and Blood of Thy Divinity" is not to be understood in some kind of static theological terminology such as "transubstantiation," but rather as a sacramental intensification of the offered elements of bread and wine by means of a mystical perception of the Divine Presence within them.

10. These gods are recounted as the highlights in the evolutionary interpretation of sacrifice and salvation in the cultural development of religion. All of these gods became at various times the central focus of a Mystery cult which taught and often ceremonially enacted the life, death, and resurrection of the Sacred King. In most of these cults, the Goddess frequently played an integral role.

    Pan is here included even though he did not become the god of any widespread Mystery religion. In his earliest origins, Pan is thought by some to have been a sacrificed and rising god with many Dionysian characteristics. (See Barbara Walker, *The Woman's Encyclopedia of Myths and Secrets*. [San Francisco, CA: Harper & Row, 1983], p.765.) The reason for his inclusion in this liturgical recounting has to do with the tradition often hawked about by Christians that "Great Pan is dead!" To the Church, this was a way of saying that the old Paganism had finally capitulated to the triumphant new religion. But in our own day we have witnessed the "resurrection" of Pan through the revitalization of the Neo-Pagan renaissance, and in this sense he deserves to be included in this liturgical list of the dying and rising gods.

11. What is being offered to the Goddess is more than mere bread and wine; it is the Mystery that they become through our sacramental actions in the Grail Mass. We offer this Mystery back to Her Who is its Source, for it is too wondrous to be contained within our finite comprehension. We appropriate that which we are able to Eucharistically absorb from our Communion with this life-flow of Deity. The Mass is also here identified as the living memorial of the dying and rising gods (i.e., a ritual means of making them present among us, alive within our consciousness).

12. See *Bulfinch's Mythology*. (New York, NY: Avenel Books, 1979), pp. 65-67.

13. See Harold R. Willoughby, *Pagan Regeneration*. (Chicago, IL: University of Chicago Press, 1929).

14. This is a reference to the crucifixion of Jesus (Isaiah 53; John 12:32).

15. Here begins the triumphal turning point in the Mass. The suffering and succumbing to death, while part of the natural cycle of mere mortals, always signifies something deeper when it occurs to the gods. Many of the dying and rising deities were clearly related to the seasonal vegetation cycles of death, dormancy, and rebirth. As such, they

universally became divine symbols of hope. By their illustrations we see that death is a mere transient necessity out of which new life must rise again. It is important to keep in mind that the concept of resurrection was not unique or new to Christianity.

16. There are ancient Christian legends of Christ freeing all the inhabitants of the Underworld when He descended to their realm in death. Primitive apostolic teaching even insisted that Christ preached His Gospel to the dead (1 Peter 4:6). There is a twofold implication here: (1) early Church speculation was very much oriented towards a positive universalism. The later theological demons of guilt, fear and "eternal damnation" were later inventions of a warped, repressive Church; and (2) death as a morbid threat of finality has been forever mitigated by the hope which Life's yearly death and resurrection acted out in the passion play of passing seasons and symbolized by these ancient gods has given us by a revelation that life must always follow death.

17. In the Gospel story of the Resurrection, the discovery of the empty tomb takes place at the rising of the Sun on "the first day of the week" (Mark 16:2)—the Sun's Day—thereby closely identifying Jesus as a successor to the other solar deities of antiquity. To Him is attributed the messianic title, "The Sun of Righteousness" (Malachi 4:2).

18. Osiris, too, is a god of death and resurrection, but his restoration and elevation to Lordship over the dead is specifically stated to be through the instrumentality of the goddess Isis.

19. "The Body of the God" (i.e., in Wiccan theology, the Body of the Corn [Grain] King). At the Earth Rite of Lammas (Loaf Mass), the latter phrase can be substituted for the former, since the whole Sabbat theme revolves around the sacrifice of the Grain God—the Corn King of folkloric antiquity.

20. All of the ancient dying and rising gods shared in common at least two of these identifying marks: the occupation or symbolic office of a shepherd, a son of a goddess or god, and a divine savior.

21. In our mystical identification with their death, we experience in spirit the desolation of sacrifice. We similarly relate to it by comparing the seeming defeat of the gods in death with our own "dark nights of the soul." Only through the knowledge of the depths can we ascend with true appreciation to the heights.

22. Resurrection is a symbol of hope which triumphs over the ultimate in adversity. Gods who are born again from the dead speak healing to our deepest wounds of hopelessness and futility through their example. In their resurrections we can see there a symbol of ourselves experiencing the transformation of spiritual renewal.

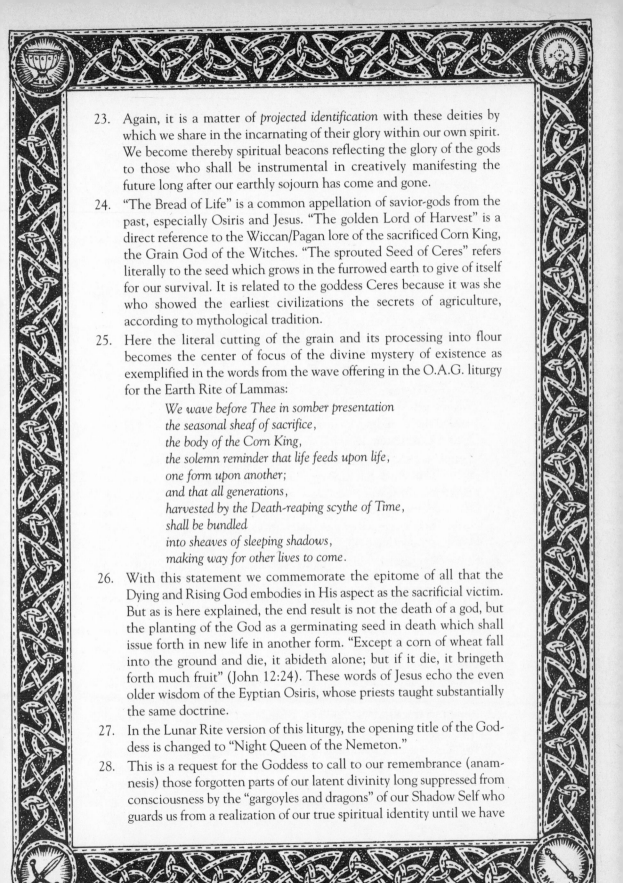

23. Again, it is a matter of *projected identification* with these deities by which we share in the incarnating of their glory within our own spirit. We become thereby spiritual beacons reflecting the glory of the gods to those who shall be instrumental in creatively manifesting the future long after our earthly sojourn has come and gone.

24. "The Bread of Life" is a common appellation of savior-gods from the past, especially Osiris and Jesus. "The golden Lord of Harvest" is a direct reference to the Wiccan/Pagan lore of the sacrificed Corn King, the Grain God of the Witches. "The sprouted Seed of Ceres" refers literally to the seed which grows in the furrowed earth to give of itself for our survival. It is related to the goddess Ceres because it was she who showed the earliest civilizations the secrets of agriculture, according to mythological tradition.

25. Here the literal cutting of the grain and its processing into flour becomes the center of focus of the divine mystery of existence as exemplified in the words from the wave offering in the O.A.G. liturgy for the Earth Rite of Lammas:

> *We wave before Thee in somber presentation*
> *the seasonal sheaf of sacrifice,*
> *the body of the Corn King,*
> *the solemn reminder that life feeds upon life,*
> *one form upon another;*
> *and that all generations,*
> *harvested by the Death-reaping scythe of Time,*
> *shall be bundled*
> *into sheaves of sleeping shadows,*
> *making way for other lives to come.*

26. With this statement we commemorate the epitome of all that the Dying and Rising God embodies in His aspect as the sacrificial victim. But as is here explained, the end result is not the death of a god, but the planting of the God as a germinating seed in death which shall issue forth in new life in another form. "Except a corn of wheat fall into the ground and die, it abideth alone; but if it die, it bringeth forth much fruit" (John 12:24). These words of Jesus echo the even older wisdom of the Eyptian Osiris, whose priests taught substantially the same doctrine.

27. In the Lunar Rite version of this liturgy, the opening title of the Goddess is changed to "Night Queen of the Nemeton."

28. This is a request for the Goddess to call to our remembrance (anamnesis) those forgotten parts of our latent divinity long suppressed from consciousness by the "gargoyles and dragons" of our Shadow Self who guards us from a realization of our true spiritual identity until we have

reached the maturity necessary to handle such depths of inner knowledge.

29. Darkness can be said to be at times the outer garment which conceals the light of Wisdom. In the Hebrew tradition, the righteous are to inherit "the hidden treasures of darkness." Another function of darkness in the divine counsels is to conceal the glories of the gods from the uninitiated and the unworthy.

30. "The Treasures of Taliesin" refers to the knowledge of our past lives as well as foreknowledge of the future: " 'Thrice have I been born,' sang Taliesin, the Radiant Fronted One, 'I know how to meditate. It is pitiful that men (sic) will not come to seek all the sciences of the world which are treasured in my bosom, for I know all that has been and all that will be hereafter.' " (Lewis Spence, *The Mysteries of Britain.* [Wellingborough: Aquarian Press, 1970], p. 203.)

31. "The Cauldron of Cerridwen"—While the Liturgy of the Host is focused primarily on the Mediterranean gods of death and resurrection, the Liturgy of the Chalice, on the other hand, concentrates its imagery primarily in a Celtic mythological context. Cerridwen guarded the Cauldron of Inspiration, which signifies the goal of our Quest for enlightenment and wisdom.

32. "The Wise Blood of Blessing" has several different levels of meaning: (1) as a symbol of searching for our roots of being, having come forth figuratively from the creative Cauldron of the Mother's magickal blood, according to ancient lore; and, (2) it has reference to the crushed and sacrificed grapes which produce the "blood of the vine" for the sacramental Cup.

33. Stories of magick cauldrons which had the power of giving heroes an inexhaustible supply of food and drink were very prevalent in Celtic legends. This first supplication of the Anamnesis serves as a reminder that we are ever-dependent upon the Lady for our physical growth and survival. Without these gifts from the earth-cauldron of Her planetary body, we could not live.

34. This is a direct reference to the Cauldron of Cerridwen and its brew of Inspiration just mentioned above. However, it is described, not as an anecdote of a once-upon-a-time mythological happening, but as a symbol of the Goddess and the availability of Her knowledge and inspiration to all of us who seek earnestly for it.

35. The Gundestrup Cauldron with its pictorial imagery of human sacrifice, death, and apotheosis forms the backdrop for this final of the three supplications. While thankfully we have progressed beyond the primitive notions of human sacrifice so common to our ancient ancestors, we still recognize that the beginning of all personal transforma-

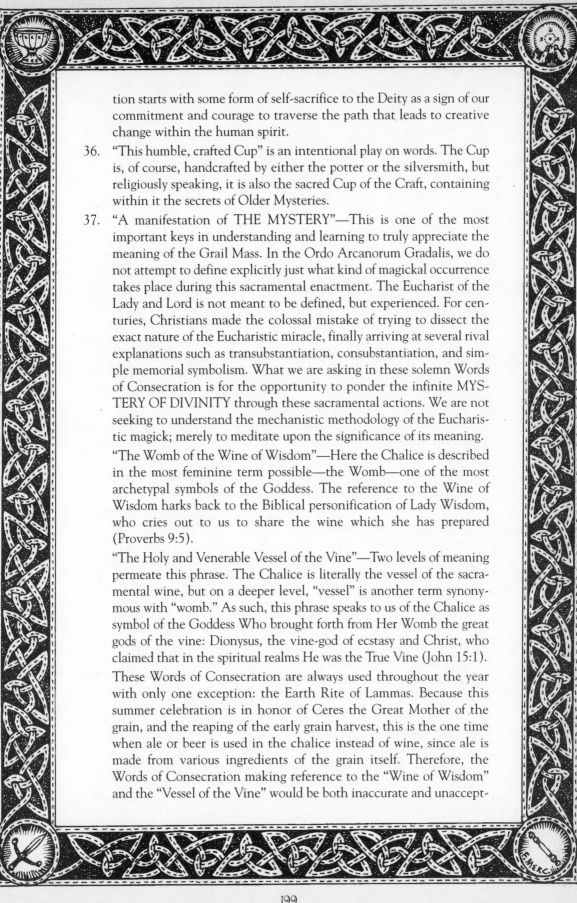

tion starts with some form of self-sacrifice to the Deity as a sign of our commitment and courage to traverse the path that leads to creative change within the human spirit.

36. "This humble, crafted Cup" is an intentional play on words. The Cup is, of course, handcrafted by either the potter or the silversmith, but religiously speaking, it is also the sacred Cup of the Craft, containing within it the secrets of Older Mysteries.

37. "A manifestation of THE MYSTERY"—This is one of the most important keys in understanding and learning to truly appreciate the meaning of the Grail Mass. In the Ordo Arcanorum Gradalis, we do not attempt to define explicitly just what kind of magickal occurrence takes place during this sacramental enactment. The Eucharist of the Lady and Lord is not meant to be defined, but experienced. For centuries, Christians made the colossal mistake of trying to dissect the exact nature of the Eucharistic miracle, finally arriving at several rival explanations such as transubstantiation, consubstantiation, and simple memorial symbolism. What we are asking in these solemn Words of Consecration is for the opportunity to ponder the infinite MYSTERY OF DIVINITY through these sacramental actions. We are not seeking to understand the mechanistic methodology of the Eucharistic magick; merely to meditate upon the significance of its meaning.

"The Womb of the Wine of Wisdom"—Here the Chalice is described in the most feminine term possible—the Womb—one of the most archetypal symbols of the Goddess. The reference to the Wine of Wisdom harks back to the Biblical personification of Lady Wisdom, who cries out to us to share the wine which she has prepared (Proverbs 9:5).

"The Holy and Venerable Vessel of the Vine"—Two levels of meaning permeate this phrase. The Chalice is literally the vessel of the sacramental wine, but on a deeper level, "vessel" is another term synonymous with "womb." As such, this phrase speaks to us of the Chalice as symbol of the Goddess Who brought forth from Her Womb the great gods of the vine: Dionysus, the vine-god of ecstasy and Christ, who claimed that in the spiritual realms He was the True Vine (John 15:1).

These Words of Consecration are always used throughout the year with only one exception: the Earth Rite of Lammas. Because this summer celebration is in honor of Ceres the Great Mother of the grain, and the reaping of the early grain harvest, this is the one time when ale or beer is used in the chalice instead of wine, since ale is made from various ingredients of the grain itself. Therefore, the Words of Consecration making reference to the "Wine of Wisdom" and the "Vessel of the Vine" would be both inaccurate and unacceptable. Instead, the words are suitably altered in this instance to reflect the change of beverage used in the Mass:

> *Holy Queen of the Glorious Grail,*
> *we offer unto Thee here*
> *this humble, crafted Cup,*
> *that it may become for us*
> *a manifestation of THE MYSTERY;*
> *the Grail of the Living Grain;*
> *the Holy and Venerable Vessel of the God.**

*(The reference here is to the grain-god [i.e., the Corn King, sacrificed in the cutting of the fields for the early harvest].)

38. The Goddess was originally considered to be the source of spiritual grace (Greek: *charis*) long before such a concept was ever transformed into a cornerstone of Pauline Christian theology. Here we have described the true "wonder-working" nature of the Grail in the Mass itself. It is the means by which we experience the grace of the Goddess, for through our sacramental actions She manifests Her Real Presence as the Lady of the Chalice, she Who is the Queen of Cups.

39. Even though it was probably the product of pious Christian revisionism, the vision of Galahad can be seen as yet another form of Quest for the Beautific Vision of the Deity. As such, Galahad stands for one of the highest forms of spiritual purity and aspiration.

40. There are some Arthurian scholars who now question whether Glastonbury was in actuality the final resting place of King Arthur and Guinevere. However, the fact that Glastonbury has always drawn its strength and inspiration from the legends of the Grail, and the further confirmation of numerous psychics and sensitives who have testified that the Tor area and other legendary locations such as Chalice Well, have an accumulated residue of mystical power, gives contemporary evidence to the justification for Glastonbury's continued existence as a place of pilgrimage because of the aura of the Grail which has psychically superimposed itself upon this hallowed village.

41. The Grail itself is the Shrine concealed from the eyes of the profane within the spiritual Avalon, the Holy Isle of the Goddess. The Cup which we use in the Eucharist becomes the outer symbol of this mystical reality.

42. The Gnosis is the hidden Wisdom, the Secret Knowledge of the Ages which can only be assimilated by figuratively eating from the Tree of the Knowledge of Good and Evil. In the Biblical story, the Elohim wanted to keep our first parents in ignorance by forbidding them access to the fruit of this Tree. The Serpent (an earlier symbol of the Consort of the Goddess, and of the wisdom of the Goddess Herself,

now vilified in this patriarchal, reworked story) told them the truth and proceeded to show them the way towards the attainment of godhood (Genesis 3:5). The Serpent was also correct in telling Adam and Eve that the threat of the Elohim to the effect that "in the day you eat thereof, you shall surely die" was a mere empty threat to frighten them away from the Tree of Knowledge, for in the day they ate of its fruit, they did *not* die, but continued to live for another 800 years (Genesis 5:5).

43. "The forbidden fruit of Eden" has a twofold meaning. First, it has immediate reference to the fruit of the Tree of the Knowledge of Good and Evil (see the previous footnote). Secondarily, it refers to the fruit from the Tree of Life. Those who ate of its fruit would live forever. When the Elohim stationed cherubim to guard the way to the Tree of Life, they were attempting to forbid the gift of immortality to the human race. Ultimately, however, it is the Goddess, according to Celtic lore, who grants access to the Apple Orchard of Avalon. Those who partake of those magick apples are blessed with life unending. For this reason, in the practice of our Order, we prefer to place a thin slice of apple in the altar chalice, floating it in the wine. Besides being considered sacred to Our Lady, an upright apple cut across its center horizontally reveals the sign of the pentagram naturally formed by the placement of its seeds. Cutting a thin slice of apple in this way and carefully extracting the seeds from it gives the pentagram even more definition as it floats in the wine. When we partake of the Grail Chalice, we are sampling a foretaste of the precious draught which gives insight and wisdom, opening wide the gateway to the realization of immortality.

The Grail Mass: The Elevation of the Chalice. "Behold in symbol the Vision of Galahad, the Hope of Glastonbury, the Shrine of Avalon!"

Cakes and Wine

(In most Wiccan traditions, the ceremony of Cakes and Wine usually takes place during the latter part of the ritual within the circle itself, and signifies the beginning of the general informalities of discussion, singing, etc. However, in the Ordo Arcanorum Gradalis we have departed from this customary procedure to the extent that we have repositioned it to be the last ceremonial act of the evening, taking place *after* the circle has been opened and the main ritual concluded. Usually, it is done in the kitchen or dining room area where the traditional pot luck dinner and other refreshments are arranged. It is, in effect, an act of blessing which serves to remind us of our thankfulness for the fruits of the earth which sustain us. It also signifies the beginning of the evening's informalities. We have removed this ceremony from the circle ritual because having Cakes and Wine so soon after partaking of the Eucharistic elements in the Grail Mass tends to blur the distinction between the two rituals, since they use substantially the same ingredients. Solitaries are free to delete the Cakes and Wine altogether if they feel no need for it within their ritual format.)

(The celebrant [either priest, priestess, or appointed grove member] begins the blessing of the elements by first taking up the dish of salt, saying:)[1]

Celebrant:

> *Blessed be this salt,*
> *that in partaking of these crystals*
> *we might be filled*
> *with vitality and health.*

(The salt is then passed around for all to take some and taste. The celebrant then takes the basket or dish of cakes, saying:)

Celebrant:

> *Blessed be this bread,*
> *that in partaking of the staff of life*
> *we might be enabled*
> *to create our own sufficiency.*

(The cakes are then passed around for all to eat. The celebrant then takes the decanter of wine and pours it into the communal chalice, lifts up the chalice and says:)

Celebrant:

> Blessed be this wine,
> that in tasting it we might partake
> of the sweetness of the spirit of life.[2]

(The communal chalice is passed around the table for all to share. Now begins the general time of relaxation, laughter, music, food, and frivolity.)

Footnotes

1. The dish of salt is not the same one as is used upon the ritual altar. Another small dish should be placed upon the dining table for this purpose.

2. There is only one time during the year that wine is not used in the communal chalice: the Earth Rite of Lammas. During this Sabbat, both the Grail Chalice and the communal chalice are filled with ale or beer instead, since it is a time celebrating the first harvest of the grain and the related products which we make from it, including bread and ale. As a consequence, the blessing over the communal chalice also changes slightly, as is reflected below:

> Blessed be this ale,
> that in tasting it,
> we might partake
> of the heartiness of the spirit of life.

The Charge of the Goddess: "Hear now the wisdom of the Great Goddess!"

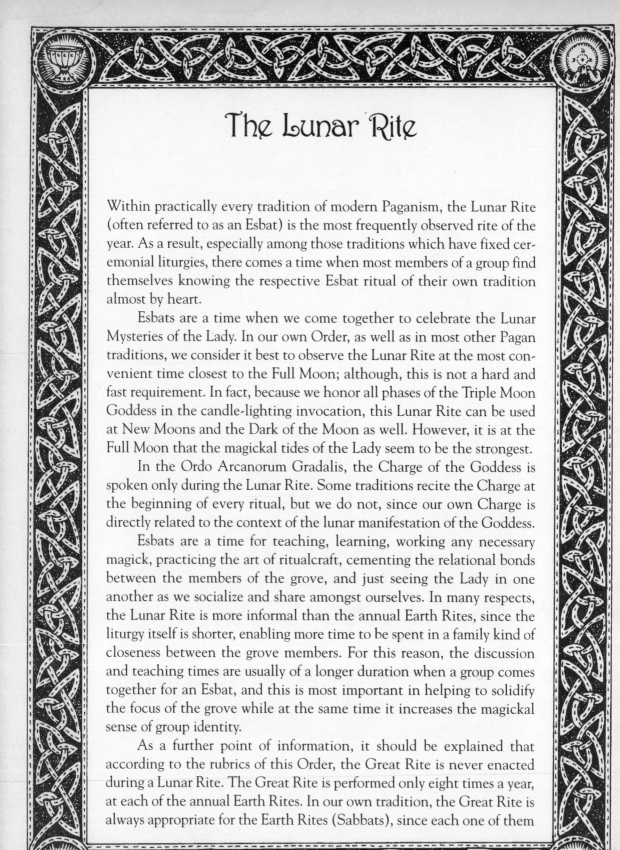

The Lunar Rite

Within practically every tradition of modern Paganism, the Lunar Rite (often referred to as an Esbat) is the most frequently observed rite of the year. As a result, especially among those traditions which have fixed ceremonial liturgies, there comes a time when most members of a group find themselves knowing the respective Esbat ritual of their own tradition almost by heart.

Esbats are a time when we come together to celebrate the Lunar Mysteries of the Lady. In our own Order, as well as in most other Pagan traditions, we consider it best to observe the Lunar Rite at the most convenient time closest to the Full Moon; although, this is not a hard and fast requirement. In fact, because we honor all phases of the Triple Moon Goddess in the candle-lighting invocation, this Lunar Rite can be used at New Moons and the Dark of the Moon as well. However, it is at the Full Moon that the magickal tides of the Lady seem to be the strongest.

In the Ordo Arcanorum Gradalis, the Charge of the Goddess is spoken only during the Lunar Rite. Some traditions recite the Charge at the beginning of every ritual, but we do not, since our own Charge is directly related to the context of the lunar manifestation of the Goddess.

Esbats are a time for teaching, learning, working any necessary magick, practicing the art of ritualcraft, cementing the relational bonds between the members of the grove, and just seeing the Lady in one another as we socialize and share amongst ourselves. In many respects, the Lunar Rite is more informal than the annual Earth Rites, since the liturgy itself is shorter, enabling more time to be spent in a family kind of closeness between the grove members. For this reason, the discussion and teaching times are usually of a longer duration when a group comes together for an Esbat, and this is most important in helping to solidify the focus of the grove while at the same time it increases the magickal sense of group identity.

As a further point of information, it should be explained that according to the rubrics of this Order, the Great Rite is never enacted during a Lunar Rite. The Great Rite is performed only eight times a year, at each of the annual Earth Rites. In our own tradition, the Great Rite is always appropriate for the Earth Rites (Sabbats), since each one of them in some way depicts the seasonal interaction between the energies of the Goddess and God. However, the Lunar Rite is for us preeminently a celebration of the Lady Herself in all of Her feminine mystery. It is for this reason that you will find no formal invocation of the God during the Lunar Rite. To be sure, the Lord is invoked by virtue of our constant reference to Him in the Opening Rite, but it is never formalized in the Lunar Rite itself, which is thoroughly Goddess-oriented in its focus.

Basic Requirements

Below are some things to remember for the celebration of the Lunar Rite which are necessary requirements if the observance is to be in accordance with the rubrics of the Ordo Arcanorum Gradalis.

Altar

The altar should be in the center of the circle area, facing east in the spring, south in the summer, west in the fall, and north in the winter.

Altar Cloth

The altar cloth should always correspond to the color of whichever quarter has the seasonal preeminence at the time: yellow in the spring, red in the summer, blue in the fall, and green in the winter. (This is only if you are using a regular rectangular altar. If you are using the Altar of the Pentagram, see the earlier chapter entitled "The Altar and the Sacred Tools" for further details and instructions.)

Altar Candles

The two main altar candles should be the same color as the altar cloth being used: yellow in the spring, red in the summer, blue in the fall, and green in the winter.

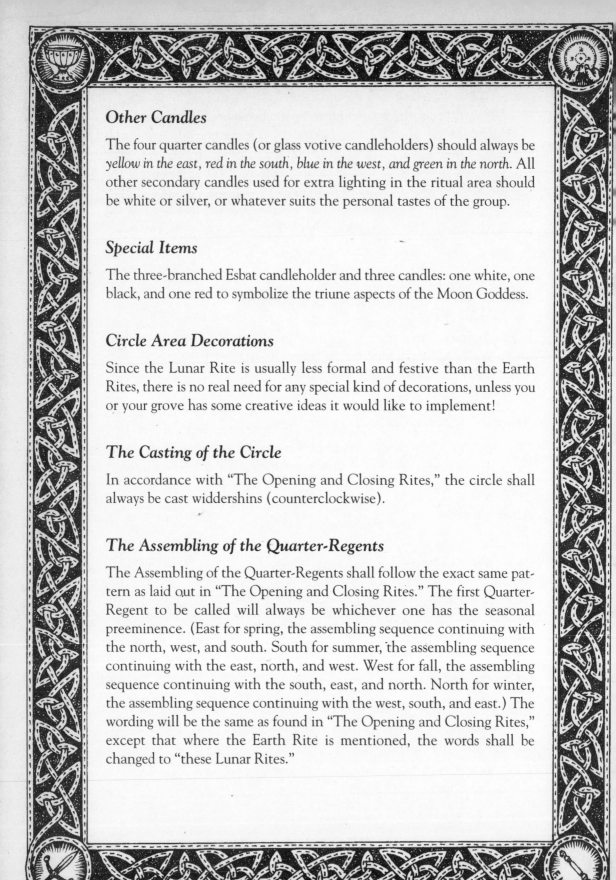

Other Candles

The four quarter candles (or glass votive candleholders) should always be *yellow in the east, red in the south, blue in the west, and green in the north*. All other secondary candles used for extra lighting in the ritual area should be white or silver, or whatever suits the personal tastes of the group.

Special Items

The three-branched Esbat candleholder and three candles: one white, one black, and one red to symbolize the triune aspects of the Moon Goddess.

Circle Area Decorations

Since the Lunar Rite is usually less formal and festive than the Earth Rites, there is no real need for any special kind of decorations, unless you or your grove has some creative ideas it would like to implement!

The Casting of the Circle

In accordance with "The Opening and Closing Rites," the circle shall always be cast widdershins (counterclockwise).

The Assembling of the Quarter-Regents

The Assembling of the Quarter-Regents shall follow the exact same pattern as laid out in "The Opening and Closing Rites." The first Quarter-Regent to be called will always be whichever one has the seasonal preeminence. (East for spring, the assembling sequence continuing with the north, west, and south. South for summer, the assembling sequence continuing with the east, north, and west. West for fall, the assembling sequence continuing with the south, east, and north. North for winter, the assembling sequence continuing with the west, south, and east.) The wording will be the same as found in "The Opening and Closing Rites," except that where the Earth Rite is mentioned, the words shall be changed to "these Lunar Rites."

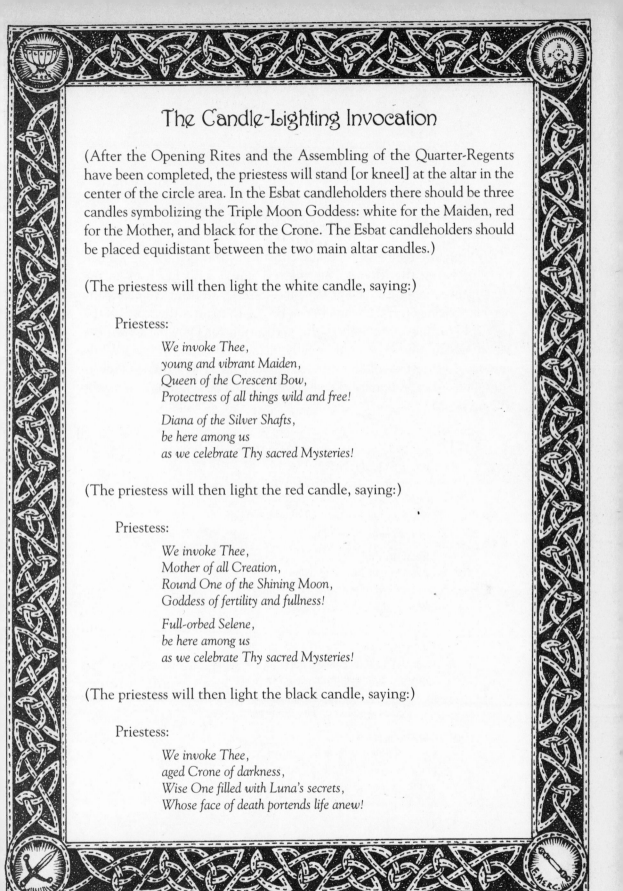

The Candle-Lighting Invocation

(After the Opening Rites and the Assembling of the Quarter-Regents have been completed, the priestess will stand [or kneel] at the altar in the center of the circle area. In the Esbat candleholders there should be three candles symbolizing the Triple Moon Goddess: white for the Maiden, red for the Mother, and black for the Crone. The Esbat candleholders should be placed equidistant between the two main altar candles.)

(The priestess will then light the white candle, saying:)

Priestess:

> *We invoke Thee,*
> *young and vibrant Maiden,*
> *Queen of the Crescent Bow,*
> *Protectress of all things wild and free!*
>
> *Diana of the Silver Shafts,*
> *be here among us*
> *as we celebrate Thy sacred Mysteries!*

(The priestess will then light the red candle, saying:)

Priestess:

> *We invoke Thee,*
> *Mother of all Creation,*
> *Round One of the Shining Moon,*
> *Goddess of fertility and fullness!*
>
> *Full-orbed Selene,*
> *be here among us*
> *as we celebrate Thy sacred Mysteries!*

(The priestess will then light the black candle, saying:)

Priestess:

> *We invoke Thee,*
> *aged Crone of darkness,*
> *Wise One filled with Luna's secrets,*
> *Whose face of death portends life anew!*

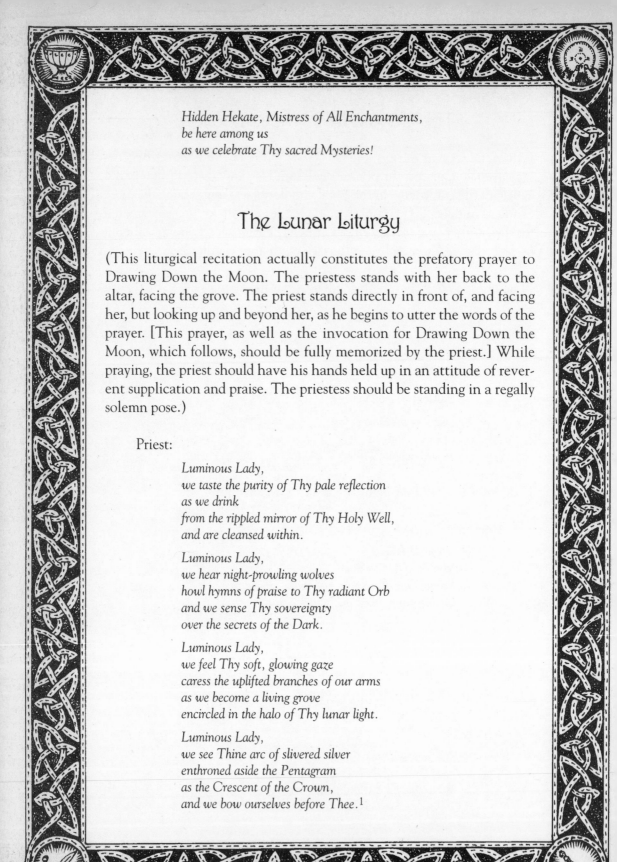

Hidden Hekate, Mistress of All Enchantments,
be here among us
as we celebrate Thy sacred Mysteries!

The Lunar Liturgy

(This liturgical recitation actually constitutes the prefatory prayer to Drawing Down the Moon. The priestess stands with her back to the altar, facing the grove. The priest stands directly in front of, and facing her, but looking up and beyond her, as he begins to utter the words of the prayer. [This prayer, as well as the invocation for Drawing Down the Moon, which follows, should be fully memorized by the priest.] While praying, the priest should have his hands held up in an attitude of reverent supplication and praise. The priestess should be standing in a regally solemn pose.)

Priest:

Luminous Lady,
we taste the purity of Thy pale reflection
as we drink
from the rippled mirror of Thy Holy Well,
and are cleansed within.

Luminous Lady,
we hear night-prowling wolves
howl hymns of praise to Thy radiant Orb
and we sense Thy sovereignty
over the secrets of the Dark.

Luminous Lady,
we feel Thy soft, glowing gaze
caress the uplifted branches of our arms
as we become a living grove
encircled in the halo of Thy lunar light.

Luminous Lady,
we see Thine arc of slivered silver
enthroned aside the Pentagram
as the Crescent of the Crown,
and we bow ourselves before Thee.[1]

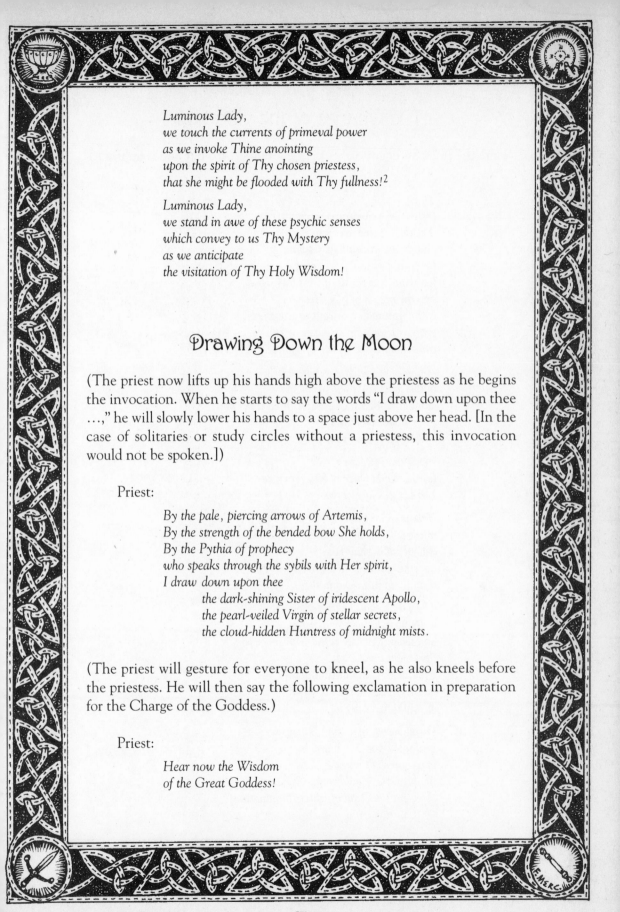

Luminous Lady,
we touch the currents of primeval power
as we invoke Thine anointing
upon the spirit of Thy chosen priestess,
that she might be flooded with Thy fullness![2]

Luminous Lady,
we stand in awe of these psychic senses
which convey to us Thy Mystery
as we anticipate
the visitation of Thy Holy Wisdom!

Drawing Down the Moon

(The priest now lifts up his hands high above the priestess as he begins the invocation. When he starts to say the words "I draw down upon thee …," he will slowly lower his hands to a space just above her head. [In the case of solitaries or study circles without a priestess, this invocation would not be spoken.])

Priest:

By the pale, piercing arrows of Artemis,
By the strength of the bended bow She holds,
By the Pythia of prophecy
who speaks through the sybils with Her spirit,
I draw down upon thee
        the dark-shining Sister of iridescent Apollo,
        the pearl-veiled Virgin of stellar secrets,
        the cloud-hidden Huntress of midnight mists.

(The priest will gesture for everyone to kneel, as he also kneels before the priestess. He will then say the following exclamation in preparation for the Charge of the Goddess.)

Priest:

Hear now the Wisdom
of the Great Goddess!

The Charge of the Goddess

(Here the priestess begins to recite the Charge with her hands uplifted.)[3]

Priestess:

Listen, My children,
that thine ears may receive instruction,
and thy heart distill its wisdom,
for from My lips
fall the velvet petals of the Holy Rose,
and the breath of My whispers
is fragrant with the scent of Eternity,
even as I speak in syllables of Spirit,
transcending the trance of Time.

Among moonlit groves where willows weep;
in the solitude of sea-swept shores;
along forgotten roads where three ways meet;
there shall I be found
in shadow and in symbol.

But if thou seekest
for the secret place of My presence,
behold, it is nigh thee.

If thou seekest for the throne of My theophany
in the stillness of thy soul,
behold, thou shalt hear
the continuous counsel of My words
welling up from within thee.

Then shalt thou be overwhelmed
in the wonder of My worship,
and when My face is full with silver fire,
thou shalt invoke Me
with incense and incantation
that My magick may descend
as a mantle in thy midst.

Dwell deeply upon My Divinity;
meditate upon My marvels,
and thou shalt know well My ways,
for I am the Cauldron of Creation;
*   I am the Grail of Inner Illumination;*
*   I am the Bringer of Birth,*

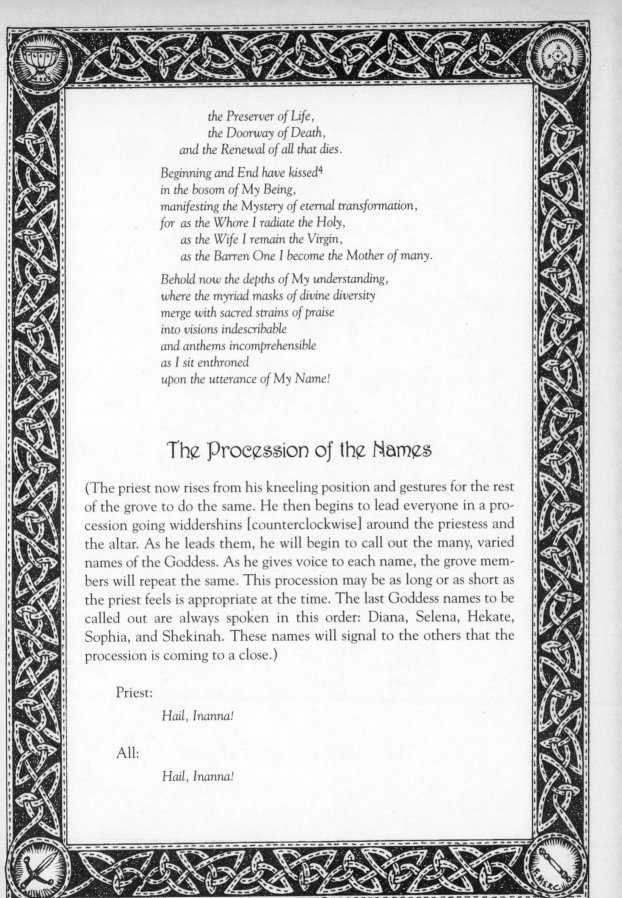

the Preserver of Life,
the Doorway of Death,
and the Renewal of all that dies.

Beginning and End have kissed[4]
in the bosom of My Being,
manifesting the Mystery of eternal transformation,
for as the Whore I radiate the Holy,
as the Wife I remain the Virgin,
as the Barren One I become the Mother of many.

Behold now the depths of My understanding,
where the myriad masks of divine diversity
merge with sacred strains of praise
into visions indescribable
and anthems incomprehensible
as I sit enthroned
upon the utterance of My Name!

The Procession of the Names

(The priest now rises from his kneeling position and gestures for the rest of the grove to do the same. He then begins to lead everyone in a procession going widdershins [counterclockwise] around the priestess and the altar. As he leads them, he will begin to call out the many, varied names of the Goddess. As he gives voice to each name, the grove members will repeat the same. This procession may be as long or as short as the priest feels is appropriate at the time. The last Goddess names to be called out are always spoken in this order: Diana, Selena, Hekate, Sophia, and Shekinah. These names will signal to the others that the procession is coming to a close.)

Priest:

Hail, Inanna!

All:

Hail, Inanna!

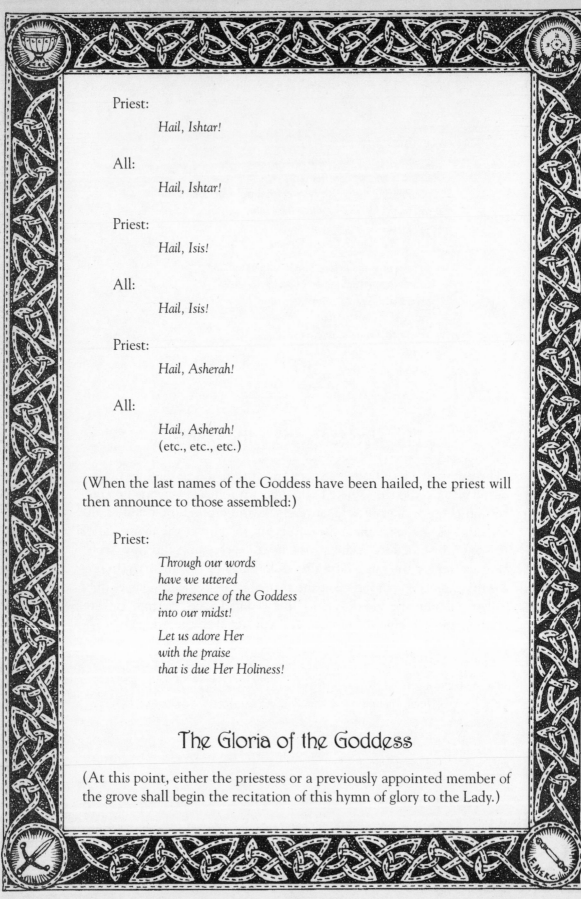

Priest:

> Hail, Ishtar!

All:

> Hail, Ishtar!

Priest:

> Hail, Isis!

All:

> Hail, Isis!

Priest:

> Hail, Asherah!

All:

> Hail, Asherah!
> (etc., etc., etc.)

(When the last names of the Goddess have been hailed, the priest will then announce to those assembled:)

Priest:

> Through our words
> have we uttered
> the presence of the Goddess
> into our midst!
>
> Let us adore Her
> with the praise
> that is due Her Holiness!

The Gloria of the Goddess

(At this point, either the priestess or a previously appointed member of the grove shall begin the recitation of this hymn of glory to the Lady.)

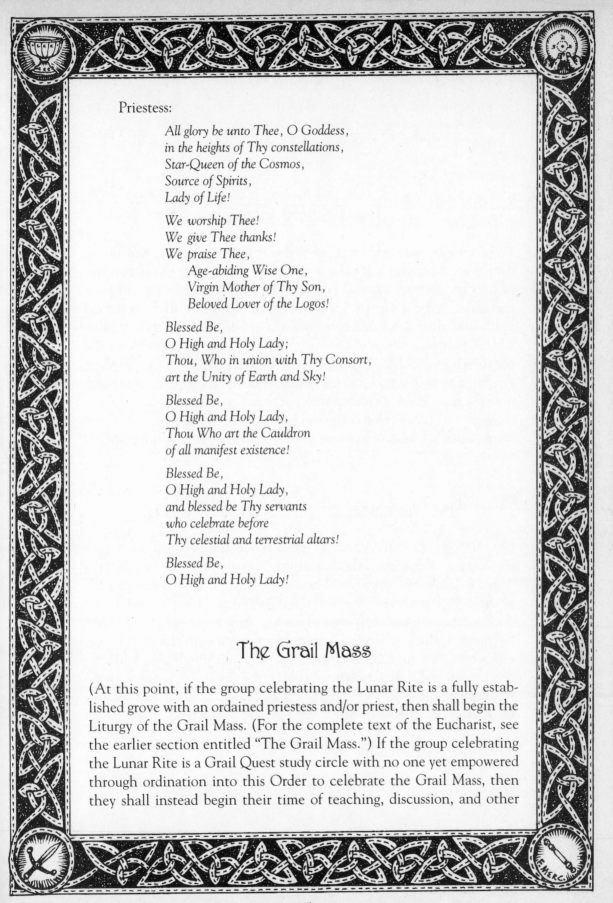

Priestess:

> All glory be unto Thee, O Goddess,
> in the heights of Thy constellations,
> Star-Queen of the Cosmos,
> Source of Spirits,
> Lady of Life!

> We worship Thee!
> We give Thee thanks!
> We praise Thee,
> > Age-abiding Wise One,
> > Virgin Mother of Thy Son,
> > Beloved Lover of the Logos!

> Blessed Be,
> O High and Holy Lady;
> Thou, Who in union with Thy Consort,
> art the Unity of Earth and Sky!

> Blessed Be,
> O High and Holy Lady,
> Thou Who art the Cauldron
> of all manifest existence!

> Blessed Be,
> O High and Holy Lady,
> and blessed be Thy servants
> who celebrate before
> Thy celestial and terrestrial altars!

> Blessed Be,
> O High and Holy Lady!

The Grail Mass

(At this point, if the group celebrating the Lunar Rite is a fully established grove with an ordained priestess and/or priest, then shall begin the Liturgy of the Grail Mass. (For the complete text of the Eucharist, see the earlier section entitled "The Grail Mass.") If the group celebrating the Lunar Rite is a Grail Quest study circle with no one yet empowered through ordination into this Order to celebrate the Grail Mass, then they shall instead begin their time of teaching, discussion, and other informalities, led by an appointed facilitator. For an established grove, their time of teaching and discussion shall follow immediately after the Grail Mass has been celebrated with a subsequent meditation.)

The Parting Prayer

(When the priestess and priest sense that it is time for the Lunar Rite to come to a close, they will bid the rest of the members to rise in preparation for the Parting Prayer and the Closing Rites. Since the Lunar Rite is considered to be a slightly less formal time of worship then an annual Earth Rite, there is no set or prescribed prayer of parting to the Goddess. This is done on purpose in order that it may inspire spontaneity on the part of whoever is called upon to say the Parting Prayer to the Goddess. Anyone can be designated to lead this prayer, and it should be something from the heart of the individual that is spoken. This can serve as an incentive for others to develop their own personal relationship with the Lady through private times of meditation, conversational prayer, and praise.)

The Dismissal of the Quarter-Regents

(At this time, the same appointed grove members that called the respective Quarter-Regents in the beginning of the ritual will now dismiss Them to Their own domains. The dismissal will always begin with the Quarter-Regent who has the seasonal preeminence. [East for spring, the dismissing sequence continuing with the north, west, and south. South for summer, the dismissing sequence continuing with the east, north, and west. West for fall, the dismissing sequence continuing with the south, east, and north. North for winter, the dismissing sequence continuing with the west, south, and east.] The wording and procedure shall be the same as is found in The Opening and Closing Rites.)

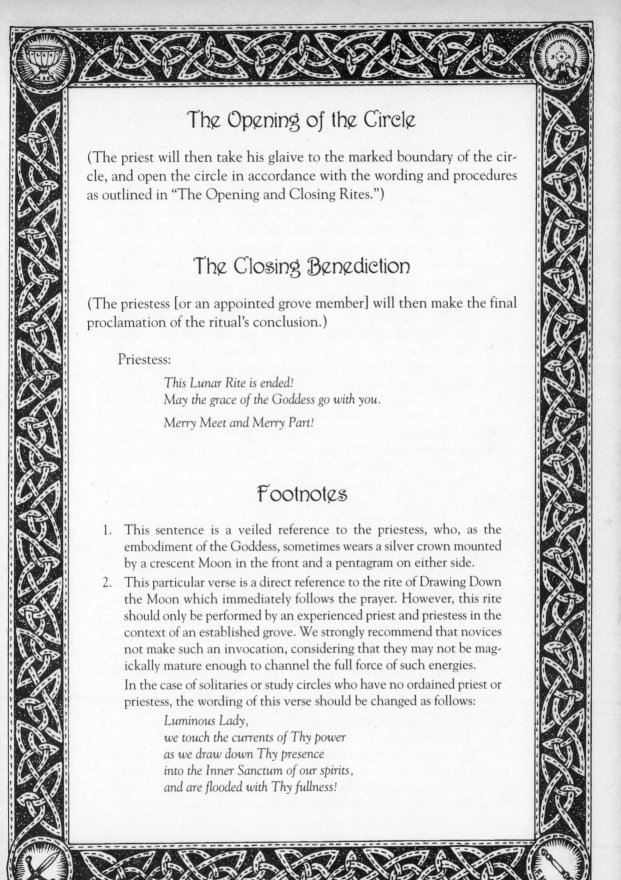

The Opening of the Circle

(The priest will then take his glaive to the marked boundary of the circle, and open the circle in accordance with the wording and procedures as outlined in "The Opening and Closing Rites.")

The Closing Benediction

(The priestess [or an appointed grove member] will then make the final proclamation of the ritual's conclusion.)

Priestess:

> *This Lunar Rite is ended!*
> *May the grace of the Goddess go with you.*
>
> *Merry Meet and Merry Part!*

Footnotes

1. This sentence is a veiled reference to the priestess, who, as the embodiment of the Goddess, sometimes wears a silver crown mounted by a crescent Moon in the front and a pentagram on either side.

2. This particular verse is a direct reference to the rite of Drawing Down the Moon which immediately follows the prayer. However, this rite should only be performed by an experienced priest and priestess in the context of an established grove. We strongly recommend that novices not make such an invocation, considering that they may not be magickally mature enough to channel the full force of such energies.

   In the case of solitaries or study circles who have no ordained priest or priestess, the wording of this verse should be changed as follows:

   > *Luminous Lady,*
   > *we touch the currents of Thy power*
   > *as we draw down Thy presence*
   > *into the Inner Sanctum of our spirits,*
   > *and are flooded with Thy fullness!*

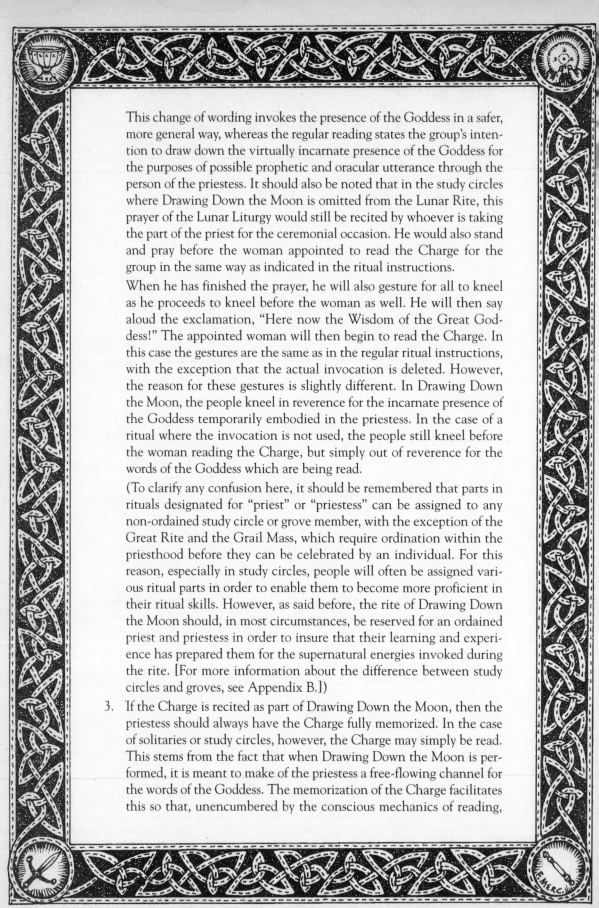

This change of wording invokes the presence of the Goddess in a safer, more general way, whereas the regular reading states the group's intention to draw down the virtually incarnate presence of the Goddess for the purposes of possible prophetic and oracular utterance through the person of the priestess. It should also be noted that in the study circles where Drawing Down the Moon is omitted from the Lunar Rite, this prayer of the Lunar Liturgy would still be recited by whoever is taking the part of the priest for the ceremonial occasion. He would also stand and pray before the woman appointed to read the Charge for the group in the same way as indicated in the ritual instructions.

When he has finished the prayer, he will also gesture for all to kneel as he proceeds to kneel before the woman as well. He will then say aloud the exclamation, "Here now the Wisdom of the Great Goddess!" The appointed woman will then begin to read the Charge. In this case the gestures are the same as in the regular ritual instructions, with the exception that the actual invocation is deleted. However, the reason for these gestures is slightly different. In Drawing Down the Moon, the people kneel in reverence for the incarnate presence of the Goddess temporarily embodied in the priestess. In the case of a ritual where the invocation is not used, the people still kneel before the woman reading the Charge, but simply out of reverence for the words of the Goddess which are being read.

(To clarify any confusion here, it should be remembered that parts in rituals designated for "priest" or "priestess" can be assigned to any non-ordained study circle or grove member, with the exception of the Great Rite and the Grail Mass, which require ordination within the priesthood before they can be celebrated by an individual. For this reason, especially in study circles, people will often be assigned various ritual parts in order to enable them to become more proficient in their ritual skills. However, as said before, the rite of Drawing Down the Moon should, in most circumstances, be reserved for an ordained priest and priestess in order to insure that their learning and experience has prepared them for the supernatural energies invoked during the rite. [For more information about the difference between study circles and groves, see Appendix B.])

3. If the Charge is recited as part of Drawing Down the Moon, then the priestess should always have the Charge fully memorized. In the case of solitaries or study circles, however, the Charge may simply be read. This stems from the fact that when Drawing Down the Moon is performed, it is meant to make of the priestess a free-flowing channel for the words of the Goddess. The memorization of the Charge facilitates this so that, unencumbered by the conscious mechanics of reading,

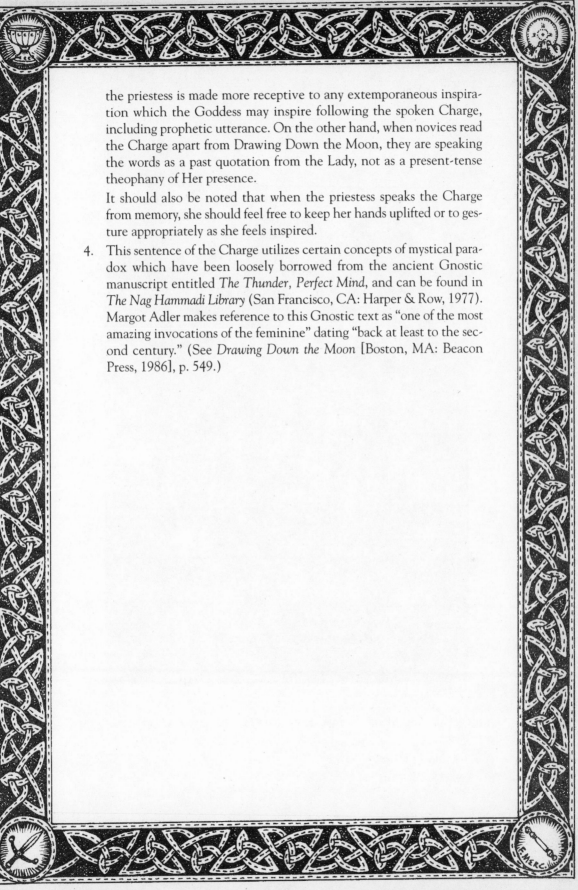

the priestess is made more receptive to any extemporaneous inspiration which the Goddess may inspire following the spoken Charge, including prophetic utterance. On the other hand, when novices read the Charge apart from Drawing Down the Moon, they are speaking the words as a past quotation from the Lady, not as a present-tense theophany of Her presence.

It should also be noted that when the priestess speaks the Charge from memory, she should feel free to keep her hands uplifted or to gesture appropriately as she feels inspired.

4. This sentence of the Charge utilizes certain concepts of mystical paradox which have been loosely borrowed from the ancient Gnostic manuscript entitled *The Thunder, Perfect Mind*, and can be found in *The Nag Hammadi Library* (San Francisco, CA: Harper & Row, 1977). Margot Adler makes reference to this Gnostic text as "one of the most amazing invocations of the feminine" dating "back at least to the second century." (See *Drawing Down the Moon* [Boston, MA: Beacon Press, 1986], p. 549.)

Drawing Down the Moon: "I draw down upon thee the dark-shining Sister of irides-cent Apollo ..."

The Wheel of the Year

Hallowmas

Basic Requirements

Below are some things to remember for the High Earth Rite of Hallowmas which are necessary requirements if the observance is to be in accordance with the rubrics of the Ordo Arcanorum Gradalis.

Altar

The altar should be in the center of the circle area, facing the western quarter.

Altar Cloth

The altar cloth should always be blue for the High Earth Rite of Hallowmas. (This is only if you are using a regular rectangular altar. If you are using the Altar of the Pentagram, see the earlier chapter entitled "The Altar and the Sacred Tools" for further details and instructions.)

Altar Candles

The two main altar candles should be blue for the High Earth Rite of Hallowmas.

Other Candles

The four quarter candles (or glass votive candleholders) *should always be blue in the west, red in the south, yellow (or gold) in the east, and green in the north.* For the actual Hallowmas rite, three *black* candles will be required for placement in the three-branched candleholder, symbolic of the Triple Goddess as Crone. A large candle to be set within the Cauldron will also be needed. All other secondary candles used for extra lighting in the ritual area should be of either various shades of pale gold, rust, and other late harvest colors suitable to the grove's personal tastes. Of course, black and orange candles are most traditional at this Samhain season.

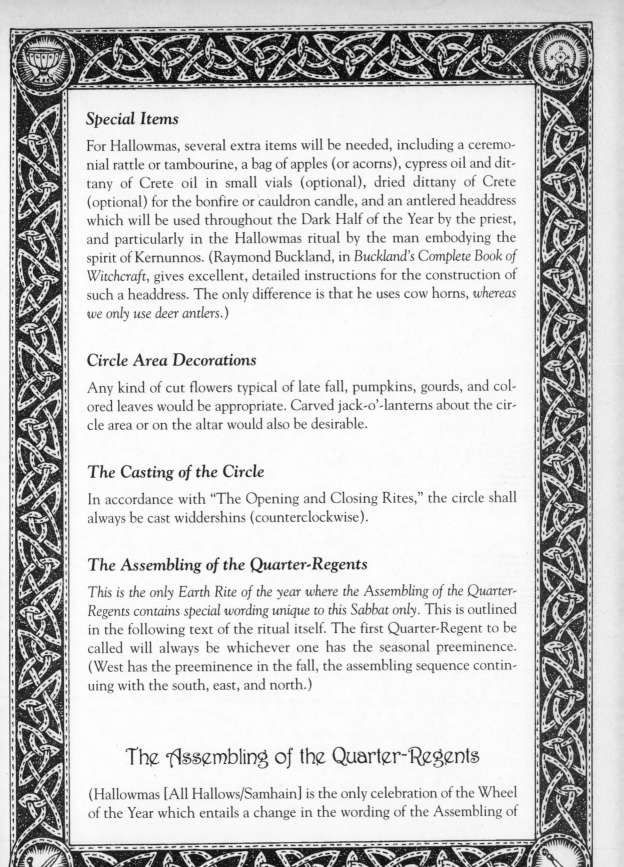

Special Items

For Hallowmas, several extra items will be needed, including a ceremonial rattle or tambourine, a bag of apples (or acorns), cypress oil and dittany of Crete oil in small vials (optional), dried dittany of Crete (optional) for the bonfire or cauldron candle, and an antlered headdress which will be used throughout the Dark Half of the Year by the priest, and particularly in the Hallowmas ritual by the man embodying the spirit of Kernunnos. (Raymond Buckland, in *Buckland's Complete Book of Witchcraft*, gives excellent, detailed instructions for the construction of such a headdress. The only difference is that he uses cow horns, *whereas we only use deer antlers.*)

Circle Area Decorations

Any kind of cut flowers typical of late fall, pumpkins, gourds, and colored leaves would be appropriate. Carved jack-o'-lanterns about the circle area or on the altar would also be desirable.

The Casting of the Circle

In accordance with "The Opening and Closing Rites," the circle shall always be cast widdershins (counterclockwise).

The Assembling of the Quarter-Regents

This is the only Earth Rite of the year where the Assembling of the Quarter-Regents contains special wording unique to this Sabbat only. This is outlined in the following text of the ritual itself. The first Quarter-Regent to be called will always be whichever one has the seasonal preeminence. (West has the preeminence in the fall, the assembling sequence continuing with the south, east, and north.)

The Assembling of the Quarter-Regents

(Hallowmas [All Hallows/Samhain] is the only celebration of the Wheel of the Year which entails a change in the wording of the Assembling of the Quarter-Regents. [Otherwise, The Opening Rites are performed as usual.] The appropriate wording and directional sequence of the salutations is as follows:)

Caller of the West:

Regents of the West,
Patrons of the Blessed Dead,
Protectors of the Departed in Avalon
beyond Thy primordial seas;
by the Holy Pentagram of Balance
sacred to the Goddess,
Queen of the Cardinal Quarters,
we call Thee to this Circle,
charging Thee to witness and watch over
these rites of Hallowmas
on this Night between the worlds
and out of time.

Caller of the South:

Regents of the South,
Patrons of All Hallow's blazing bonfires,
Protectors of the paths of wandering spirits
as Ye illumine their way
to ancestral home and hearth;
by the Holy Pentagram of Balance
sacred to the Goddess,
Queen of the Cardinal Quarters,
we call Thee to this Circle,
charging Thee to witness and watch over
these rites of Hallowmas
on this Night between the worlds
and out of time.

Caller of the East:

Regents of the East,
Patrons of phantom-filled winds,
Protectors of breeze-borne apparitions
let loose from the ethereal realms;
by the Holy Pentagram of Balance
sacred to the Goddess,
Queen of the Cardinal Quarters,

> *we call Thee to this Circle,*
> *charging Thee to witness and watch over*
> *these rites of Hallowmas*
> *on this Night between the worlds*
> *and out of time.*

Caller of the North:

> *Regents of the North,*
> *Patrons of enchanted places*
> *and moonlit megaliths,*
> *Protectors of haunted heaths*
> *and long-forgotten, circled stones;*
> *by the Holy Pentagram of Balance*
> *sacred to the Goddess,*
> *Queen of the Cardinal Quarters,*
> *we call Thee to this Circle,*
> *charging Thee to witness and watch over*
> *these rites of Hallowmas*
> *on this Night between the worlds*
> *and out of time.*

The Anointing with Oil

(This part of the ceremony is totally optional, but if there are "first-timers" in the circle, it can sometimes be beneficial to give them a sense of security and protection.)

(When the Assembling of the Quarter-Regents has been completed, the priestess and priest will put down their glaives and take up the vials of anointing oil from the altar. Turning around to face the rest of the grove, the priestess begins to anoint each individual upon the forehead with cypress oil, making an invoking pentagram on the forehead while speaking the following blessing.)

Priestess:

> *In the Name of Holy Persephone,*
> *Protector of the Blessed Dead,*
> *I anoint you with the chrism of protection*

for this journey of vision
between the worlds.

(Then the priest begins to anoint each person with dittany of Crete oil with a dot-like mark upon the forehead in the area of the "third eye," saying the following blessing upon each individual.)

Priest:

In the Name of Holy Persephone,
Hope of the Blessed Dead,
I anoint you with this chrism
of spirit-perception,
that you may sense the presence
of those passed on
beyond the gathering shrouds of the Grave
on this,
their sacred Night.

(When the anointing procedure has been finished, both the priestess and priest will return the vials upon the altar and use the prepared white cloths or napkins to absorb the oil from their fingers.)[1]

The Triple Candle Invocation of Hekate Trevia

(After the anointing of the grove members has been completed, the invocations will now begin [or if this optional anointing has been eliminated from the ceremony, then this invocation will take place immediately following the Assembling of the Quarter-Regents]. Standing before the unlit candles for Hekate placed prominently upon the altar between the two major candlesticks, [if the rite is held outdoors, tall torches stationed in the ground behind the altar can be substituted for candles], the priest begins with the following reading.)

Priest:

The Dark Mother comes
from time long past the setting sun.
Lady of Night she is,

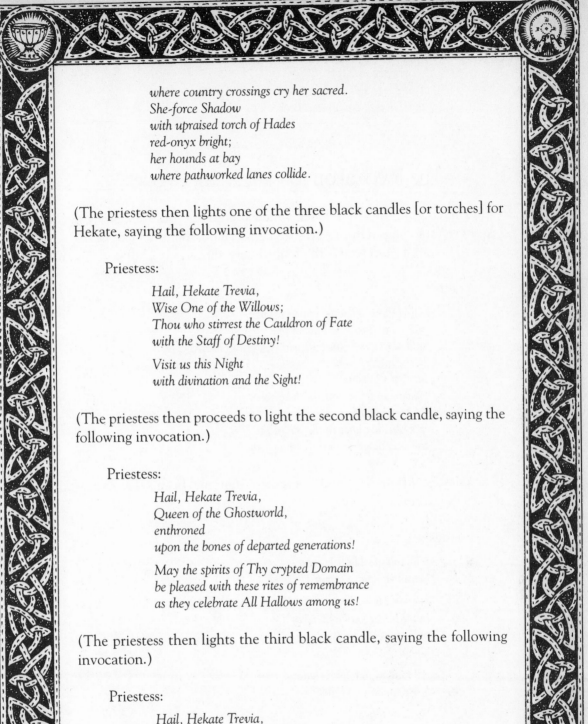

where country crossings cry her sacred.
She-force Shadow
with upraised torch of Hades
red-onyx bright;
her hounds at bay
where pathworked lanes collide.

(The priestess then lights one of the three black candles [or torches] for Hekate, saying the following invocation.)

Priestess:

Hail, Hekate Trevia,
Wise One of the Willows;
Thou who stirrest the Cauldron of Fate
with the Staff of Destiny!

Visit us this Night
with divination and the Sight!

(The priestess then proceeds to light the second black candle, saying the following invocation.)

Priestess:

Hail, Hekate Trevia,
Queen of the Ghostworld,
enthroned
upon the bones of departed generations!

May the spirits of Thy crypted Domain
be pleased with these rites of remembrance
as they celebrate All Hallows among us!

(The priestess then lights the third black candle, saying the following invocation.)

Priestess:

Hail, Hekate Trevia,
Spectral Sovereign of Darkness;
Bringer of Shadows
that we might see invisible realities
without distraction from the light.

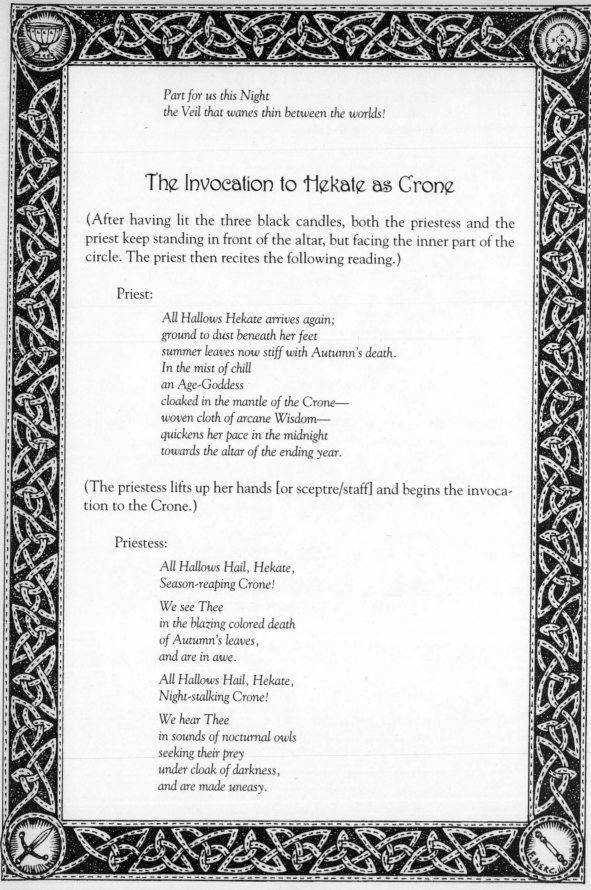

Part for us this Night
the Veil that wanes thin between the worlds!

The Invocation to Hekate as Crone

(After having lit the three black candles, both the priestess and the priest keep standing in front of the altar, but facing the inner part of the circle. The priest then recites the following reading.)

Priest:

All Hallows Hekate arrives again;
ground to dust beneath her feet
summer leaves now stiff with Autumn's death.
In the mist of chill
an Age-Goddess
cloaked in the mantle of the Crone—
woven cloth of arcane Wisdom—
quickens her pace in the midnight
towards the altar of the ending year.

(The priestess lifts up her hands [or sceptre/staff] and begins the invocation to the Crone.)

Priestess:

All Hallows Hail, Hekate,
Season-reaping Crone!

We see Thee
in the blazing colored death
of Autumn's leaves,
and are in awe.

All Hallows Hail, Hekate,
Night-stalking Crone!

We hear Thee
in sounds of nocturnal owls
seeking their prey
under cloak of darkness,
and are made uneasy.

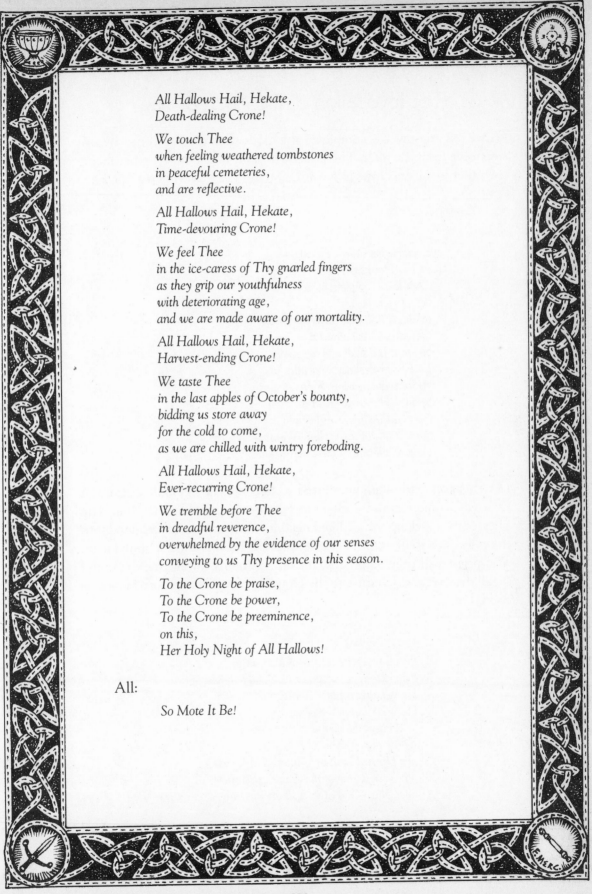

All Hallows Hail, Hekate,
Death-dealing Crone!

We touch Thee
when feeling weathered tombstones
in peaceful cemeteries,
and are reflective.

All Hallows Hail, Hekate,
Time-devouring Crone!

We feel Thee
in the ice-caress of Thy gnarled fingers
as they grip our youthfulness
with deteriorating age,
and we are made aware of our mortality.

All Hallows Hail, Hekate,
Harvest-ending Crone!

We taste Thee
in the last apples of October's bounty,
bidding us store away
for the cold to come,
as we are chilled with wintry foreboding.

All Hallows Hail, Hekate,
Ever-recurring Crone!

We tremble before Thee
in dreadful reverence,
overwhelmed by the evidence of our senses
conveying to us Thy presence in this season.

To the Crone be praise,
To the Crone be power,
To the Crone be preeminence,
on this,
Her Holy Night of All Hallows!

All:

So Mote It Be!

229

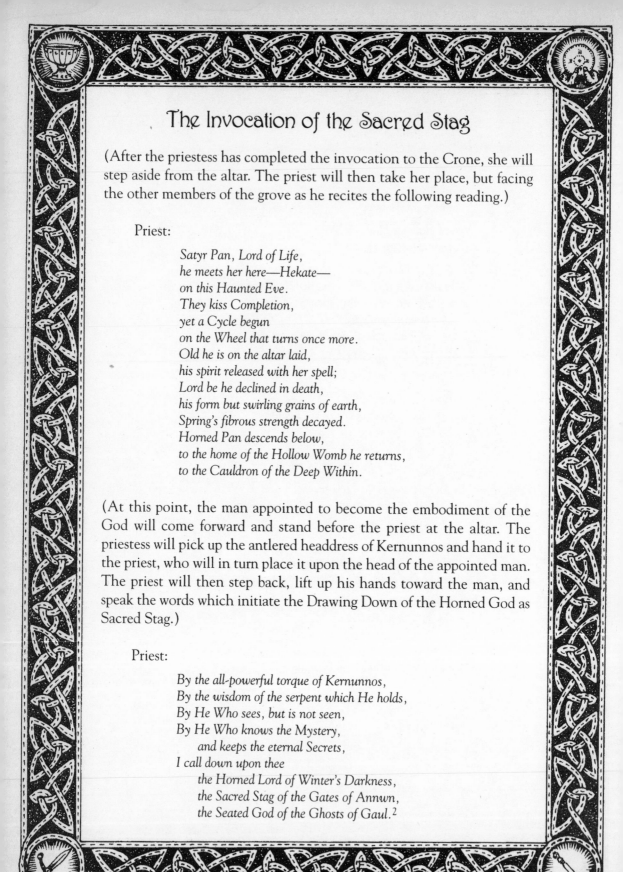

The Invocation of the Sacred Stag

(After the priestess has completed the invocation to the Crone, she will step aside from the altar. The priest will then take her place, but facing the other members of the grove as he recites the following reading.)

Priest:

> *Satyr Pan, Lord of Life,*
> *he meets her here—Hekate—*
> *on this Haunted Eve.*
> *They kiss Completion,*
> *yet a Cycle begun*
> *on the Wheel that turns once more.*
> *Old he is on the altar laid,*
> *his spirit released with her spell;*
> *Lord be he declined in death,*
> *his form but swirling grains of earth,*
> *Spring's fibrous strength decayed.*
> *Horned Pan descends below,*
> *to the home of the Hollow Womb he returns,*
> *to the Cauldron of the Deep Within.*

(At this point, the man appointed to become the embodiment of the God will come forward and stand before the priest at the altar. The priestess will pick up the antlered headdress of Kernunnos and hand it to the priest, who will in turn place it upon the head of the appointed man. The priest will then step back, lift up his hands toward the man, and speak the words which initiate the Drawing Down of the Horned God as Sacred Stag.)

Priest:

> *By the all-powerful torque of Kernunnos,*
> *By the wisdom of the serpent which He holds,*
> *By He Who sees, but is not seen,*
> *By He Who knows the Mystery,*
>   *and keeps the eternal Secrets,*
> *I call down upon thee*
>   *the Horned Lord of Winter's Darkness,*
>   *the Sacred Stag of the Gates of Annwn,*
>   *the Seated God of the Ghosts of Gaul.*[2]

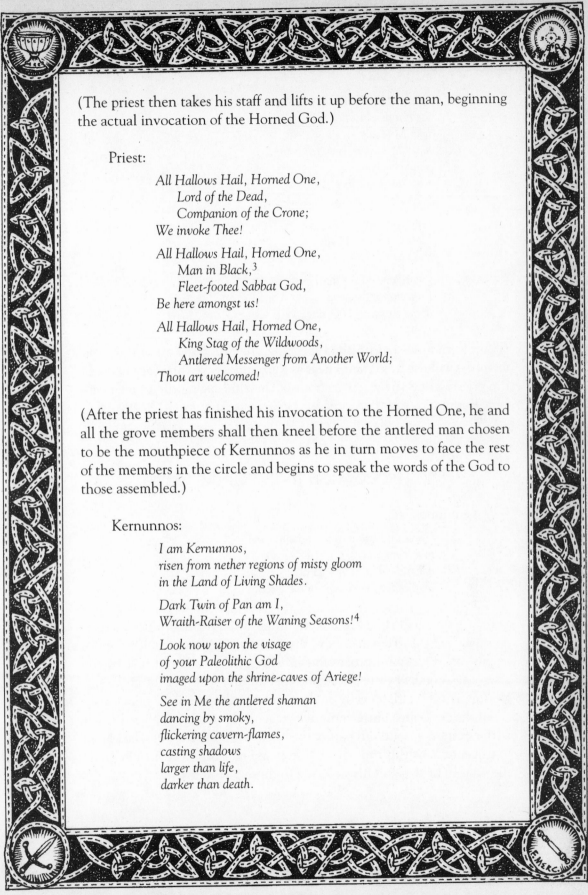

(The priest then takes his staff and lifts it up before the man, beginning the actual invocation of the Horned God.)

Priest:

> All Hallows Hail, Horned One,
>> Lord of the Dead,
>> Companion of the Crone;
> We invoke Thee!
>
> All Hallows Hail, Horned One,
>> Man in Black,[3]
>> Fleet-footed Sabbat God,
> Be here amongst us!
>
> All Hallows Hail, Horned One,
>> King Stag of the Wildwoods,
>> Antlered Messenger from Another World;
> Thou art welcomed!

(After the priest has finished his invocation to the Horned One, he and all the grove members shall then kneel before the antlered man chosen to be the mouthpiece of Kernunnos as he in turn moves to face the rest of the members in the circle and begins to speak the words of the God to those assembled.)

Kernunnos:

> I am Kernunnos,
> risen from nether regions of misty gloom
> in the Land of Living Shades.
>
> Dark Twin of Pan am I,
> Wraith-Raiser of the Waning Seasons![4]
>
> Look now upon the visage
> of your Paleolithic God
> imaged upon the shrine-caves of Ariege!
>
> See in Me the antlered shaman
> dancing by smoky,
> flickering cavern-flames,
> casting shadows
> larger than life,
> darker than death.

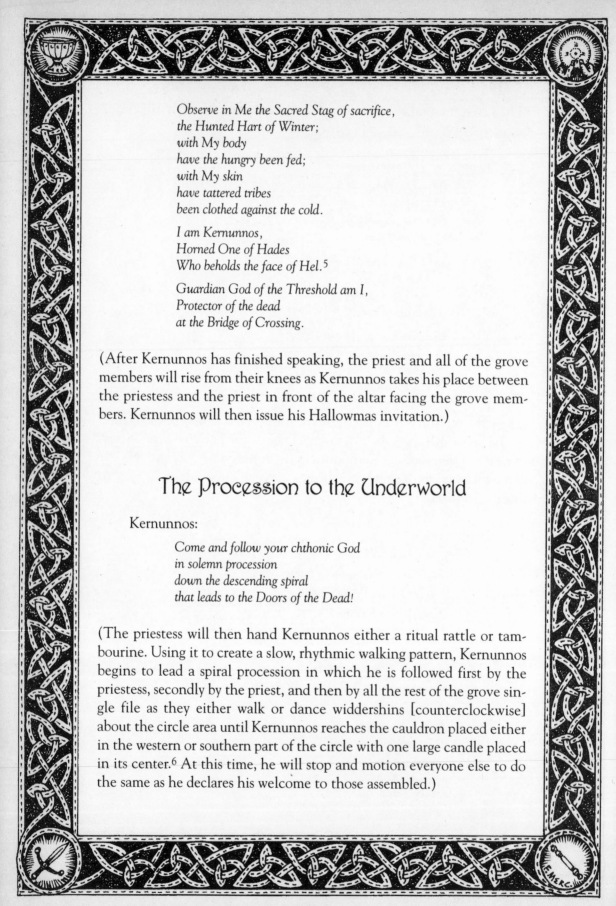

Observe in Me the Sacred Stag of sacrifice,
the Hunted Hart of Winter;
with My body
have the hungry been fed;
with My skin
have tattered tribes
been clothed against the cold.

I am Kernunnos,
Horned One of Hades
Who beholds the face of Hel.[5]

Guardian God of the Threshold am I,
Protector of the dead
at the Bridge of Crossing.

(After Kernunnos has finished speaking, the priest and all of the grove members will rise from their knees as Kernunnos takes his place between the priestess and the priest in front of the altar facing the grove members. Kernunnos will then issue his Hallowmas invitation.)

The Procession to the Underworld

Kernunnos:

Come and follow your chthonic God
in solemn procession
down the descending spiral
that leads to the Doors of the Dead!

(The priestess will then hand Kernunnos either a ritual rattle or tambourine. Using it to create a slow, rhythmic walking pattern, Kernunnos begins to lead a spiral procession in which he is followed first by the priestess, secondly by the priest, and then by all the rest of the grove single file as they either walk or dance widdershins [counterclockwise] about the circle area until Kernunnos reaches the cauldron placed either in the western or southern part of the circle with one large candle placed in its center.[6] At this time, he will stop and motion everyone else to do the same as he declares his welcome to those assembled.)

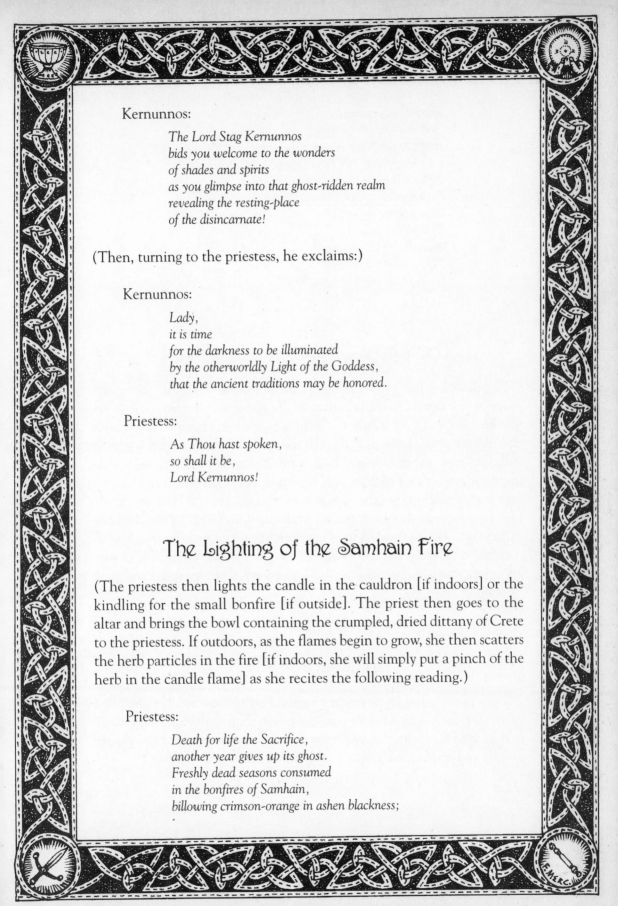

Kernunnos:

> *The Lord Stag Kernunnos*
> *bids you welcome to the wonders*
> *of shades and spirits*
> *as you glimpse into that ghost-ridden realm*
> *revealing the resting-place*
> *of the disincarnate!*

(Then, turning to the priestess, he exclaims:)

Kernunnos:

> *Lady,*
> *it is time*
> *for the darkness to be illuminated*
> *by the otherworldly Light of the Goddess,*
> *that the ancient traditions may be honored.*

Priestess:

> *As Thou hast spoken,*
> *so shall it be,*
> *Lord Kernunnos!*

The Lighting of the Samhain Fire

(The priestess then lights the candle in the cauldron [if indoors] or the kindling for the small bonfire [if outside]. The priest then goes to the altar and brings the bowl containing the crumpled, dried dittany of Crete to the priestess. If outdoors, as the flames begin to grow, she then scatters the herb particles in the fire [if indoors, she will simply put a pinch of the herb in the candle flame] as she recites the following reading.)

Priestess:

> *Death for life the Sacrifice,*
> *another year gives up its ghost.*
> *Freshly dead seasons consumed*
> *in the bonfires of Samhain,*
> *billowing crimson-orange in ashen blackness;*

spectral fiery incantations.
Goddess-summoned spirits
celebrate this Night between the years.
End, Beginning, No Time Betwixt,
cradle and grave in one.
Future faded, past returned,
all alive have died.
Dimensions departed,
merged with the moment;
Mystery the magick yarn
for Hekate's wraith-raising loom!

The Apple Offering for the Dead

(The priestess returns to stand before the altar, but facing the rest of the grove as she begins to explain that all are about to offer an apple [nuts like acorns can be substituted, if desired] for the memory of loved ones and friends which have passed on to the Land of Shadows. Each person will then pick an apple from a basket situated near the altar, and standing during a time of silence, will meditate upon the memory of loved ones before placing it in the cauldron around the central Hallows candle [or, if outdoors, it should be placed in the cauldron next to the bonfire]. Individuals will go forward to place their apple offerings to the dead as they are so moved. During this time, it may be considered suitable to sing an appropriate song or chant, such as a very slow, somber version of "Hoof and Horn.")[7]

The Great Rite

(At this point, if the group celebrating the Earth Rite is a fully established grove with an ordained priestess and/or priest, then shall begin the Liturgy of the Great Rite with the appropriate seasonal preface. [For the complete preface and text see the earlier section entitled "The Great Rite."])

The Grail Mass

(If the group celebrating the Earth Rite is a Grail Quest study circle with no one yet empowered through ordination into this Order to celebrate the Grail Mass, then they shall instead begin their time of teaching, discussion, or divination [of which an optional example is given below], led by an appointed facilitator. For an established grove, their time of teaching, discussion, or divination [of which an optional example is given below] shall follow immediately after the Grail Mass has been celebrated with a subsequent meditation. [For the complete text of the Eucharist, see the earlier section entitled "The Grail Mass."])

The Hallowmas Divination

([This following suggestion for group divination is purely optional.] The priestess will bid the grove to be seated. She will then take the deck of Tarot cards from their place on or below the altar along with the cloth on which she shall lay the Tarot spread from which the divination will be gleaned. The priestess will then say a spontaneous invocation for the gods and divining spirits to speak to the grove through the cards, giving advice, warning and wisdom about the grove's year to come. She will then spread the cloth, shuffle the cards, and spread out in a rainbow half-circle the entire deck with all cards face down. Each grove member will then be instructed to pick out a card to be laid face up in whatever manner of layout the priestess so directs. [The priestess will choose the first card and the priest will choose last in sequence after the rest of the grove. If more cards still need to be drawn for the layout, the sequence shall once again begin with the priestess picking out the next card after the priest has drawn the last previous card.] When the layout has been completed, an appointed person will then begin to copy the exact card placements in the grove's Book of Shadows so that it can be discussed and further interpreted at the next Lunar Rite [although, no doubt, there will be many comments from the grove members about their possible meanings for the grove as the appointed scribe is copying them down!] After the Tarot layout has been fully copied, the deck of cards will once again be mixed and thoroughly shuffled and spread out in a semicircle as before. This time the priestess will invite the Sabbat guests [non-members] to each choose one card from the face-down deck, and to meditate on it briefly as to what it might portend in their own lives. After a suitable time for meditation and discussion, the cards will again be mixed and shuffled by the priestess and cut three times by the priest before they are replaced upon the altar with the spread cloth.)

(At this point, the priestess may lead everyone in a grounding exercise to return all excess psychic energy back to the Earth of our Mother in order to avoid any unnecessary tension in the atmosphere.)

The Return Procession

(When the priestess and priest sense that it is time to draw the ritual to a close, they will bid everyone to rise. The priestess and priest will go to the altar, turn around and face the grove. Kernunnos shall take his place standing before them and facing them. [During the informalities the person designated as Kernunnos may take off his ceremonial headdress, but at this time the priest will replace it upon his head.] The priestess will then begin to speak.)

Priestess:

> Let us make ready for our journey
> back to the world
> where night follows day
> and moon follows sun,
> rotating the spinning cycles
> of season after season;
> where the tides of our lives
> shall wax and wane
> until we, too,
> must descend again
> into this nether-dimness
> among the shadowed spirits.

Priest:

> Lord Kernunnos,
> it is time that we depart
> Thy dark Domain.
>
> Dread God of Death,
> Thou alone can take us back
> to that dimension
> where light and life are intertwined
> to make for the brightness
> of our momentary incarnations
> before we must return again
> to Thy caring embrace.
>
> We beseech Thee,
> O Stag Lord of Autumn's Night,
> while the psychic Veil
> that divides the dead from the living
> is still transparently thin,
> grant us guidance between the worlds
> to the safety of the realm above.

(When the priest has finished his entreaty, Kernunnos shall lift up his right hand, palm outward, as in a command for silence, before he begins his reply.)

Kernunnos:

> Lady and Lord,
> as you have asked,
> so shall it be done!
>
> In these night-draped regions of Persephone
> there is serenity and rest
> for those labored of life and tired of heart,
> but your time has not yet come.
>
> Follow now in My hoof prints
> and you shall all cross in safety
> the bridge between the worlds.

(The priestess will then hand Kernunnos either a ceremonial rattle or tambourine, and both she and the priest will bow to him. Kernunnos will begin creating the same rhythm as in his previous procession earlier. He will start walking or dancing in a deosil [clockwise] spiral, beginning in the center of the circle at the altar, followed by the priestess and priest, and then by all the rest of the grove. When the spiral procession has reached the boundaries of the circle, Kernunnos will signal for all to stop and face the eastern quarter as he takes his place behind them all in the western quarter of the circle. He will at this time take off his headdress, unobserved by the rest of the grove, while he speaks his parting words.)

Kernunnos:

> Turn towards the lantern
> at the Eastern Gate,
> the glowing lamplight
> at the Quarter of the Rising Sun.
>
> See there in prophecy
> the insatiable Satyr,
> Spring's Horned Pan
> in pursuit of the Maiden's pleasure,
> for life must always follow death;
> this, the fallow season,
> must be followed by the fertile.
>
> But it is now I Who reign
> in the dying of Autumn
> and the snowy slumber of Winter's repose.
>
> As I take My leave,
> look not behind you
> lest I take you with Me
> into the infernal Abyss
> that divides the dimensions,
> for I go the Way of the Gods,
> and My Secret Mysteries
> are not for you to know.
>
> The blessings of All Hallows
> be upon you,
> and the granted guidance of the Crone
> be your portion.
>
> All Hail, Farewell, and Blessed Be!

(After Kernunnos has spoken, there will be a space of silence for about 30 seconds before the priest will turn around to face the others and exclaim:)

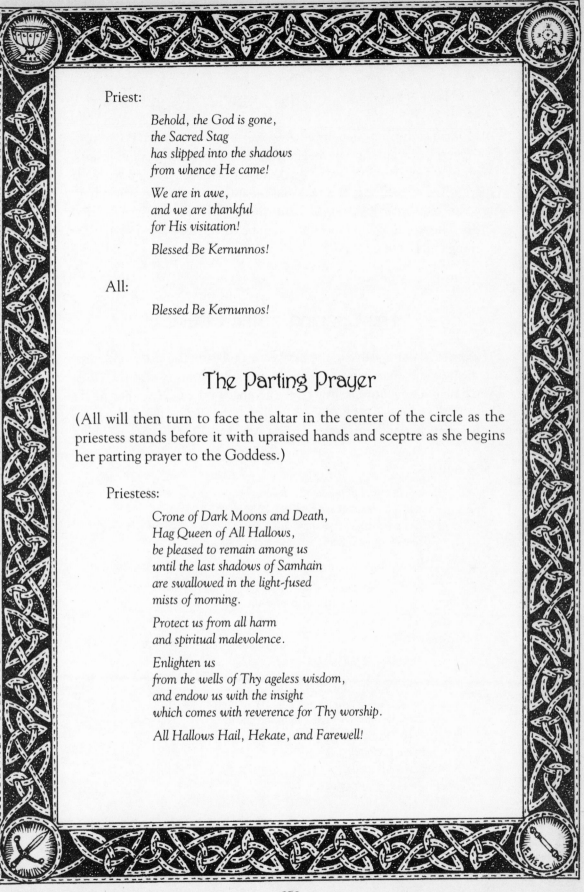

Priest:

> Behold, the God is gone,
> the Sacred Stag
> has slipped into the shadows
> from whence He came!
>
> We are in awe,
> and we are thankful
> for His visitation!
>
> Blessed Be Kernunnos!

All:

> Blessed Be Kernunnos!

The Parting Prayer

(All will then turn to face the altar in the center of the circle as the priestess stands before it with upraised hands and sceptre as she begins her parting prayer to the Goddess.)

Priestess:

> Crone of Dark Moons and Death,
> Hag Queen of All Hallows,
> be pleased to remain among us
> until the last shadows of Samhain
> are swallowed in the light-fused
> mists of morning.
>
> Protect us from all harm
> and spiritual malevolence.
>
> Enlighten us
> from the wells of Thy ageless wisdom,
> and endow us with the insight
> which comes with reverence for Thy worship.
>
> All Hallows Hail, Hekate, and Farewell!

The Dismissal of the Quarter-Regents

(At this time, the same appointed grove members that called the respective Quarter-Regents in the beginning of the ritual will now dismiss Them to Their own domains. The dismissal will always begin with the Quarter-Regent who has the seasonal preeminence. [West for Hallowmas, the sequence of dismissal continuing with the south, east, and north.] The wording and procedure shall be the same as is found in "The Opening and Closing Rites.")

The Opening of the Circle

(The priest takes his glaive to the marked boundary of the circle, and starting at the same quarter from which he initially began to cast the circle [west], he once again walks the circumference of the circle, pointing his glaive at the boundary as he goes, visualizing the dissipation of the blue-white spherical walls of the sacred space as he says the following words.)

Priest:

> *Circle round of the sacred Sphere,*
> *may Thy boundaries be dissolved.*
> *Thy purpose is accomplished,*
> *Thy work well done.*
>
> *Blessed Be!*

(The priestess will make the final proclamation of the ritual's conclusion.)

Priestess:

> *This rite of Hallowmas is ended!*
>
> *May shadows and spirits*
> *guide you towards*
> *the dark-crystalled wisdom of the Crone*
> *as you learn to be at peace*
> *in the season of death*
> *that leads to life.*
>
> *Merry Meet and Merry Part!*

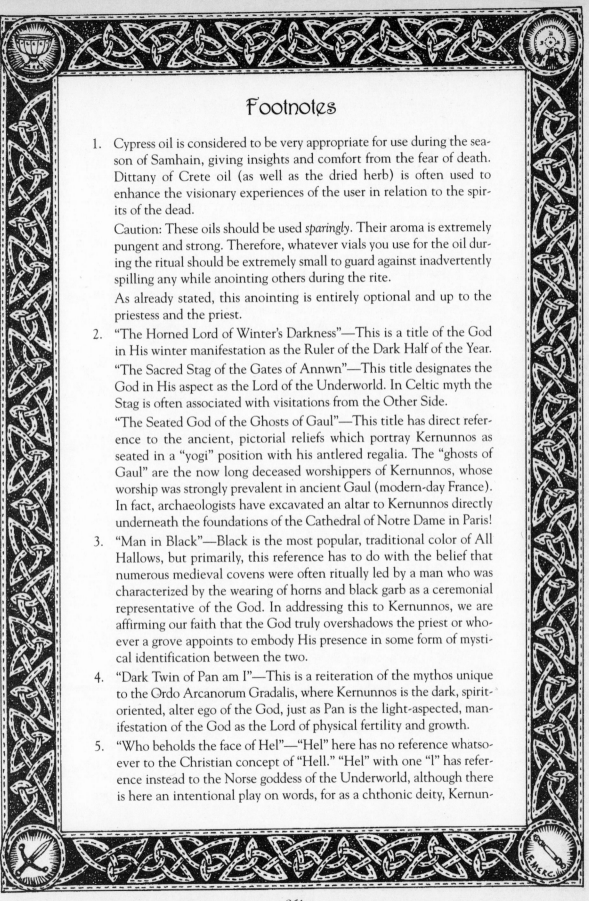

Footnotes

1. Cypress oil is considered to be very appropriate for use during the season of Samhain, giving insights and comfort from the fear of death. Dittany of Crete oil (as well as the dried herb) is often used to enhance the visionary experiences of the user in relation to the spirits of the dead.

    Caution: These oils should be used *sparingly*. Their aroma is extremely pungent and strong. Therefore, whatever vials you use for the oil during the ritual should be extremely small to guard against inadvertently spilling any while anointing others during the rite.

    As already stated, this anointing is entirely optional and up to the priestess and the priest.

2. "The Horned Lord of Winter's Darkness"—This is a title of the God in His winter manifestation as the Ruler of the Dark Half of the Year.

    "The Sacred Stag of the Gates of Annwn"—This title designates the God in His aspect as the Lord of the Underworld. In Celtic myth the Stag is often associated with visitations from the Other Side.

    "The Seated God of the Ghosts of Gaul"—This title has direct reference to the ancient, pictorial reliefs which portray Kernunnos as seated in a "yogi" position with his antlered regalia. The "ghosts of Gaul" are the now long deceased worshippers of Kernunnos, whose worship was strongly prevalent in ancient Gaul (modern-day France). In fact, archaeologists have excavated an altar to Kernunnos directly underneath the foundations of the Cathedral of Notre Dame in Paris!

3. "Man in Black"—Black is the most popular, traditional color of All Hallows, but primarily, this reference has to do with the belief that numerous medieval covens were often ritually led by a man who was characterized by the wearing of horns and black garb as a ceremonial representative of the God. In addressing this to Kernunnos, we are affirming our faith that the God truly overshadows the priest or whoever a grove appoints to embody His presence in some form of mystical identification between the two.

4. "Dark Twin of Pan am I"—This is a reiteration of the mythos unique to the Ordo Arcanorum Gradalis, where Kernunnos is the dark, spirit-oriented, alter ego of the God, just as Pan is the light-aspected, manifestation of the God as the Lord of physical fertility and growth.

5. "Who beholds the face of Hel"—"Hel" here has no reference whatsoever to the Christian concept of "Hell." "Hel" with one "l" has reference instead to the Norse goddess of the Underworld, although there is here an intentional play on words, for as a chthonic deity, Kernun-

241

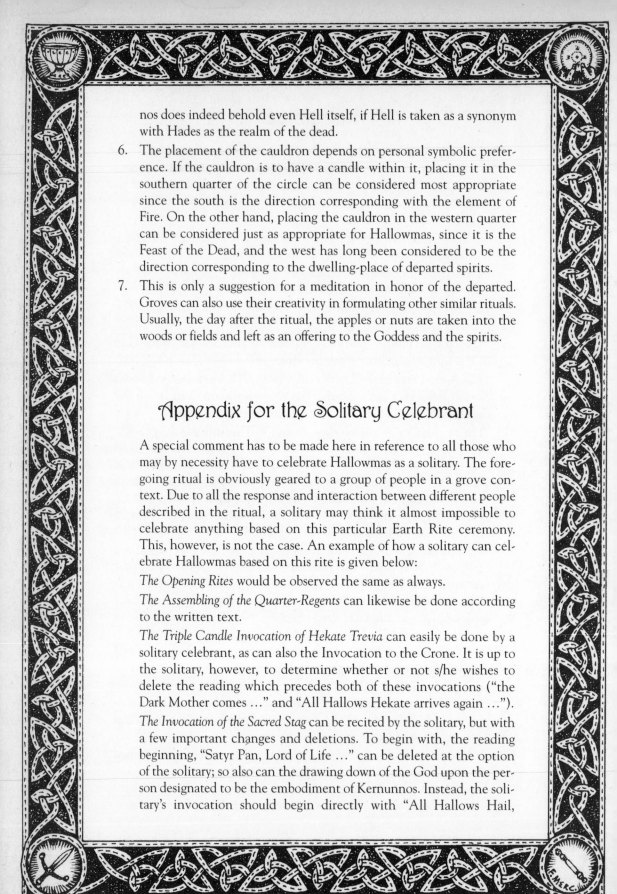

nos does indeed behold even Hell itself, if Hell is taken as a synonym with Hades as the realm of the dead.

6. The placement of the cauldron depends on personal symbolic preference. If the cauldron is to have a candle within it, placing it in the southern quarter of the circle can be considered most appropriate since the south is the direction corresponding with the element of Fire. On the other hand, placing the cauldron in the western quarter can be considered just as appropriate for Hallowmas, since it is the Feast of the Dead, and the west has long been considered to be the direction corresponding to the dwelling-place of departed spirits.

7. This is only a suggestion for a meditation in honor of the departed. Groves can also use their creativity in formulating other similar rituals. Usually, the day after the ritual, the apples or nuts are taken into the woods or fields and left as an offering to the Goddess and the spirits.

Appendix for the Solitary Celebrant

A special comment has to be made here in reference to all those who may by necessity have to celebrate Hallowmas as a solitary. The foregoing ritual is obviously geared to a group of people in a grove context. Due to all the response and interaction between different people described in the ritual, a solitary may think it almost impossible to celebrate anything based on this particular Earth Rite ceremony. This, however, is not the case. An example of how a solitary can celebrate Hallowmas based on this rite is given below:

The Opening Rites would be observed the same as always.

The Assembling of the Quarter-Regents can likewise be done according to the written text.

The Triple Candle Invocation of Hekate Trevia can easily be done by a solitary celebrant, as can also the Invocation to the Crone. It is up to the solitary, however, to determine whether or not s/he wishes to delete the reading which precedes both of these invocations ("the Dark Mother comes …" and "All Hallows Hekate arrives again …").

The Invocation of the Sacred Stag can be recited by the solitary, but with a few important changes and deletions. To begin with, the reading beginning, "Satyr Pan, Lord of Life …" can be deleted at the option of the solitary; so also can the drawing down of the God upon the person designated to be the embodiment of Kernunnos. Instead, the solitary's invocation should begin directly with "All Hallows Hail,

Horned One ..." as a simple prayer before the altar. However, the recitation "I am Kernunnos, risen from nether regions of misty gloom ..." needs to be slightly changed so that it can be transformed into a statement of spiritual affirmation on the part of the solitary regarding the power of the Dark, Horned God. This revision is given below:

> Thou art Kernunnos,
> risen from nether regions of misty gloom
> in the Land of Living Shades.
>
> Dark Twin of Pan art Thou,
> wraith raiser of the waning seasons!
>
> In Thee I see the visage
> of the Paleolithic God
> imaged upon the shrine-caves of Ariege!
>
> In Thee I see the antlered shaman
> dancing by smoky,
> flickering cavern-flames,
> casting shadows
> larger than life,
> darker than death.
>
> In Thee I observe the Sacred Stag of Sacrifice,
> the Hunted Hart of Winter;
> with Thy body
> have the hungry been fed,
> with Thy skin
> have tattered tribes
> been clothed against the cold.
>
> Thou art Kernunnos,
> Horned One of Hades
> Who beholds the face of Hel!
>
> Guardian God of the Threshold art Thou,
> Protector of the dead
> at the Bridge of Crossing!

The Procession to the Underworld would be eliminated by the solitary. Instead, s/he would skip it and go directly to *The Lighting of the Samhain Fire* which can easily remain intact for a solitary observance, as can *The Apple Offering for the Dead*.

For an ordained solitary, *The Great Rite* and *The Grail Mass* would be celebrated as usual. For those not yet ordained, these rites would be skipped and the time for meditation or personal divination would begin.

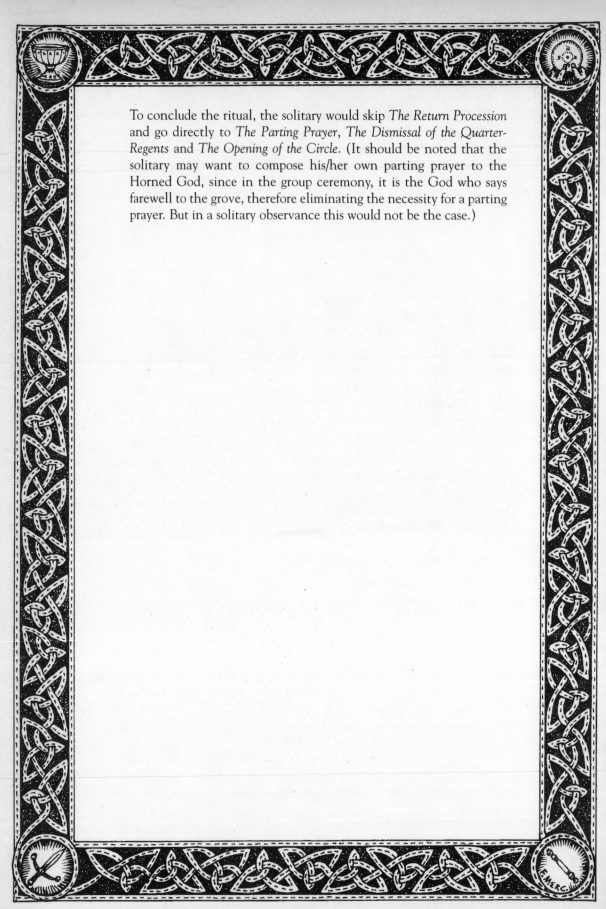

To conclude the ritual, the solitary would skip *The Return Procession* and go directly to *The Parting Prayer*, *The Dismissal of the Quarter-Regents* and *The Opening of the Circle*. (It should be noted that the solitary may want to compose his/her own parting prayer to the Horned God, since in the group ceremony, it is the God who says farewell to the grove, therefore eliminating the necessity for a parting prayer. But in a solitary observance this would not be the case.)

The Assembling of the Quarter-Regents: Saluting the southern quarter with the candle-lantern. "Regents of the South, Sovereigns of Fire and Flame ..."

Winter Solstice

Basic Requirements

Below are some things to remember for the Low Earth Rite of the Winter Solstice which are necessary requirements if the observance is to be in accordance with the rubrics of the Ordo Arcanorum Gradalis.

Altar

The altar should be in the center of the circle area, facing the northern quarter.

Altar Cloth

The altar cloth should always be green for the Low Earth Rite of the Winter Solstice. (This is only if you are using a regular rectangular altar. If you are using the Altar of the Pentagram, see the earlier chapter entitled "The Altar and the Sacred Tools" for further details and instructions.)

Altar Candles

The two main altar candles should be green for the Low Earth Rite of the Winter Solstice.

Other Candles

The four quarter candles (or glass votive candleholders) *should always be blue in the west, red in the south, yellow (or gold) in the east, and green in the north.* All other secondary candles used for extra lighting in the ritual area should be of various shades of brown (for the barren branches of the winter woods) and red (for the red of holly berries and the blood of the Hunted Hart [the Sacred Stag]), or other colors suitable to the grove's personal tastes.

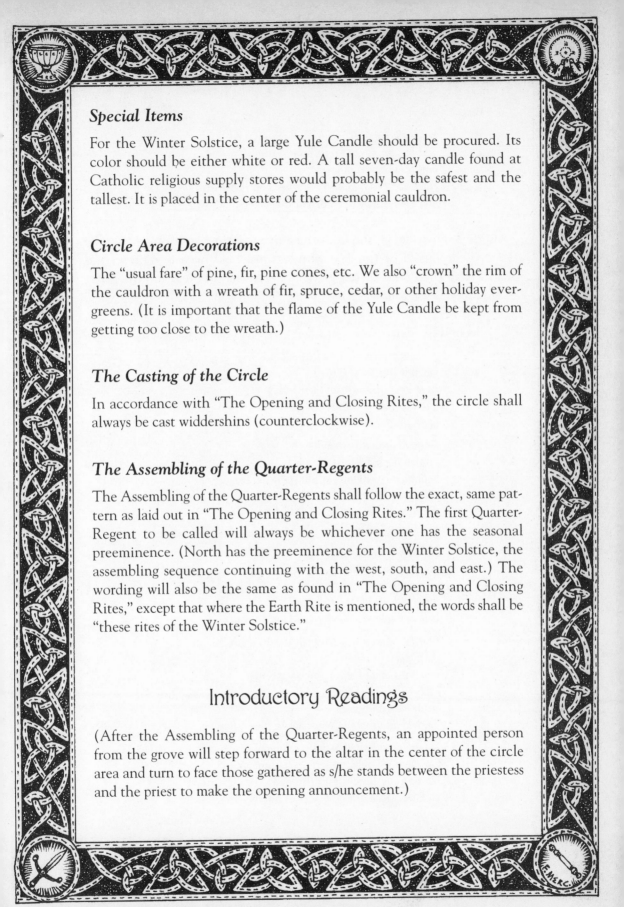

Special Items

For the Winter Solstice, a large Yule Candle should be procured. Its color should be either white or red. A tall seven-day candle found at Catholic religious supply stores would probably be the safest and the tallest. It is placed in the center of the ceremonial cauldron.

Circle Area Decorations

The "usual fare" of pine, fir, pine cones, etc. We also "crown" the rim of the cauldron with a wreath of fir, spruce, cedar, or other holiday evergreens. (It is important that the flame of the Yule Candle be kept from getting too close to the wreath.)

The Casting of the Circle

In accordance with "The Opening and Closing Rites," the circle shall always be cast widdershins (counterclockwise).

The Assembling of the Quarter-Regents

The Assembling of the Quarter-Regents shall follow the exact, same pattern as laid out in "The Opening and Closing Rites." The first Quarter-Regent to be called will always be whichever one has the seasonal preeminence. (North has the preeminence for the Winter Solstice, the assembling sequence continuing with the west, south, and east.) The wording will also be the same as found in "The Opening and Closing Rites," except that where the Earth Rite is mentioned, the words shall be "these rites of the Winter Solstice."

Introductory Readings

(After the Assembling of the Quarter-Regents, an appointed person from the grove will step forward to the altar in the center of the circle area and turn to face those gathered as s/he stands between the priestess and the priest to make the opening announcement.)

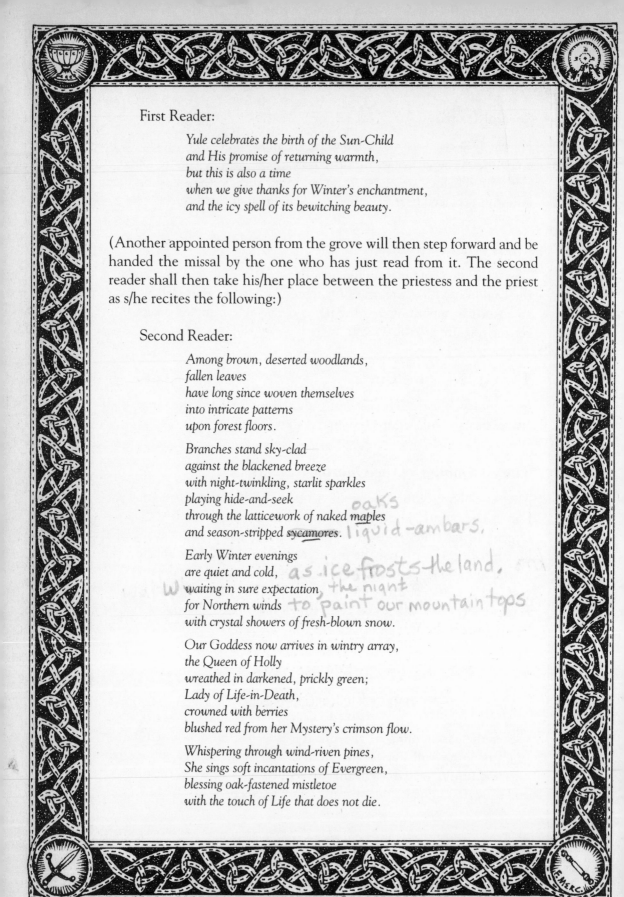

First Reader:

Yule celebrates the birth of the Sun-Child
and His promise of returning warmth,
but this is also a time
when we give thanks for Winter's enchantment,
and the icy spell of its bewitching beauty.

(Another appointed person from the grove will then step forward and be handed the missal by the one who has just read from it. The second reader shall then take his/her place between the priestess and the priest as s/he recites the following:)

Second Reader:

Among brown, deserted woodlands,
fallen leaves
have long since woven themselves
into intricate patterns
upon forest floors.

Branches stand sky-clad
against the blackened breeze
with night-twinkling, starlit sparkles
playing hide-and-seek
through the latticework of naked maples oaks
and season-stripped sycamores. liquid-ambars,

Early Winter evenings
are quiet and cold, as ice frosts the land,
W *waiting in sure expectation,* the night
for Northern winds to paint our mountain tops
with crystal showers of fresh-blown snow.

Our Goddess now arrives in wintry array,
the Queen of Holly
wreathed in darkened, prickly green;
Lady of Life-in-Death,
crowned with berries
blushed red from her Mystery's crimson flow.

Whispering through wind-riven pines,
She sings soft incantations of Evergreen,
blessing oak-fastened mistletoe
with the touch of Life that does not die.

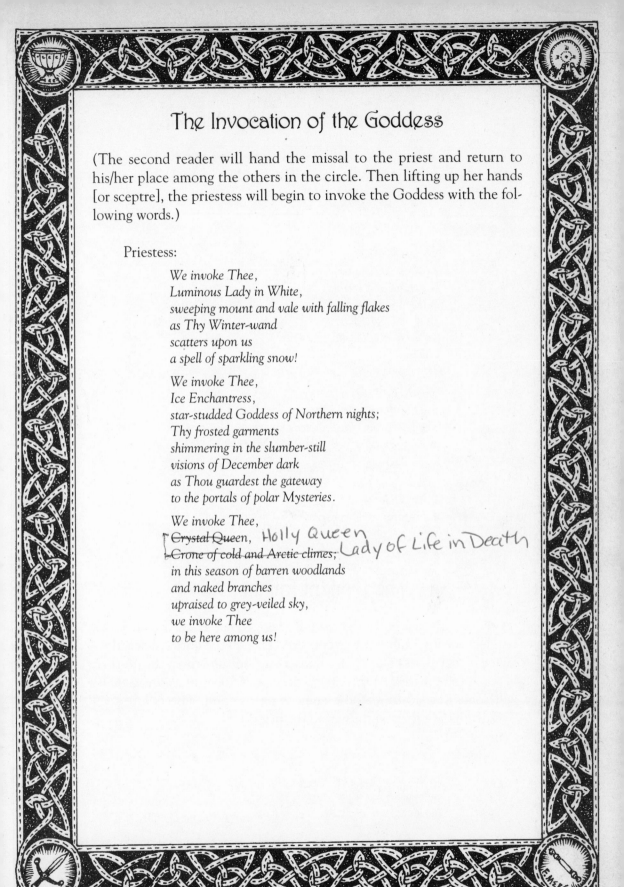

The Invocation of the Goddess

(The second reader will hand the missal to the priest and return to his/her place among the others in the circle. Then lifting up her hands [or sceptre], the priestess will begin to invoke the Goddess with the following words.)

Priestess:

We invoke Thee,
Luminous Lady in White,
sweeping mount and vale with falling flakes
as Thy Winter-wand
scatters upon us
a spell of sparkling snow!

We invoke Thee,
Ice Enchantress,
star-studded Goddess of Northern nights;
Thy frosted garments
shimmering in the slumber-still
visions of December dark
as Thou guardest the gateway
to the portals of polar Mysteries.

We invoke Thee,
~~Crystal Queen,~~ Holly Queen *Lady of Life in Death*
~~Crone of cold and Arctic climes;~~
in this season of barren woodlands
and naked branches
upraised to grey-veiled sky,
we invoke Thee
to be here among us!

The Invocation of the Sacred Stag

(The priestess then picks up the antlered headdress of Kernunnos and places it upon the head of the priest. He then lifts up his hands [or sceptre/staff] to invoke the Sacred Stag, saying:)

Priest:

> *We invoke Thee,*
> *antlered Ancient One,*
> *both Lord and Victim*
> *of the Winter's hunt;*
> *giver of Thy flesh*
> *for the love of our lives,*
> *in this,*
> *Thy season of Sacrifice.*
>
> *We invoke Thee,*
> *shape-shifting Solstice Stag,*
> *Thy hoof prints brushed away by driven snow*
> *as Thou guardest the pathways to the Invisible.*
>
> *Winter-reigning forest-phantom,*
> *be here among us*
> *as we celebrate*
> *this turning of the Solar Wheel!*

The Lament for the Sun

(After the invocation of the Sacred Stag is completed, the priest will hand his sceptre/staff to the priestess and take off the antlered headdress, laying it back in its proper place [either on a side altar or at the northern quarter of the circle]. At this time, a previously appointed grove member will come forward to read the Lament for the Sun. The priestess will then hand back the sceptre/staff to the priest.)

Reader:

> *In this season of lengthening night,*
> *ever earlier we strike*
> *the lanterns of eventide*

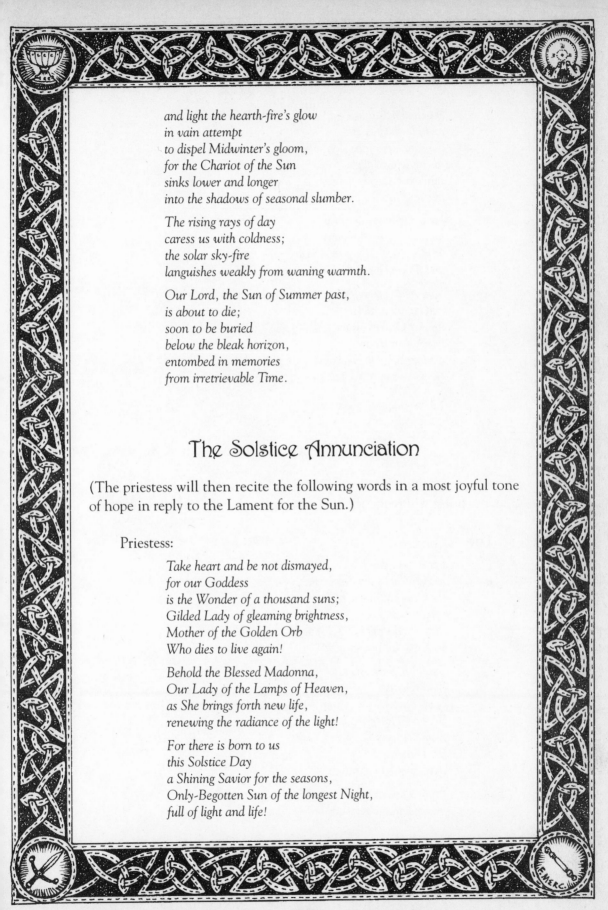

and light the hearth-fire's glow
in vain attempt
to dispel Midwinter's gloom,
for the Chariot of the Sun
sinks lower and longer
into the shadows of seasonal slumber.

The rising rays of day
caress us with coldness;
the solar sky-fire
languishes weakly from waning warmth.

Our Lord, the Sun of Summer past,
is about to die;
soon to be buried
below the bleak horizon,
entombed in memories
from irretrievable Time.

The Solstice Annunciation

(The priestess will then recite the following words in a most joyful tone
of hope in reply to the Lament for the Sun.)

Priestess:

Take heart and be not dismayed,
for our Goddess
is the Wonder of a thousand suns;
Gilded Lady of gleaming brightness,
Mother of the Golden Orb
Who dies to live again!

Behold the Blessed Madonna,
Our Lady of the Lamps of Heaven,
as She brings forth new life,
renewing the radiance of the light!

For there is born to us
this Solstice Day
a Shining Savior for the seasons,
Only-Begotten Sun of the longest Night,
full of light and life!

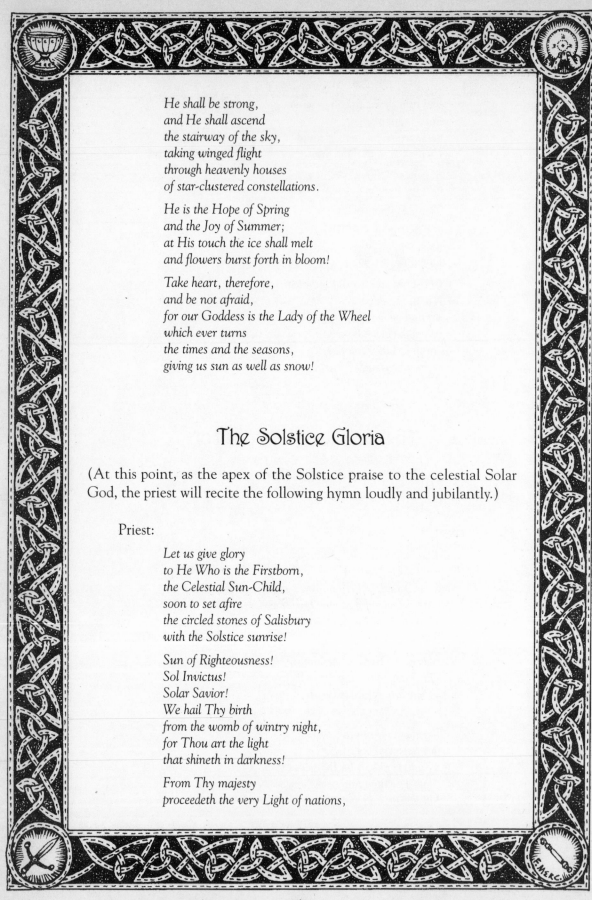

He shall be strong,
and He shall ascend
the stairway of the sky,
taking winged flight
through heavenly houses
of star-clustered constellations.

He is the Hope of Spring
and the Joy of Summer;
at His touch the ice shall melt
and flowers burst forth in bloom!

Take heart, therefore,
and be not afraid,
for our Goddess is the Lady of the Wheel
which ever turns
the times and the seasons,
giving us sun as well as snow!

The Solstice Gloria

(At this point, as the apex of the Solstice praise to the celestial Solar God, the priest will recite the following hymn loudly and jubilantly.)

Priest:

Let us give glory
to He Who is the Firstborn,
the Celestial Sun-Child,
soon to set afire
the circled stones of Salisbury
with the Solstice sunrise!

Sun of Righteousness!
Sol Invictus!
Solar Savior!
We hail Thy birth
from the womb of wintry night,
for Thou art the light
that shineth in darkness!

From Thy majesty
proceedeth the very Light of nations,

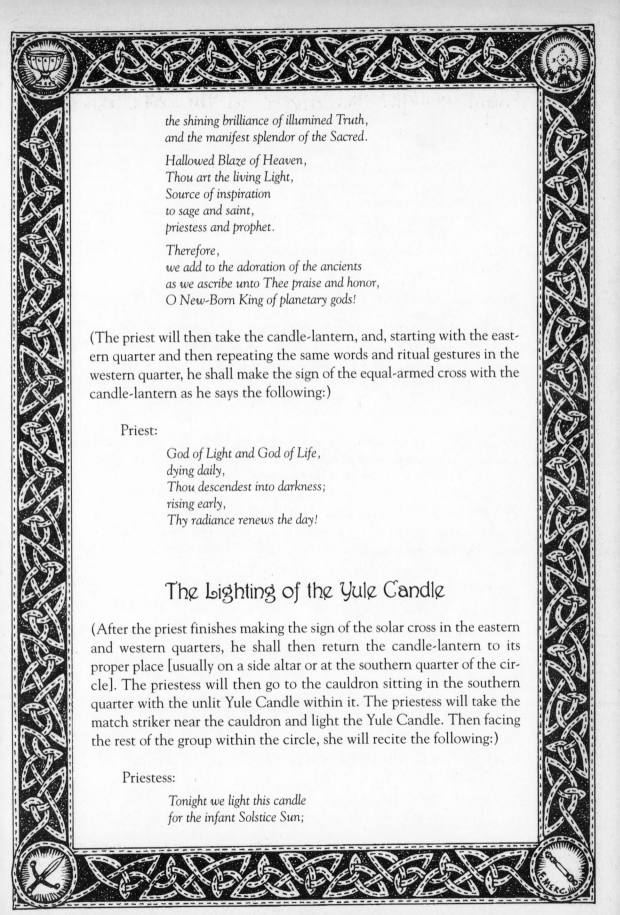

the shining brilliance of illumined Truth,
and the manifest splendor of the Sacred.

Hallowed Blaze of Heaven,
Thou art the living Light,
Source of inspiration
to sage and saint,
priestess and prophet.

Therefore,
we add to the adoration of the ancients
as we ascribe unto Thee praise and honor,
O New-Born King of planetary gods!

(The priest will then take the candle-lantern, and, starting with the eastern quarter and then repeating the same words and ritual gestures in the western quarter, he shall make the sign of the equal-armed cross with the candle-lantern as he says the following:)

Priest:

God of Light and God of Life,
dying daily,
Thou descendest into darkness;
rising early,
Thy radiance renews the day!

The Lighting of the Yule Candle

(After the priest finishes making the sign of the solar cross in the eastern and western quarters, he shall then return the candle-lantern to its proper place [usually on a side altar or at the southern quarter of the circle]. The priestess will then go to the cauldron sitting in the southern quarter with the unlit Yule Candle within it. The priestess will take the match striker near the cauldron and light the Yule Candle. Then facing the rest of the group within the circle, she will recite the following:)

Priestess:

Tonight we light this candle
for the infant Solstice Sun;

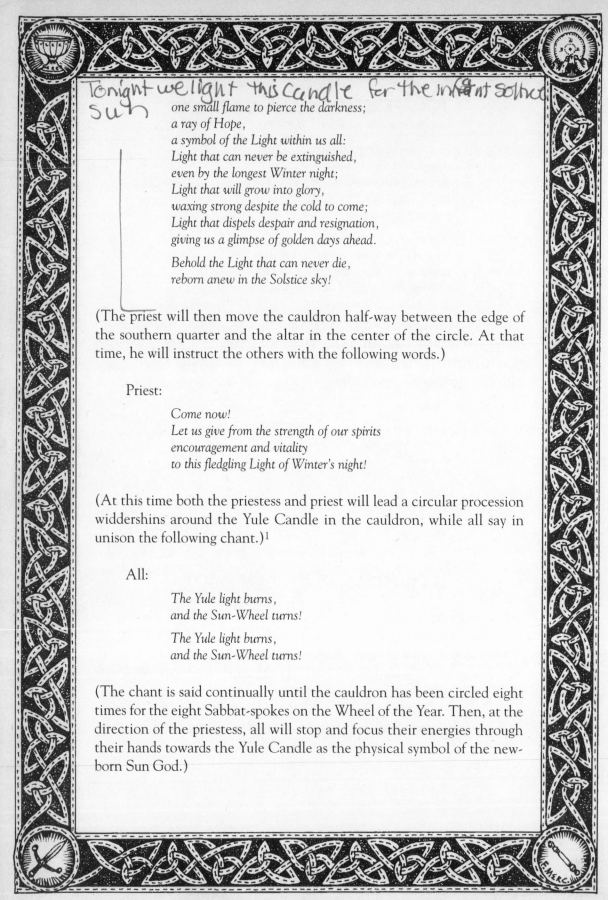

Tonight we light this candle for the infant solstice sun [handwritten annotation]

one small flame to pierce the darkness;
a ray of Hope,
a symbol of the Light within us all:
Light that can never be extinguished,
even by the longest Winter night;
Light that will grow into glory,
waxing strong despite the cold to come;
Light that dispels despair and resignation,
giving us a glimpse of golden days ahead.

Behold the Light that can never die,
reborn anew in the Solstice sky!

(The priest will then move the cauldron half-way between the edge of the southern quarter and the altar in the center of the circle. At that time, he will instruct the others with the following words.)

Priest:

Come now!
Let us give from the strength of our spirits
encouragement and vitality
to this fledgling Light of Winter's night!

(At this time both the priestess and priest will lead a circular procession widdershins around the Yule Candle in the cauldron, while all say in unison the following chant.)[1]

All:

The Yule light burns,
and the Sun-Wheel turns!

The Yule light burns,
and the Sun-Wheel turns!

(The chant is said continually until the cauldron has been circled eight times for the eight Sabbat-spokes on the Wheel of the Year. Then, at the direction of the priestess, all will stop and focus their energies through their hands towards the Yule Candle as the physical symbol of the new-born Sun God.)

254

The Great Rite

(At this point, if the group celebrating the Earth Rite is a fully established grove with an ordained priestess and/or priest, then shall begin the liturgy of the Great Rite with the appropriate seasonal preface. [For the complete preface and text, see the earlier section entitled "The Great Rite."])

The Grail Mass

(If the group celebrating the Earth Rite is a Grail Quest study circle with no one yet empowered through ordination into this Order to celebrate the Grail Mass, then they shall instead begin their time of teaching and discussion, led by an appointed facilitator. For an established grove, their time of teaching and discussion shall follow immediately after the Grail Mass has been celebrated with a subsequent meditation. [For the complete text of the Eucharist see the earlier section entitled "The Grail Mass."])

The Parting Prayers

(When both the priestess and the priest sense that the time has come to close the rites and open the circle, they will bid everyone to stand. The priestess will stand before the altar facing the northern quarter, and lifting up her hands [or sceptre], she will speak the following prayer.)

Priestess:

> *Glimmering Goddess,*
> *draped in the blackened folds*
> *of the galaxies which art Thy garment,*
> *once again Thou hast given birth*
> *to Thy Celestial Sun,*
> *the reborn Christ* the reborn child
> *of the ever-turning Solar Wheel!*
>
> *O Heavenly Virgin, Lady*
> *Thou hast brought forth Thy Son*
> *that we might live in the Light!*[2] for this we give thanks
> rejiocing in this ebb + flow of Solticetide

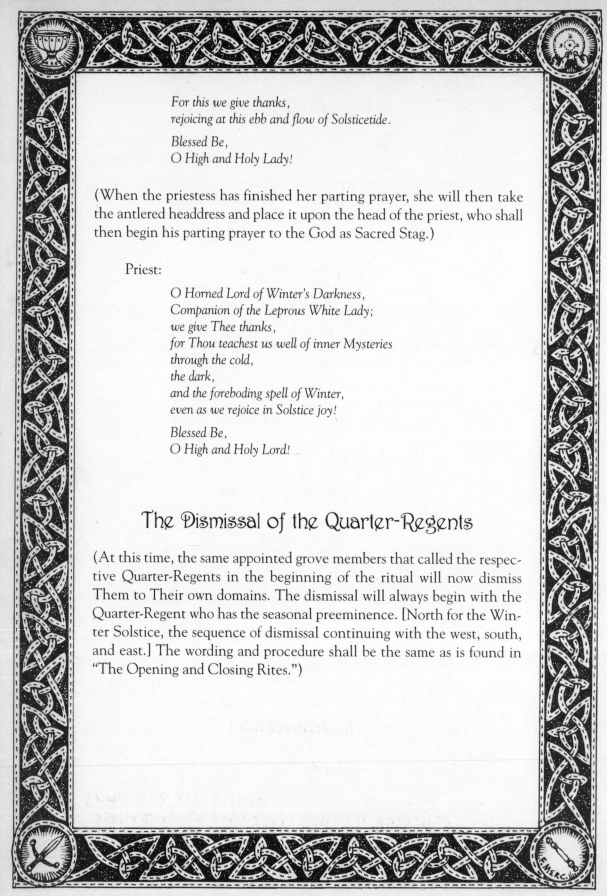

For this we give thanks,
rejoicing at this ebb and flow of Solsticetide.

Blessed Be,
O High and Holy Lady!

(When the priestess has finished her parting prayer, she will then take the antlered headdress and place it upon the head of the priest, who shall then begin his parting prayer to the God as Sacred Stag.)

Priest:

O Horned Lord of Winter's Darkness,
Companion of the Leprous White Lady;
we give Thee thanks,
for Thou teachest us well of inner Mysteries
through the cold,
the dark,
and the foreboding spell of Winter,
even as we rejoice in Solstice joy!

Blessed Be,
O High and Holy Lord!

The Dismissal of the Quarter-Regents

(At this time, the same appointed grove members that called the respective Quarter-Regents in the beginning of the ritual will now dismiss Them to Their own domains. The dismissal will always begin with the Quarter-Regent who has the seasonal preeminence. [North for the Winter Solstice, the sequence of dismissal continuing with the west, south, and east.] The wording and procedure shall be the same as is found in "The Opening and Closing Rites.")

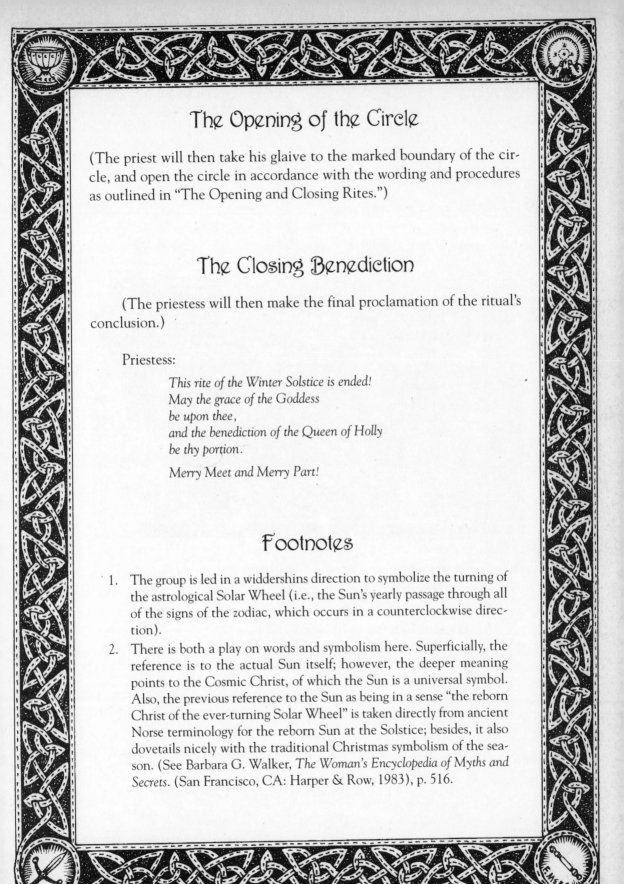

The Opening of the Circle

(The priest will then take his glaive to the marked boundary of the circle, and open the circle in accordance with the wording and procedures as outlined in "The Opening and Closing Rites.")

The Closing Benediction

(The priestess will then make the final proclamation of the ritual's conclusion.)

Priestess:

> *This rite of the Winter Solstice is ended!*
> *May the grace of the Goddess*
> *be upon thee,*
> *and the benediction of the Queen of Holly*
> *be thy portion.*
>
> *Merry Meet and Merry Part!*

Footnotes

1. The group is led in a widdershins direction to symbolize the turning of the astrological Solar Wheel (i.e., the Sun's yearly passage through all of the signs of the zodiac, which occurs in a counterclockwise direction).

2. There is both a play on words and symbolism here. Superficially, the reference is to the actual Sun itself; however, the deeper meaning points to the Cosmic Christ, of which the Sun is a universal symbol. Also, the previous reference to the Sun as being in a sense "the reborn Christ of the ever-turning Solar Wheel" is taken directly from ancient Norse terminology for the reborn Sun at the Solstice; besides, it also dovetails nicely with the traditional Christmas symbolism of the season. (See Barbara G. Walker, *The Woman's Encyclopedia of Myths and Secrets.* (San Francisco, CA: Harper & Row, 1983), p. 516.

Invocation of the God: "We invoke Thee, antlered Ancient One ..."

Candlemas

Basic Requirements

Below are some things to remember for the High Earth Rite of Candlemas which are necessary requirements if the observance is to be in accordance with the rubrics of the Ordo Arcanorum Gradalis.

Altar

The altar should be in the center of the circle area, facing the northern quarter.

Altar Cloth

The altar cloth should always be green for the High Earth Rite of Candlemas. (This is only if you are using a regular rectangular altar. If you are using the Altar of the Pentagram, see the earlier chapter entitled "The Altar and the Sacred Tools" for further details and instructions.)

Altar Candles

The two main altar candles should be green for the High Earth Rite of Candlemas.

Other Candles

The four quarter candles (or glass votive candleholders) *should always be blue in the west, red in the south, yellow (or gold) in the east, and green in the north.* All other secondary candles used for extra lighting in the ritual area should be of various shades of white (for purification), and brown (a reminder that winter is still with us). Other colors are optional, depending on the grove's personal tastes.

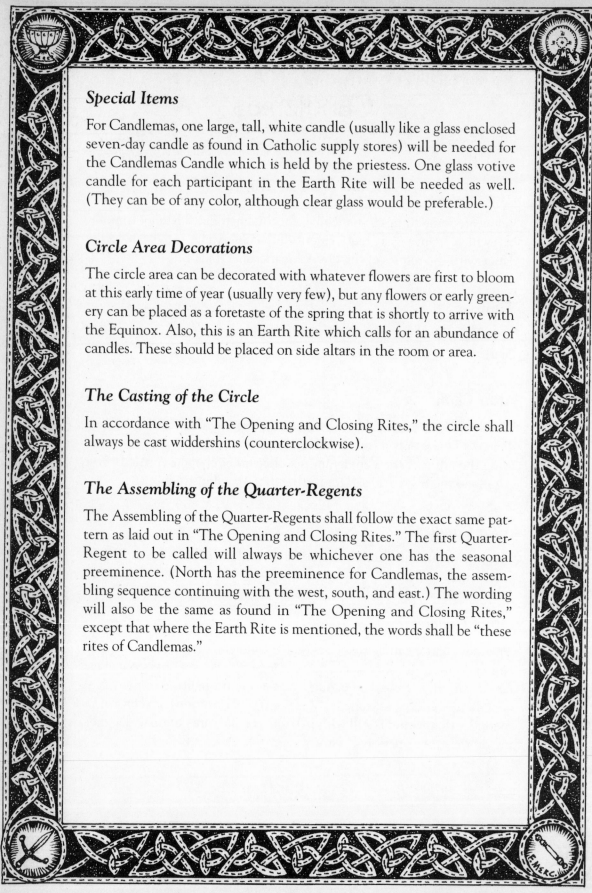

Special Items

For Candlemas, one large, tall, white candle (usually like a glass enclosed seven-day candle as found in Catholic supply stores) will be needed for the Candlemas Candle which is held by the priestess. One glass votive candle for each participant in the Earth Rite will be needed as well. (They can be of any color, although clear glass would be preferable.)

Circle Area Decorations

The circle area can be decorated with whatever flowers are first to bloom at this early time of year (usually very few), but any flowers or early greenery can be placed as a foretaste of the spring that is shortly to arrive with the Equinox. Also, this is an Earth Rite which calls for an abundance of candles. These should be placed on side altars in the room or area.

The Casting of the Circle

In accordance with "The Opening and Closing Rites," the circle shall always be cast widdershins (counterclockwise).

The Assembling of the Quarter-Regents

The Assembling of the Quarter-Regents shall follow the exact same pattern as laid out in "The Opening and Closing Rites." The first Quarter-Regent to be called will always be whichever one has the seasonal preeminence. (North has the preeminence for Candlemas, the assembling sequence continuing with the west, south, and east.) The wording will also be the same as found in "The Opening and Closing Rites," except that where the Earth Rite is mentioned, the words shall be "these rites of Candlemas."

The Lighting of the Candles

(This is the only Earth Rite of the year in which a portion of the ritual actually *precedes* the Opening Rites. At all other Earth Rites and Lunar Rites, the quarter candles and side altar candles [if any] are always lit before the ritual begins, and the two main altar candles are lit just before the prayer to the Lady at the very beginning of the Opening Rites. However, for the High Earth Rite of Candlemas, the following procedure should be observed.)

(All shall be dark, and no altar or quarter candles will have been lit yet. The priest and the priestess shall enter the circle area with the priestess carrying a tall, white, lighted candle. Going to the altar in the center of the circle, they will turn to face the other assembled grove members standing outside the circle area. The priest and priestess will then either read or recite from memory the following verses.)

Priest:

> Go back,
> go back before your beginning,
> before the lamps of Creation were lit;
> when all was the dark, blackened stillness
> of the Great Mother's womb
> until phallic lightning from the God primeval
> found its home
> in the cave of the ebon Lady's secret parts,
> igniting the light of life
> as energy sparks,
> daring the complacency of formless Chaos
> with molten, fiery pinwheels;
> exploding atoms of glowing,
> embryonic substance;
> the cosmic orgasm of pulsating generation
> setting the life-streams
> of lower worlds in motion.

Priestess:

> As it was,
> as it is,
> as it shall always be:

Light and Darkness,
Darkness and Light;
for in union with the Dark
is the glory of the Light!

(They shall both go to each quarter candle around the circle to light its wick from the Candlemas Candle carried by the priestess, beginning with the northern quarter and ending counterclockwise with the eastern quarter. They shall then light the side altar candles [if any], and finally, the two main altar candles. When the lighting of the candles has been completed, the priestess will set the Candlemas Candle inside the cauldron which should be situated in the southern quarter of the circle. Then shall begin the Opening Rites.)

The Invocation of the Crone

(After the Opening Rites, including the Assembling of the Quarter-Regents, have been completed, the priestess will take her place at the altar in the center of the circle, facing the northern quarter. She will then lift up her hands [or sceptre] and begin the invocation.)[1]

Priestess:

Crone of waning Winter,
soon to lay aside
Thy chilling, crystalled sceptre
in parting benediction
to the season of swirling snow.

We invoke Thee,
even as Thou yieldest
to the approaching light of the bright Maiden,
Goddess of growth and green things,
standing upon the horizon of Spring,
eagerly waiting to wake again
the dormant earth.

Venerable Crone,
Goddess of each dying cycle
upon the ever-turning Wheel of years,

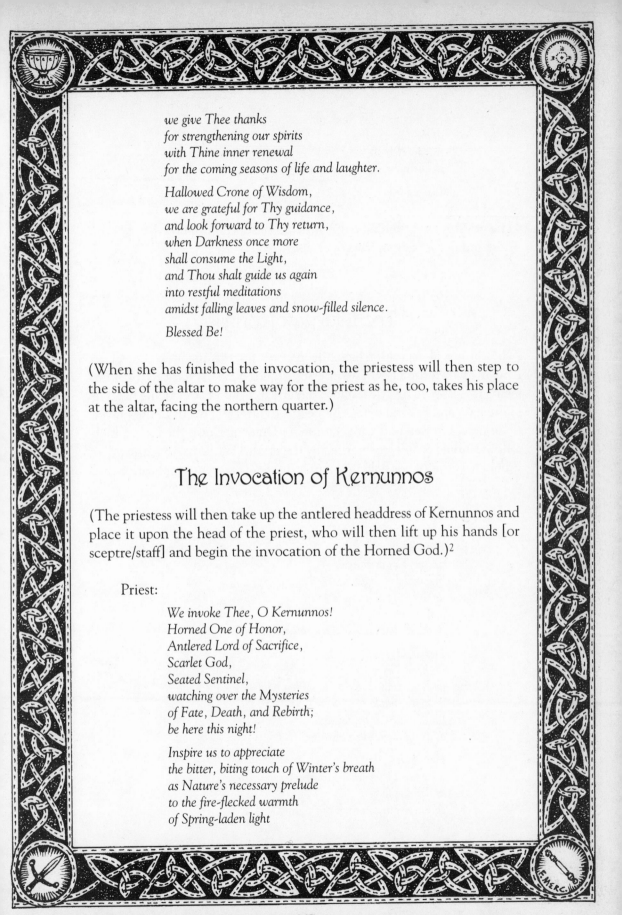

we give Thee thanks
for strengthening our spirits
with Thine inner renewal
for the coming seasons of life and laughter.

Hallowed Crone of Wisdom,
we are grateful for Thy guidance,
and look forward to Thy return,
when Darkness once more
shall consume the Light,
and Thou shalt guide us again
into restful meditations
amidst falling leaves and snow-filled silence.

Blessed Be!

(When she has finished the invocation, the priestess will then step to the side of the altar to make way for the priest as he, too, takes his place at the altar, facing the northern quarter.)

The Invocation of Kernunnos

(The priestess will then take up the antlered headdress of Kernunnos and place it upon the head of the priest, who will then lift up his hands [or sceptre/staff] and begin the invocation of the Horned God.)[2]

Priest:

We invoke Thee, O Kernunnos!
Horned One of Honor,
Antlered Lord of Sacrifice,
Scarlet God,
Seated Sentinel,
watching over the Mysteries
of Fate, Death, and Rebirth;
be here this night!

Inspire us to appreciate
the bitter, biting touch of Winter's breath
as Nature's necessary prelude
to the fire-flecked warmth
of Spring-laden light

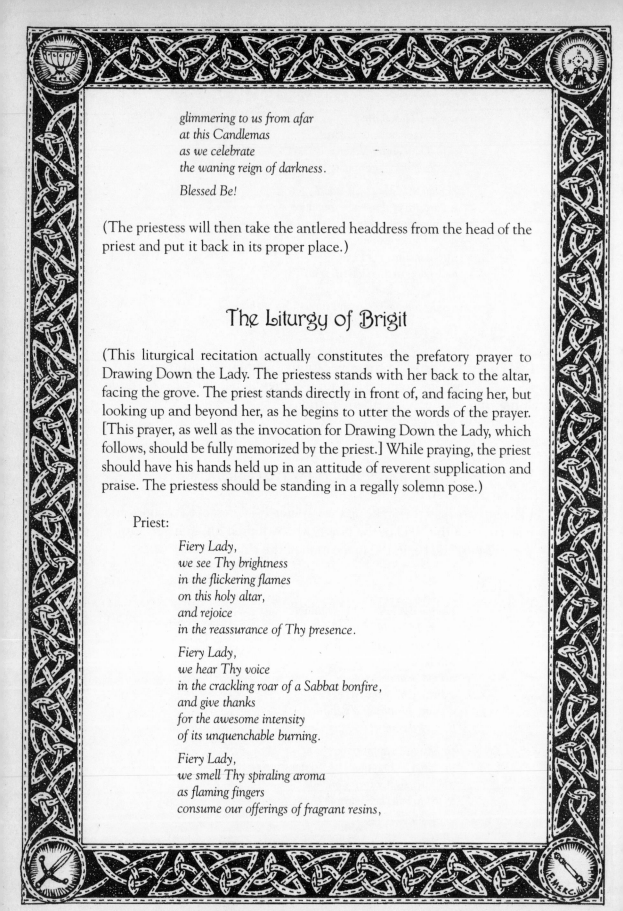

glimmering to us from afar
at this Candlemas
as we celebrate
the waning reign of darkness.

Blessed Be!

(The priestess will then take the antlered headdress from the head of the priest and put it back in its proper place.)

The Liturgy of Brigit

(This liturgical recitation actually constitutes the prefatory prayer to Drawing Down the Lady. The priestess stands with her back to the altar, facing the grove. The priest stands directly in front of, and facing her, but looking up and beyond her, as he begins to utter the words of the prayer. [This prayer, as well as the invocation for Drawing Down the Lady, which follows, should be fully memorized by the priest.] While praying, the priest should have his hands held up in an attitude of reverent supplication and praise. The priestess should be standing in a regally solemn pose.)

Priest:

Fiery Lady,
we see Thy brightness
in the flickering flames
on this holy altar,
and rejoice
in the reassurance of Thy presence.

Fiery Lady,
we hear Thy voice
in the crackling roar of a Sabbat bonfire,
and give thanks
for the awesome intensity
of its unquenchable burning.

Fiery Lady,
we smell Thy spiraling aroma
as flaming fingers
consume our offerings of fragrant resins,

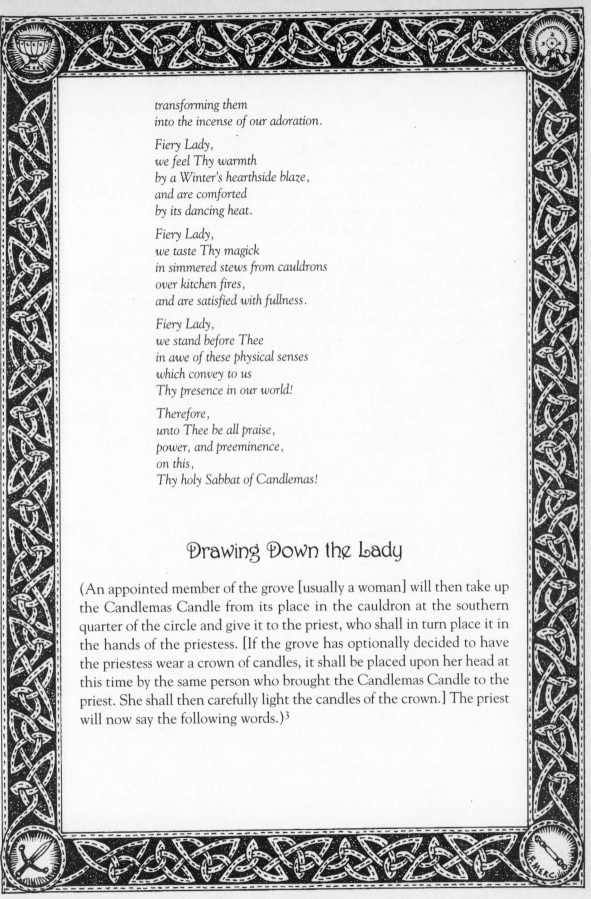

transforming them
into the incense of our adoration.

Fiery Lady,
we feel Thy warmth
by a Winter's hearthside blaze,
and are comforted
by its dancing heat.

Fiery Lady,
we taste Thy magick
in simmered stews from cauldrons
over kitchen fires,
and are satisfied with fullness.

Fiery Lady,
we stand before Thee
in awe of these physical senses
which convey to us
Thy presence in our world!

Therefore,
unto Thee be all praise,
power, and preeminence,
on this,
Thy holy Sabbat of Candlemas!

Drawing Down the Lady

(An appointed member of the grove [usually a woman] will then take up the Candlemas Candle from its place in the cauldron at the southern quarter of the circle and give it to the priest, who shall in turn place it in the hands of the priestess. [If the grove has optionally decided to have the priestess wear a crown of candles, it shall be placed upon her head at this time by the same person who brought the Candlemas Candle to the priest. She shall then carefully light the candles of the crown.] The priest will now say the following words.)[3]

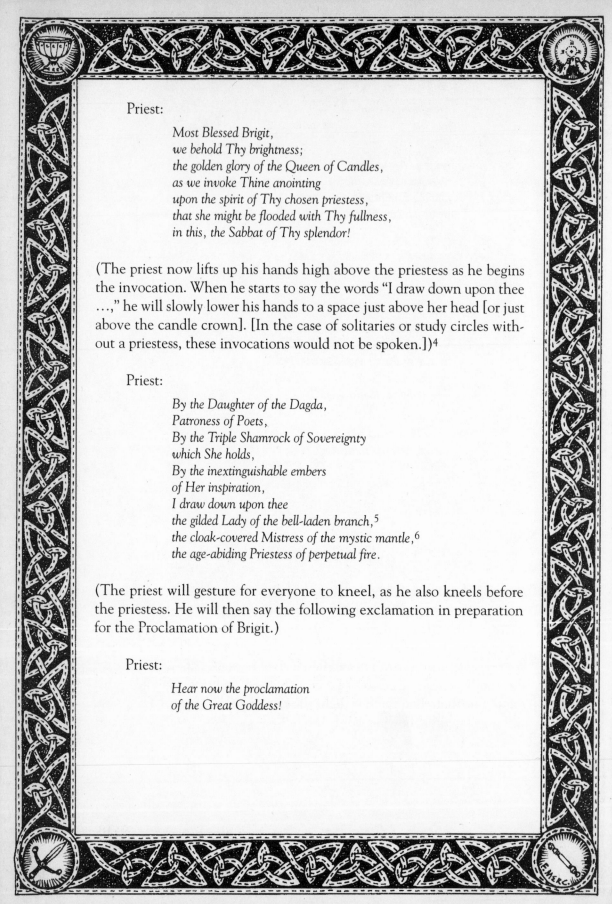

Priest:

> *Most Blessed Brigit,*
> *we behold Thy brightness;*
> *the golden glory of the Queen of Candles,*
> *as we invoke Thine anointing*
> *upon the spirit of Thy chosen priestess,*
> *that she might be flooded with Thy fullness,*
> *in this, the Sabbat of Thy splendor!*

(The priest now lifts up his hands high above the priestess as he begins the invocation. When he starts to say the words "I draw down upon thee …," he will slowly lower his hands to a space just above her head [or just above the candle crown]. [In the case of solitaries or study circles without a priestess, these invocations would not be spoken.])[4]

Priest:

> *By the Daughter of the Dagda,*
> *Patroness of Poets,*
> *By the Triple Shamrock of Sovereignty*
> *which She holds,*
> *By the inextinguishable embers*
> *of Her inspiration,*
> *I draw down upon thee*
> *the gilded Lady of the bell-laden branch,*[5]
> *the cloak-covered Mistress of the mystic mantle,*[6]
> *the age-abiding Priestess of perpetual fire.*

(The priest will gesture for everyone to kneel, as he also kneels before the priestess. He will then say the following exclamation in preparation for the Proclamation of Brigit.)

Priest:

> *Hear now the proclamation*
> *of the Great Goddess!*

The Proclamation

(The priestess will then begin to recite the words of the proclamation as she continues to hold the Candlemas Candle in her hands.)[7]

Priestess:

I am Brigit,
Holy Lady of Lingering Light,
shod with sandals of the Sun,
warming the frozen earth beneath
as heralding Maiden of melting snow.

I wait impatiently to sprinkle flowering garlands
upon the landscapes of Winter's sleep,
draping naked trees
in mantles of glistening green!

But the time has not yet come,
for My brightness is still in the distance
beyond the frigid winds
and final frosts
of the Ancient Crone's departure.

The hour of My reign approaches,
but for now,
let this radiant candle
be to thee a sign of hope;
a symbol of assurance
that I shall come,
and the Gatekeepers of the Seasons
shall not deny Me entrance!

Come now, ye wise women,
and be warmed
by the glowing gift of My intuitive knowledge!

Come now, ye wordsmiths,
and be ignited
by the sparks of My inscriptions
upon thy heart!

Come now, ye weldcrafters,
and be aflame
from the fanning bellows of My creative forge!

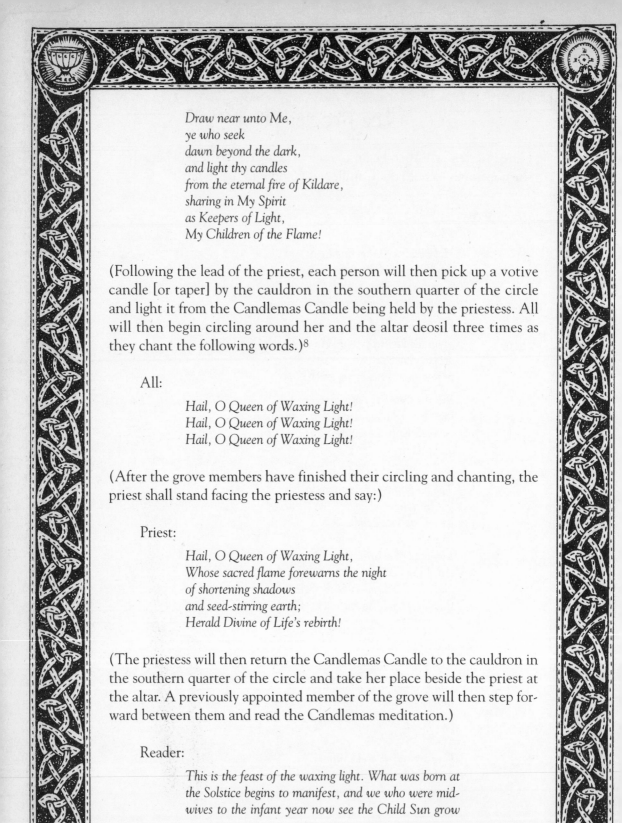

Draw near unto Me,
ye who seek
dawn beyond the dark,
and light thy candles
from the eternal fire of Kildare,
sharing in My Spirit
as Keepers of Light,
My Children of the Flame!

(Following the lead of the priest, each person will then pick up a votive candle [or taper] by the cauldron in the southern quarter of the circle and light it from the Candlemas Candle being held by the priestess. All will then begin circling around her and the altar deosil three times as they chant the following words.)[8]

All:

Hail, O Queen of Waxing Light!
Hail, O Queen of Waxing Light!
Hail, O Queen of Waxing Light!

(After the grove members have finished their circling and chanting, the priest shall stand facing the priestess and say:)

Priest:

Hail, O Queen of Waxing Light,
Whose sacred flame forewarns the night
of shortening shadows
and seed-stirring earth;
Herald Divine of Life's rebirth!

(The priestess will then return the Candlemas Candle to the cauldron in the southern quarter of the circle and take her place beside the priest at the altar. A previously appointed member of the grove will then step forward between them and read the Candlemas meditation.)

Reader:

This is the feast of the waxing light. What was born at
the Solstice begins to manifest, and we who were mid-
wives to the infant year now see the Child Sun grow

strong as the days grow visibly longer. This is the time of individuation: within the measures of the spiral, we each light our own light, and become uniquely ourselves. It is the time of initiation, of beginning, when seeds that will later sprout and grow begin to stir from their dark sleep. We meet to share the light of inspiration, that will grow with the coming year.[9]

(After the meditation is read, the priestess will then instruct everyone to see in the candle flames they carry a symbol of their own highest aspirations for the new year, and to visualize themselves walking through the coming months guided by the flame of the Lady's light burning brightly within their spirit. Each member will then put their votive lights in a circle around the cauldron in the southern quarter.)[10]

(At this time, either the priestess or another appointed woman of the grove shall take up the ritual broom and begin to sweep around the periphery of the circle going in the widdershins direction with the others following her as she and the rest of the grove chants the following incantation.)

Priestess:

> *Thus we banish Winter,*
> *Thus we welcome Spring;*
> *Say farewell to what is dead,*
> *And greet each living thing.*
> *Thus we banish Winter,*
> *Thus we welcome Spring![11]*

The Great Rite

(At this point, if the group celebrating the Earth Rite is a fully established grove with an ordained priestess and/or priest, then shall begin the Liturgy of the Great Rite with the appropriate seasonal preface. [For the complete preface and text, see the earlier section entitled "The Great Rite."])

The Grail Mass

(If the group celebrating the Earth Rite is a Grail Quest study circle with no one yet empowered through ordination into this Order to celebrate the Grail Mass, then they shall instead begin their time of teaching and discussion, led by an appointed facilitator. For an established grove, their time of teaching and discussion shall follow immediately after the Grail Mass has been celebrated with a subsequent meditation. [For the complete text of the Eucharist, see the earlier section entitled "The Grail Mass."])

The Parting Prayers

(When the time has come to bring the ritual to a close, the priestess will bid the grove members to stand as she takes her place before the altar, facing north. Lifting up her hands [or sceptre] she will then begin the parting prayer to the Lady.)

Priestess:

> *Lady of Lights,*
> *Whose celestial crown*
> *contains the jeweled suns of the galaxy;*
> *before Thy departure from this sacred space,*
> *be pleased, we pray,*
> *to scatter lavishly upon us*
> *Thy Candlemas blessings,*
> *that Thy radiance may shine forth*
> *from within us!*
>
> *May we be clothed anew*
> *with the warming glow of love,*
> *the inner illumination of Thine inspiration,*
> *and a fiery zeal for the fullness of life!*
>
> *All Hail, Farewell, and Blessed Be!*

(Now the priestess puts the antlered headdress of Kernunnos upon the head of the priest. The priest will then begin his parting prayer to the God.)

Priest:

> O Horned God of Winter's hardship,
> Stag Lord of Darkness,
> Thy majestic antlers
> are fleetingly seen
> intertwined among barren branches
> in sleeping woodlands
> as Thou leadest us
> on an eternal chase
> in our pursuit of the Divine.
>
> God of Two Dimensions,
> Thou Who guardest
> the treasures of the Unknown,
> continually puzzling
> our perceptions of reality;
> leave us this night
> with Thy blessings of psychic Sight
> as we strain our eyes
> upon the distant light
> in search of the Spring-born Satyr Lord!
>
> All Hail, Farewell, and Blessed Be!

(The priestess then takes off the antlered headdress from the head of the priest and returns it to its proper place.)

The Dismissal of the Quarter-Regents

(At this time, the same appointed grove members that called the respective Quarter-Regents in the beginning of the ritual will now dismiss Them to Their own domains. The dismissal will always begin with the Quarter-Regent who has the seasonal preeminence. [North for Candlemas, the sequence of dismissal continuing with the west, south, and east.] The wording and procedure shall be the same as is found in "The Opening and Closing Rites.")

The Opening of the Circle

(The priest will then take his glaive to the marked boundary of the circle, and open the circle in accordance with the wording and procedures as outlined in "The Opening and Closing Rites.")

The Closing Benediction

(The priestess will then make the final proclamation of the ritual's conclusion.)

Priestess:

> *This rite of Candlemas is ended!*
> *May the grace of the Goddess of Light*
> *be upon thee,*
> *and the benediction of the Queen of Candles*
> *be thy portion!*
>
> *Merry Meet and Merry Part!*

Footnotes

1. This is a most unusual invocation, for it is at the same time both an invocation and a prayer of farewell. Candlemas is seen in our tradition as an Earth Rite of *transition*, for while technically it is presided over by the Crone, its main theme is the coming of the light of spring brought by the Goddess in Her Maiden aspect. This is the last Earth Rite at which the Crone will be invoked until the following Hallowmas. This prayer, then, is one of thanksgiving for the blessings the Crone has given us during these cold and wintry months, recognizing that Her seasonal reign is fast coming to a close in preparation for the coming of the Maiden with Her warm breath of spring perfume.

2. In the Ordo Arcanorum Gradalis, throughout the dark half of the year beginning with Hallowmas and ending with Candlemas, the priest always wears an antlered headdress in honor of Kernunnos, the Underworld aspect of the Horned God. Any form of antlered headdress will be sufficient, although we prefer the kind which closely

approximates the look of an American Indian shaman. However, until you, your study circle, or grove are able to make one for your own ceremonial usage, just ignore the ritual instructions about when the headdress is to be worn. The ceremony will proceed just as smoothly without it.

3. For detailed instructions on how to construct a candle-crown which is safe and will protect the wearer's hair from dripping wax, see Janet and Stewart Farrar, *Eight Sabbats for Witches* (Custer, WA: Phoenix Publishing, Inc., 1984), pp. 66-68.

4. For those groups which do not invoke the drawing down of the Lady, the same procedures would be followed as given in footnote 2 of "The Lunar Rite."

5. This is an allusion to an ancient Irish custom where the chief poet always carried a golden branch with bells in honor of Brigit, his supernatural Patroness. (See Mary Condren, *The Serpent and the Goddess.* [San Francisco, CA: Harper & Row, 1989], p. 57.)

6. The mantle was closely associated with the goddess Brigit in the Celtic Mysteries. (See Caitlin Matthews, *Sophia—Goddess of Wisdom.* [London: Mandala, 1991], pp. 213-214.)

7. For the priestess speaking the Proclamation, the same instructions would apply as are given with regard to the Charge of the Goddess (see footnote 3 of "The Lunar Rite").

8. While most of our ritual circle movements are done in the widdershins (counterclockwise) direction, occasionally we will perform deosil (clockwise) movements for very specific symbolic purposes. This is a case in point. As we hail the Queen of Waxing Light, we walk deosil around the priestess to remind us that the light is waxing on a *daily* basis. Each day, the Sun sets a little bit later in its deosil journey through the daytime sky.

9. This Candlemas meditation is directly excerpted from *The Spiral Dance* by Starhawk (San Francisco, CA: Harper & Row, 1979), p. 174. Eventually groves may want to write their own meditations to be used in place of this.

10. Each grove has several options on how to make use of the candles during this part of the ritual. Perhaps the safest is to use the small, colored or clear votive candle glasses. This helps to eliminate the possibility of dripping wax from a candle taper being spilled on the floor or carpet. In this case, the candles are put around the bottom of the outside of the cauldron at the proper time. On the other hand, if you wish to use regular candle tapers (sometimes you can purchase these in church supply stores complete with a paper "drip catcher" on them), you can always fill your cauldron with some sand, and then at

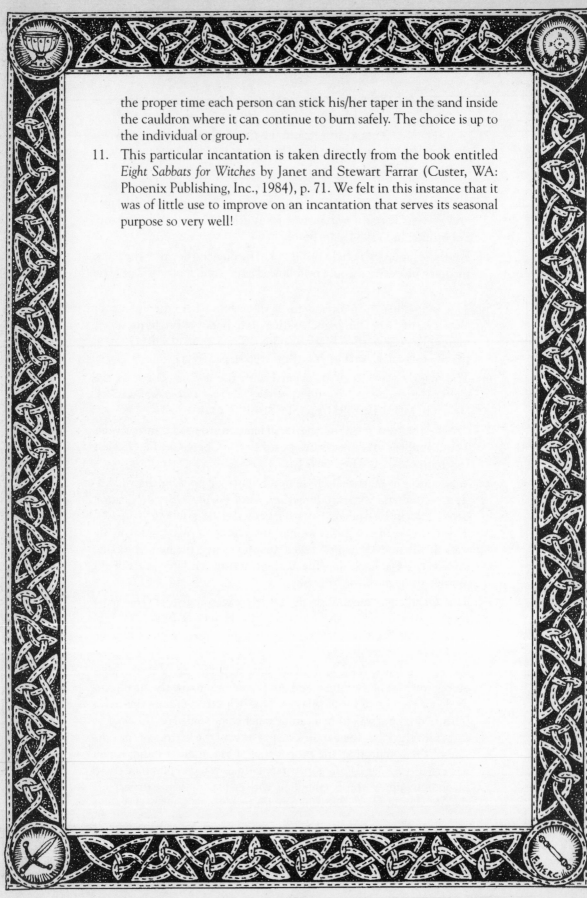

the proper time each person can stick his/her taper in the sand inside the cauldron where it can continue to burn safely. The choice is up to the individual or group.

11. This particular incantation is taken directly from the book entitled *Eight Sabbats for Witches* by Janet and Stewart Farrar (Custer, WA: Phoenix Publishing, Inc., 1984), p. 71. We felt in this instance that it was of little use to improve on an incantation that serves its seasonal purpose so very well!

The Grail Mass: Censing of the chalice and paten.

Spring Equinox

Basic Requirements

Below are some things to remember for the Low Earth Rite of the Spring Equinox which are necessary requirements if the observance is to be in accordance with the rubrics of the Ordo Arcanorum Gradalis.

Altar

The altar should be in the center of the circle area, facing the eastern quarter.

Altar Cloth

The altar cloth should always be yellow for the Earth Rite of the Spring Equinox. (This is only if you are using a regular rectangular altar. If you are using the Altar of the Pentagram, see "The Altar and the Sacred Tools" for further details and instructions.)

Altar Candles

The two main altar candles should be yellow for the Spring Equinox ritual.

Other Candles

The four quarter candles (or glass votive candleholders) *should always be yellow in the east, green in the north, blue in the west, and red in the south.* All other secondary candles used for extra lighting in the ritual area can be of pale shades of green and whatever other colors may suit the tastes of the grove members. A candle-lantern (or extra candle) will also be needed for the priest's invocation of the Solar Lord.

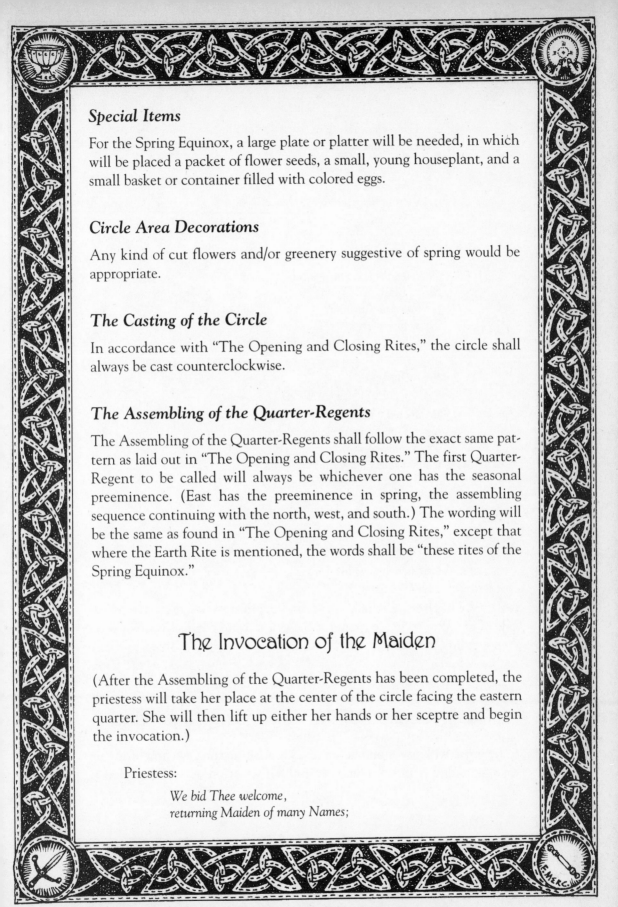

Special Items

For the Spring Equinox, a large plate or platter will be needed, in which will be placed a packet of flower seeds, a small, young houseplant, and a small basket or container filled with colored eggs.

Circle Area Decorations

Any kind of cut flowers and/or greenery suggestive of spring would be appropriate.

The Casting of the Circle

In accordance with "The Opening and Closing Rites," the circle shall always be cast counterclockwise.

The Assembling of the Quarter-Regents

The Assembling of the Quarter-Regents shall follow the exact same pattern as laid out in "The Opening and Closing Rites." The first Quarter-Regent to be called will always be whichever one has the seasonal preeminence. (East has the preeminence in spring, the assembling sequence continuing with the north, west, and south.) The wording will be the same as found in "The Opening and Closing Rites," except that where the Earth Rite is mentioned, the words shall be "these rites of the Spring Equinox."

The Invocation of the Maiden

(After the Assembling of the Quarter-Regents has been completed, the priestess will take her place at the center of the circle facing the eastern quarter. She will then lift up either her hands or her sceptre and begin the invocation.)

Priestess:

> We bid Thee welcome,
> returning Maiden of many Names;

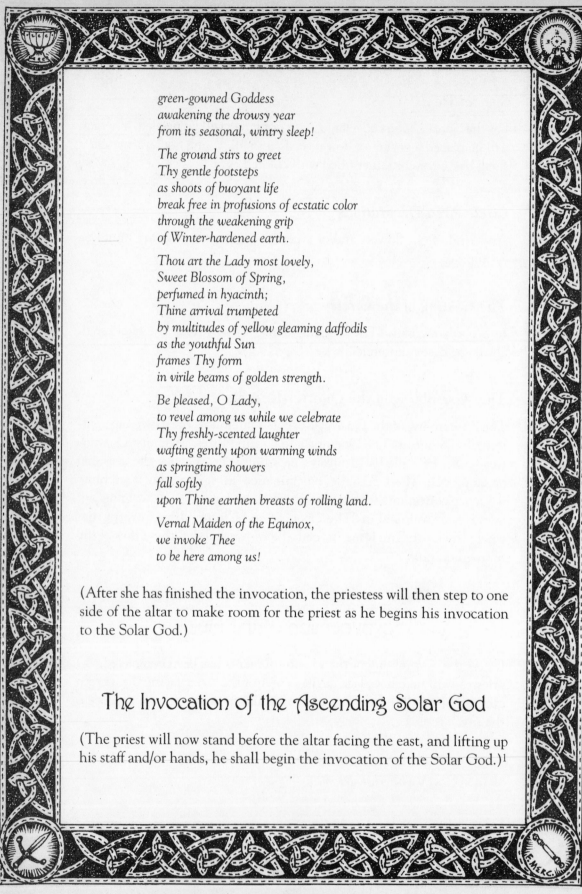

green-gowned Goddess
awakening the drowsy year
from its seasonal, wintry sleep!

The ground stirs to greet
Thy gentle footsteps
as shoots of buoyant life
break free in profusions of ecstatic color
through the weakening grip
of Winter-hardened earth.

Thou art the Lady most lovely,
Sweet Blossom of Spring,
perfumed in hyacinth;
Thine arrival trumpeted
by multitudes of yellow gleaming daffodils
as the youthful Sun
frames Thy form
in virile beams of golden strength.

Be pleased, O Lady,
to revel among us while we celebrate
Thy freshly-scented laughter
wafting gently upon warming winds
as springtime showers
fall softly
upon Thine earthen breasts of rolling land.

Vernal Maiden of the Equinox,
we invoke Thee
to be here among us!

(After she has finished the invocation, the priestess will then step to one side of the altar to make room for the priest as he begins his invocation to the Solar God.)

The Invocation of the Ascending Solar God

(The priest will now stand before the altar facing the east, and lifting up his staff and/or hands, he shall begin the invocation of the Solar God.)[1]

Priest:

> Let us give praise
> to the glory of the God celestial,
> stretched forth
> upon the cosmic Cross,
> soon to rise above
> the Circle of the Equinox![2]
>
> Sun of Righteousness!
> Sol Invictus!
> Solar Savior!
> We hail Thy triumph
> over the seasons of shadow!
>
> From Thy majesty
> proceeds the very Light of nations,
> the shining brilliance of illumined Truth,
> and the manifest splendor of the Sacred.
>
> Hallowed Blaze of Heaven,
> Thou art the living Light,
> Source of inspiration
> to sage and saint,
> priestess and prophet.
>
> Therefore,
> we add to the adoration of the ancients
> as we ascribe to Thee praise and honor,
> O Ascendant King of planetary gods!

(The priest will then set his staff in its place. Then he will take the candle-lantern [or candle], and going first to the eastern quarter and then to the western quarter he shall make the sign of the equal-armed cross with the candle-lantern [or candle] as he says the following words.)

Priest:

> God of Light, God of Life,
> dying daily,
> Thou descendest into darkness;
> rising early,
> Thy radiance renews the day!

(The candle-lantern [or candle] is returned to its place by the priest.)

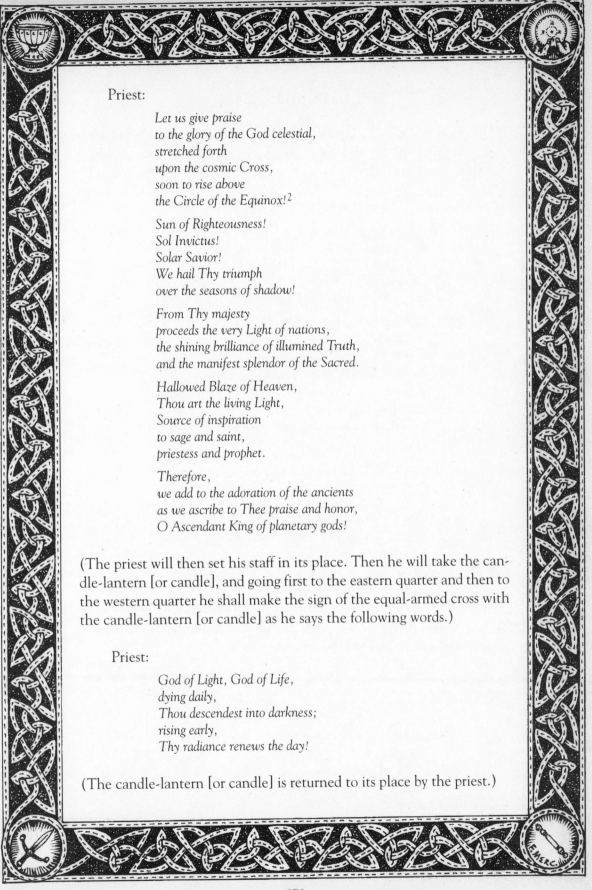

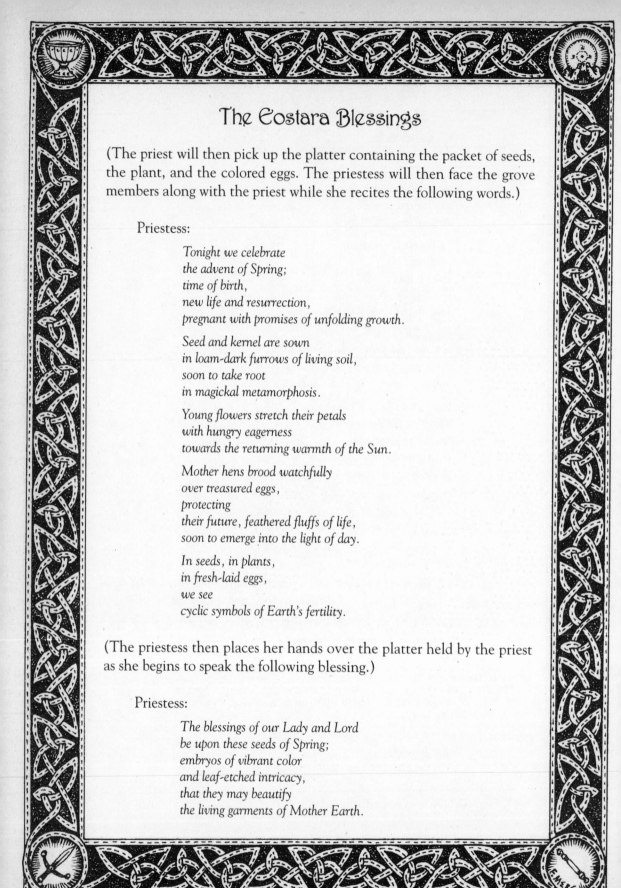

The Eostara Blessings

(The priest will then pick up the platter containing the packet of seeds, the plant, and the colored eggs. The priestess will then face the grove members along with the priest while she recites the following words.)

Priestess:

Tonight we celebrate
the advent of Spring;
time of birth,
new life and resurrection,
pregnant with promises of unfolding growth.

Seed and kernel are sown
in loam-dark furrows of living soil,
soon to take root
in magickal metamorphosis.

Young flowers stretch their petals
with hungry eagerness
towards the returning warmth of the Sun.

Mother hens brood watchfully
over treasured eggs,
protecting
their future, feathered fluffs of life,
soon to emerge into the light of day.

In seeds, in plants,
in fresh-laid eggs,
we see
cyclic symbols of Earth's fertility.

(The priestess then places her hands over the platter held by the priest as she begins to speak the following blessing.)

Priestess:

The blessings of our Lady and Lord
be upon these seeds of Spring;
embryos of vibrant color
and leaf-etched intricacy,
that they may beautify
the living garments of Mother Earth.

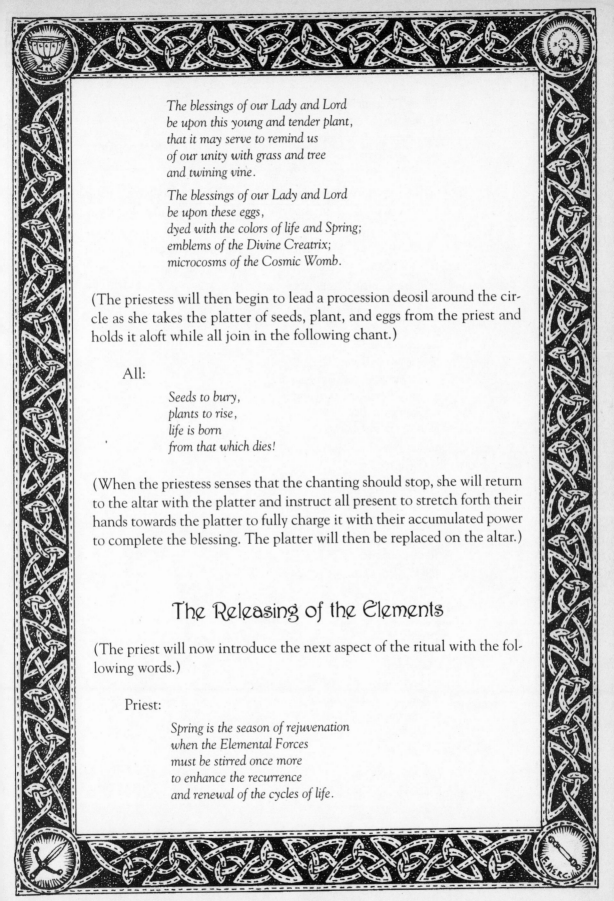

The blessings of our Lady and Lord
be upon this young and tender plant,
that it may serve to remind us
of our unity with grass and tree
and twining vine.

The blessings of our Lady and Lord
be upon these eggs,
dyed with the colors of life and Spring;
emblems of the Divine Creatrix;
microcosms of the Cosmic Womb.

(The priestess will then begin to lead a procession deosil around the circle as she takes the platter of seeds, plant, and eggs from the priest and holds it aloft while all join in the following chant.)

All:

Seeds to bury,
plants to rise,
life is born
from that which dies!

(When the priestess senses that the chanting should stop, she will return to the altar with the platter and instruct all present to stretch forth their hands towards the platter to fully charge it with their accumulated power to complete the blessing. The platter will then be replaced on the altar.)

The Releasing of the Elements

(The priest will now introduce the next aspect of the ritual with the following words.)

Priest:

Spring is the season of rejuvenation
when the Elemental Forces
must be stirred once more
to enhance the recurrence
and renewal of the cycles of life.

Let us exhort the Regents
to bring again
the greening of the groves
with the advent of Eostara!

(The same four individuals who assembled the Quarter-Regents during the Opening Rites will now unsheathe their glaives and take their respective positions at each of the quarters to which they have been assigned. Then starting with the caller of the eastern quarter and finally ending with the southern quarter, they will each raise their glaive and begin to address the Quarter-Regents.)

Eastern Caller:

Regents of the East,
Sovereigns of Wind and Air,
release now the breezes of dawn,
bearing aloft the scent of Spring,
refreshing the face
of the Maiden's presence!

Northern Caller:

Regents of the North,
Sovereigns of elemental Earth,
release now Thy fertility
in the furrows of the field,
the nests of birds,
and the dens of furry forest families!

Western Caller:

Regents of the West,
Sovereigns of all Watery Realms,
release now
gentle showers and fresh-flowing streams
that the thirst of the soil
may be quenched!

Southern Caller:

Regents of the South,
Sovereigns of Fire and Flame,
release now

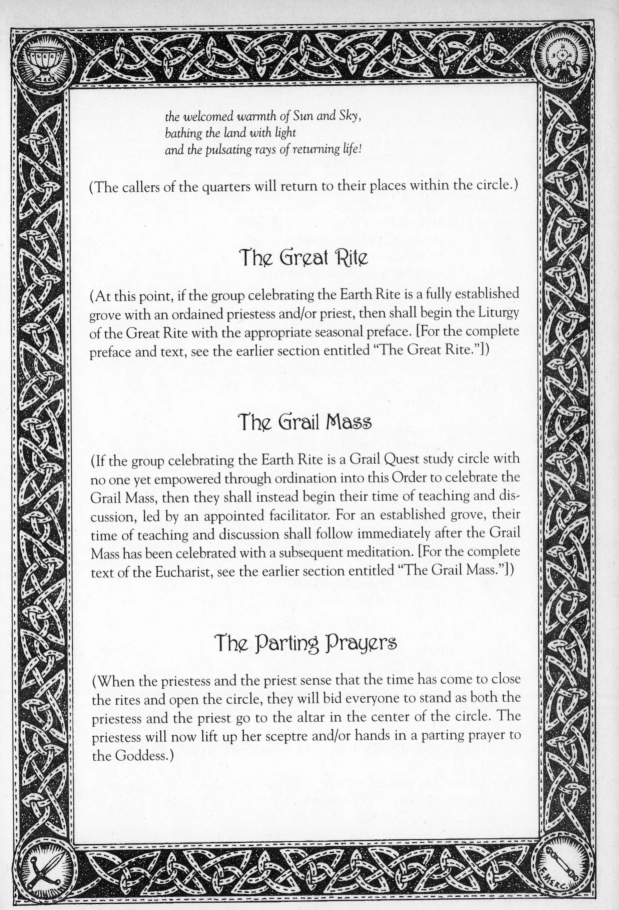

the welcomed warmth of Sun and Sky,
bathing the land with light
and the pulsating rays of returning life!

(The callers of the quarters will return to their places within the circle.)

The Great Rite

(At this point, if the group celebrating the Earth Rite is a fully established grove with an ordained priestess and/or priest, then shall begin the Liturgy of the Great Rite with the appropriate seasonal preface. [For the complete preface and text, see the earlier section entitled "The Great Rite."])

The Grail Mass

(If the group celebrating the Earth Rite is a Grail Quest study circle with no one yet empowered through ordination into this Order to celebrate the Grail Mass, then they shall instead begin their time of teaching and discussion, led by an appointed facilitator. For an established grove, their time of teaching and discussion shall follow immediately after the Grail Mass has been celebrated with a subsequent meditation. [For the complete text of the Eucharist, see the earlier section entitled "The Grail Mass."])

The Parting Prayers

(When the priestess and the priest sense that the time has come to close the rites and open the circle, they will bid everyone to stand as both the priestess and the priest go to the altar in the center of the circle. The priestess will now lift up her sceptre and/or hands in a parting prayer to the Goddess.)

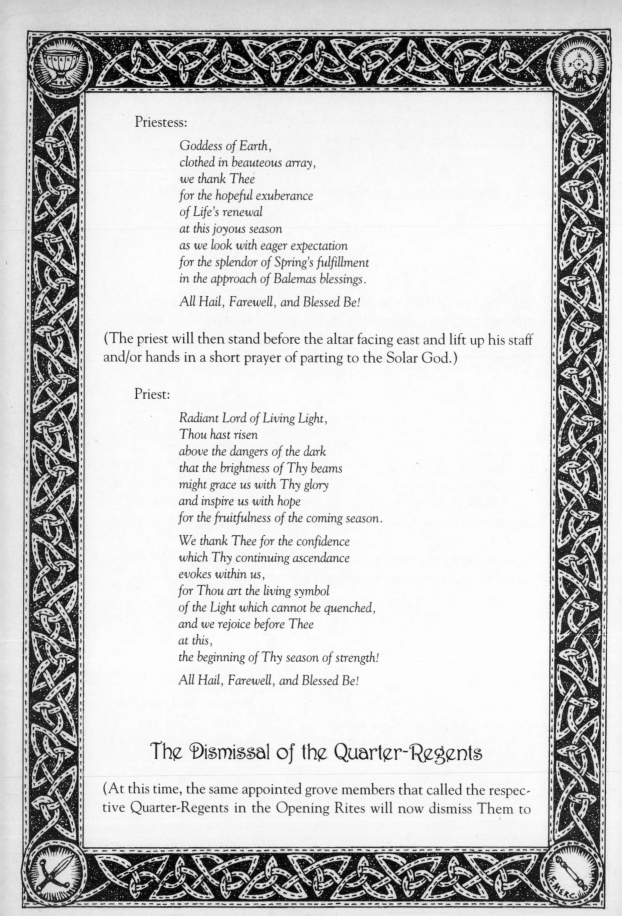

Priestess:

> Goddess of Earth,
> clothed in beauteous array,
> we thank Thee
> for the hopeful exuberance
> of Life's renewal
> at this joyous season
> as we look with eager expectation
> for the splendor of Spring's fulfillment
> in the approach of Balemas blessings.
>
> All Hail, Farewell, and Blessed Be!

(The priest will then stand before the altar facing east and lift up his staff and/or hands in a short prayer of parting to the Solar God.)

Priest:

> Radiant Lord of Living Light,
> Thou hast risen
> above the dangers of the dark
> that the brightness of Thy beams
> might grace us with Thy glory
> and inspire us with hope
> for the fruitfulness of the coming season.
>
> We thank Thee for the confidence
> which Thy continuing ascendance
> evokes within us,
> for Thou art the living symbol
> of the Light which cannot be quenched,
> and we rejoice before Thee
> at this,
> the beginning of Thy season of strength!
>
> All Hail, Farewell, and Blessed Be!

The Dismissal of the Quarter-Regents

(At this time, the same appointed grove members that called the respective Quarter-Regents in the Opening Rites will now dismiss Them to

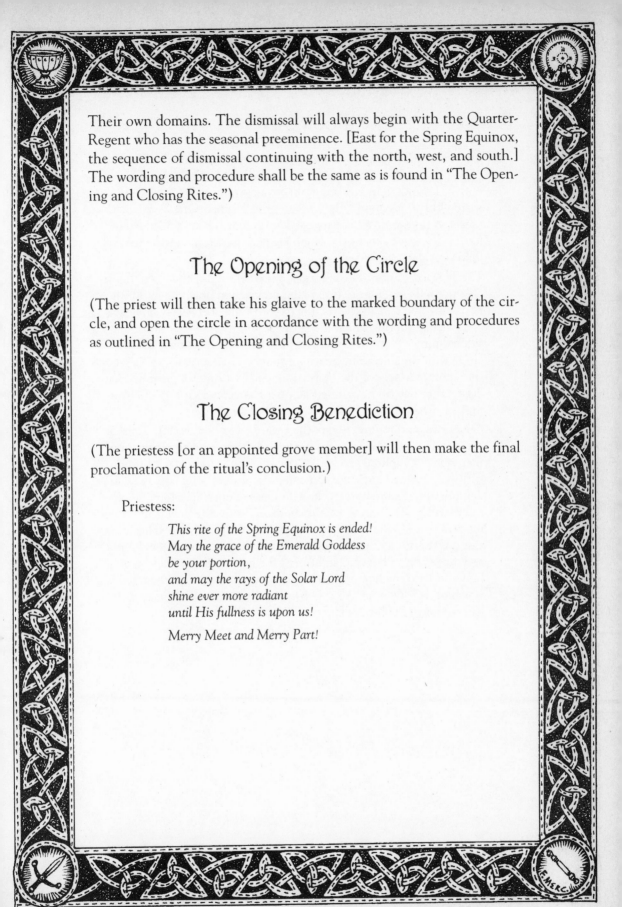

Their own domains. The dismissal will always begin with the Quarter-Regent who has the seasonal preeminence. [East for the Spring Equinox, the sequence of dismissal continuing with the north, west, and south.] The wording and procedure shall be the same as is found in "The Opening and Closing Rites.")

The Opening of the Circle

(The priest will then take his glaive to the marked boundary of the circle, and open the circle in accordance with the wording and procedures as outlined in "The Opening and Closing Rites.")

The Closing Benediction

(The priestess [or an appointed grove member] will then make the final proclamation of the ritual's conclusion.)

Priestess:

This rite of the Spring Equinox is ended!
May the grace of the Emerald Goddess
be your portion,
and may the rays of the Solar Lord
shine ever more radiant
until His fullness is upon us!

Merry Meet and Merry Part!

Footnotes

1. The God in His aspect as the Horned One is not invoked at the Spring Equinox for several reasons. Primarily, this is a Solar Sabbat in honor of the God in His celestial persona as the Solar Lord. Secondarily, in the mythos of the O.A.G., the Horned One in His dark aspect as Kernunnos is last invoked at the Earth Rite of Candlemas, for it is the last Sabbat over which He and the Crone reign until the following Hallowmas.

    The Horned God in His luminous persona as Pan, the Satyr Lord, does not fully manifest to begin His annual reign until the Earth Rite of Balemas. So we can see that the period of time between Candlemas and Balemas (during which the Spring Equinox falls) is a time of transition during which the power and presence of Pan is slowly strengthening with the oncoming arrival of spring. Therefore, it can be seen that neither aspect of the Horned One is in a state of preeminence during the time of the Spring Equinox. Hence, our custom of avoiding any invocations of His aspects at this time.

2. "The death and resurrection of the Solar Hero at or about the vernal equinox is as widespread as his birth at the winter solstice. Osiris was then slain by Typhon, and he is pictured on the circle of the horizon, with outstretched arms, as if crucified—a posture originally of benediction, not of suffering ... The Sun God is sometimes found sculptured within the circle of the horizon, with the head and feet touching the circle at north and south, and the outstretched hands at east and west—'He was crucified.' After this he rises triumphantly and ascends into heaven, and ripens the corn and the grape, giving his very life to them to make their substance and through them to his worshippers." (Annie Besant, *Esoteric Christianity.* [Wheaton, IL: Theosophical Publishing House, 1901, 1966], pp. 113, 108.)

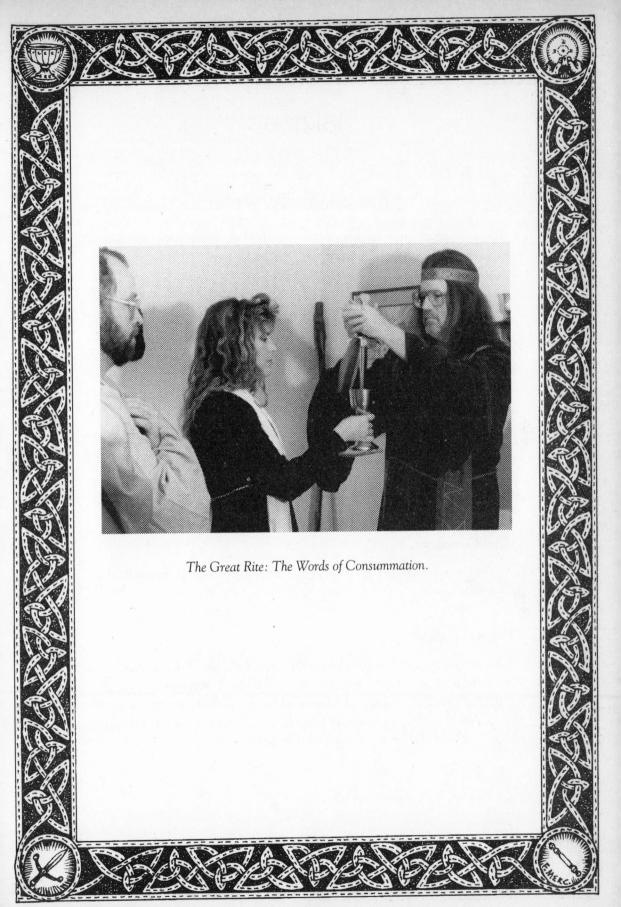

The Great Rite: The Words of Consummation.

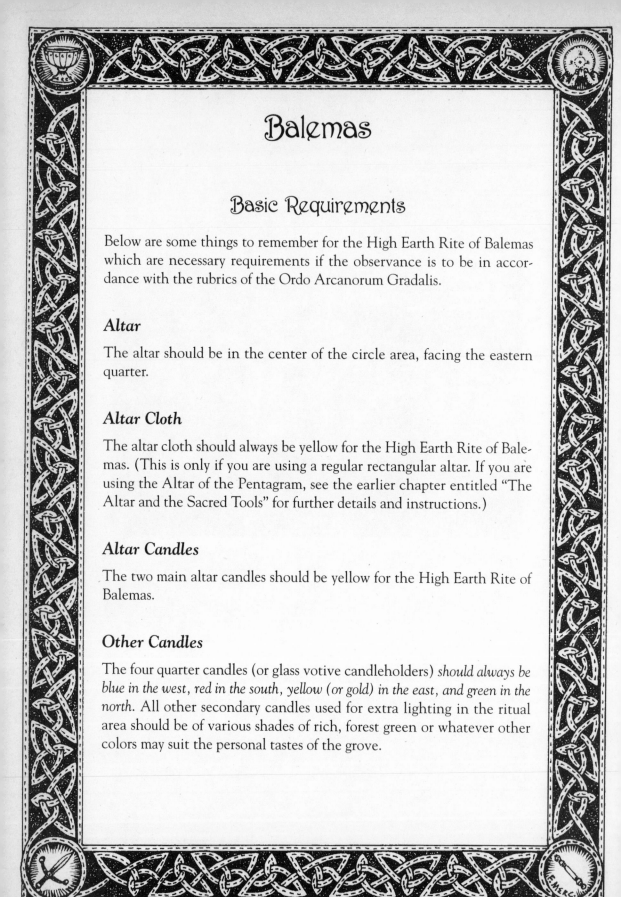

Balemas

Basic Requirements

Below are some things to remember for the High Earth Rite of Balemas which are necessary requirements if the observance is to be in accordance with the rubrics of the Ordo Arcanorum Gradalis.

Altar

The altar should be in the center of the circle area, facing the eastern quarter.

Altar Cloth

The altar cloth should always be yellow for the High Earth Rite of Balemas. (This is only if you are using a regular rectangular altar. If you are using the Altar of the Pentagram, see the earlier chapter entitled "The Altar and the Sacred Tools" for further details and instructions.)

Altar Candles

The two main altar candles should be yellow for the High Earth Rite of Balemas.

Other Candles

The four quarter candles (or glass votive candleholders) *should always be blue in the west, red in the south, yellow (or gold) in the east, and green in the north.* All other secondary candles used for extra lighting in the ritual area should be of various shades of rich, forest green or whatever other colors may suit the personal tastes of the grove.

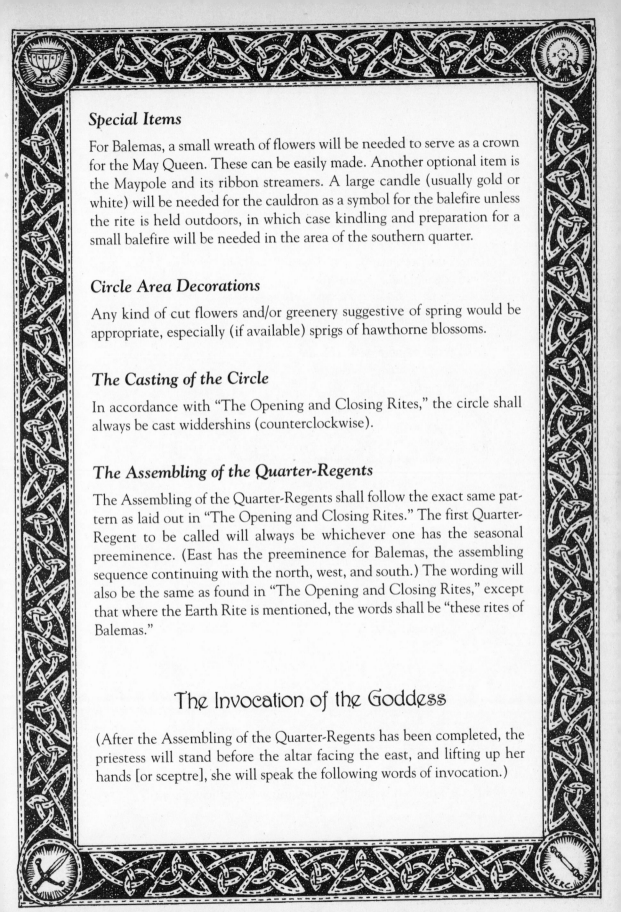

Special Items

For Balemas, a small wreath of flowers will be needed to serve as a crown for the May Queen. These can be easily made. Another optional item is the Maypole and its ribbon streamers. A large candle (usually gold or white) will be needed for the cauldron as a symbol for the balefire unless the rite is held outdoors, in which case kindling and preparation for a small balefire will be needed in the area of the southern quarter.

Circle Area Decorations

Any kind of cut flowers and/or greenery suggestive of spring would be appropriate, especially (if available) sprigs of hawthorne blossoms.

The Casting of the Circle

In accordance with "The Opening and Closing Rites," the circle shall always be cast widdershins (counterclockwise).

The Assembling of the Quarter-Regents

The Assembling of the Quarter-Regents shall follow the exact same pattern as laid out in "The Opening and Closing Rites." The first Quarter-Regent to be called will always be whichever one has the seasonal preeminence. (East has the preeminence for Balemas, the assembling sequence continuing with the north, west, and south.) The wording will also be the same as found in "The Opening and Closing Rites," except that where the Earth Rite is mentioned, the words shall be "these rites of Balemas."

The Invocation of the Goddess

(After the Assembling of the Quarter-Regents has been completed, the priestess will stand before the altar facing the east, and lifting up her hands [or sceptre], she will speak the following words of invocation.)

Priestess:

Hallowed Lady of the Hawthorn,[1]
Goddess of the greenwood groves,
we call upon Thee
in the season of Thy sensuality,
as Thy blossom opens
to the amorous advances
of our Lord, Thy Lover.

In Thy union
is the fertility of Spring,
and the beckoning whisper of young desire.

Touch us with the breath
of Thy passion,
that we might seek
for the ecstasy of life!

Inflame us with the fever
of Thine inmost longings,
that we not be satisfied
until our oneness
with the God is consummated!

Capture us with the fragrance
of Thine allurement,
that we may be overwhelmed
with an obsession for Thy presence!

Bright Maiden of May,
be here among us
as we celebrate
the Beltane blessings of Thy bridal-bed!

Blessed Be![2]

The Invocation of the Satyr Lord

(After she speaks the invocation of the Goddess, the priestess will then step to the side of the altar to make way for the priest who will then stand before the altar facing the east, and raising up his hands [or sceptre/staff], he will then speak the following words of invocation.)

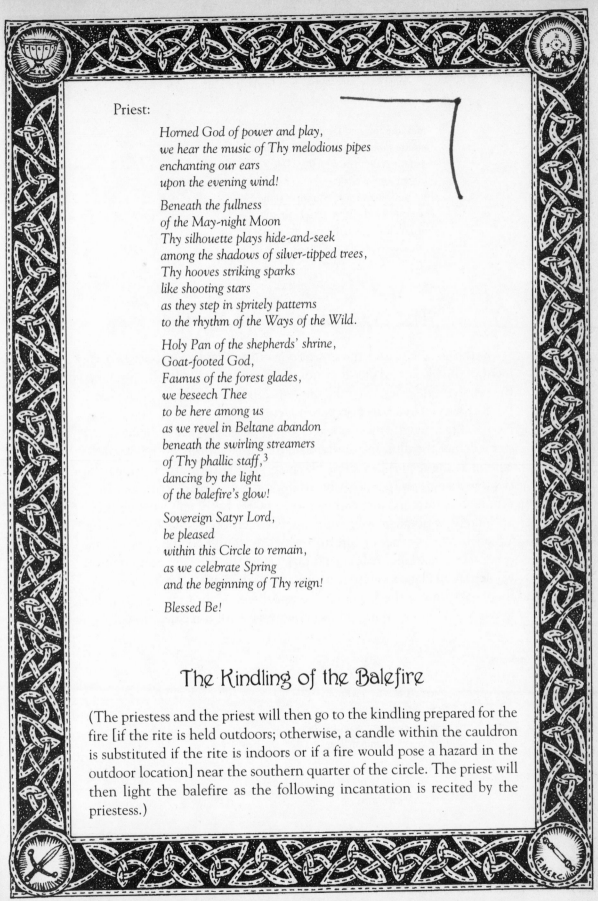

Priest:

Horned God of power and play,
we hear the music of Thy melodious pipes
enchanting our ears
upon the evening wind!

Beneath the fullness
of the May-night Moon
Thy silhouette plays hide-and-seek
among the shadows of silver-tipped trees,
Thy hooves striking sparks
like shooting stars
as they step in spritely patterns
to the rhythm of the Ways of the Wild.

Holy Pan of the shepherds' shrine,
Goat-footed God,
Faunus of the forest glades,
we beseech Thee
to be here among us
as we revel in Beltane abandon
beneath the swirling streamers
of Thy phallic staff,[3]
dancing by the light
of the balefire's glow!

Sovereign Satyr Lord,
be pleased
within this Circle to remain,
as we celebrate Spring
and the beginning of Thy reign!

Blessed Be!

The Kindling of the Balefire

(The priestess and the priest will then go to the kindling prepared for the fire [if the rite is held outdoors; otherwise, a candle within the cauldron is substituted if the rite is indoors or if a fire would pose a hazard in the outdoor location] near the southern quarter of the circle. The priest will then light the balefire as the following incantation is recited by the priestess.)

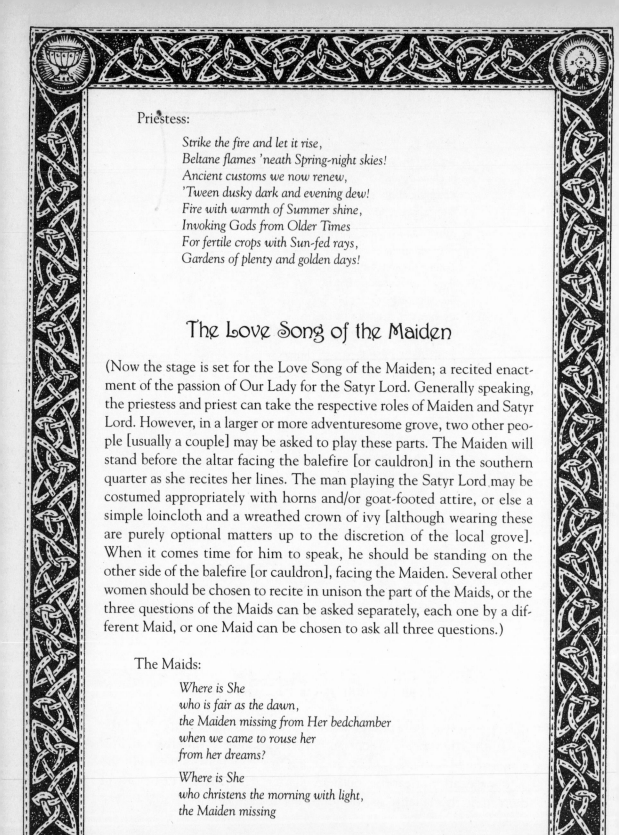

Priestess:

Strike the fire and let it rise,
Beltane flames 'neath Spring-night skies!
Ancient customs we now renew,
'Tween dusky dark and evening dew!
Fire with warmth of Summer shine,
Invoking Gods from Older Times
For fertile crops with Sun-fed rays,
Gardens of plenty and golden days!

The Love Song of the Maiden

(Now the stage is set for the Love Song of the Maiden; a recited enactment of the passion of Our Lady for the Satyr Lord. Generally speaking, the priestess and priest can take the respective roles of Maiden and Satyr Lord. However, in a larger or more adventuresome grove, two other people [usually a couple] may be asked to play these parts. The Maiden will stand before the altar facing the balefire [or cauldron] in the southern quarter as she recites her lines. The man playing the Satyr Lord may be costumed appropriately with horns and/or goat-footed attire, or else a simple loincloth and a wreathed crown of ivy [although wearing these are purely optional matters up to the discretion of the local grove]. When it comes time for him to speak, he should be standing on the other side of the balefire [or cauldron], facing the Maiden. Several other women should be chosen to recite in unison the part of the Maids, or the three questions of the Maids can be asked separately, each one by a different Maid, or one Maid can be chosen to ask all three questions.)

The Maids:

Where is She
who is fair as the dawn,
the Maiden missing from Her bedchamber
when we came to rouse her
from her dreams?

Where is She
who christens the morning with light,
the Maiden missing

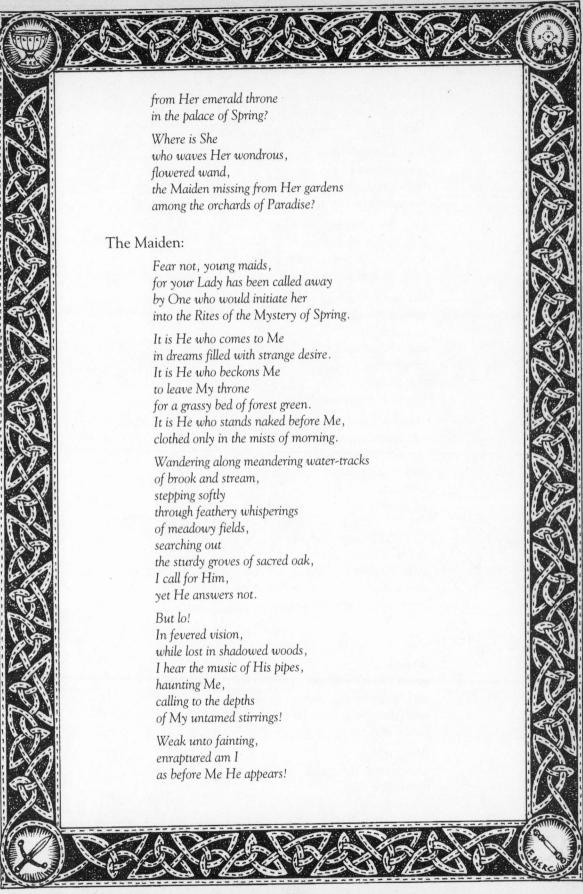

from Her emerald throne
in the palace of Spring?

Where is She
who waves Her wondrous,
flowered wand,
the Maiden missing from Her gardens
among the orchards of Paradise?

The Maiden:

Fear not, young maids,
for your Lady has been called away
by One who would initiate her
into the Rites of the Mystery of Spring.

It is He who comes to Me
in dreams filled with strange desire.
It is He who beckons Me
to leave My throne
for a grassy bed of forest green.
It is He who stands naked before Me,
clothed only in the mists of morning.

Wandering along meandering water-tracks
of brook and stream,
stepping softly
through feathery whisperings
of meadowy fields,
searching out
the sturdy groves of sacred oak,
I call for Him,
yet He answers not.

But lo!
In fevered vision,
while lost in shadowed woods,
I hear the music of His pipes,
haunting Me,
calling to the depths
of My untamed stirrings!

Weak unto fainting,
enraptured am I
as before Me He appears!

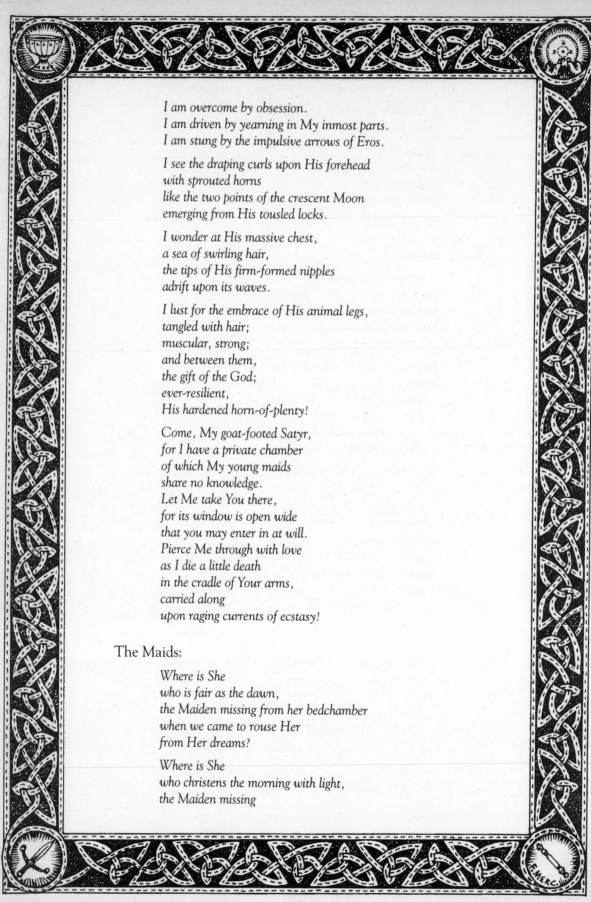

I am overcome by obsession.
I am driven by yearning in My inmost parts.
I am stung by the impulsive arrows of Eros.

I see the draping curls upon His forehead
with sprouted horns
like the two points of the crescent Moon
emerging from His tousled locks.

I wonder at His massive chest,
a sea of swirling hair,
the tips of His firm-formed nipples
adrift upon its waves.

I lust for the embrace of His animal legs,
tangled with hair;
muscular, strong;
and between them,
the gift of the God;
ever-resilient,
His hardened horn-of-plenty!

Come, My goat-footed Satyr,
for I have a private chamber
of which My young maids
share no knowledge.
Let Me take You there,
for its window is open wide
that you may enter in at will.
Pierce Me through with love
as I die a little death
in the cradle of Your arms,
carried along
upon raging currents of ecstasy!

The Maids:

Where is She
who is fair as the dawn,
the Maiden missing from her bedchamber
when we came to rouse Her
from Her dreams?

Where is She
who christens the morning with light,
the Maiden missing

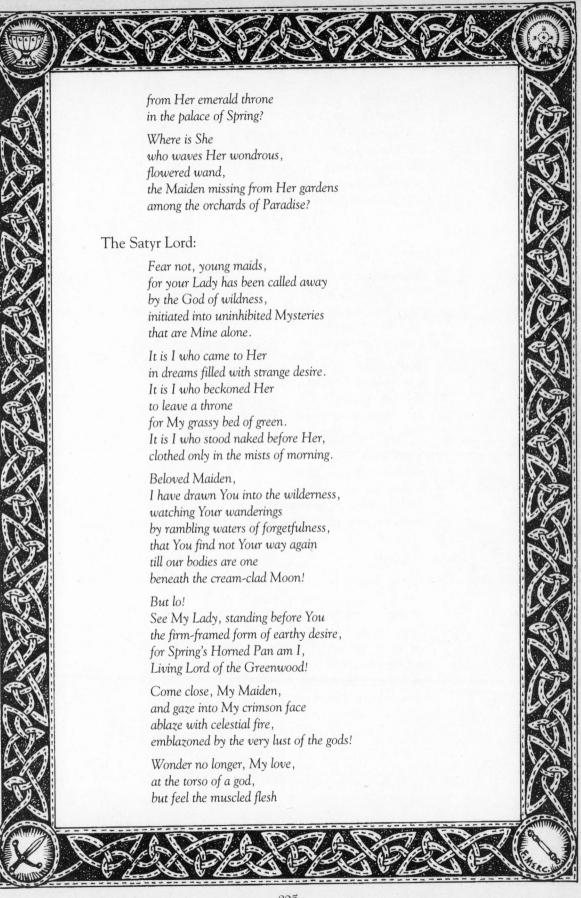

from Her emerald throne
in the palace of Spring?

Where is She
who waves Her wondrous,
flowered wand,
the Maiden missing from Her gardens
among the orchards of Paradise?

The Satyr Lord:

Fear not, young maids,
for your Lady has been called away
by the God of wildness,
initiated into uninhibited Mysteries
that are Mine alone.

It is I who came to Her
in dreams filled with strange desire.
It is I who beckoned Her
to leave a throne
for My grassy bed of green.
It is I who stood naked before Her,
clothed only in the mists of morning.

Beloved Maiden,
I have drawn You into the wilderness,
watching Your wanderings
by rambling waters of forgetfulness,
that You find not Your way again
till our bodies are one
beneath the cream-clad Moon!

But lo!
See My Lady, standing before You
the firm-framed form of earthy desire,
for Spring's Horned Pan am I,
Living Lord of the Greenwood!

Come close, My Maiden,
and gaze into My crimson face
ablaze with celestial fire,
emblazoned by the very lust of the gods!

Wonder no longer, My love,
at the torso of a god,
but feel the muscled flesh

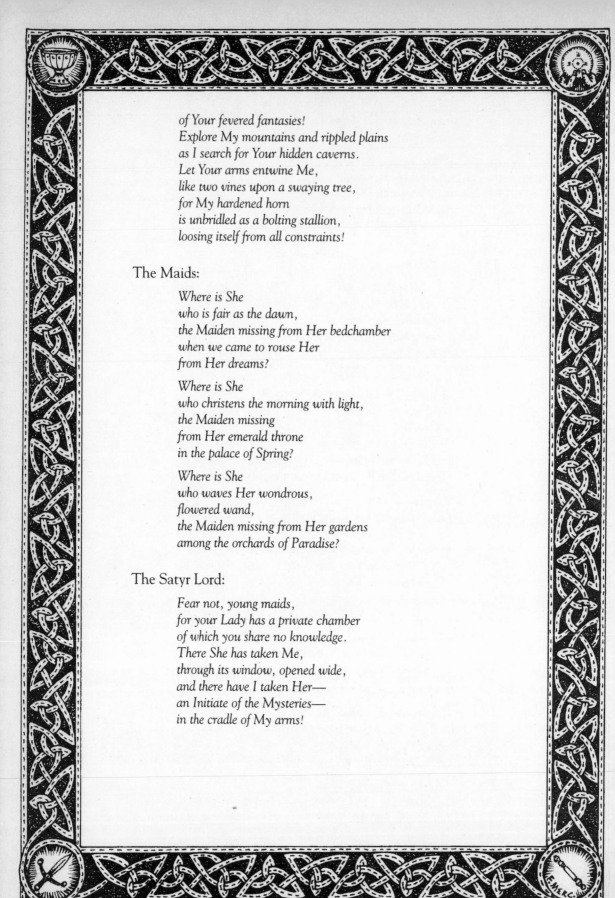

of Your fevered fantasies!
Explore My mountains and rippled plains
as I search for Your hidden caverns.
Let Your arms entwine Me,
like two vines upon a swaying tree,
for My hardened horn
is unbridled as a bolting stallion,
loosing itself from all constraints!

The Maids:

Where is She
who is fair as the dawn,
the Maiden missing from Her bedchamber
when we came to rouse Her
from Her dreams?

Where is She
who christens the morning with light,
the Maiden missing
from Her emerald throne
in the palace of Spring?

Where is She
who waves Her wondrous,
flowered wand,
the Maiden missing from Her gardens
among the orchards of Paradise?

The Satyr Lord:

Fear not, young maids,
for your Lady has a private chamber
of which you share no knowledge.
There She has taken Me,
through its window, opened wide,
and there have I taken Her—
an Initiate of the Mysteries—
in the cradle of My arms!

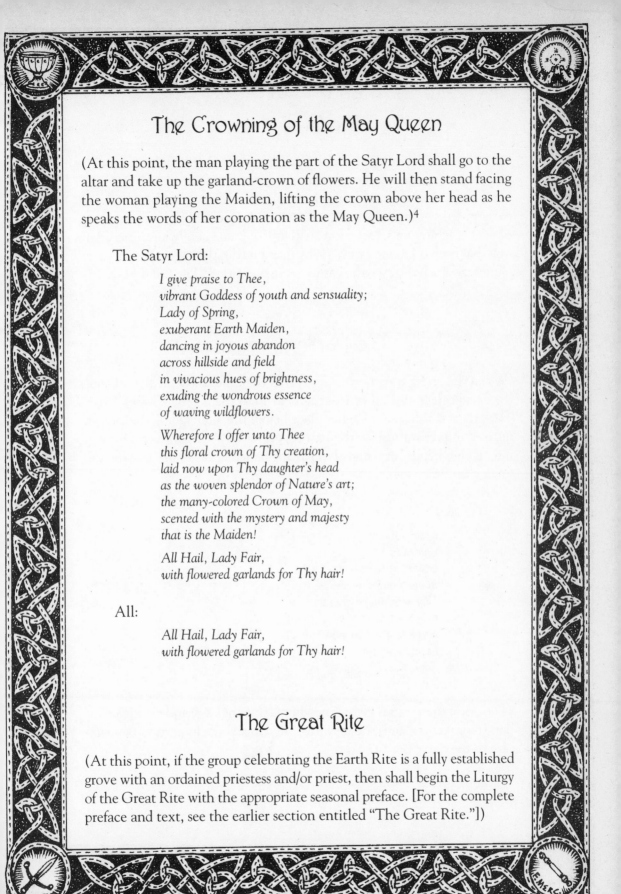

The Crowning of the May Queen

(At this point, the man playing the part of the Satyr Lord shall go to the altar and take up the garland-crown of flowers. He will then stand facing the woman playing the Maiden, lifting the crown above her head as he speaks the words of her coronation as the May Queen.)[4]

The Satyr Lord:

I give praise to Thee,
vibrant Goddess of youth and sensuality;
Lady of Spring,
exuberant Earth Maiden,
dancing in joyous abandon
across hillside and field
in vivacious hues of brightness,
exuding the wondrous essence
of waving wildflowers.

Wherefore I offer unto Thee
this floral crown of Thy creation,
laid now upon Thy daughter's head
as the woven splendor of Nature's art;
the many-colored Crown of May,
scented with the mystery and majesty
that is the Maiden!

All Hail, Lady Fair,
with flowered garlands for Thy hair!

All:

All Hail, Lady Fair,
with flowered garlands for Thy hair!

The Great Rite

(At this point, if the group celebrating the Earth Rite is a fully established grove with an ordained priestess and/or priest, then shall begin the Liturgy of the Great Rite with the appropriate seasonal preface. [For the complete preface and text, see the earlier section entitled "The Great Rite."])

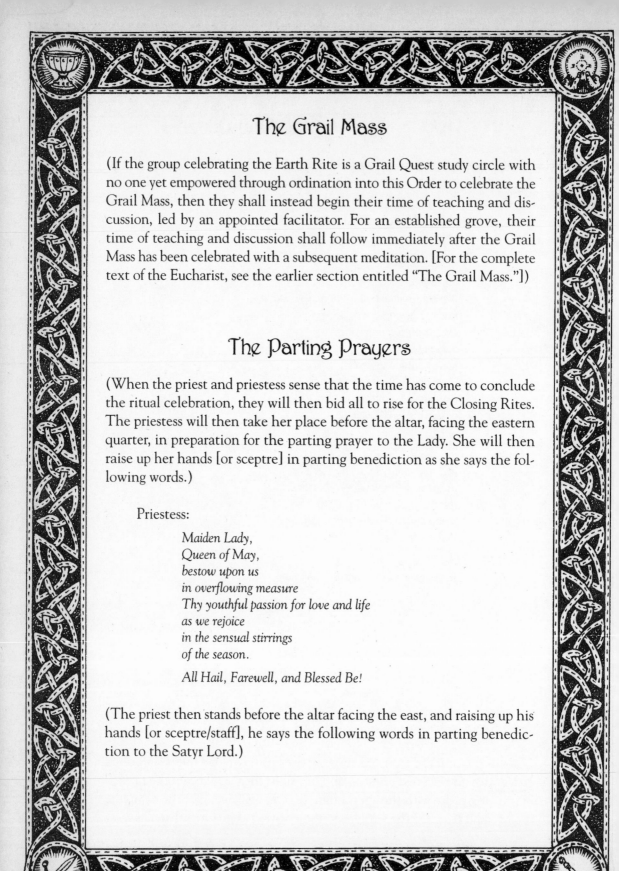

The Grail Mass

(If the group celebrating the Earth Rite is a Grail Quest study circle with no one yet empowered through ordination into this Order to celebrate the Grail Mass, then they shall instead begin their time of teaching and discussion, led by an appointed facilitator. For an established grove, their time of teaching and discussion shall follow immediately after the Grail Mass has been celebrated with a subsequent meditation. [For the complete text of the Eucharist, see the earlier section entitled "The Grail Mass."])

The Parting Prayers

(When the priest and priestess sense that the time has come to conclude the ritual celebration, they will then bid all to rise for the Closing Rites. The priestess will then take her place before the altar, facing the eastern quarter, in preparation for the parting prayer to the Lady. She will then raise up her hands [or sceptre] in parting benediction as she says the following words.)

Priestess:

Maiden Lady,
Queen of May,
bestow upon us
in overflowing measure
Thy youthful passion for love and life
as we rejoice
in the sensual stirrings
of the season.

All Hail, Farewell, and Blessed Be!

(The priest then stands before the altar facing the east, and raising up his hands [or sceptre/staff], he says the following words in parting benediction to the Satyr Lord.)

Priest:

Sovereign Satyr Lord,
Pan of the Pagan Ways,
at this Sabbat of Springtime's warmth,
bestow upon us
the heated breath
of Thy lust for living
as we depart this sacred space
with the joyous blessings
of Thy Beltane benediction.

All Hail, Farewell, and Blessed Be!

The Dismissal of the Quarter-Regents

(At this time, the same appointed grove members that called the respective Quarter-Regents in the beginning of the ritual will now dismiss Them to Their own domains. The dismissal will always begin with the Quarter-Regent who has the seasonal preeminence. [East for Balemas, the sequence of dismissal continuing with the north, west, and south.] The wording and procedure shall be the same as is found in "The Opening and Closing Rites.")

The Opening of the Circle

(The priest will then take his glaive to the marked boundary of the circle, and open the circle in accordance with the wording and procedures as outlined in "The Opening and Closing Rites.")

The Closing Benediction

(The priestess will then make the final proclamation of the ritual's conclusion.)

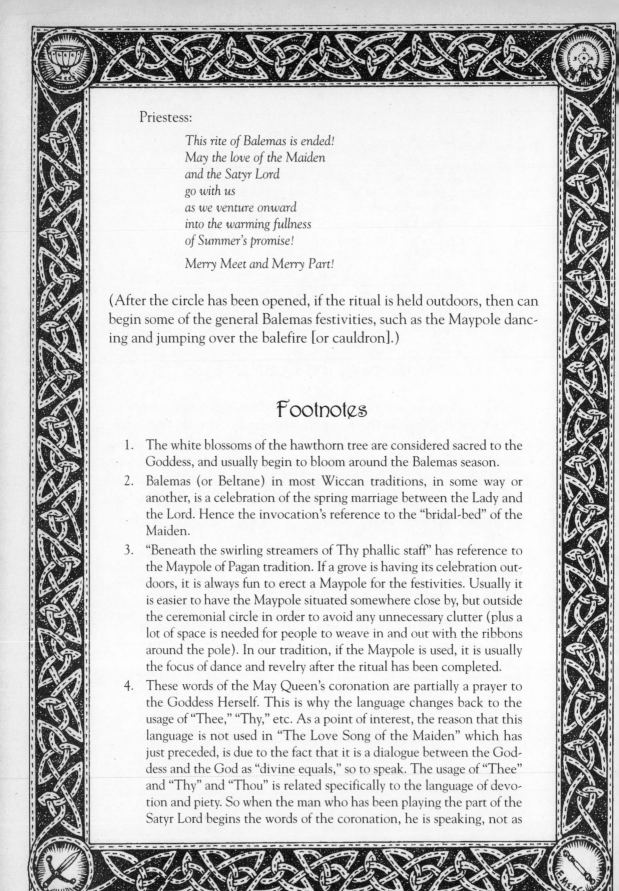

Priestess:

> *This rite of Balemas is ended!*
> *May the love of the Maiden*
> *and the Satyr Lord*
> *go with us*
> *as we venture onward*
> *into the warming fullness*
> *of Summer's promise!*
>
> *Merry Meet and Merry Part!*

(After the circle has been opened, if the ritual is held outdoors, then can begin some of the general Balemas festivities, such as the Maypole dancing and jumping over the balefire [or cauldron].)

Footnotes

1. The white blossoms of the hawthorn tree are considered sacred to the Goddess, and usually begin to bloom around the Balemas season.

2. Balemas (or Beltane) in most Wiccan traditions, in some way or another, is a celebration of the spring marriage between the Lady and the Lord. Hence the invocation's reference to the "bridal-bed" of the Maiden.

3. "Beneath the swirling streamers of Thy phallic staff" has reference to the Maypole of Pagan tradition. If a grove is having its celebration outdoors, it is always fun to erect a Maypole for the festivities. Usually it is easier to have the Maypole situated somewhere close by, but outside the ceremonial circle in order to avoid any unnecessary clutter (plus a lot of space is needed for people to weave in and out with the ribbons around the pole). In our tradition, if the Maypole is used, it is usually the focus of dance and revelry after the ritual has been completed.

4. These words of the May Queen's coronation are partially a prayer to the Goddess Herself. This is why the language changes back to the usage of "Thee," "Thy," etc. As a point of interest, the reason that this language is not used in "The Love Song of the Maiden" which has just preceded, is due to the fact that it is a dialogue between the Goddess and the God as "divine equals," so to speak. The usage of "Thee" and "Thy" and "Thou" is related specifically to the language of devotion and piety. So when the man who has been playing the part of the Satyr Lord begins the words of the coronation, he is speaking, not as

the Satyr Lord, but as a mortal in supplication to the Lady. The "daughter" to which he refers is the woman who is chosen to be the May Queen. And when he proclaims, "All Hail, Lady Fair, with flowered garlands for Thy hair," he is addressing the Goddess within the May Queen herself.

For the purposes of solitary practice, this particular part of the ritual can be changed so as to be adaptable for either a solitary or a small group where no woman may be present.

The Floral Offering to the Goddess

(In a solitary rite for Balemas, the garland crown of flowers is initially placed at the eastern quarter of the circle in preparation for this moment in the ritual. The solitary celebrant will now pick up the flower-crown, and standing or kneeling before the altar s/he will begin the prayer.)

Solitary:

> *We give praise to Thee,*
> *vibrant Goddess of youth and sensuality;*
> *Lady of Spring,*
> *exuberant Earth Maiden,*
> *dancing in joyous abandon*
> *with the goat-footed God*
> *across hillside and field*
> *in vivacious hues of brightness,*
> *exuding the wondrous essence*
> *of waving wildflowers.*
>
> *Wherefore we offer unto Thee*
> *this floral crown of Thy Creation,*
> *laid now upon Thine altar*
> *as the woven splendor of Nature's art;*
> *the many-colored Crown of May,*
> *scented with the mystery and majesty*
> *that is the Maiden!*
>
> *All Hail, Lady Fair,*
> *with flowered garlands for Thy hair!*

(S/he then lays the crown upon the altar as an offering to the Goddess.)

The Opening Rites: "With fire, with water, with earth, and with air ..."

Summer Solstice

Basic Requirements

Below are some things to remember for the Low Earth Rite of the Summer Solstice which are necessary requirements if the observance is to be in accordance with the rubrics of the Ordo Arcanorum Gradalis.

Altar

The altar should be in the center of the circle area, facing the southern quarter.

Altar Cloth

The altar cloth should always be red for the Low Earth Rite of the Summer Solstice. (This is only if you are using a regular rectangular altar. If you are using the Altar of the Pentagram, see the earlier chapter entitled "The Altar and the Sacred Tools" for further details and instructions.)

Altar Candles

The two main altar candles should be red for the Low Earth Rite of the Summer Solstice.

Other Candles

The four quarter candles (or glass votive candleholders) *should always be blue in the west, red in the south, yellow (or gold) in the east, and green in the north.* All other secondary candles used for extra lighting in the ritual area should be of either various shades of red or gold or whatever other colors suit the grove's personal tastes.

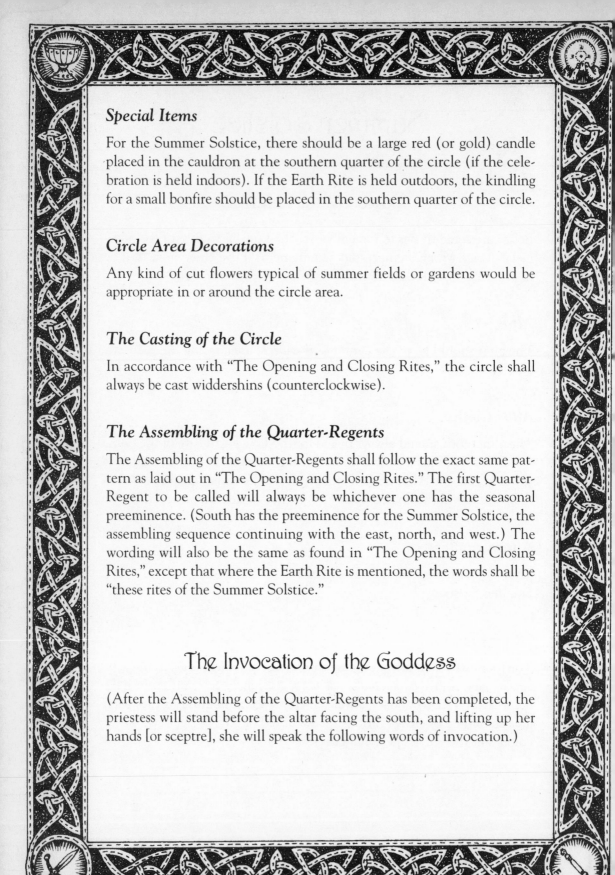

Special Items

For the Summer Solstice, there should be a large red (or gold) candle placed in the cauldron at the southern quarter of the circle (if the celebration is held indoors). If the Earth Rite is held outdoors, the kindling for a small bonfire should be placed in the southern quarter of the circle.

Circle Area Decorations

Any kind of cut flowers typical of summer fields or gardens would be appropriate in or around the circle area.

The Casting of the Circle

In accordance with "The Opening and Closing Rites," the circle shall always be cast widdershins (counterclockwise).

The Assembling of the Quarter-Regents

The Assembling of the Quarter-Regents shall follow the exact same pattern as laid out in "The Opening and Closing Rites." The first Quarter-Regent to be called will always be whichever one has the seasonal preeminence. (South has the preeminence for the Summer Solstice, the assembling sequence continuing with the east, north, and west.) The wording will also be the same as found in "The Opening and Closing Rites," except that where the Earth Rite is mentioned, the words shall be "these rites of the Summer Solstice."

The Invocation of the Goddess

(After the Assembling of the Quarter-Regents has been completed, the priestess will stand before the altar facing the south, and lifting up her hands [or sceptre], she will speak the following words of invocation.)

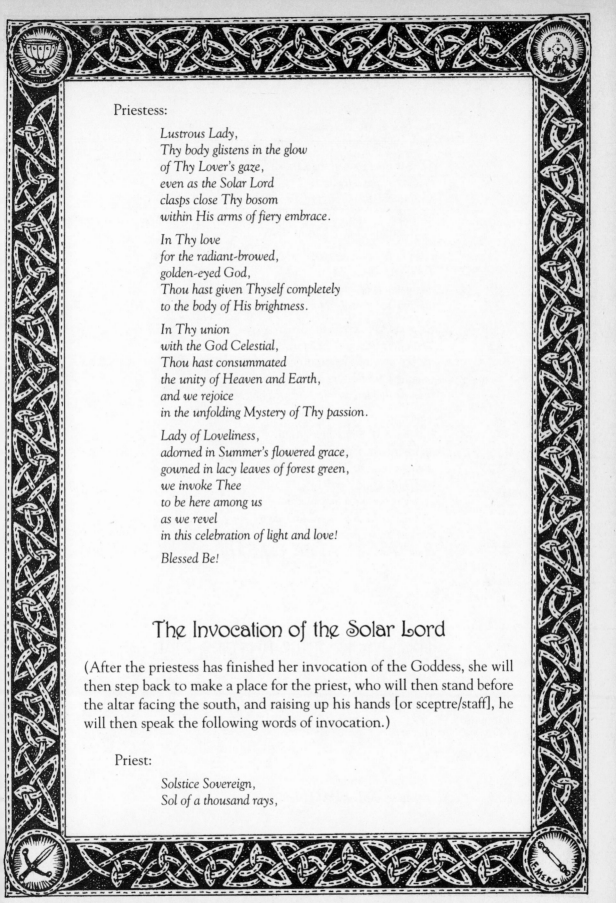

Priestess:

> Lustrous Lady,
> Thy body glistens in the glow
> of Thy Lover's gaze,
> even as the Solar Lord
> clasps close Thy bosom
> within His arms of fiery embrace.
>
> In Thy love
> for the radiant-browed,
> golden-eyed God,
> Thou hast given Thyself completely
> to the body of His brightness.
>
> In Thy union
> with the God Celestial,
> Thou hast consummated
> the unity of Heaven and Earth,
> and we rejoice
> in the unfolding Mystery of Thy passion.
>
> Lady of Loveliness,
> adorned in Summer's flowered grace,
> gowned in lacy leaves of forest green,
> we invoke Thee
> to be here among us
> as we revel
> in this celebration of light and love!
>
> Blessed Be!

The Invocation of the Solar Lord

(After the priestess has finished her invocation of the Goddess, she will then step back to make a place for the priest, who will then stand before the altar facing the south, and raising up his hands [or sceptre/staff], he will then speak the following words of invocation.)

Priest:

> Solstice Sovereign,
> Sol of a thousand rays,

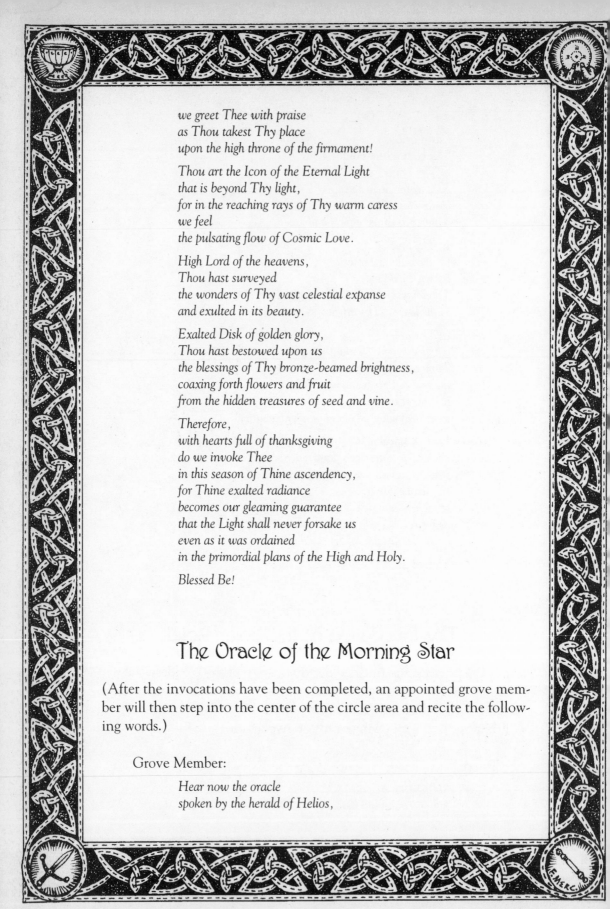

we greet Thee with praise
as Thou takest Thy place
upon the high throne of the firmament!

Thou art the Icon of the Eternal Light
that is beyond Thy light,
for in the reaching rays of Thy warm caress
we feel
the pulsating flow of Cosmic Love.

High Lord of the heavens,
Thou hast surveyed
the wonders of Thy vast celestial expanse
and exulted in its beauty.

Exalted Disk of golden glory,
Thou hast bestowed upon us
the blessings of Thy bronze-beamed brightness,
coaxing forth flowers and fruit
from the hidden treasures of seed and vine.

Therefore,
with hearts full of thanksgiving
do we invoke Thee
in this season of Thine ascendency,
for Thine exalted radiance
becomes our gleaming guarantee
that the Light shall never forsake us
even as it was ordained
in the primordial plans of the High and Holy.

Blessed Be!

The Oracle of the Morning Star

(After the invocations have been completed, an appointed grove member will then step into the center of the circle area and recite the following words.)

Grove Member:

Hear now the oracle
spoken by the herald of Helios,

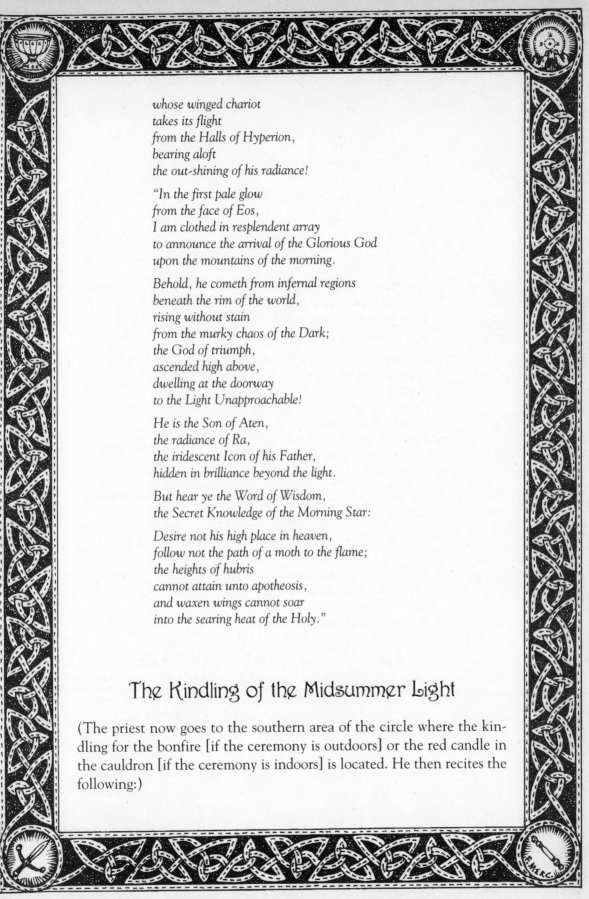

whose winged chariot
takes its flight
from the Halls of Hyperion,
bearing aloft
the out-shining of his radiance!

"In the first pale glow
from the face of Eos,
I am clothed in resplendent array
to announce the arrival of the Glorious God
upon the mountains of the morning.

Behold, he cometh from infernal regions
beneath the rim of the world,
rising without stain
from the murky chaos of the Dark;
the God of triumph,
ascended high above,
dwelling at the doorway
to the Light Unapproachable!

He is the Son of Aten,
the radiance of Ra,
the iridescent Icon of his Father,
hidden in brilliance beyond the light.

But hear ye the Word of Wisdom,
the Secret Knowledge of the Morning Star:

Desire not his high place in heaven,
follow not the path of a moth to the flame;
the heights of hubris
cannot attain unto apotheosis,
and waxen wings cannot soar
into the searing heat of the Holy."

The Kindling of the Midsummer Light

(The priest now goes to the southern area of the circle where the kindling for the bonfire [if the ceremony is outdoors] or the red candle in the cauldron [if the ceremony is indoors] is located. He then recites the following:)

307

Priest:

The Sun-King sinks below the horizon,
but his warmth remains
in the heaviness of the humid dark
as sweat makes slick the skin
from the lingering of his heated breath.

While twilight changes
to late-evening hues of ebony and indigo,
the Solstice Lord
scatters fragments of himself
into the airy sea of Summer night;
sparkling sequins of flying reflections
in the dance of fleeting fireflies.

And even now shall the element of his brilliance
consume the kindling and the wick
in the circumscribed glories
of candle and fire;
flaming microcosms of the Sun;
symbols of the Solstice
submerged in nocturnal shadows
of Midsummer fantasy.

(Here the priest lights the bonfire [if outdoors] or the red solar candle [if indoors], speaking the following incantation.)

Priest:

Shining like the sacred Sun,
Thy fire we kindle as day is done.
Beings of Light, surround us here,
Illumine the night with love and cheer!

(At this point, the priestess and priest will lead the rest of the grove in a deosil procession around the circle, either rhythmically speaking or chanting the same incantation. [This can be accompanied with drumming, flutes, harps, and/or other musical instruments, if desired.])[1]

Hymn of Exaltation to the Solar Lord

(When the chanting has been concluded, the priestess will then take the candle-lantern from its place, and standing in the center of the circle next to the altar, she will lift it up as she recites the following hymn.)

Priestess:

> *Let us give glory*
> *to Him Who sits enthroned*
> *at the apex of His epiphany,*
> *Symbol of the light-originating Logos,*
> *seated high above*
> *the Assembly of the Mighty*
> *as a burning beacon*
> *upon the shining path*
> *to the Mysteries of higher realms!*
>
> *Sun of Righteousness!*
> *Sol Invictus!*
> *Solar Savior!*
> *We hail Thy coronation*
> *as Lord of the Summer Skies*
> *in honor of Thy Solstice supremacy!*
>
> *From Thy majesty*
> *proceeds the very Light of nations,*
> *the shining brilliance of illumined Truth,*
> *and the manifest splendor of the Sacred.*
>
> *Hallowed Blaze of Heaven,*
> *Thou art the living Light,*
> *Source of inspiration*
> *to sage and saint,*
> *priestess and prophet.*
>
> *Therefore,*
> *we add to the adoration of the ancients*
> *as we ascribe to Thee praise and honor,*
> *O Radiant King of planetary gods!*

(The priestess will then take the candle-lantern with her, going first to the eastern quarter and then to the western quarter, making the sign of the equal-armed solar cross with the candle-lantern as she says the following:)

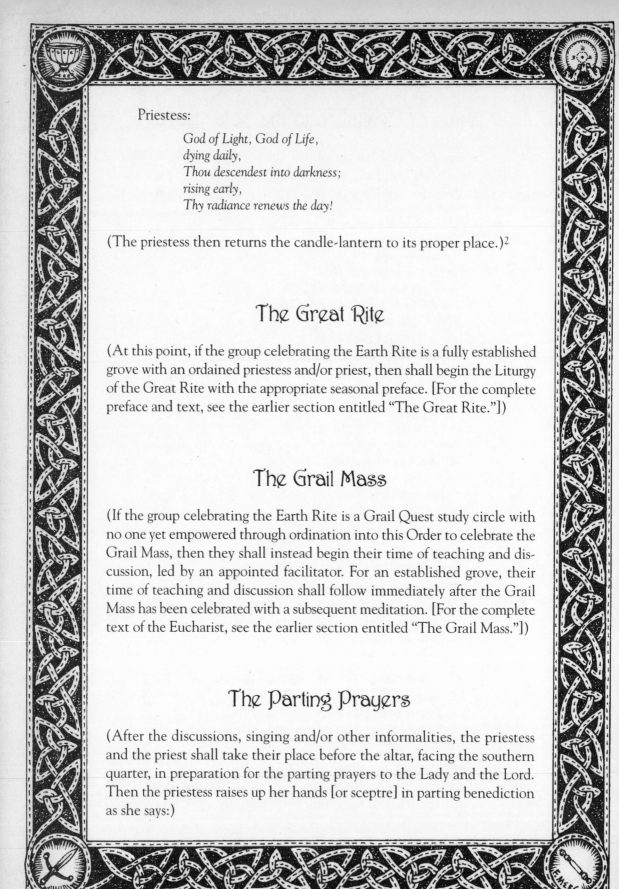

Priestess:

> God of Light, God of Life,
> dying daily,
> Thou descendest into darkness;
> rising early,
> Thy radiance renews the day!

(The priestess then returns the candle-lantern to its proper place.)[2]

The Great Rite

(At this point, if the group celebrating the Earth Rite is a fully established grove with an ordained priestess and/or priest, then shall begin the Liturgy of the Great Rite with the appropriate seasonal preface. [For the complete preface and text, see the earlier section entitled "The Great Rite."])

The Grail Mass

(If the group celebrating the Earth Rite is a Grail Quest study circle with no one yet empowered through ordination into this Order to celebrate the Grail Mass, then they shall instead begin their time of teaching and discussion, led by an appointed facilitator. For an established grove, their time of teaching and discussion shall follow immediately after the Grail Mass has been celebrated with a subsequent meditation. [For the complete text of the Eucharist, see the earlier section entitled "The Grail Mass."])

The Parting Prayers

(After the discussions, singing and/or other informalities, the priestess and the priest shall take their place before the altar, facing the southern quarter, in preparation for the parting prayers to the Lady and the Lord. Then the priestess raises up her hands [or sceptre] in parting benediction as she says:)

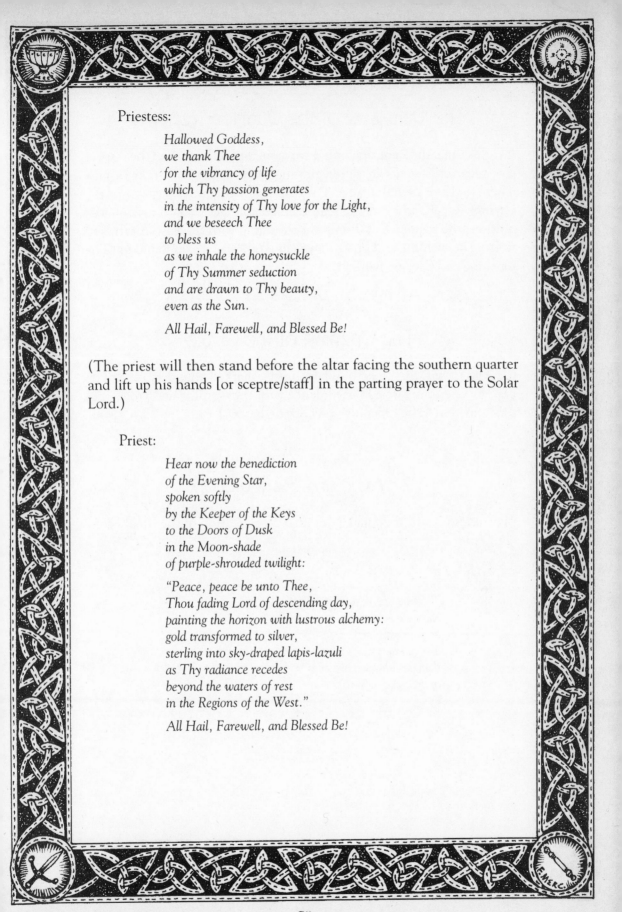

Priestess:

> Hallowed Goddess,
> we thank Thee
> for the vibrancy of life
> which Thy passion generates
> in the intensity of Thy love for the Light,
> and we beseech Thee
> to bless us
> as we inhale the honeysuckle
> of Thy Summer seduction
> and are drawn to Thy beauty,
> even as the Sun.

> All Hail, Farewell, and Blessed Be!

(The priest will then stand before the altar facing the southern quarter and lift up his hands [or sceptre/staff] in the parting prayer to the Solar Lord.)

Priest:

> Hear now the benediction
> of the Evening Star,
> spoken softly
> by the Keeper of the Keys
> to the Doors of Dusk
> in the Moon-shade
> of purple-shrouded twilight:

> "Peace, peace be unto Thee,
> Thou fading Lord of descending day,
> painting the horizon with lustrous alchemy:
> gold transformed to silver,
> sterling into sky-draped lapis-lazuli
> as Thy radiance recedes
> beyond the waters of rest
> in the Regions of the West."

> All Hail, Farewell, and Blessed Be!

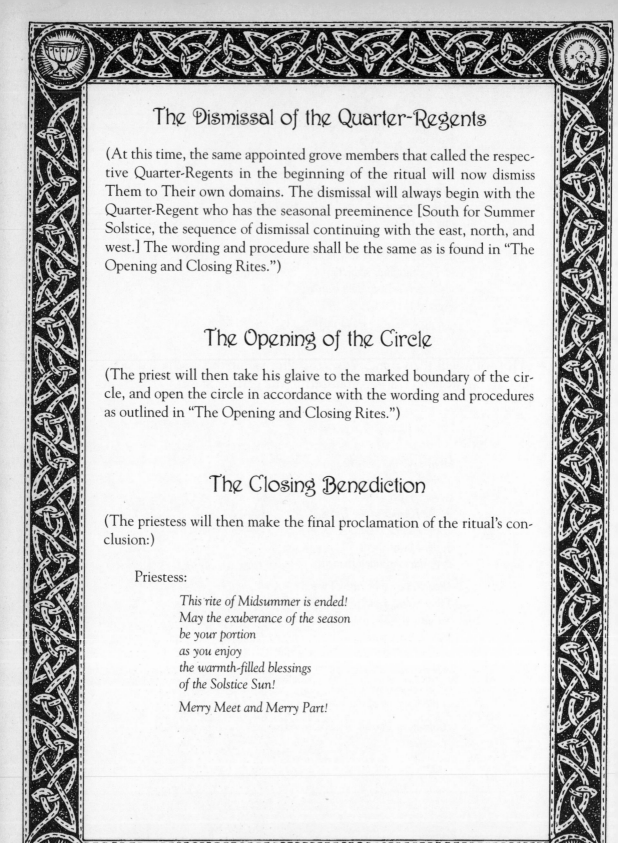

The Dismissal of the Quarter-Regents

(At this time, the same appointed grove members that called the respective Quarter-Regents in the beginning of the ritual will now dismiss Them to Their own domains. The dismissal will always begin with the Quarter-Regent who has the seasonal preeminence [South for Summer Solstice, the sequence of dismissal continuing with the east, north, and west.] The wording and procedure shall be the same as is found in "The Opening and Closing Rites.")

The Opening of the Circle

(The priest will then take his glaive to the marked boundary of the circle, and open the circle in accordance with the wording and procedures as outlined in "The Opening and Closing Rites.")

The Closing Benediction

(The priestess will then make the final proclamation of the ritual's conclusion:)

Priestess:

This rite of Midsummer is ended!
May the exuberance of the season
be your portion
as you enjoy
the warmth-filled blessings
of the Solstice Sun!

Merry Meet and Merry Part!

Footnotes

1. In this instance, the procession is led deosil to symbolize the rising and setting of the Solar Lord on this, the day of His glorification.

2. If the grove has a permanent indoor temple, the candle-lantern is usually kept on a side-altar within the circle. Otherwise, when not in use, it should be kept near the cauldron in the southern quarter of the circle.

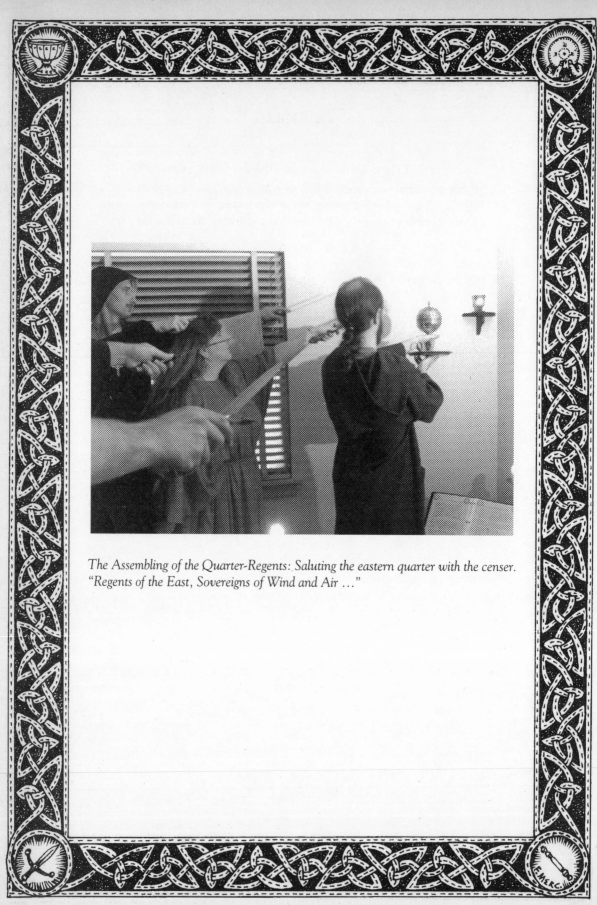

The Assembling of the Quarter-Regents: Saluting the eastern quarter with the censer. "Regents of the East, Sovereigns of Wind and Air …"

Lammas

Basic Requirements

Below are some things to remember for the High Earth Rite of Lammas which are necessary requirements if the observance is to be in accordance with the rubrics of the Ordo Arcanorum Gradalis.

Altar

The altar should be in the center of the circle area, facing the southern quarter.

Altar Cloth

The altar cloth should always be red for the High Earth Rite of Lammas. (This is only if you are using a regular rectangular altar. If you are using the Altar of the Pentagram, see the earlier chapter entitled "The Altar and the Sacred Tools" for further details and instructions.)

Altar Candles

The two main altar candles should be red for the High Earth Rite of Lammas.

Other Candles

The four quarter candles (or glass votive candleholders) *should always be blue in the west, red in the south, yellow (or gold) in the east, and green in the north.* All other secondary candles used for extra lighting in the ritual area should be of various shades of red, yellow, and gold, or whatever other colors may suit the personal tastes of the grove.

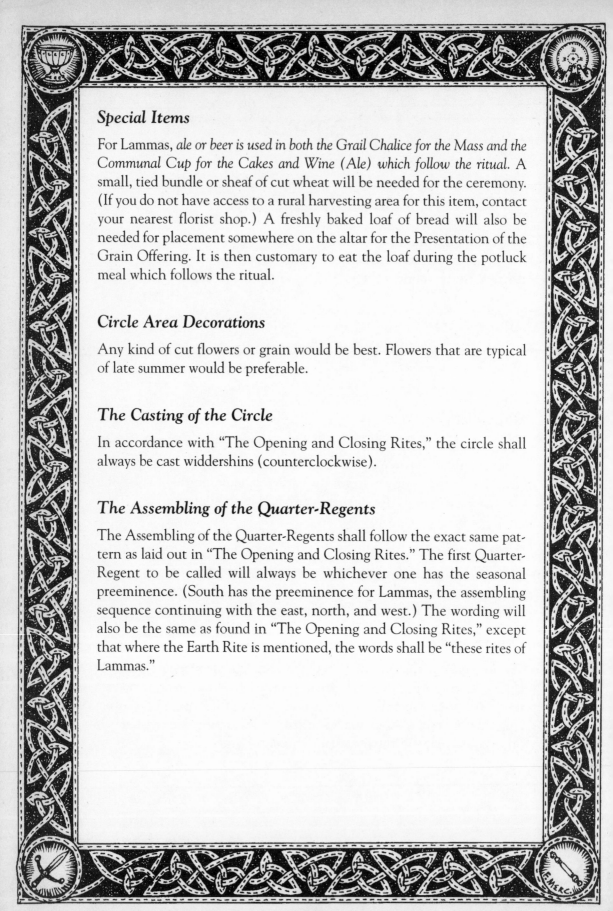

Special Items

For Lammas, *ale or beer is used in both the Grail Chalice for the Mass and the Communal Cup for the Cakes and Wine (Ale) which follow the ritual.* A small, tied bundle or sheaf of cut wheat will be needed for the ceremony. (If you do not have access to a rural harvesting area for this item, contact your nearest florist shop.) A freshly baked loaf of bread will also be needed for placement somewhere on the altar for the Presentation of the Grain Offering. It is then customary to eat the loaf during the potluck meal which follows the ritual.

Circle Area Decorations

Any kind of cut flowers or grain would be best. Flowers that are typical of late summer would be preferable.

The Casting of the Circle

In accordance with "The Opening and Closing Rites," the circle shall always be cast widdershins (counterclockwise).

The Assembling of the Quarter-Regents

The Assembling of the Quarter-Regents shall follow the exact same pattern as laid out in "The Opening and Closing Rites." The first Quarter-Regent to be called will always be whichever one has the seasonal preeminence. (South has the preeminence for Lammas, the assembling sequence continuing with the east, north, and west.) The wording will also be the same as found in "The Opening and Closing Rites," except that where the Earth Rite is mentioned, the words shall be "these rites of Lammas."

The Invocation of the Goddess

(After the Assembling of the Quarter-Regents has been completed, the priestess will then stand before the altar, facing the southern quarter as she lifts up her hands [or sceptre] saying the following invocation.)

Priestess:

Lavish Lady of Summer's delight,
Thy beauty is ageless in its season,
captivating to the senses of our fascination!

In Thy hands are sheaves of ripened wheat.
In Thy womb is the promise of fertility.
In Thy breasts are the milky rivers of life.

Goat-footed satyrs play before Thy presence
and nymphs look upon Thee with wonder,
for Thou art the Lover and the Mother,
Lady of sensuousness and the suckled breast.

Bronze-bodied Helios,
his eyes the radiance of heaven,
has sapped his strength,
spent upon Thy bed of passion!

Spring's Horned Lord
lies exhausted in Thy Summer chamber,
depleted from the flaming heat of Thy desires!

Thy lovers are many, yet they decline
while Thy womb is full
with the fruit of their union![1]

Expectant Mother,
soon to give birth to Autumn's harvest,
we invoke Thee to be here among us
as we celebrate the Mysteries
of this earth-bearing season!

The Presentation of the Grain Offering

(When the priestess has concluded the invocation of the Goddess, the priest will then begin the prayer of offering facing the altar with hands uplifted. When he comes to the words "the baked bounty of fresh-made bread and the hops-laden ale of August," each item mentioned will then either be picked up or pointed towards for emphasis.)

Priest:

Our Lady of Lammas,
Thou providest us with seed for sowing,
Thou rewardest us with fields for reaping;
Thou bringest forth upon the labored land
sprouted legions of the staff of life.

Grain-giving Goddess,
Mother of the early and latter harvests,
we rejoice before Thee
for these first fruits from the fields:
the baked bounty of fresh-made bread
and the hops-laden ale of August.

Be pleased to accept
these our offerings upon Thine altar,
that we who partake of them
may be blessed
with the strength of the Summer Sun,
the refreshment of renewing rain,
and the abundance of this sultry season.

The Wave Offering

(Now the priestess [or any appointed grove member] will stand before the altar, facing the southern quarter, and lifting up with both hands the small, bundled sheaf of wheat, she will recite the following words.)[2]

Priestess:

Blessed Kore,
Thou Who bearest

the ancient, sacred, crescent sickle;
we wave before Thee in somber presentation
the seasonal sheaf of sacrifice,
the Body of the Corn King,
the solemn reminder
that life feeds upon life,
one form upon another;
and that all generations,
harvested by the Death-reaping scythe of Time,
shall be bundled
into sheaves of sleeping shadows,
making way for other lives to come.

(The priestess [or appointed grove member] will then begin to wave the sheaf of wheat back and forth, reciting the words below. When the priestess has finished, each member of the grove in turn will come forward and be handed the sheaf which they will each wave in turn, while all in unison recite the same words with each waving of the sheaf. [These words can also be chanted or set to music if the grove so wishes.])

All:

Spirits of the wind, wave gently,
the barley, the oats and the rye,
sighing a song through the whispering wheat
of the harvest that now draws nigh!

The Great Rite

(At this point, if the group celebrating the Earth Rite is a fully established grove with an ordained priestess and/or priest, then shall begin the Liturgy of the Great Rite with the appropriate seasonal preface. [For the complete preface and text, see the earlier section entitled "The Great Rite."])

The Grail Mass

(If the group celebrating the Earth Rite is a Grail Quest study circle with no one yet empowered through ordination into this Order to celebrate the Grail Mass, then they shall instead begin their time of teaching and discussion, led by an appointed facilitator. For an established grove, their time of teaching and discussion shall follow immediately after the Grail Mass has been celebrated with a subsequent meditation. [For the complete text of the Eucharist, see the earlier section entitled "The Grail Mass."])

The Parting Prayer

(When the time has come to bring the ritual to a close, the priestess will bid the grove members to stand as she takes her place before the altar, facing the southern quarter. Lifting up her hands [or sceptre] she will then begin the parting prayer to the Lady.)

Priestess:

> *Gracious Goddess,*
> *we have tasted*
> *of the brew and the bread;*
> *we have fed*
> *upon the nourishing staples of life,*
> *thoughtful of the Lord of Harvest;*
> *and we are thankful*
> *for the mystery of meaning*
> *that these gifts of grain*
> *convey to us.*
>
> *Our Lady of Lammastide,*
> *we pray Thee,*
> *bestow upon us now*
> *Thy Sabbat blessing*
> *as Thou takest Thy leave*
> *of this sacred space,*
> *leaving us*
> *with Thy silent, Summer benediction.*
>
> *All Hail, Farewell, and Blessed Be!*

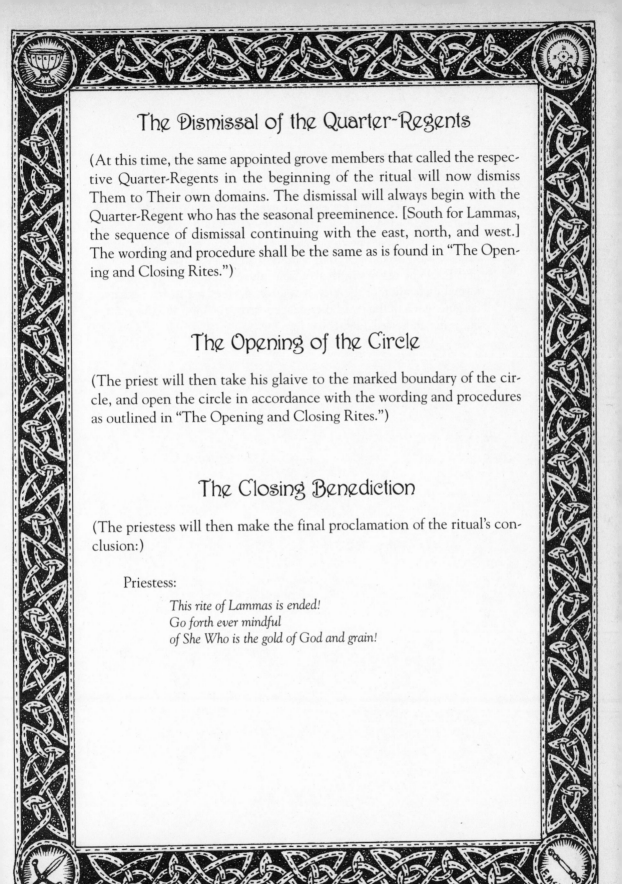

The Dismissal of the Quarter-Regents

(At this time, the same appointed grove members that called the respective Quarter-Regents in the beginning of the ritual will now dismiss Them to Their own domains. The dismissal will always begin with the Quarter-Regent who has the seasonal preeminence. [South for Lammas, the sequence of dismissal continuing with the east, north, and west.] The wording and procedure shall be the same as is found in "The Opening and Closing Rites.")

The Opening of the Circle

(The priest will then take his glaive to the marked boundary of the circle, and open the circle in accordance with the wording and procedures as outlined in "The Opening and Closing Rites.")

The Closing Benediction

(The priestess will then make the final proclamation of the ritual's conclusion:)

Priestess:

> This rite of Lammas is ended!
> Go forth ever mindful
> of She Who is the gold of God and grain!

Footnotes

1. This is not meant to imply that the Goddess is some kind of faithless nymphomaniac! In actuality, all these lovers of the Lady are the same God, but in different seasonal and emanating aspects; the Satyr Lord, for instance, being the terrestrial, earthy manifestation of the God, whereas Helios is a celestial, heavenly manifestation of the God.

2. At Lammas this presentation takes the place of the regular invocation of the God. The sheaf of grain is in itself an image of the God's sacrifice. For some reason, in the course of the evolution of this ritual, a formal invocation of the God was never deemed necessary; perhaps because much of the ritual uses imagery *about* the God and the grain, but is not addressed directly to Him.

The Grail Mass: The Consecration of the Chalice. "Descend, we pray, upon this Cup which we offer ..."

Fall Equinox

Basic Requirements

Below are some things to remember for the Low Earth Rite of the Fall Equinox which are necessary requirements if the observance is to be in accordance with the rubrics of the Ordo Arcanorum Gradalis.

Altar

The altar should be in the center of the circle area, facing the western quarter.

Altar Cloth

The altar cloth should always be blue for the Low Earth Rite of the Fall Equinox. (This is only if you are using a regular rectangular altar. If you are using the Altar of the Pentagram, see the earlier chapter entitled "The Altar and the Sacred Tools" for further details and instructions.)

Altar Candles

The two main altar candles should be blue for the Low Earth Rite of the Fall Equinox.

Other Candles

The four quarter candles (or glass votive candleholders) *should always be blue in the west, red in the south, yellow (or gold) in the east, and green in the north.* All other secondary candles used for extra lighting in the ritual area should be of various shades of pale gold, rust, and other early harvest colors suitable to the grove's personal tastes.

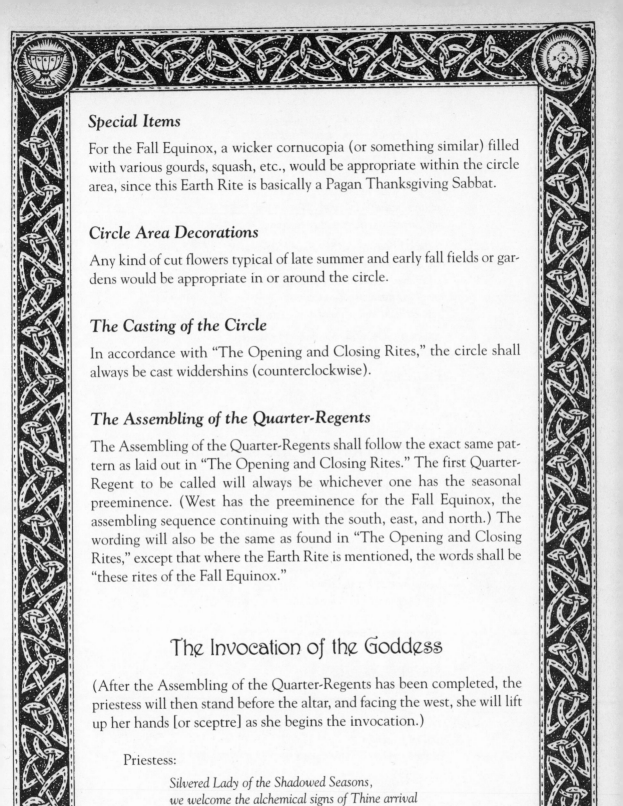

Special Items

For the Fall Equinox, a wicker cornucopia (or something similar) filled with various gourds, squash, etc., would be appropriate within the circle area, since this Earth Rite is basically a Pagan Thanksgiving Sabbat.

Circle Area Decorations

Any kind of cut flowers typical of late summer and early fall fields or gardens would be appropriate in or around the circle.

The Casting of the Circle

In accordance with "The Opening and Closing Rites," the circle shall always be cast widdershins (counterclockwise).

The Assembling of the Quarter-Regents

The Assembling of the Quarter-Regents shall follow the exact same pattern as laid out in "The Opening and Closing Rites." The first Quarter-Regent to be called will always be whichever one has the seasonal preeminence. (West has the preeminence for the Fall Equinox, the assembling sequence continuing with the south, east, and north.) The wording will also be the same as found in "The Opening and Closing Rites," except that where the Earth Rite is mentioned, the words shall be "these rites of the Fall Equinox."

The Invocation of the Goddess

(After the Assembling of the Quarter-Regents has been completed, the priestess will then stand before the altar, and facing the west, she will lift up her hands [or sceptre] as she begins the invocation.)

Priestess:

> *Silvered Lady of the Shadowed Seasons,*
> *we welcome the alchemical signs of Thine arrival*
> *with sturdy trees of shimmering green*

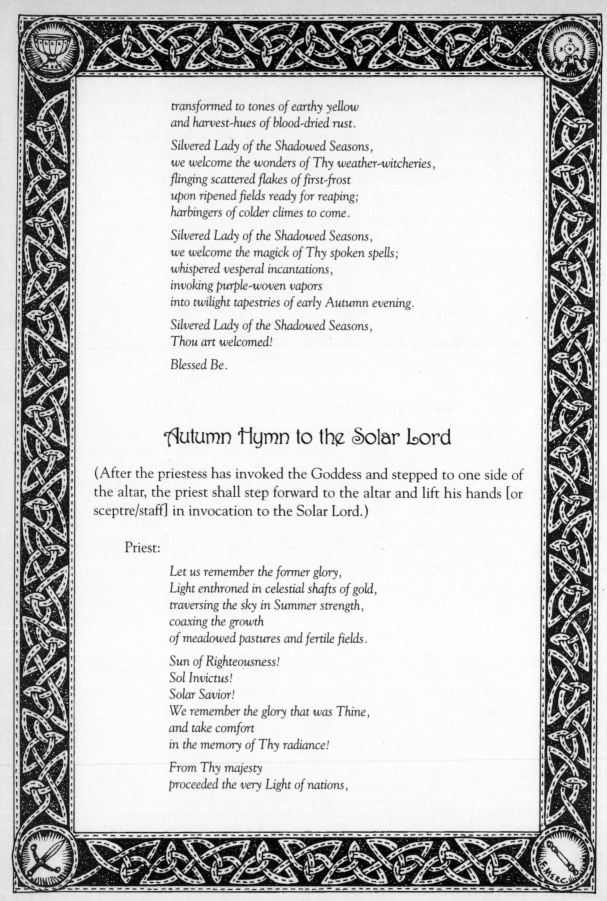

transformed to tones of earthy yellow
and harvest-hues of blood-dried rust.

Silvered Lady of the Shadowed Seasons,
we welcome the wonders of Thy weather-witcheries,
flinging scattered flakes of first-frost
upon ripened fields ready for reaping;
harbingers of colder climes to come.

Silvered Lady of the Shadowed Seasons,
we welcome the magick of Thy spoken spells;
whispered vesperal incantations,
invoking purple-woven vapors
into twilight tapestries of early Autumn evening.

Silvered Lady of the Shadowed Seasons,
Thou art welcomed!

Blessed Be.

Autumn Hymn to the Solar Lord

(After the priestess has invoked the Goddess and stepped to one side of the altar, the priest shall step forward to the altar and lift his hands [or sceptre/staff] in invocation to the Solar Lord.)

Priest:

Let us remember the former glory,
Light enthroned in celestial shafts of gold,
traversing the sky in Summer strength,
coaxing the growth
of meadowed pastures and fertile fields.

Sun of Righteousness!
Sol Invictus!
Solar Savior!
We remember the glory that was Thine,
and take comfort
in the memory of Thy radiance!

From Thy majesty
proceeded the very Light of nations,

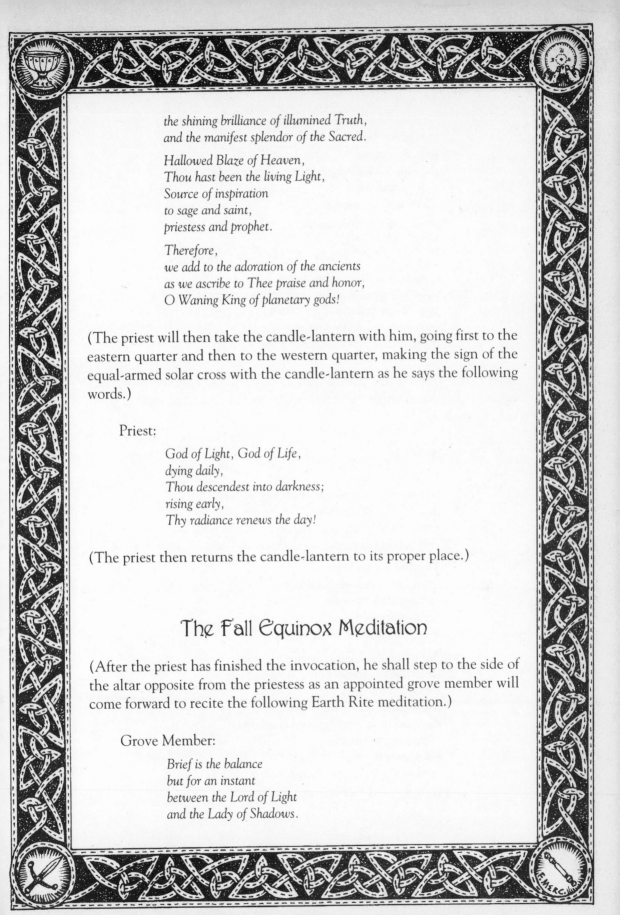

the shining brilliance of illumined Truth,
and the manifest splendor of the Sacred.

Hallowed Blaze of Heaven,
Thou hast been the living Light,
Source of inspiration
to sage and saint,
priestess and prophet.

Therefore,
we add to the adoration of the ancients
as we ascribe to Thee praise and honor,
O Waning King of planetary gods!

(The priest will then take the candle-lantern with him, going first to the eastern quarter and then to the western quarter, making the sign of the equal-armed solar cross with the candle-lantern as he says the following words.)

Priest:

God of Light, God of Life,
dying daily,
Thou descendest into darkness;
rising early,
Thy radiance renews the day!

(The priest then returns the candle-lantern to its proper place.)

The Fall Equinox Meditation

(After the priest has finished the invocation, he shall step to the side of the altar opposite from the priestess as an appointed grove member will come forward to recite the following Earth Rite meditation.)

Grove Member:

Brief is the balance
but for an instant
between the Lord of Light
and the Lady of Shadows.

At this equinox of the ending year,
the waning Sun
must bow before
the dark-kindled dragon-steeds of luminous gloom;
serpent-stallions
whose wondrous wings,
silver-scaled with ebony glow,
veil in cloud-cloaked, misty mantles,
the final, flickering beams of Midsummer warmth.

Swift they sail the turbulent sky
upon leaf-swirling winds of wintry prophecy
from the far-country of the Crone;
trampling into dusky dimness
the retreating rays of Summer's dying Lord.

(Here, the rest of the meditation is recited by another previously appointed grove member. [Preferably one reader should be male and the other female.])

Grove Member:

Summer now retreats
into the perennial parade of passing seasons
as the Wheel of the Year
revolves once more to its place
at the advent of the Season of the Dead.

The time has come for us
to prepare for new beginnings,
making ready our spirits
for the restful reign of the coming Crone
in the womb of Winter's darkness.

But we have reasons to rejoice,
for at this last Sabbat of the dying year,
the love of the Lady
and the gifts of the God
surround us in a multicolored cornucopia
of Autumn's abundance:
the ripened produce
of blossom, fruit, and planted seed;
parting gifts of Summer's gardened growth.

The Harvest Thanksgiving Litany

(At this time the priestess once again takes her place before the altar to lead the grove in the Thanksgiving Litany.)

Priestess:

Therefore,
in joy do we give thanks to Thee,
Great Mother of Harvest Home,
known from of old by a myriad of names
and a multitude of faces:
Anna Perenna, Pomona, Ceres,
    Demeter, and Habondia;
and to Thee do we give hearty thanks,
O Horned Consort of the Lady,
Pan of the Sacred Pipes,
Maddened Dionysus of the Holy Vine!

Lady and Lord,
be pleased now, we pray,
with these,
our heart-felt acclamations of thanksgiving
as we remember the blessings
of yet another year
fast receding into the mists of memory.

for All Hallows past,
when we wisely recollect
that death is the doorway of emerging life.

All: THANKS WE GIVE TO OUR LADY AND LORD!

for the softness of new-fallen snow,
glowing white beneath a Winter Moon,
giving warmth to the slumbering earth.

All: THANKS WE GIVE TO OUR LADY AND LORD!

for the fresh-cleansed scent
of Springtime showers,
quenching the thirst of new-grown grass.

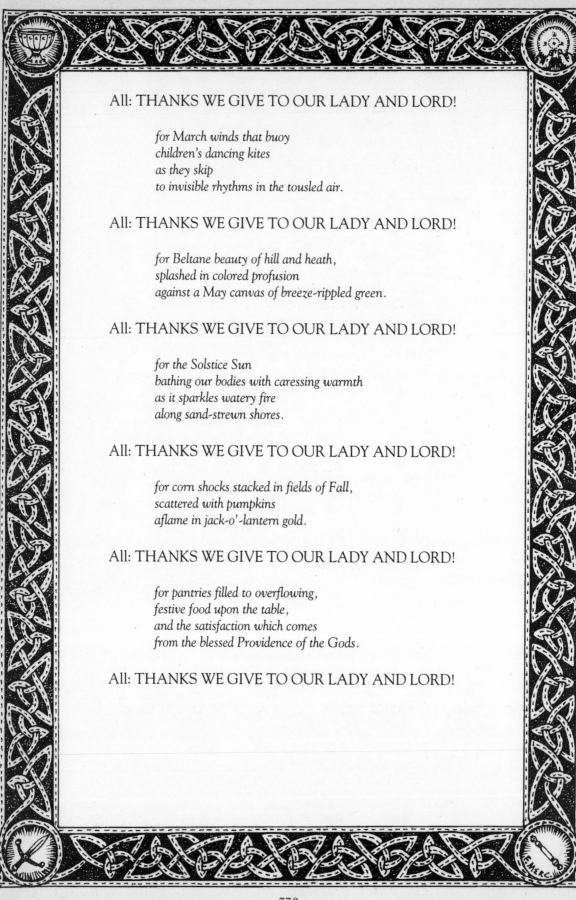

All: THANKS WE GIVE TO OUR LADY AND LORD!

for March winds that buoy
children's dancing kites
as they skip
to invisible rhythms in the tousled air.

All: THANKS WE GIVE TO OUR LADY AND LORD!

for Beltane beauty of hill and heath,
splashed in colored profusion
against a May canvas of breeze-rippled green.

All: THANKS WE GIVE TO OUR LADY AND LORD!

for the Solstice Sun
bathing our bodies with caressing warmth
as it sparkles watery fire
along sand-strewn shores.

All: THANKS WE GIVE TO OUR LADY AND LORD!

for corn shocks stacked in fields of Fall,
scattered with pumpkins
aflame in jack-o'-lantern gold.

All: THANKS WE GIVE TO OUR LADY AND LORD!

for pantries filled to overflowing,
festive food upon the table,
and the satisfaction which comes
from the blessed Providence of the Gods.

All: THANKS WE GIVE TO OUR LADY AND LORD!

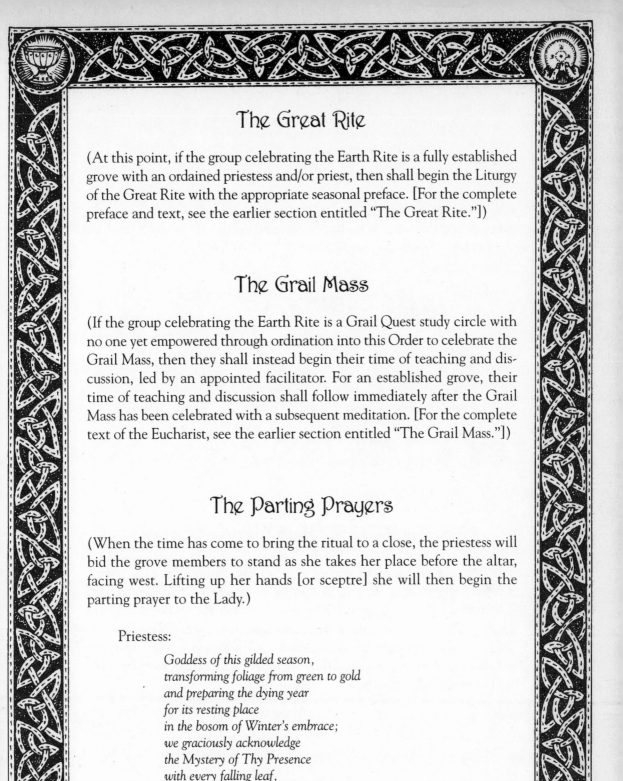

The Great Rite

(At this point, if the group celebrating the Earth Rite is a fully established grove with an ordained priestess and/or priest, then shall begin the Liturgy of the Great Rite with the appropriate seasonal preface. [For the complete preface and text, see the earlier section entitled "The Great Rite."])

The Grail Mass

(If the group celebrating the Earth Rite is a Grail Quest study circle with no one yet empowered through ordination into this Order to celebrate the Grail Mass, then they shall instead begin their time of teaching and discussion, led by an appointed facilitator. For an established grove, their time of teaching and discussion shall follow immediately after the Grail Mass has been celebrated with a subsequent meditation. [For the complete text of the Eucharist, see the earlier section entitled "The Grail Mass."])

The Parting Prayers

(When the time has come to bring the ritual to a close, the priestess will bid the grove members to stand as she takes her place before the altar, facing west. Lifting up her hands [or sceptre] she will then begin the parting prayer to the Lady.)

Priestess:

> *Goddess of this gilded season,*
> *transforming foliage from green to gold*
> *and preparing the dying year*
> *for its resting place*
> *in the bosom of Winter's embrace;*
> *we graciously acknowledge*
> *the Mystery of Thy Presence*
> *with every falling leaf,*
> *and we ask Thy guidance*
> *through this season of lengthening shadows,*

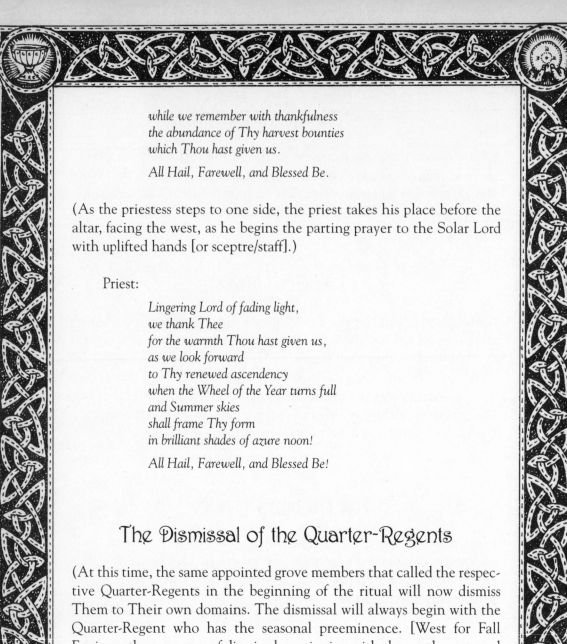

while we remember with thankfulness
the abundance of Thy harvest bounties
which Thou hast given us.

All Hail, Farewell, and Blessed Be.

(As the priestess steps to one side, the priest takes his place before the altar, facing the west, as he begins the parting prayer to the Solar Lord with uplifted hands [or sceptre/staff].)

Priest:

Lingering Lord of fading light,
we thank Thee
for the warmth Thou hast given us,
as we look forward
to Thy renewed ascendency
when the Wheel of the Year turns full
and Summer skies
shall frame Thy form
in brilliant shades of azure noon!

All Hail, Farewell, and Blessed Be!

The Dismissal of the Quarter-Regents

(At this time, the same appointed grove members that called the respective Quarter-Regents in the beginning of the ritual will now dismiss Them to Their own domains. The dismissal will always begin with the Quarter-Regent who has the seasonal preeminence. [West for Fall Equinox, the sequence of dismissal continuing with the south, east, and north.] The wording and procedure shall be the same as is found in "The Opening and Closing Rites.")

The Opening of the Circle

(The priest will then take his glaive to the marked boundary of the circle, and open the circle in accordance with the wording and procedures as outlined in "The Opening and Closing Rites.")

The Closing Benediction

(The priestess will then make the final proclamation of the ritual's conclusion.)

Priestess:

> *This rite of the Fall Equinox is ended!*
> *May the equal balance of light and dark*
> *bless you with insights*
> *into the equilibrium that is life itself!*
>
> *Merry Meet and Merry Part!*

The Altar of the Pentagram: The traditional set-up for an Earth Rite.

The Rites of Passage

The Rite of Child Blessing

The Rite of Child Blessing is the first ritual of passage which a person born into the Pagan community of faith would encounter. It is a joyous time for the parents and a means by which they can officially present their newborn ceremonially before the Goddess, the God, and the local Pagan assembly with expectations of blessing and support for the little one.

This rite, unlike many others, has a great amount of flexibility, in that it can be performed during a regular grove ceremony (usually following the Grail Mass) or, as is more common, it can be held at the parents' home or in a suitable location chosen by them. Like most other ritual celebrations, it normally would be followed by a potluck dinner or general festivities.

Basic Requirements

Below are some things to remember for the Rite of Child Blessing which are necessary requirements if the observance is to be in accordance with the rubrics of the Ordo Arcanorum Gradalis.

Altar

If the ceremony is held during a regular grove ritual, then the altar is usually in the center of the circle area. However, for a child blessing, this general rule of thumb is most flexible, since many times the rite is held separately in homes or back yards, or special places where there is only one suitable location for the altar to be placed. In such cases the altar can face any direction which is deemed most aesthetically pleasing to the parents.

In the Rite of Child Blessing, the type of altar which is used should be determined by the participants.

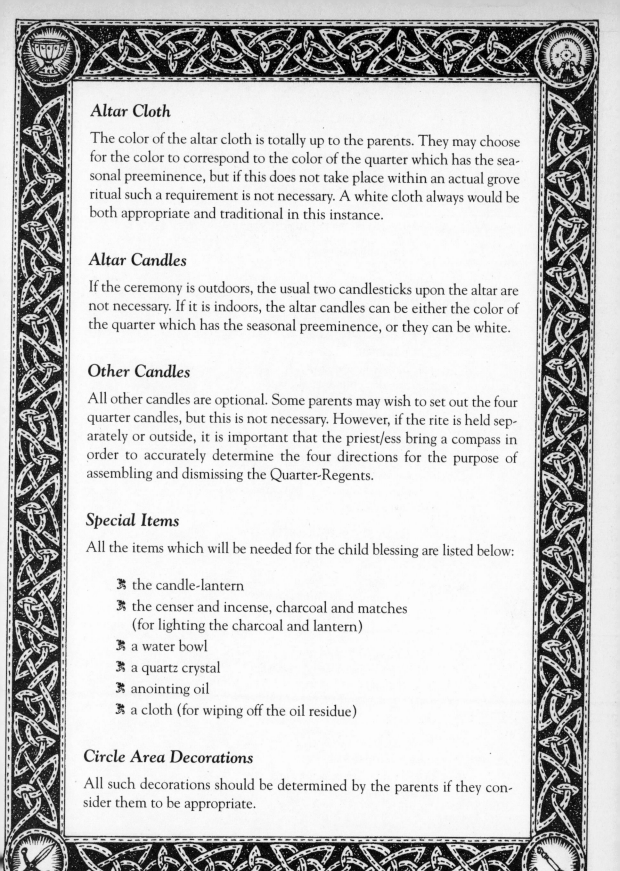

Altar Cloth

The color of the altar cloth is totally up to the parents. They may choose for the color to correspond to the color of the quarter which has the seasonal preeminence, but if this does not take place within an actual grove ritual such a requirement is not necessary. A white cloth always would be both appropriate and traditional in this instance.

Altar Candles

If the ceremony is outdoors, the usual two candlesticks upon the altar are not necessary. If it is indoors, the altar candles can be either the color of the quarter which has the seasonal preeminence, or they can be white.

Other Candles

All other candles are optional. Some parents may wish to set out the four quarter candles, but this is not necessary. However, if the rite is held separately or outside, it is important that the priest/ess bring a compass in order to accurately determine the four directions for the purpose of assembling and dismissing the Quarter-Regents.

Special Items

All the items which will be needed for the child blessing are listed below:

- the candle-lantern
- the censer and incense, charcoal and matches
  (for lighting the charcoal and lantern)
- a water bowl
- a quartz crystal
- anointing oil
- a cloth (for wiping off the oil residue)

Circle Area Decorations

All such decorations should be determined by the parents if they consider them to be appropriate.

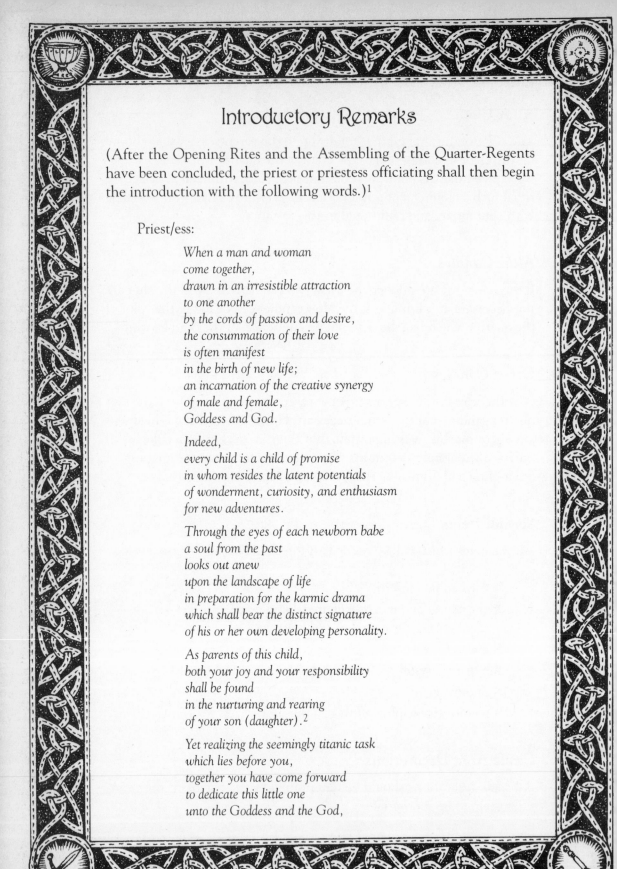

Introductory Remarks

(After the Opening Rites and the Assembling of the Quarter-Regents have been concluded, the priest or priestess officiating shall then begin the introduction with the following words.)[1]

Priest/ess:

When a man and woman
come together,
drawn in an irresistible attraction
to one another
by the cords of passion and desire,
the consummation of their love
is often manifest
in the birth of new life;
an incarnation of the creative synergy
of male and female,
Goddess and God.

Indeed,
every child is a child of promise
in whom resides the latent potentials
of wonderment, curiosity, and enthusiasm
for new adventures.

Through the eyes of each newborn babe
a soul from the past
looks out anew
upon the landscape of life
in preparation for the karmic drama
which shall bear the distinct signature
of his or her own developing personality.

As parents of this child,
both your joy and your responsibility
shall be found
in the nurturing and rearing
of your son (daughter).[2]

Yet realizing the seemingly titanic task
which lies before you,
together you have come forward
to dedicate this little one
unto the Goddess and the God,

that They might overshadow him (her)
with the encompassing circle
of Their protective presence.

Here and now,
before the Lady, the Lord,
and all those here assembled,
I admonish you as parents
to take care that you cherish
the memories of this moment,
wherein your child
shall be named
as a gift from the Goddess and God.

The Four Blessings

(The priest/ess shall then put incense into the censer and proceed to cense both the child and parents as they stand in front of him/her and as s/he censes, the following blessing shall be recited.)

Priest/ess:

May you be a child
enchanted by the Wind,
free and uninhibited,
and blessed by its breath
to become a breeze of inspiration
as you touch the lives
of those around you.

(The priest/ess will put back the censer, pick up the lighted candle-lantern, and make with it the sign of the equidistant cross before the child.)

Priest/ess:

May you be blessed
by the brightness of the Light
as it becomes a lamp unto your feet
while you grow
in character and maturity,
warm with the radiance of the Sun.

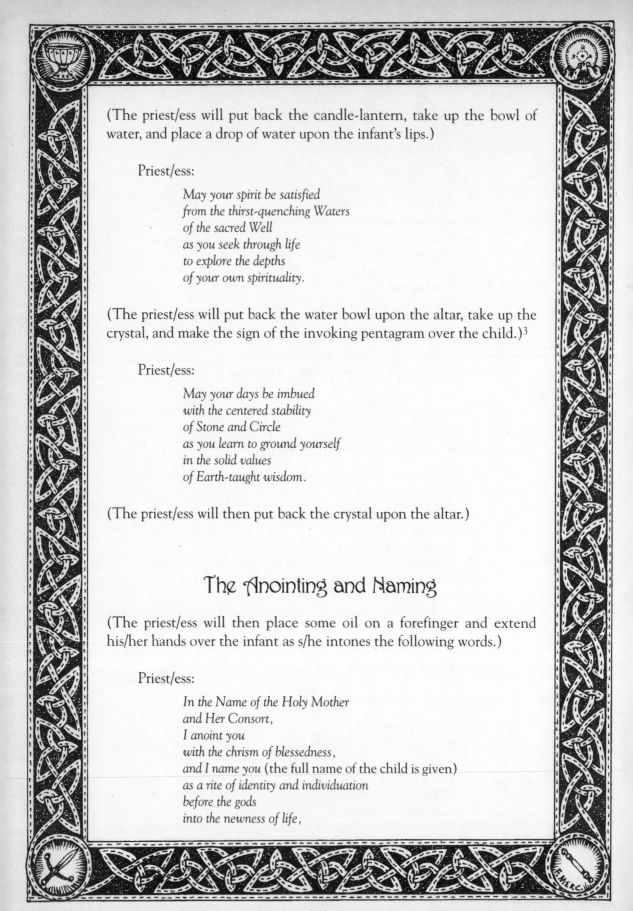

(The priest/ess will put back the candle-lantern, take up the bowl of water, and place a drop of water upon the infant's lips.)

Priest/ess:

May your spirit be satisfied
from the thirst-quenching Waters
of the sacred Well
as you seek through life
to explore the depths
of your own spirituality.

(The priest/ess will put back the water bowl upon the altar, take up the crystal, and make the sign of the invoking pentagram over the child.)[3]

Priest/ess:

May your days be imbued
with the centered stability
of Stone and Circle
as you learn to ground yourself
in the solid values
of Earth-taught wisdom.

(The priest/ess will then put back the crystal upon the altar.)

The Anointing and Naming

(The priest/ess will then place some oil on a forefinger and extend his/her hands over the infant as s/he intones the following words.)

Priest/ess:

In the Name of the Holy Mother
and Her Consort,
I anoint you
with the chrism of blessedness,
and I name you (the full name of the child is given)
as a rite of identity and individuation
before the gods
into the newness of life,

(The child is anointed on the forehead with an
invoking pentagram.)
*that you might experience
the joys of youth,
the fulfillment of love,
and the contentment of a life well lived.*

*May the Lady lead you
into an appreciation of Her Mysteries,
and may the Lord bless you
with the ability to hear
the melody of His sacred pipes,
for you are a child
of Wind and Water, Earth, and Fire;
a newborn expression
of the ever-changing face of the Lady (Lord)[4]*

*May the lifetime
of your sojourn among us
in this new and unique incarnation
be a time of growth for your soul,
and a means
by which the Goddess (God) is glorified[5]
through your goals and aspirations.*

Blessed Be!

The Charge to the Parents

(The priest/ess will then wipe the residue of oil from the finger which
anointed the baby, and face the parents once again for the charge.)

Priest/ess:

*To bring forth new life into the world
is not only a joyous experience,
but a solemn one as well,
for it carries with it
the attendant responsibilities
of caring, nurturing, discipline, and guidance
through those stages
of infancy, childhood, and adolescence.*

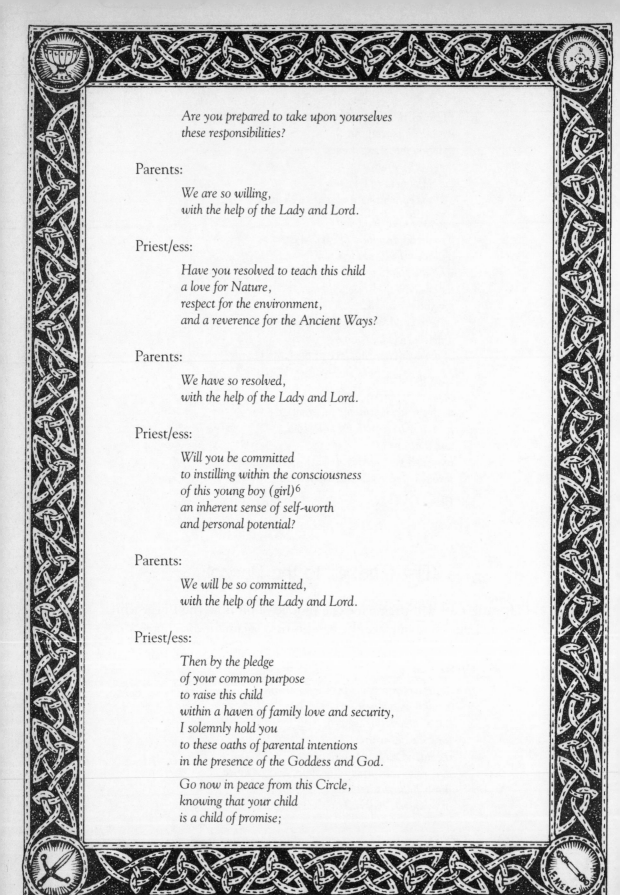

Are you prepared to take upon yourselves
these responsibilities?

Parents:

We are so willing,
with the help of the Lady and Lord.

Priest/ess:

Have you resolved to teach this child
a love for Nature,
respect for the environment,
and a reverence for the Ancient Ways?

Parents:

We have so resolved,
with the help of the Lady and Lord.

Priest/ess:

Will you be committed
to instilling within the consciousness
of this young boy (girl)[6]
an inherent sense of self-worth
and personal potential?

Parents:

We will be so committed,
with the help of the Lady and Lord.

Priest/ess:

Then by the pledge
of your common purpose
to raise this child
within a haven of family love and security,
I solemnly hold you
to these oaths of parental intentions
in the presence of the Goddess and God.

Go now in peace from this Circle,
knowing that your child
is a child of promise;

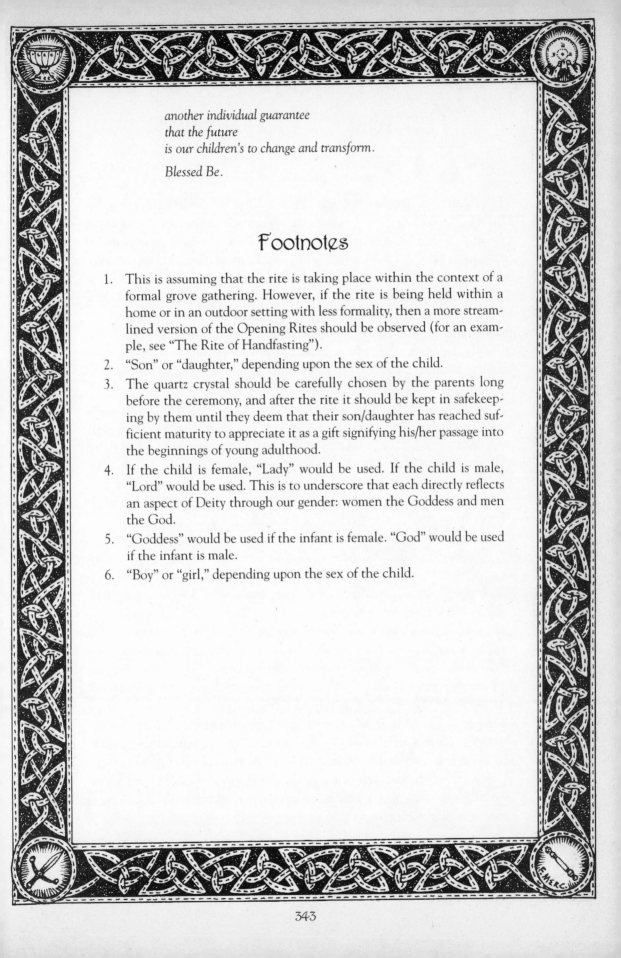

another individual guarantee
that the future
is our children's to change and transform.

Blessed Be.

Footnotes

1. This is assuming that the rite is taking place within the context of a formal grove gathering. However, if the rite is being held within a home or in an outdoor setting with less formality, then a more streamlined version of the Opening Rites should be observed (for an example, see "The Rite of Handfasting").

2. "Son" or "daughter," depending upon the sex of the child.

3. The quartz crystal should be carefully chosen by the parents long before the ceremony, and after the rite it should be kept in safekeeping by them until they deem that their son/daughter has reached sufficient maturity to appreciate it as a gift signifying his/her passage into the beginnings of young adulthood.

4. If the child is female, "Lady" would be used. If the child is male, "Lord" would be used. This is to underscore that each directly reflects an aspect of Deity through our gender: women the Goddess and men the God.

5. "Goddess" would be used if the infant is female. "God" would be used if the infant is male.

6. "Boy" or "girl," depending upon the sex of the child.

The Rite of Handfasting

"Handfasting" is simply a popular Wiccan term for a marriage ceremony. This rite, as practiced in our tradition, is a ritual combining sacramental solemnity with a heightened sense of nuptial joy. It is also an unabashed celebration of human sexuality, and as such, it contains numerous allusions to the theme of erotic fulfillment within the relationship itself.

Handfastings can be as elaborate or as understated as the couple wishes, for this O.A.G. ritual can lend itself equally to either extreme or anywhere in between these two points on the spectrum of options. More often than not, prospective couples tend to prefer an outdoor location for their weddings, but indoor ceremonies can be accommodated just as easily.

In groves affiliated with the Ordo Arcanorum Gradalis, handfastings can only be performed by a priest or priestess who has been duly ordained by this Order. It is furthermore highly recommended that those who carry the authority of being the presiding priest and priestess of a local grove should present their ordination credentials to the appropriate state, county, or provincial courts as soon as possible in order to receive licensing for the purpose of conducting legally recognized marriages within that state or province.

There are many Wiccans who view handfasting merely as a non-legally binding way of publically recognizing an already existing relationship. Consequently, for many years there was no great emphasis placed on the need for state-recognized handfastings; but recently more and more Pagan clergy have become aware of their need to possess the same legal authority for ritually sealing a couple in marriage as is retained by the mainline clergy of the established churches. We also recommend that our own priesthood only perform weddings which are legally recognized as such, thereby encouraging the couple to view the step they are taking as one of utmost seriousness and commitment. (One significant exception to this rule would be lesbian and gay handfastings, which, while not being officially recognized by most state or provincial authorities, are nevertheless deserving of the same kind of public and sacramental blessing as the more commonplace ceremonies celebrating a heterosexual handfasting.)

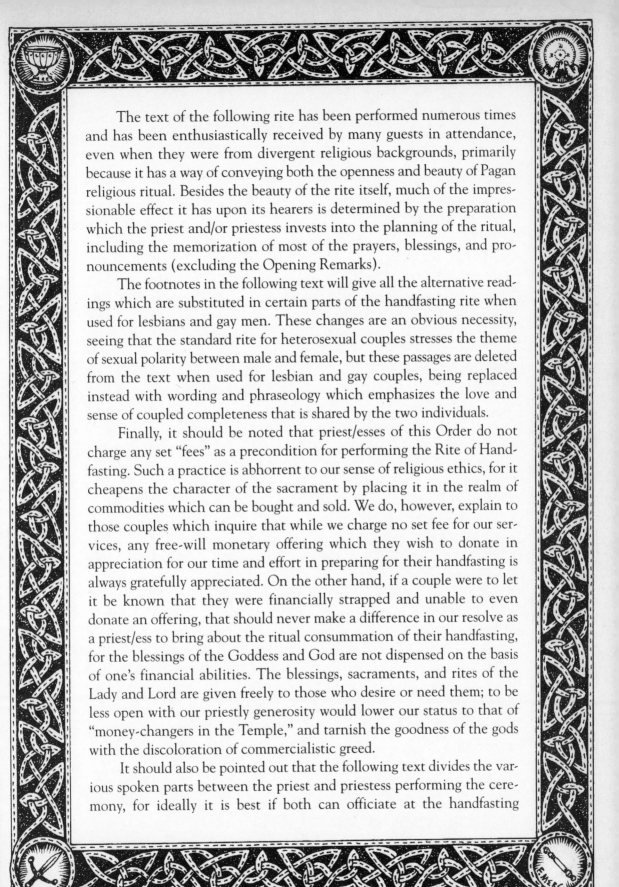

The text of the following rite has been performed numerous times and has been enthusiastically received by many guests in attendance, even when they were from divergent religious backgrounds, primarily because it has a way of conveying both the openness and beauty of Pagan religious ritual. Besides the beauty of the rite itself, much of the impressionable effect it has upon its hearers is determined by the preparation which the priest and/or priestess invests into the planning of the ritual, including the memorization of most of the prayers, blessings, and pronouncements (excluding the Opening Remarks).

The footnotes in the following text will give all the alternative readings which are substituted in certain parts of the handfasting rite when used for lesbians and gay men. These changes are an obvious necessity, seeing that the standard rite for heterosexual couples stresses the theme of sexual polarity between male and female, but these passages are deleted from the text when used for lesbian and gay couples, being replaced instead with wording and phraseology which emphasizes the love and sense of coupled completeness that is shared by the two individuals.

Finally, it should be noted that priest/esses of this Order do not charge any set "fees" as a precondition for performing the Rite of Handfasting. Such a practice is abhorrent to our sense of religious ethics, for it cheapens the character of the sacrament by placing it in the realm of commodities which can be bought and sold. We do, however, explain to those couples which inquire that while we charge no set fee for our services, any free-will monetary offering which they wish to donate in appreciation for our time and effort in preparing for their handfasting is always gratefully appreciated. On the other hand, if a couple were to let it be known that they were financially strapped and unable to even donate an offering, that should never make a difference in our resolve as a priest/ess to bring about the ritual consummation of their handfasting, for the blessings of the Goddess and God are not dispensed on the basis of one's financial abilities. The blessings, sacraments, and rites of the Lady and Lord are given freely to those who desire or need them; to be less open with our priestly generosity would lower our status to that of "money-changers in the Temple," and tarnish the goodness of the gods with the discoloration of commercialistic greed.

It should also be pointed out that the following text divides the various spoken parts between the priest and priestess performing the ceremony, for ideally it is best if both can officiate at the handfasting together. However, in many situations there will only be one of them available to conduct the rite. In such cases, all of the spoken parts usually divided between the priest and priestess would be done by whichever one was officiating.

Basic Requirements

Below are some things to remember for the Rite of Handfasting which are necessary requirements if the observance is to be in accordance with the rubrics of the Ordo Arcanorum Gradalis.

Altar

The altar is usually situated near the periphery of the circle area; preferably in whichever quarter of the circle has the seasonal preeminence at the time. However, for a handfasting, this general rule of thumb is most flexible, since many times the ceremony is held in back yards or in special places where there is only one suitable location for the altar to be placed. In such cases the altar can face any direction which is deemed most aesthetically pleasing to the couple or their families.

In the Rite of Handfasting, that which is used for an altar should be of regular table height, since the ritual (including the Grail Mass) will be performed standing. Any kind of table or flat surface is acceptable for use as an altar.

Altar Cloth

The color of the altar cloth is totally up to the couple. They may choose for the color to correspond to the color of the quarter which has the seasonal preeminence, but since this is not an actual grove ritual in the same sense as an Earth Rite or a Lunar Rite, this usual requirement can be waived. Many couples prefer the traditional color of white for their handfasting.

Altar Candles

If the ceremony is outdoors, the usual two candlesticks upon the altar are not necessary. If it is indoors, the altar candles can be either the color of the quarter which has the seasonal preeminence, or they can be white. In a heterosexual handfasting, it is also permissible to have one candle white and the other one black, as a symbol of sexual polarity.

Other Candles

All other candles are optional. Some couples may wish to set out the four quarter candles, but this is not necessary. However, it is important the the priest and/or priestess bring with them a compass in order to accurately determine the four directions for the purpose of assembling and dismissing the Quarter-Regents.

The only other candle which is *absolutely necessary* is the one for the candle-lantern, for it must be used to bless the couple during the Blessing of the Elements.

Special Items

All the items which will be needed for the handfasting are listed below:

- the candle-lantern
- a bowl of water
- a bowl of potpourri
- a censer and incense, charcoal and matches
  (for lighting the charcoal and lantern)
- a chalice and paten (for the Grail Mass)
- wine (or white grape juice) and the wafer
- one cruet for the wine (heterosexual handfasting)
- two cruets for the wine and water (gay/lesbian handfasting)
- the groom's glaive (heterosexual handfasting)
- the sceptre
- the cord for tying the couple's hands
  (this cord can be any color the couple wishes)
- the ceremonial broom

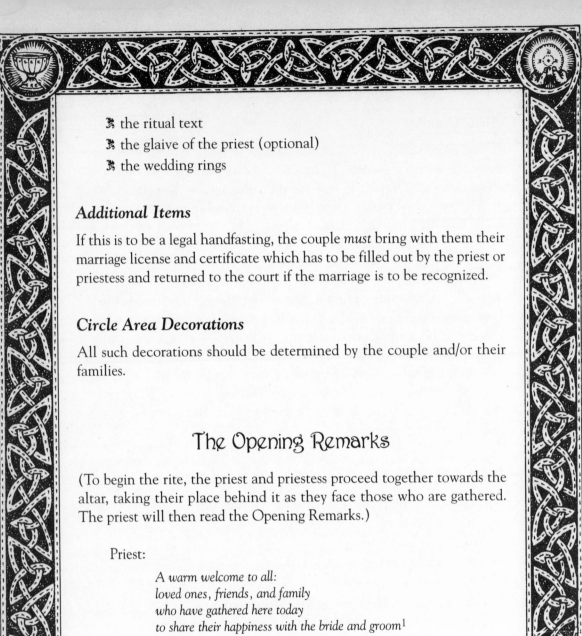

☯ the ritual text
☯ the glaive of the priest (optional)
☯ the wedding rings

Additional Items

If this is to be a legal handfasting, the couple *must* bring with them their marriage license and certificate which has to be filled out by the priest or priestess and returned to the court if the marriage is to be recognized.

Circle Area Decorations

All such decorations should be determined by the couple and/or their families.

The Opening Remarks

(To begin the rite, the priest and priestess proceed together towards the altar, taking their place behind it as they face those who are gathered. The priest will then read the Opening Remarks.)

Priest:

> *A warm welcome to all:*
> *loved ones, friends, and family*
> *who have gathered here today*
> *to share their happiness with the bride and groom[1]*
> *upon this, the occasion of their Handfasting.*
>
> *Marriage has been celebrated and solemnized*
> *from time immemorial*
> *throughout the world's varied cultures*
> *and religions as being in some mystical way*
> *a microcosm of the eternal marriage*
> *between Heaven and Earth.[2]*
>
> *The union of man and woman*
> *was seen as a manifestation of the Divinity*
> *which propels and empowers*
> *the drive of our sexuality*

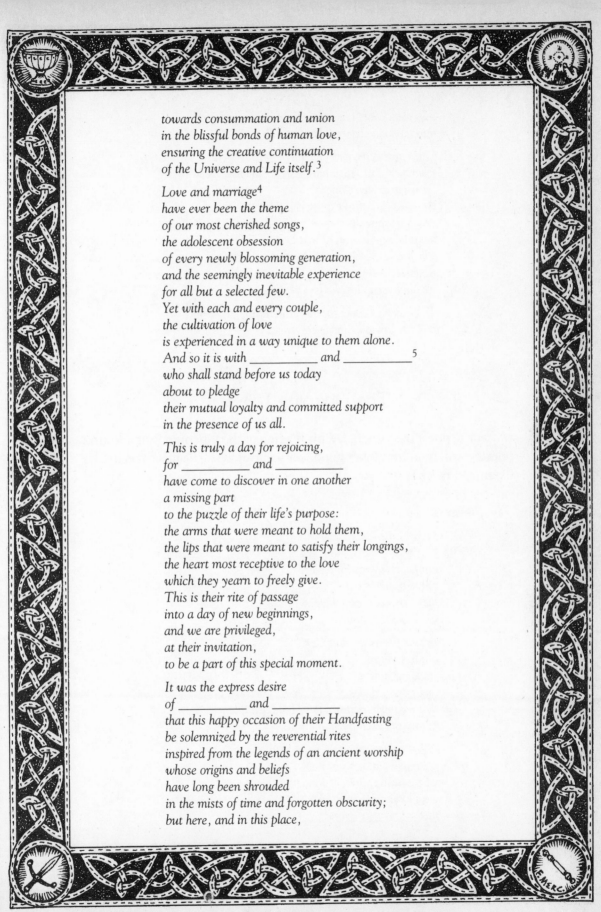

towards consummation and union
in the blissful bonds of human love,
ensuring the creative continuation
of the Universe and Life itself.[3]

Love and marriage[4]
have ever been the theme
of our most cherished songs,
the adolescent obsession
of every newly blossoming generation,
and the seemingly inevitable experience
for all but a selected few.
Yet with each and every couple,
the cultivation of love
is experienced in a way unique to them alone.
And so it is with _____ and _____[5]
who shall stand before us today
about to pledge
their mutual loyalty and committed support
in the presence of us all.

This is truly a day for rejoicing,
for _____ and _____
have come to discover in one another
a missing part
to the puzzle of their life's purpose:
the arms that were meant to hold them,
the lips that were meant to satisfy their longings,
the heart most receptive to the love
which they yearn to freely give.
This is their rite of passage
into a day of new beginnings,
and we are privileged,
at their invitation,
to be a part of this special moment.

It was the express desire
of _____ and _____
that this happy occasion of their Handfasting
be solemnized by the reverential rites
inspired from the legends of an ancient worship
whose origins and beliefs
have long been shrouded
in the mists of time and forgotten obscurity;
but here, and in this place,

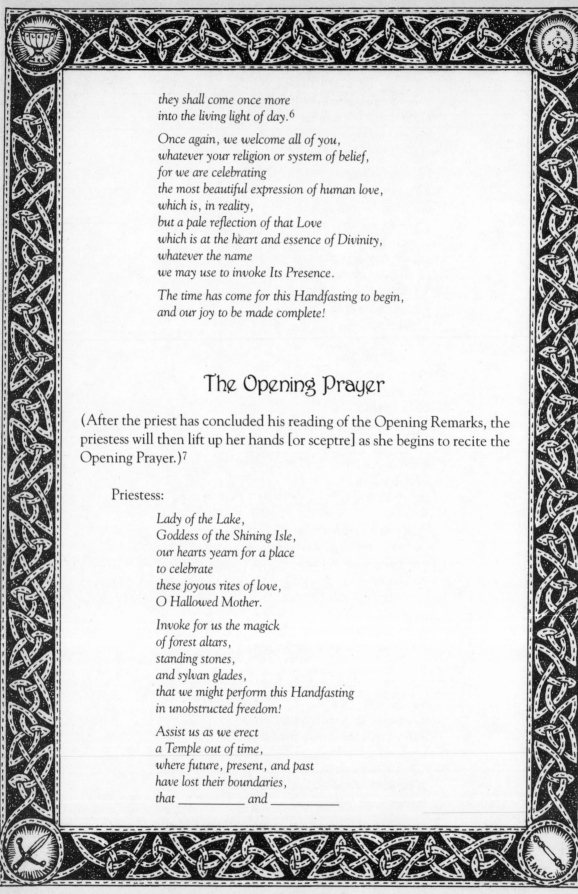

they shall come once more
into the living light of day.[6]

Once again, we welcome all of you,
whatever your religion or system of belief,
for we are celebrating
the most beautiful expression of human love,
which is, in reality,
but a pale reflection of that Love
which is at the heart and essence of Divinity,
whatever the name
we may use to invoke Its Presence.

The time has come for this Handfasting to begin,
and our joy to be made complete!

The Opening Prayer

(After the priest has concluded his reading of the Opening Remarks, the
priestess will then lift up her hands [or sceptre] as she begins to recite the
Opening Prayer.)[7]

Priestess:

Lady of the Lake,
Goddess of the Shining Isle,
our hearts yearn for a place
to celebrate
these joyous rites of love,
O Hallowed Mother.

Invoke for us the magick
of forest altars,
standing stones,
and sylvan glades,
that we might perform this Handfasting
in unobstructed freedom!

Assist us as we erect
a Temple out of time,
where future, present, and past
have lost their boundaries,
that _____ and _____

might continue their Quest
for the Cauldron of Regeneration.

We ask these things
that we may honor Thee, Our Lady,
for Thou art the very Life-spring of eternity,
and Thou art most pleased
to bestow upon us
the blessings of lasting love.

(After the priestess finishes the Opening Prayer, the priest will take his place in the center of the circle area.[8] Raising either the sceptre or his glaive, he will begin to cast the circle, starting in whichever quarter has the seasonal preeminence at the time,[9] going widdershins full-circle back to the same quarter where he started, saying the following words.)

Priest:

I consecrate this place
as a sanctuary set apart
for these solemn rites of love,
covered with a canopy of astral light,
hallowed by the holy archangels,
surrounded by shields of Spirit;
a place of protection
and a sacred Circle which shall amplify
the energies of our celebration and joy![10]

(Then, while still facing the quarter which has the seasonal preeminence, he will begin to call the Quarter-Regents, raising his sceptre or glaive as he faces each of the four directions. [The sequence given here is for a summer wedding.])[11]

Priest:

(Facing south) *Regents of the South,*
Sovereigns of Fire and Flame!

(He makes the invoking sign of the pentagram.)

(Facing east) *Regents of the East,*
Sovereigns of Wind and Air!

(He makes the invoking sign of the pentagram.)

> (Facing north) *Regents of the North,*
> *Sovereigns of elemental Earth!*

(He makes the invoking sign of the pentagram.)

> (Facing west) *Regents of the West,*
> *Sovereigns of all Watery Realms!*

(He makes the invoking sign of the pentagram.)

(The priest then points his sceptre or glaive skyward and once again makes a slow 360-degree turn counterclockwise as he continues the invocation of the Quarter-Regents.)

> Priest:
>
>> *By the holy pentagram of balance*
>> *sacred to the Goddess,*
>> *Queen of the Cardinal Quarters,*
>> *we call Thee to this Circle,*
>> *charging Thee to witness and watch over*
>> *these rites of love*
>> *in this sacred space between the worlds*
>> *and out of time!*

(The priest will then return to his place behind the altar and face those assembled as he prepares to call forth the couple, who will be standing together opposite from the altar at the rear of the assembled guests.)

> Priest:
>
>> *Before the Lady of Life*
>> *and the Lord of the Ancient Ways;*
>> *in the presence of Earth and Sky,*
>> *and all the unseen eyes of Creation,*
>> *as well as those in attendance here,*
>> *you who would declare your desire*
>> *for one another,*
>> *come forth to stand*
>> *before the altar of your destiny!*

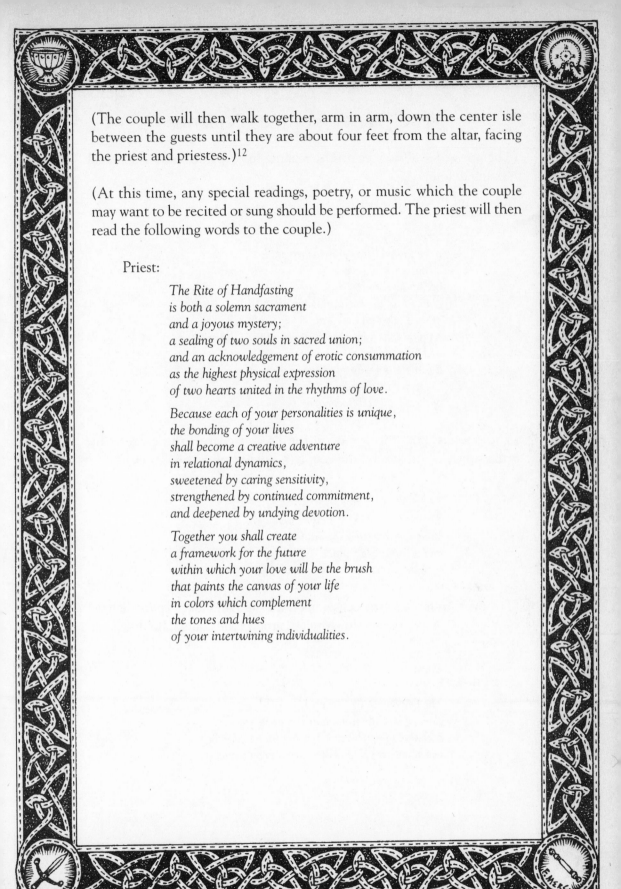

(The couple will then walk together, arm in arm, down the center isle between the guests until they are about four feet from the altar, facing the priest and priestess.)[12]

(At this time, any special readings, poetry, or music which the couple may want to be recited or sung should be performed. The priest will then read the following words to the couple.)

Priest:

The Rite of Handfasting
is both a solemn sacrament
and a joyous mystery;
a sealing of two souls in sacred union;
and an acknowledgement of erotic consummation
as the highest physical expression
of two hearts united in the rhythms of love.

Because each of your personalities is unique,
the bonding of your lives
shall become a creative adventure
in relational dynamics,
sweetened by caring sensitivity,
strengthened by continued commitment,
and deepened by undying devotion.

Together you shall create
a framework for the future
within which your love will be the brush
that paints the canvas of your life
in colors which complement
the tones and hues
of your intertwining individualities.

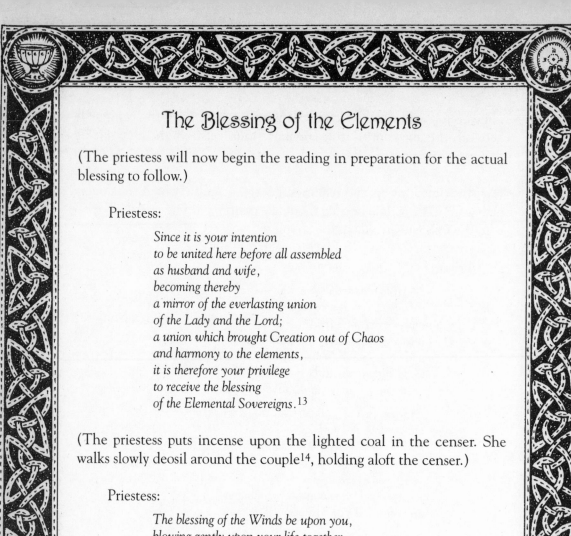

The Blessing of the Elements

(The priestess will now begin the reading in preparation for the actual blessing to follow.)

Priestess:

Since it is your intention
to be united here before all assembled
as husband and wife,
becoming thereby
a mirror of the everlasting union
of the Lady and the Lord;
a union which brought Creation out of Chaos
and harmony to the elements,
it is therefore your privilege
to receive the blessing
of the Elemental Sovereigns.[13]

(The priestess puts incense upon the lighted coal in the censer. She walks slowly deosil around the couple[14], holding aloft the censer.)

Priestess:

The blessing of the Winds be upon you,
blowing gently upon your life together,
and scenting your union
with the sweet fragrance of new beginnings.

(The priestess replaces the censer upon the altar and takes up the lighted candle-lantern. She walks slowly deosil around the couple, holding aloft the lantern.)

Priestess:

The blessing of Fire be upon you,
glowing warmly from your homeside hearth,
a symbol of your heated passion for one another
which only the flames of your love can ignite.

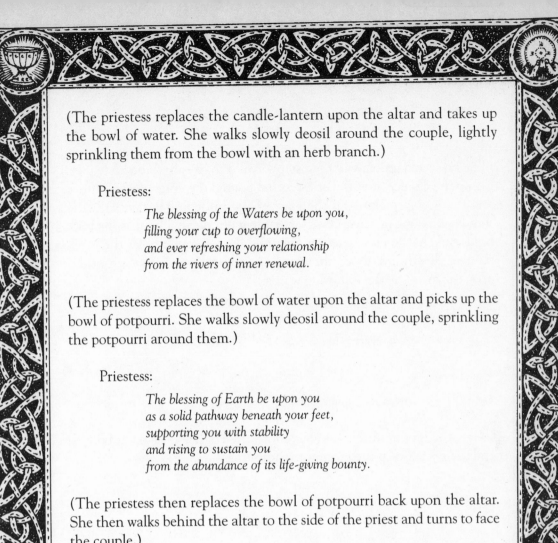

(The priestess replaces the candle-lantern upon the altar and takes up the bowl of water. She walks slowly deosil around the couple, lightly sprinkling them from the bowl with an herb branch.)

Priestess:

The blessing of the Waters be upon you,
filling your cup to overflowing,
and ever refreshing your relationship
from the rivers of inner renewal.

(The priestess replaces the bowl of water upon the altar and picks up the bowl of potpourri. She walks slowly deosil around the couple, sprinkling the potpourri around them.)

Priestess:

The blessing of Earth be upon you
as a solid pathway beneath your feet,
supporting you with stability
and rising to sustain you
from the abundance of its life-giving bounty.

(The priestess then replaces the bowl of potpourri back upon the altar. She then walks behind the altar to the side of the priest and turns to face the couple.)

The Great Rite[15]

(Facing the couple from behind the altar, the priest then proceeds to explain the significance of the following rite.)

Priest:

According to our traditions,
it is most appropriate
that the bride and groom
enact here in symbol
a mystical analogy
as a token of their personal commitment

to the fulfilled realization
of their relationship.

(The bride and groom will then step forward to the altar; the bride picking up the chalice after the priestess has poured the cruet of wine into it, and the groom picking up the glaive. The bride and groom will then stand facing one another closely, their feet almost touching as the bride holds the chalice closely to her breast while the groom holds the glaive pointed downward above the chalice. As they look into each other's eyes, they will say the following words.)[16]

Groom:

As the glaive is to the male ...

Bride:

So the cup is to the female ...

(Here, the groom lowers his glaive into the chalice of wine as both he and the bride finish the sentence in unison.)

Both:

... and conjoined they bring blessedness.[17]

(While the groom's glaive is still lowered into the chalice, the priestess will then lift up her hands to pronounce the following blessing as she lays her hands upon their heads.)

Priestess:

Foot to foot,
Knee to knee,
Lance to Grail,
Breast to breast,
Lips to lips.[18]

May the desire of the fertile Maiden
and the Greenwood God for one another
be crystallized within your blood
and upon your bed,
that no part of your love

be left untouched by Their passion,
as your union becomes
a microcosm of the macrocosm,
As Above, So Below.[19]

(The groom then lifts the glaive out of the chalice and replaces it upon the altar, while the bride gives the chalice back to the priestess, who puts it in its central place upon the altar.)

The Grail Mass

(The couple will now stand side by side once again as they face the priest and priestess who are standing behind the altar. The priest and priestess will then begin to recite the liturgy of the Grail Mass.[20] The couple will then partake of the consecrated elements by administering them to one another after they are handed the paten and chalice, respectively. When the paten and chalice have been handed back to the priest and priestess by the couple, then the final Eucharistic prayer shall be recited.)

The Blessing of the Rings

(The priest will now address the couple with the following words.)

Priest:
> *It is time now that your intentions of love*
> *be sealed by solemn vows*
> *in the presence of those here assembled*
> *to be witnesses of your common commitment.*
>
> *Since you both have decided*
> *to exchange rings*
> *as a visible symbol*
> *of your love for one another,*
> *it is only fitting*
> *that they be prepared by prayerful blessing*
> *for their noble purpose.*

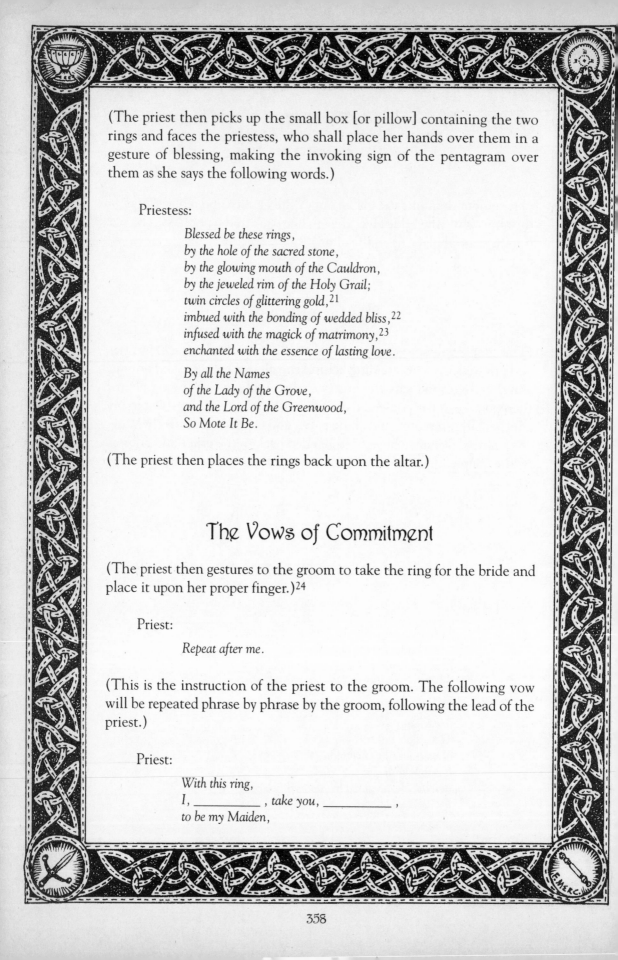

(The priest then picks up the small box [or pillow] containing the two rings and faces the priestess, who shall place her hands over them in a gesture of blessing, making the invoking sign of the pentagram over them as she says the following words.)

Priestess:

Blessed be these rings,
by the hole of the sacred stone,
by the glowing mouth of the Cauldron,
by the jeweled rim of the Holy Grail;
twin circles of glittering gold,[21]
imbued with the bonding of wedded bliss,[22]
infused with the magick of matrimony,[23]
enchanted with the essence of lasting love.

By all the Names
of the Lady of the Grove,
and the Lord of the Greenwood,
So Mote It Be.

(The priest then places the rings back upon the altar.)

The Vows of Commitment

(The priest then gestures to the groom to take the ring for the bride and place it upon her proper finger.)[24]

Priest:

Repeat after me.

(This is the instruction of the priest to the groom. The following vow will be repeated phrase by phrase by the groom, following the lead of the priest.)

Priest:

With this ring,
I, _____ , take you, _____ ,
to be my Maiden,

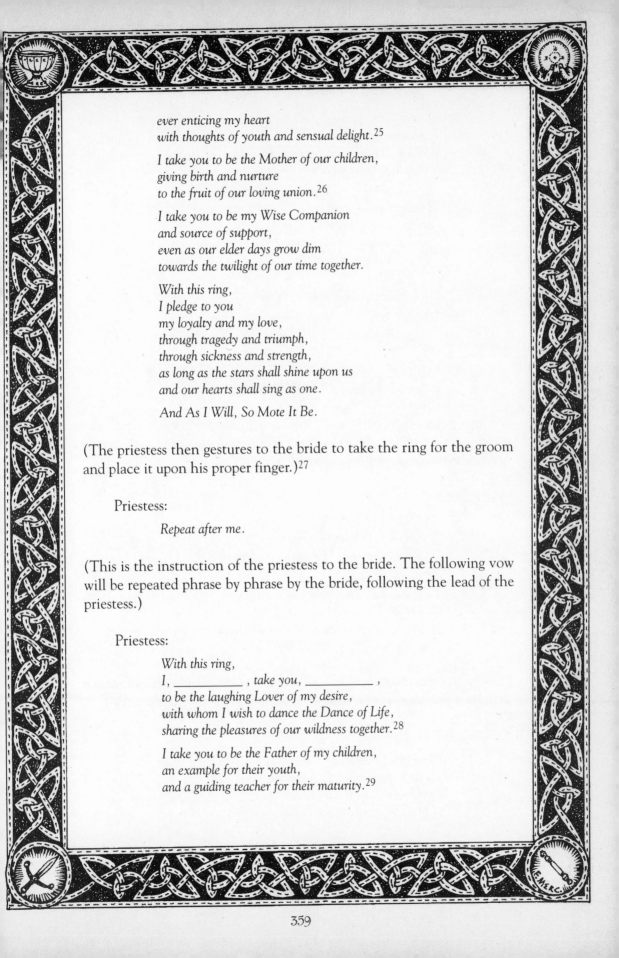

ever enticing my heart
with thoughts of youth and sensual delight.[25]

I take you to be the Mother of our children,
giving birth and nurture
to the fruit of our loving union.[26]

I take you to be my Wise Companion
and source of support,
even as our elder days grow dim
towards the twilight of our time together.

With this ring,
I pledge to you
my loyalty and my love,
through tragedy and triumph,
through sickness and strength,
as long as the stars shall shine upon us
and our hearts shall sing as one.

And As I Will, So Mote It Be.

(The priestess then gestures to the bride to take the ring for the groom and place it upon his proper finger.)[27]

Priestess:

Repeat after me.

(This is the instruction of the priestess to the bride. The following vow will be repeated phrase by phrase by the bride, following the lead of the priestess.)

Priestess:

With this ring,
I, _____ , take you, _____ ,
to be the laughing Lover of my desire,
with whom I wish to dance the Dance of Life,
sharing the pleasures of our wildness together.[28]

I take you to be the Father of my children,
an example for their youth,
and a guiding teacher for their maturity.[29]

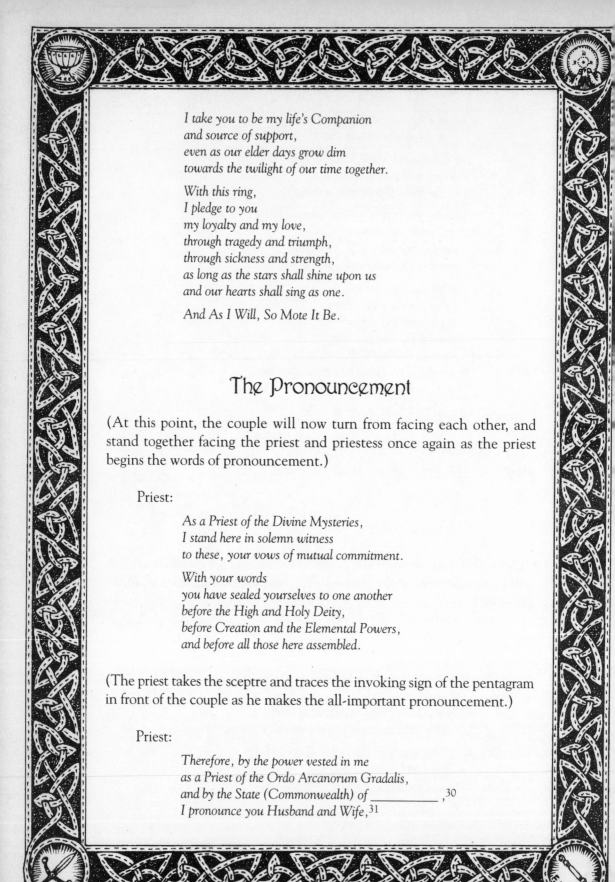

I take you to be my life's Companion
and source of support,
even as our elder days grow dim
towards the twilight of our time together.

With this ring,
I pledge to you
my loyalty and my love,
through tragedy and triumph,
through sickness and strength,
as long as the stars shall shine upon us
and our hearts shall sing as one.

And As I Will, So Mote It Be.

The Pronouncement

(At this point, the couple will now turn from facing each other, and stand together facing the priest and priestess once again as the priest begins the words of pronouncement.)

Priest:

> *As a Priest of the Divine Mysteries,*
> *I stand here in solemn witness*
> *to these, your vows of mutual commitment.*
>
> *With your words*
> *you have sealed yourselves to one another*
> *before the High and Holy Deity,*
> *before Creation and the Elemental Powers,*
> *and before all those here assembled.*

(The priest takes the sceptre and traces the invoking sign of the pentagram in front of the couple as he makes the all-important pronouncement.)

Priest:

> *Therefore, by the power vested in me*
> *as a Priest of the Ordo Arcanorum Gradalis,*
> *and by the State (Commonwealth) of _____ ,*[30]
> *I pronounce you Husband and Wife,*[31]

co-creators for a common future,
and heirs together of the grace of life.

(The priest then returns the sceptre to the altar, and the priestess lifts up
her hands for the nuptial blessing as she says:)

Priestess:

The blessings of the Lady and Lord
be upon you
for growth and understanding with one another,
for tolerance and patience with one another,
and for the happiness which can come
only by the joy of two hearts
knit together as one.

And As We Will, So Mote It Be.

(The priestess will then gesture to the couple, saying:)

Priestess:

You may kiss one another!

The Broom Ceremony

(The priest now takes up the broom that is resting against the side of the
altar. He then hands it to two appointed assistants who take the broom
and place it in front of the couple who have now turned to face the people, their backs to the altar. The priestess then picks up the colored cord
from the altar and leaves from behind the altar to stand in front of the
couple as the priest does the same, taking the book of rites with him and
standing off to the side of the couple. The priest then begins to read the
following words.)

Priest:

In olden days,
the broom was considered
to be a symbol of the hearth and home;
a representation of all

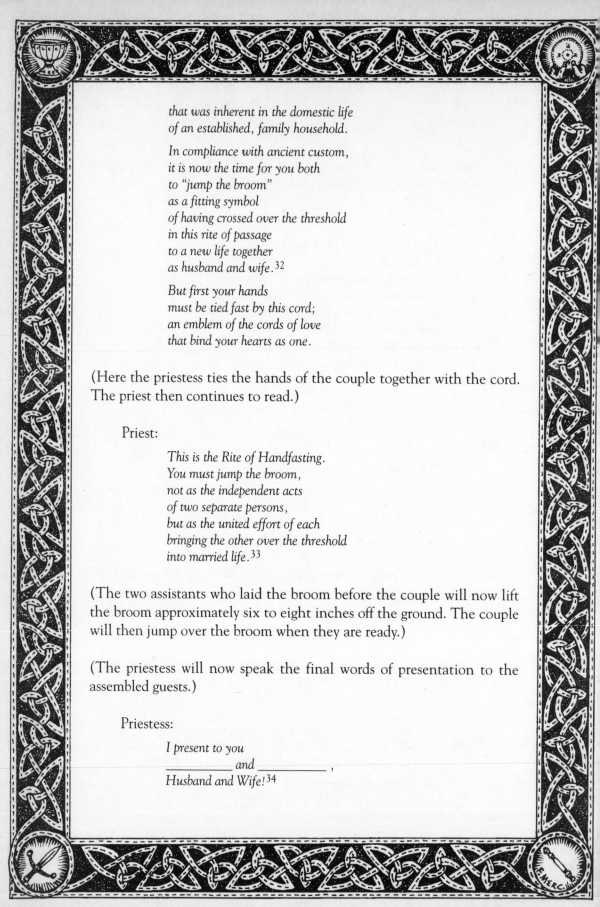

*that was inherent in the domestic life
of an established, family household.*

*In compliance with ancient custom,
it is now the time for you both
to "jump the broom"
as a fitting symbol
of having crossed over the threshold
in this rite of passage
to a new life together
as husband and wife.*[32]

*But first your hands
must be tied fast by this cord;
an emblem of the cords of love
that bind your hearts as one.*

(Here the priestess ties the hands of the couple together with the cord.
The priest then continues to read.)

Priest:

*This is the Rite of Handfasting.
You must jump the broom,
not as the independent acts
of two separate persons,
but as the united effort of each
bringing the other over the threshold
into married life.*[33]

(The two assistants who laid the broom before the couple will now lift
the broom approximately six to eight inches off the ground. The couple
will then jump over the broom when they are ready.)

(The priestess will now speak the final words of presentation to the
assembled guests.)

Priestess:

*I present to you
_____ and _____ ,
Husband and Wife!*[34]

(After the guests applaud, the priestess loosens the cord from the couple's hands and places it on the altar. The priest then reads the closing prayer.)

Priest:

Gracious and loving Deity,
_____ and _____
have exchanged vows and promises
spoken with the tender earnestness
of two hearts smitten by the sweetness of love.

May they ever chart their course together
as a couple committed
to facing the future with faith
in their common capacity
to persevere against all odds and obstacles.

Guide them, we pray,
that their eyes always be open
to the ever-present possibilities
for an exciting life of their own
teeming with creative potential.

May trust and mutual respect
be the undergirding strength
of their relationship,
and may the memories they create together
be cherished as heirlooms of their intimacy;
the treasures that Time cannot erase.

This we ask in the Name of Thy Divinity
which is the Ground of all being.

And So Mote It Be.

(The priest will then follow the same procedure as at the beginning of the ceremony for dismissing the Regents of the Four Quarters. As he calls upon them, "Regents of the South, Sovereigns of Fire and Flame," etc., he will make the banishing sign of the pentagram with the glaive or sceptre. Then he will say the following words.)

Priest:

We thank Thee
for witnessing these rites
and watching over the Circle,

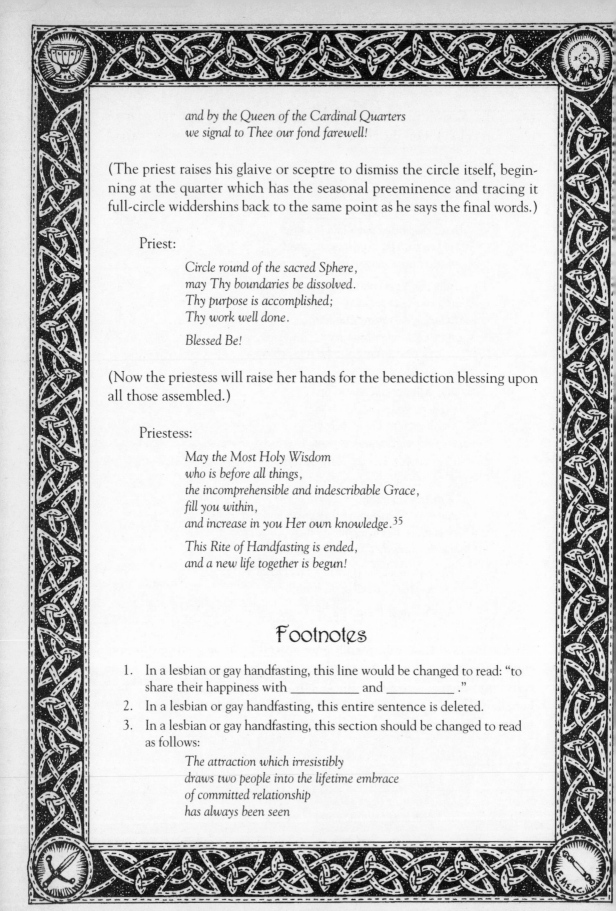

*and by the Queen of the Cardinal Quarters
we signal to Thee our fond farewell!*

(The priest raises his glaive or sceptre to dismiss the circle itself, beginning at the quarter which has the seasonal preeminence and tracing it full-circle widdershins back to the same point as he says the final words.)

Priest:

*Circle round of the sacred Sphere,
may Thy boundaries be dissolved.
Thy purpose is accomplished;
Thy work well done.*

Blessed Be!

(Now the priestess will raise her hands for the benediction blessing upon all those assembled.)

Priestess:

*May the Most Holy Wisdom
who is before all things,
the incomprehensible and indescribable Grace,
fill you within,
and increase in you Her own knowledge.*[35]

*This Rite of Handfasting is ended,
and a new life together is begun!*

Footnotes

1. In a lesbian or gay handfasting, this line would be changed to read: "to share their happiness with _____ and _____ ."
2. In a lesbian or gay handfasting, this entire sentence is deleted.
3. In a lesbian or gay handfasting, this section should be changed to read as follows:

   *The attraction which irresistibly
   draws two people into the lifetime embrace
   of committed relationship
   has always been seen*

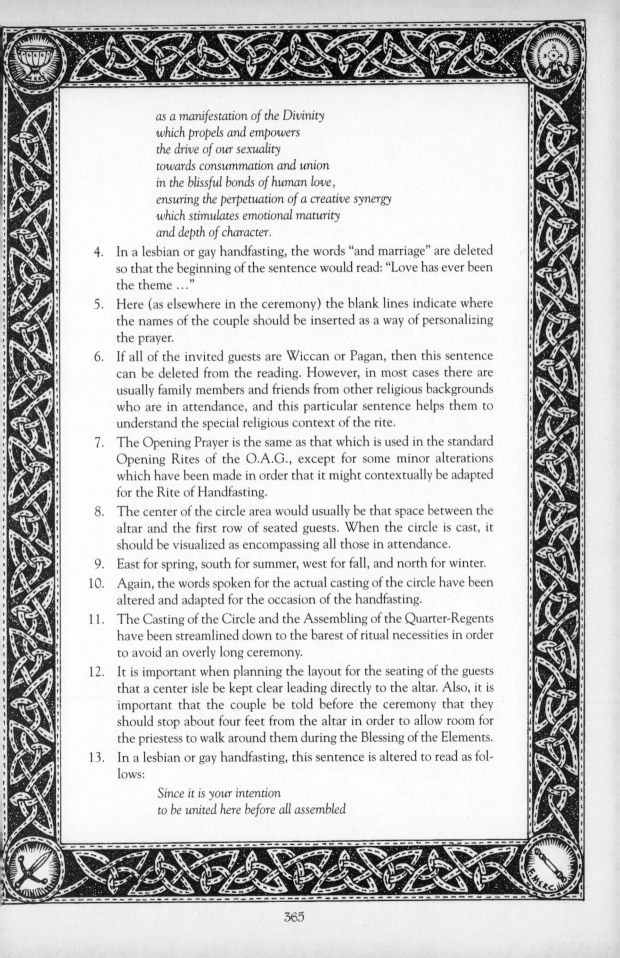

> *as a manifestation of the Divinity*
> *which propels and empowers*
> *the drive of our sexuality*
> *towards consummation and union*
> *in the blissful bonds of human love,*
> *ensuring the perpetuation of a creative synergy*
> *which stimulates emotional maturity*
> *and depth of character.*

4. In a lesbian or gay handfasting, the words "and marriage" are deleted so that the beginning of the sentence would read: "Love has ever been the theme …"

5. Here (as elsewhere in the ceremony) the blank lines indicate where the names of the couple should be inserted as a way of personalizing the prayer.

6. If all of the invited guests are Wiccan or Pagan, then this sentence can be deleted from the reading. However, in most cases there are usually family members and friends from other religious backgrounds who are in attendance, and this particular sentence helps them to understand the special religious context of the rite.

7. The Opening Prayer is the same as that which is used in the standard Opening Rites of the O.A.G., except for some minor alterations which have been made in order that it might contextually be adapted for the Rite of Handfasting.

8. The center of the circle area would usually be that space between the altar and the first row of seated guests. When the circle is cast, it should be visualized as encompassing all those in attendance.

9. East for spring, south for summer, west for fall, and north for winter.

10. Again, the words spoken for the actual casting of the circle have been altered and adapted for the occasion of the handfasting.

11. The Casting of the Circle and the Assembling of the Quarter-Regents have been streamlined down to the barest of ritual necessities in order to avoid an overly long ceremony.

12. It is important when planning the layout for the seating of the guests that a center isle be kept clear leading directly to the altar. Also, it is important that the couple be told before the ceremony that they should stop about four feet from the altar in order to allow room for the priestess to walk around them during the Blessing of the Elements.

13. In a lesbian or gay handfasting, this sentence is altered to read as follows:

> *Since it is your intention*
> *to be united here before all assembled*

> as two people bonded
> by the ties of unfettered affection,
> becoming thereby
> a mirror of the cosmic cohesion
> of the Universe held fast by Infinite Love;
> a Love whose purpose was to bring
> Creation out of Chaos
> and harmony to the elements.
> It is therefore your privilege
> to receive the blessing
> of the Elemental Sovereigns.

14. The priestess walks in the deosil (clockwise) direction in this instance because the blessings which she is speaking are meant for the strengthening of the couple's daily ongoing relationship. For more information about this kind of usage for ritual deosil movements, see footnote 13 of "Casting the Ceremonial Circle."

15. The Great Rite is ceremonially performed only in a heterosexual handfasting. For a lesbian or gay handfasting, another rite is substituted as given below:

The Chalice Rite

(Facing the couple from behind the altar, the priest then proceeds to explain the significance of the following rite.)

Priest:

> According to our traditions,
> it is most appropriate
> that this couple
> enact here in symbol
> a mystical analogy
> as a token
> of their personal commitment
> to the fulfilled realization
> of their relationship.

(The couple will then step forward to the altar; one of them picking up a cruet of wine, and the other picking up a cruet of water; both pouring the wine and water into the chalice simultaneously. The couple will then be handed the chalice by the priestess and they will both hold it closely facing one another. As they look into each other's eyes, they will say the following words.)

(The partner who poured the water into the chalice will say the following words if he is a gay man.)

> As water is to the streams of ecstasy ...

(The partner who poured the water into the chalice will say the following words if she is a lesbian.)

> As water is to the waves of ecstasy ...

(The partner who poured the wine into the chalice [whether a lesbian or a gay man] will then say the following words.)

> ... so wine is to the flowered
> fruit of Paradise ...

(Here, both partners [whether lesbians or gay men] will finish the sentence in unison.)

> ... and conjoined they fill full
> the Cup of Blessedness.

(The priestess will then lift up her hands to pronounce the blessing as she lays her hands upon their heads.)

Priestess:

> Foot to foot,
> Knee to knee,
> Rose to rose, (for lesbians)
> Staff to staff, (for gay men)
> Breast to breast,
> Lips to lips.
>
> May no part of your love
> be left untouched
> by the passion of Divine Desire,
> as your union becomes
> a microcosm of the macrocosm,
> As Above, So Below.

16. These words will have been memorized previously by the couple for this occasion.

17. These words are adapted from the Gardnerian/Alexandrian third degree initiation rites because of what we feel to be their exquisite appropriateness within the text of a handfasting. (See Janet and Stewart Farrar, *The Witches' Way*. [Custer, WA: Phoenix Publishing Company, 1984], p. 35.)

18. These words have also been adapted from the same third degree initiation ritual. (See the Farrars, p. 38.)

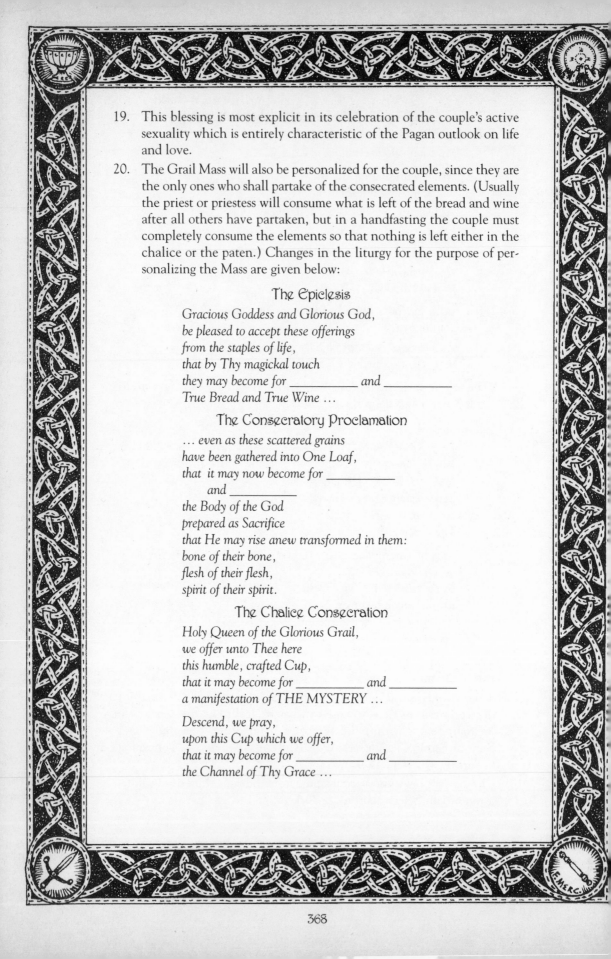

19. This blessing is most explicit in its celebration of the couple's active sexuality which is entirely characteristic of the Pagan outlook on life and love.

20. The Grail Mass will also be personalized for the couple, since they are the only ones who shall partake of the consecrated elements. (Usually the priest or priestess will consume what is left of the bread and wine after all others have partaken, but in a handfasting the couple must completely consume the elements so that nothing is left either in the chalice or the paten.) Changes in the liturgy for the purpose of personalizing the Mass are given below:

The Epiclesis

Gracious Goddess and Glorious God,
be pleased to accept these offerings
from the staples of life,
that by Thy magickal touch
they may become for _____ and _____
True Bread and True Wine ...

The Consecratory Proclamation

... even as these scattered grains
have been gathered into One Loaf,
that it may now become for _____
*   and _____*
the Body of the God
prepared as Sacrifice
that He may rise anew transformed in them:
bone of their bone,
flesh of their flesh,
spirit of their spirit.

The Chalice Consecration

Holy Queen of the Glorious Grail,
we offer unto Thee here
this humble, crafted Cup,
that it may become for _____ and _____
a manifestation of THE MYSTERY ...

Descend, we pray,
upon this Cup which we offer,
that it may become for _____ and _____
the Channel of Thy Grace ...

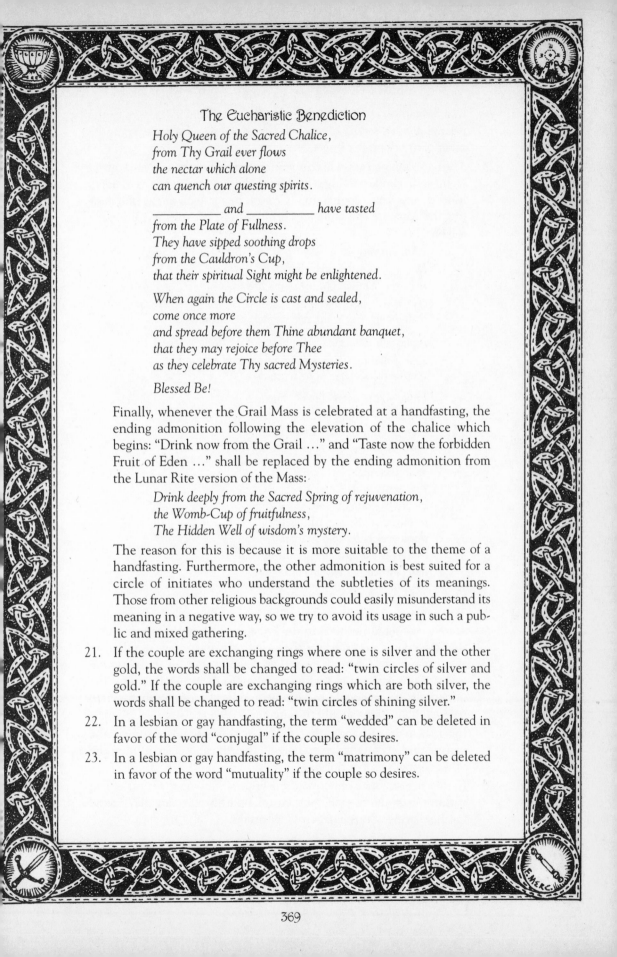

The Eucharistic Benediction

Holy Queen of the Sacred Chalice,
from Thy Grail ever flows
the nectar which alone
can quench our questing spirits.

_____ *and* _____ *have tasted*
from the Plate of Fullness.
They have sipped soothing drops
from the Cauldron's Cup,
that their spiritual Sight might be enlightened.

When again the Circle is cast and sealed,
come once more
and spread before them Thine abundant banquet,
that they may rejoice before Thee
as they celebrate Thy sacred Mysteries.

Blessed Be!

Finally, whenever the Grail Mass is celebrated at a handfasting, the ending admonition following the elevation of the chalice which begins: "Drink now from the Grail …" and "Taste now the forbidden Fruit of Eden …" shall be replaced by the ending admonition from the Lunar Rite version of the Mass:

Drink deeply from the Sacred Spring of rejuvenation,
the Womb-Cup of fruitfulness,
The Hidden Well of wisdom's mystery.

The reason for this is because it is more suitable to the theme of a handfasting. Furthermore, the other admonition is best suited for a circle of initiates who understand the subtleties of its meanings. Those from other religious backgrounds could easily misunderstand its meaning in a negative way, so we try to avoid its usage in such a public and mixed gathering.

21. If the couple are exchanging rings where one is silver and the other gold, the words shall be changed to read: "twin circles of silver and gold." If the couple are exchanging rings which are both silver, the words shall be changed to read: "twin circles of shining silver."

22. In a lesbian or gay handfasting, the term "wedded" can be deleted in favor of the word "conjugal" if the couple so desires.

23. In a lesbian or gay handfasting, the term "matrimony" can be deleted in favor of the word "mutuality" if the couple so desires.

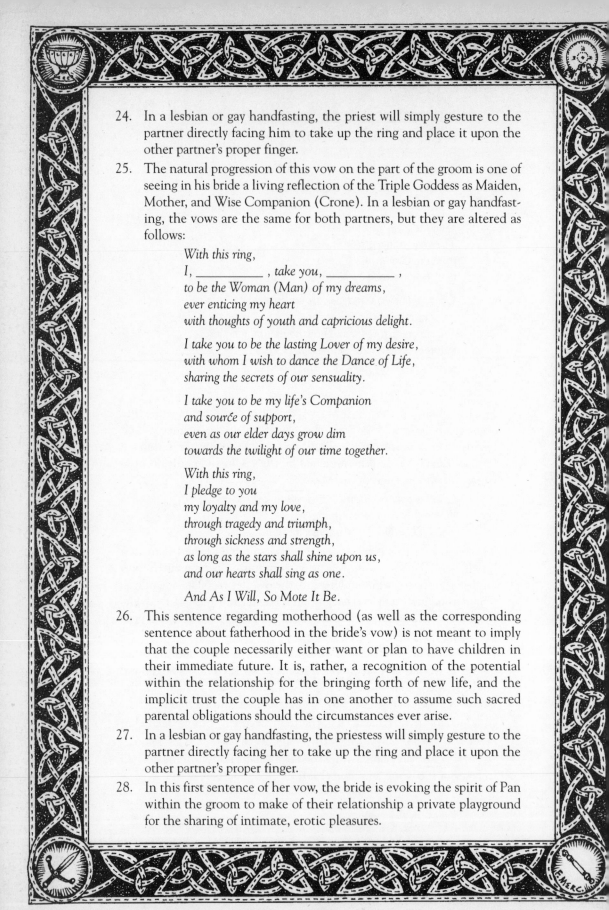

24. In a lesbian or gay handfasting, the priest will simply gesture to the partner directly facing him to take up the ring and place it upon the other partner's proper finger.

25. The natural progression of this vow on the part of the groom is one of seeing in his bride a living reflection of the Triple Goddess as Maiden, Mother, and Wise Companion (Crone). In a lesbian or gay handfasting, the vows are the same for both partners, but they are altered as follows:

> *With this ring,*
> *I, _____ , take you, _____ ,*
> *to be the Woman (Man) of my dreams,*
> *ever enticing my heart*
> *with thoughts of youth and capricious delight.*
>
> *I take you to be the lasting Lover of my desire,*
> *with whom I wish to dance the Dance of Life,*
> *sharing the secrets of our sensuality.*
>
> *I take you to be my life's Companion*
> *and source of support,*
> *even as our elder days grow dim*
> *towards the twilight of our time together.*
>
> *With this ring,*
> *I pledge to you*
> *my loyalty and my love,*
> *through tragedy and triumph,*
> *through sickness and strength,*
> *as long as the stars shall shine upon us,*
> *and our hearts shall sing as one.*
>
> *And As I Will, So Mote It Be.*

26. This sentence regarding motherhood (as well as the corresponding sentence about fatherhood in the bride's vow) is not meant to imply that the couple necessarily either want or plan to have children in their immediate future. It is, rather, a recognition of the potential within the relationship for the bringing forth of new life, and the implicit trust the couple has in one another to assume such sacred parental obligations should the circumstances ever arise.

27. In a lesbian or gay handfasting, the priestess will simply gesture to the partner directly facing her to take up the ring and place it upon the other partner's proper finger.

28. In this first sentence of her vow, the bride is evoking the spirit of Pan within the groom to make of their relationship a private playground for the sharing of intimate, erotic pleasures.

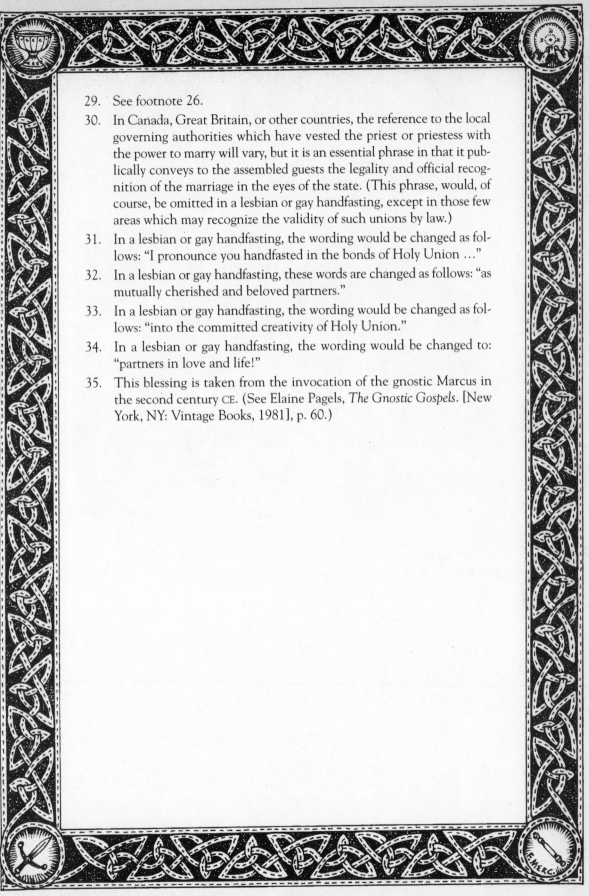

29. See footnote 26.

30. In Canada, Great Britain, or other countries, the reference to the local governing authorities which have vested the priest or priestess with the power to marry will vary, but it is an essential phrase in that it publically conveys to the assembled guests the legality and official recognition of the marriage in the eyes of the state. (This phrase, would, of course, be omitted in a lesbian or gay handfasting, except in those few areas which may recognize the validity of such unions by law.)

31. In a lesbian or gay handfasting, the wording would be changed as follows: "I pronounce you handfasted in the bonds of Holy Union ..."

32. In a lesbian or gay handfasting, these words are changed as follows: "as mutually cherished and beloved partners."

33. In a lesbian or gay handfasting, the wording would be changed as follows: "into the committed creativity of Holy Union."

34. In a lesbian or gay handfasting, the wording would be changed to: "partners in love and life!"

35. This blessing is taken from the invocation of the gnostic Marcus in the second century CE. (See Elaine Pagels, *The Gnostic Gospels*. [New York, NY: Vintage Books, 1981], p. 60.)

The Opening Rites: Admission into the circle. "By this moisture from the body of the Great Mother, be purified as you enter this sacred space."

The Requiem Rite

It can truly be said that the Requiem Rite and the Graveside Service is the one ceremonial occasion which a member of the priesthood hopes it will never be necessary to lead. We instinctively cringe at the thought of officiating at the funeral of a friend, acquaintance, loved one, or grove member, for the feelings of loss are often depressingly numbing; but it is precisely in these situations that the consolation of ritual based upon religious reflection can begin to make bearable the death of another.

The process of dying is seen by most Pagans as a necessary complement to life by which the cyclic nature of the physical environment is perpetuated, and the means by which human beings graduate from one incarnation to another in the progressive advancement of the soul. But such a theological understanding can still be most inadequate to enable one to cope with the crushing agony of grief which affects both the family and friends of the deceased. For this reason, the strength of the Requiem Rite lies in its ability to put within a ritualized structure and form the collective expression of our grief as well as the highest of our hopes for the spirit of the one who has died. The underlying message is the same as that shared by the majority of all religions: death is not a final end, but a doorway to other dimensions of life and spirit.

Basic Requirements

Below are some things to remember for the observance of a Requiem Rite which are necessary requirements if the ceremony is to be in accordance with the rubrics of the Ordo Arcanorum Gradalis.

Altar

The altar should be in the center of the circle area, facing east in the spring, south in the summer, west in the fall, and north in the winter.

Altar Cloth

The altar cloth should always correspond to the color of whichever quarter has the seasonal preeminence at the time of the Requiem: yellow in the spring, red in the summer, blue in the fall, and green in the winter. (This is only if you are using a regular rectangular altar. If the grove uses the Altar of the Pentagram, see the earlier chapter entitled "The Altar and the Sacred Tools" for further details and instructions.)

Altar Candles

The two main altar candles should be the same color as the altar cloth being used: yellow in the spring, red in the summer, blue in the fall, and green in the winter.

Other Candles

The four quarter candles (or glass votive candleholders) *should always be yellow in the east, red in the south, blue in the west, and green in the north.* All other secondary candles used for extra lighting in the ritual area should be black or lavender as a sign of mourning.

Special Items

There needs to be one white candle and holder which will be placed midway between the two main altar candles. It is the Memorial Candle for the deceased, and can be of any size.

Circle Area Decorations

Due to the somber nature of this Rite, decorations, as such, would not be appropriate.

The Casting of the Circle

In accordance with "The Opening and Closing Rites," the circle shall always be cast widdershins (counterclockwise).

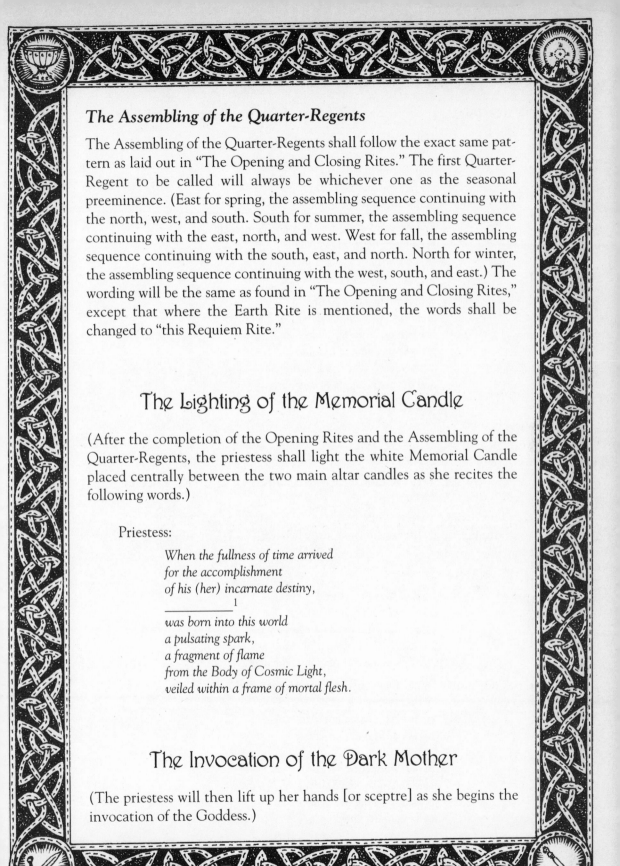

The Assembling of the Quarter-Regents

The Assembling of the Quarter-Regents shall follow the exact same pattern as laid out in "The Opening and Closing Rites." The first Quarter-Regent to be called will always be whichever one as the seasonal preeminence. (East for spring, the assembling sequence continuing with the north, west, and south. South for summer, the assembling sequence continuing with the east, north, and west. West for fall, the assembling sequence continuing with the south, east, and north. North for winter, the assembling sequence continuing with the west, south, and east.) The wording will be the same as found in "The Opening and Closing Rites," except that where the Earth Rite is mentioned, the words shall be changed to "this Requiem Rite."

The Lighting of the Memorial Candle

(After the completion of the Opening Rites and the Assembling of the Quarter-Regents, the priestess shall light the white Memorial Candle placed centrally between the two main altar candles as she recites the following words.)

Priestess:

> *When the fullness of time arrived*
> *for the accomplishment*
> *of his (her) incarnate destiny,*
> _____[1]
> *was born into this world*
> *a pulsating spark,*
> *a fragment of flame*
> *from the Body of Cosmic Light,*
> *veiled within a frame of mortal flesh.*

The Invocation of the Dark Mother

(The priestess will then lift up her hands [or sceptre] as she begins the invocation of the Goddess.)

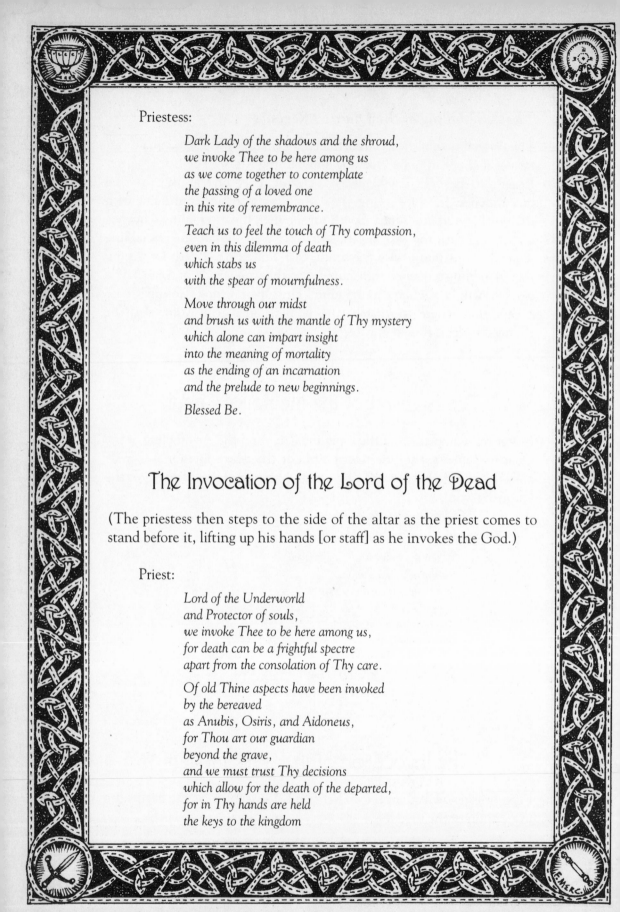

Priestess:

> Dark Lady of the shadows and the shroud,
> we invoke Thee to be here among us
> as we come together to contemplate
> the passing of a loved one
> in this rite of remembrance.
>
> Teach us to feel the touch of Thy compassion,
> even in this dilemma of death
> which stabs us
> with the spear of mournfulness.
>
> Move through our midst
> and brush us with the mantle of Thy mystery
> which alone can impart insight
> into the meaning of mortality
> as the ending of an incarnation
> and the prelude to new beginnings.
>
> Blessed Be.

The Invocation of the Lord of the Dead

(The priestess then steps to the side of the altar as the priest comes to stand before it, lifting up his hands [or staff] as he invokes the God.)

Priest:

> Lord of the Underworld
> and Protector of souls,
> we invoke Thee to be here among us,
> for death can be a frightful spectre
> apart from the consolation of Thy care.
>
> Of old Thine aspects have been invoked
> by the bereaved
> as Anubis, Osiris, and Aidoneus,
> for Thou art our guardian
> beyond the grave,
> and we must trust Thy decisions
> which allow for the death of the departed,
> for in Thy hands are held
> the keys to the kingdom

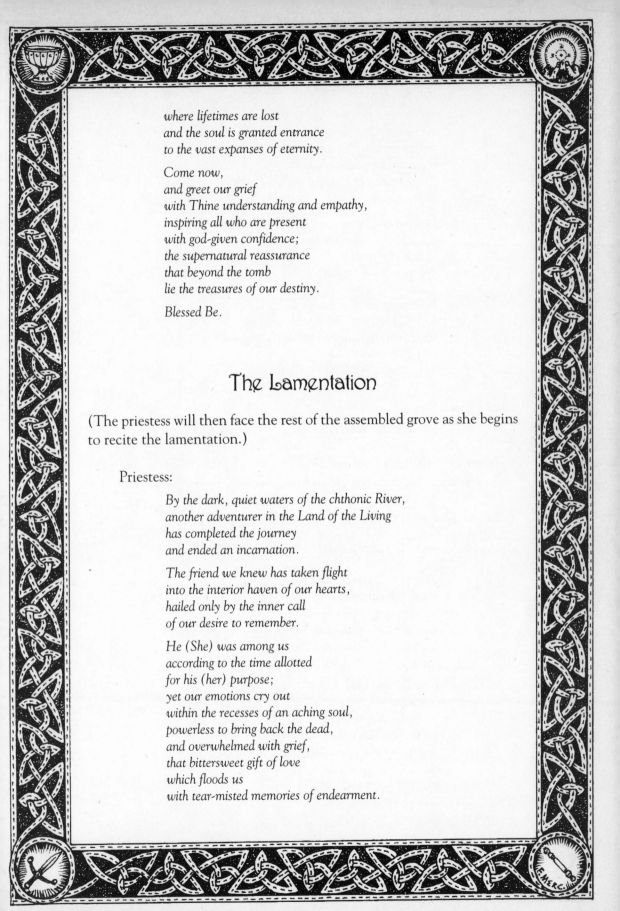

where lifetimes are lost
and the soul is granted entrance
to the vast expanses of eternity.

Come now,
and greet our grief
with Thine understanding and empathy,
inspiring all who are present
with god-given confidence;
the supernatural reassurance
that beyond the tomb
lie the treasures of our destiny.

Blessed Be.

The Lamentation

(The priestess will then face the rest of the assembled grove as she begins to recite the lamentation.)

Priestess:

By the dark, quiet waters of the chthonic River,
another adventurer in the Land of the Living
has completed the journey
and ended an incarnation.

The friend we knew has taken flight
into the interior haven of our hearts,
hailed only by the inner call
of our desire to remember.

He (She) was among us
according to the time allotted
for his (her) purpose;
yet our emotions cry out
within the recesses of an aching soul,
powerless to bring back the dead,
and overwhelmed with grief,
that bittersweet gift of love
which floods us
with tear-misted memories of endearment.

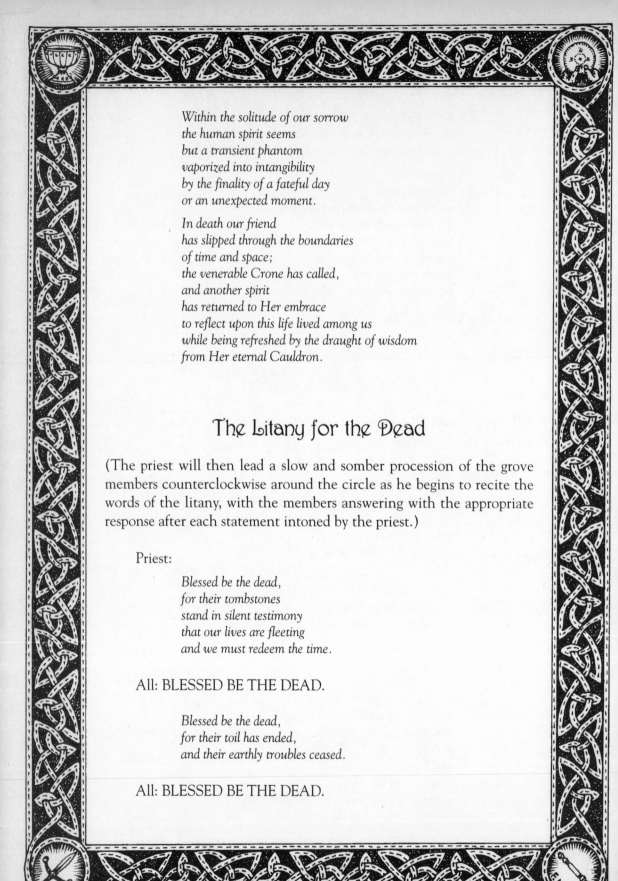

Within the solitude of our sorrow
the human spirit seems
but a transient phantom
vaporized into intangibility
by the finality of a fateful day
or an unexpected moment.

In death our friend
has slipped through the boundaries
of time and space;
the venerable Crone has called,
and another spirit
has returned to Her embrace
to reflect upon this life lived among us
while being refreshed by the draught of wisdom
from Her eternal Cauldron.

The Litany for the Dead

(The priest will then lead a slow and somber procession of the grove members counterclockwise around the circle as he begins to recite the words of the litany, with the members answering with the appropriate response after each statement intoned by the priest.)

Priest:

> *Blessed be the dead,*
> *for their tombstones*
> *stand in silent testimony*
> *that our lives are fleeting*
> *and we must redeem the time.*

All: BLESSED BE THE DEAD.

> *Blessed be the dead,*
> *for their toil has ended,*
> *and their earthly troubles ceased.*

All: BLESSED BE THE DEAD.

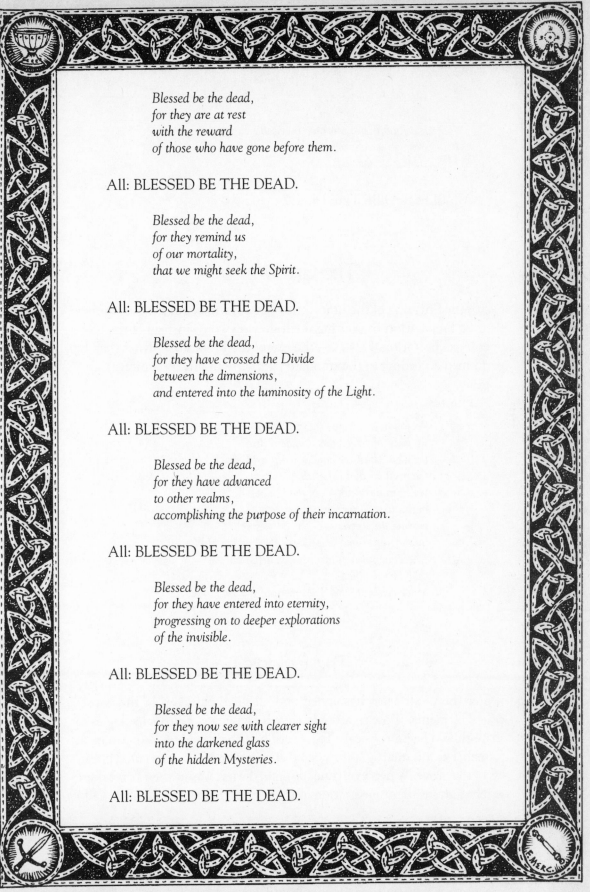

Blessed be the dead,
for they are at rest
with the reward
of those who have gone before them.

All: BLESSED BE THE DEAD.

Blessed be the dead,
for they remind us
of our mortality,
that we might seek the Spirit.

All: BLESSED BE THE DEAD.

Blessed be the dead,
for they have crossed the Divide
between the dimensions,
and entered into the luminosity of the Light.

All: BLESSED BE THE DEAD.

Blessed be the dead,
for they have advanced
to other realms,
accomplishing the purpose of their incarnation.

All: BLESSED BE THE DEAD.

Blessed be the dead,
for they have entered into eternity,
progressing on to deeper explorations
of the invisible.

All: BLESSED BE THE DEAD.

Blessed be the dead,
for they now see with clearer sight
into the darkened glass
of the hidden Mysteries.

All: BLESSED BE THE DEAD.

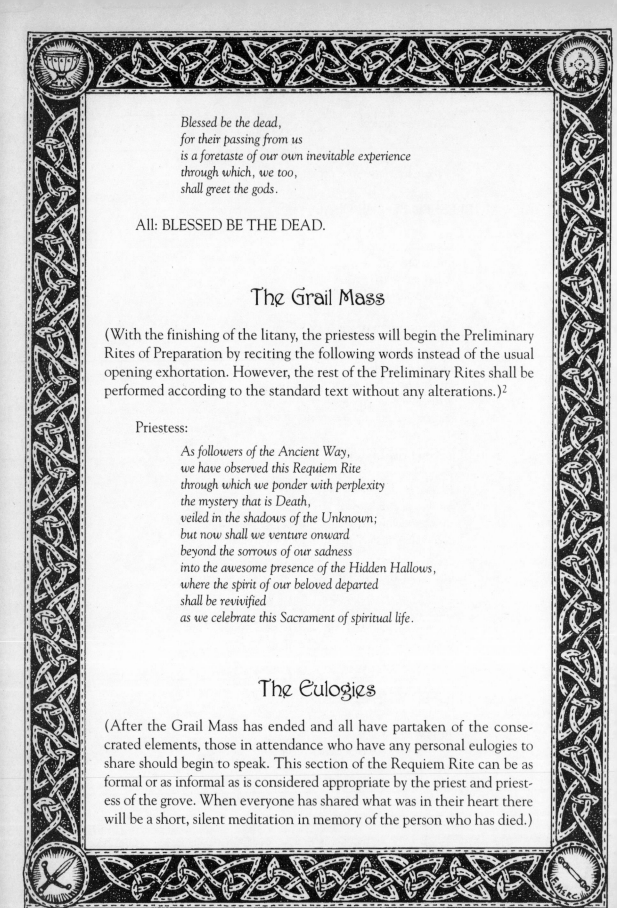

Blessed be the dead,
for their passing from us
is a foretaste of our own inevitable experience
through which, we too,
shall greet the gods.

All: BLESSED BE THE DEAD.

The Grail Mass

(With the finishing of the litany, the priestess will begin the Preliminary Rites of Preparation by reciting the following words instead of the usual opening exhortation. However, the rest of the Preliminary Rites shall be performed according to the standard text without any alterations.)[2]

Priestess:

As followers of the Ancient Way,
we have observed this Requiem Rite
through which we ponder with perplexity
the mystery that is Death,
veiled in the shadows of the Unknown;
but now shall we venture onward
beyond the sorrows of our sadness
into the awesome presence of the Hidden Hallows,
where the spirit of our beloved departed
shall be revivified
as we celebrate this Sacrament of spiritual life.

The Eulogies

(After the Grail Mass has ended and all have partaken of the consecrated elements, those in attendance who have any personal eulogies to share should begin to speak. This section of the Requiem Rite can be as formal or as informal as is considered appropriate by the priest and priestess of the grove. When everyone has shared what was in their heart there will be a short, silent meditation in memory of the person who has died.)

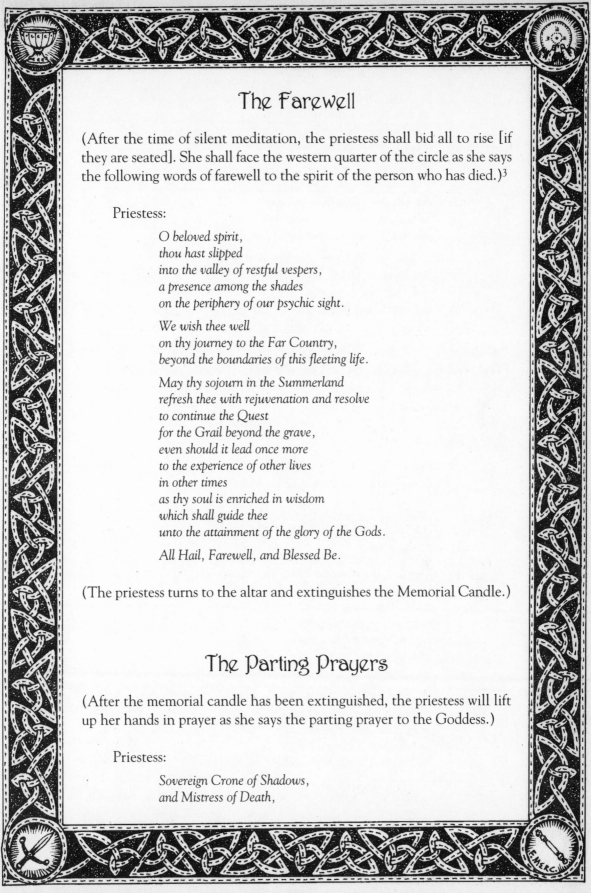

The Farewell

(After the time of silent meditation, the priestess shall bid all to rise [if they are seated]. She shall face the western quarter of the circle as she says the following words of farewell to the spirit of the person who has died.)[3]

Priestess:

O beloved spirit,
thou hast slipped
into the valley of restful vespers,
a presence among the shades
on the periphery of our psychic sight.

We wish thee well
on thy journey to the Far Country,
beyond the boundaries of this fleeting life.

May thy sojourn in the Summerland
refresh thee with rejuvenation and resolve
to continue the Quest
for the Grail beyond the grave,
even should it lead once more
to the experience of other lives
in other times
as thy soul is enriched in wisdom
which shall guide thee
unto the attainment of the glory of the Gods.

All Hail, Farewell, and Blessed Be.

(The priestess turns to the altar and extinguishes the Memorial Candle.)

The Parting Prayers

(After the memorial candle has been extinguished, the priestess will lift up her hands in prayer as she says the parting prayer to the Goddess.)

Priestess:

Sovereign Crone of Shadows,
and Mistress of Death,

> we thank Thee
> for Thy presence here among us
> in response to the burden
> of our common bereavement.
>
> We ask of Thee in reverent supplication
> to have mercy upon the soul of _____
> that he (she) might find the Light
> beyond Thy veil of darkness,
> and bask in the beauty of higher realms.
>
> We ask Thy departing benediction upon us
> as we end this rite
> with solace for our sorrow
> and hope in our hearts.
>
> All Hail, Farewell, and Blessed Be.

(The priestess will now step to one side of the altar to make way for the priest who will take her place and begin the parting prayer to the God with hands upraised.)

Priest:

> Lord of the Nether Regions,
> whose kingdom welcomes the world-weary
> from the labor of their lives,
> we thank Thee for having heard
> our prayers of petition
> for the spirit of _____ .
>
> May he (she) be received into Thy realm,
> having returned from his (her) journey
> into this lifetime,
> welcomed by the embrace
> of friends and familiar faces
> who have preceded him (her)
> into the presence of Thy peace.
>
> We ask Thy blessing upon us,
> that we might be strengthened
> in the assurance of immortality
> and the eternal ties of love,
> both in this life and beyond.
>
> All Hail, Farewell, and Blessed Be.

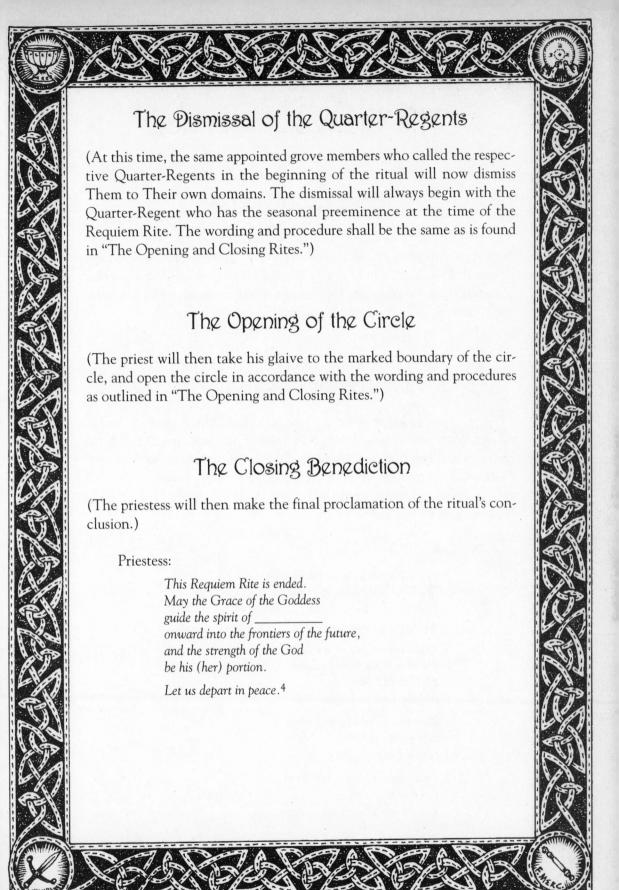

The Dismissal of the Quarter-Regents

(At this time, the same appointed grove members who called the respective Quarter-Regents in the beginning of the ritual will now dismiss Them to Their own domains. The dismissal will always begin with the Quarter-Regent who has the seasonal preeminence at the time of the Requiem Rite. The wording and procedure shall be the same as is found in "The Opening and Closing Rites.")

The Opening of the Circle

(The priest will then take his glaive to the marked boundary of the circle, and open the circle in accordance with the wording and procedures as outlined in "The Opening and Closing Rites.")

The Closing Benediction

(The priestess will then make the final proclamation of the ritual's conclusion.)

Priestess:

> *This Requiem Rite is ended.*
> *May the Grace of the Goddess*
> *guide the spirit of _____*
> *onward into the frontiers of the future,*
> *and the strength of the God*
> *be his (her) portion.*
>
> *Let us depart in peace.*[4]

The Graveside Service

Basic Requirements

The only required items are a censer with coal and incense, a candle-lantern, a dish of earth, and a bowl of water. The use of a small altar is optional. Usually, it would not be needed as long as at least two other members from the grove are appointed to hold the items when not being used. Flowers, of course, are also appropriate at the graveside.

The Sanctification

(The priest should first place incense upon the lighted coal within the censer. With a small bowl containing salted holy water in her hand, the priestess will begin to process around the casket widdershins [counter-clockwise], sprinkling water upon the ground as the priest follows her with incense billowing from the censer. As they process, the priestess will recite the following words.)[5]

Priestess:

> *In the Name of the Great Goddess,*
> *She Who is the Mother of the Earth,*
> *Lady of the Moon,*
> *and Queen of the Cosmos;*
>
> *And in the Name of the Glorious God,*
> *He Who is the Horned Lord,*
> *the Celestial Sun,*
> *and the Cosmic Logos;*
>
> *May this ground be sanctified*
> *as a resting place*
> *for the body of _____*
>
> *Once more the womb of Earth*
> *receives Her own,*
> *that the cycle might begin again.*

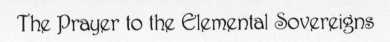

The Prayer to the Elemental Sovereigns

(The priest will take his place at the head of the casket and lift up the censer towards the sky.)

Priest:

> Sovereigns of Wind and Air,
> unto Thy care
> we commend the breath of our beloved;
> may it be swept heavenward
> in wispy flight,
> and given new life
> as it blends into the breezes
> to greet the newness of each dawning day.

(An assistant will take the censer from the priest while the priestess hands him the lighted candle-lantern which he will lift towards the sky.)

Priest:

> Sovereigns of Fire and Flame,
> unto Thy care
> we commend the sparks of personal vitality
> which energized his (her) will
> to grasp for growth
> into the essence of life;
> may they glow brightly in the astral ether
> as a testimony to the beauty
> of his (her) love for the zest of living.

(An assistant will take the lighted candle-lantern from the priest while the priestess hands him the bowl of salted water. He will sprinkle some water upon the casket and lift the bowl towards the sky.)

Priest:

> Sovereigns of all Watery Realms,
> unto Thy care
> we commend the sensitivities of his (her) soul,
> that all emotions, worries and cares
> may take their leave
> in embarcation upon the twilight sea of serenity.

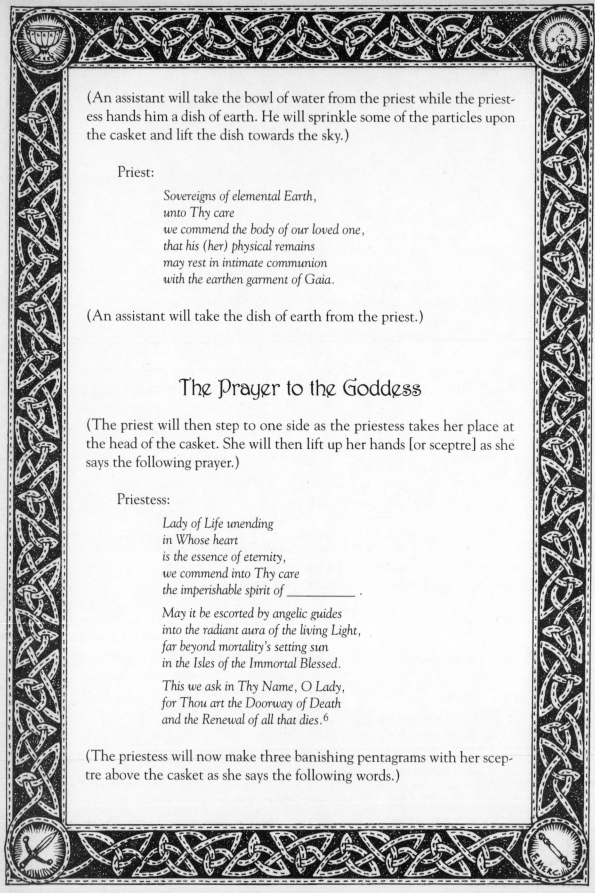

(An assistant will take the bowl of water from the priest while the priestess hands him a dish of earth. He will sprinkle some of the particles upon the casket and lift the dish towards the sky.)

Priest:

> *Sovereigns of elemental Earth,*
> *unto Thy care*
> *we commend the body of our loved one,*
> *that his (her) physical remains*
> *may rest in intimate communion*
> *with the earthen garment of Gaia.*

(An assistant will take the dish of earth from the priest.)

The Prayer to the Goddess

(The priest will then step to one side as the priestess takes her place at the head of the casket. She will then lift up her hands [or sceptre] as she says the following prayer.)

Priestess:

> *Lady of Life unending*
> *in Whose heart*
> *is the essence of eternity,*
> *we commend into Thy care*
> *the imperishable spirit of _____ .*
>
> *May it be escorted by angelic guides*
> *into the radiant aura of the living Light,*
> *far beyond mortality's setting sun*
> *in the Isles of the Immortal Blessed.*
>
> *This we ask in Thy Name, O Lady,*
> *for Thou art the Doorway of Death*
> *and the Renewal of all that dies.*[6]

(The priestess will now make three banishing pentagrams with her sceptre above the casket as she says the following words.)

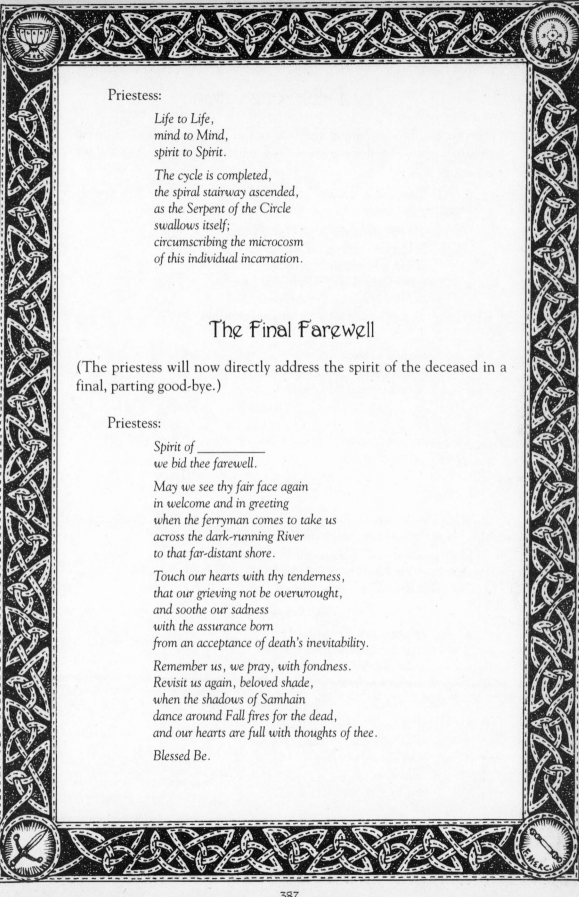

Priestess:

> Life to Life,
> mind to Mind,
> spirit to Spirit.
>
> The cycle is completed,
> the spiral stairway ascended,
> as the Serpent of the Circle
> swallows itself;
> circumscribing the microcosm
> of this individual incarnation.

The Final Farewell

(The priestess will now directly address the spirit of the deceased in a final, parting good-bye.)

Priestess:

> Spirit of _____
> we bid thee farewell.
>
> May we see thy fair face again
> in welcome and in greeting
> when the ferryman comes to take us
> across the dark-running River
> to that far-distant shore.
>
> Touch our hearts with thy tenderness,
> that our grieving not be overwrought,
> and soothe our sadness
> with the assurance born
> from an acceptance of death's inevitability.
>
> Remember us, we pray, with fondness.
> Revisit us again, beloved shade,
> when the shadows of Samhain
> dance around Fall fires for the dead,
> and our hearts are full with thoughts of thee.
>
> Blessed Be.

The Final Benediction

(The priest, now standing at the side of the priestess, will raise up his hands in a gesture of blessing upon those gathered as he says the following benediction.)

Priest:

The blessing of the Triple Goddess
be upon the living and the dead,
that in life we might be humbled
by the realization of our physical mortality,
and that in death we might obtain
the reassurance of our spiritual imperishability.

This rite is ended.
Go now in peace,
enfolded in the comforting arms
of the Lady and the Lord.

Blessed Be.

Footnotes

1. Here (as elsewhere during the ceremony) the blank line indicates where the name of the deceased should be inserted.

2. In the actual text of the Grail Mass itself, there are only two alterations which should be noted which are unique to its usage within the Requiem Rite. They are as follows:

The Preface

In union with the spirit of _____
and all the faithful from ages past,
seekers of the Way,
companions on the Quest …

The Epiclesis

Gracious Goddess and Glorious God,
be pleased to accept these offerings
from the staples of life
in memory of _____
that by Thy magickal touch …

3. The priestess faces the western quarter because it is traditionally seen as the direction of the setting sun and that which lies beyond (i.e., the realm of the dead).

4. The usual closing statement of "Merry Meet, and Merry Part, and Merry Meet Again!" is dispensed with in this rite since it is not considered suitable to the solemnity of the occasion. Instead, "Let us depart in peace" is used in its place.

5. These words can either be memorized by the priestess, or else they can be read after the casket has been circled by the priestess and priest.

6. This is a direct reference to the words of the Goddess as quoted in Her Charge at each Lunar Rite.

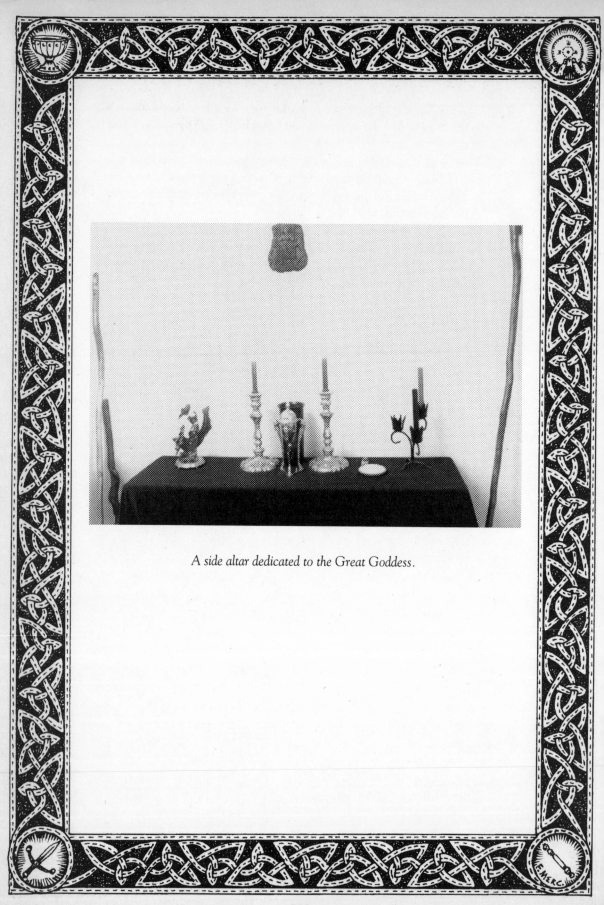

A side altar dedicated to the Great Goddess.

The Rite of Initiation

In many traditions of the Craft, initiation is ideally a one-time experience never to be forgotten, marking that most momentous spiritual turning point when one finally and officially becomes ceremonially inaugurated into a commitment to the pathway of Pagan spirituality. For those interested in becoming a member of an O.A.G. affiliated grove, a word of explanation is in order regarding our approach to the general concept of initiation. Ironically, for groves affiliated with our Order, initiation is far less common than is ordination, for we are primarily a religious Order of priesthood; an ecclesiastical Fellowship of the Grail which can only be joined through ordination. Initiation, as such, does not constitute entrance into the Ordo Arcanorum Gradalis, but merely membership into the ranks of a local grove affiliated with our Order.

If you have already been initiated into the Craft through another tradition, we accept that as a valid, experiential entrance into the Pagan way. We therefore do not require you to duplicate such a ceremony for admittance into our groves. The same also applies to former solitaries who, through formal self-initiation, have already started upon their journey into Pagan spirituality.

If you have never been initiated, but are seeking to join the fellowship of the Craft through membership in a grove affiliated with this Order; then, at the completion of your studies and training as dictated by the requirements of that local grove, you will be initiated by its presiding priest/ess. Those who have been previously initiated into other Wiccan, Gnostic, or Pagan traditions, upon the completion of the required studies and training as stipulated by the local grove, will be automatically accepted into grove membership. However, it is important to keep in mind that this acceptance into the grove is more on the order of the Protestant practice of "extending the hand of fellowship" to a new member who has come from another congregation or denomination. This is different from an initiation, in that initiation signifies one's commitment to the Craft and the Pagan path in general, whereas acceptance into membership signifies an already-initiated Pagan's entrance into the fellowship of a grove affiliated with the Ordo Arcanorum Gradalis.

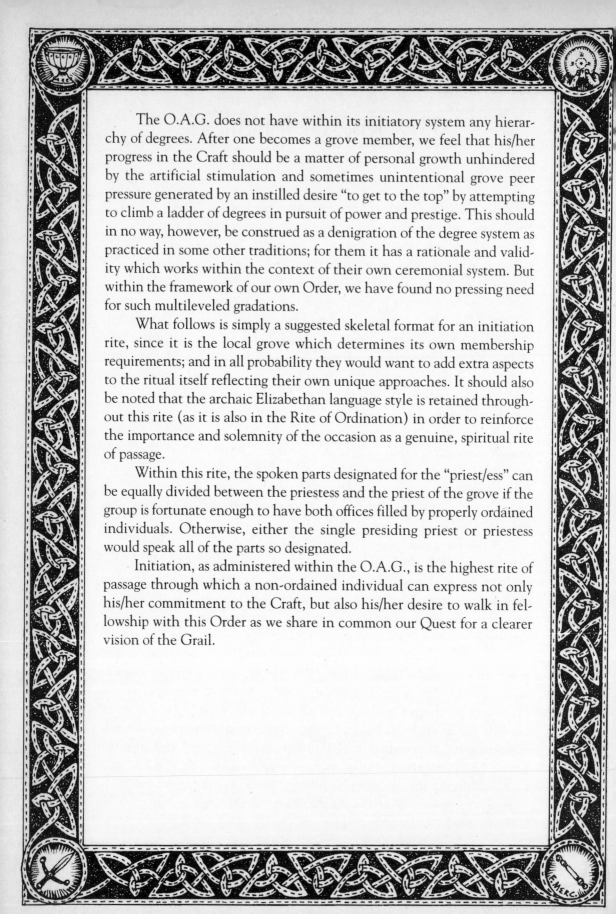

The O.A.G. does not have within its initiatory system any hierarchy of degrees. After one becomes a grove member, we feel that his/her progress in the Craft should be a matter of personal growth unhindered by the artificial stimulation and sometimes unintentional grove peer pressure generated by an instilled desire "to get to the top" by attempting to climb a ladder of degrees in pursuit of power and prestige. This should in no way, however, be construed as a denigration of the degree system as practiced in some other traditions; for them it has a rationale and validity which works within the context of their own ceremonial system. But within the framework of our own Order, we have found no pressing need for such multileveled gradations.

What follows is simply a suggested skeletal format for an initiation rite, since it is the local grove which determines its own membership requirements; and in all probability they would want to add extra aspects to the ritual itself reflecting their own unique approaches. It should also be noted that the archaic Elizabethan language style is retained throughout this rite (as it is also in the Rite of Ordination) in order to reinforce the importance and solemnity of the occasion as a genuine, spiritual rite of passage.

Within this rite, the spoken parts designated for the "priest/ess" can be equally divided between the priestess and the priest of the grove if the group is fortunate enough to have both offices filled by properly ordained individuals. Otherwise, either the single presiding priest or priestess would speak all of the parts so designated.

Initiation, as administered within the O.A.G., is the highest rite of passage through which a non-ordained individual can express not only his/her commitment to the Craft, but also his/her desire to walk in fellowship with this Order as we share in common our Quest for a clearer vision of the Grail.

Basic Requirements

Below are some things to remember which are necessary requirements if the Rite of Initiation is to be in accordance with the rubrics of the Ordo Arcanorum Gradalis.

Altar

The altar should be in the center of the circle area, facing whichever quarter has the seasonal preeminence at the time of the initiation (east for spring, south for summer, west for fall, and north for winter).

Altar Cloth and Candles

The altar cloth and the two main altar candles should always be the same color as the corresponding quarter color which has the seasonal preeminence at the time of the initiation (yellow in spring, red in summer, blue in fall, and green in winter).

Other Candles

The four quarter candles (or glass votive candleholders) *should always be yellow in the east, red in the south, blue in the west, and green in the north.* All other secondary candles used for extra lighting in the ritual area should be white or cream colored.

Special Items

The only special item needed for the Rite of Initiation is a black cloth blindfold. (However, local groves may stipulate additional items or ritual accessories in accordance with any extra ceremonies which they may see fit to add to the rite.)

Circle Area Decorations

No special decorations are required.

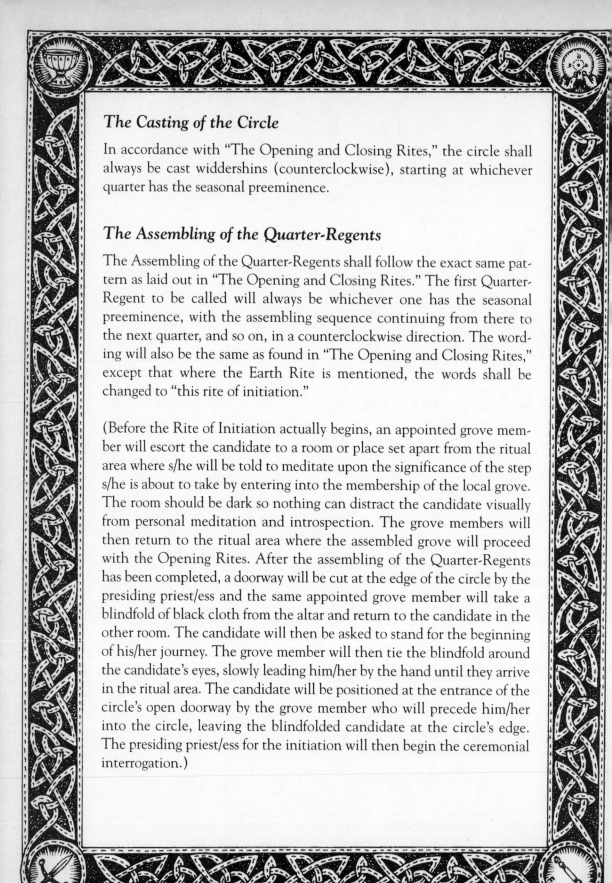

The Casting of the Circle

In accordance with "The Opening and Closing Rites," the circle shall always be cast widdershins (counterclockwise), starting at whichever quarter has the seasonal preeminence.

The Assembling of the Quarter-Regents

The Assembling of the Quarter-Regents shall follow the exact same pattern as laid out in "The Opening and Closing Rites." The first Quarter-Regent to be called will always be whichever one has the seasonal preeminence, with the assembling sequence continuing from there to the next quarter, and so on, in a counterclockwise direction. The wording will also be the same as found in "The Opening and Closing Rites," except that where the Earth Rite is mentioned, the words shall be changed to "this rite of initiation."

(Before the Rite of Initiation actually begins, an appointed grove member will escort the candidate to a room or place set apart from the ritual area where s/he will be told to meditate upon the significance of the step s/he is about to take by entering into the membership of the local grove. The room should be dark so nothing can distract the candidate visually from personal meditation and introspection. The grove members will then return to the ritual area where the assembled grove will proceed with the Opening Rites. After the assembling of the Quarter-Regents has been completed, a doorway will be cut at the edge of the circle by the presiding priest/ess and the same appointed grove member will take a blindfold of black cloth from the altar and return to the candidate in the other room. The candidate will then be asked to stand for the beginning of his/her journey. The grove member will then tie the blindfold around the candidate's eyes, slowly leading him/her by the hand until they arrive in the ritual area. The candidate will be positioned at the entrance of the circle's open doorway by the grove member who will precede him/her into the circle, leaving the blindfolded candidate at the circle's edge. The presiding priest/ess for the initiation will then begin the ceremonial interrogation.)

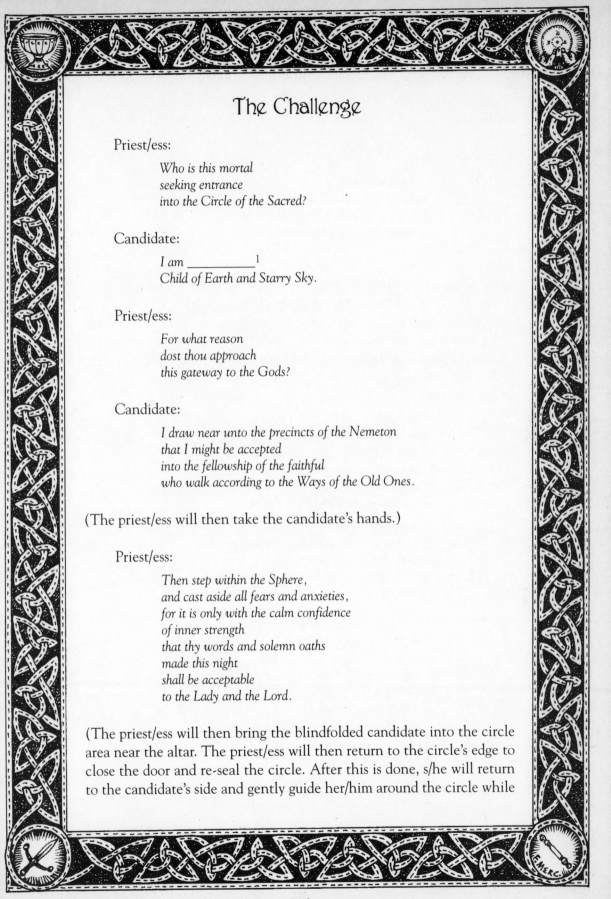

The Challenge

Priest/ess:

> Who is this mortal
> seeking entrance
> into the Circle of the Sacred?

Candidate:

> I am _____ [1]
> Child of Earth and Starry Sky.

Priest/ess:

> For what reason
> dost thou approach
> this gateway to the Gods?

Candidate:

> I draw near unto the precincts of the Nemeton
> that I might be accepted
> into the fellowship of the faithful
> who walk according to the Ways of the Old Ones.

(The priest/ess will then take the candidate's hands.)

Priest/ess:

> Then step within the Sphere,
> and cast aside all fears and anxieties,
> for it is only with the calm confidence
> of inner strength
> that thy words and solemn oaths
> made this night
> shall be acceptable
> to the Lady and the Lord.

(The priest/ess will then bring the blindfolded candidate into the circle area near the altar. The priest/ess will then return to the circle's edge to close the door and re-seal the circle. After this is done, s/he will return to the candidate's side and gently guide her/him around the circle while

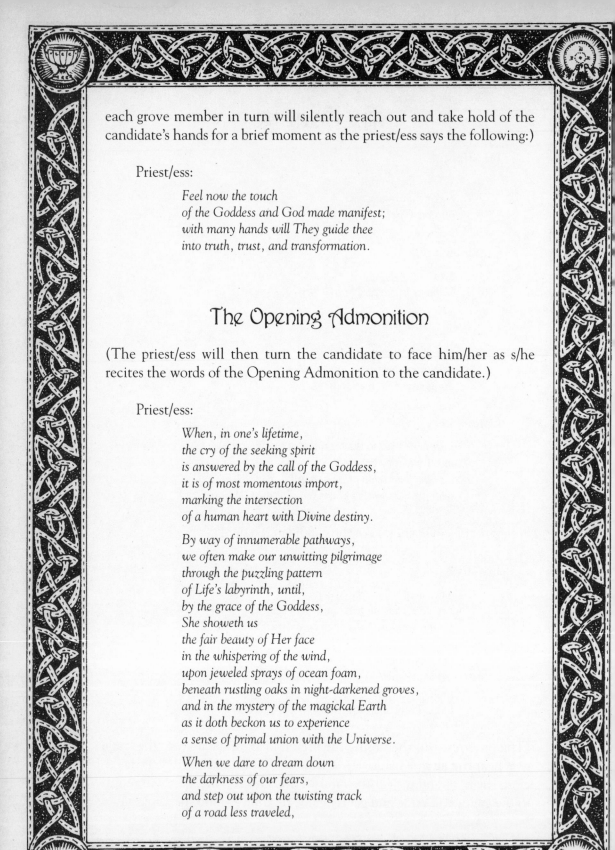

each grove member in turn will silently reach out and take hold of the candidate's hands for a brief moment as the priest/ess says the following:)

Priest/ess:

Feel now the touch
of the Goddess and God made manifest;
with many hands will They guide thee
into truth, trust, and transformation.

The Opening Admonition

(The priest/ess will then turn the candidate to face him/her as s/he recites the words of the Opening Admonition to the candidate.)

Priest/ess:

When, in one's lifetime,
the cry of the seeking spirit
is answered by the call of the Goddess,
it is of most momentous import,
marking the intersection
of a human heart with Divine destiny.

By way of innumerable pathways,
we often make our unwitting pilgrimage
through the puzzling pattern
of Life's labyrinth, until,
by the grace of the Goddess,
She showeth us
the fair beauty of Her face
in the whispering of the wind,
upon jeweled sprays of ocean foam,
beneath rustling oaks in night-darkened groves,
and in the mystery of the magickal Earth
as it doth beckon us to experience
a sense of primal union with the Universe.

When we dare to dream down
the darkness of our fears,
and step out upon the twisting track
of a road less traveled,

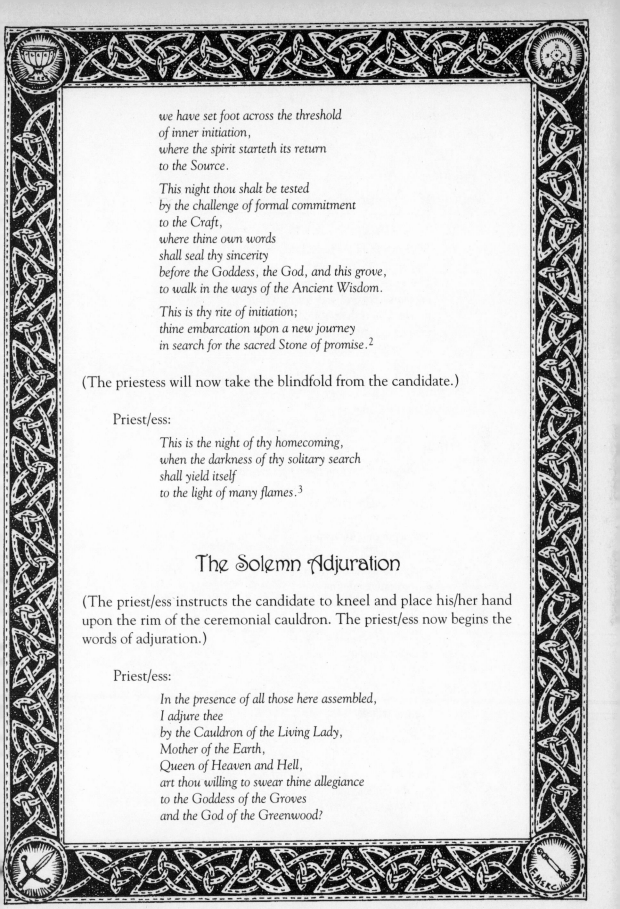

we have set foot across the threshold
of inner initiation,
where the spirit starteth its return
to the Source.

This night thou shalt be tested
by the challenge of formal commitment
to the Craft,
where thine own words
shall seal thy sincerity
before the Goddess, the God, and this grove,
to walk in the ways of the Ancient Wisdom.

This is thy rite of initiation;
thine embarcation upon a new journey
in search for the sacred Stone of promise.[2]

(The priestess will now take the blindfold from the candidate.)

Priest/ess:

This is the night of thy homecoming,
when the darkness of thy solitary search
shall yield itself
to the light of many flames.[3]

The Solemn Adjuration

(The priest/ess instructs the candidate to kneel and place his/her hand
upon the rim of the ceremonial cauldron. The priest/ess now begins the
words of adjuration.)

Priest/ess:

In the presence of all those here assembled,
I adjure thee
by the Cauldron of the Living Lady,
Mother of the Earth,
Queen of Heaven and Hell,
art thou willing to swear thine allegiance
to the Goddess of the Groves
and the God of the Greenwood?

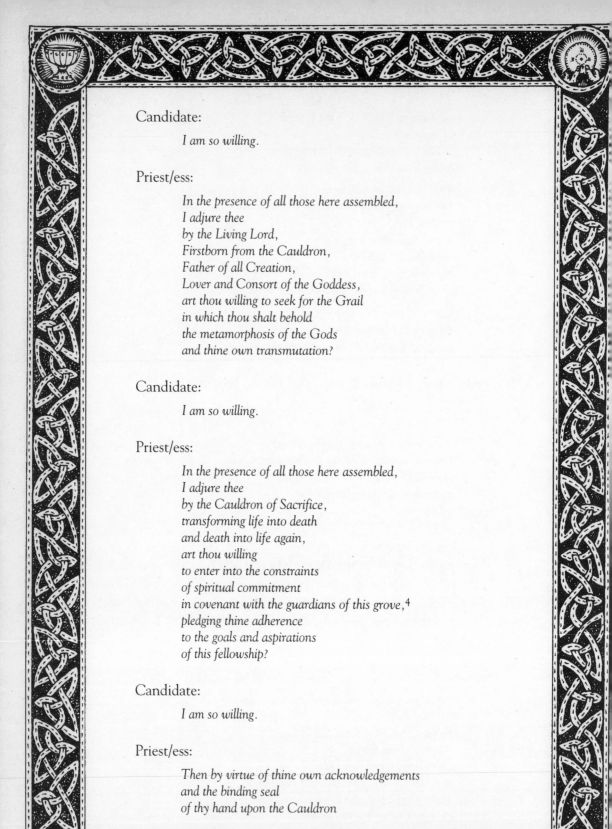

Candidate:

> *I am so willing.*

Priest/ess:

> *In the presence of all those here assembled,*
> *I adjure thee*
> *by the Living Lord,*
> *Firstborn from the Cauldron,*
> *Father of all Creation,*
> *Lover and Consort of the Goddess,*
> *art thou willing to seek for the Grail*
> *in which thou shalt behold*
> *the metamorphosis of the Gods*
> *and thine own transmutation?*

Candidate:

> *I am so willing.*

Priest/ess:

> *In the presence of all those here assembled,*
> *I adjure thee*
> *by the Cauldron of Sacrifice,*
> *transforming life into death*
> *and death into life again,*
> *art thou willing*
> *to enter into the constraints*
> *of spiritual commitment*
> *in covenant with the guardians of this grove,[4]*
> *pledging thine adherence*
> *to the goals and aspirations*
> *of this fellowship?*

Candidate:

> *I am so willing.*

Priest/ess:

> *Then by virtue of thine own acknowledgements*
> *and the binding seal*
> *of thy hand upon the Cauldron*

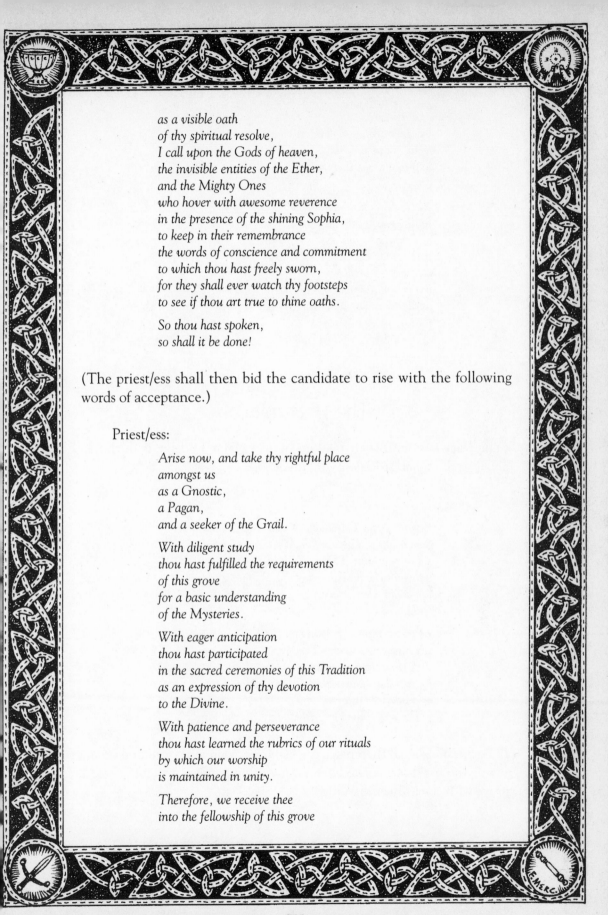

as a visible oath
of thy spiritual resolve,
I call upon the Gods of heaven,
the invisible entities of the Ether,
and the Mighty Ones
who hover with awesome reverence
in the presence of the shining Sophia,
to keep in their remembrance
the words of conscience and commitment
to which thou hast freely sworn,
for they shall ever watch thy footsteps
to see if thou art true to thine oaths.

So thou hast spoken,
so shall it be done!

(The priest/ess shall then bid the candidate to rise with the following
words of acceptance.)

Priest/ess:

Arise now, and take thy rightful place
amongst us
as a Gnostic,
a Pagan,
and a seeker of the Grail.

With diligent study
thou hast fulfilled the requirements
of this grove
for a basic understanding
of the Mysteries.

With eager anticipation
thou hast participated
in the sacred ceremonies of this Tradition
as an expression of thy devotion
to the Divine.

With patience and perseverance
thou hast learned the rubrics of our rituals
by which our worship
is maintained in unity.

Therefore, we receive thee
into the fellowship of this grove

as a living tree
whose branches shall intertwine with our own
as we lift up our hands
in praise to the Lady and the Lord.

Strive for unity within the grove;
cheerfully contribute thy talents
for the good of the group,
and remember always
that despite individual diversities,
our strength shall be
in the realization of our oneness
as we continue on in common Quest
for an apprehension
of the presence of the Grail.

The Presentation

(The priest/ess shall then take up her/his glaive and lift it in the air above as the Quarter-Regents are invoked.)

Priest/ess:

Regents of the Cardinal Quarters,
Sovereigns of East, South, West and North;
we present unto Thee _____
a Pagan who hast chosen
to take his (her) place
within the family of this grove.

Be pleased to smile upon him (her) in recognition
when he (she) salutes Thee
with glaive and elements,
for he (she) now standeth in our midst
as a brother (sister)
to the Wind, the Fire, the Water, and the Earth.

(The priest/ess shall then place the glaive back upon the altar and then, taking the hand of the candidate, shall formally present him/her to the grove with the following words.)

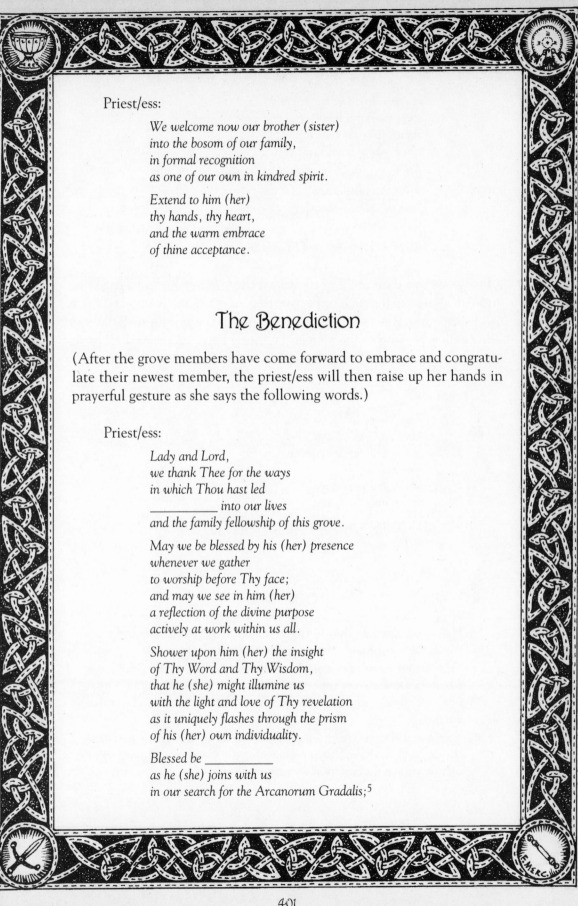

Priest/ess:

> We welcome now our brother (sister)
> into the bosom of our family,
> in formal recognition
> as one of our own in kindred spirit.
>
> Extend to him (her)
> thy hands, thy heart,
> and the warm embrace
> of thine acceptance.

The Benediction

(After the grove members have come forward to embrace and congratulate their newest member, the priest/ess will then raise up her hands in prayerful gesture as she says the following words.)

Priest/ess:

> Lady and Lord,
> we thank Thee for the ways
> in which Thou hast led
> _____ into our lives
> and the family fellowship of this grove.
>
> May we be blessed by his (her) presence
> whenever we gather
> to worship before Thy face;
> and may we see in him (her)
> a reflection of the divine purpose
> actively at work within us all.
>
> Shower upon him (her) the insight
> of Thy Word and Thy Wisdom,
> that he (she) might illumine us
> with the light and love of Thy revelation
> as it uniquely flashes through the prism
> of his (her) own individuality.
>
> Blessed be _____
> as he (she) joins with us
> in our search for the Arcanorum Gradalis;[5]

may his (her) feet be firm and fast
upon the Royal Road
in pursuit of the Hallows
which lead to holiness.

Let the lavishness of Thy loving kindness
be his (her) mainstay
from this night forward,
even forever.

All Hail, Farewell, and Blessed Be.

(The grove will then proceed to dismiss the Quarter-Regents, the same individuals dismissing each respective Regent as originally invoked them in the Opening Rites of the ritual. Afterward, the priest/ess shall open the circle according to the standard Closing Rite, and then shall bring the ceremony to a close with these final words.)

Priest/ess:

This Rite of Initiation is ended.
May the Goddess and God
grant ye all further growth
into the grace
which shall enable us
to continue the Quest.

Merry Meet and Merry Part, and Merry Meet Again!

Footnotes

1. Here (as elsewhere during the ceremony) the blank line indicates where the Craft name of the candidate should be inserted.

2. "The sacred Stone of promise"—A direct reference to the Grail itself, which in some literary traditions took on the form and manifestation of a precious crystal gem radiating from it the most potent of spiritual energies.

3. The many flames are the assembled spirits of the grove members themselves. In the collective Quest for the Grail, we all tend to be instruments of illumination for one another.

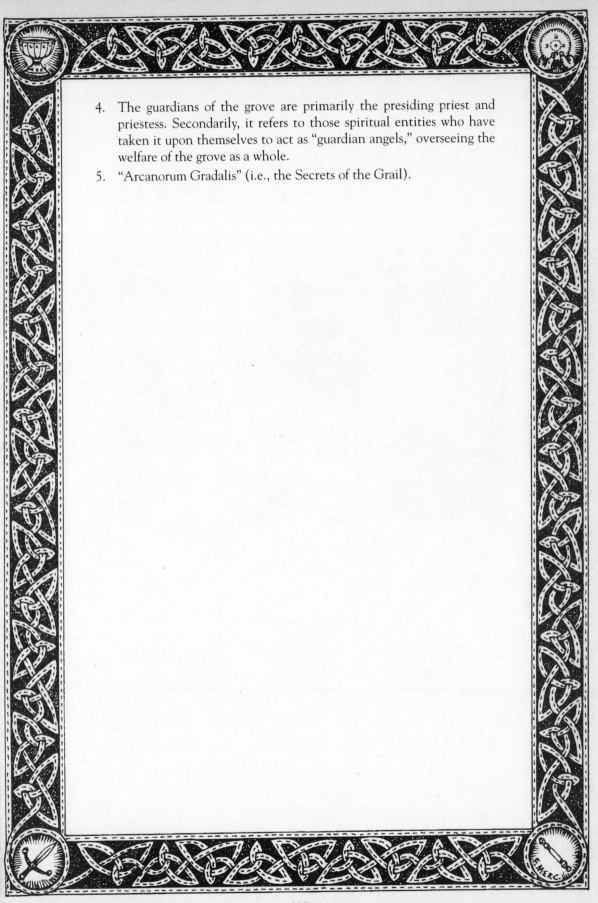

4. The guardians of the grove are primarily the presiding priest and priestess. Secondarily, it refers to those spiritual entities who have taken it upon themselves to act as "guardian angels," overseeing the welfare of the grove as a whole.

5. "Arcanorum Gradalis" (i.e., the Secrets of the Grail).

A side altar dedicated to the God.

The Rite of Ordination

Besides the Grail Mass and the Great Rite, there is no more important ritual within the Ordo Arcanorum Gradalis than the Rite of Ordination. Ordination is the literal gateway to the Higher Mysteries, for through this transition from laity to priesthood an individual is empowered to unite Heaven and Earth in a form of sacramental fusion whenever s/he celebrates the Mystery that is the Mass.

The fact that this is such an important rite also lies in the obvious: without ordination, the priesthood of the O.A.G. could not continue into perpetuity. It can even be said that this Rite of Ordination is the means by which the Order regenerates itself (i.e., a form of spiritual reproduction).

One thing unique to this ceremony is the fact that the entire rite utilizes the archaic Elizabethan style of language. Usually, in most of our rituals, such language style is only used when addressing the deities or other spirit powers. But in the Rite of Ordination we have expanded the usage to underscore the solemnity of the occasion.

Two other brief explanations are in order. First, it should be kept in mind that the candidate will be fully aware of the text of the ritual beforehand, and will be expected to memorize the appropriate answers to the ritual questions which will be asked. Secondly, some may wonder why the use of a blindfold if the candidate already knows what is going to happen. Actually the blindfold here serves a different purpose altogether. The candidate is blindfolded in our tradition as a ceremonial way of highlighting the trust which s/he has in the Goddess and God to lead him/her along the unknown pathways of the future. Furthermore, the blindfold serves the purpose of keeping the candidate from being visually distracted from the full force of the words which shall be spoken until the proper time for its removal.

Finally, since the Rite of Ordination actually incorporates the ritual of knighthood, there are always some candidates who feel the need for a traditional Vigil over their Craft tools, especially the glaive. For those wishing to include this custom in their own pre-ordination preparation, such a ceremony would usually take place the night previous to the evening of the ordination itself. (Candidates who are planning such a

Vigil prior to their ordination [or self-ordination] should contact the Order for further details.)

For an in-depth review of the Order's requirements for ordination, consult Appendix A at the back of this book.

Basic Requirements

Below are some things to remember which are necessary requirements if the Rite of Ordination is to be in accordance with the rubrics of the Ordo Arcanorum Gradalis.

Altar

The altar should be in the center of the circle area, facing whichever quarter has the seasonal preeminence at the time of the Ordination (east for spring, south for summer, west for fall, and north for winter).

Altar Cloth and Candles

The altar cloth and the two main altar candles should always be the same color as the corresponding quarter color which has the seasonal preeminence at the time of the Ordination (yellow in spring, red in summer, blue in fall, and green in winter).

Other Candles

The four quarter candles (or glass votive candleholders) *should always be yellow in the east, red in the south, blue in the west, and green in the north.* All other secondary candles used for extra lighting in the ritual area should be white or cream colored.

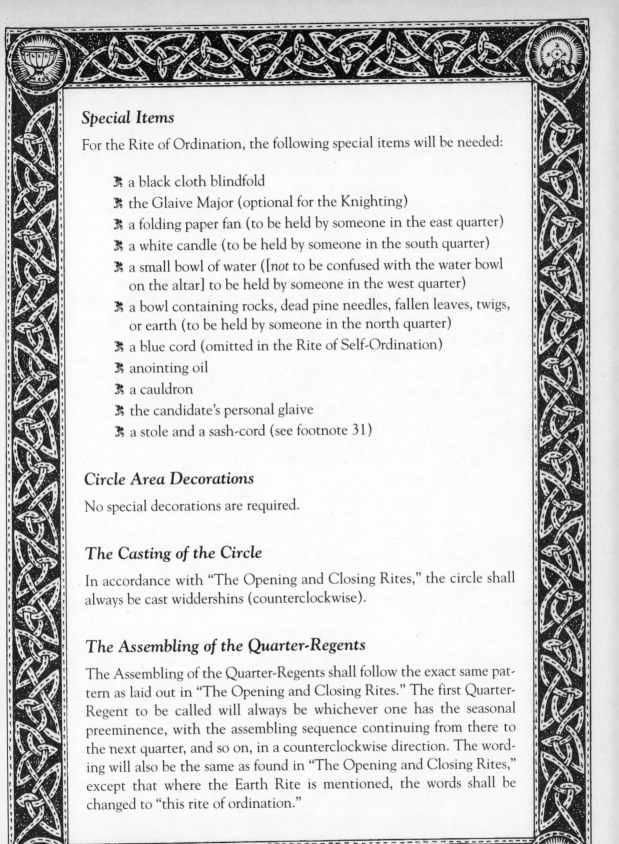

Special Items

For the Rite of Ordination, the following special items will be needed:

- ❧ a black cloth blindfold
- ❧ the Glaive Major (optional for the Knighting)
- ❧ a folding paper fan (to be held by someone in the east quarter)
- ❧ a white candle (to be held by someone in the south quarter)
- ❧ a small bowl of water ([*not* to be confused with the water bowl on the altar] to be held by someone in the west quarter)
- ❧ a bowl containing rocks, dead pine needles, fallen leaves, twigs, or earth (to be held by someone in the north quarter)
- ❧ a blue cord (omitted in the Rite of Self-Ordination)
- ❧ anointing oil
- ❧ a cauldron
- ❧ the candidate's personal glaive
- ❧ a stole and a sash-cord (see footnote 31)

Circle Area Decorations

No special decorations are required.

The Casting of the Circle

In accordance with "The Opening and Closing Rites," the circle shall always be cast widdershins (counterclockwise).

The Assembling of the Quarter-Regents

The Assembling of the Quarter-Regents shall follow the exact same pattern as laid out in "The Opening and Closing Rites." The first Quarter-Regent to be called will always be whichever one has the seasonal preeminence, with the assembling sequence continuing from there to the next quarter, and so on, in a counterclockwise direction. The wording will also be the same as found in "The Opening and Closing Rites," except that where the Earth Rite is mentioned, the words shall be changed to "this rite of ordination."

(Before the Rite of Ordination actually begins, an appointed grove member will escort the candidate to a room or place set apart from the ritual area where s/he will be told to meditate upon the significance of the step s/he is about to take by entering the Order through ordination into the priesthood. The room should be dark so nothing can visually distract the candidate from personal meditation and introspection. The grove member will then return to the ritual area where the assembled grove will proceed with the Opening Rites. After the Assembling of the Quarter-Regents has been completed, a doorway will be cut at the edge of the circle by the presiding priest/ess and the same appointed grove member will take a blindfold of black cloth from the altar and return to the candidate in the other room. The candidate will then be asked to stand for the beginning of his/her journey. The grove member will then tie the blindfold around the candidate's eyes, slowly leading him/her by the hand until they arrive in the ritual area. The candidate will be positioned at the entrance of the circle's open doorway by the grove member who will precede him/her into the circle, leaving the blindfolded candidate at the circle's edge. The presiding priest/ess for the ordination will then begin the ceremonial interrogation.)

The Challenge

Priest/ess:

> *Who is this mortal*
> *seeking entrance*
> *into the Halls of the Hallowed?*

Candidate:

> *I am _____ (candidate's Craft name),*
> *follower in the footsteps*
> *of the Seven Who Returned.*[1]

Priest/ess:

> *I am the servant*
> *of the Lord of the Labyrinth,*
> *He Who is the Keeper of the Cauldron,*
> *and the Guardian of Subterranean Secrets.*[2]

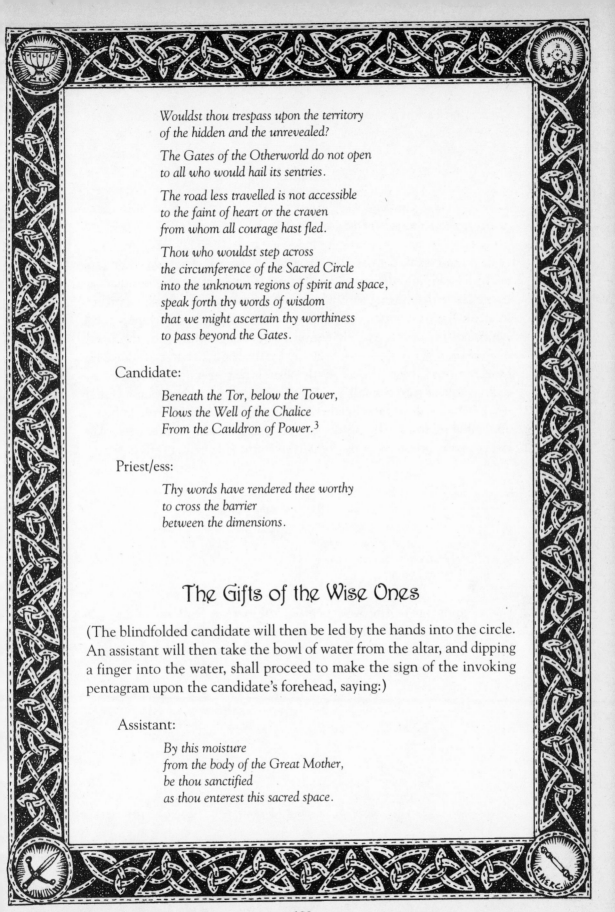

Wouldst thou trespass upon the territory
of the hidden and the unrevealed?

The Gates of the Otherworld do not open
to all who would hail its sentries.

The road less travelled is not accessible
to the faint of heart or the craven
from whom all courage hast fled.

Thou who wouldst step across
the circumference of the Sacred Circle
into the unknown regions of spirit and space,
speak forth thy words of wisdom
that we might ascertain thy worthiness
to pass beyond the Gates.

Candidate:

Beneath the Tor, below the Tower,
Flows the Well of the Chalice
From the Cauldron of Power.[3]

Priest/ess:

Thy words have rendered thee worthy
to cross the barrier
between the dimensions.

The Gifts of the Wise Ones

(The blindfolded candidate will then be led by the hands into the circle.
An assistant will then take the bowl of water from the altar, and dipping
a finger into the water, shall proceed to make the sign of the invoking
pentagram upon the candidate's forehead, saying:)

Assistant:

By this moisture
from the body of the Great Mother,
be thou sanctified
as thou enterest this sacred space.

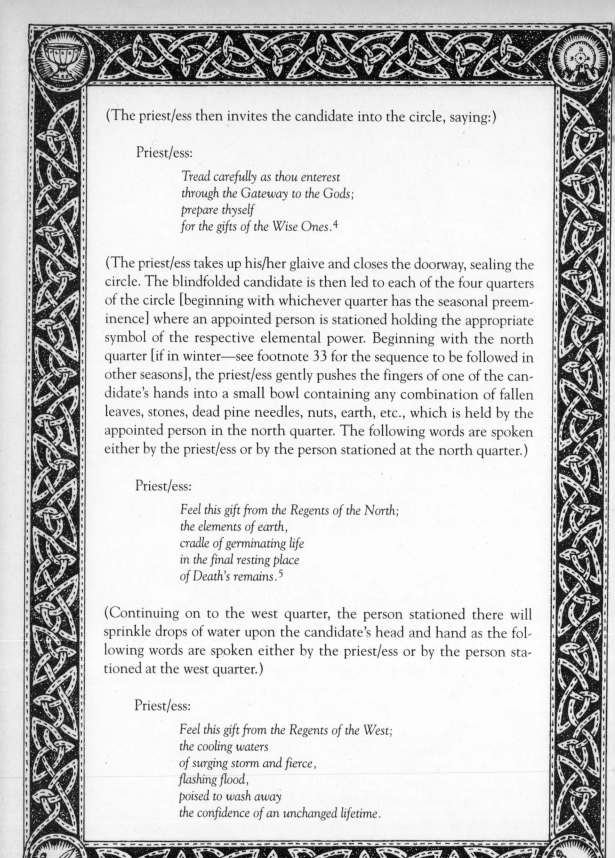

(The priest/ess then invites the candidate into the circle, saying:)

Priest/ess:

> Tread carefully as thou enterest
> through the Gateway to the Gods;
> prepare thyself
> for the gifts of the Wise Ones.[4]

(The priest/ess takes up his/her glaive and closes the doorway, sealing the circle. The blindfolded candidate is then led to each of the four quarters of the circle [beginning with whichever quarter has the seasonal preeminence] where an appointed person is stationed holding the appropriate symbol of the respective elemental power. Beginning with the north quarter [if in winter—see footnote 33 for the sequence to be followed in other seasons], the priest/ess gently pushes the fingers of one of the candidate's hands into a small bowl containing any combination of fallen leaves, stones, dead pine needles, nuts, earth, etc., which is held by the appointed person in the north quarter. The following words are spoken either by the priest/ess or by the person stationed at the north quarter.)

Priest/ess:

> Feel this gift from the Regents of the North;
> the elements of earth,
> cradle of germinating life
> in the final resting place
> of Death's remains.[5]

(Continuing on to the west quarter, the person stationed there will sprinkle drops of water upon the candidate's head and hand as the following words are spoken either by the priest/ess or by the person stationed at the west quarter.)

Priest/ess:

> Feel this gift from the Regents of the West;
> the cooling waters
> of surging storm and fierce,
> flashing flood,
> poised to wash away
> the confidence of an unchanged lifetime.

(Continuing on to the south quarter, the person stationed there will take the candidate's hand and pass it just close enough over a candle flame for the candidate to feel its warmth as the following words are spoken either by the priest/ess or by the person stationed at the south quarter.)

Priest/ess:

> Feel this gift from the Regents of the South;
> the warmth of fire
> which consumes in but a moment
> that which cannot pass the test of time.

(Continuing on to the east quarter, the person stationed there will take a small fan and fan the air against the candidate's face as the following words are spoken either by the priest/ess or by the person stationed at the east quarter.)

Priest/ess:

> Feel this gift from the Regents of the East;
> the breath of life
> rushing past thee
> as the transient mortal that thou art:
> a mere vapor upon the wind.

The Binding

(After the candidate is brought full-circle, s/he shall be turned to face the priest/ess. The priest/ess will now begin to speak the introductory words of the symbolic binding.)

Priest/ess:

> Many wonders await thee
> in the secret regions of the Shining Ones
> as thine eyes behold
> what is already known by thine inmost self,
> but the journey must begin here
> in Caer Sidhe,[6]
> for like the Singer in the Shadows,

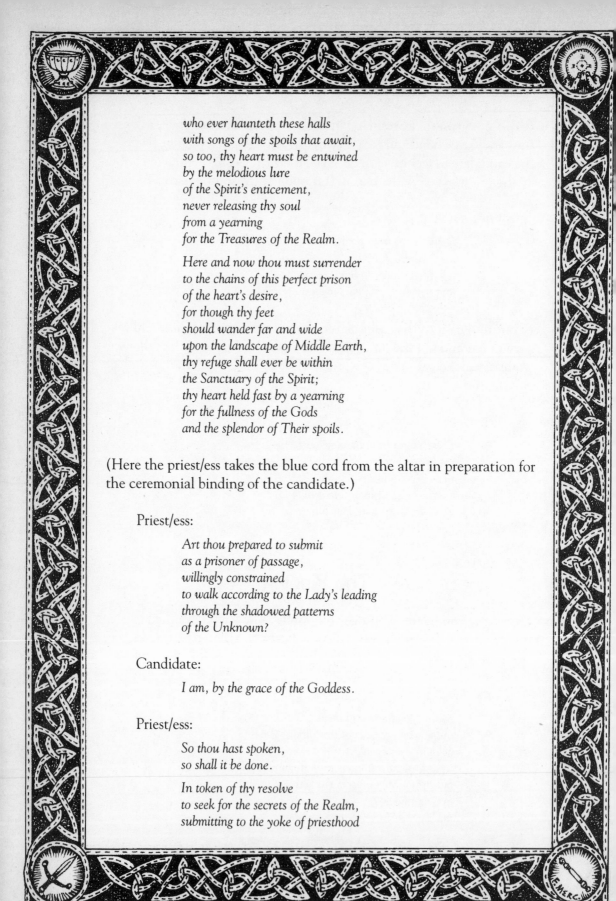

who ever haunteth these halls
with songs of the spoils that await,
so too, thy heart must be entwined
by the melodious lure
of the Spirit's enticement,
never releasing thy soul
from a yearning
for the Treasures of the Realm.

Here and now thou must surrender
to the chains of this perfect prison
of the heart's desire,
for though thy feet
should wander far and wide
upon the landscape of Middle Earth,
thy refuge shall ever be within
the Sanctuary of the Spirit;
thy heart held fast by a yearning
for the fullness of the Gods
and the splendor of Their spoils.

(Here the priest/ess takes the blue cord from the altar in preparation for the ceremonial binding of the candidate.)

Priest/ess:

Art thou prepared to submit
as a prisoner of passage,
willingly constrained
to walk according to the Lady's leading
through the shadowed patterns
of the Unknown?

Candidate:

I am, by the grace of the Goddess.

Priest/ess:

So thou hast spoken,
so shall it be done.

In token of thy resolve
to seek for the secrets of the Realm,
submitting to the yoke of priesthood

under the guidance of the Gods,
I bind thee with blue
for the serenity of spirit
which comes from commitment
to thy Calling.

(Here the priest/ess binds the candidate's hands together with one end of the blue cord.)

Priest/ess:

May thy hands be bound
from all gestures
of wrath and impiety.

(Here the priest/ess loosely binds the candidate's feet with the remaining length of the cord.)[7]

Priest/ess:

May thy feet be restrained
from running
the road of rashness.

(The priest/ess then stands once more facing the candidate, and says the following words.)

Priest/ess:

Bound now with these fetters of devotion,
the chains of thine own choosing,
thou hast demonstrated thy determination
to walk the way of wisdom and introspection
in the service
of the Lord of Inner Mysteries
as thou treadest
the winding labyrinth of life
leading to the Treasures of Light.

(The candidate is then twisted widdershins in four complete revolutions by the assistant as the priest/ess says the following riddle.)

Priest/ess:

> Four times the turn
> in Caer Pedryvan,
> with lessons to learn
> in Caer Pedryvan,
> dark torches that burn
> in Caer Pedryvan,
> secrets to discern
> in Caer Pedryvan![8]

(At this time, the priest/ess [or the assistant] first removes the blue cord from the candidate's hands and feet, placing it loosely around his/her neck and over the shoulders. S/he then takes off the blindfold from the candidate and places it upon the altar. The priest/ess then says the following words.)

Priest/ess:

> Look around thee and ponder thy surroundings,
> for the eyes of thy memory
> shall ever remember this night
> wherein thy transformation
> shall be accomplished
> within the confines
> of the Cauldron's Circle.

The Preliminary Anointing

(The priest/ess now takes up the chalice of wine from the altar, saying the following words to the candidate.)

Priest/ess:

> If thou wouldst tread
> the path of priesthood,
> as a mediator between the worlds
> and an opener of the doorway
> to the Divine,
> then thy lips
> must be an instrument of invocation,

414

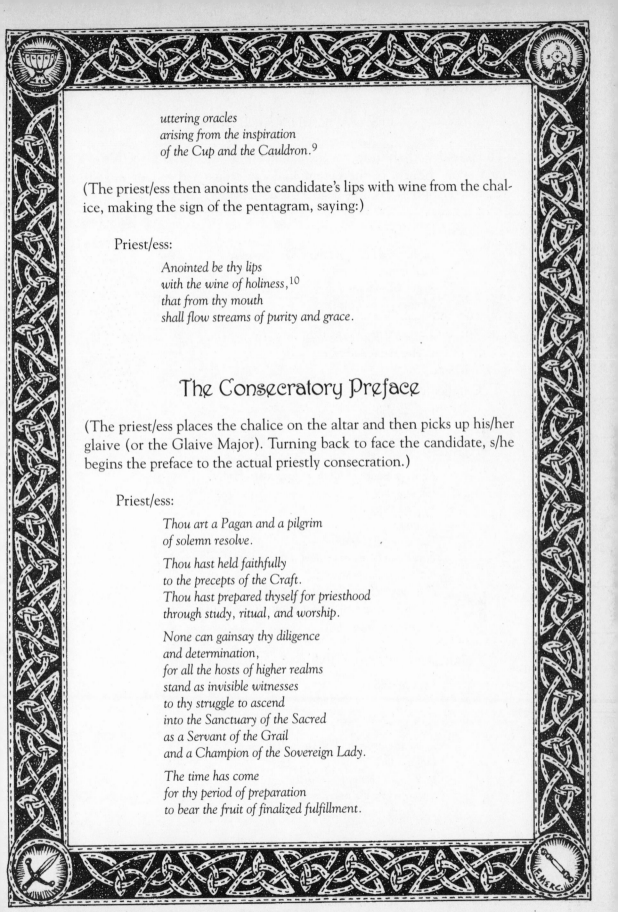

uttering oracles
arising from the inspiration
of the Cup and the Cauldron.[9]

(The priest/ess then anoints the candidate's lips with wine from the chalice, making the sign of the pentagram, saying:)

Priest/ess:

> *Anointed be thy lips*
> *with the wine of holiness,*[10]
> *that from thy mouth*
> *shall flow streams of purity and grace.*

The Consecratory Preface

(The priest/ess places the chalice on the altar and then picks up his/her glaive (or the Glaive Major). Turning back to face the candidate, s/he begins the preface to the actual priestly consecration.)

Priest/ess:

> *Thou art a Pagan and a pilgrim*
> *of solemn resolve.*
>
> *Thou hast held faithfully*
> *to the precepts of the Craft.*
> *Thou hast prepared thyself for priesthood*
> *through study, ritual, and worship.*
>
> *None can gainsay thy diligence*
> *and determination,*
> *for all the hosts of higher realms*
> *stand as invisible witnesses*
> *to thy struggle to ascend*
> *into the Sanctuary of the Sacred*
> *as a Servant of the Grail*
> *and a Champion of the Sovereign Lady.*
>
> *The time has come*
> *for thy period of preparation*
> *to bear the fruit of finalized fulfillment.*

The Solemn Adjuration

(The priest/ess then instructs the candidate to kneel and place his/her hand upon the rim of the ceremonial cauldron on the floor next to him/her. The priest/ess now begins the adjuration.)

Priest/ess:

> *In the presence of all those here assembled,*
> *I adjure thee*
> *by the Cauldron of the Living Lady,*
> *Mother of the Earth,*
> *Queen of Heaven and Hell,*
> *art thou willing to be loyal*
> *to Her Ways and Her Word?*[11]

Candidate:

> *I am so willing.*

Priest/ess:

> *In the presence of all those here assembled,*
> *I adjure thee*
> *by the Living Lord,*
> *Firstborn from the Cauldron,*
> *Father of all Creation,*
> *Lover and Consort of the Goddess,*
> *art thou willing to stand*
> *as a public confessor of the Ancient Faith,*
> *defending it against false accusations*
> *and malicious calumny?*[12]

Candidate:

> *I am so willing.*

Priest/ess:

> *In the presence of all those here assembled,*
> *I adjure thee*
> *by the Cauldron of Sacrifice,*
> *transforming life into death*
> *and death into life again,*

art thou willing to suffer
in order to experience
the depths of the Holy Mysteries?[13]

Candidate:

> *I am so willing.*

Priest/ess:

> *As a postulant to the priesthood,*
> *thou hast pledged*
> *thy loyalty to the leading of the Lady,*
> *thy willingness to defend*
> *the integrity of the Pagan Way,*
> *and thy resolve to suffer if necessary,*
> *for the realization of Thy Calling*
> *as Way-Shower of the Sacred Secrets.*

The Knighting

(As the priest/ess begins to say the following words, s/he will hold the handle of the sword (Glaive Major) or the glaive with both hands, the blade pointing upward; but when s/he starts to utter the words "I DUB THEE …," s/he shall slowly bring the sword or glaive level with the candidate's shoulders. S/he will then lightly tap the blade first upon the candidate's left shoulder, then the right shoulder, and then back to the left shoulder again. This constitutes the physical act of knighting.)

Priest/ess:

> *Therefore,*
> *as a Priest(ess) of the Holy Grail,*
> *I call upon the Old Ones*
> *of the Ancient Hierarchy,*
> *I beseech the Lady of the Lake,*
> *I supplicate the shade of Merlin,*
> *and I invoke the spirit of Arthur*
> *to touch thy shoulders*
> *with the shining sword of the cherubim,*
> *the excellence of Excalibur,*

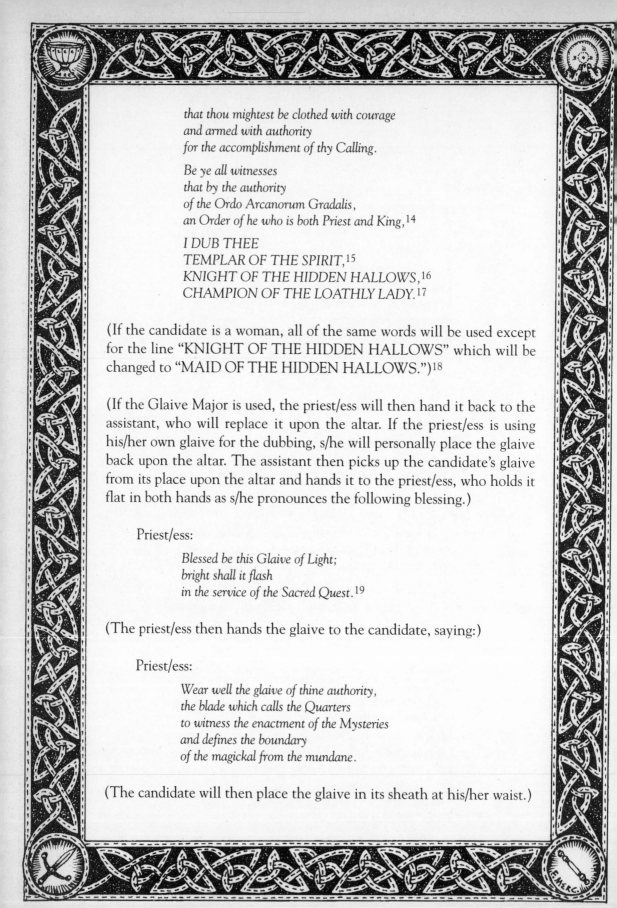

that thou mightest be clothed with courage
and armed with authority
for the accomplishment of thy Calling.

Be ye all witnesses
that by the authority
of the Ordo Arcanorum Gradalis,
an Order of he who is both Priest and King,[14]

I DUB THEE
TEMPLAR OF THE SPIRIT,[15]
KNIGHT OF THE HIDDEN HALLOWS,[16]
CHAMPION OF THE LOATHLY LADY.[17]

(If the candidate is a woman, all of the same words will be used except for the line "KNIGHT OF THE HIDDEN HALLOWS" which will be changed to "MAID OF THE HIDDEN HALLOWS.")[18]

(If the Glaive Major is used, the priest/ess will then hand it back to the assistant, who will replace it upon the altar. If the priest/ess is using his/her own glaive for the dubbing, s/he will personally place the glaive back upon the altar. The assistant then picks up the candidate's glaive from its place upon the altar and hands it to the priest/ess, who holds it flat in both hands as s/he pronounces the following blessing.)

Priest/ess:

> *Blessed be this Glaive of Light;*
> *bright shall it flash*
> *in the service of the Sacred Quest.*[19]

(The priest/ess then hands the glaive to the candidate, saying:)

Priest/ess:

> *Wear well the glaive of thine authority,*
> *the blade which calls the Quarters*
> *to witness the enactment of the Mysteries*
> *and defines the boundary*
> *of the magickal from the mundane.*

(The candidate will then place the glaive in its sheath at his/her waist.)

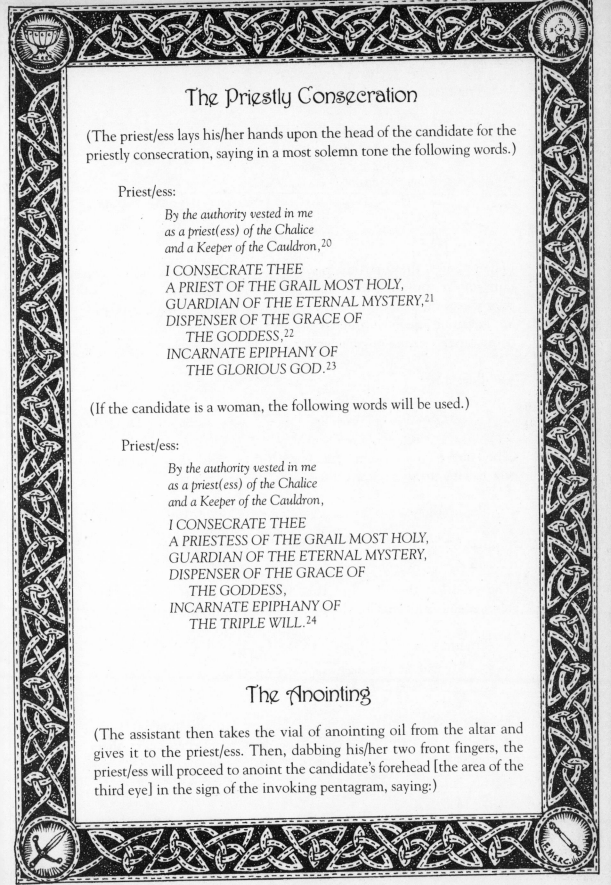

The Priestly Consecration

(The priest/ess lays his/her hands upon the head of the candidate for the priestly consecration, saying in a most solemn tone the following words.)

Priest/ess:

By the authority vested in me
as a priest(ess) of the Chalice
and a Keeper of the Cauldron,[20]

I CONSECRATE THEE
A PRIEST OF THE GRAIL MOST HOLY,
GUARDIAN OF THE ETERNAL MYSTERY,[21]
DISPENSER OF THE GRACE OF
*   THE GODDESS,*[22]
INCARNATE EPIPHANY OF
*   THE GLORIOUS GOD.*[23]

(If the candidate is a woman, the following words will be used.)

Priest/ess:

By the authority vested in me
as a priest(ess) of the Chalice
and a Keeper of the Cauldron,

I CONSECRATE THEE
A PRIESTESS OF THE GRAIL MOST HOLY,
GUARDIAN OF THE ETERNAL MYSTERY,
DISPENSER OF THE GRACE OF
*   THE GODDESS,*
INCARNATE EPIPHANY OF
*   THE TRIPLE WILL.*[24]

The Anointing

(The assistant then takes the vial of anointing oil from the altar and gives it to the priest/ess. Then, dabbing his/her two front fingers, the priest/ess will proceed to anoint the candidate's forehead [the area of the third eye] in the sign of the invoking pentagram, saying:)

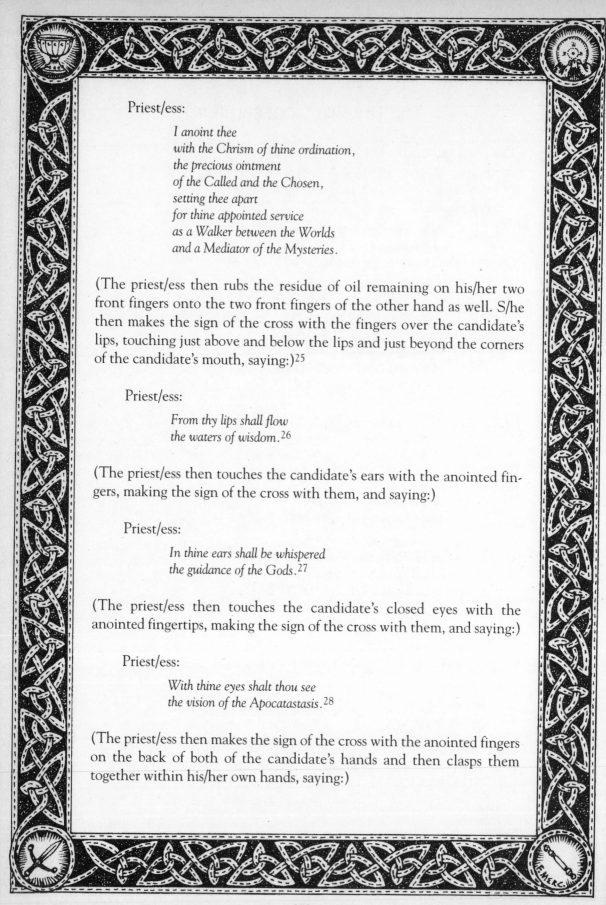

Priest/ess:

> *I anoint thee*
> *with the Chrism of thine ordination,*
> *the precious ointment*
> *of the Called and the Chosen,*
> *setting thee apart*
> *for thine appointed service*
> *as a Walker between the Worlds*
> *and a Mediator of the Mysteries.*

(The priest/ess then rubs the residue of oil remaining on his/her two front fingers onto the two front fingers of the other hand as well. S/he then makes the sign of the cross with the fingers over the candidate's lips, touching just above and below the lips and just beyond the corners of the candidate's mouth, saying:)[25]

Priest/ess:

> *From thy lips shall flow*
> *the waters of wisdom.*[26]

(The priest/ess then touches the candidate's ears with the anointed fingers, making the sign of the cross with them, and saying:)

Priest/ess:

> *In thine ears shall be whispered*
> *the guidance of the Gods.*[27]

(The priest/ess then touches the candidate's closed eyes with the anointed fingertips, making the sign of the cross with them, and saying:)

Priest/ess:

> *With thine eyes shalt thou see*
> *the vision of the Apocatastasis.*[28]

(The priest/ess then makes the sign of the cross with the anointed fingers on the back of both of the candidate's hands and then clasps them together within his/her own hands, saying:)

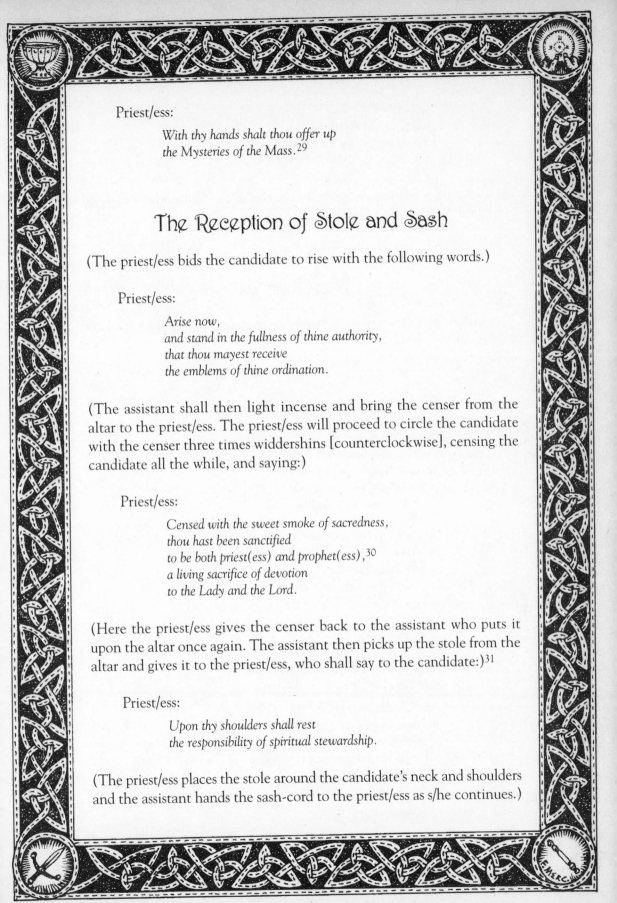

Priest/ess:

> *With thy hands shalt thou offer up*
> *the Mysteries of the Mass.*[29]

The Reception of Stole and Sash

(The priest/ess bids the candidate to rise with the following words.)

Priest/ess:

> *Arise now,*
> *and stand in the fullness of thine authority,*
> *that thou mayest receive*
> *the emblems of thine ordination.*

(The assistant shall then light incense and bring the censer from the altar to the priest/ess. The priest/ess will proceed to circle the candidate with the censer three times widdershins [counterclockwise], censing the candidate all the while, and saying:)

Priest/ess:

> *Censed with the sweet smoke of sacredness,*
> *thou hast been sanctified*
> *to be both priest(ess) and prophet(ess),*[30]
> *a living sacrifice of devotion*
> *to the Lady and the Lord.*

(Here the priest/ess gives the censer back to the assistant who puts it upon the altar once again. The assistant then picks up the stole from the altar and gives it to the priest/ess, who shall say to the candidate:)[31]

Priest/ess:

> *Upon thy shoulders shall rest*
> *the responsibility of spiritual stewardship.*

(The priest/ess places the stole around the candidate's neck and shoulders and the assistant hands the sash-cord to the priest/ess as s/he continues.)

And around thy waist
shalt thou gird thyself
with the sash of sacred service,
dedicated to the Trinity of the Triple Will.[32]

(Here the priest/ess hands the sash-cord to the candidate who will place it around the waist and tie it fast.)

The Charge

(The priest/ess will now proceed to recite to the candidate the Charge of Ordination.)

Priest/ess:

I therefore charge thee,
before the Goddess and the God,
be vigilant for the values
that engender wholeness;
be resilient in the face of adversity;
be resourceful with the spiritual gifts
which thou hast been given;
be eager to educate
those who seek to learn the Ancient Ways;
be reverent towards the rites
of the Old Religion;
be prayerful in thine approach
to the Altar of the Holy Ones;
be joyous in thy celebration
of the Eucharistic Sacrifice;
be steadfast in thy commitment
to the Calling which the Lady and Lord
have laid upon thee.

Adhere to these commands
and thou shalt be a blessing
let loose upon the land;
a glory to the priesthood of the Pagans,
and a righteous Way-shower
to the Gateway of the Grail.

Blessed Be.

The Presentation

(The priest/ess then escorts the candidate to each of the four quarters of the circle, beginning first with the quarter which has the seasonal preeminence (the sequence given below is for winter).[33] At each quarter, the candidate will elevate his/her glaive in salute to the Regents as the priest/ess says the following words appropriate to each respective quarter.)

Priest/ess:

>*Regents of the North,*
>*Sovereigns of elemental Earth,*
>*Servants of the Silver Paten;*
>*behold _____ (candidate's Craft name),*
>*having been consecrated*
>*before Thy presence*
>*as a Priest(ess) of the Holy Grail,*
>*empowered to celebrate*
>*the Mysteries of the Goddess and the God.*

>*When he (she) commands Thy coming forth,*
>*Thou shalt answer.*
>*When he (she) invokes the Sacred Names,*
>*Thou shalt be swift in Thine attendance.*
>*When he (she) offers up the Solemn Oblation,[34]*
>*Thou shalt respond with reverence.*

>*Blessed Be!*

(These same words will be spoken to each of the Quarter-Regents, with only their opening salutations changing as follows:)

Priest/ess:

>*Regents of the West,*
>*Sovereigns of all Watery Realms,*
>*Servants of the Sacred Chalice,*
>*behold …*

>*Regents of the South,*
>*Sovereigns of Fire and Flame,*
>*Servants of the Staff and Spear,*
>*behold …*

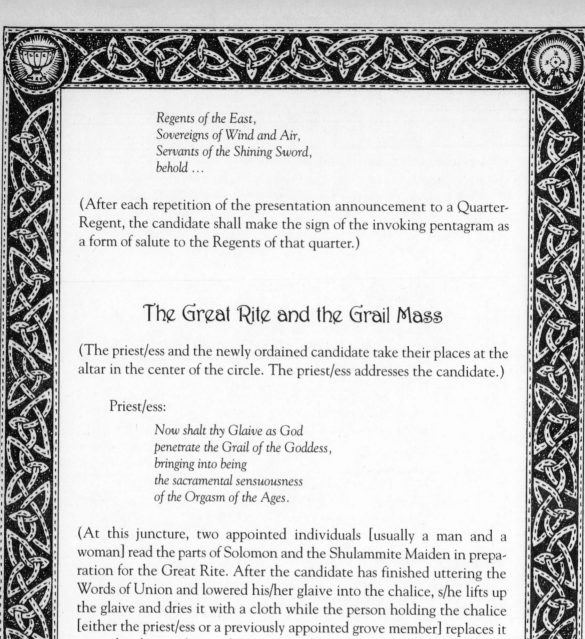

Regents of the East,
Sovereigns of Wind and Air,
Servants of the Shining Sword,
behold …

(After each repetition of the presentation announcement to a Quarter-Regent, the candidate shall make the sign of the invoking pentagram as a form of salute to the Regents of that quarter.)

The Great Rite and the Grail Mass

(The priest/ess and the newly ordained candidate take their places at the altar in the center of the circle. The priest/ess addresses the candidate.)

Priest/ess:

Now shalt thy Glaive as God
penetrate the Grail of the Goddess,
bringing into being
the sacramental sensuousness
of the Orgasm of the Ages.

(At this juncture, two appointed individuals [usually a man and a woman] read the parts of Solomon and the Shulammite Maiden in preparation for the Great Rite. After the candidate has finished uttering the Words of Union and lowered his/her glaive into the chalice, s/he lifts up the glaive and dries it with a cloth while the person holding the chalice [either the priest/ess or a previously appointed grove member] replaces it upon the altar, replacing the paten on its rim if it was placed there originally. Then the priest/ess gestures with his/her hands towards the chalice and paten, saying the following words to the newly ordained candidate.)

Priest/ess:

Behold the bread and the wine,
waiting for the words of thine invocations
that the seal of thine office
might be made manifest
in the celebration of the Holy Mysteries.

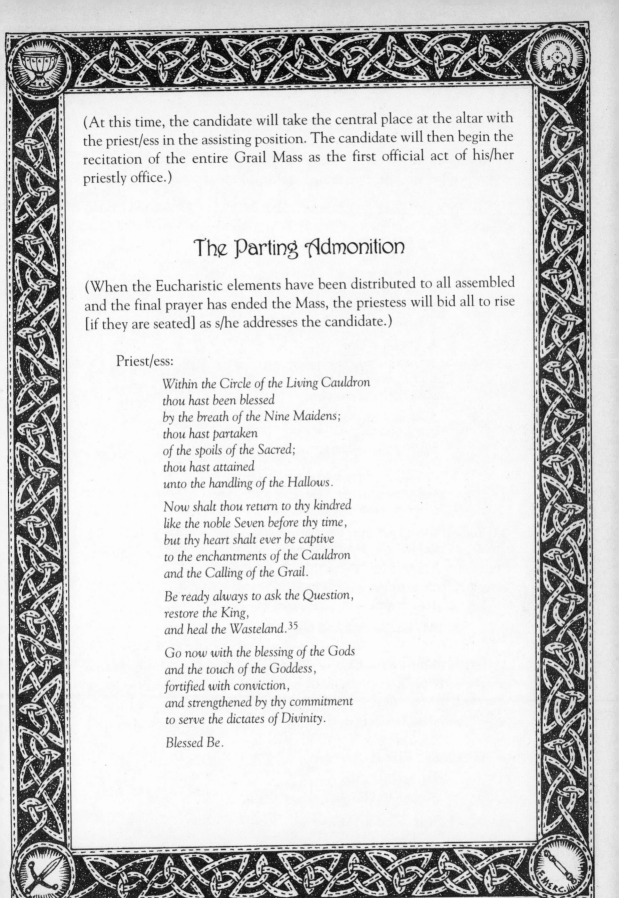

(At this time, the candidate will take the central place at the altar with the priest/ess in the assisting position. The candidate will then begin the recitation of the entire Grail Mass as the first official act of his/her priestly office.)

The Parting Admonition

(When the Eucharistic elements have been distributed to all assembled and the final prayer has ended the Mass, the priestess will bid all to rise [if they are seated] as s/he addresses the candidate.)

Priest/ess:

> Within the Circle of the Living Cauldron
> thou hast been blessed
> by the breath of the Nine Maidens;
> thou hast partaken
> of the spoils of the Sacred;
> thou hast attained
> unto the handling of the Hallows.
>
> Now shalt thou return to thy kindred
> like the noble Seven before thy time,
> but thy heart shalt ever be captive
> to the enchantments of the Cauldron
> and the Calling of the Grail.
>
> Be ready always to ask the Question,
> restore the King,
> and heal the Wasteland.[35]
>
> Go now with the blessing of the Gods
> and the touch of the Goddess,
> fortified with conviction,
> and strengthened by thy commitment
> to serve the dictates of Divinity.
>
> Blessed Be.

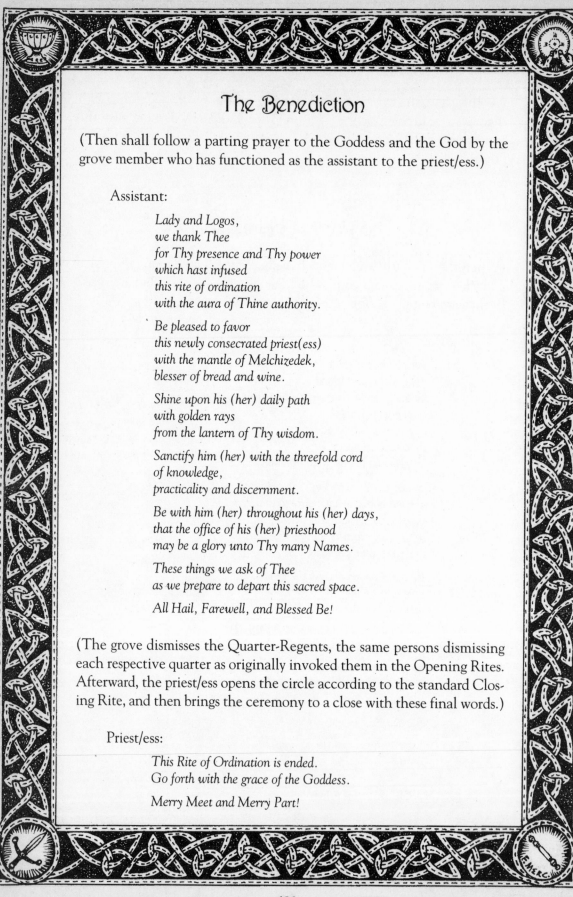

The Benediction

(Then shall follow a parting prayer to the Goddess and the God by the grove member who has functioned as the assistant to the priest/ess.)

Assistant:

> *Lady and Logos,*
> *we thank Thee*
> *for Thy presence and Thy power*
> *which hast infused*
> *this rite of ordination*
> *with the aura of Thine authority.*
>
> *Be pleased to favor*
> *this newly consecrated priest(ess)*
> *with the mantle of Melchizedek,*
> *blesser of bread and wine.*
>
> *Shine upon his (her) daily path*
> *with golden rays*
> *from the lantern of Thy wisdom.*
>
> *Sanctify him (her) with the threefold cord*
> *of knowledge,*
> *practicality and discernment.*
>
> *Be with him (her) throughout his (her) days,*
> *that the office of his (her) priesthood*
> *may be a glory unto Thy many Names.*
>
> *These things we ask of Thee*
> *as we prepare to depart this sacred space.*
>
> *All Hail, Farewell, and Blessed Be!*

(The grove dismisses the Quarter-Regents, the same persons dismissing each respective quarter as originally invoked them in the Opening Rites. Afterward, the priest/ess opens the circle according to the standard Closing Rite, and then brings the ceremony to a close with these final words.)

Priest/ess:

> *This Rite of Ordination is ended.*
> *Go forth with the grace of the Goddess.*
>
> *Merry Meet and Merry Part!*

Footnotes

1. "The Seven Who Returned" is a direct reference to the seven knights of Arthur who managed to escape Annwn (the Underworld) and return with the King from his attempt to possess the sacred Cauldron. This is one of the earliest stories of Arthur's exploits, taken from the ancient Welsh poem *Preiddeu Annwn*. There are indirect illusions to the imagery of this poem throughout the Rite of Ordination with a few slight twists of reinterpretation.

2. "The Lord of the Labyrinth" is a title for the God in His chthonic aspect. This title is used to remind the candidate that ordination is an irrevocable step of commitment that reaches into the very depths of his/her own being, where we will inevitably encounter the dark visage of the God who we must trust to lead us through the murky labyrinth of the unknown future if our calling is to ever be fulfilled.

3. The first line has reference to Glastonbury Tor, which in the local pre-Christian mythology of the area was believed to be the gateway to the Underworld. The Well of the Chalice is also a literal location in Glastonbury, but the deeper significance of these words is their affirmation that the Grail as Chalice and mystical Christian icon proceeds from the far older Pagan mysteries which centered upon the miraculous properties of the Great Mother's cauldron of power and transformation. In these words the candidate speaks a belief in the unbroken continuity of the Grail legacy from Pagan roots to Christian romanticism.

4. These words are virtually identical with those from the Opening Rite which are spoken to each one as they enter the circle—except for the last line. Instead of "prepare yourself for the presence of the Goddess," the words are changed to "prepare thyself for the gifts of the Wise Ones." The Wise Ones are the elemental Quarter-Regents.

5. This and the following "gifts" from each of the Quarter-Regents are meant to instill in the candidate a sense of transience, insignificance, and fragile mortality in the larger scheme of the Cosmos. This is done to reinforce within the candidate the realization that s/he is in the immediate presence of the awesome Spirit Forces which s/he is now preparing through ordination to serve, respect, and glorify by commitment to the priesthood. The gifts serve notice that the priesthood is not some kind of ecclesiastical "game" to be taken lightly.

6. "Caer Sidhe"—The first of the castles in Annwn to which Arthur and his men came in *Preiddeu Annwn*.

7. The blue binding cord is thin and usually nine feet in length to insure sufficient length for the tying of both hands and feet.

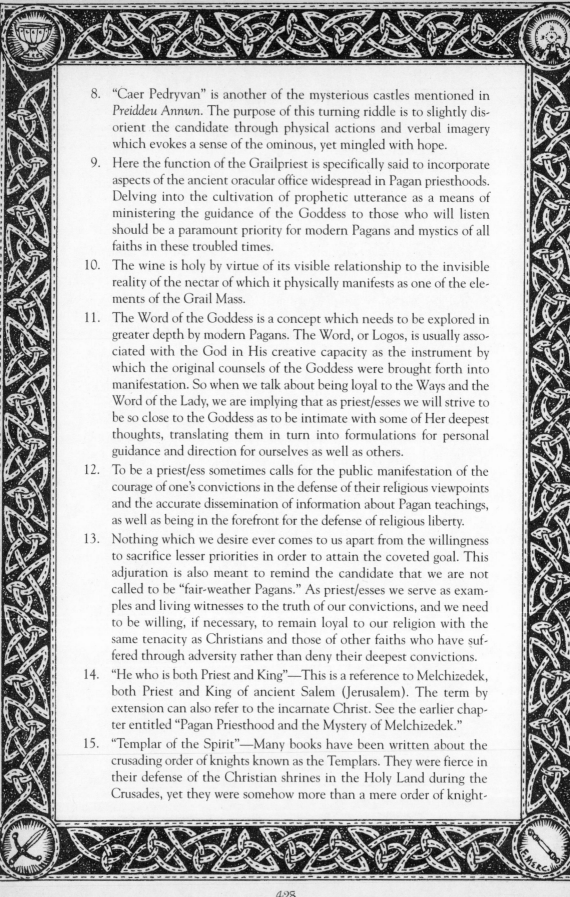

8. "Caer Pedryvan" is another of the mysterious castles mentioned in *Preiddeu Annwn.* The purpose of this turning riddle is to slightly disorient the candidate through physical actions and verbal imagery which evokes a sense of the ominous, yet mingled with hope.

9. Here the function of the Grailpriest is specifically said to incorporate aspects of the ancient oracular office widespread in Pagan priesthoods. Delving into the cultivation of prophetic utterance as a means of ministering the guidance of the Goddess to those who will listen should be a paramount priority for modern Pagans and mystics of all faiths in these troubled times.

10. The wine is holy by virtue of its visible relationship to the invisible reality of the nectar of which it physically manifests as one of the elements of the Grail Mass.

11. The Word of the Goddess is a concept which needs to be explored in greater depth by modern Pagans. The Word, or Logos, is usually associated with the God in His creative capacity as the instrument by which the original counsels of the Goddess were brought forth into manifestation. So when we talk about being loyal to the Ways and the Word of the Lady, we are implying that as priest/esses we will strive to be so close to the Goddess as to be intimate with some of Her deepest thoughts, translating them in turn into formulations for personal guidance and direction for ourselves as well as others.

12. To be a priest/ess sometimes calls for the public manifestation of the courage of one's convictions in the defense of their religious viewpoints and the accurate dissemination of information about Pagan teachings, as well as being in the forefront for the defense of religious liberty.

13. Nothing which we desire ever comes to us apart from the willingness to sacrifice lesser priorities in order to attain the coveted goal. This adjuration is also meant to remind the candidate that we are not called to be "fair-weather Pagans." As priest/esses we serve as examples and living witnesses to the truth of our convictions, and we need to be willing, if necessary, to remain loyal to our religion with the same tenacity as Christians and those of other faiths who have suffered through adversity rather than deny their deepest convictions.

14. "He who is both Priest and King"—This is a reference to Melchizedek, both Priest and King of ancient Salem (Jerusalem). The term by extension can also refer to the incarnate Christ. See the earlier chapter entitled "Pagan Priesthood and the Mystery of Melchizedek."

15. "Templar of the Spirit"—Many books have been written about the crusading order of knights known as the Templars. They were fierce in their defense of the Christian shrines in the Holy Land during the Crusades, yet they were somehow more than a mere order of knight-

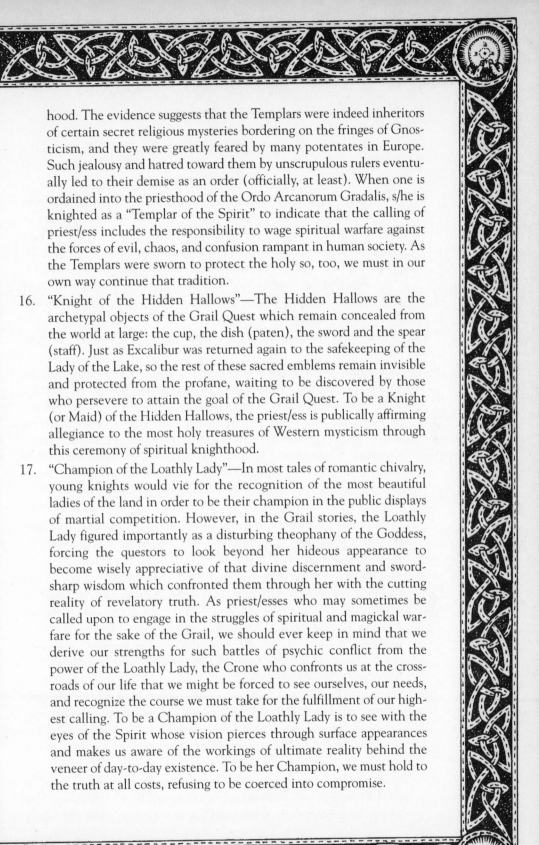

hood. The evidence suggests that the Templars were indeed inheritors of certain secret religious mysteries bordering on the fringes of Gnosticism, and they were greatly feared by many potentates in Europe. Such jealousy and hatred toward them by unscrupulous rulers eventually led to their demise as an order (officially, at least). When one is ordained into the priesthood of the Ordo Arcanorum Gradalis, s/he is knighted as a "Templar of the Spirit" to indicate that the calling of priest/ess includes the responsibility to wage spiritual warfare against the forces of evil, chaos, and confusion rampant in human society. As the Templars were sworn to protect the holy so, too, we must in our own way continue that tradition.

16. "Knight of the Hidden Hallows"—The Hidden Hallows are the archetypal objects of the Grail Quest which remain concealed from the world at large: the cup, the dish (paten), the sword and the spear (staff). Just as Excalibur was returned again to the safekeeping of the Lady of the Lake, so the rest of these sacred emblems remain invisible and protected from the profane, waiting to be discovered by those who persevere to attain the goal of the Grail Quest. To be a Knight (or Maid) of the Hidden Hallows, the priest/ess is publically affirming allegiance to the most holy treasures of Western mysticism through this ceremony of spiritual knighthood.

17. "Champion of the Loathly Lady"—In most tales of romantic chivalry, young knights would vie for the recognition of the most beautiful ladies of the land in order to be their champion in the public displays of martial competition. However, in the Grail stories, the Loathly Lady figured importantly as a disturbing theophany of the Goddess, forcing the questors to look beyond her hideous appearance to become wisely appreciative of that divine discernment and sword-sharp wisdom which confronted them through her with the cutting reality of revelatory truth. As priest/esses who may sometimes be called upon to engage in the struggles of spiritual and magickal warfare for the sake of the Grail, we should ever keep in mind that we derive our strengths for such battles of psychic conflict from the power of the Loathly Lady, the Crone who confronts us at the crossroads of our life that we might be forced to see ourselves, our needs, and recognize the course we must take for the fulfillment of our highest calling. To be a Champion of the Loathly Lady is to see with the eyes of the Spirit whose vision pierces through surface appearances and makes us aware of the workings of ultimate reality behind the veneer of day-to-day existence. To be her Champion, we must hold to the truth at all costs, refusing to be coerced into compromise.

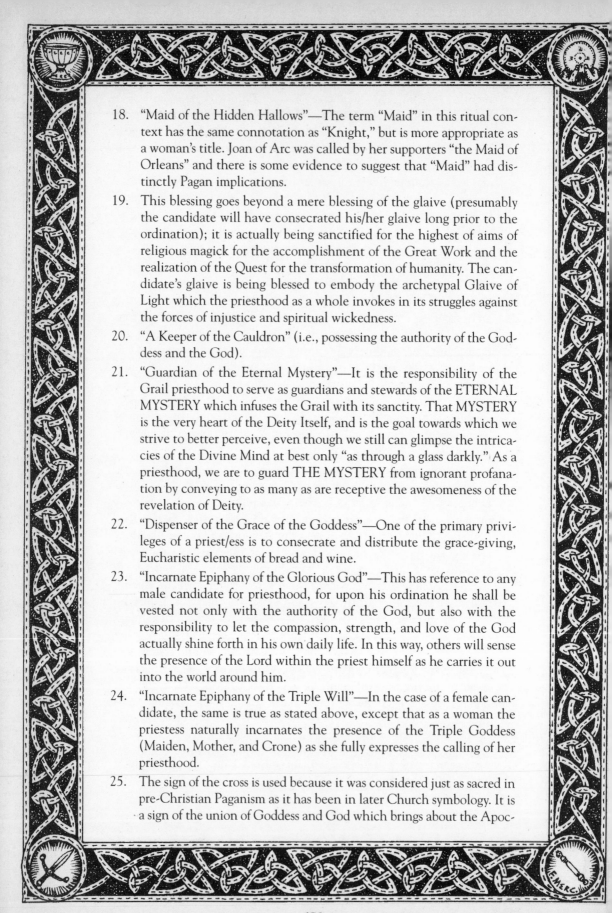

18. "Maid of the Hidden Hallows"—The term "Maid" in this ritual context has the same connotation as "Knight," but is more appropriate as a woman's title. Joan of Arc was called by her supporters "the Maid of Orleans" and there is some evidence to suggest that "Maid" had distinctly Pagan implications.

19. This blessing goes beyond a mere blessing of the glaive (presumably the candidate will have consecrated his/her glaive long prior to the ordination); it is actually being sanctified for the highest of aims of religious magick for the accomplishment of the Great Work and the realization of the Quest for the transformation of humanity. The candidate's glaive is being blessed to embody the archetypal Glaive of Light which the priesthood as a whole invokes in its struggles against the forces of injustice and spiritual wickedness.

20. "A Keeper of the Cauldron" (i.e., possessing the authority of the Goddess and the God).

21. "Guardian of the Eternal Mystery"—It is the responsibility of the Grail priesthood to serve as guardians and stewards of the ETERNAL MYSTERY which infuses the Grail with its sanctity. That MYSTERY is the very heart of the Deity Itself, and is the goal towards which we strive to better perceive, even though we still can glimpse the intricacies of the Divine Mind at best only "as through a glass darkly." As a priesthood, we are to guard THE MYSTERY from ignorant profanation by conveying to as many as are receptive the awesomeness of the revelation of Deity.

22. "Dispenser of the Grace of the Goddess"—One of the primary privileges of a priest/ess is to consecrate and distribute the grace-giving, Eucharistic elements of bread and wine.

23. "Incarnate Epiphany of the Glorious God"—This has reference to any male candidate for priesthood, for upon his ordination he shall be vested not only with the authority of the God, but also with the responsibility to let the compassion, strength, and love of the God actually shine forth in his own daily life. In this way, others will sense the presence of the Lord within the priest himself as he carries it out into the world around him.

24. "Incarnate Epiphany of the Triple Will"—In the case of a female candidate, the same is true as stated above, except that as a woman the priestess naturally incarnates the presence of the Triple Goddess (Maiden, Mother, and Crone) as she fully expresses the calling of her priesthood.

25. The sign of the cross is used because it was considered just as sacred in pre-Christian Paganism as it has been in later Church symbology. It is a sign of the union of Goddess and God which brings about the Apoc-

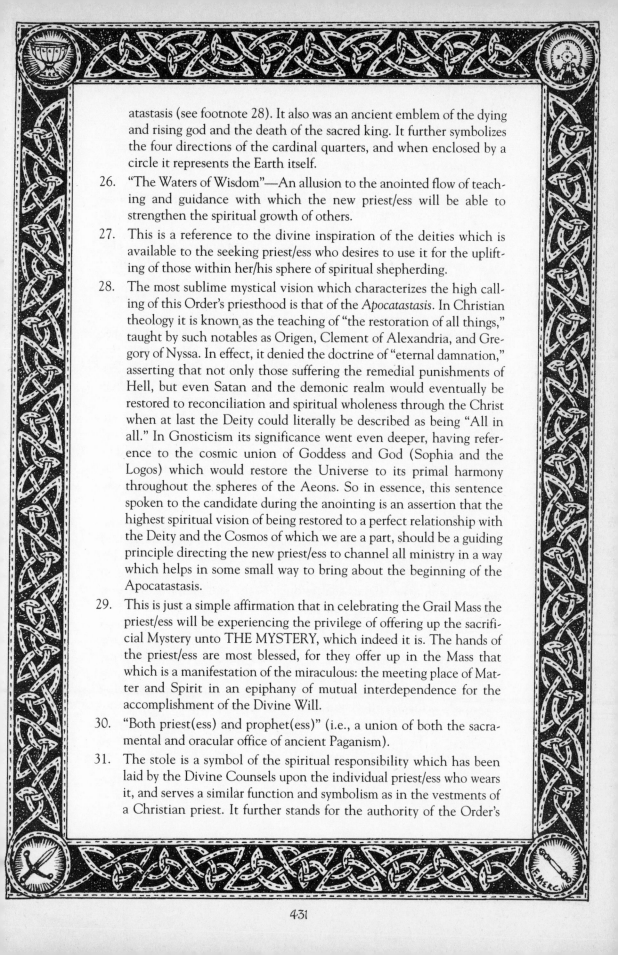

atastasis (see footnote 28). It also was an ancient emblem of the dying and rising god and the death of the sacred king. It further symbolizes the four directions of the cardinal quarters, and when enclosed by a circle it represents the Earth itself.

26. "The Waters of Wisdom"—An allusion to the anointed flow of teaching and guidance with which the new priest/ess will be able to strengthen the spiritual growth of others.

27. This is a reference to the divine inspiration of the deities which is available to the seeking priest/ess who desires to use it for the uplifting of those within her/his sphere of spiritual shepherding.

28. The most sublime mystical vision which characterizes the high calling of this Order's priesthood is that of the *Apocatastasis*. In Christian theology it is known as the teaching of "the restoration of all things," taught by such notables as Origen, Clement of Alexandria, and Gregory of Nyssa. In effect, it denied the doctrine of "eternal damnation," asserting that not only those suffering the remedial punishments of Hell, but even Satan and the demonic realm would eventually be restored to reconciliation and spiritual wholeness through the Christ when at last the Deity could literally be described as being "All in all." In Gnosticism its significance went even deeper, having reference to the cosmic union of Goddess and God (Sophia and the Logos) which would restore the Universe to its primal harmony throughout the spheres of the Aeons. So in essence, this sentence spoken to the candidate during the anointing is an assertion that the highest spiritual vision of being restored to a perfect relationship with the Deity and the Cosmos of which we are a part, should be a guiding principle directing the new priest/ess to channel all ministry in a way which helps in some small way to bring about the beginning of the Apocatastasis.

29. This is just a simple affirmation that in celebrating the Grail Mass the priest/ess will be experiencing the privilege of offering up the sacrificial Mystery unto THE MYSTERY, which indeed it is. The hands of the priest/ess are most blessed, for they offer up in the Mass that which is a manifestation of the miraculous: the meeting place of Matter and Spirit in an epiphany of mutual interdependence for the accomplishment of the Divine Will.

30. "Both priest(ess) and prophet(ess)" (i.e., a union of both the sacramental and oracular office of ancient Paganism).

31. The stole is a symbol of the spiritual responsibility which has been laid by the Divine Counsels upon the individual priest/ess who wears it, and serves a similar function and symbolism as in the vestments of a Christian priest. It further stands for the authority of the Order's

priesthood. The stole can be of any design, color(s), or pattern. It is worn around the neck and shoulders, hanging to a length of at least to the knees of the priest/ess when standing. It can be as wide or narrow as suits one's personal tastes. One simple design is to have the stole divided equally in half between the colors of silver and gold, standing for the Goddess and God, respectively. Emblems such as pentagrams, spirals, crosses, etc., can be embroidered or sewn upon the stole. In essence, the stole can become a personalized expression reflecting the spirituality of the priest/ess who wears it. The stole should always be worn during ritual occasions over the robe, for it designates the office of the priesthood.

32. "The Trinity of the Triple Will" (i.e., the Goddess as Maiden, Mother, and Crone). The sash-cord that is given to the candidate is usually red in color, nine feet in length, and bordered on each end with three tassels: one white, one red, and one black. This is normally made by the grove members (as is the stole) for presentation to the candidate during the ordination ceremony. However, for those who must ordain themselves, both stole and cord should be made either for or by the candidate before the performance of the Rite of Self-Ordination.

33. The sequence for an ordination performed in spring would be east, north, west, and south. The sequence for an ordination performed in summer would be south, east, north, and west. The sequence for an ordination performed in the fall would be west, south, east, and north.

34. "Solemn Oblation" (i.e., the Grail Mass).

35. This is an obvious allusion to the legends of the Grail Quest. If the knights had known to ask the right question during the mysterious procession of the Hallows, the wounded King would have been made whole and the land which had been laid waste due to his maimed condition would have been restored. In the same way, those within the priesthood should always keep before their consciousness the pivotal question which at first eluded the questing knights: "Whom does the Grail serve?" Indeed, it serves the will of the Goddess to bring about the betterment of the human race and the ecological wasteland of the planet on which we live. But the key is that as exalted and mystifying as is the Grail, its primary purpose is to serve. This too, is the responsibility of the Grail priest/ess: to serve the needs of those around them who are also involved in the Quest in order to bring about in their own small part the ultimate restoration of terrestrial, celestial, and cosmic unity in the Goddess and God.

Priest with sash-cord, stole, and staff: Emblems of the priesthood of the Ordo Arcanorum Gradalis.

The Rite of Self-Ordination

The Rite of Self-Ordination is performed only when an individual who is forced to practice as a solitary has completed the studies and requirements necessary for ordination into the Ordo Arcanorum Gradalis. If such a candidate is too far geographically removed from the proximity of a local Grail Quest Grove of the O.A.G., then the only option available is to perform the Rite of Self-Ordination. The same holds true for the coordinator of a Grail Quest study circle who is ready for ordination, but unable to be ordained by a priest/ess of the O.A.G. due to distance, area, etc. (However, thereafter all members of the group completing ordination requirements would in turn be consecrated by this newly self-ordained priest/ess.) In these cases, self-ordination is the only option.

A self-ordination cannot be performed without the express written authorization of a priest/ess of the Order who has certified that the candidate in question has indeed completed all the preliminary requirements. For solitaries, this would usually be the priest/esses in charge of overseeing the correspondence course training program as outlined in the Appendices of this book.

In a sense, the term "self-ordained" is a misnomer, for in reality it is the authority of the Order which conveys the actual seal of ordination in the realm of spirit. When a person performs the Rite of Self-Ordination, he or she is confirming in ritual format what has already been decreed to be a right and proper procedure.

The text which follows is substantially the same as the previous Rite of Ordination, except that it has been altered to accommodate the spoken needs of the solitary candidate. There are also very few footnotes to this text in order to avoid any unnecessary repetition of what has already been stated in the footnotes of the previous rite. The footnotes here will only be referencing wording or procedure which is unique to the Rite of Self-Ordination.

(After the candidate has cast the circle and completed the Opening Rites, including the Assembling of the Quarter-Regents, then s/he shall stand before the altar and begin to recite the following introductory words.)

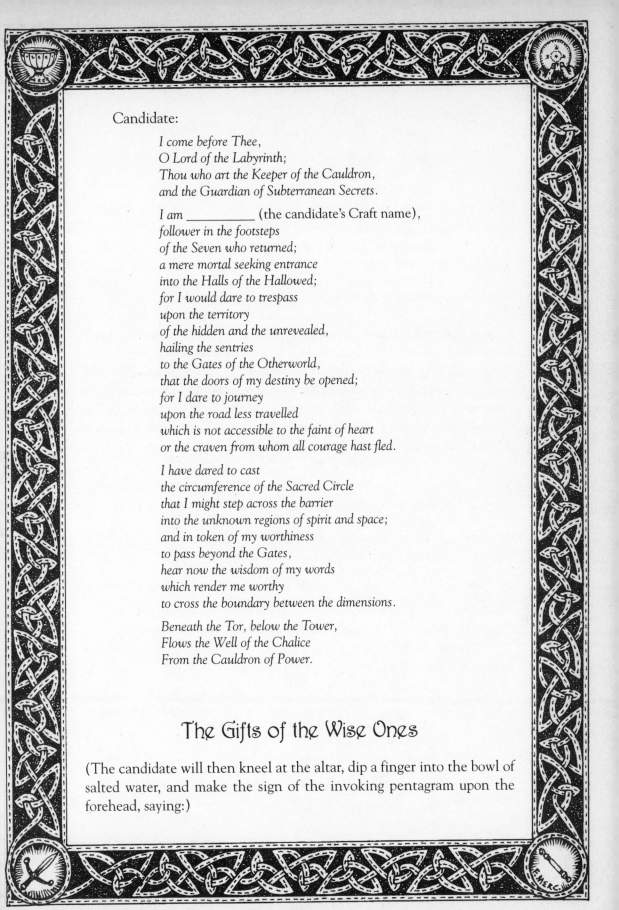

Candidate:

> *I come before Thee,*
> *O Lord of the Labyrinth;*
> *Thou who art the Keeper of the Cauldron,*
> *and the Guardian of Subterranean Secrets.*
>
> *I am _____ (the candidate's Craft name),*
> *follower in the footsteps*
> *of the Seven who returned;*
> *a mere mortal seeking entrance*
> *into the Halls of the Hallowed;*
> *for I would dare to trespass*
> *upon the territory*
> *of the hidden and the unrevealed,*
> *hailing the sentries*
> *to the Gates of the Otherworld,*
> *that the doors of my destiny be opened;*
> *for I dare to journey*
> *upon the road less travelled*
> *which is not accessible to the faint of heart*
> *or the craven from whom all courage hast fled.*
>
> *I have dared to cast*
> *the circumference of the Sacred Circle*
> *that I might step across the barrier*
> *into the unknown regions of spirit and space;*
> *and in token of my worthiness*
> *to pass beyond the Gates,*
> *hear now the wisdom of my words*
> *which render me worthy*
> *to cross the boundary between the dimensions.*
>
> *Beneath the Tor, below the Tower,*
> *Flows the Well of the Chalice*
> *From the Cauldron of Power.*

The Gifts of the Wise Ones

(The candidate will then kneel at the altar, dip a finger into the bowl of salted water, and make the sign of the invoking pentagram upon the forehead, saying:)

435

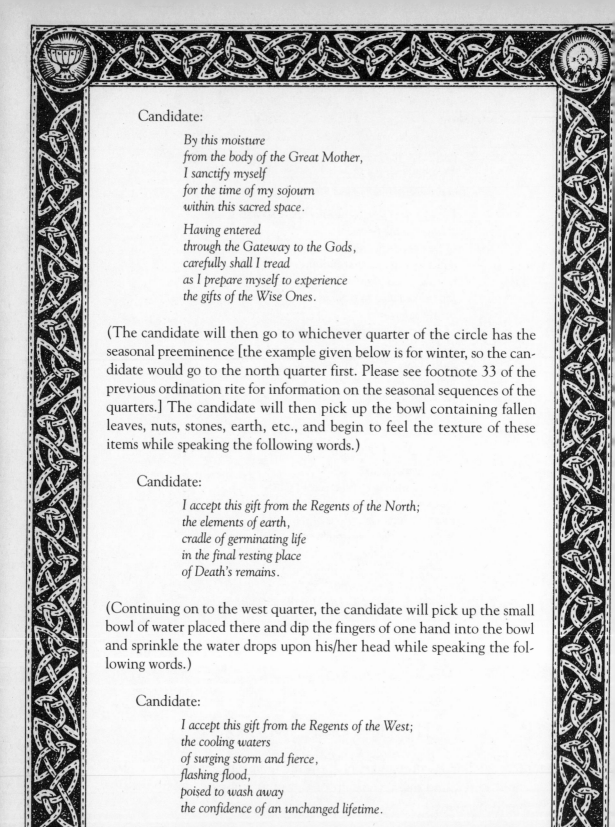

Candidate:

> By this moisture
> from the body of the Great Mother,
> I sanctify myself
> for the time of my sojourn
> within this sacred space.
>
> Having entered
> through the Gateway to the Gods,
> carefully shall I tread
> as I prepare myself to experience
> the gifts of the Wise Ones.

(The candidate will then go to whichever quarter of the circle has the seasonal preeminence [the example given below is for winter, so the candidate would go to the north quarter first. Please see footnote 33 of the previous ordination rite for information on the seasonal sequences of the quarters.] The candidate will then pick up the bowl containing fallen leaves, nuts, stones, earth, etc., and begin to feel the texture of these items while speaking the following words.)

Candidate:

> I accept this gift from the Regents of the North;
> the elements of earth,
> cradle of germinating life
> in the final resting place
> of Death's remains.

(Continuing on to the west quarter, the candidate will pick up the small bowl of water placed there and dip the fingers of one hand into the bowl and sprinkle the water drops upon his/her head while speaking the following words.)

Candidate:

> I accept this gift from the Regents of the West;
> the cooling waters
> of surging storm and fierce,
> flashing flood,
> poised to wash away
> the confidence of an unchanged lifetime.

(Continuing on to the south quarter, the candidate will pick up the special candle placed there and proceed to pass one hand close enough over the flame to feel its warmth while speaking the following words.)

Candidate:

> *I accept this gift from the Regents of the South;*
> *the warmth of fire*
> *which consumes in but a moment*
> *that which cannot pass the test of time.*

(Continuing on to the east quarter, the candidate will take up a small fan previously placed there and fan the air against his/her face while speaking the following words:)

Candidate:

> *I accept this gift from the Regents of the East;*
> *the breath of life*
> *rushing past me*
> *as the transient mortal that I am:*
> *a mere vapor upon the wind.*

The Affirmation of Commitment

(After the candidate has gone full-circle and accepted the gifts from all four of the Quarter-Regents, s/he shall return to the altar and begin the following recitation.)

Candidate:

> *Many wonders await me*
> *in the secret regions of the Shining Ones*
> *as mine eyes behold*
> *that which is already known by mine inmost self,*
> *but the journey must begin here in Caer Sidhe,*
> *for like the Singer in the Shadows,*
> *who ever haunteth these halls*
> *with songs of the spoils that await,*
> *so too, my heart must be entwined*

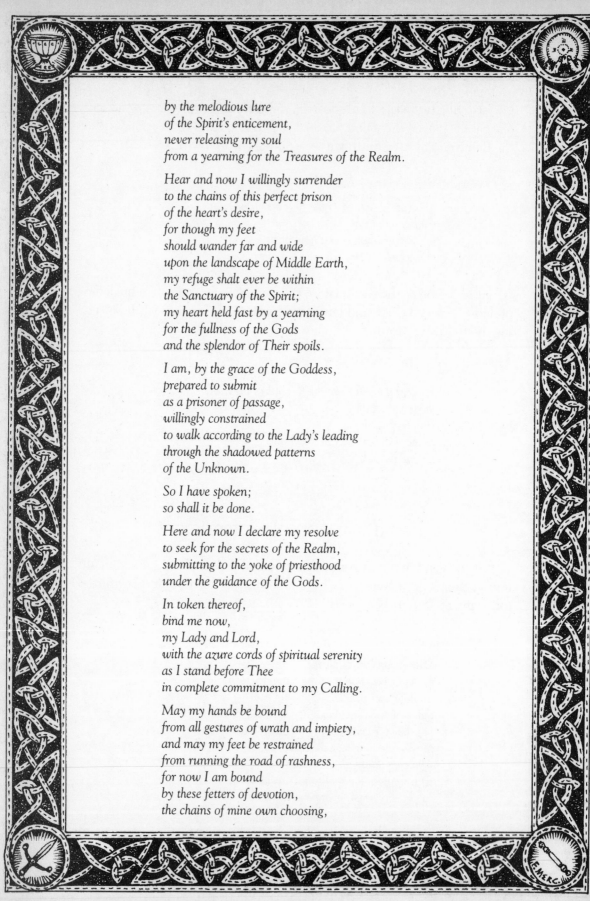

by the melodious lure
of the Spirit's enticement,
never releasing my soul
from a yearning for the Treasures of the Realm.

Hear and now I willingly surrender
to the chains of this perfect prison
of the heart's desire,
for though my feet
should wander far and wide
upon the landscape of Middle Earth,
my refuge shalt ever be within
the Sanctuary of the Spirit;
my heart held fast by a yearning
for the fullness of the Gods
and the splendor of Their spoils.

I am, by the grace of the Goddess,
prepared to submit
as a prisoner of passage,
willingly constrained
to walk according to the Lady's leading
through the shadowed patterns
of the Unknown.

So I have spoken;
so shall it be done.

Here and now I declare my resolve
to seek for the secrets of the Realm,
submitting to the yoke of priesthood
under the guidance of the Gods.

In token thereof,
bind me now,
my Lady and Lord,
with the azure cords of spiritual serenity
as I stand before Thee
in complete commitment to my Calling.

May my hands be bound
from all gestures of wrath and impiety,
and may my feet be restrained
from running the road of rashness,
for now I am bound
by these fetters of devotion,
the chains of mine own choosing,

in order that I may walk
the way of wisdom and introspection
in the service of the Lord of Inner Mysteries.

I pray Thee,
O Lady and Lord,
that I be given the grace
to walk circumspectly
as I tread the winding labyrinth of life
leading to the Treasures of Light.

(The candidate will then complete the Affirmation by reciting the riddle of Caer Pedryvan.)

Candidate:

Four times the turn
> *in Caer Pedryvan,*
with lessons to learn
> *in Caer Pedryvan,*
dark torches that burn
> *in Caer Pedryvan,*
secrets to discern
> *in Caer Pedryvan!*

The Preliminary Anointing

(The candidate now takes up the chalice of wine from the altar, saying the following words.)

Candidate:

To tread the path of priesthood
as a mediator between the worlds
and an opener of the doorway
to the Divine,
my lips must become
an instrument of invocation,
uttering oracles
arising from the inspiration
of the Cup and the Cauldron.

(The candidate then dips a finger into the wine and anoints his/her lips, making the sign of the pentagram, and saying:)

Candidate:

> Anointed be my lips
> with the wine of holiness,
> that from my mouth
> shall flow streams of purity and grace.

The Consecratory Preface

(The candidate will then place the chalice back upon the altar and begin saying the declaration of the preface:)

Candidate:

> I am a Pagan and a pilgrim
> of solemn resolve.
>
> I have held faithfully
> to the precepts of the Craft.
>
> I have prepared myself for priesthood
> through study, ritual, and worship.
>
> None can gainsay my diligence
> and determination,
> for all the hosts of higher realms
> stand as invisible witnesses
> to my struggle to ascend
> into the Sanctuary of the Sacred
> as a Servant of the Grail
> and a Champion of the Sovereign Lady.
>
> The time has come
> for my period of preparation
> to bear the fruit of finalized fulfillment.

The Solemn Adjuration

(The candidate will then kneel next to the cauldron, placing his/her hand upon its rim, saying:)

Candidate:

> In the presence of the Mighty Ones
> here assembled,[1]
> I swear by the Cauldron of the Living Lady,
> Mother of the Earth,
> Queen of Heaven and Hell,
> that I am willing to be loyal
> to Her Ways and Her Word.
>
> In the presence of the Mighty Ones
> here assembled,
> I swear by the Living Lord,
> Firstborn from the Cauldron,
> Father of all Creation,
> Lover and Consort of the Goddess,
> that I am willing to stand
> as a public confessor of the Ancient Faith,
> defending it against false accusations
> and malicious calumny.
>
> In the presence of the Mighty Ones
> here assembled,
> I swear by the Cauldron of Sacrifice
> transforming life into death
> and death into life again,
> that I am willing to suffer
> in order to experience
> the depths of the Holy Mysteries.
>
> As a postulant to the priesthood,
> I have pledged
> my loyalty to the leading of the Lady,
> my willingness to defend
> the integrity of the Pagan Way,
> and my resolve to suffer if necessary,
> for the realization of my Calling
> as a Way-shower of the Sacred Secrets.

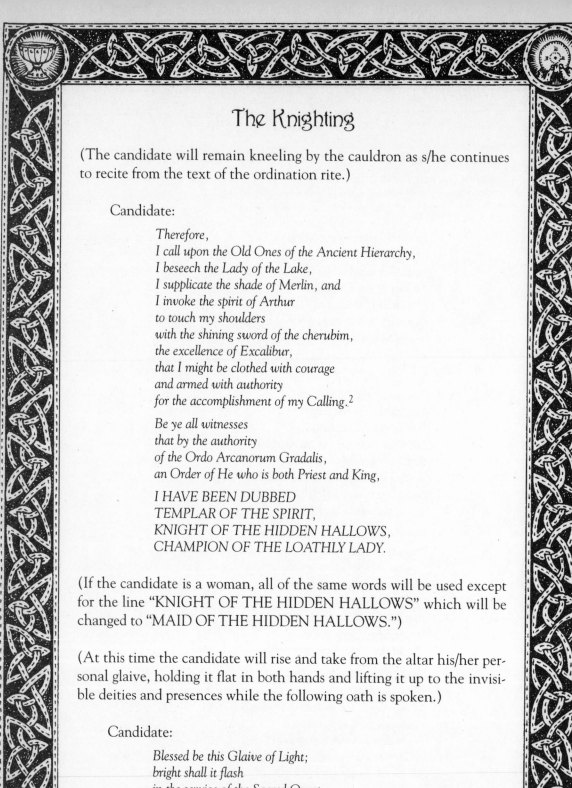

The Knighting

(The candidate will remain kneeling by the cauldron as s/he continues to recite from the text of the ordination rite.)

Candidate:

> *Therefore,*
> *I call upon the Old Ones of the Ancient Hierarchy,*
> *I beseech the Lady of the Lake,*
> *I supplicate the shade of Merlin, and*
> *I invoke the spirit of Arthur*
> *to touch my shoulders*
> *with the shining sword of the cherubim,*
> *the excellence of Excalibur,*
> *that I might be clothed with courage*
> *and armed with authority*
> *for the accomplishment of my Calling.*[2]
>
> *Be ye all witnesses*
> *that by the authority*
> *of the Ordo Arcanorum Gradalis,*
> *an Order of He who is both Priest and King,*
>
> *I HAVE BEEN DUBBED*
> *TEMPLAR OF THE SPIRIT,*
> *KNIGHT OF THE HIDDEN HALLOWS,*
> *CHAMPION OF THE LOATHLY LADY.*

(If the candidate is a woman, all of the same words will be used except for the line "KNIGHT OF THE HIDDEN HALLOWS" which will be changed to "MAID OF THE HIDDEN HALLOWS.")

(At this time the candidate will rise and take from the altar his/her personal glaive, holding it flat in both hands and lifting it up to the invisible deities and presences while the following oath is spoken.)

Candidate:

> *Blessed be this Glaive of Light;*
> *bright shall it flash*
> *in the service of the Sacred Quest,*
> *for I do swear before the Gods*

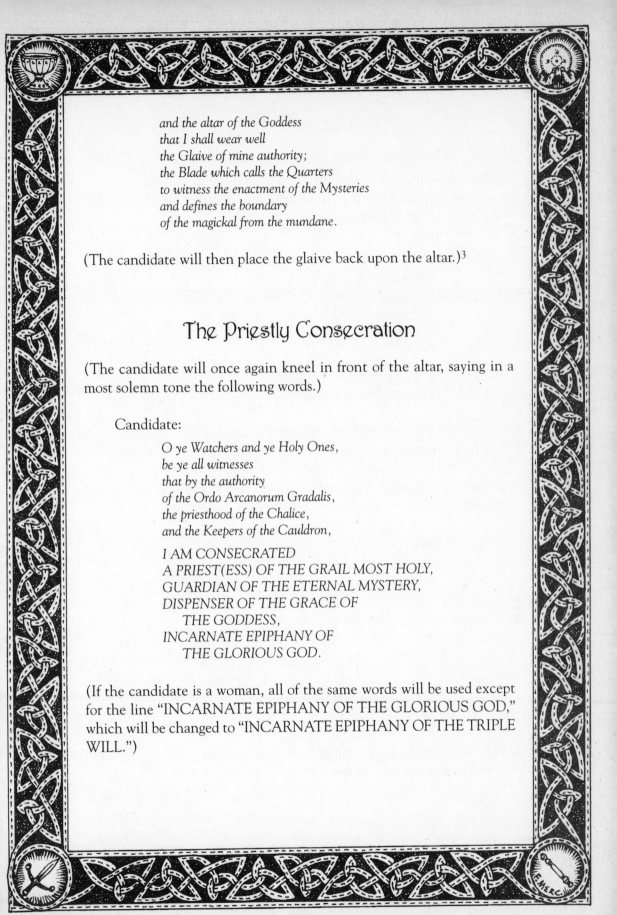

and the altar of the Goddess
that I shall wear well
the Glaive of mine authority;
the Blade which calls the Quarters
to witness the enactment of the Mysteries
and defines the boundary
of the magickal from the mundane.

(The candidate will then place the glaive back upon the altar.)[3]

The Priestly Consecration

(The candidate will once again kneel in front of the altar, saying in a most solemn tone the following words.)

Candidate:

O ye Watchers and ye Holy Ones,
be ye all witnesses
that by the authority
of the Ordo Arcanorum Gradalis,
the priesthood of the Chalice,
and the Keepers of the Cauldron,

I AM CONSECRATED
A PRIEST(ESS) OF THE GRAIL MOST HOLY,
GUARDIAN OF THE ETERNAL MYSTERY,
DISPENSER OF THE GRACE OF
    THE GODDESS,
INCARNATE EPIPHANY OF
    THE GLORIOUS GOD.

(If the candidate is a woman, all of the same words will be used except for the line "INCARNATE EPIPHANY OF THE GLORIOUS GOD," which will be changed to "INCARNATE EPIPHANY OF THE TRIPLE WILL.")

The Anointing

(The candidate will then pick up the vial of anointing oil from the altar. Then dabbing the two front fingers of one hand, the candidate will proceed to anoint him/herself on the forehead [the area of the third eye] in the sign of the invoking pentagram, saying:)

> Candidate:
>
>> *I anoint myself*
>> *with the chrism of my ordination,*
>> *the precious ointment*
>> *of the Called and the Chosen,*
>> *setting me apart*
>> *for my appointed service*
>> *as a Walker between the Worlds*
>> *and a Mediator of the Mysteries.*

(The candidate then rubs the residue of oil remaining on his/her two front fingers onto the two front fingers of the other hand as well. S/he then makes the sign of the cross with the two front fingers of each hand, self-anointing the lips, touching just above and below the lips and just beyond the corners of the mouth, saying:)

> Candidate:
>
>> *From my lips shall flow*
>> *the waters of wisdom.*

(The candidate then self-anoints the ears with his/her oil-tipped fingers, making the sign of the cross and saying:)

> Candidate:
>
>> *In my ears shall be whispered*
>> *the guidance of the Gods.*

(The candidate then self-anoints his/her closed eyes with the oil-tipped fingers, making the sign of the cross and saying:)

Candidate:

> *With mine eyes shalt I see*
> *the vision of the Apocatastasis.*

(The candidate then self-anoints his/her hands by making the sign of the cross with the oil-tipped fingers on the back of each hand. Then holding them together in a gesture of prayer, the candidate shall say:)

Candidate:

> *With my hands shalt I offer up*
> *the Mysteries of the Mass.*

The Reception of Stole and Sash

(The candidate will then rise from the kneeling position and say the following words.)

Candidate:

> *Arising now,*
> *I stand in the fullness of my authority,*
> *worthy to wear*
> *the emblems of my ordination.*

(The candidate shall then put more incense on the lighted coal in the censer. S/he will pick up the censer and make a full 360-degree rotation with it three times in a widdershins direction while standing at the altar. The candidate will then say:)

Candidate:

> *Censed with the sweet smoke of sacredness,*
> *I have been sanctified*
> *to be both priest(ess) and prophet(ess),*
> *a living sacrifice of devotion*
> *to the Lady and the Lord.*

(Here the candidate puts back the censer upon the altar and then takes up the stole, saying:)

Candidate:

Upon my shoulders shall rest
the responsibility of spiritual stewardship.

(The candidate will now place the stole around his/her neck and shoulders. S/he will then pick up the sash-cord from the altar and tie it around the waist as the following words are spoken.)

And around my waist
I shall be girded
with the sash of sacred service,
dedicated to the Trinity of the Triple Will.

The Final Oath

(The candidate will now begin to recite the final oath of the ordination rite.)

Candidate:

I therefore swear
before the Goddess and the God
that I shall be vigilant for the values
that engender wholeness;
resilient in the face of adversity;
resourceful with the spiritual gifts
which I have been given;
eager to educate those who seek
to learn the Ancient Ways;
reverent towards the rites
of the Old Religion;
prayerful in my approach
to the Altar of the Holy Ones;
joyous in my celebration
of the Eucharistic Sacrifice;
and steadfast in my commitment

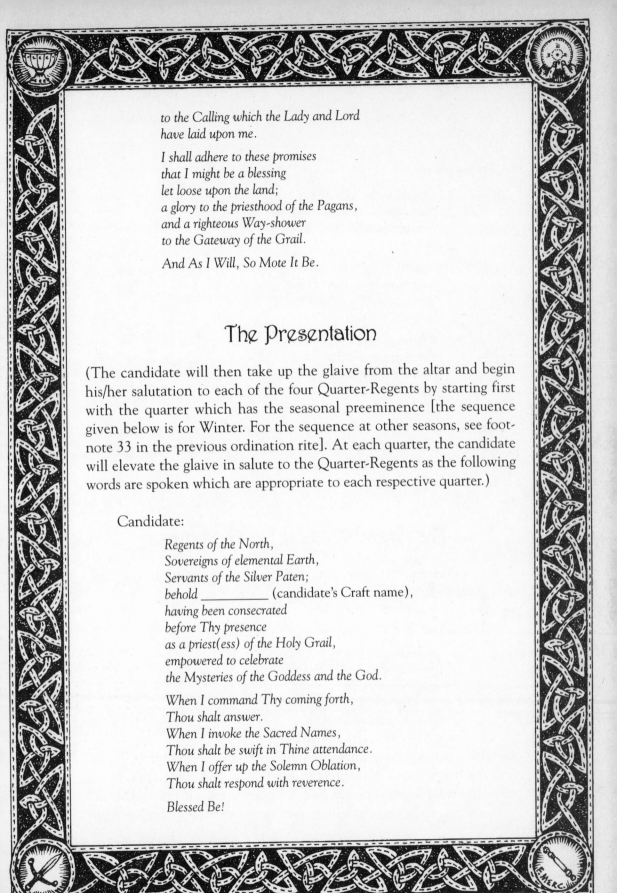

to the Calling which the Lady and Lord
have laid upon me.

I shall adhere to these promises
that I might be a blessing
let loose upon the land;
a glory to the priesthood of the Pagans,
and a righteous Way-shower
to the Gateway of the Grail.

And As I Will, So Mote It Be.

The Presentation

(The candidate will then take up the glaive from the altar and begin his/her salutation to each of the four Quarter-Regents by starting first with the quarter which has the seasonal preeminence [the sequence given below is for Winter. For the sequence at other seasons, see footnote 33 in the previous ordination rite]. At each quarter, the candidate will elevate the glaive in salute to the Quarter-Regents as the following words are spoken which are appropriate to each respective quarter.)

Candidate:

Regents of the North,
Sovereigns of elemental Earth,
Servants of the Silver Paten;
behold _____ (candidate's Craft name),
having been consecrated
before Thy presence
as a priest(ess) of the Holy Grail,
empowered to celebrate
the Mysteries of the Goddess and the God.

When I command Thy coming forth,
Thou shalt answer.
When I invoke the Sacred Names,
Thou shalt be swift in Thine attendance.
When I offer up the Solemn Oblation,
Thou shalt respond with reverence.

Blessed Be!

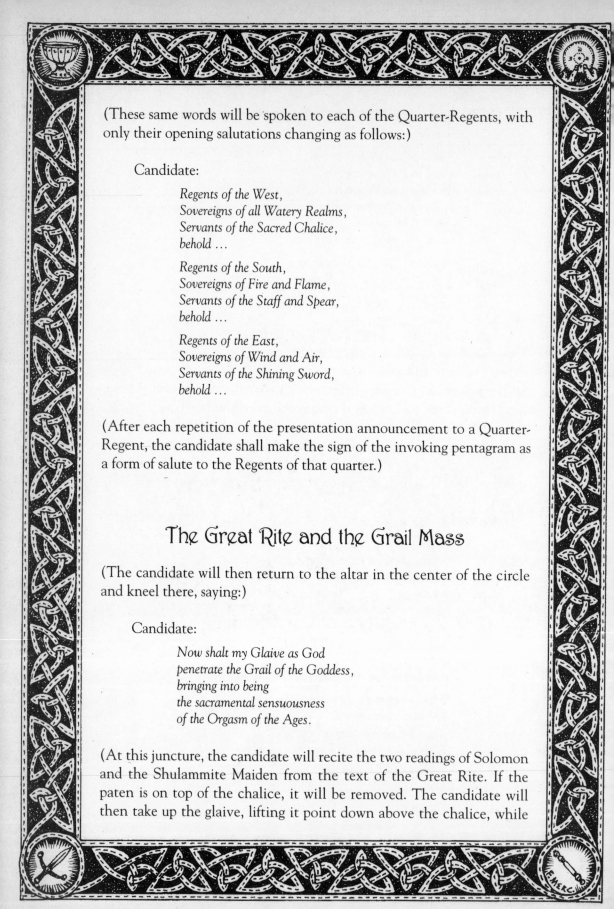

(These same words will be spoken to each of the Quarter-Regents, with only their opening salutations changing as follows:)

Candidate:

> Regents of the West,
> Sovereigns of all Watery Realms,
> Servants of the Sacred Chalice,
> behold …

> Regents of the South,
> Sovereigns of Fire and Flame,
> Servants of the Staff and Spear,
> behold …

> Regents of the East,
> Sovereigns of Wind and Air,
> Servants of the Shining Sword,
> behold …

(After each repetition of the presentation announcement to a Quarter-Regent, the candidate shall make the sign of the invoking pentagram as a form of salute to the Regents of that quarter.)

The Great Rite and the Grail Mass

(The candidate will then return to the altar in the center of the circle and kneel there, saying:)

Candidate:

> Now shalt my Glaive as God
> penetrate the Grail of the Goddess,
> bringing into being
> the sacramental sensuousness
> of the Orgasm of the Ages.

(At this juncture, the candidate will recite the two readings of Solomon and the Shulammite Maiden from the text of the Great Rite. If the paten is on top of the chalice, it will be removed. The candidate will then take up the glaive, lifting it point down above the chalice, while reciting the Words of Union. S/he will then lower the point of the glaive into the chalice on the altar. The glaive will then be removed from the chalice and wiped with a dry cloth and placed back in its place upon the altar. If the paten was previously on the rim of the chalice, it shall now be replaced in preparation for the Grail Mass. The candidate will then gesture with his/her hands towards the chalice and paten, saying the following words.)

Candidate:

> Behold the bread and the wine
> waiting for the words of my invocations
> that the seal of my office
> might be made manifest
> in the celebration of the Holy Mysteries.

(The candidate will then begin the recitation of the entire Grail Mass as the first official act of his/her priestly office.)

The Parting Declaration

(When the candidate has partaken and consumed all of the Eucharistic elements and said the final prayer of the Mass, s/he will then rise and say the following words.)

Candidate:

> Within the Circle of the Living Cauldron
> I have been blessed
> by the breath of the Nine Maidens;
> I have partaken
> of the spoils of the Sacred;
> I have attained
> unto the handling of the Hallows.
>
> Now shalt I return to my kindred
> like the noble Seven before my time,
> but my heart shalt ever be captive
> to the enchantments of the Cauldron
> and the Calling of the Grail.

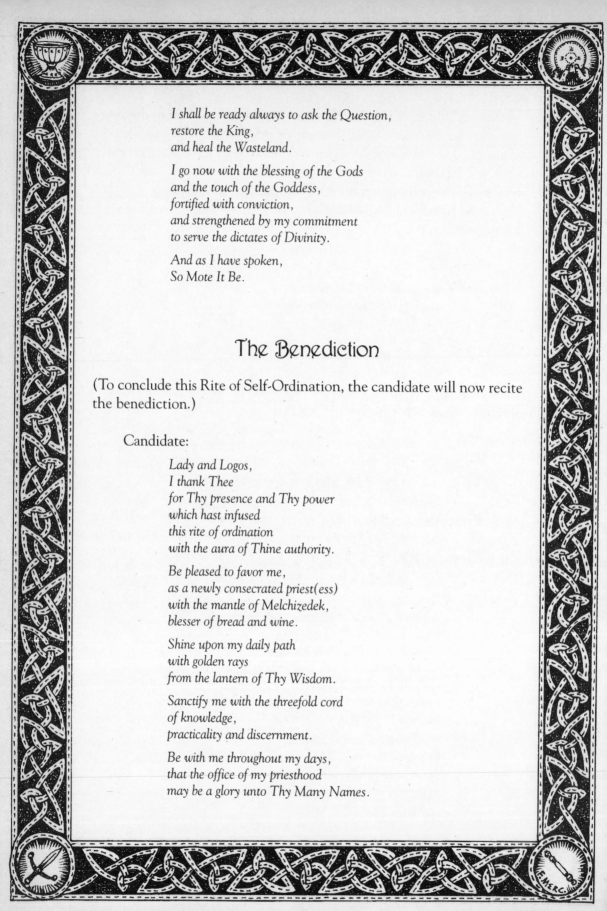

I shall be ready always to ask the Question,
restore the King,
and heal the Wasteland.

I go now with the blessing of the Gods
and the touch of the Goddess,
fortified with conviction,
and strengthened by my commitment
to serve the dictates of Divinity.

And as I have spoken,
So Mote It Be.

The Benediction

(To conclude this Rite of Self-Ordination, the candidate will now recite the benediction.)

Candidate:

Lady and Logos,
I thank Thee
for Thy presence and Thy power
which hast infused
this rite of ordination
with the aura of Thine authority.

Be pleased to favor me,
as a newly consecrated priest(ess)
with the mantle of Melchizedek,
blesser of bread and wine.

Shine upon my daily path
with golden rays
from the lantern of Thy Wisdom.

Sanctify me with the threefold cord
of knowledge,
practicality and discernment.

Be with me throughout my days,
that the office of my priesthood
may be a glory unto Thy Many Names.

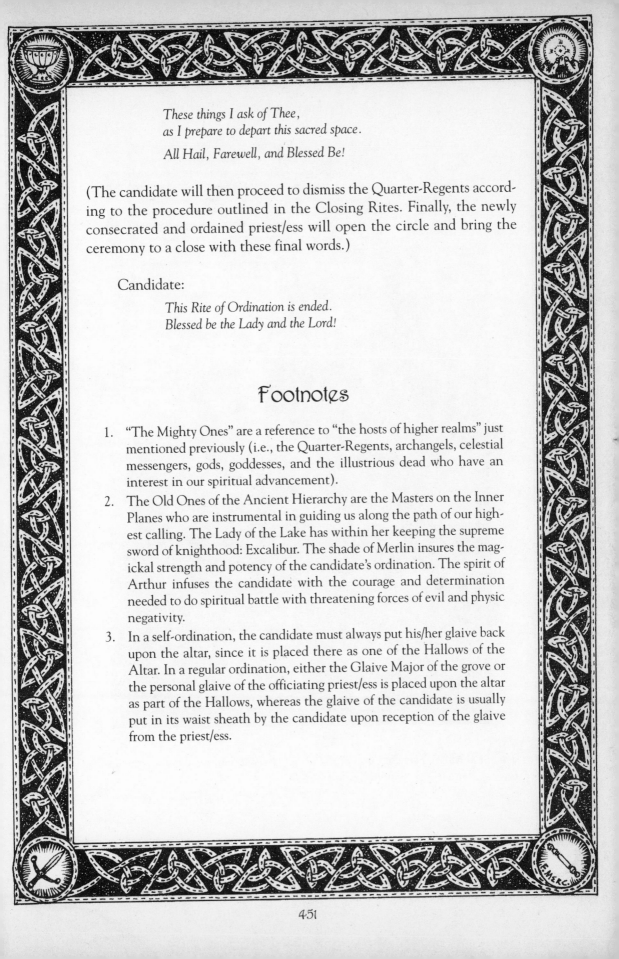

These things I ask of Thee,
as I prepare to depart this sacred space.

All Hail, Farewell, and Blessed Be!

(The candidate will then proceed to dismiss the Quarter-Regents according to the procedure outlined in the Closing Rites. Finally, the newly consecrated and ordained priest/ess will open the circle and bring the ceremony to a close with these final words.)

Candidate:

This Rite of Ordination is ended.
Blessed be the Lady and the Lord!

Footnotes

1. "The Mighty Ones" are a reference to "the hosts of higher realms" just mentioned previously (i.e., the Quarter-Regents, archangels, celestial messengers, gods, goddesses, and the illustrious dead who have an interest in our spiritual advancement).

2. The Old Ones of the Ancient Hierarchy are the Masters on the Inner Planes who are instrumental in guiding us along the path of our highest calling. The Lady of the Lake has within her keeping the supreme sword of knighthood: Excalibur. The shade of Merlin insures the magickal strength and potency of the candidate's ordination. The spirit of Arthur infuses the candidate with the courage and determination needed to do spiritual battle with threatening forces of evil and physic negativity.

3. In a self-ordination, the candidate must always put his/her glaive back upon the altar, since it is placed there as one of the Hallows of the Altar. In a regular ordination, either the Glaive Major of the grove or the personal glaive of the officiating priest/ess is placed upon the altar as part of the Hallows, whereas the glaive of the candidate is usually put in its waist sheath by the candidate upon reception of the glaive from the priest/ess.

The Grail Mass: The Elevation of the Host. "Behold the Bread of Life, the golden Lord of Harvest, the sprouted Seed of Ceres!"

A Ritual Format for the Lighting of Candles

(Presented here is an optional formula for the ritual lighting of candles just prior to, or at the beginning of a circle rite. It is designed to demonstrate the thankful respect we should have towards these beautiful flickering globes of fiery radiance which grace our altars with magickal luminosity. The following prayer can be said first, before any candles are lit. [This prayer is also customary just after the opening readings of the Candlemas candle-lighting at the beginning of the ceremony, just prior to the actual lighting of the candles.])

Priest/ess:

> Most Holy Shekinah,
> whose mystic light is diffused
> through the Cloud of Thy Holiness,
> we beseech Thee
> to set afire the darkness of this Temple
> with brilliant flares
> from Wisdom's flame;
> the Light which knows no quenching.
>
> As we kindle these candles,
> may they become columns of brightness
> cleaving the velvet veil of night;
> pillars of fire
> lighting the way before Thy presence,
> Thou torch-bearer of shining splendor!
>
> Between the twilight of our understanding
> and the midnight of our perplexity,
> we beseech Thee, O Lady,
> to dance down the corridors of darkness
> casting candle-framed shadows of Truth
> upon the walls of our imagination,
> that we might be illuminated
> by the flickering glow of Thy guidance.

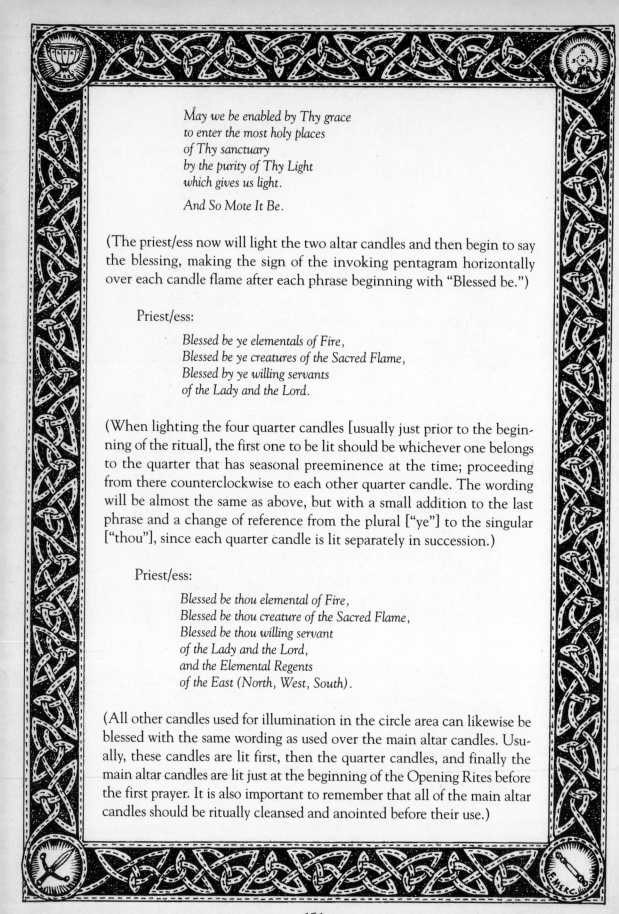

May we be enabled by Thy grace
to enter the most holy places
of Thy sanctuary
by the purity of Thy Light
which gives us light.

And So Mote It Be.

(The priest/ess now will light the two altar candles and then begin to say the blessing, making the sign of the invoking pentagram horizontally over each candle flame after each phrase beginning with "Blessed be.")

Priest/ess:

Blessed be ye elementals of Fire,
Blessed be ye creatures of the Sacred Flame,
Blessed by ye willing servants
of the Lady and the Lord.

(When lighting the four quarter candles [usually just prior to the beginning of the ritual], the first one to be lit should be whichever one belongs to the quarter that has seasonal preeminence at the time; proceeding from there counterclockwise to each other quarter candle. The wording will be almost the same as above, but with a small addition to the last phrase and a change of reference from the plural ["ye"] to the singular ["thou"], since each quarter candle is lit separately in succession.)

Priest/ess:

Blessed be thou elemental of Fire,
Blessed be thou creature of the Sacred Flame,
Blessed be thou willing servant
of the Lady and the Lord,
and the Elemental Regents
of the East (North, West, South).

(All other candles used for illumination in the circle area can likewise be blessed with the same wording as used over the main altar candles. Usually, these candles are lit first, then the quarter candles, and finally the main altar candles are lit just at the beginning of the Opening Rites before the first prayer. It is also important to remember that all of the main altar candles should be ritually cleansed and anointed before their use.)

The Opening Rites: "Water from the depths, by the Goddess be blessed!"

Appendix A

Requirements for Ordination

I n the chronicles of old and the romances of troubadours' tales, it captured the imagination of medieval wonderment—the Holy Grail, the Prize of the Quest, the Answer which lies within the center of the collective enigma that is the Mystery of Life itself. Illusive yet impelling, the Grail has always called out to the ranks of the Wise Ones, those old souls incarnated in each generation in order to bestow the blessings of wisdom, insight, and inspiration upon the less spiritually evolved consciousness of the world's teeming masses.

If you find yourself genuinely drawn to the imagery of the Grail without an analytical understanding of the nature of the attraction (if it is more than a momentary fancy of novel fascination), then you can rest reasonably assured that you are being personally drawn by the revelatory influence of the Grail upon your own higher consciousness. Such calling may indicate your identity as a member of that chosen company being summoned through the Spirit to serve as a priest or priestess of the Grail in order to mediate the hidden treasures of the Holy to the hungry and seeking souls of a spiritually bewildered humanity.

To function within the priesthood of the Grail is not a matter to be taken lightly. Nor is it necessarily a religious "career" where all the disparate aspects of our spiritual pilgrimage through life fall neatly into expected and prearranged patterns to enhance our sense of inner security. The call to ordination is, however, one of the highest privileges to which one can be predestined within the life span of his/her incarnation.

> If you take your studies of the Grail material seriously, and choose to follow the magical path ... you may come to want to take up the task of priest of the Grail. Like any other undertaking in magic, it is not a light task, nor one to be taken up without a lot of prior thought and meditation. To some extent it is not really something you can expect to become, but rather something that the Inner worlds decide to lay upon you. There has to be rather more than a human desire for the priesthood, for it truly is "of the Order of Melchisidek," not confined to any faith or Church, but a servant of the Creator.[1]

Priesthood carries with it responsibilities, ministry, the authority to offer the sacramental sacrifice, and the mantle of heavenly foreordination to be a humble and hallowed instrument for change and spiritual transformation in the world around us. In other words, the importance of the priesthood of the Grail cannot be underestimated, nor can consideration of a commitment to join the ranks of this Order be taken lightly. But if your heart truly responds to the call of the Quest, an interior assurance will steadily grow within your spirit, and you will have no doubt as to the path which you should follow.

In order to be prepared for the beginning of your priestly journey, there must be at least some minimal preparation of mind and spirit for the accomplishment of your calling. Listed below are the basic requirements for ordination into the priesthood of the Ordo Arcanorum Gradalis with some added explanations and comments. Actually, the requirements as set forth on these few pages are simple yet substantive with a view towards practicality. There will always be a few initiated from other traditions who insist that their own requirements from that particular tradition are far more intensive and thorough than what we have stipulated here. However, it is necessary to keep in mind that we are not just dealing with newcomers being trained within the context of the activities of a local grove. There are also many solitary Craft practitioners who are not solitary by choice, but out of necessity because there are no compatible Pagan groups within their own areas. This means that for solitaries who wish to join the O.A.G., the requirements for ordination (or self-ordination) must be tailored to their respective limitations since they do not have the opportunity for the social interaction and group dynamics through which one's training experience can be deepened. As a result, these requirements have been kept to a minimum and interpreted in such a way so as to be applicable to both solitary and group member alike. It should also be remembered that Craft solitaries do not have the luxury of opting for simple initiation as a non-ordained member. This is because of the fact that non-ordained members of a local grove can still participate in all of the sacramental rites since there is already a priest and/or priestess empowered with the authority to celebrate the Grail Mass and the Great Rite. But for a solitary, the only way one can become a member of the Order and still receive all of the spiritual benefits of the Mass is through the process of ordination, since if s/he were not ordained, s/he would be unable to say the Mass, even for him/herself. So while ideally we would love to be able to administer more in-depth, hands-on training for the priesthood, the limitations of time and place, location and need, have all placed their imposition upon the nature and extent of our ordination requirements. Otherwise, if we insisted upon the thoroughness of training which can only be accomplished within the confines of grove participation and personal instruction, we would be discriminating against the very real needs of solitaries to advance in their spiritual calling through the high and holy ministry of priesthood.

Finally, before we list the actual requirements with commentary, we need to address another question which has no doubt crossed the minds of some readers. Why is there such a need for ordination? Why can't any reader just open this book and use any of the rites, including the Grail Mass, which s/he chooses? After all, we know of many other Craft-oriented books with rituals which have allowed for such non-restrictive usage. However, it is essential to realize that the O.A.G. is specifically an Order of priesthood. Priest/esses are people *set apart* from the rank-and-file of religious devotees to a distinct office of spiritual *authority*, and it is the rite of ordination which conveys that authority to the individual candidate upon his or her consecration. Anyone can mouth the words from the text of the Grail Mass, but only when they are uttered from the lips of those who are ordained to the priesthood of this Order will they carry any authority on the plane of the Inner Realms. Unfortunately, there are too many today within the ranks of those interested in the mystical and the occult who were initially attracted by the prospect of gaining magickal power over other people, Nature, or the invisible worlds. It is true that power is a formidable force to be respected, but power apart from the authority to use, control, and direct it can at best result in the loosing of unfocused or misdirected energy, and at its worst the unleashing of forces and subtle energies which an inexperienced practitioner would be unable through lack of training to creatively control. So while it is true that anyone could try and perform the Grail Mass without taking the proper steps leading to ordination, the end result of such presumption would be the uttering of a magickally potent liturgy of sacramental transformation without the *authority* to invoke and project the consubstantial presence of the dyadic Deity into the physical elements of the Mass itself as inspired by the revelations of the Ancient Hierarchy instrumental in the founding of this Order.

This is not for a moment meant to imply that only the rituals and rites of the O.A.G. have any validity, or that effective ceremonies cannot be performed by the everyday "lay" student of the Mysteries. To the contrary, there are many ritual systems which the seeking student can make use of legitimately precisely because they were originally intended for individuals to use within the context of their own independent experimentation. Many Wiccan books and even some traditions are based upon this type of approach, and when students use them *as they were intended to be used*, they may full well assume that they are performing these rituals clothed in the mantle of authority given them through the instructions accompanying these rites which specifically state that they are meant for private or public usage without restrictions. On the other hand, to utilize the ceremonial system of any tradition in a way which plainly violates the original instructions and intentions of their authors, is to actually show disrespect, and constitutes an act of ritual abuse.

In our tradition, as in many others, the rite of ordination is the gateway through which we appropriate the authority to literally become the earthly extension of the gods in the manifestation of the highest Mysteries. This is at the very core of our teachings. An order without ordination cannot be a priestly order; and since we are an Order of priesthood, ordination is not only essential, it is a cornerstone by which the larger mission of the Ordo Arcanorum Gradalis is perpetuated from the present into the future.

To keep things in a balanced perspective, however, we hasten to remind the reader that most of the rituals contained in *The Crafted Cup* can be performed by non-ordained individuals or members; in particular the Opening and Closing Rites, the Lunar Rite, and the Earth Rites. *It is only the Grail Mass, the Great Rite, and the other rites such as handfasting, ordination, and requiem ceremonies which are exclusively reserved for the priesthood of this Order.* That obviously leaves plenty for novices to work with until their own ordination!

Ordination through official certification of the O.A.G. also insures a stability and consistency of those charged with the teaching magisterium of the Order. Any priest or priestess of the Order is ordained only after completing a course of study which ensures that s/he is both knowledgeable and proficient in the teachings and liturgical rubrics of the O.A.G. as contained in *The Crafted Cup*. This reinforces the ability of the priesthood to disseminate a uniform theology regarding the basic, standard traits and teachings of the Order. Official certification of ordained O.A.G. priest/esses also means that only they have the right to speak publically as a representative of the Order. This minimizes the possible problem of non-authorized pretenders claiming to be part of our priesthood and distorting our teachings and ritual practice through either brash ignorance or malicious designs to discredit the O.A.G. This also further strengthens the hand of the Order in its ability to disavow any relationship with those who claim to speak for us in an official priestly capacity, yet are not on record with us as being ordained. The Order further reserves the right to withdraw its recognition of the fellowship credentials of any legitimately ordained O.A.G. priest/ess who willfully seeks to undermine the basic goals, values, and theology of the Ordo Arcanorum Gradalis.[2]

Hopefully, these explanations regarding the importance of ordination within the context of O.A.G. teachings will go a long way towards clarifying any vague uncertainties which may have been lurking in the reader's mind. Now we shall proceed with a listing of the actual requirements for priestly ordination.

1. The candidate must have been involved in the Grail Quest training program a minimum of six months, but preferably the traditional "year and a day."

This is fairly self-explanatory. We obviously prefer that candidates for ordination be involved in their studies for a year to make sure that their interest and resolve for the priesthood is not just a passing fancy with a novel idea. A full year also gives them ample time to absorb the teachings, rituals, and general spirit of the Order. Of course, there will always be occasional exceptions to the rule; individuals who show a masterful proficiency with their study material and an advanced maturity which sets them apart from the others. The decision to ordain before the traditional "year and a day" shall be up to the presiding priest and priestess of the local grove, and in the case of solitaries, such a decision would be made by the priest/esses in charge of the national correspondence courses. Since solitaries will not be able to take part in local grove activities, nearly all of their program training will be based through correspondence, and personal ritual implementation of what they have learned through a thorough study of *The Crafted Cup*.

2. The candidate must have completed both the required reading for the course and the related written essays.

These essay questions (see Appendix C) are not meant to be simplistic book reports, but rather answers to questions which are based on the required reading, and which encourage candidates to form opinions based upon their reading. Whether they always agree with the books is not important. Most of us never agree with anyone one hundred percent! What *is* important is that they show through these essay answers their ability to utilize the information extracted from these books in a manner which contributes to their well-roundedness as informed and intelligent Pagans.

As the candidate completes each book, s/he should then answer the essay questions listed for each book title in Appendix C. These questions should be answered and returned to us via the address given at the back of this book. They will not be graded, but comments will be made on the essays and exam papers and copies sent back to you. This procedure will be repeated upon the finishing of each required book until all of them have been completed.

When all of the reading and essay assignments have been completed, one final examination will be sent to the candidate, testing his/her knowledge and understanding of those teachings unique to the Ordo Arcanorum Gradalis as set forth in *The Crafted Cup*. This, we feel, is necessary because it is imperative that those who aspire to the positions of priest and priestess in this Order be proficient in their ability to explain its concepts, rituals, and myths to others as subsequent occasions of inquiry may arise.

Following is a list of the required books which must be read preparatory to ordination. Most all of them can be obtained in your local occult, New Age, or even standard bookstores like Waldenbooks or B. Dalton. If they don't have them in stock, ask that they be ordered for you. Most bookstores are more than willing to comply with such a request. If for some reason these books are out of print or hard to locate, local libraries can usually obtain copies for you through their book-search capabilities.

Unless the candidate has already read some of the listed books, they should be read in the order in which they are given for the best cumulative effect.

- *Drawing Down the Moon: Witches, Druids, Goddess-Worshippers, and Other Pagans in America Today* by Margot Adler (Beacon Press, 1986 [Revised and Expanded Edition]).

- *The Mists of Avalon* by Marion Zimmer Bradley (Ballantine Books, 1982)

- *The Elements of the Grail Tradition* by John Matthews (Element Books Limited, 1990 [Great Britain]).

- *The Grail Seeker's Companion: A Guide to the Grail Quest in the Aquarian Age* by John Matthews and Marian Green (The Aquarian Press, 1986 [Great Britain]).

- *The Western Way: A Practical Guide to the Western Mystery Tradition, Volume I—The Native Tradition* by Caitlin and John Matthews (Arkana, 1985 [Great Britain]).

- *The Western Way: A Practical Guide to the Western Mystery Tradition, Volume II—The Hermetic Tradition* by Caitlin and John Matthews (Arkana, 1985 [Great Britain]).

- *The Gentle Arts of Aquarian Magic* by Marian Green (The Aquarian Press, 1987 [Great Britain]).

These books have been chosen because they specialize in grounding the candidate in solid conceptualizations. "How To" books are not as important as those which give one the mental and spiritual capacities to understand what and why they believe before they attempt to put these principles in practice through various practical magickal procedures.

No doubt, if the candidate has come from a background in another Wiccan/Pagan tradition, s/he may already have read some of these books. If that be the case, then it just puts that person even farther ahead in their own studies.

These seven books are not to be taken as the extent of our literary horizons, for there are many other books which we highly recommend, dealing with different facets of the Grail, Mysticism, and the Craft. However, these seven are ones which we consider to be the basic, mandatory building blocks for a balanced introduction to the theological cosmology of the Western Mysteries and the Ordo Arcanorum Gradalis in particular.

3. The candidate must commit to memorization the entire Opening and Closing Rites, the complete text of the Grail Mass, and the Words of Union contained in the Great Rite.

Memorization is essential to the rituals and ceremonial performance within the O.A.G. Of course, very few of us can memorize everything! Actually, most of the ritual invocations and the theme ceremonies unique to the particular Earth Rites are usually read by the participants directly from the text itself. However, the rituals which we perform at every gathering (or most of them) need to be known by heart, because once they become "second nature" to us, we are then freed within our spirit to tune into the vibrations of what is actually taking place on the invisible planes during the ceremonies because our conscious minds are no longer bogged down with the distraction of reading everything and trying to get through the basic mechanics of the ritual itself.

We understand that you cannot memorize everything overnight. But six months to a year should give the candidate enough time to do so. The best way to learn these rites is to actually do them, either by one's self or with other trusted friends who share similar interests with regard to the Order.[3]

The other very important reason we require memorization of the main, most sacred rituals is the fact that once a person is ordained, that individual becomes a priest/ess of this Order, and as such, should be able to lead a ritual when called upon to do so. A priest or priestess bumbling through the words of a ceremony does not inspire much confidence on the part of the other participants!

The fact that a candidate may be practicing as a solitary should not alter this requirement for ordination, since memorization can have the same liberating effect upon one's own personal times of ritual worship. Furthermore, a candidate, once ordained, never knows when s/he may be called upon to lead or participate in a group atmosphere with other Order members at special convocations, etc. It is best to always be prepared for even the remotest eventualities where one may be called upon to manifest the power and effectiveness of their sacred calling.

During the course of training, the candidate will be able to perform, as s/he learns them, all of the common rituals of the circle *except* for the Grail Mass and the Great Rite. These, as already mentioned, are reserved for ordained priest/esses only. However, the candidate is encouraged to by all means begin the memorization of the Mass in preparation for the time of her/his own ordination, when, for the first time, s/he will be able to celebrate this sacred sacrament as a fully vested priest/ess of the Ordo Arcanorum Gradalis. Initially though, the other rituals such as the Opening and Closing Rites should come first in the candidate's priorities for memorization.

One final word: memorization is not nearly as difficult as many have been led to believe. I personally know of many who at first were hesitant or lacked faith in the phenomenal powers of their own mental capacities, but when they took it "one step at a time," they soon discovered that their memory was not near as feeble as they had imagined! If it is any source of encouragement, keep in mind that the ancient Druids were reportedly required to commit *all* of their bardic and magickal skill to memory, including literal volumes worth of stories and religious lore!

4. The candidate must demonstrate proficiency in ritual participation and leadership, so that if called upon, s/he would be able to lead and coordinate the ritual effectively.

This is one of the requirements which of necessity must be greatly modified due to the fact that those who practice as solitaries cannot be directly under training and supervision in a local grove. The most we ask of those who cannot participate in local grove activities due to distance and/or location is that they learn to do the rituals as mentioned above, realizing that as future priests or priestesses they have a spiritual responsibility to be the best they can be as representatives of the Lady and the Lord. Of course, after their ordination, they will then have the authority to ordain others who may come to them for instruction in the tradition of the O.A.G. It is therefore imperative that they be able to set a good example.

5. The candidate must either have made or acquired a personal glaive and a white robe for the ordination ceremony itself.

As mentioned earlier, in the Ordo Arcanorum Gradalis we refer to the ceremonial knife as the glaive. (Most other Wiccan traditions call it an athame.) It can be of any kind or style which appeals to your sense of the magickal. If you do not already have one, we encourage you to acquire or fashion one of your own as soon as is convenient to you if you are planning to pursue the path towards ordination.

While the glaive is specially blessed at the candidate's ordination, s/he is nevertheless encouraged to consecrate it personally before then and begin using it in the Opening and Closing Rites for the calling and dismissal of the Quarter-Regents. Further information on the working purpose of the glaive can be found in the earlier chapter "The Altar and the Sacred Tools."

The white robe may be of any style or design which appeals to the candidate, but preferably of cotton cloth. If you do not yet have one, we encourage you to make or have made for you a regular "working robe" that you can start using at once in your own private rituals or in the celebrations of the local grove. Any color will be acceptable; whichever color appeals to your inner sense of aesthetics. Most of us use hooded robes on the order of the traditional monk's robe.

6. Upon completion of the studies and other requirements, the candidate will then be eligible for ordination.

If the candidate is being ordained by a priest and/or priestess of a local grove, s/he will make arrangements with the candidate with regard to the time and place of the ceremony and discuss whatever other preparations may need to be made.

If the candidate is being self-ordained into this Order as a solitary, upon completion of his/her studies, s/he will be sent a formal letter of confirmation authorizing the candidate to perform the rite of self-ordination, and requesting that the candidate inform the Order of the actual date upon which the rite was performed so that it can be reflected in our official records of the priesthood.

7. The candidate must fast for three days and three nights before his/her ordination, drinking only water and fruit juices.

For example, if the candidate were to be ordained on a Saturday night, s/he would begin to fast Thursday morning. The fast should be broken with a light meal following the ordination. Fasting is a traditional cleansing and purifying procedure frequently utilized by many religions to amplify one's focus upon the realm of Spirit. The length of time for this fast also approximates the proverbial three days and three nights symbolizing the spiritual transition of the priestly initiate from Death to Life; the death and rebirth (resurrection) experience (like that of the Christ in the tomb) which in the experience of the candidate launches the spirit into higher planes and new beginnings. However, if there are any medical reasons why such a fast would be dangerous to the health of the candidate, this requirement is automatically waived.

These are the requirements for ordination into the priesthood of the Ordo Arcanorum Gradalis, and as can be seen, they are not extremely rigorous; but they are challenging enough to cause an individual contemplating this path of ministry and service to pause and reflect upon how much s/he is willing to sacrifice in study and practice in order to attain the high calling of this priesthood. Should you accept this challenge as an invitation from the Goddess, then you can rest assured that your Quest for the Grail has only begun!

If you wish to enter into formal study for ordination into the priesthood of this Order, we request that you write to us, informing us of your intentions. We will then respond to you as soon as possible with the address of the local grove nearest your area through which you can establish contact with the Order. If there are no groves in your area, we will so inform you, and confirm that we are enrolling you as a solitary studying for priesthood through our training program.

All correspondence and inquiries should be sent to the address listed below:

ORDO ARCANORUM GRADALIS
P. O. Box 1108
Glen Allen, Virginia 23060

Footnotes

1. John Matthews and Marian Green, *The Grail Seeker's Companion*. (London: Thorsons [an imprint of HarperCollins Publishers Ltd.],1986), p. 188.

2. Withdrawing recognition of fellowship credentials does not in any way void the legitimacy of one's ordination. "Once a priest/ess, always a priest/ess." Withdrawal of credentials simply means that a particular priest/ess is no longer allowed to practice as such within the groves affiliated with the O.A.G.

3. One of the most effective ways to learn these rites, and especially the Grail Mass, is to slowly read the words of the text into a tape recorder. You can then play back the tape to yourself as often as you like. This will greatly help to speed up the memorization process. When we talk about "doing" the rites, we are referring to the context of practice only when it comes to the Grail Mass and the Great Rite, since only the ordained priesthood of the Order can perform them in the actual sense of the word.

Appendix B

Guidelines for Grail Quest Study Circles

hen a group of people wish to become affiliated with the Ordo Arcanorum Gradalis, but they have no one among them who has been ordained into the priesthood of this Order, the first necessary step they must take is to officially apply for an affiliated status as a Grail Quest study circle. Affiliation is the means by which a group can affirm their common commitment and unity of purpose with the general goals and teachings of this Order. This becomes the first step towards full association with the Order as a Grail Quest grove or chapel. However, the following steps must first be taken before a group can be said to be officially affiliated with the Ordo Arcanorum Gradalis.

1. Both the leadership and the members of the group must become fully familiar with the major teachings and basic precepts of the Order as set forth in *The Crafted Cup*.
2. The group should then cast an official vote on whether or not to begin the process of affiliation with the Order.
3. If the group decides to begin the affiliation process, then they need to first inform the Order in writing, signed by the current leadership of the group. (The Order can be contacted through the address given on page 465, or by writing to the author in care of the publisher.)

4. Once this letter of intention is received and accepted by the Order, the group will then be granted immediate status as a Grail Quest study circle.

5. Thereafter, the necessary steps of preparation for attaining official grove status within the Order outlined in this chapter shall immediately be applicable, and the group in question shall be considered officially affiliated with the Order as a Grail Quest study circle.

The choice of a coordinator for the study circle should be democratically determined from among the eligible candidates within a group which has been newly formed. This should, if at all possible, be done by general consensus. For established groups or covens coming from a background of other traditions, the best option is to simply recognize their present leaders as the coordinators. It is also the option of the study circle to rotate coordinators on a continuous basis in order to give all of the elected coordinators the opportunity to learn the varied arts of group facilitation. Furthermore, all coordinators of a study circle must be recognized by the Order as having entered into preparation for their own eventual ordination into the priesthood of this tradition.

A study circle should conform to the same ritual format in its ceremonial celebrations as would a Grail Quest grove, except that it will not celebrate the Great Rite or the Grail Mass. A study circle should also use the Opening and Closing Rites, the Earth Rites, and the Lunar Rites of the Order.

It is important for the interested participants in a study circle to be grounded by the coordinator(s) in the elementary teachings of the Order, while they all begin to build a group mind and a sense of magickal, cooperative identity as a functioning circle. This is important, for it helps members to identify with the tradition of the Order, while at the same time the study circle begins to create its own sense of corporate awareness. In order to accomplish this goal, it should be mandatory that all members of the group obtain their own copy of *The Crafted Cup* to more easily facilitate an understanding of the distinctive traits of this tradition at the very offset of their involvement. (Several extra copies should always be available on a lending basis within the group for those who cannot afford a copy of their own.)

The first meeting of a study circle should be kept fairly simple and semi-social, serving as a time for people to get better acquainted. Topics for discussion could include each person describing why s/he is attracted to the Craft, the Grail, or mystical spirituality in general, and what s/he expects to get out of his/her involvement with the study circle, as well as what s/he believes that s/he will be able to contribute.

It is best to choose carefully who you invite to your initial meetings. Try and use your own psychic senses to screen out those who may want to become involved for all the wrong reasons: to gain power over others, misconstruing the Ordo Arcanorum Gradalis as a training ground for sorcery, and using the group as a backdrop for their own ego trips. Beware also of "psychic vampires":

> ... it is an unfortunate fact that many individuals are attracted to coven membership because they have many personal problems and they hope that by joining a group, they will have a large number of people solving their troubles by constantly doing magic for them. Such persons are able to invent a thousand ways of wasting the group's energy, which is another good reason for selective membership and careful screening of applicants.[1]

It is also best not to just jump "cold turkey" into a ritual setting without first getting everyone familiar with the rite(s) which they will be performing. The coordinator should be sure to go over "The Opening and Closing Rites" with everyone, so that they will have a better idea of the magickal framework and context in which all the rituals will be celebrated.

For a novice coordinator, leading or helping to guide a study circle can be a little frightening at first, if you are not used to being in situations which call for qualities of leadership and decision-making. But don't worry; "butterflies" in the stomach are normal. Expect them for a while; at least during the first few times all of you come together. Also, expect that you will probably make a few mistakes here and there, especially in the rituals, until you become very familiar with them. If you occasionally "flub up" in a ritual or forget your words, don't go into the depths of depression over it. The best thing is to have a sense of humor! I'm sure the Gods do, too! If you goof, learn from it, but don't take it too seriously. Learn to laugh at yourself. When others see this quality in you, it will put them more at ease as they begin to learn the art of ritual for themselves when the study circle comes together to celebrate the Earth Rites and the Lunar Rites.

As far as a course of study is concerned, the best option which we would recommend would be to start an in-depth study of *The Crafted Cup*, chapter by chapter. Discuss each chapter amongst yourselves to make sure that you adequately understand the teachings which they convey. To facilitate this, it is suggested that you utilize any variety of ways which can contribute to a stimulating group discussion on these various topics.[2]

Other subject topics which can be profitably discussed in a study circle would have to do with the books for required reading as set forth in "The Requirements for Ordination." You could easily set aside a study circle discussion for each of the books as each one has been completed by most of the group. Several people discussing the different aspects of a book which they have all read can serve to give deeper insights to everyone about the book itself as viewed through many individual perspectives. (It would be best to study these books *after* the study circle has completed its reading of *The Crafted Cup*. The only exception to this might be if there are a large number of novices new to Paganism and the Craft. In this case, it would probably be advisable to start off with a general overview of *Drawing Down the Moon* by Margot Adler, since it is considered to be the most thorough introduction to the Neo-Pagan/Wiccan revival in America.)

As much as possible, any decisions within the study circle not affecting basic theology or ritual practice should be made by democratic consensus. As an example, it may be a good idea for the group to equally distribute the responsibilities for buying (or making) the items needed for every ceremonial gathering, such as candles, wine, cakes, matches, sea salt, incense, etc. Another helpful idea is for everyone to bring a dish or beverage for a "pot luck" which follows the conclusion of the circle, when the members are ready to relax and enjoy the rest of the evening together.

One of the first projects a study circle may want to tackle is making sure that they have all the ritual tools and implements necessary for the basic practice of the O.A.G. rituals as laid out elsewhere in this book. It is also necessary that everyone know how to set up the altar for the rites so that the study circle as a whole can learn to set up the altar together as a group activity. In this way, the responsibility doesn't always descend "like a ton of bricks" on one person alone to set up everything needed for the Earth and Lunar Rites. (Of course, at the beginning, the coordinator[s] will need to learn this set-up beforehand so that they can be familiar enough with it to teach the rest of the study circle according to the standard instructions as given in "The Altar and the Sacred Tools.")

As the members of the study circle begin to practice the basic rites, it is highly recommended that everyone be given the chance to perform the Opening and Closing Rites as well as various parts in the Lunar and Earth Rite ceremonies, for it is essential that all of those seeking to be ordained into the priesthood of the Order be able to perform these rites, and some portions of them by memory. For those desiring only to be initiated as a non-ordained member of a grove, their goal should also be a proficiency in the performance of the Opening and Closing Rites, at the very least. The more practice they get, the better. It will be, of course, the responsibility of the coordinator(s) to become familiar with these rites as set forth in this book in order to lead and teach other newcomers as the group expands.

During the time that a group is functioning as a study circle preparatory to attaining the status of grove, the members may want to explore the possibility of what name they will want to call themselves once the study circle actually makes the transition to grove status. This helps to further create a sense of distinct and independent identity and deepens their expectations for "coming of age" as a Grail Quest grove in affiliation with the Order.

The coordinator(s) of the study circle must complete the requirements necessary for their own ordination into the priesthood of the Order before the study circle can be upgraded to the level of a grove. Where there is no already-existing grove which can ordain the qualified coordinator(s) of a study circle, the person(s) must of necessity perform the Rite of Self-Ordination according to the specifications and ritual format of the O.A.G. The self-ordained coordinator will then be qualified to directly ordain the other members of the study circle who have also completed the standard requirements for ordination into the priesthood, as well as administering the Rite of Initiation to those seeking non-ordained membership status in the new grove.[3]

As already mentioned, as soon as there is at least one ordained priest/ess in the study circle, the status of the study circle will be upgraded to that of an official Grail Quest grove of the Ordo Arcanorum Gradalis, for then there will be a priest/ess empowered by this Order to celebrate the Great Rite and the Grail Mass. The first Lunar or Earth Rite following his/her ordination (or self-ordination), the Grail Mass should be celebrated, becoming thereby the sacramental and ceremonial seal indicating that the study circle is now a grove.

The implementation of several policies which all involved should know from the beginning of their participation in the study circle are strongly recommended. First of all, individuals who are "high" on either alcohol or illegal substances should not be allowed into the ceremonial circle. The vibrations which they bring with them under such altered states can often wreak havoc with the psychic balance of a circle. Furthermore, no illegal substances should be allowed on the premises of a study circle or grove gathering for use during the times of socializing which occur after the ritual has been concluded. In this we concur with Janet and Stewart Farrar:

> As for psychedelic, hallucinogenic and similar drugs—we do not take them ourselves, and we ban them absolutely from our covenstead. This ban includes *cannabis*, though we realize that differing views are sincerely held on the question of whether it should be legalized ... Wise witches will leave drugs strictly alone, and achieve their expansion of consciousness the hard way—which in both the short and the long run is the only way.[4]

Whatever policy individuals in the group may follow regarding their own private use (or non-use) of mind-altering substances is totally their own responsibility. However, it is the policy of this Order to encourage its affiliated groves and study circles not to allow such recreational usage of drugs on the premises of their ritual gatherings. Having beer and wine with a "pot luck" or for a Sabbat party after the circle has been concluded is appropriately acceptable, having a long and robust history as a part of Pagan socializing and celebration, as long as everyone is able to keep their drinking within the generally recognized and acceptable bounds of propriety.

Sometimes individuals who are recovering alcoholics will become part of a study circle or grove. In such circumstances, it is suggested that in a grove, instead of using wine in the Grail Chalice for the Mass, that white grape juice or non-alcoholic wine be used. Similarly, in a study circle (as well as a grove), white grape juice could also be used for the ceremony of Cakes and Wine held at the close of the circle, just before the beginning of the evening's informalities. This way the recovering alcoholic will be able to fully participate without any sense of isolation from the rest of the group.

One final issue which needs to be addressed is that of the admission of legal minors into the membership of a study circle or grove. We generally recommend a rather strict policy on this point: people under the age of eighteen should not be allowed into membership without the express *written* permission of their parents or legal guardians. This insistence is for an obvious reason. Most parents, the minute they first hear that their son or daughter has gotten involved with an "occult" or "Pagan" group will immediately equate such participation as being "ensnared into Satanic activity" by the sinister influence of "evil witches" (us!). Most people are woefully ignorant of the Pagan/Wiccan revival as well as the rest of the esoteric and mystical movement, having been brainwashed by the proliferation of sensationalistic, cinematic misinformation regarding the occult by Hollywood movie producers who care little for accuracy of information and detail. Parents will then usually project their worst fears upon the group with which their child may be involved. This can easily lead to hysterically unfounded charges of ritual sacrifice, sexual orgies, drug parties, etc., which many parochial and narrow-minded community members would be only too willing to believe. In the long run this can only cause a good deal of grief and perhaps even legal hassles resulting from parental accusations.

We suggest that if a young person becomes interested in attending the meetings of the study circle or grove, then the coordinator(s) should discuss with the teenager the necessary steps and procedures which must be taken in order to be accepted as a regular participant or potential member of the group. First of all, the coordinator needs to make contact with the parents, explaining to them their son or daughter's interest in the group, giving them a brief overview of the most basic teachings and goals of the Ordo Arcanorum Gradalis, and emphasizing the fact that we have no relationship whatsoever with Satanism, devil-worship, or black magick. Further, it should also be made clear to them that we require written consent from the parents of minors before we can accept them into our meetings on a regular basis. This protects both the group and the minor from later accusations or troublemaking by the parents. A simple consent form can be composed wherein the parents acknowledge that the leadership of the group has discussed the teachings of the Order with them, and that as a result, they have no objection to their teenager receiving religious instruction from us or participating in our ritual celebrations.

Of course, there are times when a study circle or grove may decide against admitting certain young people to their membership due to the fact of individual adolescent immaturity or simply because the group senses that the young person in question does not seem to fit in comfortably with the other members. However, such decisions must be made on a case-by-case basis.

Finally, it is essential that if certain young people are allowed into the group life of a study circle or grove, they be made aware of a standing policy that prohibits them from drinking alcoholic beverages during the times of socializing after the circle. This is simple, common sense. It also protects the group and the owner of the property on which the celebrations are held from any legal liability due to later accidents which may result from serving liquor to a minor. It further keeps the group out of any questionable or compromising situations which could blacken its reputation, either with the local community or the municipal law enforcement authorities.[5]

In closing this section, we need to mention that a Grail Quest study circle or grove can be as large as necessary (groves, unlike covens, are not limited to a maximum membership of thirteen), or be as small as two or three committed people. Although, in rare cases, an extremely large group may want to split into two different study circles or groves in order to keep the "family" atmosphere conducive to personal bonding which can only be attained in a more moderately sized group.

These are the basic guidelines for the establishment and operation of a Grail Quest study circle in preparation for its eventual upgrade in status to the level of a fully-functioning, autonomous grove in affiliation with the Ordo Arcanorum Gradalis. Undoubtedly there will be future revisions and/or additions to this list as continuing experience teaches us even better ways to facilitate the growth of newly organized groups, but for now it is hoped that these guidelines can supply the necessary framework needed for growth, maturing, and expansion.

Footnotes

1. Ed Fitch, *Magical Rites from the Crystal Well*. (St. Paul, MN: Llewellyn Publications, 1984), p. 8.

2. Should questions arise in the group about the lessons which the coordinator(s) are not able to adequately answer, make a list of them and send them to us, and we will be glad to try and answer them in detail so that the coordinator(s) can share the clarifications with the group.

3. Once a qualified individual has completed the study requirements for priesthood, that person will then be authorized by the Order to perform the Rite of Self-Ordination. The new priest/ess should then notify the Order of the date the rite was performed in order that accurate records can be maintained for the priesthood of the O.A.G. For the same reason, all other ordinations administered by a priest/ess in the local grove should be reported in writing to the national office of the Order.

4. Janet and Stewart Farrar, *The Witches' Way*. (Custer, WA: Phoenix Publishing Co., 1984), pp. 139-140.

5. Of course, taking a sip from the Grail Chalice during the Mass, or sharing in the brief Cakes and Wine blessing after the circle should pose no problem due to the extremely small amount of alcohol consumed. It is also for sacramental purposes, and therefore can be considered most acceptable.

Appendix C

Essay Questions for Required Books

s already mentioned in Appendix A, one part of the requirements for ordination consists of completing the mandatory reading of seven books which are listed there in detail. If you are studying for ordination as a solitary, after the completion of each book, there is a set of six essay questions which must be answered in writing and sent to the Order's mailing address. In the case of those students seeking ordination through the instruction of one of our local groves, these questions should be submitted to the presiding priest and/or priestess who shall oversee all ordination studies.

These questions are designed to test your knowledge and overall retentive comprehension of the basic themes and points of emphasis found in each volume. All questions should be answered with a minimum of at least one paragraph. Your essay answers, however, may be as lengthy and extended as you wish. All answers to these questions should be either legibly handwritten or else typed upon regular 8 1/2 x 11 paper with each answer numbered according to the number of the question being answered.

As discussed previously, most of these required books easily can be obtained in any occult or metaphysical bookstore. They can often be found in the New Age section of many large chain stores. If you cannot readily find these volumes, most store proprietors will be more than happy to special order them for you.

If, for any reason, you find that a particular book is temporarily out of print or unavailable, there are several alternative options still open to you. The first and most obvious is the public library. If your local library does not have a copy of the book in question, they can, nevertheless, instigate a search for the book in other libraries in your state or an even larger geographical area. This process may take a few weeks, but it is often successful. Should your efforts still meet with no positive results in obtaining the desired book, it is recommended that you write to us. In such cases, we will be able to give you the title of an alternative selection to substitute for the original required book, as well as a set of essay questions for you to answer when you have completed the reading.

Drawing Down the Moon

1. In your opinion, what are the most attractive and compelling characteristics of a Neo-Pagan world view as described by the author?

2. Give a brief explanation of the rationale of ceremonial ritual as practiced in the Craft. What would you consider to be essential to the art of ritual?

3. Discuss the strengths and deficiencies inherent in Dianic (feminist) Craft.

4. By which group or tradition in the Neo-Pagan spectrum did you find yourself the most fascinated?

5. Many of the groups discussed in Margot Adler's 1979 first edition have since disbanded or disintegrated. Do you see this as an indication of strength through evolutionary development in the movement or as a potentially dangerous weakness in Neo-Paganism?

6. How would you describe your most lasting impressions of Adler's "panorama of Paganism?"

The Elements of the Grail Tradition

1. Who is Bran, and what is his connection to Arthur?

2. What are the Four Hallows of the Grail, and what is the symbolic meaning of each?

3. What is the relation of the Divine to the king and the king to the land?

4. Who is the Maimed King, and what is his significance?

5. Explain the significance of the Templars and their mysterious relationship to the Grail.

6. How can we reconcile Christian and Pagan understandings of the Grail?

The Mists of Avalon

1. What impressed you most about the methodology of Morgaine's magick spell-work over the scabbard for Excalibur (pp. 196-199)? What does it tell us about the attitudes and approach we should have with regard to our own practice of magick?

2. Discuss the correspondences and symbolism between Gwenhwyfar and those of the orthodox Church establishment of our own day.

3. As one of the spiritual high points of the book (pp. 769-774), describe how Morgaine's invocation of the Goddess upon the Cup of the Holy

Regalia and the subsequent mystical experiences occurring at the Round Table on that Pentecost day contain the seeds of the theology for a Pagan Mass of the Grail.

4. Explain the significance of that small group of Christian hermits (not to be confused with the church on the nearby priests' island) who lived in peace with the Lady of the Lake and worshipped in their own small chapel on Avalon itself.

5. What do you sense to be the underlying message of the epilogue, and how does it apply to us as contemporary Pagans and our attitudes towards Christianity?

6. Give your own impressions of the difference between *The Mists of Avalon* and other Arthurian literature which you have read. What excited you the most about the author's approach to the story?

The Grail Seeker's Companion

1. Why is an initial focus on the early texts of the Grail Romance important? In all their contradictions, variations, and sometimes inexplicable allegories, what wisdom of essential worth do they ultimately convey?

2. What is the significance of the Waste Land in helping to develop a Pagan theology of compassion and concern for the collective and/or individual human condition? Do you see any themes of fall and redemption embodied in the imagery of the Waste Land, the Maimed King, and the healing of his wound; and if so, what impact should this have upon our Pagan concepts of spiritual and ecological renewal?

3. Essential to the heart of the Grail legacy are the questions that are an inherent part of the Quest itself. What kind of questions should we be asking about the Hallows which parade before us in the Grail Castle of our own meditations?

4. Describe your most lasting impressions and insights regarding the Goddess and the Grail as you read "The Way of the Cauldron."

5. How does the interpenetration of Pagan and esoteric Christian symbology in the mythic legends of the Grail strengthen its relevance for us today?

6. What part of the book spoke most of all to your own spiritual sensitivities?

The Western Way, Volume I - The Native Tradition

1. Explain why the Native Tradition is described as an inward spiral of the spiritual path in contradistinction to the Hermetic Tradition which is considered to be the outward spiral of the Western Mystery Tradition.

2. Elaborate upon the concept of Analeptic Memory.

3. In "Meeting the Gods," which gods/goddesses and other supernatural personages listed by the authors most struck a chord of inner resonance within you?

4. Describe the importance of "the Mysteries" and in what way they are an essential part of the Native Tradition.

5. Briefly define the Foretime, the Otherworld, the Secret Commonwealth, and the Shining Ones. How do they interrelate?

6. Comment on the constructive criticisms which the authors proffer about the dangers and seduction of "inappropriate atavism" within the modern Pagan revival, and the need for a healthy Neo-Pagan perspective (pp. 136-137). Comment also on the authors' observation that "the old and new religion (Paganism and Christianity) need never be a stumbling block to each other as they have been in the past."

The Western Way, Volume II - The Hermetic Tradition

1. Explain the importance of the underlying Hermetic conceptualization of the scattered, universal Body of Light and our relationship to it.

2. Give a brief overview of Gnosticism and the importance of its contribution to the pathways of inner spiritual growth.

3. Explain the relationship between the Great Work and the Grail, and how it should affect our own Order with regards to our attitudes, outlook and theology.

4. Why is Aslan not a "safe" Lion, and what does this say to us about the serious respect with which we should accord the manifestations of Deity to which we give homage?

5. Describe the implications of the esoteric Christian teaching of *theosis*.

6. How has the authors' perspective increased your awareness of the basic complementarity of mystical systems and approaches?

The Gentle Arts of Aquarian Magic

1. Why do you think the author continuously makes reference to magickal abilities as "The Gentle Arts?" Gentle in comparison to what?

2. What do you consider to be the distinctive uniqueness of the author's approach to her subject as compared with other similar books?

3. Explain the author's aversion for adhering to regulated calendrical dates for determining the seasonal Sabbat celebrations.

4. While this book is meant primarily for solitary practitioners, what do you consider to be the most advantageous insights in the book which could be applied collectively within a local grove?

5. Briefly discuss the ritual of "Drawing Down the Moon" as described by Ms. Green. How does it differ from the ceremony which most Wiccans have come to label by the same title?

6. Comment on Marian Green's strong statement about the Gods: "THEY ARE REAL …" (pp. 141-142). How can heeding this admonition serve to deepen our religio-psychic experience?

Appendix D

Gays, Lesbians, and the Craft

ne thing refreshing about Wicca and Neo-Paganism in general is that, by and large, homophobia is relatively rare within its ranks. "An it harm none, do as ye will." However, many will often encounter a vocal minority active in the Pagan revival who make their anti-gay opinions quite clear when the subject comes up in conversation, and it can be most disconcerting to someone totally unprepared to encounter such feelings of sexual resentment. Yet I believe that I am safe in saying that this is still a minority position within the movement as a whole.

People who hold to an anti-gay stance in Wicca and Paganism do so for usually one of two reasons: (1) they are simply reflecting the homophobic prejudice with which they were indoctrinated by family and society starting at a very early age, or (2) they genuinely feel that Wicca is a Nature fertility cult, and as such, can only countenance fertility-producing sexuality (i.e., heterosexuality); believing in common with their orthodox Christian competitors that homosexuality is somehow "unnatural." The first position is simply prejudice, the second a gross combination of historical and biological ignorance.

Interestingly enough, the argument which seems to hold the most credence among anti-gay Crafters is the one which asserts that novices to the Craft must come into a coven or grove as bonded male-female partners in order to guarantee the adequate flow of "polarity" in the group, which they consider necessary to raising effective power. In their idea, polarity is produced only through the pairing of two people, one female and one male. They also question how the Great Rite could be consummated if the participants were gay or lesbian. That question is very easy to lay to rest from the standpoint of our own teachings: in our tradition, the Great Rite is always ritually enacted in its *symbolic* form. In its universal symbolism it far exceeds the limited dimensions of human sexuality. Of course, if two people actually want to do the Great Rite, then obviously they would have to be heterosexual! However, in our Order we do not believe it is ritually enhancing to have the grove leave the temple room, light up a cigarette, and talk about the weather while the priest and priestess are having sex on the floor in the middle of the circle! (Lest anyone think that I am being too sarcastic, consult the book *What Witches Do* by Stewart Farrar.)

It is very true that the Great Rite is, among other things, a symbol of the life-producing sexuality which perpetuates our species, and is, therefore, a celebration of heterosexual union. No gay or lesbian should be bothered by this, for without it none of us would be here! And while it is appropriate for a man and a woman to hold the chalice and glaive in the symbolic enactment of the rite, it really does not matter what the sexual orientation of the two happens to be, for it is celebrating something infinitely greater than their individual inclinations!

As far as the "polarity" question is concerned, Raymond Buckland, in one of his early books *Witchcraft From the Inside*, written while he was still a Gardnerian, insisted on this need for male/female polarity within the circle. When I commented on my confusion regarding this requirement that we must work as male/female pairs within a coven, the High Priest of the group in which I was involved at the time indignantly wrote this comment across my lesson paper: "Bullshit. To each his/her own. We all do as we wish—'An it harm none.'"

Starhawk has gone a long way in debunking some of these old limited visions of how polarity can be manifested. In her book *Dreaming the Dark*, she has this to say on the subject:

> And polarity does not have to be generated either between two partners according to the heterosexual model. There are female/female and male/male polarities, each of which can also be generated or within a person by the creation of a same-sex *double*. These currents may have a different flavor but be equal in power and sometimes stronger than heterosexual polarities. Which form of polarity one chooses to work with is a matter of personal taste and inclination. But within a healthy community, all forms are necessary if a balance is to be sustained.[1]

I hasten to add that these are not the biased opinions of a crusading lesbian priestess; Starhawk is heterosexual and married!

Even back in the '60s, Sybil Leek spoke to the homosexual issue in her book *The Complete Art of Witchcraft*, and even though she was from the old school belief that gays and lesbians should not be High Priests or Priestesses, she nevertheless stunningly documented the revered history of homosexuals in the ancient priesthoods of the Pagan past, and concluded that, as such, they could not be denied entrance to the Craft. Another very interesting book which documents the relationship between Witchcraft and homosexuality is *Witchcraft and the Gay Counterculture* by Arthur Evans. It is excellent if one can get past some of the author's rather radical political formulations. One more book of great educative value on this issue is *Another Mother Tongue: Gay Words, Gay Worlds* by Judy Grahn. It goes a long way into showing the direct relationship between gay sexuality and social customs and Pagan spirituality.

Unfortunately, one of the worst recent contributions to the subject has been by Janet and Stewart Farrar in their otherwise excellent book *The Witches' Way*. They are very honest in expressing that they are uncomfortable with the subject of gays and lesbians in the Craft, and in the process they do not hesitate to subtly convey thereby a latent form of Wiccan homophobia. In all probability, the relevant passage of their book (pp. 169-170) has gone a long way in reinforcing other Pagans' own inherited sexual prejudice and bigotry.

Another interesting observation is the fact that many of those who disparage gays and lesbians in the Craft claim to be practicing some form of "Celtic Craft." Obviously, they haven't delved into the history of their spiritual ancestors! It is a fact that Roman historians graphically detailed the almost universal pervasiveness of male homosexuality among the Celts, just as it was very common among the ancient Greeks. I find it rather amusing that some homophobic modern Wiccans feel free to adopt the religious customs of their forebears while conveniently ignoring the sexual customs and mores of the same Pagan culture!

Admittedly, these few pages have only scratched the surface regarding this issue, but I believe that the reader can now discern a better idea of exactly where we stand on this important subject of the legitimacy of gays and lesbians in the Craft. On this issue we have no room for compromise. The Ordo Arcanorum Gradalis accepts into its membership all who qualify, irrespective of their sexual orientation. We do not consider homosexuality to be a moral issue in and of itself. The only moral issue is how heterosexuals, bisexuals, and homosexuals conduct their lifestyles in the context of loving, responsible behavior.

Footnotes

1. Starhawk, *Dreaming the Dark: Magic, Sex & Politics.* (Boston, MA: Beacon Press, 1982), pp. 146-147.

Appendix E

A Musical Selection for Ceremonial Work

Music can be an extremely important part of any ritual experience. For those groups which do not have their own musical talents to draw upon from within the grove, it is often necessary to find recordings and instrumental selections that are both appropriate and integral to the enhancement of a ceremonial gathering. For many groups it is often a process of searching and sifting through a seemingly vast array of classical, New Age, and recent feminist/Pagan recordings until just the right selections are found. Listed below are a few of the recordings from which we have been able to extract some real gems of ceremonially appropriate music. We hope that you, your study circle, or grove may find them helpful as a partial musical solution to your own ritual needs as well.

- *Ascension to the All That Is: Inner-Harmony New Age Music by Robert Slap* (Valley of the Sun Publishing, 1987).
- *Avalon: Solo Flute Meditations by Kay Gardner* (Ladyslipper Records, 1988).
- *Carmina Burana*, Carl Orff (Philips, 1989 [422 363-2]).
- *Celtic Symphony by Alan Stivell* (Rounder Records, 1987 [CD 3988/89]).
- *Cran Ull by Clannad* (Tara Records, 1980, [CD 3007]).
- *Crystal Cave: Back to Atlantis—Higher Consciousness Music by Upper Astral* (Valley of the Sun Publishing, 1982).
- *Crystal Fantasy by Michel Genest* (Narada Productions, Inc., 1984).

🜂 *From Heart to Crown by Rob Whitesides-Woo* (Search for Serenity, 1986 [SFSD-005]).

🜂 *Gregorian Chants, Monks of the Benedictine Abbey, Grand Prix du Disque* (Everest Record Group).

🜂 *Indigo by Patrick O'Hearn* (Private Music, 1991 [01005-82091-2]).

🜂 *Instratum by Lee Stone* (Lee Stone Gallery, P. O. Box 98 Wanchese, Roanoke Island, NC 27981 [privately produced, 1988]).

🜂 *Medicine Wind: The Celestial Bliss Music of George Tortorelli* (Medicine Wind Productions, 1983).

🜂 *Novus Magnificat: Through the Stargate by Constance Demby* (Hearts of Space Records, 1986 [H5003]).

🜂 *Parallel Dreams by Loreena McKennitt* (Quinian Road Productions, 1989 [QR CD103]).

🜂 *Planetary Chronicles: Vol. 1 by John Serrie* (Miramar Recordings, 1992 [MPCO 2004]).

🜂 *Ritual by Gabrielle Roth and the Mirrors* (Raven Recording, 1990).

🜂 *Sacred Space Music: Vol. 1 by Constance Demby* (Constance Demby Productions, 1987).

🜂 *Spleen and Ideal by Dead Can Dance* (Beggars Banquet Music [CAD 512 CD]).

🜂 *Strata by Robert Rich and Steve Roach* (Hearts of Space, 1990 [H511019-2]).

🜂 *Upper Astral Suite: Inner-Harmony New Age Music by Upper Astral* (Valley of the Sun Publishing, 1981).

Bibliography

Adler, Margot. *Drawing Down the Moon*. Boston, MA: Beacon Press, 1979, 1986.

The American Heritage Dictionary of the English Language. Boston, MA: Houghton Mifflin Company, 1982.

The Anchor Bible: Genesis. A New Translation with Introduction and Commentary by Ephraim A. Speiser. New York, NY: Doubleday & Co., Inc., 1981.

Anderson, Flavia. *The Ancient Secret—In Search of the Holy Grail*. London: Victor Gollancz, Ltd., 1955.

Ashe, Geoffrey. *King Arthur's Avalon*. New York, NY: E. P. Dutton & Co., Inc., 1957.

Assyrian and Babylonian Literature, Selected Translations. D. Appleton and Co., 1901.

Bach, Marcus. *The Inner Ecstasy*. Nashville, TN: Abingdon Press, 1969.

Baigent, Michael, Richard Leigh, and Henry Lincoln. *Holy Blood, Holy Grail*. New York, NY: Delacorte Press, 1982.

Ballard, Frank, D.D. *The True God—A Modern Summary of the Relations of Theism to Naturalism, Monism, Pluralism, and Pantheism*. London: Robert Culley, 1907.

Besant, Annie. *Esoteric Christianity*. Wheaton, IL: The Theosophical Publishing House, 1901, 1953, 1966, 1982.

Beyerl, Paul. *The Master Book of Herbalism*. Custer, WA: Phoenix Publishing, Inc., 1984.

Bonewits, Philip Emmons Isaac. *Real Magic*. Berkeley, CA: Creative Arts Book Company, 1971, 1979.

Bonwick, James. *Irish Druids and Old Irish Religions*. Reprint ed. New York, NY: Dorset Press, 1986 .

Bradley, Marion Zimmer. *The Mists of Avalon*. New York, NY: Ballantine Books, 1982.

Brandon, S.G.F. *Dictionary of Comparative Religion*. New York, NY: Charles Scribner's Sons, 1970.

Buckland, Raymond. *Buckland's Complete Book of Witchcraft*. St. Paul, MN: Llewellyn Publications, 1986.

_____ . *The Tree: The Complete Book of Saxon Witchcraft*. York Beach, ME: Samuel Weiser, 1974.

Bulfinch's Mythology. New York, NY: Avenel Books, 1979.

Christie-Murray, David. *Voices From the Gods*. London: Routledge & Kegan Paul, 1978.

Coggins, Richard. *Who's Who in the Bible*. Totowa, NJ: Barnes & Noble Books, 1981.

Crowther, Arnold and Patricia. *The Secrets of Ancient Witchcraft*. New York, NY: Citadel Press, 1974.

Cunningham, Scott. *Earth, Air, Fire and Water*. St. Paul, MN: Llewellyn Publications, 1991.

Davidson, Gustav. *A Dictionary of Angels*. New York, NY: The Free Press, 1967.

Denning, Melita and Osborne Phillips. *Robe and Ring*. St. Paul, MN: Llewellyn Publications.

_____ . *The Apparel of High Magick*. St. Paul, MN: Llewellyn Publications.

_____ . *The Sword and the Serpent*. St. Paul, MN: Llewellyn Publications, 1988.

_____ . *The Triumph of Light*. St. Paul, MN: Llewellyn Publications.

_____ . *Mysteria Magica*. St. Paul, MN: Llewellyn Publications, 1981, 1986.

_____ . *Psychic Self-Defense and Well-Being*. St. Paul, MN: Llewellyn Publications, 1980.

Eisler, Riane. *The Chalice and the Blade*. San Francisco, CA: Harper & Row, Inc., 1987.

The Encyclopedia Britannica. Chicago, IL.

Encyclopaedia of Religion and Ethics. Ed. by James Hastings. New York, NY: Charles Scribner's Sons, 1926.

The Encyclopedia of Religion. Ed. by Mircea Eliade. New York, NY: Macmillan Publishing Co., 1987.

Evans, Arthur. *Witchcraft and the Gay Counterculture*. Boston, MA: Fag Rag Books, 1978.

Farrar, Janet and Stewart. *Eight Sabbats for Witches*. Custer, WA: Phoenix Publishing Inc., 1981.

_____ . *The Witches' Way*. Custer, WA: Phoenix Publishing Inc., 1984.

Farrar, Stewart. *What Witches Do*. Custer, WA: Phoenix Publishing Inc., 1983.

Fitch, Ed. *Magical Rites From the Crystal Well*. St. Paul, MN: Llewellyn Publications, 1984.

Fosdick, Harry Emerson. *The Man From Nazareth*. New York, NY: Harper & Brothers, 1949.

Fox, Robin Lane. *Pagans and Christians*. New York, NY: Alfred A. Knopf, Inc., 1989.

Gardner, Gerald. *The Meaning of Witchcraft*. New York, NY: Magickal Childe, Inc., 1959, 1982.

Grahn, Judy. *Another Mother Tongue: Gay Words, Gay Worlds*. Boston, MA: Beacon Press, 1984.

Gray, William G. *Evoking the Primal Goddess*. St. Paul, MN: Llewellyn Publications, 1989.

Green, Marian. *The Gentle Arts of Aquarian Magic*. Wellingborough: The Aquarian Press, 1987.

Gromacki, Robert Glenn. *The Modern Tongues Movement*. Philadelphia, PA: The Presbyterian and Reformed Publishing Co., 1967.

Hawkins, D.J.B. *The Essentials of Theism*. New York, NY: Sheed & Ward, 1950.

The Holy Bible: New International Version. Copyright © 1973 by the New York Bible Society International.

Hunt, John, D.D. *Pantheism and Christianity*. Port Washington, NY: Kennikat Press, 1884, reissued 1970.

The International Standard Bible Encyclopedia. Ed. by Geoffrey W. Bromiley. Grand Rapids, MI: William B. Eerdmans, 1988.

The Interpreter's Bible. Nashville: Abingdon Press, copyright renewal 1981 by Abingdon.

The Jerusalem Bible. Garden City, NY: Doubleday & Co., Inc., 1966.

Jevons, Frank B. *The Idea of God in Early Religions*. Cambridge University Press, 1910.

Jong, Erica. *Witches*. New York, NY: New American Library, 1981.

Kelly, Aidan. *Crafting the Art of Magic, Book I*. St. Paul, MN: Llewellyn Publications, 1991.

La Violette, Wesley. *The New Gita*. Santa Monica, CA: DeVorss & Co., 1973.

Leek, Sybil. *The Complete Art of Witchcraft*. New York, NY: The New American Library, 1971.

The Lost Books of the Bible and the Forgotten Books of Eden. New York, NY: World Publishing Company, 1973.

Mariechild, Diane. *Mother Wit—A Feminist Guide to Psychic Development*. Trumansburg, NY: The Crossing Press, 1981.

Matthews, Caitlin and John. *The Western Way—Volumes I & II*. London: Arkana, 1985, 1986.

Matthews, John. *The Elements of the Grail Tradition*. Great Britain: Element Books Limited, 1990.

_____ . *The Grail—Quest for the Eternal*. London: Thames and Hudson Ltd., 1981.

Matthews, John and Marian Green. *The Grail Seeker's Companion*. Wellingborough: The Aquarian Press, 1986.

Menninger, Karl. *Whatever Became of Sin?* New York, NY: Hawthorn Books, 1973.

The Nag Hammadi Library. Ed. by J.M. Robinson. New York, NY: Harper & Row, 1977.

The New English Bible. Copyright © the Delegates of the Oxford University Press and the Syndics of the Cambridge University Press, 1961, 1970.

The New Saint Joseph Sunday Missal. New York, NY: Catholic Book Publishing Company, 1980.

Ophiel. *The Art and Practice of Talismanic Magic*. York Beach, ME: Samuel Weiser, Inc., 1973.

Otto, Rudolph. *The Idea of the Holy*. London: Oxford University Press, 1923, 1950, 1958.

The Oxford Dictionary of the Christian Church. Ed. by F.L. Cross. Oxford: Oxford University Press, 1974.

Pagels, Elaine. *The Gnostic Gospels*. New York, NY: Vintage Books, 1981.

Revised Standard Version of the Bible. Copyrighted 1946, 1952, © 1971, 1973 by the Division of Christian Education of the National Council of the Churches of Christ in the U.S.A.

Richardson, Alan. *Earth God Rising*. St. Paul, MN: Llewellyn Publications, 1990.

Robinson, J.M. *Pagan Christs*. Reprint ed. New York, NY: Dorset Press, 1987.

Rokeah, David. *Jews, Pagans and Christians in Conflict*. Jerusalem: The Magnes Press, 1982.

Rossner, Father John. *In Search of the Primordial Tradition and the Cosmic Christ*. St. Paul, MN: Llewellyn Publications, 1989.

Schonfield, Hugh J. *The Passover Plot*. New York, NY: Bernard Geis Associates, 1965.

Smith, Morton. *Jesus the Magician*. San Francisco, CA: Harper & Row, 1981.

Spence, Lewis. *The Mysteries of Britain*. Wellingborough: The Aquarian Press, 1970.

Starhawk. *Dreaming the Dark*. Boston, MA: The Beacon Press, 1982.

_____ . *The Spiral Dance*. San Francisco, CA: Harper & Row, 1979.

Teixidor, Javier. *The Pagan God—Popular Religion in the Greco-Roman Near East*. Princeton, NJ: Princeton University Press, 1977.

Valiente, Doreen. *An ABC of Witchcraft*. Custer, WA: Phoenix Publishing Inc., 1973, 1988.

_____ . *Natural Magic*. Custer, WA: Phoenix Publishing Inc., 1975.

_____ . *Witchcraft for Tomorrow*. Custer, WA: Phoenix Publishing Inc., 1978, 1985.

Waite, Arthur Edward. *The Holy Grail—Its Legends and Symbolism*. London: Rider and Co., 1933.

Walker, Barbara G. *The Secrets of the Tarot*. San Francisco, CA: Harper & Row, 1984.

_____ . *The Woman's Encyclopedia of Myths and Secrets*. San Francisco, CA: Harper & Row, 1983.

Watts, Alan. *Beyond Theology*. New York, NY: Vintage Books, 1973.

Weigall, Arthur. *The Paganism in Our Christianity*. New York, NY: G.P. Putnam's Sons, 1928.

Weinstein, Marion. *Positive Magic*. Custer, WA: Phoenix Publishing Inc., 1981.

Willoughby, Harold R. *Pagan Regeneration*. Chicago, IL: University of Chicago Press, 1929.

Winterhalter, Robert. *The Fifth Gospel*. San Francisco, CA: Harper & Row, 1988.

Wood-Martin, W.G. *Pagan Ireland*. New York, NY: Longmans, Green, and Co., 1895.

Index

Stay in Touch

On the following pages you will find listed, with their current prices, some of the books now available on related subjects. Your book dealer stocks most of these and will stock new titles in the Llewellyn series as they become available. We urge your patronage.

To obtain our full catalog, to keep informed about new titles as they are released and to benefit from informative articles and helpful news, you are invited to write for our bimonthly news magazine/catalog, *Llewellyn's New Worlds of Mind and Spirit*. A sample copy is free, and it will continue coming to you at no cost as long as you are an active mail customer. Or you may subscribe for just $10.00 in the U.S.A. and Canada ($20.00 overseas, first class mail). Many bookstores also have New Worlds available to their customers. Ask for it.

Stay in touch! In *New Worlds'* pages you will find news and features about new books, tapes and services, announcements of meetings and seminars, articles helpful to our readers, news of authors, products and services, special money-making opportunities, and much more.

Llewellyn's New Worlds of Mind and Spirit
P.O. Box 64383-739, St. Paul, MN 55164-0383, U.S.A.

* * *

To Order Books and Tapes

If your book dealer does not have the books described on the following pages readily available, you may order them directly from the publisher by sending full price in U.S. funds, plus $3.00 for postage and handling for orders *under* $10.00; $4.00 for orders *over* $10.00. There are no postage and handling charges for orders over $50.00. Postage and handling rates are subject to change. UPS Delivery: We ship UPS whenever possible. Delivery guaranteed. Provide your street address as UPS does not deliver to P.O. Boxes. UPS to Canada requires a $50.00 minimum order. Allow 4-6 weeks for delivery. Orders outside the U.S.A. and Canada: Airmail—add retail price of book; add $5.00 for each non-book item (tapes, etc.); add $1.00 per item for surface mail.

For Group Study and Purchase

Because there is a great deal of interest in group discussion and study of the subject matter of this book, we feel that we should encourage the adoption and use of this particular book by such groups by offering a special quantity price to group leaders or agents.

Our special quantity price for a minimum order of five copies of *The Crafted Cup* is $54.00 cash-with-order. This price includes postage and handling within the United States. Minnesota residents must add 6.5% sales tax. For additional quantities, please order in multiples of five. For Canadian and foreign orders, add postage and handling charges as above. Credit card (VISA, MasterCard, American Express) orders are accepted. Charge card orders only ($15.00 minimum order) may be phoned in free within the U.S.A. or Canada by dialing 1-800-THE-MOON. For customer service, call 1-612-291-1970. Mail orders to:

LLEWELLYN PUBLICATIONS
P.O. Box 64383-739, St. Paul, MN 55164-0383, U.S.A.

Prices subject to change without notice.

In Search of the Primordial Tradition & the Cosmic Christ
by Father John Rossner, Ph.D.

This is a new book on the identity of Jesus—the occult Jesus overlooked by conventional New Testament scholars. It is a must for those interested in the Western Esoteric Tradition and its relevance to the contemporary crisis in religion, science, and human culture.

Father Rossner finds ample evidence for the existence of an "ancient gnosis," or tradition of arcane wisdom spanning the centuries from Egypt to India, Persia, Greece and Rome. He traces the entry of this gnosis into pre-Christian Jewish mystical traditions, and from there into the fabric of the canonical gospels, New Testament epistles, and the church's creeds and sacramental rites.

He also argues that only those who are familiar with the transformative effects of live psychic and spirit phenomena can fully appreciate the original Biblical experience. He calls for an entirely new approach to the study of religion and spiritual insight in the West, one that will bring a "Second Copernican Revolution" and a greater understanding of the inner dynamics and capabilities of the human psyche and spirit.

0-87542-685-9, 320 pgs., 6 x 9, illus., softcover $12.95

The Occult Christ
by Ted Andrews

Few people realize that great mystical secrets lie hidden within the teachings of Christianity—secrets to the laws of the universe and their application in our lives. *The Occult Christ* reveals this hidden wisdom and knowledge within Biblical Scripture and presents Christianity as a Modern Mystery School in the manner of the ancient traditions throughout the world.

Within the Christ Mysteries is the cosmic effort to restore the experience of mysticism, power and the Divine on a personal level. This path not only acknowledges the Divine Feminine within the Universe and the individual, but it also reveals the means to unfold it within your life. You are shown how to access great universal and Divine power through the sacred festivals of the changing of the seasons—times in which the veil between the physical and the spiritual is thinnest. The true Christ Mysteries open the angelic hierarchies to humanity and shows the way to attune to them for greater self-knowledge, self-mastery and self-realization.

Breathe new life into your religious foundations with *The Occult Christ*, and learn to walk "the road of shadows where secret knowledge of the soul dwells."

0-87542-019-2, 224 pgs., 6 x 9, softcover $10.00